EVERYDAY GARDENING

THE SUNK GARDEN

E.G.

[Frontispiece

EVERYDAY
GARDENING

J. COUTTS, A.H.R.H.S.

FORMERLY CURATOR
OF THE
ROYAL BOTANIC GARDENS
KEW

8 PLATES IN COLOUR
32 FULL-PAGE ILLUSTRATIONS FROM PHOTOGRAPHS
AND MANY DIAGRAMS

WARD, LOCK & CO., LIMITED
LONDON AND MELBOURNE

First Published 1931
Second Impression (Revised) 1937
Reprinted 1942

MADE IN ENGLAND
Printed in Great Britain by Butler & Tanner Ltd., Frome and London

PREFACE

THE position held by the author at the Royal Botanic Gardens, Kew, enables him to understand to the fullest degree the needs of the practical gardener, and when his unique horticultural knowledge is also taken into account, it will be realized that he is exceptionally qualified to write an accurate, practical and up-to-date book covering every phase of gardening.

EVERYDAY GARDENING tells in simple, straightforward language, in which technical terms are reduced to a minimum, how to plan and make a modern garden and how to maintain it. It embodies the very latest horticultural methods and recommends the newest and most desirable varieties of flowers, shrubs, vegetables and fruit trees. The first aim of the Author has been to ensure accuracy and up-to-dateness; secondly, he has striven for comprehensiveness, and the Publishers feel confident that the book will meet the requirements of the keenest and most exacting gardeners.

The work is thoroughly practical, and as a gardening volume is essentially a book of reference, the information it imparts should be quickly and easily accessible ; for this reason the work has, as far as possible, been arranged alphabetically and much of the matter is in the form of lists and tables.

The first few chapters describe the general principles of gardening, soil improvement, draining and levelling, manuring, laying out the garden, making beds, paths and lawns. Next follow chapters on the Herbaceous Border, the Rock Garden, the Wall and Paved Gardens, the Water and Bog Gardens and then Propagation. In the Alphabetical List of Flowering Plants and Shrubs will be found the detailed culture of well over 600 different species ; annuals, biennials, perennials, bulbs, shrubs, climbers, etc.—how and when to propagate them, soils and situations most suited to them, and lists of best species and varieties to grow, showing their heights, colour of flowers and times of blooming. The detailed culture of all fruit, vegetables and salads is described in the same practical and comprehensive manner, and in the chapter on Gardening under Glass are instructions for the care of greenhouse plants, together with lists of plants that will make a show in the house throughout the year.

It will be seen that every branch and phase of gardening has been considered in detail. Moreover, the common mistake of assuming that the reader has at least some knowledge of the point in question has been avoided, and the subjects are treated in a most detailed, yet concise, manner. The beginner will, therefore, find the book invaluable because of its clearness of expression and detailed instructions, while owing to its scope, accuracy, and authoritativeness, to the expert it will be of the greatest use for reference.

The very large number of colour plates, photographs and diagrams, which have been selected with a view to making the instructions in the text, if possible, yet more clear, will be found an extremely valuable feature.

THE EDITOR.

WARWICK HOUSE,
   SALISBURY SQUARE,
      E.C.4.

CONTENTS

LIST OF COLOUR PLATES

11

LIST OF ILLUSTRATIONS

DIAGRAMS IN THE TEXT

From the Coloured Photograph by]

[Reginald Malby

DELPHINIUMS

E.G.

B

CALENDAR OF WORK

THE reader should bear in mind that locality has a decided influence on the operations advocated herein. For instance, Scotland and the North are always about a fortnight behind the Midlands in cropping, while the Southern Counties are a fortnight or so ahead of the Midlands. Many half-hardy plants, usually raised under glass in less favoured localities, will grow equally well if sown outdoors in warm, sheltered situations in the South-west. Readers south of the Equator must take into consideration the difference in the seasons. For example, in Australia May is equivalent to November in England. This inversion is quite in favour of the Antipodes, and most of the subjects mentioned for sowing in heat in this calendar can safely be treated in the open air in Australia and countries in similar latitudes. The forcing of vegetables, fruit, etc., is fully dealt with in the section on Frames and Forcing in the chapter on Gardening under Glass.

JANUARY

General Garden Work

All digging and trenching should already have been completed. If not finished, this should be done without further delay. No work should be attempted, however, when the ground is covered with snow or muddy. Protection for growing crops must be provided where necessary. Plants against walls and on other supports should be nailed up, and lawns and paths should receive attention.

The Flower Garden

General Operations.—All vacant ground should be thrown up into ridges; the borders, new and old, should be trenched. Vacant ground should be constantly forked or "pointed," so that the surface is loosened and the air permitted to permeate the soil. Any alterations in the flower-beds that are deemed necessary should be made. New catalogues should be obtained so that seeds may be ordered early.

Annuals.—Autumn-sown annuals in the reserve garden should be protected with mats during severe frosts.

E.G.   17   B

Bedding Plants.—All ground which is to be planted later with bedding plants should be well manured.

Bulbs.—Great care must be taken when forking or hoeing in places where bulbs are planted ; in fact, it is better to leave such places entirely alone for the time being.

Climbing Plants.—Thin out the dead wood of climbing plants and fasten up where necessary.

Herbaceous Plants.—The frost has the effect of raising herbaceous plants, such as the *Arabis, Alyssum, Carnations, Daisies, Forget-me-nots, Pansies, Phloxes, Polyanthuses,* for example, above the ground-level. When this has happened, these should be firmly pressed down and a little fine soil should be drawn round them.

Protection.—Protection should be afforded to all young and tender shoots now showing, except those of the hardiest of herbaceous and bulbous plants.

Seeds to Sow.—A few early *Antirrhinums (Snapdragons), Petunias* and *Verbenas* may now be sown in gentle heat.

Planting.—All hardy bulbs may be planted this month for a succession of bloom ; the main crops will have been planted earlier.

Under Glass (Flowers).—The greenhouse should be kept clean. All dead leaves being removed from the plants. Plants must be kept free from draughts, air being given from above or by means of bottom ventilators. Pots, boxes, and soil composts should be prepared for the reception of seeds and cuttings. To preserve flowers in bloom for as long as possible, the atmosphere must be kept moist and genial, but not wet. Water should be given regularly when necessary, especially to bulbs—as much water, of the same temperature as the greenhouse, as they can assimilate.

Achimenes and *Gloxinias* for early flowering may be started.

Bulbs may be introduced into heat.

Hard-wooded Plants require plenty of water at the roots.

Heaths are best kept in a cold house, provided it is frost-proof.

Roses in pots should be pruned.

Seeds to Sow.—*Asparagus plumosus, Cannas, Freesias, Fuchsias, Gloxinias, Sweet Peas,* etc.

Cuttings.—*Bedding stock* to produce cuttings should be placed in heat. Cuttings of *chrysanthemums, tree carnations, heliotropes* and *verbenas* may be put in now. Place scarce varieties of *dahlias* in heat so as to secure plenty of cuttings. *Fuchsias* may now be started.

Potting.—*Calceolaria* seedlings should be shifted into larger pots, and those sown for late blooming should be pricked-off. *Hippeastrums* may be re-potted and started. *Pelargoniums,* if strongly rooted, should be moved into larger pots. *Soft-wooded plants* should be re-potted into the larger pots in which they will ultimately flower.

The Vegetable Garden

General Operations.—All vegetable refuse and leaves should be collected and allowed to rot for future use. If infested with insects, it must be burned, the ashes being dug in. The hoe should be kept moving between growing crops.

SEEDS TO SOW.—*Broad Beans and Peas.*—Some may be sown towards the end of this month in warm, sheltered situations. A few *cauliflowers, radishes* and other early crops may be sown on a hot-bed, or in a south border, being protected with hand-lights. *Lettuces* should be sown every fortnight for a succession. *Onions* may be sown in boxes.

PLANTING.—*Potatoes* may be placed to sprout in the light in some shed free from frost. *Rhubarb* may be planted in deeply dug, heavily manured soil.

Under Glass (Vegetables).—Hot-beds should be made up for forcing *asparagus, broad beans, carrots, herbs, onions, radishes,* etc. A start can be made with forcing *cauliflowers, chicory, lettuces, rhubarb* and *seakale.*

Cucumbers may be had at any time by planting the seed in a hot-bed or under glass about three months before the fruit is required.

SEEDS TO SOW.—*Beans (Broad), beans (French), beetroot (Globe), carrots (stump-rooted), aubergines, leeks, mustard and cress, onions, peas (early), radishes, seakale,* and *tomatoes.*

The Fruit Garden

General Operations.—The pruning of all the hardier kinds of trees should be carried out. *Apricots, cherries, figs, nectarines* and *peaches* must not be pruned this month. Trees that are to be grafted should be cut back, and the scions for grafting should be cut, carefully labelled and heeled into the ground ready for subsequent use. The stems of old fruit trees should be lime-washed, or sprayed with caustic soda, dead bark being removed. It is not wise to plant trees this month; if essential, open weather should be selected and no time should be lost when once the trees are out of the ground. When planting is complete, cover the ground surrounding the trees with a two- to three-inch mulch of manure.

Shrubs and Trees

General Operations.—Evergreens and deciduous shrubs may still be planted. Hedges of *beech, hawthorn* and *privet* should be pruned; also all deciduous shrubs. Cuttings of hardy deciduous shrubs may be planted in open weather and layers made of young branches. Rooted suckers should be taken from *roses, lilacs* and other shrubs for transplantation. Preparations for grafting should be made.

FEBRUARY

General Garden Work

All vacant ground should be weeded and trenched, and a dressing of manure and leaf-mould should be applied to vacant beds.

The Flower Garden

General Operations.—Herbaceous borders should be given a light top-dressing with manure and litter. Any digging that has had to be postponed should be carried out whenever the weather permits.

BULBS.—*Crocuses, Hyacinths* and *Tulips* should be protected against mice, snails and sparrows. See section on Pests.

Roses.—Manure the rose trees well, preferably with cow-dung. All hardy varieties may be planted this month. Rose trees put in now should not be pruned when planted, but after an interval of a month or six weeks. Climbers should be trimmed and trained.

Rock Garden.—Top-dress with a compost of gritty loam and leaf-mould, firming all plants thrown out by frost and dividing and transplanting any of the coarser plants that require it.

SEEDS TO SOW.—Sow seed of *antirrhinums* (*snapdragons*), *begonias, lobelias, petunias* and *verbenas* in gentle heat.

PLANTING.—*Anemones* and *ranunculuses* may be planted out. Provided the weather is mild, all autumn-sown *annuals* may be transplanted. *Box Edging* and other living edgings, such as *pinks* or *thrift,* may be planted now.

Under Glass (Flowers).—A night temperature of from 40° to 50° F. should be maintained. Unless frosty, air must be given daily, if only for an hour at noon. Watering should be carefully attended to.

Azaleas and *Heaths* should have their leaves washed and the soil should be kept moist. *Bedding-out Plants* should be propagated now. *Dahlias* may be started in heat. *Fuchsias* should be given a little bottom heat after re-potting. *Geranium* roots which have been stored should be subjected to bottom heat and cuttings taken.

SEEDS TO SOW.—*Balsam, begonia, canna, celosia, cobæa, cyclamen, fuchsia, thunbergia,* etc. Also bedding plants such as : *golden feather, lobelia, petunia* and *pyrethrum.*

CUTTINGS.—Strike cuttings of *tree carnations* and *gardenias.*

POTTING.—Plants should be moved into larger pots as needed. *Achimenes* tubers may be potted up. Also *calceolarias* sown last August. Clumps of *cannas* should be divided and started in pots. *Border carnations, ferns* and *fuchsias* should be re-potted, also *hydrangeas* (if not done in autumn), and *palms* require attention.

The Vegetable Garden

General Operations.—Hoeing should be carried out whenever the weather permits. Old beds of *Brussel sprouts* and *cabbages* must be cleared off. *Pea* and *bean* sticks should be got ready as they will soon be required. *Broccoli* that has not been cut should have the leaves bent over the flower. *Leeks* should be dug up and should be planted close together in a cool spot. *Onions.*—The ground should be well trenched for the main crop. *Peas* should be earthed up and given an occasional dusting with lime. *Potatoes.*—Continue to sprout these in boxes.

SEEDS TO SOW.—*Broad beans, Brussel sprouts* (for autumn use), *cabbages* (*early*), *carrots, cauliflowers, mustard and cress, lettuces, onions, leeks, parsley, parsnips, peas, radishes, spinach, tomatoes* and *turnips.*

PLANTING.—*Artichokes* (*Globe*), *garlic, shallots, lettuces* (*winter*), *early potatoes, rhubarb* and *seakale.*

Under Glass.—*Cauliflowers* and *lettuces* that have been wintering under frames or under cloches should not be coddled ; the frames should only be closed when the weather is frosty. This applies to all plants in frames. *Early lettuces* can be pricked out on rich beds in frames. *Onions* sown in boxes last month will require thinning out. Hot-beds should be prepared under glass for *cucumbers, marrows* and *melons.*

SEEDS TO SOW.—*Aubergines, broad beans, beans* (*French*), *beetroot* (on a mild hot-bed in a frame), *Brussel sprouts, capsicums, cauliflowers, celery, leeks, peas* (*early*), *radishes, tomatoes, turnips* and *vegetable marrows.* *Potatoes* for forcing may be planted.

The Fruit Garden

General Operations.—Pruning of all fruit trees should be completed this month. All trees in borders should have the ground either well mulched with manure or covered with mould and treated with liquid manure. Stocks for grafting may still be headed back this month. Scions for grafting should be taken from the parent tree, being placed in earth under a north wall. *Damsons* are best pruned this month. *Pear* and *plum* trees should be pruned. *Quince* trees are best pruned this month. *Strawberries.*—New beds should be made where necessary.

Under Glass (Fruit).—The pruning, cleaning and training of all fruit trees indoors should be completed. If no bees are present, fruit trees should be fertilized by means of transferring pollen from flower to flower with a feather, rabbit's tail, or camel-hair brush. Fumigation with a tobacco or nicotine vaporizing compound should be carried out if green-fly are present.

MARCH

General Garden Work

Ground which has been roughly dug up or left ridged through the winter should be prepared for seed sowing. The lawn should receive attention, manure being applied where the grass is thin. Grass seed may be sown, and an application of soot is useful. Where necessary, grass paths should be re-turfed, crazy paving being laid or repaired.

The Flower Garden

General Operations.—Vacant borders must be cleaned up and forked over and the soil for sowing biennials and perennials next month should be prepared. Superfluous dead leaves should be removed, only a few where slight protection is still desirable being left. All dead and broken shoots of *alyssum, forget-me-nots, wallflowers* and similar plants that have come through the winter must be cut away, the plants being made firm where necessary, exposed roots being covered and a top-dressing of suitable soil added if the weather is suitable. Work may now be commenced on transplanting and dividing many Alpines, any thrown out by frost being firmed in again.

Bulbs.—Protect early-flowering bulbs from birds, and take general precautions against frost. *Hyacinths* and *narcissi* should be tied to short stakes.

Seeds to Sow.—Sowings should be made early in the month (if dry) of *hardy annuals, clarkias, coreopsis, cosmos, delphiniums (larkspur), godetia, gypsophila, lavatera, lupins, nigella, poppies, sweet peas, sweet sultan,* etc., and later in the month of *alyssum, anemone, asperula, bartonia, brachycome, calendula, campanulas, China asters, gaillardias, gilia, limnanthes, mignonette, nasturtiums, nemesia, statice, stocks, sunflowers, veronica, Virginian stocks, viscaria.*

Planting.—*Bedding plants* (protect from wind), *carnations* (layered last year), *chrysanthemums, dahlias* (stored through the winter), *late-flowering gladioli, montbretias, pansies* and *violas, ranunculus, roses* (if frosts are over), *summer-flowering creepers, sweet peas* (sown in pots), *winter-sown annuals* and *rock plants.* Many of these rock plants may be propagated by means of division towards the end of the month.

Pruning.—All creepers should be finally pruned. Old, worn-out and leggy shrubs must be cut back to within about 12 inches from the ground. The pruning of *roses* should be commenced (if frosts are over). *Box Edging* must be trimmed, being broken up and replanted where necessary. *Hollies, laurels, bays, rhododendrons* and *conifers* may be cut back, and can be moved where necessary.

Under Glass (Flowers).—The temperature should be from 45° to 50° F. by night. Growing plants should be given ample air and water. Bulbs that have lost vitality through early flowering must be discarded. *Cinerarias* that have flowered, except choice varieties, should be thrown away. Plants, if drooping, must be shaded and, where necessary, *azaleas, camellias* and *marguerites* should be potted on. *Begonias* sown last month should be pricked-off, and tubers started in heat. *Calceolarias* should have crowded leaves thinned out and their shoots staked out. A start should be made with the hardening-off of bedding plants. Keep a sharp look-out for scale and other insect pests and destroy them.

SEEDS TO SOW.—A sowing should be made early in the month of *abronias, ageratums, antirrhinums (snapdragon), cannas, carnations, celosias (cockscomb), China asters, chrysanthemums, delphiniums, dianthus, freesias, gloxinias, heliotropes, hollyhocks, lobelias, pansies, pentstemons, petunias, polyanthus, portulacas, primulas, salvias, stocks* and *verbenas.* And later on in the month : *alyssum, anagallis, anchusas, androsaces, anemones, arabis, aralias, arenaria, asparagus, asters, balsams, calceolarias, calendulas, celmisia, cinerarias, clivias, coleus blumei, draba, eryngiums, fuchsias, grevilleas, linums, nasturtiums, nemesia, nicotiana, perilla, phloxes, pyrethrums, salpiglossis, scabious, stocks (ten-week), streptocarpus, sweet peas, tagetes (African marigolds), thunbergias, zinnias,* and further sowings of those already sown earlier in the month.

CUTTINGS.—Cuttings may be taken of *abutilons, acacias, carnations (winter-flowering* or *perpetual), chrysanthemums (single late-flowering), fuchsias gardenias, geraniums* and *petunias.* Rooted cuttings of *fuchsias, geraniums, heliotropes, marguerites,* etc., should be potted on. *Dahlia roots, Marvels of Peru* and old *pelargoniums* should be placed in the warm, so that cuttings can be obtained.

POTTING.—Re-potting should be continued, plants being moved on into larger pots where necessary. *Agapanthus* and *cannas* will require attention this month.. Pot-up *abutilons, cacti* and *ferns.*

The Vegetable Garden

General Operations.—Dug-over soil should be forked up, pulverized and made ready for seed sowing. *Winter greens* that have run to seed should be taken up, being planted close together in some odd corner. The hoe must be used freely among growing crops, and to keep the birds away young plants should be dusted with soot until they are well up.

Asparagus.—New asparagus beds should, if necessary, be made. *Mint* may be lifted where necessary, being separated and replanted.

SEEDS TO SOW.—Sow in warm, sheltered positions : *Broad beans, broccoli, Brussel sprouts, cabbages, carrots, cauliflowers, corn salad, dwarf French beans, kale, kohl rabi, leeks, lettuces, mustard and cress, onions, parsley, parsnips, peas, radishes, rampion, seakale, shallots, spinach, swedes, tomatoes* and *turnips.*

PLANTING.—*Artichokes (Chinese)* and *asparagus.* Chives should be divided and planted in a sunny position. *Early peas* should be hardened off and planted out about the second week in the month in a warm, sheltered position. Also *early potatoes, horse-radish, rhubarb* and *seakale.*

Under Glass (Vegetables).—*Broad beans* sown in January and February should be planted out under glass. *Leeks* sown in January and February must now be pricked-off into fresh boxes (2 inches apart). *Mint* for forcing may be planted in a heated frame.

SEEDS TO SOW.—*Asparagus, broccoli, cucumbers, dwarf French beans, leeks, lettuces, melons, mustard and cress, onions, parsley, peas, rhubarb, seakale* and *tomatoes.* Towards the end of the month *vegetable marrows* may be sown in pots for frame or house culture.

The Fruit Garden

General Operations.—Any wall fruit coming into blossom should be protected from frost by means of canvas, netting, or by bracken fixed among the branches, and from the birds. The surface of the ground around the dwarf fruit trees should be hoed. This is the last month, until the autumn, for planting. Towards the end of the month, *apples, cherries, pears* and *plums* which were cut back in January may be grafted. The grafts should have been taken quite a month beforehand. All pruning of fruit trees, if not completed in February, should be finished early this month. New plantations of bush fruit should be made. As a general protection against insects, fruit trees should be syringed with tepid water with sulphur and soot added. Newly planted apple trees are best pruned now.

Under Glass (Fruit).—Fruit trees forced under glass must be protected against sudden changes of temperature and from cold draughts. Great care must be taken in ventilating, as the weather this month is unusually changeable.

Shrubs and Trees

General Operations.—Clean up the shrub border thoroughly. Top-dress rhododendron beds with a mixture of equal parts of decayed cow-dung and leaf-mould, and protect tender shrubs against the wind by means of boughs of evergreens and mats. Towards the end of the month various shrubs and trees may be grafted and propagation by means of division can be carried out. Deciduous shrubs and trees may be planted.

APRIL

General Garden Work

The time for digging and trenching is past, but the hoe should be kept constantly at work destroying weeds and breaking up the surface between growing plants. If there is any sign of frost, early plants and fruit blossom still require a little protection. A keen look-out must be kept for green-fly. Slugs and snails are very prevalent and must be searched for and destroyed. The lawn should be swept, cut and rolled, and paths and walks should receive attention where necessary.

The Flower Garden

General Operations.—Preparations should be made for summer bedding and bulbs should, where possible, be lifted. Staking where necessary should be seen to. *Azaleas* and tender shrubs should be protected from cold winds ; also *polyanthuses*. Tender seedlings must be protected from insects and birds, all weeds being destroyed.

Auriculas.—The trusses of auriculas which are in bloom should be thinned, deformed pips being removed. Apply weak manure water in the mornings and shade from the sun. *Ranunculuses.*— Loosen the soil around the plants as they appear above ground and water with weak manure water. *Tulips.*—Expose tulips during sunshine, but protect from frost, snow and heavy rain.

SEEDS TO SOW.—This is the chief month for sowing all *hardy annuals*, and towards the end of the month *half-hardy annuals* (except the tenderest) may be sown in the open. So may *biennials* and *perennials*, and all seeds intended to flower during the summer. Sow also *auriculas* (*Alpine*), *mignonette, polyanthuses, primroses* and *ten-week stocks. Carnation* seeds may be sown in boxes or pots and placed in a west aspect covered with a sheet of glass.

PLANTING.—*Hardy perennials* propagated by means of division. (To obtain the newest varieties, however, seed must be sown.) *Antirrhinums* (autumn sown), *aquilegias, calceolarias, carnations, dahlias, dianthus, hardy ferns, hollyhocks, irises, pansies, pentstemons, pinks, stocks, summer-flowering bulbs* (*gladiolus, tigridia,* etc.), *sunflowers, water lilies* and all other hardy plants. Continue the propagation of rock plants by means of division.

THINNING OUT.—*Autumn-sown hardy annuals*, and transplant *biennials.*

PRUNING.—*Roses* and many *shrubs* should be pruned.

STAKING.—Staking, where necessary, must be attended to, and creepers should be tied up and trained.

Under Glass (Flowers).—The temperature should be maintained at from 45° F. by night to 65° F. by day. Air should be admitted freely in mild weather and growing plants must be given plenty of water. Shade must be provided on hot days and plants requiring more space should be re-potted. All plants breaking into flower will be better for a dose of weak liquid manure. To retard the blooming of *azaleas* and similar plants, and to secure a succession, the plants should be placed on the shady side of the house. A sharp look-out for insect pests must be kept, measures to combat them being at once taken.

Aspidistras.—These may be divided up and re-potted. *Asters* and *Stocks.*—These should be pricked-off.

BEDDING PLANTS.—Preparations should be made to harden-off summer bedding plants sown in March. The tops should be pinched out to make them strong and bushy. *Begonias* and *Gloxinias.*—Should start into growth. *Calceolarias* and *Carnations.*—Calceolarias should receive their final shift and carnations should be put into their flowering pots.

CLIMBING PLANTS.—These should be trimmed and fastened up.

SEEDS TO SOW.—*Ageratum, asters, auriculas* (in shallow pans), *balsam, cinerarias, freesias, nemesia, petunias, phloxes, stocks, tree carnations* and other *half-hardy annuals* in boxes.

CUTTINGS.—Cuttings of all soft-wooded plants may now be struck. *Fuchsias* may still be started in heat and cuttings obtained.

POTTING.—Re-potting should be continued where necessary. *Azaleas* should be re-potted after they have finished flowering.

The Vegetable Garden

General Operations.—The ground must be prepared for the reception of *Brussel sprouts, cauliflowers, lettuces,* etc., grown in frames. The ground should also be got ready for *runner beans,* and *celery* trenches should be dug. There is still a danger of frost and provision should be made for this. Young plants should receive protection from birds.

Asparagus.—New beds may still be made. *Cabbages.*—Spring cabbages should be given a stimulant in the form of nitrate of soda (1 oz. to the square yard). *Cucumbers, Marrows* and *Tomatoes.*—Beds should be prepared for these. *Mushrooms.*—Beds for these may be made up now. *Peas.*—Early peas will appreciate a dusting of sulphate of ammonia 1 oz. and sulphate of potash ½ oz. to the square yard. *Potatoes.*—These should have the soil drawn up to protect them from frost.

SEEDS TO SOW.—All kinds of herbs, salading, and vegetables may now be sown in the open. *Beetroot* or *Red Beet* should be sown where it is not shaded from the sun at any time. A late sowing of *broccoli* should be made ; also of *kale*. *Chicory* should be sown in chalky soil. About the middle of the month the main crop

of *carrots* should be sown. If a warm corner is available, a sowing
of *French beans* may be made. *Salading* may be sown with protection. *Spinach* may still be sown in the shade, and in drills *kohl
rabi, rampion* and *salsify.*

PLANTING.—*Artichokes (Globe)* [suckers], *artichokes (Jerusalem)* if
not already done, *asparagus* (one year old), *borecole* or *kale* (six weeks
old), *Brussel sprouts, cabbages, potatoes* (main crop), *rhubarb, seakale,*
and *early vegetable marrows.* *Marjoram, mint, pennyroyal, sage,
thyme,* etc., should be lifted, divided and planted out.

THINNING OUT.—*Carrots, onions, parsnips,* etc., as necessary.

Under Glass (Vegetables).—SEEDS TO SOW.—*Beans (runner),
cardoons, cucumbers, marrows* and *melons.*

PRICKING-OFF.—Main *celery* crop and *tomato* seedlings.

HARDENING-OFF.—*Brussel sprouts, cauliflowers, lettuces,* etc.

The Fruit Garden

General Operations.—Grafting should be finished early this
month. All trees should have been pruned. Protection to blossom
on wall fruit should be continued, and syringing with quassia-
chips and soft-soap solution should be carried out. The planting
of fruit trees should be over; if absolutely essential to do this now,
roots should be well protected by covering the ground with long
stable manure or pebbles laid on a bed of sand. Keep the roots
of wall trees moist, and attend to staking where necessary.

Apple and *Pear Trees.*—Syringe with a summer wash to destroy
apple sucker and midge. *Black Currants.*—Dust or spray bushes
affected with big-bud with lime and sulphur mixture every other
week.

Peaches and *nectarines* may be summer-pruned.

Under Glass (Fruit).—Constant vigilance must be exercised in
maintaining the temperature, since the weather is changeable.

Apricots, nectarines and *peaches* should be fertilized by means
of a feather or rabbit's tail passed from flower to flower.

Figs should have their leaves syringed daily, and the temperature
should be kept at 60° F. *Grapes* require thinning, the seedless
and small berries being removed first. *Strawberries* under glass
should be given plenty of air when in bloom.

Shrubs and Trees

General Operations.—As last month. Certain shrubs and trees
may still be grafted and propagated by means of division. Gaps
in *Box Edging* should be made good, the plants being well watered
and trimmed. *Azaleas* and the shrubs mentioned for planting
last month may still be put in.

MAY

General Garden Work

May is the last month during which any considerable amount of planting out should be done. The work entails much labour in thinning out seedlings, planting out, and hoeing. If the weather should turn dry, watering may have to be done, but this should be left as long as possible, as the plants will thrive better. It should not be undertaken unless absolutely essential.

The Flower Garden

General Operations.—Towards the end of the month many half-hardy annuals which have been raised under glass will have to be planted out.

Bulbs.—All spring-flowering bulbs which are to be taken up must be lifted and replanted in some odd corner until the foliage has died down. They should be lifted again and stored as soon as the foliage is dried.

Carnations, Picotees and *Pinks.*—These should be kept free from dead leaves, the surrounding soil being stirred occasionally and a little fresh mould added. Side stalks should be removed from the main stems, nothing but top buds being left. *Sweet Peas.*— These will require attention as regards supporting and tying up.

Climbing Plants.—Fasten up and support where necessary.

Roses.—A little manure forked into the soil will benefit roses.

Seeds to Sow.—*Aquilegia, asters, auriculas, Brompton stocks, cobæa, delphiniums, eccremocarpus, forget-me-nots, foxgloves, gypsophila, hardy annuals* (for succession), *night-scented stocks, polyanthus* and *primroses.*

Planting.—*Abronias, antirrhinums, begonias, calceolarias, dahlias* (in pots), *hydrangeas* (in pots), *half-hardy bedding plants, scabious, violets,* etc. Spring-flowering plants such as *arabis, aubrietia, daisies* and *primroses* should be divided. Late-flowering *annuals* should be planted out.

Staking.—All plants which require it should be staked and pegged down as planting proceeds.

Thinning Out.—All *annuals* must be thinned and transplanted where necessary.

Under Glass (Flowers).—If the greenhouse is not used very much during the summer months, it should be cleaned thoroughly at any convenient time from now onwards. Pits and frames, also, should be cleaned as they become vacant. The temperature should remain at 45° F. by night and 65° F. by day. Water must be given regularly and a moist atmosphere maintained by means of damping floors, syringing, etc. Plenty of air and shade must be given where necessary. A sharp look-out for insect pests must be kept.

Azaleas should have old flowers and seed-vessels picked off. Re-pot if necessary. *Balsams* and *celosias* should be plunged in a frame or pit. *Calceolarias* coming into bloom require ample water. *Carnations.*—Malmaison Carnations should be given a little liquid manure twice a week and should be shaded when they begin to form flower buds. *Pelargoniums* should have their shoots tied out as far apart as possible to admit the air freely. They require plenty of liquid manure twice a week.

BULBS.—Move bulbs that have done flowering out of doors.

SHRUBS.—Wood that has borne flowers must be cut away and the bushes should be thinned out. Shrubs in the house should be hardened off for planting out.

SEEDS TO SOW.—*Achimenes, begonias, cinerarias* (in cold frame), *herbaceous calceolarias, coleuses, gloxinias, primulas,* etc.

CUTTINGS.—Cuttings of most plants may be taken now.

POTTING.—All plants should be re-potted as it becomes necessary.

THINNING.—Carefully thin out all seedlings that are fit to handle.

The Vegetable Garden

General Operations.—The hoe must be kept moving between rows of growing plants, and a sharp look-out for insects and pests must be maintained. *Artichokes (Globe).*—The soil should be well stirred and the shoots reduced to three. The offsets should be planted and watered copiously. *Asparagus.*—When cutting asparagus, the shoots should be cut as they reach about 6 inches in height. *Herbs.*— *Balm, mint, marjoram, savory, thyme* and other herbs may be increased by means of slips.

SEEDS TO SOW.—Seeds of all vegetables sown in March and April may still be sown for succession. *Runner beans* may be sown in quantity, and if the weather is good, *French* or *kidney beans* also. *Broccoli* and *globe beetroot* may be sown right on into July. *Peas* may be sown for August picking. *Saladings.*—A successional sowing of *lettuces, mustard and cress, radishes,* etc., may be made. *Herbs.*—Sow *chervil* and *parsley* for winter use.

PLANTING.—*Brussel sprouts* (in well-limed land), *cauliflowers* (early sown), *celery, celeriac, kohl rabi, leeks, onions* (sown in boxes in January), *marrows* (if weather is favourable, but protect on cold nights), *potatoes* (a few late ones may still be planted), *pumpkins, savoys* and *tomatoes.*

Under Glass (Vegetables).—*Carrots, potatoes* and other vegetables, which have been grown in frames, will be ready for table. After replacing the old soil with fresh and re-lining, similar crops may be planted again, or the frames may be employed for raising *tomatoes* prior to planting out in the open. *Borecole* or *kale* (six weeks old), *beans* (*runner*), sown last month, should be planted out. *Cucumbers.*—The frames in which cucumbers are growing should be closed about 4.30 p.m., and should be opened as early in the morning as the weather allows. They should be watered before closing at night, for they require a moist atmosphere. Pinch back the undergrowth and peg down the stems. *Melons.*—The pits for the principal summer crop of melons should be prepared now, the plants being put out when the bed is ready. They should be settled with warm water and afterwards watered twice a week. *Vegetable marrows* may be planted under hand-lights.

The Fruit Garden

General Operations.—All fruit trees on dry ground will be benefited by a mulch of manure round the roots. The fruit should be thinned out to half a dozen on newly planted trees. *Apricot* shoots should be pinched back. *Gooseberries.*—A look-out should be kept for the eggs of the Gooseberry Moth and the leaves should be dusted with Hellebore Powder. *Morello cherries* should be disbudded, also *peaches* and *nectarines*. *Raspberry* suckers should be thinned out, leaving only 4–6 to each stool. *Strawberry* runners not required for making young plants should be cut off, strawy litter being placed between the plants.

Under Glass (Fruit).—In hot weather, trees should be syringed with water. *Peaches.*—If the trees were put forward in December, they will stand forcing freely—the house being kept fairly dry, but as much air as possible being given. To ripen the fruit, any leaves that may shade it should be taken off. *Figs.*—Watering should be discontinued if the fruit has started to ripen. If in tubs and a second crop is coming on, manure water should be given in moderation. *Grapes.*—The early crop will now be colouring; a temperature of about 65° F. should be maintained. Air should be given freely and the fruit kept perfectly dry. The later crop will be flowering; the temperature should be kept at 65° F. to 70° F., according to variety, until the fruit is wholly set.

Shrubs and Trees

General Operations.—Evergreens and hedges should be clipped before the young growth has advanced too far. Spring-flowering shrubs must be pruned. *Azaleas* and numerous other shrubs may still be planted. If planting in the autumn was impossible, broadleaved evergreens and conifers, such as *hollies, red cedars, evergreen oaks* and *Portugal laurels*, may be planted. They root more freely now than in the early spring.

JUNE

General Garden Work

Hoeing and watering are both of the utmost importance. The hoe must be kept constantly at work between the rows of growing plants, since weeds now grow very rapidly and will soon choke the crops. Generous watering is essential in very dry weather. The soil must be kept as moist as possible by mulching and by stirring the surface. The remains of all crops which have been gathered should be removed. A sharp look-out for pests should be maintained, the pest being dealt with immediately.

The Flower Garden

General Operations.—Bedding-out, if not already finished, should be completed as early as possible. *Anchusas, delphiniums, doronicums, lupins,* etc., should be cut down as the flowers fade, the roots being mulched with manure and watered regularly. The best kinds should be marked for obtaining seed. Failures must be removed, being replaced by new plants. *Carnations (early)* require disbudding and staking. *Dahlia* shoots require thinning out. *Pinks* should have their top bud pinched out. *Ranunculus* should be shaded as soon as they begin to show colour. *Roses* require the application of liquid manure, and towards the end of this month may be budded. *Sweet peas* should have an occasional dose of liquid manure and should be attended to generally. *Violets* should have their runners pinched back as soon as they appear.

Bulbs.—If not already taken up, should be lifted, dried off and stored.

Seeds to Sow.—All kinds of *biennials* and *perennials* can be sown, also quick-flowering *annuals* for late blooming.

Planting.—*Half-hardy annuals* raised in frames. Spring-flowering plants should be divided and planted out. *Begonias* may also be planted out. *Irises* which have finished flowering should be divided and replanted.

Cuttings.—A plot should be prepared in the reserve garden for cuttings of *rockets, sweet williams* and *double wallflowers* for next spring's blooming. Cuttings of *Alyssum saxatilis* may be inserted under a hand-glass.

Thinning Out.—Seedlings of all kinds.

Staking.—*Carnations* should be staked and tied loosely. *Dahlias* and *sweet peas* require attention.

Under Glass.—Plenty of air should be given. Fumigation and syringing for insects should be attended to. The greenhouse must

31

be shaded unless the roof is covered with creepers, the floor being damped to keep the atmosphere moist, and all faded blooms should be removed. Artificial heating should no longer be needed, unless the weather turns very damp and cold. *Achimenes* and *gloxinias* should be moved to more airy quarters. *Azaleas* and *camellias* should have a damp growing heat all the time they are making wood. Towards the end of the month, they may be stood outdoors on ashes in a semi-shaded position. *Ferns* should be stood in a place where they will receive plenty of light, but not too much sun. *Gladioli* and *Japanese lilies* should have the glass taken off unless very early blooms are desired. A number should be kept in the shade of a north wall to secure a succession of bloom. *Heaths* and numerous *tender shrubs* may be hardened-off and stood outdoors.

SEEDS TO SOW.—*Calceolarias* (*herbaceous*) for next year's flowering, *cinerarias, cyclamen, primula malacoides* and *p. obconica*, also various *rock plants* for autumn planting : *aubrietia, alyssum, campanulas, candytuft* (*Iberis*), *carnations, dianthus, geraniums, linaria, saxifrages,* etc.

CUTTINGS.—Cuttings of *pelargoniums* may be taken, also root cuttings of *verbenas* in a close frame.

POTTING.—All plants that require more room should be re-potted. *Begonias* sown in February may be potted up. *Carnations, chrysanthemums* and *fuchsias* should be moved into their flowering pots.

CLEANING AND REPAINTING.—Now is probably the most convenient time for renovations and decorations.

The Vegetable Garden

General Operations.—Hoeing and watering are of the utmost importance, and pests must be guarded against. *Asparagus.*—This should not be cut later than the middle of this month. *Broad Beans.*—The main crop should be gathered and the plants watered to promote a further crop. *Cauliflowers.*—A little liquid manure should be given to early cauliflowers, a leaf being broken over the flower to shade it. *Lettuces.*—If watered copiously, these are not so likely to run to seed. *Mushroom* beds may be made outdoors, and will bear by August. *Onions* (autumn-sown).—A final topdressing of nitrate of soda should be given. *Peas.*—These should be picked off regularly. The more you pick, the more the plants will produce. *Potatoes* may still be earthed-up. Any cleared this month may be followed by late *celery* or *winter turnips*. *Runner beans* need supports. *Seakale* should be dressed with salt. *Shallots.*—These should be dressed with nitrate of soda (2 oz. to the square yard). *Vegetable marrow* plants which were planted out last month should be stopped to encourage them to make shoots.

From the Painting by]   [Flora Pilkington

A CORNER OF THE PAVED GARDEN

SEEDS TO SOW.—*Beans.*—A last sowing of these should be made early in the month. *Cardoons, chicory* and *colewort* should also be sown. *Cucumbers* may be sown on ridges outdoors. *Endive* and *Lettuce.*—Every fortnight a sowing should be made. *Mustard and cress, peas, radishes, spinach* and *swedes* may be sown. *Turnips.*— The main sowing should be made.

PLANTING.—*Borecole* (six weeks old), *broccoli, cardoons, cauliflowers* and *celery.* They should be planted out in wet, showery weather. *Leeks, ridge cucumbers, savoys,* for October use, should also be planted. *Tomatoes* may still be planted out. *Vegetable Marrows.*— Plant these if not already out.

THINNING OUT.—The main crops of *beetroots, carrots, onions,* also *parsley, salsify* and *scorzonera.*

The Fruit Garden

General Operations.—All trees require mulching. Any superfluous growths on fruit trees of every kind should be thinned out and stopped. Over-vigorous shoots on young trees should be cut back. Heavily laden trees need support. If Mildew makes its appearance, spray with a liver of sulphur solution ($\frac{1}{2}$ oz. to a gallon of water). Green-fly should be attended to, insecticides being applied where necessary. *Cherry trees* should have the shoots stopped and nets arranged to save the fruit. *Currant* and *Gooseberry Bushes.*— If caterpillars appear, the bushes should be sprayed with lime water or soot water. Some green gooseberries may be picked, but a proportion should be allowed to ripen for dessert. Young side shoots on currant bushes must be pinched back. *Grapes.*—Any wood that is not wanted should be thinned out on outdoor vines and leading shoots should be fastened to the wall. *Loganberries* may be propagated by means of layering. *Peaches* and *apricots* should be thinned if necessary. *Pear, plum,* and *cherry trees* will require disbudding. *Raspberries.*—All surplus and weak canes should be pulled to ensure a good crop. *Strawberries.*—These must be watered copiously, runners being layered.

Shrubs and Trees

General Operations.—Tie up and support trees where needed. Syringe the foliage of newly-planted shrubs (especially evergreens) every evening in hot, dry weather, and mulch whenever possible. Remove seed-vessels from *rhododendrons* and other similar plants as soon as they go out of bloom; give a good soaking with manure-water made from cow-dung and mulch the roots. Propagation of most shrubs can now be carried out by means of cuttings of young shoots in a frame.

E.G.   C

JULY

General Garden Work

Hoeing, weeding and watering will be necessary throughout the month. Top-dressing round the bases of shrubs and trees and between growing crops is of great value.

The Flower Garden

General Operations.—All dead flowers should be picked off. Plants as they grow will require staking and tying. *Carnations* may be layered. *Chrysanthemums* that are growing too tall should have the tops pinched out. *Dahlias* should be given a mulch of manure and staking requires attention. Flowering plants, such as *fuchsias* and *geraniums*, should be watered regularly. *Rock plants* may be propagated by means of cuttings. *Roses* should be budded. A mulch of stable manure will help them on.

BULBS which have not already been shifted should be taken up and any offsets should be prepared for planting.

SEEDS TO SOW.—*Perennial* and *biennial* plants for flowering the following year, as *Hollyhocks*, for example. *Pansies* may be sown outdoors in boxes.

PLANTING.—Seedlings of all kinds. All *bedding plants* in the reserve garden should be planted out. *Biennials* and *perennials* should be transplanted, and seedling *ranunculus* should be planted out.

CUTTINGS.—Cuttings of hardy plants may be taken and placed under hand-lights, so may *rose* cuttings.

Under Glass (Flowers).—Copious watering will be required by all plants under glass. It is generally possible to give air all night without risk. A sharp look-out for pests must be kept. Plants that have finished flowering should be cut down, and bulbs should be matured and ripened. If the greenhouse has not already been thoroughly cleaned, an attempt should be made at the beginning of this month. *Carnations* that have flowered should be layered. *Carnations* in pots and *chrysanthemums* will need staking and tying. *Climbing plants* require a lot of attention ; new shoots should be tied up, never being allowed to straggle. *Roses* may be pruned.

SEEDS TO SOW.—*Border carnations*, also *Brompton* and *Intermediate stocks* for winter-flowering in greenhouse. *Herbaceous calceolarias* for spring-flowering, also *pinks*.

PRICKING OUT.—*Cinerarias* sown two months previously.

POTTING.—All those plants which need it should be re-potted. *Cyclamen* should be moved into flowering pots, old plants being started in fresh soil. *Primulas* should be moved into their flowering pots. *Rhododendrons* and *azaleas* should be stood outdoors.

The Vegetable Garden

General Operations.—After the crops have been gathered, all *cabbage* stalks, *bean* stalks, and *pea* haulms should be removed. *Artichokes* (*Globe*).—The head should be cut when about three parts open. *Carrots.*—These should be mulched (in wet weather) with well-rotted manure and soot. *Mint* and other *Sweet Herbs* should be cut for drying. *Mushroom* beds should be made in the open. *Parsley* that is running to seed should be pulled out. *Potatoes.*—A final earthing-up should be given. *Runner Beans.*—Sticks or strings must be provided and ample water given. *Shallots.*—All loose soil that may be covering these should be pulled away and they will ripen well. *Tomatoes.*—Tops and side shoots must be pinched off. *Vegetable Marrows.*—An abundance of tepid water should be given.

SEEDS TO SOW.—*Cabbages, coleworts, mustard and cress, endive, kohl rabi, lettuces, onions, parsley, radishes* (as catch crop), *spinach* (*prickly-seeded*), and *turnips*.

THINNING OUT.—The *beetroot* crop must be kept thinned out and the hoe busy.

PLANTING.—*Borecole* or *kale* (six weeks old), *broccoli, celery, colewort* and *endive*. *Sage, savory*, etc., can be propagated by cuttings or division and planted out.

The Fruit Garden

General Operations.—Fruit on all overcrowded trees should be thinned, all unnecessary growths being removed. Water should be given generously if the weather is very dry, the surface of the ground being kept well hoed and mulched. Fruit trees may be budded when the weather is moist. Espalier and dwarf fruit trees should be trained, and ripening fruit protected from birds. Before fruit begins to ripen, *apricots, cherries, figs* and *plums* on walls should be attended to, all shoots that are not required being removed. *Apple trees* attacked by mildew must be sprayed with Bordeaux Mixture and diseased branches cut off. *Cherries* and *plums* may be budded. *Loganberries* and *strawberries* may be layered.

Shrubs and Trees

General Operations.—Hoeing, hand-weeding and raking are essential throughout this month. Cut away all dead foliage. Trim *privet* and *quick* hedges with the shears ; but cut back large-leaved plants, such as *laurels*, with a knife. Shrubs of *box* and *yew* that are to be grown in eccentric forms should be clipped now and trained in the desired directions. Propagation of most shrubs can be carried out by means of layering and by cuttings in a frame.

AUGUST

General Garden Work

All dead flowers, stalks and leaves should be removed. Watering, mulching and hoeing constitute the chief work in the garden during the summer months.

The Flower Garden

General Operations.—Hoeing, weeding, watering and mulching, etc. *Antirrhinums.*—Dead flower spikes must be cut down. *Carnations* and *pinks* should be layered. *Clematis, honeysuckle* and *wistaria* should be trained before the shoots become too long. *Dahlias.*—Show plants should be disbudded, staking should be seen to and earwigs trapped. *Lavender* hedges may be trimmed. *Pentstemons.*—Dead flower spikes must be cut down. *Roses* may still be budded. *Sweet peas* require ample water and doses of liquid manure. All dead flowers must be picked off. *Tulip* beds should be cleared, the bulbs being placed on one side in boxes or drawers for future use.

SEEDS TO SOW.—All sorts of *annuals* may be sown for spring flowering. *Antirrhinums, pansies, Iceland poppies,* and *violas.* Early in the month *Intermediate stocks* should be sown ; about the middle of the month *Ten-week stocks.*

CUTTINGS.—Cuttings of all kinds of hardy plants and bedding plants may be struck in sandy soil. *Geraniums* should be propagated now. *Pansies* and *Violas.*—Cuttings may still be struck. *Roses.*—Cuttings of *Bourbon, China, Hybrid Perpetual* and *Noisette Roses* may be struck. *Saxifrages.*—The offsets arising from the sides of the plants should be taken off and planted in borders or pots.

PLANTING.—*Amaryllis, colchicum, cyclamen, Guernsey lily* and *narcissi* in beds, borders or pots. First-struck cuttings of *carnations* and *picotees* may now be planted out ; some should be potted to fill vacant spaces. Seedlings of *biennials* must be pricked-off and transplanted. Seedlings of *perennials* should be transplanted where crowded, and spring-flowering *perennials* should be divided and replanted. Old bulbs and bulbs in grass should be replanted.

Under Glass (Flowers).—Work should be continued as for June and July. Plants stood outdoors require constant attention ; every evening they should be well syringed. *Achimenes.*—As these go out of bloom, they should be placed in a frame to ripen the tubers. *Azaleas* (late-flowering).—These must be re-potted and so trained that the foliage is properly drawn out before winter. *Chrysanthemums* should be disbudded. *Climbing plants* should be cut back to keep the place in order. *Lilies* that have flowered require less water. *Pelargoniums.*—Preparatory to cutting these down, those which have gone out of flower should be stood outdoors to ripen the wood.

SEEDS TO SOW.—All sorts of *annuals* for winter flowering. *Clarkia, cyclamen, geraniums* and *pelargoniums, schizanthus* and *stocks.*

CUTTINGS.—Cuttings of *arabis* and various other hardy rock plants may now be struck. Also *fuchsias, geraniums, heliotrope, hydrangeas* and all *half-hardy* plants.

POTTING.—*Camellias.*—If these were not shifted last month, this should be done now. *Calceolarias, Chinese primroses* and *cinerarias* should be potted off from seed-boxes when large enough. *Chrysanthemums.*—The potting-up should be completed. *Cyclamen* should be re-potted into flowering pots, old plants being started. *Freesias* and *Roman Hyacinths* should be potted for flowering in December. *Lachenalias* benefit by early potting. *Primulas* should be divided and should be replanted in 6-inch pots.

The Vegetable Garden

General Operations.—*Bean* stalks and the remains of gathered crops should be removed. A row or two of *French beans* should be left for seed. Pests demand continual attention and must be exterminated. *Globe Artichokes.*—These must be cut down as the heads are gathered. They must not be allowed to flower. *Asparagus.*—Beds must be kept clear of weeds. Unless seed is wanted, the bearing heads should be cut off. *Broccoli* that are heading should be given plenty of water. *Cabbages.*—To make cabbages heart, give a pinch of sulphate of ammonia at the base and hoe it in. *Cauliflowers.*—Break a leaf over the head to protect the flower. *Celery.*—Any side shoots should be cut away, and ample water and liquid manure should be applied. *Cucumbers, ridge tomatoes* and *vegetable marrows* require the same attention as during July. *Garlic* may be taken up this month. It should be ripened in the same way as onions and shallots. *Mint* and other *herbs* may still be picked. *Onions* that are ripe may be harvested. *Potatoes (early),* which are being reserved for seed, should be dug up and spread in the sun. *Runner beans* should be stopped when they reach the top of the sticks, the beans being picked as soon as ready. *Shallots* can be harvested in many places. *Turnip* seedlings may be dusted with slaked or ground lime to keep the fly in check. *Vegetable marrows* can be cut when 7 or 8 inches long ; they are excellent for table at this stage and the plants will prove more productive.

EARTHING-UP.—*Cardoons* (end of the month), *celery* and *leeks.*

SEEDS TO SOW.—*Cauliflowers* (for early summer), *colewort, corn salad, endive* (a few rows for early crop), *lettuce* (every fortnight), *onions* (for next season). *Radishes, small saladings, red cabbage* (on tilled ground) and *spinach* (for winter use), also *turnips*.

PLANTING.—*Broccoli, cabbages, celery* (do not earth-up until November), *coleworts, endive, late greens* (in shady beds).

Under Glass (Vegetables).—*General Operations.—Cucumbers.*—Bottom heat in frames should be renewed if it is declining and mildew must be kept down by means of sulphur. If cucumbers are started on beds now, they will continue bearing until Christmas. *Melons.* —As the fruit approaches ripeness the beds should be gradually dried off.

SEEDS TO SOW.—*Cauliflower* (sow seed in a frame, but uncover as soon as the seed is up).

The Fruit Garden

General Operations.—Wall fruit, as it ripens, should be protected from wasps and birds. Earwigs and snails should be trapped. The fruit should be exposed to the sun as much as possible. Summer-pruning may be continued, and fruit trees may be budded. Bands round fruit trees should be examined, the pests being destroyed. Nets used for protecting strawberries, raspberries and currants can be used for loganberries and plums. *Apples, pears* and *plums* require thinning out if the crop is too heavy. *Apricots, peaches* and *nectarines* should be exposed to the sun as much as possible. *Cherry* trees should be washed as soon as the fruit has been gathered. *Loganberries* and *Raspberries.*—Canes that have borne fruit should be cut down. *Plums* are best ripened off in a semi-dark store. *Strawberries.*—All unwanted runners must be taken off, the straw litter being removed to allow the sun to get to the crowns. New beds may now be planted.

Under Glass (Fruit).—*Peaches* and *Nectarines.*—After the fruit has been gathered the plants should be syringed well daily and given free ventilation. Fruit trees in pots should be stood outdoors after the fruit has been gathered. *Strawberries* for forcing may be moved into 6–7 inch pots and should have ample water. Precautions against wasps must be taken.

Shrubs and Trees

General Operations.—Dead flowers and stalks should be removed (except, of course, in the case of berry-bearing species and varieties), straggling shoots being shortened or tied down, all weeds being raked off and water applied when required. Hedges may now be clipped and trimmed, and propagation may be carried out by means of cuttings and layering.

SEPTEMBER

General Garden Work

Keeping the garden tidy is the principal work of the month. Dead flowers should be picked off. *Pea*-haulms and vegetable refuse must be collected, being then covered with earth and allowed to rot. The collection and drying of certain seeds needs to be done. As ground becomes vacant, it should be dug and manured. Lawns need sweeping, and this is the best month for sowing grass and for making new lawns.

The Flower Garden

General Operations.—Peat, leaf-mould and other soils should be collected and stacked for future use. The tall flowering-plants should have plenty of support ; they will need it, for heavy winds are prevalent this month. The hoe should be kept busy and weeds should be destroyed. *Climbing plants* should be cut back, being fastened up where necessary. *Dahlias* should be tied up, disbudded, and the shoots should be thinned. Earwigs should be trapped and choice blooms should be protected against the sun's rays. *Hollyhocks* should be treated in the same way. *Rock plants* require attention. They should be trimmed and cut back where necessary, being propagated by means of division or by cuttings. *Roses.*— Perpetual roses may still be cut back, and late briars may still be budded. *Stocks* that were budded early in the season should have the ligatures loosened so that growth will not be retarded ; wild shoots from the stock being shortened back to about ten leaves if the bud is still dormant.

SEEDS TO SOW.—For flowering the following spring or early summer suitable hardy *annuals* should be sown. A few *antirrhinums* sown now may last through the winter. *Sweet peas* may be sown.

CUTTINGS.—Cuttings of *ageratums, antirrhinums, blue marguerites, centaureas, fuchsias, gazanias, hollyhocks, lobelias, zonal pelargoniums* (geraniums), *heliotropes, pentstemons, petunias, roses,* all *bedding plants*, and many Alpines can now be struck.

PLANTING.—*Anemones* and *spring-flowering bulbs*, such as *crocuses, montbretia, narcissi, scillas, snowdrops,* etc., but not *tulips. Irises* and hardy *liliums* can also be planted. The transplanting of numerous early-flowering *herbaceous plants* and *evergreen shrubs* and *conifers* may now be carried out. *Box Edging* may be replanted. *Carnations.*—Rooted layers and seedlings may be planted out. *Pansies.*—Early-rooted pansy cuttings may be planted out and seedlings can be pricked out in the reserve garden. Offsets of *polyanthuses* and *auriculas,* and seedlings of the former, should be planted out in the reserve garden.

39

Under Glass.—Damping down should not be effected quite so often in the greenhouse. The assistance of a little heat will be needed for plants like *coleuses* and *iresines*. The plants can do with the sun now, so the shading may be washed off. Ventilation should be given freely during warm periods, water being applied carefully. *Achimenes*, *begonias* and *gloxinias* should be watered until the foliage fades. *Achimenes* and *gloxinias* may then be removed from pots to be stored. *Begonia* tubers should remain in the soil and should be kept frost-proof. *Climbers.*—Any climbers that have finished flowering should be trimmed. *Sub-tropical plants* outdoors should be brought inside now. *Chrysanthemums* for winter decoration should be brought indoors. *Heaths* should be examined for mildew. *Violets* should be lifted and planted near the glass in frames, plenty of air being given. Syringing should be attended to daily.

SEEDS TO SOW.—*Clarkia, godetia* and *schizanthus*. Also *pansies* and *violas*.

CUTTINGS.—Cuttings of *bedding* and *rock plants* may now be taken. *Buddleias* and *ceanothus* cuttings should be struck in a cold frame. All cuttings taken last month should be hardened off.

POTTING.—*Calceolarias* and *Cinerarias*. Suckers from old shoots should be potted off and seedling plants should be potted on. Hardy and half-hardy plants for room and conservatory should also be potted up. *Chrysanthemums* should be shifted and other plants potted on as necessary. *Pelargoniums* intended to flower the following May or June should be ready for removal to flowering pots. As soon as they are sufficiently ripe, plants for late summer and autumn flowering should be potted off or placed in frames. *Stocks* which were sown in pans, or in reserve garden, in August, should also be potted up.

The Vegetable Garden

General Operations.—Frequent hoeing between growing crops is still important. *Onions* should have their necks bent down. Those which are ripe should be harvested. *Potatoes* should be lifted when the haulms decay. *Tomatoes.*—Leaves shading the fruit from the sun should be picked off and fruit should be thinned if necessary.

SEEDS TO SOW.—*Borecole* or *kale* (spring varieties), *cauliflowers, chervil, corn salad, mustard and cress* (for succession), *onions, radishes, spinach* and *watercress*.

PLANTING.—*Cabbages* (on ground vacated by onions), *coleworts, endive, kohl rabi, lettuces* (sheltered spot), *savoys* (sown towards end of July or early August), *winter greens*, etc.

EARTHING-UP.—*Celery* and *onions*.

Under Glass (Vegetables).—*Cucumbers* should be cut as soon as fit for use. The management of the frames will depend upon the stage of growth of the plants. *Melons* approaching ripeness should be placed on slates or boards to keep the fruit from contact with the ground. *Endive* and *lettuce* should be pricked out. *Parsley* may be lifted now and planted in a cold frame. *Tomatoes* sown in August should be potted off singly into small pots.

SEEDS TO SOW.—*Cauliflowers* and *lettuce* may be sown. Also *parsley* and *tomatoes* (for early spring).

The Fruit Garden

General Operations.—All wall fruit which is now ripening should be protected. Fruit trees may still be budded ; summer pruning may be continued. Trees that need root pruning should be attended to. This is a good time to buy new fruit trees. *Apples*, *pears* and *plums.*—If the crops are too heavy, they should be thinned, and grease bands should be applied where necessary. Early varieties of *apples* and *pears* which do not keep must be gathered, and all young shoots on *pear trees* should be stopped. *Apricots*, *peaches* and *nectarines* should have their future bearing shoots nailed in closely. A final thinning should be made, any leaves that shade the fruit being removed. *Cherries* require very little shortening back, but cut away cross and interior shoots in standard trees and spur back those shoots which are too close together. *Currants.*—These should have all side sprays pruned away. *Gooseberries.*—All shoots should be stopped and thinned. *Raspberry* canes that have fruited should be cut down and the young growths thinned out to from four to six. These should be stopped when sufficiently high. *Strawberries.*—All superfluous runners should be removed ; these may be replanted if new plants are wanted.

Under Glass (Fruit).—*Grapes.*—A dry atmosphere and a cool temperature should be maintained in the vinery. *Peaches.*—The early Peach house should have the lights removed for four or six weeks ; if this is not possible, ample ventilation must be afforded.

Shrubs and Trees

General Operations.—September is generally a fairly busy month in the garden, but if time can be spared, it pays to go over the shrub border. All weeds should be removed, the ground around shrubs and trees should be forked over in order to let in air ; all dead or weak-growing shrubs should be cleared out. Cuttings of numerous shrubs may be taken and propagation carried out by means of division and layering. *Evergreen Shrubs* and *Conifers* may be planted.

OCTOBER

General Garden Work

Leaves should be swept from lawns and paths, being heaped up in an odd corner of the garden, where they are left to decay after being covered lightly with moist earth. All vacant ground should be made ready for planting. The first frosts may make their appearance this month, hence the need for taking all tender plants indoors or otherwise protecting them. Preparation should be made for any alterations in the design of the rock garden or the flower garden, the plants being removed to the reserve garden. Gravel paths and walks should be rolled and repaired where necessary. Turf should be laid this month.

The Flower Garden

General Operations.—*China asters* and plants of a similar nature that have flowered can be lifted, put into pots, and taken indoors to bloom. *Carnations, pinks, auriculas, polyanthuses,* etc., should be placed in winter quarters. *Anemone* beds should be prepared and the tubers may be planted this month. *Bulbs.*—The main planting of *tulips* should be made; practically all spring bulbs that have not been planted should be got in without delay. *Dahlia* and *hollyhock* seed should be gathered. *Dahlia* tubers must be lifted and stored. Choice *hollyhocks* should be potted up and wintered under glass. *Eranthis* (winter aconite) may be planted or propagated by division. *Gladioli* corms should be lifted.

Propagation.—All kinds of *herbaceous* plants may be divided and replanted.

Cuttings.—Cuttings of *anagallis, bouvardias, calceolarias, cerastiums, periwinkles, phloxes, ragwort, roses, salvias, various shrubs, verbenas,* etc., can now be struck.

Seed to Sow.—*Sweet peas* may be sown.

Planting.—*Biennial* and *perennial* seedlings, *spring-flowering* plants of all descriptions, also seedling *pansies.*

Under Glass (Flowers).—The nights are apt to be frosty, so the temperature of the greenhouse must be watched carefully. Air must be cautiously given and cold winds avoided. All plants before being taken into the greenhouse should be thoroughly examined and carefully cleaned. *Pelargoniums.*—Great care must be exercised in watering as the leaves must be kept dry. No syringing or sprinkling is permitted. Seedlings, such as *clarkia, schizanthus* and *sweet peas,* should have their tops pinched out. *Begonia* tubers may now be stored. *Calceolarias* (shrubby).—Cuttings of these may be taken. *Camellias* require attention. *Carnations* (*perpetual*) and *chrysanthemums* require disbudding.

42

POTTING.—*Arum lilies* should be re-potted. After *bulbs* have been potted for forcing, they should be left plunged in ashes until the shoots are ¼ inch long, when they should be removed to a cold frame, being shaded from strong light for a few days. *Hardy* and *half-hardy* plants for indoor flowering should be potted up. Pot *roses* should be brought in from the open. Cuttings of *pansies* may be potted up for indoor flowering.

The Vegetable Garden

General Operations.—The hoe must be kept busy between growing crops. The ground should be cleared after *beans* and *peas* and dug or trenched so that it may lie fallow during the winter. All roots to be stored must be sound. *Asparagus.*—Asparagus foliage should be well-ripened before being cut down. *Beetroot* and *carrots* should be lifted when the tops fade. *Cauliflowers* grown from seed in August should be pricked out and protected with a hand-glass. *Onions* and *Turnips.*—Seed-beds should be thinned. *Potatoes.*—Any remaining potatoes should be dug and stored for winter use.

EARTHING-UP.—*Cardoons* (choosing dry weather), *celery* and *leeks*.

SEEDS TO SOW.—*Corn salad* and *early peas* (under a fence or on a warm south border). *Radishes* and *spinach* may still be sown.

PLANTING.—*Cabbages*, *endive* and *lettuces* may be transplanted to a warm border or into cold frames. *Rhubarb* may be planted.

Under Glass (Vegetables).—*Cauliflowers.*—Cauliflower seedlings should be pricked out and placed in frames. Those sown in frames last month should be thinned. *Endive* and *lettuces* can be had until Christmas by successional pricking-out. *Rhubarb* may be forced by means of lifting roots of plants two or more years old and packing them in boxes in a warm, dark place. *Mustard and cress* may be sown for succession, *Parsley* may be lifted and planted in a cold frame.

SEEDS TO SOW.—*Radishes* may be sown in a frame or on a gentle hot-bed between rows of potatoes or other crops. *Tomatoes* may now be sown.

The Fruit Garden

General Operations.—Preparations should be made for planting and towards the end of the month planting itself may be commenced. Transplanting may take place, or old trees can be lifted so that the soil may be replenished. A commencement should be made with root-pruning those trees which require it. Grease banding should be done at once. *Apples* and *pears* may be gathered on fine days, the fruit being handled carefully. *Apricots*, *cherries*, *currants* and *gooseberries* should be pruned this month. *Figs.*—The old fruit, leaves and the naked old wood should be cut away to give ample room for the new shoots. *Loganberries.*—Growths which have borne fruit must be cut away to ground-level. *Raspberries.*—Canes which have fruited must be cut out, three or four young ones being left to the stool. New plantations may now be made. *Strawberries.*—All runners should be removed from the plants.

Shrubs and Trees

General Operations.—Planting of new shrubs and trees is general during this month. The sooner all deciduous shrubs and trees are transplanted, if this has to be done, the better ; there will be greater chance of success. If the weather is open, fresh roots will be formed during the winter months. Large evergreens may also be moved this month. Cuttings of most kinds strike well in the open during this month, and layering and division may be carried out where necessary.

NOVEMBER

General Garden Work

All ground as it becomes vacant should either be deeply dug or trenched, a liberal application of manure being given to all soils, with the exception of those which are very light, which should be manured in the spring. Land requiring it should be drained this month, and all alterations to the garden design should be commenced as early as possible. Paths may be re-made or new ones created. All rubbish must be collected, burnt, and dug in.

The Flower Garden

General Operations.—The flower-beds should be well manured or treated with fresh loam ; the soil should be dug before the frosts appear. Herbaceous borders must be forked over, and the stalks of all plants that have finished blooming should be cut down. *Carnations, picotees* and *pinks* which were layered in September or October should be potted off and placed in their winter quarters. *Dahlias* should be taken up and stored. Seedlings that have bloomed late will be the better for being potted and kept dry through the winter. *Hollyhocks* should be propagated from the whole stools or by eyes from the flowering stems, but should not be forced. *Pansies* may be potted off as a reserve for filling up vacancies or for making new beds in the spring. *Peonies (herbaceous).* —Propagate these by means of lifting the roots and pulling the stocks apart.

CUTTINGS.—The stock of cuttings should be sorted, and those which require similar treatment during the winter should be placed together in separate frames.

PLANTING.—*Anemones* (*tubers*), *Canterbury bells, pansies, primroses, sweet williams, violets, wallflowers*, etc., may still be planted in suitable situations. *Flags* and *English* and *Spanish irises* should be planted. *Roses* should be planted or transplanted, stocks for next season's budding being now collected and planted. *Tulip* bulbs may be planted.

Under Glass (Flowers).—The temperature should be kept at from 40° to 45° F. at night. Ventilation must be given when weather is favourable. Water is only required in moderation now. *Auriculas.* —The pots should be looked over occasionally for worms, and if present, lime-water should be poured over the soil. *Calceolarias* and *Cinerarias* should have any dead leaves removed, being shifted when necessary into larger pots. Late seedlings should be pricked out and potted up. *Camellias* require careful attention for the buds will be swelling. *Pansies* should be placed in the warmest part of the house. *Pelargoniums* should have dead leaves removed, the shoots should be thinned out and trained, and late-blooming plants should be moved into their flowering pots.

SEEDS TO SOW.—*Cyclamen* may be sown for the following year.

POTTING.—*Azaleas, deutzias* and similar shrubs for forcing may be potted up now. Bulbs may still be potted for flowering in late spring. *Dielytras, spiræas, lilies-of-the-valley*, etc., should be potted up.

The Vegetable Garden

General Operations.—The soil should be prepared for spring sowing and the hoe should be kept busy among growing crops. All vegetable refuse should be collected and burnt, the ashes being preserved. *Artichokes.*—Some of these should be lifted and stored in sand for future use. The crowns of globe artichokes should be protected with a good mulching of leaves. *Asparagus* should be cut down, if not already done, the bed being dressed with rotten dung. *Beetroots* and *carrots* should be lifted. *Broccoli* should be heeled over early in the month. *Cauliflowers* should have the leaves tied loosely together in a point over the crown. *Celery* and *leeks* require earthing up. *Endive* should be blanched in successive lots. *Parsnips* should be covered with a little litter. *Potatoes.* —The seed potatoes should be gone over carefully. *Roots.*—All roots should be taken up before the end of the month. *Scorzoneras* must be left in the ground until wanted. *Spinach* will continue to grow if thinned properly.

SEEDS TO SOW.—*Beans* and *peas* can be sown.

PLANTING.—*Cabbages, leeks, savoys* and other late plants that will stand through the average winter.

Under Glass (Vegetables).—Vegetables in frames should not be kept in too close an atmosphere. The plants should be exposed as much as possible, being treated almost as though they were growing out-of-doors. The object of keeping *carrots, cauliflowers, endive, onions, radishes,* etc., in frames is that they stand the winter better, but they will stand in the open and, therefore, it must not be considered that they are more tender than they really are. *Rhubarb* may be lifted and forced as last month, and *seakale* may be treated in the same way towards the end of the month.

SEEDS TO SOW.—*Beans (French)* may be sown. *Lettuces, mustard and cress, radishes* and small salading may be sown any time during the month.

The Fruit Garden

General Operations.—During this month the greater part of the planting and transplanting of fruit trees should be carried out, mild days being chosen for the work. When pruning dwarf trees, make up your mind as to the exact form the tree is to assume when it attains full size, and prune accordingly. The shortening of the shoots will depend largely upon this. Orchard trees, if covered with mosses and lichens, should have these scraped off and should then be sprayed with hot lime-wash, a solution of caustic soda, or tar distillate wash, applied in accordance with the instructions of the vendors. *Cherries* should be pruned as soon as the last of the fruit has been gathered. *Currants* and *gooseberries* may be planted and pruned while the weather is favourable. *Figs* on walls should have the superfluous shoots thinned out, the points of the wood selected for bearing being pinched out. *Strawberries.*—Young plantations of strawberries should have some short dung spread between the rows.

Under Glass (Fruit).—*Grapes.*—Vines which were started last month should now be breaking. A temperature of 50°–55° F. should be maintained throughout this month. Vines in pots may be started in a bottom heat of 55° F., and should be moved to their fruiting quarters after breaking. *Peaches* and *Nectarines.*—These should be started now if the fruit is wanted in May. A temperature of 45° F. should be maintained.

Shrubs and Trees

General Operations.—Flowering shrubs and trees may still be planted. The shrub border should be thinned out and any alterations that have been decided upon should be carried out this month. New borders may be made.

DECEMBER

General Garden Work

Digging and trenching should be continued ; the sooner this work is completed the better. Days when the ground is not too wet must be chosen. Planting, transplanting and pruning may still be carried on, but mild days should be selected. Leaves and stems should be collected, being allowed to rot for future use. This is the best month for repairing frames, houses, and for overhauling tools, flower-pots, seed-boxes, etc.

The Flower Garden

General Operations.—This is the best month for planting climbers. Every vacant space in the reserve garden should be dug and manured. *Annuals*, or *biennials*, which are wintering in the reserve garden may need protection. *Carnations, pansies, pinks*, etc., should be pressed firmly into the ground after each severe frost. *Christmas roses* should be protected with hand-lights. *Dahlia* roots which are in store should be examined ; choice sorts may be placed in heat towards the end of the month for flowering in May. *Michaelmas daisies* should be planted. *Roses.*—It is still possible to plant rose trees, but the sooner this is done the better.

BULBS.—Beds of *anemones* and bulbs must be sheltered in bad weather.

Under Glass (Flowers).—The greenhouse which is used for flowers in general should be run at a minimum temperature of from 40° to 45° F., as much air as possible should be given, and occasional smokings, washings and dippings will prove beneficial. A fire may be put on in the morning with the object of expelling the damp. Plants as they come into flower may be removed to the conservatory, young plants being shifted into their blooming pots as they require it. All bad leaves should be picked off plants. The advice given last month as to watering applies with equal force this month. A start may be made with the forcing of *azaleas, deutzias, lilac* and similar shrubs. *Cacti* should be kept quite dry this month. *Chrysanthemums* and *salvias* should be cut back as they go out of flower until sufficient cuttings have been secured ; then the old plants should be destroyed. *Freesias, Roman hyacinths* and *narcissi* must be very gently forced. *Lilies-of-the-valley* may be potted up for succession. *Pelargoniums.*—The general stock require careful treatment this month. The latest-flowering varieties should have their final shift, and all will need careful training. A temperature of 45° F. should be maintained, the plants being kept within two or three feet of the glass to prevent their drawing-up. Fumigation is necessary if green-fly is present.

The Vegetable Garden

General Operations.—The ground between growing crops should be hoed on fine days. Beds of *sweet herbs* should be cleared. Any plot where *celery* has been grown can be trenched and prepared for *onions.* Sprouting trays should be got ready for *potatoes.* Stored *potatoes* and *onions* should be carefully examined occasionally.

Protection.—*Celery* and *parsnips* need protecting with litter. *Endive* by means of pots covered with litter. *Lettuces* under hand-lights or cloches. If frost is severe, loose litter should be placed round the protectors. *Rhubarb* and *seakale* should be covered for forcing.

Seeds to Sow.—A few *beans* and *peas* of the earliest kinds.

Under Glass (Vegetables).—The treatment of plants in frames is the same during December as during November. *Seakale* may be lifted and forced as last month. *Asparagus* may be forced and *tomatoes* may be sown.

Seeds to Sow.—*Beans* (*French*) may be sown for forcing. A few early *peas* and *radishes*, also *mustard and cress.*

The Fruit Garden

General Operations.—The pruning of fruit trees may still be continued until the end of this month, except on frosty days. The trunks of trees may be sprayed with insecticide, and if all the trees have not yet been planted, it will be better to prepare the ground only, leaving the actual planting until the spring. Large standard fruit trees need pruning every second or third year only. This should be done now if due. *Apple* and *pear* trees (established) should be thinned out and pruned. *Currants* and *gooseberries*, if not already pruned, should be attended to at once. *Grapes.*—Outdoor vines should be pruned this month. *Raspberries* should have suckers removed from stools, no pruning until March.

Under Glass (Fruit).—*Peaches.*—In the *peach-house* the trees should be started this month, according to directions given last month. *Strawberries.*—The first batch of strawberries should be introduced ; plants in 48-sized pots invariably do best for early work.

Shrubs and Trees

General Operations.—The principal work in the shrub border during this month is digging, pointing, top-dressing and cleaning. The pruning of deciduous shrubs and trees should be proceeded with, except in times of hard frost.

CARNATIONS AND PINKS

D. Allwoodii "Sylvia" (*Pink*).　　D. Heddewigii (*Various*).　　　D. Allwoodii "Alice"
Border Carnation "Mrs. E. Charrington"　　　　　　　(*White, with Crimson Eye*).
　　(*White, Lilac Stripes*).　　Border Carnation "Mary Murray" (*Yellow*).
　　　Carnation Seedling.　　　　　　Carnation "Dorcas" (*Red Perpetual*)
Perpetual Border Carnation　　　　　　　Perpetual-flowering Car-
"Yeoman" (*Crimson, veined*　　D. chinensis (*Various*).　　nation "Wivelsfield
　　White).　　　　　　　　　　　　　　Buttercup" (*Yellow*).

E.G.　　　　　　　　　　　　　　　　　　　　　　　　　　　　　D

DAHLIAS

Photos]   [*Alexander & Brown (Perth)* ; *R. H. Bath, Ltd.* ; *Dobbie & Co., Ltd.* ; *Kelway & Son* ; *C. Jones* ; *J. E. Tyler.*

Singles.	Orchid-flowered.	Single "Union Jack."
Pæony-flowered	Pompons "Glow" and	Collarette.
"Romance."	"Tommy Laing."	Decorative "W. D.
Cactus "Golden Sun."	Charm "Kitty."	Cartwright."

CHAPTER I

SOILS AND THEIR TREATMENT

CHARACTERISTICS AND CLASSIFICATION

Types of Soil

MANY different soils can be told by visible signs. A loose open soil shifts beneath the feet, and does not adhere to the boots; a clay, or heavy soil, impedes walking and clings to the boots. A clay soil, especially when wet, can be moulded in the hand; a loose soil will pass through the fingers. The texture of a soil can be told by rubbing between the fingers. If it has a greasy or soapy feeling it is a clay soil; if gritty, a sandy soil.

The natural plant growth on the soil also denotes its nature. Heather, bracken, larches, fir-trees, appear on poor, barren soils; oak trees and cowslips grow on clay soils; birch, alders and cotton-grass grow on wet and marshy land.

CLASSIFICATION OF SOILS

Soils are composed of two great groups of compounds : namely, inorganic matter, i.e. material derived from the decay of rocks; and organic matter, i.e. material derived from the decay of vege-table and animal matter. The organic matter is termed humus.

Practically all soils contain sand, clay, limestone, and humus, but in very differing proportions. The preponderating ingredient determines the nature of the soil. Thus :—

Calcareous soils contain upwards of 20 per cent of lime in their composition. They are formed largely of lime with clay loam or sand, and humus in very small proportion.

Clay soils contain 50 per cent of stiff unctuous clay. They are composed chiefly of clay with a little sand, and are lacking in lime and humus.

Loamy soils are soils in which the proportion of clay varies from 20 to 40 per cent, sand and various kinds of alluvium making up the remainder, with a little lime and humus. When the loam con-tains a large proportion of sand, it is known as *Sandy Loam* ; when it contains a large proportion of lime, it is called a *Calcareous Loam*. A gravel loam and a chalk loam are loams in which there is a considerable proportion of gravel and chalk respectively.

Marly soils are the *débris* of limestone rock decomposed and reduced to a paste. They contain from 5 to 20 per cent of carbonate of lime, and humus is found in them. They are distinguished as *Argillaceous*, *Loamy*, and *Sandy* Marls, according to the predominance of clay, loam, or sand among their constituents.

Peaty soils, or vegetable mould, the richest of all garden soils, contain from 5 to 12 per cent of humus, that is, decomposed vegetable and animal matter. *Peat* and *Bog Soil* is composed of fibrous insoluble vegetable matter, mixed with sand and humus.

Sandy soils contain 80 per cent, or thereabouts, of *silica*, that is, the crumbling *débris* of granite or sandstone rock. In other words, they consist chiefly of sand, with a little clay and lime, and a small proportion of humus.

Indications of Good and Poor Soils

A good soil is indicated by—

Gentle slopes; strong woodlands, but no birch or fir; good strong hedges; rich green pasturage with an abundance of white clover; deep soil of a good brown or reddish colour; and strong healthy weeds.

A poor soil is indicated by—

Prevalence of birch and fir trees; stunted hedges and trees; sedges plentiful; thin soil, wet and spongy; and the presence of various weeds, such as quaking grass, Yorkshire fog, broom, heath, and moss.

The Perfect Garden Soil

The perfect soil for general garden use should be composed of the various elements in the following proportions : $\frac{1}{12}$ lime, $\frac{1}{6}$ humus, $\frac{1}{4}$ clay, and $\frac{1}{2}$ sand. Soil containing constituents in these ratios will rarely be found, but many loams will not be far from the ideal, and a little judicious improvement will, in many cases, furnish a compost in which most plants will thrive beyond expectation. Where facilities are available for improving the soil by the addition of other constituents as clay, sand, lime, or humus (which must be well decayed), these should be evenly spread over the soil in autumn and then be dug in in the spring.

SOIL IMPROVEMENT
Preparation of the Soil

To some extent different soils naturally need different treatment if they are to be rendered fertile, but there are certain general principles which are more or less applicable to all. In relation to a plant's life the soil can be considered from various standpoints. In the first place it furnishes root-hold by means of which the plant is able to fix itself in space. Then, again, it acts as a store-house from which the plant absorbs, as required, the greater part of the nourishment on which its continued life depends. Clearly, therefore, we must see to it that if our garden soil is to be fertile it must be of such a texture as shall be compatible with the healthy life and development of the roots and rootlets, and shall contain within reach of those rootlets in an assimilable form the necessary food elements for the plant's growth, and a sufficient supply of moisture at all seasons to present those elements in a dissolved form for absorption.

Drainage

Water-logged soil will not allow the continual life of the majority of plants. Very sandy soil so unretentive of moisture as rarely to contain enough water for dissolving plant foods is equally hope-less. What most plants require is a soil which, while efficiently drained and containing within a few feet of the surface no body of stagnant water, shall yet be of such a texture and shall include a sufficient proportion of organic material as to retain for an appre-ciable time a moderate degree of water. If the soil is naturally very heavy, that is to say, if it consists very largely of clay, and especially if it rests at a comparatively shallow depth below the surface on an almost impervious layer, it is almost certain to be more or less water-logged. And it is necessary in such a case to dig it deeply and to provide adequate drainage, in bad cases by means of pipes, in less bad cases by means of stones and broken bricks, and at the same time to lighten the upper layers of the soil by the addition of sand, leaf-mould, organic manures such as stable manure, and the like (*see chapter on* Drainage, p. 55.). In a similar way very light, sandy soils should be improved by the liberal addition of clay, fibrous loam such as is obtained from the top spit of meadow land, leaf-mould, and cow or pig manure. These latter, which, in the case of the heavy soils, serve to keep open the clay which would tend otherwise to form a solid block, help, in the case of sandy soils, to bind them together, and enable them to retain a greatly increased volume of water.

In the case of practically all soils one of the first things to do, over and above such special measures as have been suggested above, is to trench the ground or to dig it deeply. The processes of trenching, though extremely simple, are not always well understood by amateur gardeners. They essentially aim at the breaking-up of the soil.

For the methods of digging, trenching, and bastard trenching or double digging, *see* Garden Operations, p. 66.

SOIL FUMIGATION AND STERILIZATION

Fumigation

Newly-broken land is nearly always infested with wireworms, leather-jackets, and other pests, and a dressing with some soil fumigant such as naphthalene, or carbide refuse is invariably necessary before successful crops can be obtained.

Soils that have been under cultivation for some time also frequently become pest-ridden. The presence of these pests is indicated by the poorness of crops, and by the weak and sickly state of individual plants whose roots are perhaps attacked.

It is in the autumn that most of these pests will be present in the soil; at this time not only those that dwell in the earth all the year round will be found, but those that descend from plants and trees to pass the winter in the soil can also be here destroyed at this period, if properly treated.

For this reason soil fumigants should be used in the autumn or early winter; another reason for application at this time is that seeds and plants cannot be inserted until most of the fumigants have lain in the soil for at least three months, or they will be damaged. Use the fumigants in December at the latest, therefore, so that crops may be sown in March. Where bushes and herbaceous perennials are left standing in or near the soil to be treated, naphthalene will be found the safest fumigant to use, as it can be employed with impunity quite near the stems of plants. Other chemicals must be kept well away from the roots.

Most of the chemicals used are very poisonous and give off gases when exposed to the air and moisture. The fumigant should be applied to the surface of the soil either as a powder or a liquid, as the case may be, and must be dug in at once so that the fumes may be retained in the soil, as they are the chief agencies in destroying the pests. Fumigants left lying about on the surface of the soil, for one day even, soon lose their strength and efficiency.

Sterilization

This process consists in burning, or heating the soil to such a degree that all pests and seeds of weeds are destroyed and plant growth is stimulated. Sterilization cannot, save the process of burning to be described later, be applied to any great extent to ground in the open, and is generally confined to soil used in pots and the borders of glass houses.

Plants in sterilized soil will at first be slow in growth, as numbers of the bacteria which promote this are destroyed with the pests. Those remaining, however, are free from the influence of pests and quickly multiply, so that after a time the growth of the plants becomes surprisingly vigorous and rapid. There are several methods of effecting this sterilization ; that by which the largest area can most easily be treated is by :—

Burning.—In this method, all available combustible garden refuse, such as straw, hard and fibrous vegetable matter, and leaves are collected and spread evenly over the soil to be treated. This refuse is set fire to and encouraged to smoulder, rather than to burn fast, so that the process of burning is spread over the longest possible period. This method is best pursued in the late autumn or early winter, at which time the pests will be nearest the surface of the soil. Apart from the sterilization effected by the heat, the ashes will greatly benefit the soil.

Where the area of soil to be treated is not so extensive, other methods can be used.

(1) *Baking.*—Here the soil is placed in a shovel, or is spread thinly on a metal sheet over an open fire, and is heated until the soil cannot be grasped and held in the hand. The moisture will evaporate in steam, but the soil must be removed from the fire before actual smoke appears. After baking, the soil should be well mixed and must have nothing planted in it until two days have elapsed.

Another method of baking the soil is to insert red-hot bricks in it. Sufficient bricks must be used to heat the soil adequately, or they must be re-heated and moved about in the compost until every corner has been sterilized.

(2) *Steaming.*—This is a more difficult process, but a very effective one. A wooden box is constructed with several parallel pipes running at intervals across the bottom ; these pipes are riddled with holes. The box is filled with soil and covered over the top, and steam at the pressure of 70 lb. to the square inch is forced along the pipes and up through the soil until it is heated to a temperature of 210° F. or as near that as possible. This temperature should be maintained for about 20 minutes.

(3) *Scalding.*—When this method is adopted the pots filled with compost ready for planting have boiling water poured over them until the soil is thoroughly heated all through. They are then well drained and allowed to cool before planting. Should a larger quantity of soil require treatment, put it in a wooden box and proceed as described for the single pots. The process should be lengthened considerably in order that the larger quantity of soil may be thoroughly sterilized.

A better method, perhaps, is to stand a pail full of the soil in a bath of boiling water and to leave it there until the soil is thoroughly heated through and through; a fire must be kept burning under the bath or the water will cool before sterilization is complete.

On a larger scale in the open, fumigation is far preferable to sterilization.

Soil Fumigants

Chemical.	Rate of Application.	Remarks.
Carbide Refuse	30 lb. per square rod	Applied as powder. Useful for small pests.
Carbolic Acid .	Mix 2 oz. concentrated acid with each gallon of water. Apply 25 gallons of mixture to each square rod of soil	Applied as liquid from watering-can. Poison; all liquid should, therefore, be used up.
Formaline . .	Mix 2 oz. with each gallon of water. Apply 25 gallons of mixture to each square rod of soil	Stir the mixture just before application and use in can. Containers of formaline should be opened in open air, or the operator may be gassed. It is advisable to use a gas-mask during application.
Naphthalene .	1½ lb. per square rod	Store in air-tight containers. Harmless to plants.
Salt	25 lb. per square rod	Effective for pests at surface only.
Soot . . .	25 lb. per square rod	Should be fresh. Must not touch leaves of plants. Effective for pests at surface only.

CHAPTER II

DRAINING AND LEVELLING

Is Artificial Drainage Necessary ?

WHETHER garden land requires draining or not depends on the type of soil and on the situation. If the land has a good slope, artificial draining will probably be unnecessary, and there is rarely any need to drain lands with gravelly, sandy, or stony subsoils. Where this consists of a stiff clay, and in low-lying situations, artificial drainage is almost always essential. The following are two simple tests for ascertaining whether drainage is required. Dig a hole 3 to 3½ feet deep in winter ; if water percolates quickly into the cavity the land must be drained. Soil where the water hangs about in pools on the surface for more than a couple of hours after the cessation of heavy rain will also require attention.

Drainage by Trenching

There are some lands that have a thin stratum of material impermeable to water some 18 inches below the surface. It is obvious that such land cannot be drained by a system of land-drains and trenches, as the water, over the greater part of the surface, would not be able to percolate into the drains. It is here that trenching shows up in its true value. By digging to a depth of 2 to 3 feet over the whole surface the hard crust is thoroughly broken up and the water from the top-soil is enabled to sink down through it. This may be found to provide adequate drainage ; if it does not, pipe- or trench-drainage must be installed.

Draining Small Gardens

This is often a very difficult problem—at least the carrying away of the surplus water is no easy matter, as the natural slope is probably towards a neighbour's garden, and the small garden rarely has a ditch into which the drains can run. Pipe-drainage is also a somewhat expensive and laborious matter ; the cost and difficulties, therefore, often lead to the small garden not being drained at all, which is, of course, the worst possible policy, as nothing save a few sickly-looking specimens will thrive in saturated and water-logged land. Some attempt must, therefore, be made at drainage, where necessary, and when cost makes the use of pipes prohibitive, quite efficient drainage can be effected by cutting parallel trenches about 3 feet deep and 1 foot wide across the ground to be drained. Into the bottom of these trenches should be thrown 9 inches of broken bricks, old rubble, and ballast,—in fact any hard material that will keep the soil open and allow the water to percolate through. Brush-wood and heather may be used, but are not so lasting as clinkers and rubble. Over this drainage material place turves bottom-side-up to prevent the finer soil from silting through and clogging up the drainage. The remaining 18 inches or so should be filled in with the excavated soil; this must not be rammed down, but should be allowed to sink naturally, otherwise the drain will be rendered useless and might as well not be there.

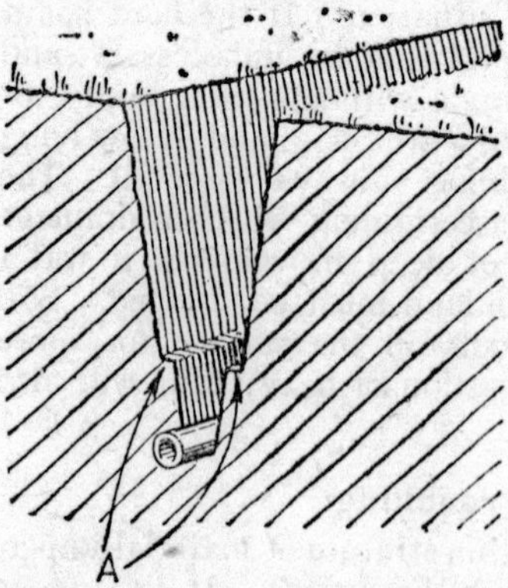

FIG. 1.—SECTION OF A DRAIN.

Drains are best dug V-shaped, as shown in the above diagram; and at the bottom, along the narrowest part below the shoulders *A*, are placed the pipes end to end.

These drains must either empty themselves into a ditch that will carry off the water, or, where this is not possible, a large sump must be dug in the lowest part of the garden and filled in with drainage material in the same way as the drains. Into this the water will flow and be gradually disposed through the soil.

Laying out Drains in Ground

There are various ways of laying out the drains in ground, according to the configuration of the surface. If the ground has a clay subsoil and has a uniform slope, as is often the case with garden ground, it will be sufficient to lay parallel lines of 2 or 3 inch pipes at a distance of from 15 feet to 20 feet apart, provided always that pipes are used in making the drains. When the land slopes slightly on either side to a depression in the middle, a main drain of 3 or 4 inch pipes should be laid along this depression from the head to the outfall, and lateral drains of 3-inch pipes entering the main drain and connected with it by junction-sockets and elbow-joints. No precise directions can be given in this matter as the construction and disposition of the drains must in every case depend on the nature of the soil and the contour of the surface. The depth, too, will also depend upon circumstances, but a main drain will vary in depth from 2½ feet to 4½ feet, being shallowest at the head and deepest at the outfall. The depth of lateral drains will of course depend upon that of the main drain   All lateral drains should enter a main drain obliquely and not at right angles, and the fall should be greater

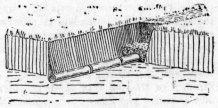

FIG. 2.—THE PIPE DRAIN.

The pipes are placed end to end so that they lie fitted closely together and all evenly at a uniform angle. If improperly laid, soil and débris will find their way into the pipes and will obstruct the drainage.

when the lateral approaches the main drain than at any other portion of its course. From 15 feet to 20 feet should be allowed between the feeders to a main drain on clay soils. The fall of a main drain should never be less than 1 in 200.

Laying the Pipes

Sometimes the drain-pipes are laid with collars, that is, short pieces of piping sufficiently large to receive the ends of two pipes, thus keeping them firmly in their place.   In other cases the pipes are joined together by bands of tempered clay, which answer very well, but when this method is adopted the upper sides of the pipes should be perforated with holes for the reception of the water, so that the solid junction of the pipes is no detriment. It is not usual, however, to do more than lay the pipes end to end in a straight line, or just fit the end of one pipe into the socket made for its reception at the end of the pipe that comes next to it, if pipes of this construction are used.   In this case no clay or cement must be used to bind the pipes together, but at the junction of any feeder with a main drain the union should be carefully made by clay or cement where permanent drainage is expected.

A straight-edge and spirit-level should always be used to ensure that the pipes are laid truly. This will save many clogged or ineffective drains in future years.

Cover the pipes for a few inches with rough

FIG. 3.—THE BUSH DRAIN.

In this type of drain brushwood, laid lengthwise, is used in place of pipes; heather, bracken and similar material may also be employed, but are not so lasting.

porous rubbish or broken crockery, heather, or gorse, or any such material, and the drains will be effective and permanent : this is especially necessary in heavy clay soils. An excellent plan is to lay soles or flat tiles, and on these to set half-pipes or bridge-pipes which are of a tunnel shape, the rough stuff is then laid over these and the trench is filled in with earth, which should not be rammed or trodden very tight, but merely allowed to settle. (*See also* Draining the Lawn, p. 93, *and* Draining Paths, p. 86.)

LEVELLING

In view of the work entailed and the cost, levelling should not be undertaken on anything but a very small scale, unless the scheme has been carefully considered and the site very thoroughly reconnoitred with reference to the probable effect on the drainage system. Where the surface is raised there will be little need for hesitation, but when the levelling consists largely in excavating a considerable portion of the soil in the lower part of the garden, the site, if the soil is a heavy and retentive clay, may quite possibly become waterlogged and may require extensive draining, which may not be easy in comparatively low-lying sections of the garden. As levelling is to a great extent carried out in the autumn and winter, the gardener may not have long to wait for a few heavy showers of rain, which will soon prove what drainage, if any, is necessary.

Levelling Tools

A number of flat-headed pegs, a garden line, a rake, a heavy roller, a spirit-level, a straight-edge at least 10 feet long, and a set of boning rods will be required.

Moving the Soil

As has already been said, the contour, texture, and situation of the ground must be very carefully considered before any work is undertaken. Once the plan of operations has been decided upon, commence by staking out the area to be levelled, then select one corner as a starting-point, drive in a peg so that its head lies at the level to be worked to, and, if the ground is undulating, from it dig trenches, the bottoms of which are all in the same horizontal plane. These trenches

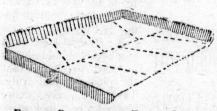

FIG. 4.—DRAINING THE TENNIS COURT.

The above diagram shows "the herring-bone" system of laying drains. The dotted lines indicate the laterals running into the main drain ; they should enter the main drain at an angle of about 60° and not at right angles.

should radiate over the
whole of the surface to
be levelled and will
show where soil must
be cut away and where
it should be added,
also in what quan-
tities. In these
trenches start driving

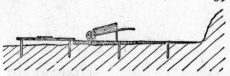

FIG. 5.—MOVING THE SOIL.

The earth is made up to the tops of the pegs, across which
a straight-edge and spirit-level have been placed to ascertain
that they are all in the same horizontal plane.

in pegs 6 to 9 feet apart, so that the heads of all of them are
exactly level with the top of the first peg in the corner whence a
start was made. To make sure that the pegs are level the straight-
edge is laid across from peg to peg, and the last inserted peg is
knocked in until the bubble of the spirit-level resting on the straight-
edge is in the centre of its run. Where a depression is to be filled
in, or where the slope is even and not undulating, there is no need
to dig these "trial" trenches, as the lie of the ground is obvious
and the pegs can be put in at once, still working, of course, from
one guiding peg.

If the slope is considerable such rough masses or materials as
can be got out of the higher portion of the ground should be piled
in a line along the lower end so as to furnish something in the shape
of a containing wall to hold in the earth afterwards thrown into
the intervening space. If there are no stones or rough earth that
can be utilized, a few rows of short stakes may be driven in to
sustain the earth, which must be dug out and thrown if the distance
is short enough, or wheeled if it is too far to throw, until the hollow
has been filled and all the earth removed from the higher portion.
Before the so-called rough levelling is commenced, however, all
the top-soil should be removed and stacked clear of the field of
operations, otherwise the subsoil will, in some places, get thrown
on top of the top-soil, in other parts the subsoil will be left uncovered
and will be of little use in growing either flowers or turf.

As the earth is gradually cut away more pegs can be driven in,
all with their heads on the same level, until the site to be levelled
is studded with pegs. The earth thrown between the stakes should
be rammed with the rammer to give consistency to it and prevent
it from falling out. The rough levelling completed, the garden-line
should be tightly stretched from post to post—from the very tops,
of course—and then the top-soil can be brought back and spread
evenly over the surface and raked fine and levelled up to the level
of the line between the pegs. The surface should then be rolled
firm. When the soil has settled sufficiently, trial must be made
by means of a level to see that the surface is true.

CHAPTER III

MANURES AND MANURING

MANURES, as the term is commonly applied, have two great functions in promoting the life and health of plants. In the first place, they are a source of actual food elements, which they directly contribute to the plants' necessities, and secondly —and this is true particularly of so-called organic manures, such as farmyard manure—by reason of the fermentation which takes place in the manure, chemical changes take place in the surrounding soil which liberate materials required by the plants.

Organic Manures.—It is because it fulfils both these functions that farmyard manure, or its equivalent, is so especially valuable.

Not only does it directly add to the soil constituents needed for the healthy life of plants, but also through the fermentation which it undergoes, and the acids produced thereby, it liberates from the soil itself plant foods which would not otherwise be available.

By its texture, and by the gases produced in the process of its fermentation, moreover, it tends to lighten the soil and keep its texture open. For similar reasons there is considerable value in such manurial substances as leaves, lawn cuttings, road sweepings, vegetable refuse, fish guano and seaweed. All organic waste, indeed, has some manurial value. It is very great in the case of such substances as cow manure, fowl manure, pig manure, and night soil. Wood-ashes and soot are also useful, the former largely on account of the potash it contains, the latter for its ammonia.

Artificial Manures.—It is, however, not always convenient to obtain a sufficiency of stable or farmyard and organic manure for the requirements of one's garden. In such cases resort must be had to various so-called artificial manures, most of which provide plant food in a highly concentrated form. These, for the most part, have but little effect—at any rate directly—on the structure or chemical activity of the soil itself. They add no humus to the soil and do not affect the tilth, and for this reason, if for no other, they cannot entirely replace organic manures.

The three elements which it is generally necessary to add to soil in the form of manure if crops, whether vegetable, fruit or flowers, are to be raised year after year on the same ground, are phosphates, potash, and nitrogen. And it must be remembered that these have not only to be added to the soil, but to be added in such a form that they are or readily become soluble and so capable of being absorbed by the fine rootlets of plants.

Nitrogenous Manures.—The most expensive of these elements is nitrogen, that is to say, nitrogen in a form available for plant food. Apart from guano and other mixed-elements manures, the most useful nitrogenous manures are nitrate of soda and sulphate of ammonia, the latter should be applied early in the spring at the rate of 2 lb. to the rod. The former fertilizer is often applied at the rate of 1 lb. to the rod as a top-dressing during the growing season. Nitrate of potash is also good, but is much more expensive. In well-drained soils certain bacteria exist, especially round the roots of leguminous plants such as peas, beans, and clover, which, by their activity, collect nitrates from the air and add them to the soil. Thus it is often possible to furnish a soil with both humus and nitrates by growing a crop of clover and lucerne and digging it in. Nitrogenous manures act very rapidly and appreciable growth is often visible a few days after application. The plants become noticeably greener and more vigorous. Nitrates must, however, not be added to excess, or rank growth will follow, accompanied by lack of flowers and fruit and susceptibility to attack by fungus.

Potash Manures help the development of sugar and starch in seeds, tubers, and fruit, and improve the colour and size of the blooms. Of potash manures kainit is, on the whole, the cheapest and most useful; it should be dug well into the soil at the rate of 2½ lb. to the rod early in the spring. On heavy soils, sulphate of potash applied at the rate of 1½ lb. to the rod in the early spring is also valuable. A simple way of providing potash for a small plot of ground is to add wood ashes and the ashes from burnt weeds in generous quantities.

Phosphatic Manures.—These assist the correct development of the plant, its fruit or seed, and its roots. The three commonest forms of phosphatic manure are superphosphate of lime, dissolved bones, and basic slag. Superphosphate is the quickest acting, whilst basic slag is the cheapest, slowest acting, and therefore most enduring. It is best applied in autumn. Superphosphate is usually applied just before the plants are mature at the rate of 5 lb. to the square rod, and should be thoroughly mixed with the top 4 inches of the soil.

Basic slag is a chemical manure much used of late years, consisting largely of lime, phosphoric acid, and various iron oxides. It contains other constituents as well as these, but in small proportions. Its effects are much those of superphosphate, but almost twice the quantity is required to produce a given result. It does not succeed mixed with ammonia salts, as it sets free the ammonia and wastes valuable material, but is useful with nitrates. It is most useful on medium or heavy soils which are deficient in lime, or are too wet and stiff ; but to obtain the full advantage the soil must already be fairly well provided with organic matter. As a manure it is good for flowering shrubs, roses, fruit trees, lawns, and pastures. It should be applied and well dug in in the autumn at the rate of 15 lb. to the rod.

Phosphates encourage the formation of fibrous roots, cause earlier development of the plants, and counteract rank, sappy growth caused by excess of nitrogen in the soil. They should be applied every third year.

Where chemical manures are applied to trees and plants which have made full root growth, so that the soil is filled with roots, the best plan, in order to avoid injury to the plants, is to scatter the manure where it is required, and then lightly to " point it in " with a small fork, only placing the manure just under the surface of the ground. In this way the manure is protected from loss by wind or rain, while the delicate roots are not liable to suffer, as they are if the manure is dug in with a spade.

Requirements of Different Crops and Soils.—Different crops have naturally different manurial requirements. Thus potatoes and tomatoes, for example, have special need of potash, whilst leguminous plants, such as peas and beans, and certain roots such as turnips, are particularly influenced by the addition of phosphates.

The requirements of each soil can only be ascertained after individual consideration, experiment, and possibly analysis. But there are certain rough rules. Farmyard manure in reasonable quantities improves almost all soils, heavy or light. It is usually unnecessary to add potash to clay soils, and usually necessary to add it to sandy soils. At the same time it may be necessary in order to liberate the potash in the clay soil, to add lime. Gravelly and sandy soils are nearly always deficient in nitrogen, and are much less retentive of manures generally. Soils that are peaty, or that have become sour from excessive humus from constant year-by-year manuring with organic manure, are much improved by the addition of quicklime applied frequently in small doses and dug in at once.

Then again different manures in each class differ in their action ; nitrate of soda, for instance, works more rapidly than sulphate of ammonia. Some fertilizers suit one crop, others another. The requirements of both soil and crops must be studied when applying manures. (*See* Manuring Vegetables, p. 372, and Fruit, p. 327.)

Stable manure and, indeed, all animal manures, should **not** be left exposed to rain and air. They are best mixed with a little soil, and covered with about another 6 inches of soil until they are required for use.

Amount of Manure Required.—As some guide to the amount of various artificial manures to apply in average cases, we may say that it is safe, as a rule, to add to a square rod of ground needing that particular manure, $2\frac{1}{2}$ lb. of kainit or $1\frac{1}{2}$ lb. of sulphate of potash, 5 lb. of superphosphate, 4 lb. of dissolved bones, 5 lb. of steamed bone flour, 12 to 15 lb. of basic slag, 2 lb. of guano, quarter of a load of stable manure, 10 lb. of fowl manure, 1 lb. of nitrate of soda, 2 lb. of sulphate of ammonia.

The fertilizers must be spread evenly over the soil and must be crushed fine and be free from lumps, so that every inch of soil receives its proportion of the fertilizer. If this is not done parts of the ground will receive an excess amount, which may kill the plants. The manure should be well worked into the soil.

When to Apply the Various Manures.—Slow-acting manures such as bone-meal, basic slag, farmyard and poultry manure are best applied while the digging is being done in the autumn and early winter. Quicker-acting fertilizers, as dissolved bones, kainit, nitrate of soda, sulphate of ammonia, sulphate of potash, must be applied in the spring or when the crops are growing. It is obviously useless to apply quick-acting manures in autumn or winter as the rain would wash away all their properties before the plants were ready to assimilate them. Conversely slow-acting fertilizers would provide little benefit if applied while the plants were growing.

APPLICATION AND USES OF MANURES

Showing the Soils to which they are most Suitable and the Time and Quantity to Apply.
Note.—A Dressing of $2\frac{3}{4}$ cwt. per Acre is equal to 2 lb. to the Square Rod, or 1 oz. per Square Yard.

Manure	Soil to which best Suited	When to Apply	Rate per Sq. Rod	Remarks
Ammonia, Nitrate of .	Any	Growing Season	2 lb.	Fruit and Vegetables
Ammonia, Phosphate of Ammonia, Sulphate of	Clay and Chalk	Spring and Early Summer	2 lb.	Cabbage Tribe, Cucumbers, etc. Never on soil deficient in Lime
Basic Slag	Heavy or Light	Autumn (Heavy) Spring (Light)	15 lb.	Best for slow-growing plants. Do not use on Chalk or Sand
Blood, Dried . . .	Any	Growing Season	6 lb.	Good for Flowers and Vegetables
Bone-meal . .	Light	Autumn	5 lb.	Excellent for Lawn, Fruit, Shrubs and Herbaceous Plants
Bones Dissolved . .	Chalk	Spring or Summer as Top-dressing	4 lb.	Never on soil deficient in Lime. Good for all plants.

APPLICATION AND USES OF MANURES—*continued*.

Manure	Soil to which best Suited	When to Apply	Rate per Sq. Rod	Remarks
Farmyard Manure .	(Horse) Heavy (Cow) Light	Autumn or Winter Spring	3 Large Barrows	All crops
Fish Meal	Light or Medium	Autumn and Winter	3 lb.	Good for nearly all plants, especially Potatoes, Turnips, etc.
Guano	Any	Growing Season	2 lb.	Never on soil deficient in Lime
Hop Manure . . .	Clay, Chalk, Gravel and Sand	Autumn	30 lb.	Good for all Fruit Trees, Shrubs and Herbaceous plants
Horn Shavings, Feathers, Hair, etc.	Any	Autumn	15 lb.	Useful only for slow-growing plants
Kainit Salts . . .	Heavy or Light	Autumn (Heavy) Spring (Light)	2½ lb.	All Vegetables and Fruit
Leaf Mould . . .	Heavy Clay	Winter or Early Spring	3 Large Barrows	Adds Humus to the soil
Lime, Nitrate of . .	Any	Growing Season	2 lb.	Especially good for Cabbage Tribe, but suitable to all crops
Lime, Sulphate of .	Clay or Medium	Spring or Early Summer	12 lb.	Fruit and Vegetables
Nitrate of Potash . .	Any	Spring	2 lb.	All Plants
Nitrate of Soda . .	Light and Dry	Spring or Early Summer	1 lb.	Helps on leaf growth in cold weather or after attack by insect pests
Potash, Muriate of .	Light and Medium	Spring or Early Summer	3 lb.	Fruit and Vegetables
Potash, Phosphate of	Light	Spring or Early Summer	2½ lb.	All Flowers and Vegetables, and all Fruit under glass
Potash, Sulphate of .	Light or Heavy	Spring or Early Summer	1½ lb.	All Flowers ; Asparagus, Carrots, Cauliflowers, Onions, Potatoes
Poultry Manure . .	Any	Growing Crops or Autumn	10 lb.	All plants, especially Root Crops
Salt	Light	Spring or Early Summer	2 lb.	Salt-loving plants such as Asparagus, Beet, Cabbage Tribe, Celery, Leeks, Onions, etc.
Seaweed (fresh) .	Light	Spring or Autumn	6 Barrow Loads	All salt-loving plants as above
Soot	Sandy or Light	Summer	1 Peck	All young plants
Superphosphate of Lime	Medium or Light	Autumn (Medium) Spring (Light)	5 lb.	Never on soil deficient in Lime
Vegetable Ashes . .	Any	Spring	10 lb.	Beans, Carrots, Onions, Peas, Potatoes, etc.
Vegetable Refuse .	Medium to Light	Winter	4 Barrow Loads	Adds Humus to the soil
Wood Ashes . .	Heavy and Rich	Autumn or as Top-dressing in Spring, Summer and Autumn	10 lb.	Excellent for Beans, Carrots, Onions, Peas, Potatoes and Fruit Trees
Wool Waste (Shoddy)	Any	Winter	14 lb.	Slow growing crops. Manurial value lasts over three years

LIME

The nitrates, phosphates, and potash supplied by manures are quite inaccessible to plants in a soil deficient in lime. Lime, too, assists the bacteria which render organic matter in the soil available to crops, and is itself an essential plant food. It makes heavy

HOW TO DIG

1. Keep the spade upright. 2. Do not take too large a spit; one 5 to 6 inches in width is ample. 3. In raising or turning the soil, get well down to the work. 4. This is wrong; the digger is too far above his work. See page 66.

GARDEN TOOLS

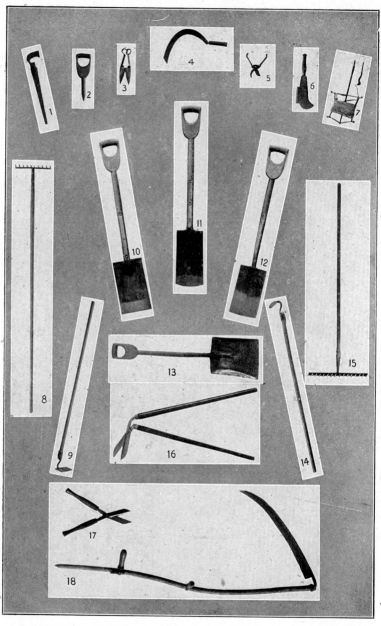

1. Pruning Saw. 2. Dibber or Dibble. 3. Grass Shears. 4. Bagging Hook.
5. Secateurs. 6. Bill-hook. 7. Garden Line and Reel. 8. Rake. 9. Swan-
necked Hoe. 10-12. Spades. 13. Shovel. 14. Hoe. 15. Rake. 16. Border
Shears. 17. Garden Shears. 18. Scythe.

soils more porous and, therefore, better drained and warmer, cleanses the soil of insect and fungoid pests, and sweetens sour soil, which has become deficient in lime either through the action of smoke, as in towns, through the dissolving action of rain, or because the roots of plants have absorbed all lime from it.

On soil naturally deficient in lime, heather, gorse and bracken will be found to flourish. The first sign that cultivated land is becoming sour, that is, deficient in lime, is the prevalence of " club-root " or " finger-and-toe " disease among cruciferous crops such as turnips. In sour soil crops become weakly, are unable to resist the attacks of disease and insect pests, and are prone to wither long before they attain maturity. When soil has thus become sour the state should be rectified as soon as possible by the application of lime at the rate of 10 oz. to the square yard, the dressing being repeated every 4 to 5 years. If the soil is not sour, but merely deficient in lime, dressings equal in amount to those shown in the table below will be sufficient. Lime must never be applied at the same time as farmyard manure. When applied it should be perfectly dry and powdered as finely as possible, must be evenly dusted over the ground, and immediately well pricked into the top 3 to 4 inches of the soil, which must also be dry. Whether the lime is applied in the form of slaked lime or carbonate of lime depends on the nature of the soil, and the time of the year.

The following table will show the forms calculated to prove most effective under the various conditions prevailing.

Form of Lime.	Nature of Soil.	When to Apply.	Amounts to Apply.	Remarks.
Slaked Lime	Heavy	Before ground is dug over in autumn or winter, unless soil is manured. In the latter case apply 3 weeks before sowing in spring.	12 lb. per sq. rod	Use immediately after slaking. Useless on Light Soils.
Carbonate of Lime	Light and Sandy	Three weeks before sowing, at any season. Will not hurt if applied at sowing time or while seedlings are growing.	20 lb. per square rod	Useless on Heavy Soils.

E.G.   E

CHAPTER IV

GARDEN OPERATIONS

Banding

(*See* Grease-banding, p. 403.)

"Bastard Trenching" or "Double Digging"

Trenching to three spades' depth, as described in the article on *Trenching*, is not often performed, as unless the top soil is very deep and good there is always the danger of bringing dead, useless subsoil to the top. On only moderately deep ground bastard trenching, that is, to two spades' depth, is usually adopted. The process is the same except that the second spit is not removed but is broken up in the same way as the third spit in trenching proper. The top spit of the second portion of ground is not wheeled away, but is placed over the first trench.

Blanching

Several vegetables require blanching to be made tender and to have the green colouring matter and consequent bitterness removed from them—celery, leeks, seakale, cardoons, chicory, endives, lettuces. The first two of these are blanched by the process of earthing-up, which is dealt with on page 67. Seakale is blanched under pots prepared for this purpose, and covered over with litter, sand, ashes or leaves.

The best plan with endive is to place over each plant, when full-grown, a large tile or slate, which will effectually exclude all light and blanch the endive in a few days. With lettuces there is no better plan than tying.

(*See also the culture of the individual plants in the chapter on* Vegetables.)

Single Digging

In digging with the fork, little can be done beyond breaking and turning over the ground and reducing the clods thus turned up. In digging with the spade the soil can be transferred more readily from one position to another. Shallow digging is of very little value, and to enable the soil to be deeply worked the spade should be inserted in as nearly an upright position as possible. The digger

66

should stand well over his spade, and must not try to dig out more than 5 to 6 inches of soil each time—that is to say in width —he must always dig to the full depth of the spade. The first thing to be done is to mark the ground out into strips each some 10 feet wide, if trenches longer than this are dug it will be found difficult to keep the soil level. Next take out a trench about a spade deep and a spade wide, or, in other words, about 12 inches in depth, the same in width, and the full width of the strip. The sides of this trench must be cut straight and square, and all loose earth must be removed from the bottom, which must be flat and even. The soil from this trench should be removed to the other end of the ground to be dug over. Another trench of the same size is now taken out, and the soil is transferred into the first trench and is left as rough as possible, thus exposing as large a surface as may be to the action of the weather during the winter months. This process is carried on until the whole ground has been dug over and the last trench taken out is filled with the soil taken from the first trench.

Digging should be completed before the soil becomes too wet. If left over-late, the ground may become quite unworkable and the digging may have to be deferred until the early spring—a very bad policy as the soil is thereby deprived of the beneficial action of air, rain, and frost through the long winter. Digging when the soil is very wet does more harm than good as the earth becomes trodden down and compressed and loses all its porosity, which is the very characteristic that digging is meant to increase. Two-thirds of the cultivated soil in a garden should be dug over each year ; the other third should be bastard trenched (*see* p. 66).

In digging, all roots of perennial weeds should be carefully picked out, but vegetable stems and leaves and all annual weeds can be dug in as manure, provided they are deeply buried. In manuring during digging, the manure should be thrown with the fork along the bottom of the trench, and the earth from the next trench must be thrown on top of it. (*See also* Double Digging, p. 66, and Trenching, p. 75).

Earthing-Up

A term employed to describe the drawing up of soil about the stems or stalks of any growing plant, as, for example, peas, beans, potatoes, celery, leeks, and many other plants. It induces the growth of rootlets from the stem in some cases, and affords greater shelter for the roots. It is desirable also to draw up the soil round the stalks of cabbages of all kinds. (*See also* Blanching.)

Mulching

This operation, which saves much watering in dry weather, consists in spreading a 3-inch layer of half-decayed stable manure, well-decayed vegetable refuse, leaf-mould, coco-nut fibre, hop manure, or other material over the soil occupied by the roots of plants, especially those which have been recently transplanted, and in times of drought watering thoroughly before the mulch is laid down. The mulch will then prevent the water from evaporating too quickly. During very dry weather the lawn may also be well watered in the evening, the following day the mower is run over without the grass-box; the cut grass will act as a mulch and preserve the moisture. Rain falling or water applied on a mulch soaks through and carries nourishment through to the roots and thus performs an additional service. Where a mulch of manure or other matter is unsightly and unpleasant, as on some flower borders, coco-nut fibre can be used as a mulch or can be sifted over to hide the mulch used. A mulch is of little benefit unless it is at least 3 inches in thickness, if deeper it is liable to make the roots too cold. After a time the material used, whatever it may be, may be forked into the soil; a new mulch should then be applied, four or five being needed during an ordinary summer. A mulch should be very retentive of moisture; certain mulches are more suitable to one soil than another. For instance, rich loamy or clayey soils are best mulched with well-decayed leaf-mould, freshly mown grass, or with well-rotted horse manure; on light sandy soils a mulch of vegetable matter should always be well-decayed and cow-dung should be used in preference to horse manure. The mulch must not be placed close up to the stems of the plants, as it is apt to damage them and cause them to rot, besides it is the roots that benefit by the mulching and these often extend a considerable way out from the stem.

A word of caution is, however, necessary as there are several materials that should not be used as mulches; some because they soon " cake " and form a hard crust, others because of chemical properties they would impart to the soil, or because they encourage insect pests. The following are a few substances that should not be used : mud from the bottom of ponds and streams, road-sweepings, pine needles, and newly fallen leaves. Such materials as soot and wood ashes should not be employed as they soon sink into the soil and are useless as mulches. Mulching is usually carried out during the months of May, June, and July; it should not be confused with top-dressing (which see), which only aims at providing nourishment to the roots, and does not prevent evaporation in hot weather. Every newly planted tree, and all wall fruit trees, should have a mulching of some sort spread around them. Plants whose roots lie near the surface of the soil, such as beans, cauliflowers, peas, raspberries, and roses, are those that suffer first in a drought, and these are the ones that most require mulching. With plants of this nature a mulch is put down in the spring ; with other plants many gardeners wait until the drought has arrived. Where mulching is impossible, hoeing will go a long way towards making up for it.

Nailing

This is a rather difficult operation, for nailing is no ornament, and the less it shows itself the better. The gardener's skill must be exerted to conceal his nails and shreds as much as possible. For use in brick or stonework cast-iron nails are best as these will pierce very hard substances without bending. Cloth list or shreds of old cloth are generally used ; but strips of leather or black tape are preferred by some, under the supposition that they not only have a neater appearance, but afford less harbour for insects. The shreds vary from $\frac{1}{2}$ to $\frac{3}{4}$ of an inch in width and from 4 to 6 inches in length, according to the size of the twig or branch on which they are to be used. Fruit-trees should be nailed close in to the wall, but ornamental shrubs, etc., should be merely fastened in for the sake of support.

Planting

Unless well planted the tree, shrub, vegetable, or flower cannot thrive. Firm planting is essential in almost all cases ; another vital matter is the preparation of the soil and the site for planting.

Detailed instructions will be found in the chapters on *Bedding Plants*, *The Herbaceous Border*, *Climbing Plants*, *Ornamental and Flowering Shrubs and Trees*, *Fruit*, *Bulbs*, *Vegetables*, *and Potting*, and to these we refer the reader.

Pointing

This consists in thrusting the garden fork some 5 or 6 inches into the soil, which is lifted and turned over. The process is useful in beds and borders filled with plants whose roots run near the surface and where it would be harmful to dig to a spade's depth. By pointing, manure is worked into the herbaceous and shrub borders in the autumn, the manure being first laid evenly over the surface, and is then worked in around the plants. The surface of a bed or border is usually pointed over when it has become unduly caked and hard.

Protection

If the garden is very much exposed to certain prevalent winds, belts of trees or dense-growing shrubs must be planted to break its force, and to protect the tenderer plants in the borders. (*See chapters on* Hedges, page 157, and Trees and Shrubs, page 149.) Where the garden is walled this protection is, of course, not needed as the walls, as well as helping to ripen the fruit grown on them, will make a most efficient protection against wind. For protecting early spring flowers, such as tulips, in very exposed positions temporary screens of coarse canvas, scrim, or coco-nut matting can be erected on poles 4 to 5 feet high or straw or wattle hurdles can be used to break the force of the wind. If branches of fir or other evergreens are available these can be stuck into the ground on the windward side of the plants, and make an excellent screen. Against cold weather and frosts individual protection of the more tender plants will be required, and there are many ways of affording this, varying with the plant. In exposed localities dwarf roses, especially teas, are best protected by a small mound of clean dry straw, bracken, coco-nut fibre or some similar material heaped round them for a few inches above the ground. The taller roses, standards and half-standards, should have dry bracken fronds tied in among their heads. The ordinary garden mat is the most useful thing for tying round other tender shrubs, and for covering frames during hard weather. It may be tied into a cone shape, and supported on small sticks like a " wigwam " over small plants, or spread over trees trained against walls. The more tender herbaceous perennials in the open borders may need protection from frost in severe winters. The means by which this is supplied is described in the chapter on *The Herbaceous Border*, to which the reader is referred. The great thing is to keep the plants dry during cold weather, it is when a plant gets wet and is subsequently frozen that the damage occurs. In the early spring protection is chiefly needed for the blossoms of early flowering fruit trees, such as the peach and apricot, during the period when there is risk of night frosts. This is best given by means of cheap calico, netting or garden tiffany suspended by means of hooks or rings attached to nails in the wall.

Many plants in the greenhouse will need shading from the sun during the summer months, and the reader is referred to the chapter on the *Greenhouse* where this is fully discussed.

Where individual blooms in the open require shading from the sun, or protecting from the weather the gardener may either make or purchase a cone-shaped shade of calico from 6 to 12 inches in diameter, stiffened and supported by a galvanized wire framework and mounted by a clip on a wooden stake so that it can be moved up and down until at the right height to give the necessary protection. Such a shade is especially useful for protecting roses from the sun and thus enabling them to keep their colour. Where sweet peas for exhibition have to be protected these individual shades are not practicable, and in this case large strips of cheap calico, canvas, or scrim should be arranged on poles over the rows of peas to protect the blooms from the sun.

Shading and Sheltering Plants

(*See article on* Protecting Plants *in this chapter, also the section on* Shading *in the chapter dealing with* Gardening under Glass.)

Staking and Tying-up Plants

As the plants in the beds and borders begin to grow, all that attain a height of over, say, $2\frac{1}{2}$ feet and many more of a less robust nature will require staking, otherwise wind and rain will soon break them down. Rather than use one large stake, to which all the stems of the plant are tied in a tight bush, quite spoiling its natural shrubbiness and contour, it is better to support each of the stronger shoots of the plant with a separate stick and so preserve the natural contour of the plant. Bamboo canes are excellent for this work.

Time will, however, rarely be available for this treatment to be given to smaller plants; with these it will usually suffice if three or four sticks are driven in round the plant and bass or string is tied from stick to stick to support the flower stems. The stakes should slope slightly outwards and away from the plant and the string must not be drawn too tight. This is a good method of supporting plants with delicate stems that would be damaged if individually tied to stakes.

The stakes must be hidden as much as possible, and should be placed behind the stems and foliage, and where natural branches and twigs of hazel or birch, which are the least unsightly, are not used they should be stained green or brown. Stakes will be very unsightly if allowed to overtop the flower stems; they should, on an average, be three-quarters of the length of the stem to be supported, excluding, of course, the portion of the stake thrust into the ground. It must not, however, be forgotten that this refers to when one is staking the mature stalk, and that when supporting young flower-spikes allowance must be made for growth. It must not be forgotten that the plants continue to grow and that further tying and staking will be necessary at intervals.

The tying material naturally varies with the plant and the weather conditions to which it will be subjected. For trees in the open, tarred cord of thickness to suit the size of the trees is used. Perennial border plants are tied up with soft tarred string if it is to last for more than a season. For annuals in the open, for most greenhouse plants, for all tying, in fact, that need not last for more than a year raffia or bass, worsted, or soft string, will be found most suitable and convenient.

Whatever the method of staking adopted, the material should always be first tied securely round the stake and is then looped round the stem sufficiently tightly to hold it in position, but not tightly enough to cut into the bark or stem, due allowance being made for the future growth of the branches. Stems should be so tied that they maintain their natural distances apart; if bunched tightly together they will be deprived of a large amount of sun and air and will suffer heavily in consequence. They should be able to sway naturally with the wind, if they cannot the blooms will offer resistance and may be torn and damaged.

(*See* Staking and Tying *in the chapter on* Fruit Growing, and Training Plants *in this chapter.*)

Tidying-up

The primary object of tidying-up may be to keep the garden neat, but it is most beneficial to the plants. Firstly the collecting and burning of waste materials, such as dead leaves and twigs, does much to stop the propagation of fungoid diseases and insect pests. Secondly, the hoeing and pointing-in of the soil does untold good. These processes, together with the benefits they confer, are fully explained in other paragraphs in this chapter. But it is more with the removal of dead shoots after flowering and the picking off of dead flowers and seed-pods that we have to deal here. Many think that these things are done purely to make the beds appear tidier; this is certainly a useful function, but the main reason is a far more important one. To reproduce its species is the foremost aim of every plant, and as a rule once this has been ensured, the plant ceases to bear more flowers, and in the case of an annual, dies down altogether. For this reason all annuals should have their dead blooms and seed-pods picked off as soon as possible to encourage the production of fresh flowers; this will greatly extend the period of blooming. With early flowering herbaceous perennials, such as delphiniums and lupins, the same process should be carried out, except that the whole of the stem supporting the dead blooms should be cut away; this will enable the plants to put forth a second crop of bloom in the early autumn.

About mid-summer, or slightly later, it will be found that border plants will require additional treatment to that mentioned above. Many of them will have grown unwieldy and may be suffocating less vigorous plants; these must be trimmed back. Plants of a trailing and creeping nature will require pegging down to lead them into the way they should go and to make them cover their allotted space. (*See* Staking and Tying-up *in this chapter.*)

Top-dressing

Although some mulches are at the same time top-dressings, these two preparations are applied for entirely different purposes. Mulches are used primarily to prevent over-rapid evaporation and to keep the roots warm, the aim of the top-dressing is to enrich the soil and furnish new food for the roots.

Most of the organic manures and artificial fertilizers mentioned in the chapter on *Manures* may be used as top-dressings ; those most generally employed for this purpose are bone-meal, kainit, leaf-mould, old lawn mowings, old hot-bed manure, nitrate of soda, sulphate of ammonia, superphosphate of lime and wood-ashes. For flower beds and borders a dressing of 75 per cent. old hotbed manure, or if this cannot be obtained the same proportion of well-decayed farmyard manure, and 25 per cent. leaf-mould or other well-rotted vegetable matter is excellent. Rock plants will need an additional 25 per cent. of leaf-mould and a liberal sprinkling of coarse sharp sand ; granite or limestone chippings may also be used. The reader is referred to the table showing the *Application and Uses of Manures*, p. 63, and to the sections on *Manuring Vegetables*, p. 372, and *Fruit Tree Manuring*, p. 327, where the manures, either organic or artificial, most suitable to each fruit or vegetable are shown, together with the amount to give and the season of application.

Top-dressings are used to augment the plant food supplied by the manure dug-in at planting time or when it is not feasible to disturb plants so that manure may be dug-in, as in the case of the herbaceous border or the rock garden. They are usually employed in spring or early summer, or in the autumn, the coarser organic manures are generally applied in even layers an inch to two thick and are then forked into the soil. Artificial fertilizers are usually very fine in texture and must be well raked into the soil and then watered.

In the case of pot plants that occupy the same pot for some time the top inch or two of soil may be removed so that a fresh top-dressing of compost may be added, usually without any stimulant, or in the case of plants known to be " gross-feeders " sufficient room is left in the pot at potting time, to enable one or more top-dressings of fresh soil and fertilizer to be given as the roots fill the old soil and seek nourishment on the surface. Where stimulants are required, one of the artificial fertilizers will be found more suitable than the more bulky organic manures, and is best applied in three or four dressings at intervals.

Top-dressings for the Lawn

(See chapter IX.)

Training

is necessary in the case of flowers, climbers, and ornamental shrubs to help to produce the greatest number of really good blooms ; to keep the plants neat and within bounds ; and, as far as possible, to make them cover a required space while still retaining a natural habit of growth and appearance. The habits and growth of each plant are described in the paragraphs dealing individually with them (chapter XXIV), and the reader is advised to study these before starting to train his plants. (*See also* Pruning and Training Shrubs, p. 151.)

Fruit and vegetables are, of course, trained and pruned with a view to quality and quantity in production. (*See* Training *and* Pruning *in the chapter on* Fruit Growing.)

Ornamental trees should be carefully trained from the outset ; it is very difficult to recast the shape of a tree badly trained or neglected when young. Keep the tree well-balanced by trimming and lopping equally on both sides, and where it is necessary to let in more air cut out a complete branch here and there rather than shorten a number. A clean straight stem should always be encouraged, and the supporting stakes (*see* Staking Fruit Trees) must be inserted where necessary.

A brick wall is by no means improved by having a mass of nails driven into it ; other means of supporting a climber are, therefore, often used. Wires can be stretched horizontally in staples across the wall at intervals of, say, 18 inches, and to these the climbers are loosely tied by means of tarred string. A better plan, however, is to make a wooden trellis, with square meshes, which can be fastened against the wall, and the climber is tied to this. Climbers should be trained regularly and not be allowed to run rampant, when the stems will become weak and will be unable to support the heads in future years. Especially is it necessary to cut back the growths of young and newly planted climbers to encourage the formation of strong sturdy stems ; it is a wise plan to cut all new growth on young climbers back by two-thirds each year.

(*See also the paragraphs on* Staking and Tying-up, *and* Nailing *in this chapter.*)

Transplanting

Most of the remarks on planting in this chapter refer equally well to the process of transplanting.

In transplanting—whatever the subject may be—the great thing is to keep the roots out of the ground for as short a time as possible, and for this reason, when transplanting trees and large plants, it is advisable to prepare the sites and dig the holes they are to occupy in advance. Keep the roots " heeled-in " if possible, but if they *must* remain out of the soil for some little time moisten and cover them with litter and matting to keep them from the frost and from becoming dried up, as once the small fibrous roots dry up they perish and the plant must form new ones before it can again take up nourishment from the soil. It, therefore, takes a long time to become established and receives a severe check. If the roots have become dry, soak them well before planting. The " ball " of earth round the roots should be kept intact, although this is not feasible with large shrubs and trees, in view of the weight of the soil that would have to be moved with it.

Every care must be taken not to damage the roots. Seedlings should not be roughly pulled up with the hand, a trowel or handfork should be used ; herbaceous plants and small shrubs are best lifted by inserting two garden forks to their full depth vertically one on each side and close into the plant, and then levering the handles gently downwards and away from the plant. This method will lift the plant from the soil with the roots intact. Large shrubs and trees are a more difficult matter ; the best way is to dig a trench round the tree and from 2 to 3 feet from it, then dig inwards towards the tree until the roots are reached, next dig downwards under the tree and it will be found possible to remove it without much damage to the roots. Trees and shrubs should be well watered after transplanting, and if the weather becomes dry before they are thoroughly established evergreens should have their foliage thoroughly syringed every evening as long as the drought lasts.

The method of setting the plants in their new sites is fully set forth in the chapters devoted to the various kinds of plants.

(*See also* Thinning and Transplanting *in the chapter on* Propagation.)

Trenching

The immediate object of trenching is to deepen the soil, and prepare the subsoil to nourish the fibres of deep-rooting plants ; the subsoil is not brought to the surface. The operation is commenced by digging a trench 2 to $2\frac{1}{2}$ feet wide and a foot deep, throwing out the top spit, and wheeling it to the farther end of the bed, the second spit is treated in the same manner if the trenching is to be three spades deep. This done, the bottom of the trench is dug over to the full depth of the fork, well broken up and is left level. The top spit of a second portion of the ground is now removed and placed alongside the first, and the second spit of this portion is dug up and placed

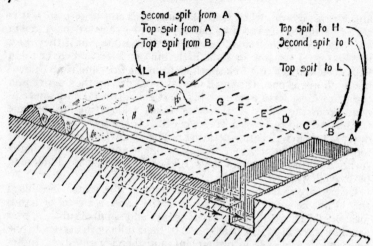

FIG. 6. —Trenching—Commencement.

The top spit of trench *A* is wheeled away to *H* and the second spit to *K* ; the top spit of the second trench *B*, to *L*. The second spit of *B* replaces the second spit of *A*, and the second spit of *C* that of *B* ; the top spit of *C* replacing that of *A*, and so on.

roughly over the first trench.   The first spit of a third portion is now removed and placed in as large masses as possible over the first trench ; the bottom of the second trench is then dug up in the same manner as the first, and so on till the whole is finished.   Heavy soils

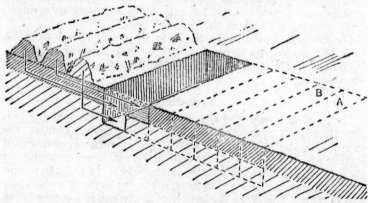

FIG. 7. —Trenching—Completion.

K (the second spit from *A*) replaces the second spit of the last trench ; *H* (the top spit from *A*) the top spit of the last trench but one ; and *L* (the top spit from *B*) takes the place of the top spit of the last trench.

are best trenched in the autumn, throwing the soil up in ridges, thus exposing a large surface to the action of frost and air during the winter. Treated in this way, the ridges should in the spring break down to a fine tilth. Light soils may be trenched in the early winter or dug at almost any time.

Watering

Rainwater is by far the best for plants as the carbonic acid and the nitrates that it contains make it a soil fertilizer. Even pump water, apparently clear, is often far too hard to do well for watering plants, but this hardness may be removed by keeping it in shallow tanks and exposed to the air for some time before using. Plants under glass should always be watered from tanks kept at the same temperature as the plants are growing in; therefore some vessel must always be kept in the house. Nothing does much greater mischief to plants than chilling them with water of lower temperature than the atmosphere they are in.

Water supplied by pipe from the main is not usually so cold as well-water, but it is often equally hard. If possible it should be stored in a tank, exposed to the air for at least twenty-four hours before use to soften it and to raise it to the required temperature.

It is impossible to make hard and fast rules for watering for many points have to be considered; first the nature of the plants, then their situation, whether in sun or shade, on a high well-drained spot or in a low-lying and damp locality; plants on light soils on a well-drained sub-soil, such as gravel or chalk, will suffer from drought far sooner than those growing on heavy loams with retentive clay beneath them. Watering is best done when the sun has gone down; if watering is done while the sun is up and hot the flowers and foliage will be scorched, as some moisture is sure to find its way on to them, and the globules will act as microscopes to magnify the power of the sun's rays. This leads us to make the point that watering is best done with the uncapped spout of the hose or can and not through a rose, which tends to cause the surface of the soil to "cake." A rose should only be used when watering seeds, seedlings, newly potted plants to settle the soil, and when spraying the foliage. Water should be applied direct to the roots of each plant and not over the foliage. Hold the hose or can so that the spout is close to the ground; if water is given from a height the soil will be disturbed overmuch.

Watering in the open should never be undertaken until essential. When commenced sufficient must be given thoroughly to moisten the top 30 inches of the soil, this takes a good deal more water and longer than most people imagine. A little water over the surface merely chills the soil, and draws the roots to the surface where they are quickly scorched unless water is frequently given, which soon "cakes" the surface, and prevents the air from penetrating to the roots. It pays to give a thorough watering once a week rather than a daily sprinkling. Constant hoeing, or better still mulching (*see* p. 68), will eliminate the need for frequent watering. If a bed is thoroughly forked up and is then well watered one evening, and mulched the following morning with well-rotted dung, decayed vegetable material, or coco-nut fibre refuse, or well hoed—the latter is, of course, not so effective—it will require little further moisture for a considerable time, even in very dry weather.

There are several classes of plants that are often overlooked as far as the question of watering goes, and among these are : pot-plants stood out in the open during the summer ; a large surface of the soil is exposed to the air and heat so that the compost quickly becomes dry and needs frequent attention, unless the pots are "plunged" in the soil, in ashes, or in coco-nut fibre ; the leaves of evergreens perpetually keep much rain from reaching the roots even in winter when other plants receive a good store of moisture ; in the same way climbers, shrubs, and trees trained on a wall often suffer during the summer, unless watered and mulched, as the position of the wall will frequently keep off much rain.

In watering newly-potted plants, it is important that the whole of the soil shall be thoroughly and evenly moistened all through, which can only be accomplished by filling up two or three times with water, or by soaking thoroughly by immersing the pot to above the brim in a pail of water and then standing it to drain in the shade. This process of watering is especially useful in the case of hard-wooded plants, such as azaleas, deutzias, heaths, and myrtles, which have fine fibrous roots and are very firmly potted in light sandly soil or peat. If at any time allowed to become too dry the inner "ball" round the roots will not readily absorb water which will flow round the "ball" leaving it unmoistened, although the surface soil may seem to be sufficiently moist. Such plants will need a thorough soaking, and to prevent them from getting into such a state it is a wise policy to immerse them in a pail of water for five or ten minutes every week or ten days. No fear need be entertained of over-watering ; if the plants have been rightly potted (*see chapter on* Potting, p. 177), all surplus water, beyond what the soil can conveniently retain, will drain away. Irregular watering is frequently the cause of failure in plant-culture, even with experienced growers.

Water each individual plant as it requires it ; because one plant in a batch needs water it does not mean that all are too dry. Plants in full growth and coming into bloom always require

more water than plants past their prime and "going-off." It
is of immense importance to bear in mind that the lower the
temperature in which greenhouse plants are placed the less *water*
they require, and *vice versâ*. Cold, which stimulates man's digestive
organs to the utmost, paralyses those of plants in the exact ratio of
its intensity. Hence the necessity of a stinted supply of water in
cold weather if plant life is to be preserved in full vigour.

Plants should never be watered overhead when in bloom or
in cold weather, or, rather, while they are in a cold atmosphere ;
and never, except to wash off dust, should those having a soft or
woolly foliage be so treated ; but some plants, as azaleas, myrtles,
heaths, and others with hard leaves, may be plentifully syringed, or
watered overhead from a fine rose, in warm weather, especially when
in full growth, or to soften the bark and encourage the formation of
new shoots. Syringing should not be overdone as it tends to weaken
the plants ; if a moist atmosphere is required this is better obtained
by keeping the walls and floor well damped rather than by excessive
overhead watering. The best time to syringe is in the early morning before the sun is up and again after the sun has lost its strength
in the late afternoon and after the house has been closed. (*See also*
Watering *in the chapter on* Gardening under Glass, Watering Seeds
in the chapter on Propagation, *and* Watering the Lawn, *p.* 102.)

Other gardening operations will be found under the chapters and
paragraphs devoted to those subjects, for example :

Under the chapter on PROPAGATION	*Under the chapter on* FRUIT-GROWING	*Under the chapter on* DISEASES AND PESTS
BUDDING	DISBUDDING	GREASE BANDING
CUTTINGS	GATHERING FRUIT	
DIVIDING	PRUNING, ROOT-PRUNING	*Under the chapter on*
GRAFTING	STORING FRUIT	SOILS AND THEIR
HARDENING-OFF	THINNING FRUIT	TREATMENT
LAYERING		FUMIGATION OF SOILS
LEAF-CUTTINGS	*Under the chapter on*	STERILIZATION OF SOILS
PRICKING-OUT	GARDENING UNDER	
RINGING	GLASS	*Under the chapter on the*
ROOT-CUTTINGS	DAMPING-DOWN	LAWN
SOWING	FUMIGATION, STOKING-UP	EDGING THE LAWN
THINNING-OUT	SYRINGEING	FEEDING THE LAWN
	VENTILATING	MOWING, ROLLING

Special chapters are devoted to such subjects as :

BEDDING-OUT	LEVELLING LAND	POTTING
DRAINING LAND	MANURING	WEEDING
FORCING	PATH-MAKING	

CHAPTER V

WEEDS AND WEEDING

APART from their unsightliness weeds do great damage in the garden, for they exclude the sun and air from the soil and deprive plants of much needed nourishment and moisture. They also harbour and encourage insect pests and fungoid diseases. As a rule gardeners do not begin weeding sufficiently early in the season, they give the weeds a start which they later find impossible to overtake. Weeding should be commenced in the early spring—early in April—and must be continued all through the summer and autumn, even till the beginning of November, it being remembered that all weeds grow apace in warm weather after rain.

Weeds on Beds

The hoe is undoubtedly the best implement with which to control weeds on beds, and if this is used early in the season and is kept in constant use, weeds will get little chance to multiply; by its aid annual weeds will be destroyed, and biennial and perennial weeds, owing to the frequent cutting down, will be so weakened that in the course of two, three, or more years they will die.

All weeds that have flowered or seeded, likewise all those with " runner " roots with " eyes " on them, which will grow again if they come into contact with the soil, must be burned, and must not be used, unburned, as vegetable manure over the soil. This latter procedure would surely spread the weeds; the ashes may safely be used as a manure. Other weeds can be put on the refuse heap and can later safely be used as manure. In hot dry weather, if the weeding is done early in the day, this class of weed may be left lying on the soil to wither and die, but in damp weather and when the soil is wet they must be removed to the rubbish heap, as there is danger of their again taking root.

Hand-weeding—gripping the weeds as near the soil as possible and twisting them out with as many of their roots as one can—must be resorted to where the plants are too close to permit of the use of the

80

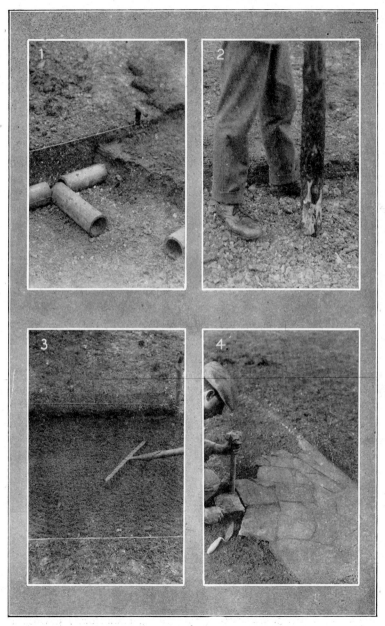

1. Laying the drainage pipes. 2. Ramming firm the hard core of rubble, clinkers or ballast. 3. Levelling the layer of sand or fine ashes in which the stone is bedded. 4. Laying the paving stone. See page 89.

GARDEN APPLIANCES

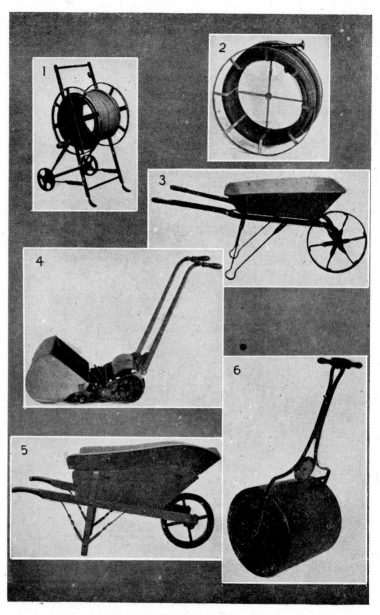

1 & 2. Hose Reels. 3. Galvanised-iron Barrow. 4. Lawn Mower. 5. Wooden
Barrow. 6. Roller.

hoe. If this method is adopted shortly after a good shower of rain, many perennial weeds may be destroyed.

As weeds spread so readily, it is most necessary to keep all rough grass near the garden cut, especially before it has time to seed. The weeds in grass-paths, grass-edgings and on the lawn must also be kept well in check for the same reason, this also applies to all neighbouring banks and hedgerows, which must be kept clean and weed-free.

Weeds on Paths

It is a mistake to hoe up weeds on paths, they may be banished temporarily, but the turned-up gravel is in a more favourable condition for their increase later on. The best method of destroying weeds on paths is to apply one of the following weed-killers in spring and in fine weather after a good shower of rain. A thorough soaking should be given, and if no rain falls for a few days after, good results can be confidently expected.

Weed-Killing Solutions

(1) Salt 1 lb. in Hot Water 1 gallon.
(2) Copper Sulphate 1 lb. in Water 6 gallons.
(3) Sulphate of Iron 1 lb. in Water 2 gallons.
(4) Caustic Soda 1 lb. in Water 8 gallons.
(5) Carbolic Acid 1 lb. in Water 10 gallons.

The solutions should be thoroughly stirred and kept well mixed while in use, and must be applied through a fine rose. A galvanized can should be used, as the chemicals are not so likely to affect it. Do not allow the mixtures to touch the skin or clothes, and label all bottles or receptacles containing the solutions " *Poison* " and keep them locked away in a safe place.

In spraying the paths care must be taken not to treat areas covering the roots of edging plants or these will be poisoned, and no dogs or domestic animals should be allowed to use the paths for at least three days after the application of the weed-killer.

Use up *all* the solution, as it is poison ; wash the can and mixing utensils thoroughly, and store the tin or bottle of weed-killer out of harm's way.

Weeds on Lawns

(*See chapter on* The Lawn, p. 98.)

E.G. P

CHAPTER VI

HOW TO PLAN A GARDEN

THE whole art of simple gardening consists really in thoughtful adaptation, in thinking out a scheme which will make the most of the natural facilities of the site. For example, the actual laying-out of the garden determines to a great extent the amount of labour necessary to keep it neat and flourishing.

In the case of a very small garden it is sometimes a mistaken enterprise to devote much time or space to vegetables. As a rule, they can be bought for less than it costs the amateur to grow them, and their presence in such gardens is seldom an attraction from the picturesque or the economical point of view.

Avoid Overcrowding.—While bareness should be avoided, the other extreme of planting the garden too generously with trees and shrubs is also a great mistake. Snugness and seclusion are two very desirable qualities in a garden, but they should be achieved without too dear a sacrifice of air and sunshine. The garden as a whole should seem compact without in any way presenting a cramped appearance ; and this desirable effect is most easily obtained by preserving a unity between its successive and varying features. The range of such variety in the different parts of a garden should lie between the definite bounds set by the style of the house itself, on the one hand, and by the paddock or surrounding landscape on the other. That is to say, that the outlying parts of the garden should be wilder and less artificial both in plan and detail than those which more closely approach the house ; and the actual transition from formal to free and from free to wild should be gradual, synthetic, and all but imperceptible. All attempts at striking contrasts should be confined to details, leaving the large and comprehensive plan of the garden a complete and harmonious whole.

House and Garden.—So many houses are, from an artistic point of view, utterly divorced from their gardens because no care has been taken to graduate their relations one to the other. House and garden are treated as essentially separate and unrelated problems, and an abrupt, unmitigable line shows exactly where the house ends and the garden begins. After all, a garden in most cases is merely a setting for the house, and those parts of it which actually approach the house should be laid out with a certain restraint which may be absent from its more remote situations. Whether one approaches the house from the garden, or the garden from the house, the change should be led up to and not suddenly insisted upon.

Too many people insist upon revealing the smallness of their garden by laying out most of it with gravel. Indeed, in many cases, the lawn itself might be but a decorative appendage to the bare stretches of gravel which circumvent it. While nothing gives a greater sense of space than breadth of lawn, nothing is more cramping in appearance than bare stretches of gravel. Paths are, of course, a necessity, but their extent and number should be restricted purely to necessity.

The Lawn.—The lawn should often be the chief feature of the small garden, even at a sacrifice of flowers. It is a permanent beauty, the hardiest of perennials, the most capable of adaptation and, from every point of view, offers the most rewarding prospect. It is both useful and ornamental, far more decorative—if imaginatively treated—than any amount of prim flower-beds, while at the same time lending itself to an infinitude of practical uses (*see* Chapter IX).

The Use of Natural Features.—Nothing is to be more deprecated than the habit of mere paper planning, that is, of drawing up a hard and fast disposition of the garden without practical reference to the site itself, and of forcing extremes of fashion upon an uncongenial locality. From all of which it must not be understood that any particular style of gardening—the formal, the natural, and so on—is condemned as such. Certain situations demand a formal, even as others call for a freer, treatment. The character of the site and its architectural and rural surroundings should give the general lines upon which the plan should be formed. Many people insist upon making a clean sweep of everything with which nature has already endowed the proposed site. Such drastic treatment is almost always a great mistake. In the case of such natural features as trees, clumps of shrubs, etc., thought should be given to decide how far these original tenants can be utilized in the gardener's scheme.

Commencing the Work.—The actual spade work should not be embarked upon until the plan of the garden is complete in every important detail, its boundaries fenced, and the walks and leading features decided upon. For it is here, in the early stage of carrying out a plan in practice, that proper methods must be understood and followed.

CHAPTER VII

DESIGNING AND MAKING BEDS AND BORDERS

IN designing the flower-beds in a garden it must always be borne in mind that the first aim is not that the bed itself shall be beautiful in shape but that it shall be so constructed and situated that it can display the flowers planted in it to the best advantage. The more simple the shape the better it will, as a rule, fulfil its purpose, and will at the same time be all the more easy to construct, plant, and keep in order. Elaborate geometrical designs have, except in the more formal Dutch and French gardens, gone right out of fashion. Many of these older designs had sharp-pointed extremities, which were very awkward to plant and care for ; the most useful shapes are circles, ellipses, squares, and rectangles. Rectilinear beds are generally used in the more formal parts of the garden, near the house, as they best harmonize with the straight lines of the architecture of the house ; if they are laid out on the lawn they should be so placed that their longer sides run parallel with those of a neighbouring straight path, or with the edge of the lawn. Except when they are permanently to accommodate shade-loving plants the beds should be so placed that they are open to the sun, but should at the same time have shelter from cold or strong prevailing winds. When beds are made on a lawn they must be so designed and placed that the lawn-mower can operate easily ; grass verges or walks between beds should never be less than 18 inches or 2 feet wide, otherwise even a small machine will have difficulty in cutting them well.

Making the Beds

Having pegged out the design to the required size and shape, the turf should be removed on a dry day with a turfing-iron in turves 2 inches deep, and the soil should then be bastard-trenched, that is, the surface must be thoroughly dug over to a depth of two spades, the top layer being kept on top, and the subsoil below this being forked over, but left in position. If the soil is very heavy, the top 2 or 3 feet should be removed, the subsoil should be broken up as before, and upon it should be placed 5 to 6 inches of broken bricks or large stones as drainage. When the top-soil is moderately good it may have loam added to it and then be returned to the bed, or if the soil is quite unsuitable, that is clayey or stony, all should be removed and fresh loam must be introduced. In either case, a liberal dressing

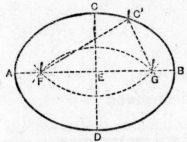

FIG. 8.—MAKING AN ELLIPTICAL BED.

AB equals the length and *CD* the width of the required bed. These lines bisect each other and cut at right angles at *E*. With radius *AE* and centres *C* and *D* describe the dotted arcs cutting each other in *F* and *G*. Set stakes in ground at *F* and *G*, and with a stick tighten a cord with its ends fixed to *F* and *G* and equal in length to *AB* until it touches point *A* ; then, keeping it tight, trace required ellipse *ACBDA*.

of well-rotted manure should be well dug into the top-soil. If these beds are being made in a new garden, lime at the rate of 14 oz. per square yard, should also be worked into the soil, as insect pests and fungi are certain to be present in quantities in any newly-broken grassland.

Each autumn the beds should be dressed with manure, as bedding plants are, as a whole, voracious feeders, like a rich soil, and soon exhaust it when spring and summer bedders are, as is usually the case, grown in the same bed. If manuring cannot be carried out in the autumn it should be done in April or May when the summer-bedding is put in. Every three or four years the soil should be thoroughly dug over to a depth of two spades, and if it appears at all sour and greasy should be dressed with lime.

The addition of new soil, manure, and drainage material will raise the bed somewhat above the level of the surrounding ground. The soil should slope neatly up to the centre of the bed, and will thus best display plants of equal height when bedded out, and will provide drainage. A bed 4 feet wide should be about 4 inches higher at the centre than at the edges ; beds of other sizes, of course, varying in height at the centre in proportion to their width. If on a lawn, the edging of the bed should be neatly trimmed round with an edging-iron. (*See also* Chapter XI.)

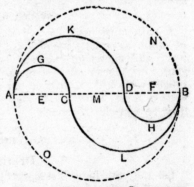

FIG. 9. —MAKING THE SERPENTINE BED.

Divide *AB*, the length of the bed, into three equal parts in the points *C* and *D*; subdivide *AC* and *DB* each into two equal parts in the points *E* and *F*. From *E* and *F* as centres, with radii *EA* and *FB*, the semicircles *AGC* and *BHD* are described, and from *C* and *D* as centres, with radii *CA* and *DB*, the semicircles *AKD*, *BLC* are described, completing the outline of the bed. Divide *AB* into two equal parts at *M* and with *M* as centre and radius *AM* describe circle *ANBO*, thus forming a pear-shaped bed *AGCLBO*.

CHAPTER VIII

PATHS AND EDGINGS

THE enjoyment of a garden is greatly increased, as also is its utility, by the provision of good and well-kept paths. The essentials of a good path are that it shall be in appearance harmonious with the rest of the garden, and that it shall afford a dry surface in wet weather. Cement, concrete, ashes, brick-dust, and asphalte are sometimes employed for the purpose ; but in general we may say that the three most suitable surfaces for garden paths are afforded by gravel, bricks, and broken paving stones.

It will be sufficient to describe the construction of the gravel path, the crazy path and the grass walk. Save for the different materials used, the principles of construction are the same for the ash, brick, concrete, or asphalte path as those described for gravel paths.

Width of Paths

A path must never be less than 2 feet in width, even if it is of quite secondary importance. A good average width is 4 feet ; this allows for the easy passage of the barrow and other garden implements, and for two people to walk abreast, an amenity often overlooked. Entrance drives and tracks which must bear horse or motor traffic should be 8 feet wide, at least ; rather should they be considerably more.

CONSTRUCTING THE PATH

Drainage

Let the path be well designed and carefully made ; if so constructed it will last many years, and will not only serve its purpose as a means of communication, but will also be a great help in draining the garden.

Whether it will be necessary to lay a pipe-drain or not depends upon the nature of the soil and the lie of the land. In light, porous soils the rough stones, bricks, or clinkers used as a foundation will provide sufficient drainage, but in heavy, retentive clays a pipe-drain will invariably be advisable ; this may run directly below the centre of the path, or else on either side of the path ; on the

86

lower side when the path is on a side slope, and always at the lowest point below the clinker or brick foundation, and resting on a firm base. Where there is any doubt as to the porosity of the soil, always lay a drain. As has been said above, a single drain down the centre or down one side will be found adequate for ordinary paths of 4 feet in width; but paths wider than this and drives should have drains down each side. The pipes used for draining should be 3 or 4 inches in diameter and must be laid from $1\frac{1}{2}$ to 2 feet deep, according to the nature of the soil and the width of the path. (*See chapter on* Draining Land, p. 55.) The drains must slope gently towards the outlet, which may be into a garden main drain or into a ditch or pond. The pipes being in position, cover them with 12 to 15 inches of broken bricks or rough stones through which the water can trickle.

The Foundations

The chief thing to be done in every case is to provide a solid, but yet porous substratum, which will afford sufficient support to the materials of which the upper part of the walk, or rather its surface, is made, and yet allow of the rapid passing away of the water that may fall on the path in the form of rain. Of course, we are now supposing that the walk is to be made in the ordinary way, and coated—if a road, with broken stones, technically called "metalling"—and if a garden path, with gravel.

The Gravel Path

The course of the path or road must first be marked out with stakes, and the surface soil removed to the depth of 9 to 18 inches if there is no lack of materials to fill it; the wider the path the deeper the excavation necessary. The nature of the soil also affects the depth of excavation necessary: in heavy clay at least 18 inches should be removed, in light soil 9 inches to a foot will suffice. There is a point that must be stressed here, and that is the importance of eradicating all perennial weeds, especially those with long creeping roots, from the soil at the bottom and sides of the path. If this is not done all kinds of weeds will soon make

FIG. 10. —THE GRAVEL PATH.

Over the drain is placed 6–9 inches of coarse clinker or rubble, rammed firm; over this is laid 4 to 6 inches of coarse gravel, and on top of this again 2 inches of gravel "hogging."

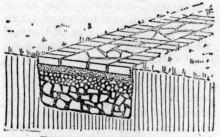

FIG. 11.—CRAZY PAVING.

For crazy paving the foundations are the same as for the gravel path, but they need not be quite so deep, and in place of the gravel "hogging" is a 1 to 2-inch layer of sand or fine ashes in which the paving is set.

their appearance through the new path, and will be very difficult to get rid of. Weed-killer *will* kill these perennial weeds, but it takes three or four years to effect a thorough clearance. From one-third to one-half the depth must then be filled up with rough stones, brickbats, clinkers from the brickfields, slag and scoriæ from the iron-works, or any coarse, hard rubbish that can be gathered together; the greater part of the remainder must then be filled up with coarse gravel, shingle, etc., which may be mixed with a little earth to give consistency to the whole, and finally coated with gravel to the depth of 2 or 3 inches, which must be raked level and be constantly rolled with a heavy garden roller until the path is hard and solid. The gravel must not be made too wet or it will adhere to the roller, and any large stones should be screened out of the gravel and used in the foundation. The correct level for the crown of the path can be marked by wooden pegs driven in to the right depth. (*See* Levelling, p. 58.) Allow the path to set for a few days before using it and then fill up any hollows with gravel and roll again. Gravel taken from the beach should not be used if other is obtainable, as it does not bind and always remains loose. If, however, it must be used, mix a quarter part of clean dry clay with the gravel before it is laid; when moistened the mixture will bind well. Supposing, as is sometimes the case, that the ground is of a loose, porous character, or wet and marshy, and, therefore, not calculated to afford a solid basis to the pathway; it is then a good plan to make the trench deeper, and to lay brushwood at the bottom before throwing in the rough rubbish.

Gutters and Drainage.—In some cases it is desirable to have a solid facing to a garden path so that it may be impervious to rain, and in this case it is of importance that the surface of the walk should be rounded—higher in the centre, and sloping down on either side. The water will escape into the earth or turf by which the walk is bordered, or, if desired, gutters can be formed to carry the water to a tank formed for its reception in some part of the garden. The gutters may either be moulded in the material of which the path is made or they may be constructed below the surface, like a drain, and hidden from view. In this case catch-pits with iron gratings should be made on each side of the path at distances of about 30 feet apart. In no case, however, should these gratings communicate directly with the drains, as the sand soon chokes them up. They should consist of a well, formed of brick, a foot or 18 inches square, and of sufficient depth to leave a space of 1 foot or 18 inches (for a 4-foot path) below the level of the drain, which should be directly below the grating and at the top of the pit. This allows ample space for collecting the sediment. The main drain, into which these side drains empty, usually runs down the centre of the path below the hard core.

Where the path lies on a steep slope, a heavy shower of rain may soon cause havoc with the gravel, the surface-water rushing down and ploughing great furrows in the path. This can be prevented by constructing brick, tile, or cement gutters, 6 inches to a foot in width, down both sides of the path, and by inserting catch-pits at regular intervals to carry away the water.

Large bricks or pieces of rock placed in the gutter just below the catch-pits will do much to impede the rush of water and will enable the drains to carry it off more easily.

Another way of getting over this " washing-out " trouble is to mix cement with the gravel when laying it down in the proportion of six parts of gravel to one of cement. Add water and mix until the consistency of a thick paste is obtained, then immediately lay the mixture down over the path, flatten out with the back of the spade, and level off with a lath of wood or with the back of a rake, and allow it to set thoroughly.

Crazy Paving

Crazy paving must be well and evenly laid, otherwise it is very unpleasant to walk on and will always be giving trouble by the loosening and rising of the stones. In the initial stages of construction the procedure is the same as for a gravel path, that is to say, the same remarks apply as to drainage: the foundation of large stones or broken bricks is laid down in the same way, but need not be quite so deep, likewise

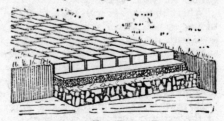

FIG. 12.—THE BRICK PATH.

Here the foundations are made as for the crazy path, but in place of the top layer of sand or ashes is a layer of mortar in which the bricks are set.

the layer of clinkers or smaller stones. The one great aim is to afford a sound and level surface for the paving, and the straight-edge and spirit-level will therefore be constantly in use with a view to this. The foundations must be rammed and rolled absolutely firm; if there is the slightest fear of any settlement in the base, as may well happen in clay, an inch layer of cement in which to lay the paving had better be laid down. Over the hard core spread a 2-inch layer of sand or ashes, if cement is not used; make this quite level and then lay down the paving, fitting the pieces carefully together so that small pieces are not required, as these always tend to work loose. No crevices of much more than an inch in width should be left between the stones or the path will be uncomfortable to walk on and will not remain firm. Where there is likely to be much traffic, the main stones, and all those at the sides of the walk, should be set in mortar. Fill the interstices with sandy loam, so that rock plants, such as saxifrages, thymes, and other creepers and trailers, may be planted. (*See* The Paved Garden, p. 139.)

Grass Walks

Grass walks running between gay borders are a delight, but ought never to be depended upon as necessary routes to or from any given place. When of great length, and 12 or 18 feet wide, they are most imposing. They should never be less than 2 feet in width, otherwise there will be difficulty in handling the mowing machine; rather should they be well over 6 feet wide; the wider they are, within reason of course, the more imposing they will be. Where there is likely to be much traffic on grass walks, their foundations should be formed and drained as if for gravel; but it will be more satisfactory to make good gravel walks for the general traffic, and to reserve the grass walks and keep them closely cut for occasional use only, their beauty providing ample justification for their existence.

Where these grass walks are likely to be much used a single row of flag-stones, either edge to edge or some 2 feet apart, sunk in level with the surface of the turf, will not only make the walk more substantial and lasting, but will also, in many cases, greatly enhance its charm. Equally pleasing and more useful, because the borders can be approached in wet weather, will be two paved walks, 18 inches to 2 feet wide, down both sides of the grass way.

In newly-laid-out gardens the grass walks are usually formed of the existing turf, and it is surprising what consistent weeding, rolling, and cutting will accomplish. Where, however, the walks are to be seeded, a variety of seed that will stand much wear should be chosen. If the barrow is to be used on turf walks in winter, boards must be laid down to prevent the wheel from sinking into and ruining the turf.

For details as to the upkeep of grass walks, *see the chapter on* The Lawn.

EDGINGS

Edgings to paths resolve themselves into two classifications—formal and informal. As formal we include edgings of stone, bricks, tiles, and wood; also grass verges, and miniature hedges of box. Edgings made of plants (*see* list, p. 92) are, of course, informal. Where suitable stones can be obtained the most interesting borders of all are afforded by irregular blocks of stone, bedded in cement if large, with alpines growing between and over them. The stones must never project more than 6 inches from the border.

Formal Edgings

Below will be found brief descriptions of the best formal edgings.

Tiles.—This word seems to conjure up the exceedingly ugly borders of fancy tiles seen in some gardens. A tile border, however, need not be ugly; it should be severely plain and nondescript in colour, and must never attract the eye, its function being utility pure and simple. The tiles must be firmly set in the soil and should be even and regular. Some have hollow heads through which canes or wires may be inserted to keep the tiles straight and in line. To lay the tiles, dig a straight-sided trench to the required depth and with its bottom cut level with the incline of the path. On the inner (border) side of the trench place a long and straight board and against it set the tiles evenly. Now fill in the earth and gravel on the path side of the tiles, ram it very firm, then remove the board, fill the space with soil and firm the tiles from that side.

Bricks.—Bricks make excellent border edgings, but they must be of a good hard variety; those that will crumble under the action of frost, when lying in the damp ground, are worse than useless and soon become ragged and unsightly. The bricks should be laid on edge, that is to say, with one of the shorter sides in the ground, and sloping slightly inwards towards the border and away from the path. If they are set vertically, or incline outwards over the path, they are more liable to be damaged by the passage of the barrow or roller. Nearly half the brick should be buried in the soil, or it may be set in a 2-inch layer of mortar, when only one-third of the brick need be below the surface level.

Concrete.—This makes a good edging, and is easily constructed. Two boards of wood one-half to an inch in thickness, a foot high, and of any length, are set up 4 inches apart, with 6 inches of their height covered by the soil. The soil between them is excavated to the full 12-inch depth of the boards, which are held firm and upright by stout pegs driven into the soil on the outer sides and nailed into the boards. A series of boards of similar size are laid in this way, in line, where the edging is required. Now mix the concrete (see p. 143) and fill up the space between the boards, making the top flat and neat with a trowel. When the concrete has set (four to five days) remove the boards and a neat permanent edging will remain. An iron rod is often laid in the centre of the concrete edging, while in the course of construction, to reinforce it.

Wood.—Wood edgings are neat and last a considerable time if creosoted or tarred. They should be made of planks 1 inch thick and 12 inches wide. Six inches of the width should lie in the soil and they must be kept firm and upright by strong wooden pegs, about 2 inches square and some 2 feet in length, driven in on the inner (border) side till they are flush with the top of the board. The pegs should be driven in about every yard, and should be fixed to the planks with long galvanized iron nails.

Grass Edgings or verges are the neatest and most pleasing of all the formal edgings. They entail a good deal of labour if they are to be kept properly trimmed and cut, but if time can be spent on them they well repay the gardener for it. They are out of place in the small garden and should only be used as edgings to large beds or borders, as they must be at least 2 feet wide to enable the mower to work properly on them. If they are too small to cut with the mower, the gardener must then have ample time and patience to spare to keep them in anything like good order.

SOME GOOD EDGING PLANTS.

NOTE.—For details as to Colour, Height, Season of Flowering and Culture, *see* the Alphabetical List of Flowering Plants and Shrubs, page 207.

Achillea umbellata (H.P.)
Ageratum (dwarf)(H.H.A.)
Alyssum saxatile compactum (H.P.)
Antirrhinums (dwarf, various) (H.P.)
Arabis (various) (H.P.)
Armeria maritima (syn. vulgaris) (H.P.)
Aubrietia (H.P.)
Bellis perennis (Daisy) (H.P.)
Campanula (dwarf, various) (H.P.)
Cerastium Biebersteinii (H.P.)
Dianthus deltoides (H.P.)

Echeveria (H.H.P.)
Erica darleyensis, kevernensis and vagans (H.S.)
Genista pilosa (H.P.)
Gypsophila repens (H.P.)
Hypericum (H.S.)
Iberis sempervirens (H.P.)
Lavendula Spica (H.S.)
Linum (various) (H.P.)
Lobelia (dwarf) (H.H.A.)
Lysimachia (Creeping Jenny) (H.P.)
Malcolmia (Virginia Stock) (H.A.)
Myosotis (Forget-Me-Not) (H.P.)

Phlox sublata (H.P.)
Polyanthus (H.P.)
Portulaca grandiflora (H.H.A.)
Primulas (various) (H.P.)
Saponaria ocymoides (H.P.)
Saxifraga (various) (H.P.)
Sedum (various) (H.P.)
Silene pendula compacta (H.A.)
Tagetes (dwarf) (H.H.A.)
Verbena (various)(H.H.A.)
Veronica (various) (H.P.)
Viola (various) (H.P.)
Zauschneria californica (H.P.)

NOTE.—H.A. = Hardy Annual; H.H.A. = Half-hardy Annual; H.P. = Hardy Perennial; H.H.P. = Half-hardy Perennial; H.S. = Hardy Shrub.

CHAPTER IX

THE LAWN

MAKING THE LAWN

TO make a lawn takes a considerable time. It is possible to obtain a covering of grass in a single season, but anything that could reasonably be called a lawn is a work of years. Of course a grass plot on which one may walk almost at once may be prepared by transplanting blocks of turf from a neighbouring field, common or hillside, and rolling it into place. But more and more gardeners have come to the conclusion that a perfect lawn of uniform colour and even surface, free from plantain and other weeds, can only be obtained by careful preparation of the soil, and by sowing carefully selected grass seed mixture. The seeded lawn is cheaper than one laid down with good turves, but cannot be used—as a tennis-court, for instance—during the first year after sowing as the turved lawn can be.

Site

Where there is any choice of situation a northern aspect is to be preferred to a southern one, especially where the water supply is limited. A fairly moist soil is indeed essential to a good lawn, though it is equally necessary that the soil should be well-drained, and must not remain soft and spongy for long after a shower of rain. Deep drainage is not necessary, seeing that the roots of grasses do not penetrate far below the surface ; but on heavy clay, pipe-drains are usually necessary, and a 4- to 5-inch layer of ashes must be placed immediately below the top-soil, which should be from 6 to 9 inches in thickness. Whatever the nature of the soil the whole surface should be trenched over to a depth of 18 inches to 2 feet, the best soil being kept on top. A point to remember is that the final dressing of soil over the drains must be much poorer than that covering other parts, otherwise the grass will grow better and greener over the drains than elsewhere and a patchy lawn will result. (*See chapter on* Draining Land, p. 55.)

Levelling

It is more than likely that it will be necessary to level the lawn ; this is, of course, essential in the case of the tennis-lawn. Levelling should be commenced as early as possible so that the land may have ample time to settle before the sowing or turfing is done. Unless the soil is very porous a lawn should not be dead level, or the water may hang on it after rain ; even a tennis-court should be from 3 to 4 inches higher on one side than the other ; this will not be apparent and will in no way affect the play. Where levelling is necessary, however, the reader is referred to the chapter on *Levelling*.

Soil

The soil itself should be a good fibrous loam, rich in humus, the ordinary soil excavated in making the foundations of a house, which it is often desired to employ for a lawn, being altogether unsuitable. Where suitable soil, from 18 inches to 2 feet in depth, is not already *in situ* it should be obtained, and used to replace, at any rate, the top foot of the existing earth. A deep root-run like this will assist the drainage of the lawn and will prevent the grass from becoming scorched up in hot, dry weather. In introducing soil from outside it is, however, important to remember that it is likely to contain the seeds of many weeds which would be fatal to a satisfactory lawn. A certain time should therefore be allowed to elapse in order to afford opportunity for these seeds to germinate, and the resulting weeds to be destroyed before any grass seed is sown. As an alternative the introduced soil may be burned, and then enriched with a liberal dressing of manure. If fresh mould cannot be introduced the top-soil, if heavy, must be well broken up, weeds and stones must be removed, and with it should be incorporated plenty of finely sifted ashes or coarse sand and grit, to render the soil porous and enable the roots to work through it. If the soil is too light, well-decayed manure and leaf-mould should be added, until the top 10 inches of the compost consists of one part of these ingredients to four parts of soil. In any event, a good dressing of farmyard manure, say twenty cartloads to the acre, should be incorporated with the top-spit of soil and should not lie more than 4 inches below the surface. Where lime is found to be lacking, powdered lime must be dug in at the rate of 6 oz. to the square yard. If this preparation is made in the autumn, the ground should be allowed to lie fallow through the winter. In the spring the surface should be again carefully tested for level with a straight-edge and spirit-level, so that any inequalities may be made up ; the upper 4 inches of the soil is then made as fine as possible by repeated rakings and thorough rollings, until the surface is so firm that it scarcely shows the mark of a boot when trodden on and is entirely devoid of stones and weed-free.

Sowing the Seed

Seed can be sown early in April or about the end of August or the beginning of September. Spring-sown seed will take between a fortnight and three weeks to germinate, but in autumn—the better time to sow—the soil is warm and the seed may be expected to show above the ground in a week or ten days. Seed should be sown on a day when there is no wind and when the soil is dry enough not to stick to the boots or the rake, and great evenness should be aimed at, two sowings being made at right angles to one another. This even distribution of seed is best obtained by marking the lawn out into squares whose sides are from a yard to 2 yards in length. The seed, which should have been mixed with twice its quantity of fine mould, is then divided into as many portions as there are squares so that each square may receive an equal amount of seed.

Care after Sowing

A very light raking is then desirable, just cover with a $\frac{1}{4}$ of an inch of finely sifted soil, and afterwards the ground should be rolled over, lengthwise and across, provided the soil is not damp enough to stick to the roller. To protect the seeds from the birds, black cotton should be stretched on short sticks, or old netting can be thrown over small tree branches spread over the seeded surface. As soon as the grass is an inch or so high roll it with a light wooden roller—in fine, dry weather—and when it has grown to 2 to 3 inches above the ground weeds must be removed and regular cutting with the scythe and rolling must be begun. A top-dressing of an ounce of guano to the square yard will help on the young grass. The scythe must continue to be used for several months until the grass is sufficiently secure in the ground to bear the mowing machine, which has a tendency to pull young grass up by the roots. It should be possible to use the mower in June, but the blades must be raised an inch above the normal level for the first two or three cuttings. That is to say, the grass should be cut so that it is from 1 to 2 inches in length, instead of the $\frac{1}{2}$ to $\frac{3}{4}$ of an inch necessary for mature grass. From 2 to 4 oz. per square yard is the quantity of seed to sow, and special seed should be obtained for the purpose from a first-rate firm of seedsmen. No economy should be attempted in this important matter, as the seed must be good ; and it is difficult to sow too thickly as the thicker the sowing the less chance weeds will have of growing through, and the young seedlings, when closely massed together, are not so liable to damage by frost or scorching sun. When autumn sowing is practised, the lawn should, if possible, be drained, levelled and should have the surface prepared in spring. Then if the soil is thoroughly and consistently weeded throughout the summer, there should be an absolutely weed-free seed bed for sowing in August or September.

When sowing a lawn care should be taken to see that the seed sown is suitable for the soil, the situation, and for the use to which the lawn is to be put. Grasses vary just as other plants do in their tastes, and careful selection will do much to secure a permanently satisfactory lawn.

Grass Seeds for Different Situations

The following list will enable the reader to choose seed suitable for sowing on a lawn in practically any situation that he is likely to encounter:

GENERAL USE:
  Festuca ovina tenuifolia
  Cynosurus cristatus
  Poa nemoralis sempervirens
  Poa pratensis
  Poa trivialis

LIGHT SOIL:
  Cynosurus cristatus
  Festuca duriuscula
  Festuca ovina tenuifolia
  Festuca rubra
  Poa pratensis

DRY SOIL:
  Festuca rubra

POOR AND SHALLOW SOIL:
  Festuca duriuscula

UNDER TREES OR MOIST, SHADY SITUATIONS:
  Poa trivialis

TOWN GARDENS:
  Poa annua
  Poa nemoralis

SPORTS GROUNDS:
  Festuca rubra

NEAR SEA:
  Festuca rubra

LARGE AREAS:
  Lolium perenne

Lawns from Turf

The turves laid down should be of good quality, that is to say, the texture of the grass must be fine and the turves moderately weed-free. Turves of coarse grass and full of weeds will give endless trouble and never make a good lawn; if really good turf cannot be obtained it is far better to sow seed. Cumberland turf is among the best, but the cost of the carriage makes it expensive and out of reach of most pockets. The best possible turves, however, should be obtained and all the largest weeds should be removed before laying down. In preparing a piece of ground for turfing, the soil should be well dug to a depth of about 9 inches, and a light dressing of well-rotted manure may with advantage be incorporated with it. The soil should then be well rolled and levelled, any hollows being filled with soil and again rolled. Immediately before the turves are laid down the top ½ inch of the soil should be raked up so that the roots of the grass may work into it and bind the turf to the soil. The turves are usually cut in slabs 3 feet long, 1 foot wide, and 1½ or 2 inches thick. In this form they are easily torn and will require to be very carefully laid if the lawn is to be level and even. Turves

1. Preparing the site. 2. Testing the depth of planting. 3. Spreading out
the roots. 4. The correctly planted bush. See page 69.

1. How to protect seedlings from frost by means of hooped sticks and sacking.
2. Protection by "thatching" with straw. 3. Keeping off bitter winds by means of boards. See page 69.

1 foot square and the same thickness as the above are often used as they are far more easy to handle and give much better results. They should be placed turf side down in a wooden frame or gauge-box 1½ inches deep, made so that they lie tightly in position. A two-handed knife with a long curved blade, or an old scythe, is then passed straight across the frame to cut off any inequalities, so that the turf shall be exactly 1½ inches thick all through. If the turves are not to be laid down immediately they should be stacked in a sheltered position out of the sun. They should not, however, be stacked for longer than is necessary, and should be laid down while the grass is still green and bright in colour. When put down they should be fitted very close together, should be laid diagonally across the lawn, and must be " bonded " as bricks are in a wall, that is to say, the junction between two in one row must come opposite the middle of a turf in the rows before and after it. Finely sifted soil must be worked in to fill the crevices and the turf should at once be watered well and then thoroughly and evenly pounded with the turf-beater and rolled, a spirit-level and straight-edge being used to ensure evenness. Water should be given daily for some time, and rolling both across and up and down the lawn with a light roller should be almost constant, provided the soil is not too wet. A dressing, ½ an inch thick, of fine sharp sand, after the rolling has been completed, will be found to improve the texture of the grass and should be well-brushed in. Turves may be laid in fine weather, either in spring or autumn, the latter being perhaps the better time. Turf must never be laid later in the spring than April, otherwise it is liable to suffer from drought. For the first three weeks the grass should be cut twice a week with the scythe, after that time it should be cut at least once a week with the machine, being rolled after each cutting during the first year. Lawns laid down in turf wear better than a seeded lawn during the first two or three years.

CARE OF THE LAWN

In the autumn, the lawn should be well swept and raked to drag out all possible moss, weeds, and dead grass. It should then be rolled with a spiked roller, or the prongs of a garden fork should be thrust perpendicularly into the turf to a depth of 6 inches, to aerate it and help to surface-drain it through the winter. The holes made by the fork should not be more than 3 to 4 inches apart, and should stud the whole surface of the lawn. If the grass, from the nature of the soil, is inclined to grow rank and coarse, it will be much improved by a good dressing early in February of clean sharp sand all over it ; if, on the other hand, it has a tendency to scald and burn up, it will receive great benefit from a dressing of equal parts

Dressings for Killing Weeds on Lawns

Type of Weed.	Dressing to be Used	Quantity applied per square yard	When to Apply	Remarks
Clover	Nitrate of Soda *or* Anti-clover Mixture	¼ oz. } ¾ oz. }	March. Repeat Dressing in 3 Weeks	Besides discouraging clover, this fertiliser encourages the growth of grass in cold weather. Clover may also be raked out and is weakened by very close cutting with the machine in dry weather. Most seedsmen sell a special anti-clover mixture with full directions on the container.
Daisies	3 parts Ammonium Sulphate, 1 part Sulphate of Iron, and 30 parts Fine, Sharp Sand	2½ oz.	September in Dry Weather, with a Second Dressing early in April.	Mix the ingredients of this lawn-sand thoroughly together.
	or Weed-killer	A Drop in Heart of Each Weed	Spring or Autumn	Apply on a dry, still day.
Dandelions	Weed-killer or Carbolic Acid (1 oz. to a gallon of water) in a weed-killer ejector or on a skewer	A Drop in Heart of Each Weed	October and November	Pierce the heart of each weed and apply weed-killer.
Moss	2 parts Kainit to 3 parts Superphosphate of Lime	2½ oz.	January	Give this dressing two or three years running.
	or Sulphate of Iron	¼ oz.	October	Rake out all possible moss before applying the weed-killer, which must be mixed with twenty times its bulk of sand or fine mould and well raked into the surface. Ten days after application again rake out all dead moss.
Plantains	*See Daisies*			

Fertilizers and Dressings for the Lawn

State of Lawn.	Nature of Soil.	Fertilizer or Top-Dressing Required.	Amount to Apply per Square Yard.	When to Apply.	Remarks.
Grass Poor and Weak	Light	Sulphate of Potash, or Kainit	1 oz.	March	
" "	Heavy	Bone Meal, or equal parts of Bone Meal and Superphosphate of lime	2 oz.	October or February	Bone Meal should not be used too freely as it encourages the growth of clover. Superphosphate is more suitable to a medium soil than to a heavy clay and is best applied in autumn, but never on soils deficient in lime.
" "	Damp and Sour	Slaked Lime (fresh), or Pulverized Chalk	10 oz.	November or December	This dressing sweetens the soil. Ten days after application thrust the prongs of the fork vertically 6 inches into the surface, all over, to let the air into the soil.
Grass, Rank and Coarse	Heavy	Clean, Sharp Sand (well-screened Sea or River Sand is best, never use soft-binding Sand)	Dressing ½-inch Thick	Early February	
Grass Scorched	Light Sandy or Gravelly	Equal parts of well-sieved fibrous Loam and Leaf-mould with a sprinkling of good guano, soot or horn-meal finely powdered	Dressing ½-inch Thick	February	The compost should be very finely sifted. If well-sieved the compost soon works down into the roots and allows the fine grass to grow.
" "	Heavy	Nitrate of Soda	½ oz.	March	Discourages clover, but encourages growth of grass in cold weather.
Young Seedling Grass	Any	Guano	1 oz.	May	Never apply guano on soils deficient in lime.
Lawn, Mossy	Any	Soot	Sufficient just to Blacken Grass	October and November Before rain if possible	The soot should have been exposed to the atmosphere for 6 months before application. Encourages growth of young grass. Wood ashes applied in December also help towards the elimination of moss.

of leaf-mould and fibrous loam together with a sprinkling of good guano, soot, or finely-powdered horn-meal. The loam must be free of fungi, the eggs of insect pests, and of the seeds of weeds ; if there is room this may be ensured by spreading out the soil for six months or so before use, so that any seeds may have time to germinate. A sprinkling of naphthaline will invariably dispense with fungi and insect pests.

Mowing

The two methods of lawn-mowing—mowing by machine and with the scythe—are best done at different times in the day. The mechanical lawn-mower works best and most quickly when the grass is dry, but for cutting with the scythe the early morning, when the dew is still on the grass, is the best and easiest time. In the cool of the morning the grass is fuller of moisture and stiffer in the stem, thus standing up more firmly against the scythe. The exact times of the year at which mowing should be commenced and ended vary, of course, with seasons, but as a general rule mowing is necessary from March until about the middle of November. The lawn should be well swept before the first mowing of the season to clear it of all stones, twigs, and worm casts that would otherwise injure the machine. Mowing should be commenced as soon as the ground will stand it, and the grass, unless newly sown, should not be allowed to grow so long that the first cutting has to be by the scythe. In spring and autumn it will be sufficient to mow the lawn once in ten days ; in summer it will be necessary once a week and even twice a week when the weather is warm and showery. In very hot, dry weather, the knives should be raised and the collecting box should be left off so that the cut grass may act as a mulch to the roots. If during the winter the weather is very mild the grass may start growing, and should it become over 2 inches in length the mower should be run over it if the ground is firm enough, otherwise the grass will tend to become thin and straggly.

Rolling

Great mistakes are made in rolling, and lawns otherwise in excellent condition are often ruined through ignorance of the proper methods of doing this. The roller should be used periodically from September to May, when the lawn is not too wet and sodden ; if rolled with a heavy roller when in the latter condition, a hard crust is formed on the surface, surface-drainage is impeded and the air is prevented from reaching the roots of the grass. Roll, therefore, when the lawn is rather on the dry side, and not directly after rain, and remember that two rollings with a light roller are far more beneficial than one with a heavy roller. Rolling is intended to keep the surface even and to spread the roots of the grass, but it is *not* intended, and *cannot* make the lawn level; this should have been done when the lawn was laid out. Never, therefore, use a heavy roller in wet weather. Rolling should be more frequent on a newly-laid lawn than on an older one, when a few rollings in the early autumn and another three or four in the spring just before mowing commences should be sufficient. The roller should never be used directly after frost; allow the turf to become thoroughly thawed out before either rolling or even walking on the grass.

Edgings

These should be kept neat and must be cut regularly with the edging shears; if they are neglected an edging iron has to be used. This implement requires great skill in its manipulation and often results, in amateur hands, in ragged and uneven edges. Do not, therefore, neglect the edgings. During the summer the edgings may, in places, be trodden down; in autumn, therefore, as soon as the ground becomes softer, a spade should be driven under them to raise them to the correct level.

Feeding the Lawn

No lawn, however good the soil, can go on looking its best year after year unless it receives occasional stimulant in one form or another. In the natural state the grass remains long, and in the autumn dies down to form plant-food in the soil. This natural process does not occur in the lawn, as the grass is cut weekly, if not more often, and the cuttings are caught in the cutting-box and removed from the lawn, which is deprived of their nourishment.

Lawns must, therefore, be fed every two or three years or the grass will become weak and thin and will gradually give place to moss and weeds, which are always ready to force their way even into the best-kept lawn. The grass should, therefore, be carefully watched, and when it becomes off-colour it should be dressed three or four times in one season with intervals of three weeks between the feedings. Little and often should be the motto in dressing the lawn. Too heavy a dressing at one time may scorch up the grass, and it must be remembered that the fertilizer must be chosen to suit the condition of the grass and the nature of the soil. Fertilizers must not be applied indiscriminately; a chemical good for one lawn may ruin another. All fertilizers are best applied in showery weather and the lawn should afterwards be well brushed with a hard birch broom to work the dressing well into the roots. If no rain is likely, give the lawn a good soaking with the sprinkler or the hose. Mix the fertilizers with twice the quantity of finely sifted loam if dressing a lawn on a sandy and rather poor soil, and with the same amount of sand when working on a clay soil ; this makes even distribution of the fertilizer more easy. Stimulants are, as a rule, applied at any time from April to September, two or three dressings being applied during that period. (For rates to apply the various fertilizers *see* table, p. 99.) Dressings of freshly slaked lime or powdered chalk, used to sweeten a sour soil and to keep down moss, can be given in November or December, at the rate of 10 oz. to the square yard. These dressings should not be rolled into the lawn, as they would form a hard covering and would exclude air from the roots. They must not be allowed to lie about on the lawn, but must be raked and swept backwards and forwards, first in one direction and then in another, with a stiff broom, so that they are worked well down into the roots, and any dressing left lying on the surface after three weeks or so should be cleared away before a subsequent one is put on. If farmyard manure is used as a dressing it must be well-decayed, finely sieved, and must not be applied too thickly or it will smother and kill the fine grass. It should be mixed with twice its bulk of finely-sieved loam, which must be absolutely weed-free. About twenty-five barrow-loads would be required for a full-size tennis-lawn, and should be applied in December or January. Any dressing remaining in March or early April should be swept off the lawn, as it will hinder the growth of young grass.

Many advise the use of road-sweepings, but these are, in most cases, undesirable, since they are bound to contain the seeds of weeds, in addition to being contaminated with tar and oil in these days when most of the roads are tarred.

Watering

Water should never be applied unless necessary. To begin with, grass seed should not be watered after sowing, and the established lawn should not receive water until a long drought makes this necessary, as once begun, watering must be continued, at least once a week, as long as the dry weather lasts. Watering seems to encourage the increase of weeds and clover rather than grass ; at the same time grass seems to stand dry weather better than the weeds. Brown, scorched and apparently dead grass recovers remarkably quickly after a shower or two of rain, and as the weeds do not make so quick a recovery, many lawns are greatly benefited by a drought, if the burnt up appearance can be countenanced for a short time. If the drought becomes serious, and the top soil is thin and sandy, watering will become essential, and must then be applied liberally by means of the garden hose or sprinkler. The ideal way is to apply water through a fine spray over a long period so that it can permeate several inches into the ground, rather than to flood the area in a short time by using a coarse nozzle ; in the latter case the water soon runs off, much of it being of little value to the grass. When mowing during the period that water must be applied, the machine should be run over the grass the day after watering, and the collecting-box should be left off so that the cut grass may form a mulch to preserve the moisture at the roots.

Weeding the Lawn

Before regular mowing commences, it will be well to go over all grass and carefully remove rank and unsightly weeds, such as daisies, plantains and dandelions. There is only one way of doing this thoroughly, and that is to stretch two garden lines across the lawn parallel to each other and from 3 to 4 feet apart, and to work steadily along between these lines until every weed is out. The worker should have a bucket of fine soil with which grass seed has been mixed, and should fill up any large holes left by the removal of the weeds. He must ram the soil down hard, so that a cup or depression is not left when the soil settles, and should roll each strip thoroughly as soon as weeding has been completed. This can be done at any time in autumn or spring, provided it is possible to get on the lawn without damaging it : the autumn is perhaps the better time, as the grass has longer to recover before the following summer.

Removing Worms from the Lawn

There is a very general opinion that worms are beneficial to the lawn in that the burrowings provide natural drainage. This may to some extent be true, but they do far more harm than good; they make the surface muddy and soft to walk upon, the grass becomes weakly and easily wears out if much used, and their evil-smelling casts, with which they cover the ground in autumn, winter, and spring, stifle fine grass and encourage the growth of coarse grasses and weeds. Worm casts should always be swept off the lawn before the roller is used—never roll them in. On an ordinary lawn as many as one thousand worms to the square yard may be found. Every effort must therefore be made to exterminate them.

The only way to get rid of worms on a lawn is to use a worm-killing solution. A ready-made mixture can be obtained from any seedsman ; full instructions for use are sent with the mixture and these should be closely followed.

CHAPTER X

THE FLOWER GARDEN

WHEREVER it is possible the flower garden should have a southern or western aspect, which is sheltered from cold winds. Such shelter, whether natural or artificial, should be sufficient to protect quite tall-growing shrubs without excluding light and air. It is an almost hopeless enterprise to attempt very much in the way of flower culture in a soil that is heavy and impervious, or in an exposed situation, unless shrubs can be grown to afford shelter, and the impervious soil either replaced by one of light texture or so improved by the addition of some element such as sand, leaf-mould, lime, chalk, or charred garden *débris* that the tender roots may be able to penetrate it easily.

Drainage

too, is a very important consideration, and one which such a treatment of heavy soil as is recommended above makes doubly necessary. It will be obvious that if certain portions of the soil are broken up and lightened, they become automatically drains for the heavier surrounding land, and all the surface water which such land is unable to absorb will just drain down into the beds that have been rendered pervious, turning them into a sort of natural reservoir. The foundation of such beds must, therefore, be constructed of such loose yet durable ingredients as will permit the accumulation of water to drain through. For this purpose nothing is better than broken brick or flints, but even this precaution needs support from a drain which will collect and convey the surface water away. It will be seen, therefore, how essential it is that the land to be used for a flower garden should be properly prepared before anything very elaborate in the way of cultivation is begun.

Backgrounds and Settings

An important consideration in the arrangement of the garden is that of form; the selection of plants beautiful in themselves, and their arrangement singly or in groups, as backgrounds for smaller flowers, as screens, boundaries, and hedges. When one speaks of form in the matter of plants, one's mind turns instinctively to such outstanding examples as the cypress whose telling silhouette is so beautiful a feature of the Italian landscape, to the tropical palm, to the poplar groves of France, and last but not least to the many beautiful varieties of English trees which at any season of the year present such lovely appearances.

Among the plants whose foliage is beautiful and whose presence in the garden is of the utmost value from the point of view of backgrounds are the willow, the acacia, the asparagus, various specimens of bamboo, reeds, pampas grass, the cypress, cedar, yew, and fir, and a host of hardy evergreens and flowering shrubs. Such plants, indeed, lend themselves to a variety of decoration and practical purposes. The larger of them can be used as screens for unsightly corners, and to afford shelter to more delicate specimens; others to break up the monotony of a lawn and to maintain the beauty of the garden through even the most trying winters. Others again require no such practical warrant. Their mere beauty is sufficient reason in itself for their inclusion. The azalea, magnolia, rhododendron (in moderation), broom, pyrus japonica, to mention but a few, whose flowering periods but crown their common life as elegant shrubs, should need no recommendation. In the use of evergreens discretion should be exercised, and their hardy and enduring qualities must not be favoured to the detriment of more vulnerable plants. In moderation their usefulness cannot be too highly praised, but it must be remembered that most evergreens are greedy feeders; their roots are voracious and spread very widely; and when, as is often the case, they are used to border flower beds, if planted there too generously or allowed to multiply unchecked, they impoverish the soil and weaken the chances of the flowers.

Flowering Shrubs

The many varieties of beautiful flowering shrubs which grow well in this climate should appeal to the gardener for more than their purely outdoor qualities. Most people who have gardens like also to decorate their houses with flowers, and, in this connection, nothing lends itself more charmingly to indoor use than single sprays of some small flowering shrub.

As an immediate setting for the house, also, no form of planting is more satisfactory than groups of flowering evergreens. Here, above all other places in the garden, permanence is a quality to aim at, for this is the view which is most constantly in evidence. In winter weather it may, perhaps, be regretted but not deplored that the remoter places of the garden are not bright with flowers, but if the immediate view from the windows is equally barren then the dreariness of the whole garden will weigh more heavily.

For this reason, then, the use of flowering evergreens near the house is to be recommended.

Annuals

The class of plants which flower and fruit in the same year as that in which its seeds are sown, or, at any rate, complete the series of those processes within twelve months of the time of sowing, is known as that of Annuals. In the flower garden it includes some of the most beautiful, as well as undoubtedly the most easily grown of all those things which make up a typical English garden.

Hardy Annuals.—Any ordinary garden soil is suitable for hardy annuals, and in fact for annuals generally. It does not require to be at all rich, since this encourages luxuriance of growth, which is incompatible with the production of flowers. Annuals do best, however, in light, sandy soil, and they should have this where possible, though not necessarily. Good drainage is essential.

In almost all cases it is wise to incorporate with the natural earth a very generous allowance of humus or of leaves or other decomposing vegetable matter which will help to create humus. In the process of decomposition of leaves or other organic matter, various acids and other products are created, which tend to liberate from the mineral elements in the soil certain foods essential to the life of plants. Gases also are generated, which help to keep the soil in a porous, spongy condition, which is agreeable to the roots, and which assists in the maintenance of that moist condition so essential to healthy growth.

Very hardy annuals may be sown in autumn, not earlier than the last week in August, and not later, even in sheltered spots, than the last week in September. Autumn-sown plants, if they survive the winter's frosts, will bloom early in spring. The situation best suited for autumn sowing is one that is sheltered from strong and cutting winds, but free from shade and well exposed to the sun. Spring sowings for blooming in summer may be made at any time from the middle of March to the middle of April. Later sowings for flowering in autumn should be made from the middle of May to the middle of June. The different conditions and climates prevailing in the various districts make it impossible to give exact times and details.

To raise annuals for transplanting, they may be sown in V-shaped drills about ½ an inch deep and 10 inches apart in the reserve garden or elsewhere, and removed when about half-grown to the position in which they are intended to flower; on an average about 9 inches should be left between each plant. They should be firmly planted then well watered to fix the soil round the roots, The transplanting of annuals, unless very carefully done, is always

attended with some danger.   This may be obviated if they are raised
in pots, from which they can be turned out without disturbing the
roots, or sown on pieces of turf turned grass downwards, the seeds
being covered with a thin coating of mould after they have been
sprinkled thinly on the turf.   Hardy annuals sown in spring, and
some kinds sown in autumn, need no protection from the weather.
(*See* Sowing Seed, p. 183, and Bedding Plants, p. 109.)

Half-Hardy Annuals.—The seeds should be sown in March or
April in well-drained pots or pans, in a mixture of loam, leaf-mould,
well-decayed manure and silver sand, and sheltered in a frame, or
else the pots should be plunged in moderate bottom-heat, such as
a hot-bed that is gradually cooling.   The temperature should not
rise above 75° Fahrenheit by day or fall below 55° at night.   (*See*
Sowing Seed, p. 187.)   Harden-off gradually and remove to flowering quarters about the middle of May, but delay the removal to
the end of the month if the weather is cold and unfavourable.

Biennials

The difference between annuals and biennials consists in their
nature and habit only.   The former grow flowers, yield seeds for
their reproduction, and die in the same year ; biennials, on the
contrary, are sown and grow in the first year, but do not come to
maturity until the second, when they flower, seed and die.

Hardy biennials may be sown at a later period of the year than
annuals, that is to say in May, June, or July, sometimes in August,
though not later than the middle or end of September, for plants
sown at this time will bloom the following year as freely as those
that have been sown at an earlier date.   It is wise to sow as
early as possible, as this enables the plants to become well-
established before the colder weather sets in, and to ensure well-
developed plants for flowering the next year.   If a frame is
available early sowing is not so important, as the plants will
continue development in the frame at a time when cold and
bad weather would impede any growth in the open.   Biennials
should be raised in drills 8 to 10 inches apart in partially shaded
beds in the reserve garden ; as soon as they are tall enough to be
handled they should be thinned out to 6 inches apart or transplanted
to the same distance between plants.   Plant out in moderately
good deeply-worked soil in their blooming quarters in the spring,
or in October if planted in early summer and sufficiently grown.

Half-hardy biennials should be sown in boxes from March to
June.   They should be protected during the winter in a frame or
in the greenhouse and be planted out in their flowering positions the
following spring, from April to June.   (*See* Sowing Seed, p. 187.)

Hardy Perennials (*See*** chapter XIII)**

SOME USEFUL ANNUALS AND BIENNIALS

For Notes on Colour, Height, Season of Flowering, Culture, and the best Species and Varieties, *see* Alphabetical List of Flowering Plants, page 207.

Half-hardy Annuals

Ageratum mexicanum
Alonsoa Warscewiczii
Amaranthus caudatus gibbosus (Love-lies-Bleeding)
Arctotis grandis
Brachycome iberidifolia
Callistephus chinensis (China Aster)
Celosia plumosa aurea (Prince of Wales' Feathers or Cockscomb)
Dianthus Heddewigii and D. chinensis
Dimorphotheca aurantiaca
Gaillardia (Single and Double)

Helichrysum bracteatum, etc.
Heliotropium (Heliotrope or Cherry Pie)
Helipterum
Impatiens Balsamina
Ipomœa (various)
Kochia trichophila
Lobelia Erinus vars.
Matthiola annua (Ten-week Stock)
Mesembryanthemum crystallinum
Mimulus tigrinus
Nemesia strumosa
Nicotiana (Tobacco Plant)
Petunia

Phlox Drummondii
Portulaca grandiflora
Salpiglossis sinuata
Salvia carduacea and S. coccinea
Scabiosa atropurpurea
Schizanthus
Statice Bonduellii
Statice sinuata
Tagetes (various) (African and French Marigolds)
Tropæolum aduncum (Canary Creeper)
Verbena
Viola
Zinnia elegans, etc.

Hardy Annuals

Alyssum maritimum
Calendula officinalis (Pot Marigold)
Centaurea Cyanus (Cornflower or Bluebottle)
Centaurea suaveolens (Sweet Sultan)
Clarkia elegans and C. pulchella
Collinsia bicolor, etc.
Convolvulus major and C. minor
Coreopsis bicolor nana, etc.
Delphinium Gayanum,syn. Ajacis, etc. (Larkspur)
Eschscholzia californica (Californian Poppy)
Gaillardia Lorenziana and G. picta
Gilia tricolor and G. aurea

Godetia (Single and Double)
Gypsophila elegans
Helianthus annuus and H. cucumerifolius (Sunflower)
Iberis (Candytuft)
Lathyrus odoratus (Sweet Pea)
Lavatera trimestris
Limnanthes Douglasii
Linaria maroccana, etc.
Linum grandiflorum, etc.
Lupinus (various) (Lupins)
Malcomia maritima (Virginian Stock)
Malope grandiflora, etc.
Matthiola bicornis (Night Scented Stock)
Nemophila (various)

Nigella damascena and N. hispanica (Love-in-a-Mist)
Papaver Rhœas (Shirley Poppy) and P. somniferum and vars. (Opium Poppy)
Reseda odorata (Mignonette)
Salvia Horminum
Senecio elegans
Silene pendula compacta
Statice Suworowii and S. sinuata and vars.
Tropæolum aduncum (Canary Creeper)
T. majus (Climbing Nasturtium)
T. minus and vars. (Dwarf Nasturtium)

Biennials

Althæa rosea (Hollyhock)
Anchusa capensis
Antirrhinum majus (Snapdragon)
Campanula medium (Canterbury Bells)
Campanula pyramidalis
Cheiranthus Cheiri (Wallflower)
Coreopsis grandiflora

Dianthus barbatus (Sweet William) [(Foxglove)
Digitalis purpurea, etc.
Lavatera arborea
Lunaria annua (Honesty)
Lychnis Flos-jovis (Rose Campion)
Matthiola (Intermediate Stock) [Stock)
Matthiola (East Lothian

Matthiola incana (Giant or Brompton Stock)
Myosotis (Forget-Me-Not)
Œnothera (various) (Evening Primrose)
Papaver (Iceland Poppy)
Scabiosa caucasica
Silene compacta
Trachelium cæruleum
Verbascum (Mullein)

NOTE.—Although some two or three of the species included in this list are not actually biennials, in a true sense, they are most satisfactory when grown as such.

CHAPTER XI

BEDDING PLANTS

SUMMER bedding has been criticized as old-fashioned and monotonous; it certainly is monotonous if no imagination is used in its arrangement, and the beds are filled year after year with geraniums, calceolarias and lobelia. Although these are excellent flowers if used with discretion, and should never be forgotten, there are so many other beautiful flowers that may be used, and which if tastily combined and laid out will give brilliant masses of colour all through the summer.

There need be no monotony, almost all flowers can be used to furnish beds, and it is now a common practice to use for this purpose such beautiful annuals as saponaria and forget-me-nots, or such hardy plants as pansies and violas. Still, the old term of " bedding plants " is commonly used to refer to certain half-hardy or tender flowering plants which are grown under glass during the winter and spring, and are merely planted out during summer to be again lifted as soon as the hot months are over. Pelargoniums or geraniums, as they are commonly called, begonias, verbenas, petunias, calceolarias and lobelias are the plants perhaps most frequently grown in this way.

Making the Beds (*See* chapter VII.)

Manure

As soon as the summer bedding is cleared away in the autumn some well-rotted manure (old hot-bed manure is excellent), leaf-mould, and thoroughly decayed vegetable refuse should be forked into the beds to a depth of about 12 inches, this will draw the roots well down. In addition to this the plants benefit by a weekly dressing with weak liquid manure made from a diluted solution of phosphate of ammonia or phosphate of potash or from some farm-yard manure water. The mixture must not be allowed to touch the foliage.

Bedding Schemes

Great care must be taken in the colour schemes, so as to avoid clashing colours, the colours must harmonize or else the gardener must aim at getting a contrast. Do not use too many colours, two, or at the most three, are best massed together; likewise only two or three kinds of flowers should be used in each bed. It is necessary, too, to remember the height and habit of the plants associated together; some make ideal carpet plants, others are excellent for use as the principal plants or for "dot" plants, while, a point sometimes forgotten, all subjects in a bedding-scheme must flower together. Never overcrowd, as this leads to weak, straggly plants with poor and scarce blooms. No plant, unless very small, should be planted nearer than 6 inches to its neighbour, while the average sized plants need to be some 10 to 15 inches apart. Dot plants are placed about 3 feet apart, while edging plants are best set about 10 inches from the edge of the bed, otherwise they are liable to be damaged when the grass is cut.

For colour schemes we would refer the reader to the *Summer and Spring Bedding Schemes*, page 115, and to our remarks as to colour grouping in the chapter on *Herbaceous Borders*, page 125. The plants used must depend chiefly on individual taste and largely on the glass available to raise them.

As to the bedding designs they should be as simple as possible, especially in small beds, and should aim at providing masses of one colour rather than small patches of highly contrasting shades in a small bed. Where the plants themselves are very small, more complicated designs may be attempted.

Cannas or tall fuchsias make very striking "dot" plants in a large bed of begonias, as do standard heliotropes or kochias in a bed of salmon pink geraniums. Abutilons and plumbagoes also make excellent "dot" plants. Bear in mind the beauty of pale pink flowers thrown up by a groundwork of mauve, dark blue or purple; a group of dark blue or purple flowers if edged with yellow violas makes a most striking display. Beware of associating colours like magenta or pink with scarlet; these colours need very careful handling. We will content ourselves with these cursory remarks as the tables of *Spring and Summer Bedding Schemes*, page 115, will be found to be replete with suggestions.

Summer Bedding

Although it is unwise to bed-out too early, this does not mean that the preparation of the beds should be left until just before it is time to put the plants in. The beds should be prepared as soon as the spring bedding is over. All bulbs used in bedding schemes should be lifted and planted in the reserve garden and watered occasionally until the " grass " has turned yellow. They should then be dried off and stored ; if care is taken of them they may be used for three or four years in succession without any appreciable deterioration in the blooms. The amateur is often worried as to what he should do with the spring bedding he takes out ; should he save any of it or should he destroy it all ? As space is usually a consideration, all plants that are easily raised from seed should be destroyed, but such perennials as arabis, daisies, erysimum, polyanthus, or violas should be divided into small plants and placed in the reserve garden where they are shaded from the hottest rays of the sun to be grown on for the next year's spring bedding.

After the beds have been dug over, they should be made thoroughly firm by treading, if the soil is light, and should then be raked over, drawing the soil well up towards the centre of the bed. This will not only drain the bed, but will display the plants to better advantage.

Antirrhinums, calceolarias, marguerites and violas are among the most hardy of our summer bedding plants and a start can be made with these as soon as the beds have been cleared of the spring bedding. This will not only help to get the work forward at this heavy time, but will give these plants time to become established before the hot weather comes.

Pot plants make better bedding subjects than those grown in boxes, as the roots are not so liable to be damaged when removed for bedding-out. In planting, use a trowel to scoop out just sufficient earth to make a hole to take the roots without crushing. Do not use a dibble as this is apt to make a hole so deep as to leave an air pocket under the roots, which will be parched and will also not have a hole wide enough to accommodate them. Press the soil *very firmly* round the roots with the hands after planting or the plants will be slow in becoming established and will be greatly handicapped. If the weather is warm, bedding-out should be done in the late afternoon or in the evening, and after planting the bed should receive a thorough soaking with warm water through a fine rose—which operation should be repeated daily for a week or so if the weather is very dry. If the nights tend to be cold, water should not be applied through a rose, but a little water should be given to the roots of each plant by means of a can with the rose removed. This will save possible chilling of the foliage and consequent checking of growth, or even the death of the plants. Do not bed-out while the soil is very dry either in the case of summer bedding or when planting the spring bedding. Give the bed a good soaking with water the evening previous to the planting, before the final raking down of the soil, and, as stated above, after the bedding-out has been completed. (*See* Mulching, p. 68; *and* Watering, p. 77.) Care must be taken to insert the plant to about the same depth as it stood in its pot or in the box. Keep the " ball " intact and plant so that the top of it is just $\frac{1}{2}$ an inch below the ground level. If the plant is set in too low there is the possibility of it " damping-off." Always remove the crocks at the bottom of the pot before the plants are bedded-out, otherwise the bed, in the course of time, will become littered with these bits of broken pots.

Care of the Bed

For the care of the bed during the summer—that is to say, weeding, removal of dead flowers, staking and training—we would refer the reader to the *Care of the Herbaceous Border*, page 127.

Spring Bedding

Spring-bedding requires much the same treatment as summer bedding. It should be done as early as possible so that the plants may establish themselves before the severe weather sets in. Plant them, therefore, early in October, as soon as the summer bedding has been cleared away; this should be done immediately the flowers are over. The question of what plants to discard and what to save again arises. As summer bedding plants are nearly all either half-hardy or tender they will require the protection of glass through the winter. The amount of glass available, therefore, usually largely decides the question. Glass space is always very valuable, therefore it would be folly to preserve any plants that can easily be raised from seed or from cuttings; such plants as the following can, therefore, be thrown away: alyssums, antirrhinums, asters, calceolarias, coreopsis, gaillardias, geraniums, geums, heliotropes, lobelia, pentstemons, petunias, stocks, and verbenas; these, however, must not be discarded until cuttings have been taken from them. Woody plants such as abutilons, fuchsias, standard heliotropes, hydrangeas and plumbagoes; cannas, centaureas, cinerarias and other foliage plants that take several years to grow to the most effective size should be taken up with as complete a ball of roots as possible and planted in suitably sized pots, the branches being trimmed if space is at a premium. If the branches are trimmed, the roots may also be reduced. Store the plants in a frost-proof frame or on shelves in the greenhouse and water occasionally. Bulbous and tuberous-rooted plants such as begonias, dahlias and gladioli must, of course, be saved. (*See* paragraphs on individual plants, chapter XXIV.) Do not leave the bedding-out until the early spring when bloom is coming and the roots are not in a favourable condition to establish themselves. As soon as the summer bedding has been removed dig over the bed to two spades' depth and manure it as described on page 66, then put in the plants that are to form the ground-work, and let them be just far enough apart so that, when grown, they will cover the surface of the bed. In the interstices between these insert the bulbs, at the correct depth for the kind planted. (*See* chapter XXIV, and chapter on Bulbs, p. 116.)

At one time bulbs were practically the only plants used by the gardener for spring bedding. This use of bulbs alone had many drawbacks; firstly the beds were plain and bare all through the winter, then as soon as the bulbs had flowered the beds would become untidy and uninteresting. To-day we use a groundwork of alyssum, arabis, aubretia, daisies, myosotis, polyanthus, silenes, violas, wallflowers, and other dwarf hardy plants, through which the bulbs rise to form a mass of colour over a carpet that is chosen either to harmonize or contrast with them. This ground-work clothes the ground and looks neat all the winter and also keeps the bed tidier and interesting for some time after the bulbs have flowered. Spring bedding is thus rendered less formal and stiff, and the period of bloom is also extended. In addition, small shrubs and dwarf conifers are often used to relieve the bareness of the bed during the winter. These are best sunk into the bed in pots, they are then easily removed when the summer bedding has to be put in. The best time to buy bulbs is in September, and care should be taken to see that they are plump and firm to the touch, of good but not excessive size, and free from disease. No growth should be visible.

Both with spring and summer bedding it is best to mark the positions of each plant by means of stakes and string, before a start is made with the actual planting.

If planting a round bed, a stake should be inserted at the exact centre and to this stake is attached a piece of string; by fixing a peg of wood at different distances down this string, the gardener can trace out circles of different diameter, on which the plants, still in their pots, should be spaced out evenly. The gardener can then see more or less how his scheme will look when planted, also the number of each kind of plant required to fill the bed.

In bedding-out small beds most gardeners find it easiest to work from the edges inwards to the centre; in large beds, however, mark the centre accurately and work outwards from this, using a board to stand on so that the feet do not tread down the soil. If this plank can span the bed and rest on two or three bricks on each side, it will be raised above the bed and will save any pressure on the soil.

E.G.   H

Carpet Bedding

Carpet bedding consists in arranging masses of low, compact-growing plants with various coloured leaves in such a manner as to show patterns. It is usual to arrange a background of plants of some one colour, and through this to run plants of other colours in masses, stripes or ribbons, so as to produce the artificial result desired. Among the commoner plants used for this purpose are Sempervivum of various colours (grey and green), Echiverias, Sedum glaucum (grey), Cerastium tomentosum (silver), Herniaria glabra (green) and Pyrethrum aureum (yellow).

Propagation of Bedding Plants

It is advantageous to have bedding plants as well advanced as possible; late and consequently undeveloped plants bear poor flowers. Sow the annuals in heat, if possible, in February or in the open, if hardy, in March or April. Biennials should be sown from May to August and wintered under glass. Annuals, too, may be treated as biennials, sown in September, and wintered under glass.

Cuttings of most half-hardy plants, as pelargoniums and verbenas, are taken in July and August; ageratums, calceolarias and salvias in September, and may be kept in the open till the end of September, when they must be wintered in a cold frame or better still near the glass in a greenhouse in slight heat. For cuttings in early spring old stocks must be placed in gentle heat and induced to grow, and when sufficiently large the young shoots may be taken off as cuttings, to be rooted also in gentle heat. (*See* Propagation, p. 183.) Begonias and similar tuberous-rooted plants need to be "started" in heat early in February and will then be ready for planting out with the other bedding plants at the end of May or early in June.

Hardening-Off

Never bring the plants straight out of the frame or warm house into the beds, harden-off by giving gradually more and more air for three weeks to a month before the time for bedding-out, which is usually about the middle of May. Planting out without adequate hardening-off is responsible for much failure and usually results in checked growth, and consequently late and poor flowering, or often complete loss of the more tender plants.

For further information as to the propagation of bedding-plants see the chapter on *The Propagation of Plants*, and for cultural details peculiar to each species see the *Alphabetical List of Flowering Plants and Shrubs*, page 207. *See also* Designing and Making Beds and Borders, chapter VII.

COLOUR SCHEMES FOR BEDDING.

NOTE.—For details as to Colour, Height, Time of Flowering and Culture, *see* the Alphabetical List of Flowering Plants and Shrubs, page 207.

Summer Bedding

Principal Plant	Ground, Edging or "Dot" Plant
Ageratum mexicanum (Pale Blue)	Geranium Madame Crousse (Rose-pink)
Ageratum mexicanum Swanley Blue	Alyssum maritimum minimum (White)
Antirrhinum nanum Golden Queen	Ageratum mexicanum Swanley Blue
Antirrhinum nanum Enchantress (Pink)	Browallia viscosa (Blue)
Antirrhinum nanum White Queen	Gladiolus primulinus Vanessa (Salmon)
Begonia semperflorens Triumph (White)	Lobelia Erinus Cambridge Blue
Begonia tuberous-rooted vars. (Various)	Alyssum maritimum (White)
Calceolaria Camden Hero (Brown)	Phlox Drummondii nana Snowball
Calendula officinalis Orange King	Anchusa capensis (Blue)
Cineraria maritima Diamond (Grey Leaves)	Gladiolus America (Lilac-rose)
Dahlia Coltness Gem (Scarlet)	Viola White Swan (White)
Fuchsia Ballet Girl (Red and White)	Phlox Drummondii nana (Mixed vars.)
Geranium Paul Crampel (Scarlet)	Abutilon Thompsonii (Yellow)
Geranium Madame Crousse (Rose-pink)	Antirrhinum White Queen (White)
Gladiolus Flaming Sword (Scarlet)	Antirrhinum nanum Golden Queen
Gladiolus War (Crimson)	Antirrhinum nanum Golden Queen
Godetia Rosy Morn (Coral-pink)	Dianthus chinensis Purity (White)
Heliotropium peruvianum Giant vars.	Eucalyptus globulus (Silver-blue Leaves)
Kochia trichophylla (Burning Bush)	Tagetes erecta nana Orange Prince
Lobelia fulgens Queen Victoria (Scarlet)	Antirrhinum White Beauty (White)
Nicotiana sylvestris (White)	Polygonum orientale (Crimson)
Nigella damascena Miss Jekyll (Blue)	Verbena Miss Willmott (Rose)
Pentstemon Southgate Gem (Carmine)	Phlox Drummondii compacta Snowball
Petunia Countess of Ellesmere (Rose)	Callistephus chinense Comet (White)
Phlox Drummondii (Rose and Pink Shades)	Gaura Lindheimeri (White, tinted Red)
Salvia patens Cambridge Blue	Leucophyta Brownii (Silvery Leaves)
Tagetes erecta (Orange)	Lobelia Erinus Sapphire (Sapphire-blue)
Tropæolum minus Golden King (Yellow)	Pentstemon Pink Beauty (Pink)
Verbena Mammoth Firefly (Scarlet)	Antirrhinum majus Yellow King
Verbena venosa (Rosy Purple)	Alyssum maritimum minimum (White)
Verbena venosa (Rosy Purple)	Artemisia Prushiana (Grey Leaves)
Zinnia elegans (Scarlet and Yellow vars.)	Gazania longiscapa (Golden Brown)

Spring Bedding

Principal Plant	Ground, Edging or "Dot" Plant
Alyssum saxatile compactum (Yellow)	Wallflower Dwarf Blood Red
Anemone St. Brigid (Mixed)	Iris Spanish (Mixed)
Hyacinth City of Haarlem (Yellow)	Myosotis alpestris Victoria (Blue)
Hyacinth Gertrude (Rose-pink)	Aubrietia Lavender
Hyacinth La Grandesse (White)	Polyanthus (Red)
Hyacinth Marconi (Rose)	Viola William Robb (Lavender)
Iris Dutch (Mixed)	Violas, Blue, Yellow and White
Iris Spanish (Mixed)	Violas, Blue, Yellow and White
Muscari Heavenly Blue (Blue)	Tulip Early Prince de Ligne (Yellow)
Narcissus Empress (Yellow and White)	Muscari Heavenly Blue (Blue)
Narcissus Seagull (White)	Myosotis dissitiflora Perfection (Blue)
Polyanthus (White)	Bellis perennis Mammoth Etna (Red)
Polyanthus (Orange)	Crocus Maximilian (Azure-blue)
Tulip Keizerskroon (Early) (Scarlet-yellow)	Arabis albida (White)
Tulip Early Vermilion Brilliant (Scarlet)	Pansy Winter-flowering Winter Sun (Yellow)
Tulip Early Double Tea Rose (Primrose)	Myosotis alpestris Victoria (Blue)
Tulip Darwin Clara Butt (Pink and Rose)	Myosotis dissitiflora Perfection (Sky)
Tulip Darwin King Harold (Blood-red)	Iberis sempervirens (White)
Tulip Darwin Princess Elizabeth (Rose)	Silene pendula Bijou (Salmon-rose)
Tulip Darwin William Pitt (Scarlet)	Narcissus Leedsii White Lady (White)
Tulip Breeder Bacchus (Royal Purple)	Wallflower Golden Monarch
Tulip Breeder Panorama (Chestnut red)	Wallflower Ivory White
Tulip Cottage Inglescombe Scarlet	Wallflower Fire King (Orange-scarlet)
Tulip Cottage Picotee (White and Rose)	Viola Kitty Bell (Lavender)
Viola Jersey Gem (Purple)	Tulip Cottage Inglescombe Yellow
Wallflower Vulcan (Crimson	Tulip Cottage Orange King

CHAPTER XII

BULBS

Bulbs in Beds and Borders

THE generality of bulbs are of the easiest cultivation, needing but to be planted in the early autumn at about two or three times their own depth, in reasonably good and light garden soil, with which a good amount of leaf-mould has been mixed. They should be planted at a uniform depth and should not come into contact with recent manure. Good drainage is essential. If the soil is inclined to be at all heavy it is desirable to lighten it by working in sand at and around each spot in which a clump of bulbs is to be planted. Bulbs, as a rule, should be planted deeply, rather than shallowly, especially crocuses, gladioli and lilies, because the bulbs are then less likely to suffer from the effects of frost.

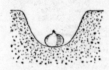

FIG. 13. — CORRECT WAY OF PLANTING A BULB.

The hole for the bulb should be scraped out with a trowel—not made with a dibber.

Plant the bulbs as early in the autumn as possible, especially the spring-flowering ones, they then have ample time to develop their roots before the strain of flowering makes its demands on them. Early planting promotes larger blooms. It is advisable always to plant the bulbs with a trowel and to press them firmly, but gently, into the earth before they are covered up. Never plant bulbs with a dibber; this makes a narrow " V "-shaped hole in which it is difficult to set the bulb straight and in which an air space, which will parch the roots, will be left.

FIG. 14. — INCORRECT WAY OF PLANTING A BULB.

If the bulb is planted with a dibber, the inevitable air-space beneath the bulb will parch the roots.

Most bulbs, having been planted in suitable soil at a reasonable distance apart, may be allowed to remain for several years without being taken up, divided and replanted. But there are certain exceptions. Tulips and hyacinths, for example, should be lifted when the leaves die down, carefully dried, stored in a cool dry place, and replanted in October and September respectively. For individual cultural details of the various bulbs see the *Alphabetical List of Flowering Plants*, p. 207.

Bonemeal is a good artificial manure for bulbs, and should be dusted round the bulbs at the rate of 2 oz. to the square yard and thoroughly forked in in February; an equal amount of superphosphate may, with advantage, be added at the same time.

Various spring bedding schemes for planting bulbs are given on page 115. Here will be found a list of dwarf plants that will form a suitable ground-work, and that will harmonize in colour with the bulbs forming the main feature.

Removing Withered Foliage

No attempt should be made to remove leaves or flower-stalks until they have withered and decayed to such an extent that they may be removed by a very slight effort. The long sword-like leaves of crocuses, hyacinths, etc., should be neatly plaited together, to obviate untidiness of appearance, and should be allowed to remain until they are quite decayed. The dead flowers ought to be cut off just below the spike of bloom, unless it is wished to save the seed. This holds good for all bulbs that have a woody or strong flower stem.

Lifting and Storing the Bulbs

When the leaves have completely died away, but not before, bulbs may be taken up and allowed to dry. When the tops are dry and withered they should be cut off an inch above the bulbs, and the roots should also be cut away; the bulbs should then be kept in a dry, dark and frost-proof place to which the air has free access until the time for planting comes round again, which commences in September for hyacinths, etc., and ends in March for late-flowering varieties of the gladiolus, the period of planting being regulated in a degree by the period of flowering.

Most bulbs may, however, remain where they are from year's end to year's end, provided that the soil is suitable, the drainage sufficient and that they are planted deeply. (*See individual cultural details in* Alphabetical List, chapter XXIV.) Bulbs have a tendency to rise to the surface, especially corms, for in the crocus and gladiolus, though not in the cyclamen, the new corms are formed every year on the top of the old corms which perish. The continuance of bulbs in the places in which they are first planted leads to the formation of splendid masses, from which at the proper season rise glorious flower spikes.

Naturalizing Bulbs in Grass

Most of our spring bulbs are far more beautiful when viewed in their natural surroundings among the grass and in the meadows, woodlands, or wild garden than when planted, however naturally and artistically, in borders. Most of them, too, especially daffodils, crocuses and scillas, do much better in this natural state than in beds or borders where they are constantly being disturbed.

Do not plant them on lawns, as the grass cannot be cut until the leaves of the bulbs have turned yellow and dried up. Another word of caution ; do not plant daffodils in pastureland as they are somewhat poisonous to cattle.

The bulbs are best planted in long, narrow oval strips some 30 to 40 feet in length, shaped like patches of snow driven by the wind into long slender drifts on the ground. They should be scattered on the grass over an area shaped as above, so that they lie thicker towards the centre of the " drift," and should be planted with a trowel or bulb planter just where they fall. There should be no regular, well-defined margin to the " drift," the edges should be indistinct and gradually merging into the surrounding grass.

August and September is the best planting time ; small bulbs like the crocus and scilla should be set some 3 inches apart, while daffodil bulbs should have about 10 inches between them. Bulbs that have been used for beds and borders are equally as good as new bulbs for naturalizing in grass and should be replanted immediately after being lifted from the beds and while their foliage is still green and succulent.

Some seven years, at least, may be allowed to elapse before it is necessary to disturb naturalized bulbs, provided they receive an annual top-dressing of leaf-mould each autumn.

The bulbs most suitable for planting in grass are : Allium moly, Anemone appennina, Chionodoxas, Crocuses, Cyclamen coum and C. europæum, Daffodils (Golden Spur, Barri Conspicuus, Poeticus), Erythroniums, Fritillarias (imperialis), Irises, Muscari (azureus or plumosum), Scillas, Snowdrops, and Winter aconites.

Bulbs in Pots

These should be planted in autumn and the crowns should just appear above the surface of the soil, which should come up to within $\frac{3}{4}$ inch of the top of the pot. After planting, the pots should be well soaked in water and placed in the open on boards or slates so that worms cannot get up into the soil. The pots should be surrounded and covered with a layer of 5 inches of fibre or ashes, and left for seven to nine weeks until the roots will have formed and the tops have made an inch of growth, when they may be moved to a frame or a cold greenhouse, if the roots have made sufficient growth, and should be liberally supplied with water but not saturated. The less forward plants should be put back in the ashes and will furnish a succession of later blooms if brought into the greenhouse at successive intervals. The darkness encourages growth of the roots, which is so essential to good blooms. Bulbs should never be forced on before their roots have sufficiently developed.

The pots should not be subjected to full light until two or three days after the covering of fibre has been removed, that is, until the pale yellow shoots have turned green. When this has happened the pots should be placed close to the glass and be brought on gradually till the flower buds are well advanced, when liquid manure-water may be used and the plants forced on with moderate heat. A good compost consists of a mixture of equal parts of loam, leaf-mould and well-rotted cow-manure, together with a little sand.

As to the number of bulbs that may be planted in a pot, this, of course, depends on the species of bulb and on the size of pot used. Snowdrops, crocuses and scilla may be planted so that they practically touch one another, that is, about nine bulbs in a 5-inch pot ; larger bulbs, such as those of the daffodil and tulip, may be planted six in a 5-inch pot, while only three hyacinths should be grown in a 6-inch pot.

Depth to Plant

The bulbs of the daffodil, hyacinth, tulip, and similar flowers should be potted so that their tips are just above the surface of the soil ; a few other bulbs should only be half-buried ; while others again must be buried one, three or even more inches below the surface. Crocuses and scilla, for instance, should be just covered with soil. For the depth to plant each species of bulb, *see* the *Alphabetical List of Flowering Plants*, page 207.

After forcing, which cannot be done for more than one year running, bulbs may be planted out in borders or used for naturalizing ; they should be dried off and planted out in July or August. The year after forcing, the bloom may not be very fine, but in subsequent years a wealth of bloom will be provided.

Bulbs in Fibre

When growing bulbs in this way in small numbers it is obvious that it is false economy to buy any but the best bulbs for treatment. In ordering the bulbs it is best to tell the people from whom they are procured that they are required for this form of culture, and they will select suitable bulbs. At the same time order the fibre, which will be found on experiment to be the best material for filling the bulb bowls. These latter should be simple in shape and colour, so that they may not distract attention from or clash with the flowers growing in them, and should be shallow, some 5 inches deep, and glazed; porous bowls are not good. Mixed with the fibre will be found a certain proportion of lumps of charcoal, and a few of them should be placed at the bottom of the bowl. If the fibre is at all lumpy pick it over and rub out the lumps between the fingers, then soak it for a day or so and drain it thoroughly until only a drop or two of water comes out when the fibre is squeezed in the hand. Then fill your bowls to a depth of about one-half for large bulbs, such as the narcissus and hyacinth; three-quarters for the smaller, such as crocuses and scillas. On this layer, which should not be pressed down too tightly, place your bulbs; if the bowl is very large grouping them in small clumps, not spacing them regularly over it; if it is small the bulbs may nearly, but not quite touch. Then fill the bowl nearly to the top with the fibre, so that the extreme tips of the bulbs just show above it, and the planting process is complete.

The bowls should be kept for the first six weeks in a dark place, preferably an airy one, and certainly not near a fire. A cool, airy cupboard or cellar will do. Once a week or so examine the bowls to see whether the fibre is dry, and if it shows signs of dryness plunge them in a tub or basin of lukewarm water, which should cover them completely. When the fibre is well soaked take out the bowls and turn them carefully sideways, so that any superfluous water may drain off. While this is being done care must be taken that the whole of the contents of the bowl do not fall out; the fibre should be supported by the open hand during the operation. The fibre should be just damp, never sodden. When the bulbs have made shoots about an inch long the bowls should be brought out into the light, but they should not be exposed to full air and sunshine until the shoots have turned a healthy green. While this is happening the bowls should be kept in a shady corner of the room. When the shoots are green the more light and air they have the better, but when they are placed in a window they should always be removed to the middle of the room if there is the smallest likelihood of a frost during the night. It should also be remembered that the plants will naturally grow towards the light, so that to ensure good straight plants and flower stalks the bowls should be turned each day. No manure should be used. Crocuses, daffodils, tulips, hyacinths, chionodoxas, fritillarias and grape hyacinths may all be successfully grown in fibre, as described above, each kind being raised in a separate bowl.

SOME USEFUL BULBS AND TUBERS

NOTE.—For Cultural Details, for Colour, Height, Season of Flowering and the best Species and Varieties, *see* the Alphabetical List of Flowering Plants, page 207.

Achimenes
*Agapanthus
Allium (various)
Alstrœmeria aurantiaca
Amaryllis Belladonna
Anemone (tuberous)
Begonia (tuberous)
Brodiæa (various)
Bulbocodium vernum
Calochortus (various)
Camassia (various)
Chionodoxa
*Clivia miniata
Colchicum (various)
Commelina cœlestis
Convallaria majalis
Corydalis bulbosa
Crinum (various)
Crocus (various)
Cyclamen (various)

Dicentra spectabilis
Eranthis hyemalis
Erythronium
*Freesia (various)
Fritillaria (various)
Galanthus (Snowdrop)
Gladiolus (various)
*Gloxinia (various)
*Habranthus pratensis
Hyacinth (various)
Iris (various)
*Ixia (various)
*Ixiolirion montanum
*Lachenalia (various)
Lapeyrousia cruenta
Leucojum (various)
Lilium (various)
*Mirabilis (various)
Muscari (various)
Narcissus (various)
Nerine (Guernsey Lily)

Ornithogalum (various)
Oxalis (various)
Pancratium illyricum
Paradisia Liliastrum
*Phædranassa chloracea
*Polianthes tuberosa
Polygonatum multiflorum
Puschkinia scilloides
Ranunculus (various)
Schizostylis coccinea
Scilla (various)
*Sparaxis tricolor
Sternbergia lutea
Tigridia (various)
Trillium grandiflorum
Tritonia (Montbretia)
Tulips (various)
*Vallota purpurea eximia
*Watsonia Meriana
Zephyranthes candida

NOTE.—* Denotes half-hardy bulbs or tubers only suitable for growing in the open in warm, sheltered situations or in the greenhouse.

Some Bulbs and Tubers for the Rock Garden

Allium azureum, A. Moly, A. neapolitanum, etc.
Anemone (tuberous)
Bulbocodium vernum
Calochortus Howellii, C. pulchellus, C. venustus
Chionodoxa
Colchicum autumnale and C. montanum

Crocus (various)
Cyclamen coum, C. europæum, C. neapolitanum
Eranthis hyemalis
Erythronium (various)
Fritillaria (various)
Galanthus (Snowdrop)
Iris (various)
Leucojum æstivum, etc.

Muscari azureus and M. conicum
Narcissus Bulbocodium, N. cyclamineus, N. minimus and N. triandrus
Puschkinia scilloides
Scilla bifolia, S. peruviana, S. sibirica, S. præcox and S. verna

Bulbs and Tubers suitable for Naturalizing in Grass

Allium Moly
Anemone apennina
Chionodoxas
Colchicum autumnale and C. montanum (Autumn Crocus)

Crocus (various)
Cyclamen (various)
Fritillaria (various)
Galanthus (Snowdrop)
Leucojum æstivum and L. vernum

Muscari azureus and M. conicum
Narcissus (various)
Ornithogalum
Scilla bifolia, S. sibirica, S. præcox and S. verna

Bulbs and Tubers suitable for Growing in Pots

Agapanthus
Allium neapolitanum
Brodiæa (various)
Calochortus (various)
Chionodoxas
Clivia miniata
Convallaria majalis
Crocus (various)
Freesia (various)
Fritillaria meleagris, F. persica and F. recurva
Galanthus (Snowdrop)
Gladiolus (various)
Hyacinthus (Hyacinth)

Hyacinthus candicans
Iris (various)
Ixia speciosa, etc.
Lachenalia (Cape Cowslip)
Lapeyrousia cruenta
Lilium (various)
Mirabilis longiflora
Muscari azureus and M. conicum
Narcissus (various)
Nerine (Guernsey Lily)
Ornithogalum arabicum
Oxalis Bowei
Polianthes tuberosa

Ranunculus asiaticus and vars. ; Persian, French
Schizostylis coccinea
Scilla bifolia, S. peruviana, S. sibirica, S. præcox and S. verna [tricolor
Sparaxis grandiflora and S.
Sternbergia lutea
Tigridia conchiflora and T. Pavonia
Trillium grandiflorum
Vallota (Scarborough Lily)
Watsonia Meriana
Zephyranthes candida

CHAPTER XIII

THE HERBACEOUS BORDER

THE herbaceous border is justly a popular feature of the garden, chiefly because of the glorious masses of colour which, if careful and skilful planting has been resorted to, may be had from early spring until November. It entails very little labour as compared with the upkeep of beds filled with annuals, or with the laying out of the more severe bedding designs. Once planted the herbaceous border lasts for many years, merely requiring weeding, staking, occasional mulching, and forking over annually.

The width of the border must naturally vary according to the size of the garden and many other considerations. But where possible it should be not less than 4 feet wide, and where there is plenty of space it should be at least double that width.

Site

The herbaceous border may occupy almost any position in the garden, but the best results will be obtained if it faces due south and has some protection in the form of a wall or a hedge from the cold winds from the north and east, though care should be taken that the hedge is far enough away for its roots not to take nourishment from the flowers in the border. Much thought should be bestowed on the choice of a background, as it can make or mar the border. A wall or trellis covered with roses is good, so also is a wall planted with fruit trees, but the dark green background provided by a yew hedge is very hard to beat.

Most perennials will grow in almost any soil, but a deep, rich, well-drained loam is preferred by most.

Preparing the Border

The ground intended to be devoted to this purpose should be thoroughly prepared in advance. This is even more important than in the case of beds of annuals or of tender plants, which will occupy the ground but for a single season. For the properly-prepared and properly-planted border should not require thorough

122

remaking or replanting for several years to come ; for one of its chief charms consists in the " settled-down " appearance, which is only possible with plants which have occupied the same ground for some time.

The border may be prepared either in September or in early January.   In the first case the plants should be put in in October or November and in the second in March or April.

The ground should be well drained and then thoroughly trenched to a depth of 2 to 3 feet, care being taken not to bring any sour or heavy subsoil to the top. With the bottom spit should be mixed good stable manure when the soil is heavy, or cow or pig dung if the land should be light, while some substance such as ashes of burnt vegetable matter, bone meal, or basic slag—in fact anything that will help to break up and lighten the soil—should be added to the top spit.   If the soil is too light it may be improved by the addition of leaf-mould and a little thoroughly pulverized clay.   Should the earth prove too heavy, coarse sand and wood ashes will serve to lighten it.

The border should be left for a month or so after trenching in order that it may settle down before the plants are put in.

Planting

As a general rule the best time to plant the border is in October or November, but in the north and very exposed positions it is often advisable to defer the planting until March or April.   The plants that bloom early should of course, if possible, be planted in the autumn so that the roots may get well-established before they have to bear the strain of flowering.   This applies to such plants as lupins and peonies. Autumn planting is also advisable in light soils, as very dry weather in late spring may prove disastrous to plants newly inserted in a light soil that will soon dry and parch the unestablished roots.   In wet, cold soils spring planting is best ; if plants must be put in in the autumn, let it be done in September. Thick succulent-rooted plants are more apt to decay if planted in autumn ; these should be spring-planted whenever possible.

In planting, holes should be dug sufficiently deep to allow the roots to be placed in without being doubled up, and wide enough to admit of the roots being well-spread out, and covered with fine soil which should be pressed firmly round the crowns.   Firm planting is essential and care must be taken that the crowns are not placed lower than ground level, as there is every possibility of their rotting off if this is done ; the plants should be so inserted that the crowns are just on the surface of the soil.   Some herbaceous plants are " tap-rooted," as the anchusa and sun-flower, and these demand an extra deep hole for planting, otherwise their long roots will be bent up and prevented from penetrating deeply into the soil and so obtaining the necessary nourishment and moisture. When planting, study the habits of the roots, and allow them to follow what seems to be their natural course, rather than direct them in one special way. Some roots want to run perpendicularly downward, others grow horizontally; each should be assisted and humoured.

Height Gradation

As a general rule the taller growing plants, as the rudbeckia, sunflower, hollyhock and delphinium should be placed at the back of the border and there should be a gentle gradation down through plants of medium height, as the phloxes, campanulas and carnations, to the violas, daisies, silenes and dwarfer species in front, but this procedure must not be adopted invariably or a stiff and severe effect will ensue, and the freedom and irregularity which are the chief charms of a herbaceous border will be lost. Here and there clumps of the taller flowers should be grouped in outstanding positions well to the front of the border, and some small-growing and creeping plants should seem to find their way right to the back, at the base of the taller ones, so as to break up the general outline and to introduce some element of surprise, for a border loses much of its charm if it can all be seen at a glance from one end. The flowers should be planted in groups of from four or five to eight or nine of each kind in a clump, but not too closely together; the dwarfer the plants the more in a group. It is one of the greatest mistakes to plant perennials singly in various parts of the border as this gives a patchwork effect which is not at all pleasing; the ideal to aim at is masses of striking, but well-harmonized colours.

The distance at which plants should be planted from one another depends on the height to which the plants may be expected to grow, and on their "bushiness." But as a guiding principle it can be taken that the dwarfer kinds should be planted about 8 inches apart, the medium sorts 15 inches apart; and the tallest kinds some 2 feet from one another. So far as space provision is concerned, the aim should be to show practically no bare earth during the period of active growth, and at the same time to avoid any overcrowding which interferes with individual development. There is thus great scope for knowledge of the habits of plants, as well as for taste in arrangement of colours and forms.

Each plant should be clearly labelled as it is planted, or confusion either in the colour scheme or in the gradation of height will be sure to ensue. When all the plants are in, the soil around them should be neatly forked over, so that the border may have a tidy and "finished" appearance.

Colour Grouping

We now come to colour grouping; this is perhaps the most difficult problem that has to be solved in the construction of the border. So much depends on the correct solution, and infinite pains will have to be expended in order that the best result may be obtained. Aim at large splashes of colour; do not go out for contrasts, but let the tints merge gently from the one into the other and with a gentle crescendo lead up from the paler shades to the most vivid colours at the summit. Let us first of all plan our red group. Start with the pale pinks, next to them put the deeper shades, and so on until the most vivid and powerful reds are reached; from this zenith of colour work gradually back to the palest of pink.

The purples, blues, and yellows can be arranged in the same way as described for the reds. We cannot, however, place these groups up against one another indiscriminately or we shall have hard lines and in places clashing colours, but we know that pink harmonizes delightfully with pale yellow so we may join our red group to the yellow group. Similarly pink is exquisite alongside lilac so we can link these up with our purple group, and our blue group with our yellows for pale yellow blends delightfully with pale blue.

We should also remember that tints may be made to lead the one from the other so as to blend harmoniously. The yellows will run into orange, the orange through orange-scarlet to scarlet, thence to the deepest crimson. Similarly through the pale blues we reach dark blue, then purple and down again through lilac to pale blue or lavender grey or white. Plants with ample green foliage must not be neglected as nature uses green very liberally in her colour schemes. White, if not used to excess, is invaluable as it will always help us out of difficulties for it may be placed next to the strongest colours equally as well as against the palest; if too much white is used the border will present a " patchy " effect.

Many of the strong colours may be associated without going through a gradation of their paler tints. Deep blue or purple, for instance, blends well with gold, orange or yellow, but care must be taken not to use any clashing colours in close proximity. The ultra vivid colours should be held in check as they strike the eye so quickly and are apt, if used too freely, to submerge the more delicate tints.

Do not fall into the common mistake of placing all the bright colours at the back and middle of the border, let there be some groups of vivid colouring well to the front; there are innumerable edging plants such as aubretias, pinks, and saxifrages that afford brilliant tints for this purpose. These groups of colour must not be bounded by hard straight lines, each group must be irregular in shape and should merge gradually and imperceptibly into the group next to it.

The novice must not feel disheartened if the colour scheme is not perfect the first year ; few, if any, are infallible in their colour grouping, and there are the subsequent years in which errors may be corrected.

Continuity of Bloom

In this we have a problem nearly as difficult as that provided by the colour scheme. Our aim is to secure a continuity of bloom from early spring until late in the autumn. Thus the plants we choose for the border must be not only brilliant in their colours, but should have as long as possible a period of bloom. If the border is wisely planned, there is no reason why there should not be plenty of colour from the beginning of April right up to the end of October.

Bulbs such as the snowdrop, the crocus, the tulip, the scilla, the chionodoxa, and the anemone, and such early flowering plants as the alyssum, the anchusa, the aubretia, and the earlier delphiniums will give a good show in spring. During May, June and July pæonies, lupins, delphiniums, irises, inulas, erigerons, antirrhinums, and many others will furnish all the colour needed ; there is no trouble at this period. In August and September we have sweet peas, thalictrums, phloxes, sunflowers, pentstemons, antirrhinums, and late delphiniums ; while gladioli, red hot pokers, aconitums, rudbeckias, dahlias, sunflowers, chrysanthemums, and Michaelmas daisies will carry on the bloom well to the end of October.

Replacements

The designer of the herbaceous border has still other things to think about. He must remember that by midsummer, or even before, the early flowering plants will have finished blooming and will be beginning to look untidy however carefully dead flowers have been picked off. He must, therefore, endeavour to plant later-flowering and taller-growing flowers which as they grow up will screen these. This, however, is more difficult than it at first appears, for a plant that will grow tall enough totally to obscure the plant behind it, but not until that plant has flowered, must be chosen. It will not do to plant *any* later-flowering plant to replace an early bloomer, even though it grows to the correct height to continue the uniformity of the scheme and flowers at the right time, for it must be remembered that the substitute plant must also fulfil the requirements of the colour scheme; it being necessary to replace a yellow flower by a yellow one or by one whose flowers harmonize with it.

Annuals may be used to fill vacant spaces, and for this purpose alyssum, asters, centaurea, clarkia, stocks, mignonette and nemophila are hard to rival.

Care of the Border

Let us say that the border has been constructed and planted in the autumn. Through the winter little attention will be necessary, but it will be wise to cover the crowns of the less hardy perennials, such as pentstemons and aquilegias, with fibre or small mounds of ashes to protect them from hard frosts in case the weather should be too severe. In the winter too, when there is little foliage and most pests are dormant, is the time to wage war on slugs and other pests infesting the borders. (*See chapter on* Diseases and Pests.)

At the beginning of spring, weeds will have begun to grow and a great deal of labour later on will be saved if these are kept down from the beginning. During the summer it is necessary to keep the hoe busy, not only to keep down the weeds, but to keep the soil well turned and to conserve the moisture in hot, dry weather. When the buds are forming the plants should be assisted by the application of a little artificial manure, applied just before rain, if possible; if no rain comes the chemicals should be well hoed in. A suitable mixture is one of 1 part of sulphate of ammonia to 2 parts of nitrate of soda, and applied at the rate of 2 oz. to the square yard. If preferred, a top-dressing of two-thirds well-decayed stable manure and one-third leaf-mould may be given in spring in lieu of the artificial manure. **Staking,** *see* page 71.

Tidying-up and Manuring

During the very dry weather, the plants will benefit if watered about every other day. Dead flowers should be cut off at once as this will prolong the flowering; once a plant is allowed to go to seed, it soon stops flowering. As the plants die and turn yellow, they must be cut down to within 3 inches of the ground, this keeps the border tidy and gives room to other plants; and in November when all flowers are over, all the plants should be cut down like this and be clearly labelled. Evergreen plants, such as red hot pokers, should, of course, not be cut down. At this time, or late in February, dig some well-decayed manure and leaf-mould in between the plants, but do not let the manure cover the crowns or they may rot off, and mind that the digging fork does not injure the roots.

Renewing the Border

About every three to four years the border will be all the better for a thorough retrenching and manuring; many of the plants, too, will be getting over-bulky and will need dividing, partly because they will overcrowd less vigorous neighbours, and partly because their flowers will have deteriorated both in size and colour. The border is best renewed in November, when all the plants, with the exception of such as pæonies, delphiniums, lilies, daffodils, and irises, should be removed, carefully labelled as to colour, height, species, etc., and laid aside in a warm and sheltered position. If they are to be left out of the border for more than a couple of days or so, they should be " heeled-into " the reserve garden. The border must be thoroughly trenched, digging as close as possible up to the plants left in position, and the subsoil should be well manured. If the soil is at all sour it should be dressed with lime at the rate of 10 oz. to the square yard. The plants should be divided, the inner and older stems being discarded, and the outer and younger crowns being replanted as when the border was first made. This work may also be done in February or March; this is wiser in colder localities where the plants might not stand an extra severe winter directly after replanting.

Propagation of Herbaceous Perennials

Herbaceous perennials may be propagated from seeds, cuttings, offsets, layers, and root divisions. The latter method is the most generally used. The use of seeds, however, is becoming increasingly popular, especially in the case of new species, although it is a somewhat lengthy process, as the plants do not attain to their best for three years. Seed is best sown in the open in May or June, or if preferred, in shallow boxes in a cold frame. First-year plants must not be allowed to flower at all; second-year plants may be permitted to bloom in moderation, but they must not be allowed to go to seed. In the chapter on *The Propagation of Plants*, p. 183, will be found full instructions for the various methods of propagation mentioned above.

PREPARING SEED DRILLS

1. Fining down the soil with the rake. 2. Making the drill with the hoe.
3. Sowing the seed. 4. Covering the seed with soil by means of the back of
the rake. See page 184.

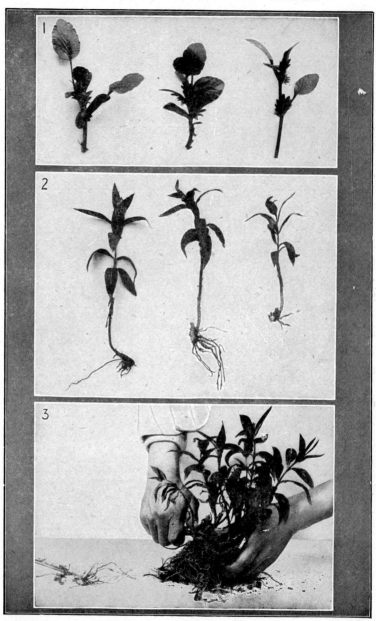

1. Viola cuttings; cuttings should be taken of new but vigorous growth from the centre of the plant, preferably in September, and struck in a shady frame. See page 316. 2. Phlox are best propagated by division of roots in March or October; root divisions ready for planting. 3. Dividing the roots of phlox; a sharp knife should be used so as to damage the roots as little as possible; never divide them with a spade. See page 286.

SOME HARDY HERBACEOUS PERENNIALS

NOTE.—For details as to Colour, Height, Season of Flowering, Culture, and the best Species and Varieties, *see* the Alphabetical List of Flowering Plants and Shrubs, page 207.

Acanthus longifolius
A. mollis and spinosus
Achillea filipendulinum
A. Ptarmica fl. pl. var. " The Pearl "
Aconitum japonicum
A. Napellus and A. Wilsonii
Adenophora liliifolia
Adonis amurensis and A. vernalis
Alstromeria aurantiaca
Althæa rosea (Hollyhock)
Anchusa italica (Dropmore, Opal and Pride of Dover)
Anemone alpina
A. apennina, A. coronaria, A. fulgens, A. Hepatica, A. japonica, and its vars.
Anthemis tinctoria and A. t. var. alba
Anthericum Liliago, " St. Bernard's Lily "
Aquilegia cœrulea (Rock Columbine)
A. chrysantha, A. vulgaris and others
Armeria latifolia, A. plantaginea and varieties
Artemisia lactiflora
Aspodelus lutea and A. ramosus (" King's Spear ")
Aster Amellus and vars.
Aster Novi-belgii and vars.
Astilbe Davidii
Aubrietia
Auricula (various)
Bellis perennis (Daisy)
Bocconia (syn. Macleaya) cordata and B. macrocarpa
Buphthalmum salicifolium
Campanula (various)
Catananche cœrulea
Centaurea babylonica and C. montana
Centranthus ruber and vars. (Valerian)
Cephalaria tartarica
Cheiranthus Cheiri (Wallflower)
Chelone Lyonii and C. obliqua

Chrysanthemum arcticum, C. uliginosum and others
Cimicifuga cordifolia, etc.
Coreopsis lanceolata, etc.
Corydalis solida, etc.
Delphinium (various)
Dianthus barbatus (Sweet William)
D. Caryophyllus (Carnation)
D. plumarius, etc. (Pink)
Dicentra spectabilis (Bleeding Heart)
Dictamnus albus
Dodecatheon Hendersonii, D. Meadia, etc.
Doronicum plantagineum var. excelsum, etc.
Echinacea purpurea
Echinops Ritro and others
Eremurus (various)
Erigeron speciosus, etc.
Erodium Manescavi
Eryngium (various)
Erysimum (various)
Funkia lancifolia and vars.
Gaillardia grandiflora
Galega officinalis, etc.
Gaura Lindheimeri
Geranium (various)
Geum (various)
Gypsophila paniculata, etc.
Hedysarum (various)
Helenium (various)
Helianthus (Sunflower)
Helleborus niger, etc. (Christmas Rose)
Hemerocallis flava, etc.
Heuchera sanguinea, etc.
Horminum pyrenaicum
Hypericum olympicum
Iberis sempervirens, etc. (Candytuft)
Incarvillea Delavayi
Inula ensifolia, etc.
Iris (various)
Kniphofia (various) (Red-Hot Poker)
Lathyrus grandiflorus, etc.
Linaria dalmatica, etc.
Linum flavum, L. narbonense, and L. perenne
Lobelia (various)
Lupinus (various) (Lupin)
Lychnis (various)
Lythrum (various)

Malva moschata, etc.
Meconopsis cambrica, etc.
Mimulus luteus and many garden vars.
Monarda didyma, etc.
Myosotis palustris, etc. (Forget-Me-Not)
Nepeta Mussinii, etc.
Œnothera glauca var. Fraseri, etc. (Evening Primrose)
Pæonia (Herbaceous)
Papaver (various) (Poppy)
Pentstemon (various)
Phlox (various)
Physalis Franchettii, etc.
Physostegia virginiana, P. v. var. speciosa
Polemonium (various)
Potentilla (various)
Primula elatior, P. vulgaris and many garden vars.
Pyrethrum (syn. Chrysanthemum)
Rudbeckia laciniata and many garden vars.
Salvia virgata, S. superba, etc.
Saponaria officinalis, S. o. var. flore plena, etc.
Saxifraga (various)
Scabiosa caucasica, etc.
Sedum spectabile and S. s. var. variegatum, etc.
Senecio (various)
Sidalcea candida, S. neomexicana, S. spicata, etc.
Solidago canadense, etc. (Golden Rod)
Spiræa palmata, etc.
Stokesia cyanea, and S. c. var. alba
Thalictrum aquilegifolium, T. Delavayi, etc.
Tradescantia virginiana and vars., etc.
Trillium grandiflorum, etc.
Trollius asiaticus, T. europæus and vars., etc.
Valeriana officinalis
Veronica incana, V. spicata and vars., etc. (Speedwell)
Viola (various) (Viola and Pansy)

CHAPTER XIV

THE ROCK GARDEN

THERE are few features in the ordinary garden which are so neglected and so ill understood as the rock garden. The horrible mass of shiny, glazed lumps of brickwork in the cracks of which half-starved ferns and plants struggle for existence is nothing but a disfigurement. The chief uses of the rocks and stones in a rock garden are the provision of coolness for the roots and the storing of moisture in crevices for the use of the plants. But the idea that rock plants grow best in practically nothing but rock is a mistaken one. A generous allowance of good soil between, amongst, and beneath the stones is essential for the healthy growth of the plants. As the function of the rocks is to provide shelter for roots, it is clearly useless to plant slabs of rock or stone perpendicularly in the soil. No protection is afforded in this way : the roots cannot get beneath them, and they do not preserve any moisture. Large masses of stone, two or more feet in length, should be used, where possible, and should be sunk well and firmly in the earth in a slightly slanting direction—tilted backwards, not forwards, so that the rain may trickle down to the roots of the plants. If the rocks lean forward, over the plants, the roots will be sheltered from the rain and probably parched. Although the visible portions of the rocks in the garden should be as pleasing as may be to the eye, and should all slant in the same direction to represent a natural outcrop or stratum of stone, it should never be forgotten that they are not there for the sake of picturesque effect, but to protect the roots of the plants growing among them. The slopes of the mounds in which the boulders are set must not be too steep and should be as natural in appearance as possible ; there should be miniature ranges and mountain peaks and dividing them valleys into which spurs from the hills project. Winding paths, 18 inches to 2 feet in width, with stepping stones, should be cut through these gorges so that every part of the rock garden is easily accessible. The pockets in which the alpines are to be planted should be irregular in shape and may vary from a few inches in diameter to as many feet across ;

they must be from a foot to 18 inches in depth, and so constructed that the soil will not wash out of them. If there is any chance of the soil in the pockets becoming sodden, clinker and rubble drainage must be provided.

Soil

The great mass of rock plants, particularly the alpines, like a rich soil, even where they need little of it. A soil full of coarse sand or grit, leaf-mould and other decayed vegetable matter, mixed in some cases with old spent manure from a hotbed, is excellent for rock gardening. As a whole these plants are not faddy as to soil and most thrive well in the compost mentioned above, but some grow best in certain soils. (*See Alphabetical List of Flowering Plants*, p. 207.) For these it is quite easy to scoop out a hollow and to substitute a little special compost in which the rock plant may be inserted.

Alpine plants in their native habitat receive a yearly top-dressing of vegetable matter from the material carried down by the melting snows, and alpines in a rock garden are all the better for a top-dressing artificially applied in imitation of this natural process.

Where rock plants are studied in their natural conditions it will be found that in most cases the soil around the roots is completely covered by the stalks and leaves, each plant touching its neighbours, and that practically no soil is left exposed. This arrangement is of the greatest use to the plants, as by preventing the exposure of the soil to the action of sun and wind, its natural moisture is preserved, so that so far as we can we should provide this protection. This is, however, rather difficult to do at first, as while the plants are still small and most need protection they are unable to cover the surface of the ground, and to plant them closer together would merely mean starving and overcrowding them. In such a case the best thing to do is to cover the intermediate surface of soil with chips of stone, small enough to be easily pushed aside by a shoot, but sufficient to prevent the over-drying of the earth.

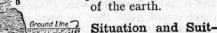
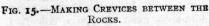

Fig. 15.—Making Crevices between the Rocks.

A shows a vertical crevice; B a horizontal fissure. The small stones C C give space for soil between the rocks.

Situation and Suitable Stone

As regards the situation of the rock garden, it should, where possible, have an open, sunny position, away

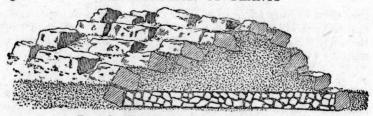

FIG. 16.—CONSTRUCTING THE ROCK GARDEN.

The rocks should be set at a uniform angle to simulate the strata of a natural outcrop of rock; they should tilt slightly backwards and the higher rocks must not overhang those below them, or no moisture will find its way into the horizontal fissures. The brick or rubble drainage is clearly shown.

from walls and trees. The rock garden always looks best where it has not to bear contrast with any formal arrangement of garden or shrubbery; a wild and "natural-looking" site, and, where possible, one where the natural rock of the district crops up here and there, is the most favourable, where there is choice. In making the garden the stone of the district should always be used if it can, but any stone will do well enough, except, perhaps, the very crumbling slates or magnesian limestone. Two of the best are weathered limestone and sandstone. It is essential that there be no spaces and hollows under and around the stones, and that the earth be well bedded round them, or the air within the hollow spaces will dry up the soil and drain the moisture from the roots of the plants.

The Selection of Plants.

When making a selection of plants for the rock garden there are several points to be borne in mind. The first is that we should aim at having bloom over the longest possible period of the year. In this connection some of the smaller-growing bulbs (*see* List of Bulbs, p. 121) which bloom in the winter and early spring are invaluable, while those later autumn-flowering alpines, such as the *Astilbe simpliciflora* and the *Wahlenbergia vincæflora* furnish colour long after the great majority of rock plants have finished blooming.

Some of the stronger growers soon over-run the rock garden and smother other plants less luxuriant, perhaps, but more beautiful and useful. These vigorous growers must, therefore, be limited in number and those that are chosen must be sternly cut back and kept in check. To add interest to the rock garden as many of the various genera as possible should be selected, but the garden must never be overcrowded. Bulbs are often overlooked when planting the rock garden. This should not be, for few sights are more lovely than some of the smaller-growing bulbs blooming above a carpeting of Acæna microphylla, Globularia nana, Arenaria balearica, or other dwarf trailer. For a selection *see* list on page 136.

Planting

Rock plants should be planted out either in the spring or, better still, in the early autumn, but not later than September, since the roots make but little growth after that month and the plant is liable to be washed out of the earth by heavy rain, or lifted from the soil by the action of the frost. If care is taken, however, all alpines can be planted out at any time between early April and the end of September. Plants from pots may, of course, be planted at any time provided a sufficient " ball " of soil from the pot is allowed to remain round the roots, and provided the weather is neither too dry nor too wet.

When planting in a crevice, it is essential that there shall be no air-pocket at the bottom; this would drain all moisture from the roots and parch them. To avoid this, first ram plenty of good gritty soil well into the crevice and make sure that the bottom is well filled, then scrape out some of the mould at the top and set the plant in firmly, pressing the soil well down round the root, and fix it in tightly by means of a smaller wedge of stone. Care should be taken that shade lovers, like the aquilegia and hepatica, are given congenial situations ; plants which prosper in the sun, as alyssum, arabis, etc., should be given the sunniest spots in the rock garden. Such plants as alyssum and aubretia should be planted in the crevices among the rocks ; on the flat, lower-lying situations the saxifrages and all such creeping plants will thrive, while an occasional dwarf evergreen shrub, in accordance with the position it occupies, will accentuate or detract from the heights and will add naturalness to the landscape.

THE MORAINE GARDEN

Many of the more fastidious of the alpines will not prosper in the ordinary rock garden. The plants to which we refer grow on mountain slopes covered with loose stones, where the melting of the snow during summer provides them with plenty of ice-cold water and where a blanket of snow protects them during the winter. The conditions we have to endeavour to reproduce are, therefore, adequate moisture for the roots in summer while the plants are growing, but at the same time good drainage, and secondly protection from damp and excessive cold in winter.

Making the Moraine

An ideal and natural position for the moraine would be at the lower end of a valley between two rocky spurs, the gorge gradually expanding into a flat bed of scree with occasional boulders strewn over it. To make the moraine, dig out about $2\frac{1}{2}$ feet of the soil and make the bottom of the basin or trench slope slightly towards the front : the slope must not be too steep or the moraine will become over dry in summer. The lower 10 inches of this basin must be made water-tight by means of puddling with clay or cement. Make an outlet in front, which when closed keeps about 10 inches of water, but not more, in the lowest part of the basin, while when the outlet is open none at all remains. Now cover the bottom of the trench with about 10 inches of rubble, stones or any material that will afford good drainage. Above this place another 3 inches or so of smaller stones roughly 1 inch in diameter, these will fill the gaps between the larger stones and prevent the small grit above from sinking through and blocking the drainage. The hollow must then be filled up with a mixture of stone chips and gravel, good loam, leaf-mould, and small stone chips similar to those used in frosty weather for sprinkling on wood-paved roads. Cover this, again, with a 2-inch layer of chips. Granite or limestone chips are excellent and easily obtained ; flint chips should not be used as they do not conserve moisture. Place a few boulders in the moraine in order to break up the surface and to give the plants some protection. A natural trickle of water may be led into the top of the moraine, or sufficient moisture given from a watering can each day to cause an overflow from the outlet at the bottom. From November to May when no additional moisture is needed in the moraine the outlet should be left open. Many plants that have proved failures in the rock garden proper will, on transplantation to the moraine, flourish beyond all expectations.

Protection of Plants in Winter

Plants whose leaves are covered with fluff or down are, when in their natural haunts, usually protected from frost and damp during the winter by a coat of snow. When they are grown out of doors in this country, they must, therefore, be given a covering of glass during the winter months. When the plant is a small one nestling in a crevice between the rocks, it is often possible to cover it with a sheet of glass resting on the surrounding rocks, but when this cannot be done, four pieces of stiff galvanized wire should be inserted firmly in the ground and bent over at the top to hold the glass plate firmly in position over the plant. If the weather is especially severe or the plant very delicate, four other pieces of glass may be firmly set in the soil and supported by the wires so as to form four walls protecting the plant. Sufficient space between the glass roof and the tops of the four walls should be left for adequate ventilation (but not enough to admit the rain or snow) or the plant will be liable to damp-off. The frost will often raise the plants from the soil, especially those planted the previous autumn. In spring, therefore, each plant should be carefully scrutinized, and if necessary, gently pressed down into the soil.

Care of the Rock Garden

All through the summer months the rock garden must be periodically weeded and all dead flower heads should be cut away. Water the choicer species during dry spells and in May top-dress with a thin layer of sandy loam and leaf-mould. By July most of the plants will have borne the best of their bloom, and many of the most vigorous will now be pushing forth new growth and will commence to overcrowd the less rampageous inmates. These plants, including the shrubby subjects, should, therefore, be trimmed back and at the same time the older portions of the plants and all dead stems and foliage should be removed. Do not, however, trim the plants back so evenly that they have the symmetrical and formal aspect of shrubs in a topiary garden; rather endeavour to foster the wild and natural appearance of the rock garden, and where a plant is not throttling its neighbours and has ample space, let it ramble over the rocks at will.

The Propagation of Rock Plants

Rock plants may be increased by seed sown under glass as soon as ripe or in March, by cuttings or by division in April or September. It is better to raise alpines from cuttings or division of the roots, rather than from seed, which is a lengthy, and in some cases a difficult process. *See also* Propagation, Chapter XXIII.

THE ALPINE HOUSE

There are some choice alpines that cannot be cultivated in the open to the best advantage in our uncertain climate. To say that they are choice does not necessarily mean that they are delicate, but that the blooms of many are apt to be spoilt by inclement weather, and it is to these subjects that the alpine house affords protection while they are in bloom ; it will also prolong their season of flowering. Most of the inmates can be brought on in pans sunk to their rims in ashes in the open or in frames until they are about to flower, when they should be transferred to the alpine house to be removed again to the open after flowering. After the beginning of October all the plants should be housed in a frost-proof frame and must be removed to the house as the blooms become visible. The alpine house does not require artificial heating and is best of the low span-roofed type, so situated that it runs north and south ; both sides then get their fair share of the sun. For management, *see* The Cold House, p. 167.

Compost and Potting

Two-thirds fibrous loam and leaf-mould with one-third coarse, gritty sand makes an excellent compost for most of these plants. Many of the finer saxifrages like a little splintered limestone in their soil, which plants, of course, require a peaty compost.

Individual tastes must be studied as far as possible. Pot-up in pans from 6 to 9 inches in diameter and about 5 inches deep, and as ample drainage is required place 2½ to 3 inches of broken crocks in the bottom of the pots for plants like the androsaces and the saxifrages. For plants of a more vigorous nature and for bulbs 1 to 2 inches of crocks will suffice. Repotting is only needed every second or third year. The stagings should be covered with a 2-inch layer of shingle or ashes so that the atmosphere may be kept moist. For the treatment of bulbs, *see* Bulbs in Pots, p. 118.

SOME GOOD ROCK PLANTS

NOTE.—For details as to Colour, Height, Season of Flowering, Culture and the best Species and Varieties, *see* the Alphabetical List of Flowering Plants and Shrubs, p. 207.

*Acæna (various)
†Achillea argentea, A. rupestris, A. tomentosa
Adonis vernalis
Alyssum montanum, etc.
*Anchusa myosotidiflora
†Androsace lanuginosa, etc.
*†Anemones
*Aquilegia glandulosa
Arabis (various)
*Arenaria (various)
†Armeria cæspitosa
†Aubrietia (various)
*†Campanula (various)
Cerastium tomentosum
Coronilla cappadocica
*Cyclamen (Hardy vars.)
Cytisus kewensis and C. Beani
†Dianthus (various) (Pink)
†Draba (various)
Dryas octopetala
Erica carnea (Heath)
†Erodium (various)

Erysimum Perofskianum, etc.
Gaultheria procumbens
Genista pilosa
†*Gentiana (various)
Geum (various)
Gypsophila repens
*Haberlea rhodopensis
Helianthemum(Sun Rose)
Heuchera sanguinea vars.
†Hypericum (various)
*Iberis (Candytuft)
*Iris (Dwarf Bearded, Hybrid, and Bulbous)
†Linaria alpina
Linum (Flax)
Lithospermum prostratum
Lychnis alpina (Campion)
*Lysimachia nummularia aurea
†*Mertensia primuloides
†Morisia hypogœa
Nierembergia rivularis

†*Omphalodes verna, etc.
Onosma albo-roseum, etc.
*Ourisia coccinea
Oxalis enneaphylla, etc.
†Papaver alpinum
Phlox (Dwarf Alpine)
†Potentilla (various)
†*Primula (various)
Pulmonaria (various)
*Ramondia pyrenaica
†*Ranunculus alpestris
Saponaria ocymoides
†*Saxifraga (various)
Sedum (various)
Sempervivum (various)
Silene (various)
Soldanella alpina, etc.
Thymus (various)
*Viola (various)
†Wahlenbergia serpyllifolia
†*Waldsteinia trifolia
Zauschneria californica splendens

NOTE.—In addition to the flowers named in this list there are many dwarf annuals which, though not rock plants in the true sense, deserve a position in the rock garden. It should not be forgotten that hardy bulbs afford masses of colour in the early spring; and suitable species are shown on p. 121; many ferns are also suitable. For dwarf shrubs for the rock garden, *see* list of Flowering Shrubs and Trees.

Those plants that will grow in the shade are marked *; those suitable for the Moraine Garden are marked †.

CHAPTER XV

WALL AND PAVED GARDENS

THE WALL GARDEN

The Dry Wall

THE " dry wall," as it is called, consists of stones, usually sandstone or limestone, from 2 to 8 inches in thickness, of any size within reason, rectangular and more or less untrimmed. Stones are better than bricks as they provide cooler and moister root-beds for the wall plants. They should be bonded, that is laid in layers, so that the lateral extremities of a stone lie over the centres of the two stones in the row immediately below it. This structure serves to keep the wall secure and firm. The stones are best when their upper surfaces are flat, or even cupped, and when placed in position they should be inclined slightly backwards so that they are lower at the back than at the front ; the rain will then be collected and drained into the soil at the back of the wall to furnish moisture for the roots. No cement is used, but earth is rammed firmly into the crevices between the stones, sufficient mould being used to keep the stones about an inch apart, vertically. This soil must be rammed well into the back of the wall so that there is soil from the very front to the earth supporting the wall at the back. The earth should be well " firmed " after each row of stones has been laid and no " air-pockets " must be left in the crevices, or the roots of the plant will be dried up.

The Compost

A mixture of good loam, cow manure, and leaf-mould makes the best compost for the wall garden. The first essential is to make a good foundation for the wall. This should be about 10 inches deep and a shade wider than the base of the wall. Here the earth is rammed well down till a solid footing is provided. Now lay the first layer of stones, using the largest available, and place them so that their upper sides form one straight horizontal line. If the stones are of moderate size, the gaps left laterally between them may be about 3 inches, the smaller the stones the smaller the gaps between them. Next pack the crevices between the stones tightly with the compost of good loam, leaf-mould and cow dung.

137

On this is placed the next layer of stone, properly bonded in the manner already explained (see also diagram Fig. 17) ; and the process is repeated over and over again until the wall has reached the required height. If a stone is occasionally inserted length-wise from back to front, the wall will be secure. The wall should not be built exactly vertical but the top should incline slightly back at an angle of about 1 in 6, that is to say, in a wall 4 feet high the base will project 8 inches further forward than the top. The top of the wall is best left flat so that the rain may soak through to the roots beneath.

FIG. 17. — How to Plant the "Dry" Wall.

A plant should never be placed at the *top*, (a) of a vertical joint between the stones; it should be set in the crevice (b), at the *bottom* of a vertical fissure.

Planting the Wall

It is, of course, easiest to plant the wall as it is constructed, the roots may then be spread out as they should be, and can be well covered with soil. Larger plants may thus be employed than when the planting is done when the wall is completed. March and April, when root growth is very vigorous, are the best months in which to construct and plant the wall-garden. Seed may be sown in the crevices in spring. The best way to do this is to mix the seeds with a little well-sieved moist sandy soil and to press it into the chink in the wall. A small piece of moss inserted into the crevice will keep the seed moist and will prevent it from being dislodged.

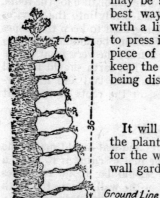

FIG. 18.—Constructing the "Dry" Wall.

The wall should incline slightly back at an angle of about 1 in 6 from bottom to top; that is, in a wall 3 feet high the base will project 6 inches beyond the top.

Selecting the Plants

It will be noted that the great majority of the plants given in our list (p. 140) as suitable for the wall garden thrive best in the sun. A wall garden situated in the shade, however, can be made anything but drab and uninteresting as the names of the shade lovers will testify. For the shady wall in a cool position such hardy ferns as the asplenium, polypodium, or the scolopendrium must not be overlooked.

In planting, every effort should

be made to insert the plants with their roots well spread out; and so that they may penetrate well into the soil at the back of the wall. A little well-rotted cow-manure inserted with the roots will prove beneficial. A plant should never be placed at the *top* (*a*) of a vertical joint between the stones, its roots would then be likely to become dried up. Rather should it be planted in the crevice (*b*) just above the centre of a stone.

A good 6 inches of compost should be firmly rammed down on to the top of the wall, and in this soil, at intervals, should be placed large stones; these will help to keep the soil in place and will furnish moist, cool sites for the roots of such plants as rock roses, wallflowers, geraniums, snapdragons, sedums, and saxifrages—all ideal plants with which to crown the wall garden.

THE PAVED GARDEN

Only certain plants are suitable to the paved garden; these are dwarf in nature and many of them will thrive although trodden on and walked over to a considerable degree, for it must be remembered that the prime reason for a path is its utility as a means of progress. A limited number of plants only, therefore, must be planted in the interstices of the paving, and these must appear to have seeded naturally from surrounding borders or from the rock garden and must in no way impede the pedestrian, although the paved garden should not be subject to constant traffic. More paved gardens are spoiled by indiscriminate and excessive planting than by any other cause. If rock work of any kind forms the boundary to the path or the paved garden, allow the plants covering it to encroach a little way and in an irregular manner over the flagstones; this informality will add a touch of nature and help to erase the traces of the handiwork of man.

As to the stones used, the majority should not be less than about 10 inches in diameter or the paving will have a patchy appearance. Stones rectangular in shape are best for paths, but for squares, circles, and ovals, the flags may be of any shape and size provided they are irregular.

The site of the paved garden, must, of course, be well drained, in fact the foundation should be similar to that of any ordinary pathway. Over this base is placed a layer of sand some 3 to 6 inches in thickness and on this the flags are laid in an irregular pattern and so that there are gaps of some 2 or 3 inches between the stones. (*See* Crazy Paving, p. 89.) These spaces should be filled with good loamy soil mixed with a quarter part well-decayed manure, preferably cow dung, and an eighth part old mortar, and in this are inserted the plants in small groups or in isolated tufts.

PLANTS FOR THE WALL AND PAVED GARDENS

NOTE.—For Cultural Details and for Colour, Height, and Time of Flowering, *see* the Alphabetical List of Flowering Plants, p. 207.

Wall Garden

*Acæna adscendens, A. Buchananii and A. microphylla
Acantholimon glumaceum
Achillea (various)
Æthionema grandiflorum
Alyssum alpestre, A. montanum, A. saxatile
Androsace (various)
Antirrhinum (various)
Aquilegia (various)
Arabis albida fl. pl. and A. androsacea
*Arenaria balearica
Asperula Gussoni
Aubrietia (various)
Campanula cæspitosa, C. fragilis, C. Hostii
Centranthus ruber
Cerastium tomentosum
Chieranthus (Wallflower)
Cortusa Matthioli
*Corydalis lutea
*Cotyledon Umbilicus
Dianthus alpinus

Dianthus cæsius, D. deltoides, D. plumaris
Draba aizoon
Erigeron mucronatus
*Erinus alpinus
Erodium macradenum and E. Manescavi
Gypsophila prostrata and G. repens
Helianthemum (various)
Helichrysum bellidioides
Hypericum fragile and H. tomentosum
Iberis sempervirens
Leontopodium alpinum
Lewisia rediviva
*Linaria alpina and L. Cymbalaria
Linum alpinum
Lychnis alpina
*Mertensia primuloides
Morisia hypogœa
Nepeta Mussini
Œnothera missouriensis and O. acaulis
Onosma tauricum

Origanum pulchrum, etc.
Pentstemon Menziesii, P. Scouleri
Phlox amœna, P. subulata
Phyteuma comosum
*Primula Allionii, P. Auricula, and P. viscosa
*Ramondia pyrenaica
Santolina incana
Saponaria cæspitosa and S. ocymoides
*Saxifraga (various)
Sedum (various)
Sempervivum (various)
Silene alpestris and S. Schaftæ
Teucrium Polium
Thymus serpyllum coccineus
Tunica Saxifraga
Veronica Guthreana
Wahlenbergia serpyllifolia
Zauschneria californica

NOTE.—Those plants suitable for growing in the shade are marked *.

Paved Garden

*Acæna Buchananii, A. microphylla and A. myriophylla
Achillea rupestris and A. tomentosa
Alyssum montanum
Antennaria dioica, A. d. var. tomentosa
Anthyllis montana
Arabis bellidifolia variegata
*Arenaria balearica, A. laricifolia
Armeria maritima
Aubrietia (various)
Bellium minutum
Calamintha alpina
Campanula cæspitosa, C. garganica, C. muralis and C. pusilla
Cerastium arvense and C. tomentosum
*Corydalis lutea

Dianthus deltoides
Dryas octopetala
*Erinus alpinus (various)
Erodium chamædryoides
Globularia cordifolia
Gypsophila cerastioides
Helianthemum croceum
Herniaria glabra
Hutchinsia alpina
Hypericum nummularium and H. reptans
Leontopodium alpinum
*Linaria alpina, L. repens
Lippia nodiflora
Lithospermum prostratum
Lotus corniculatus fl. pl.
*Mazus Pumilio
*Mentha Requienii
*Mimulus radicans
Morisia hypogœa
Myosotis cæspitosa var. Rehsteineri

Œnothera rosea
Oxalis corniculata var. atropurpurea and O. Acetosella rosea
Paronychia argentea and P. serpyllifolia
Pentstemon Menziesii
Potentilla alba and nitida
Saponaria ocymoides
*Saxifraga (various)
Sedum album, S. anglicum
Sempervivum montanum and S. tectorum
Silene acaulis
Thymus Serpyllum, and T. S. var. lanuginosus
Tunica Saxifraga
Veronica alpina, V. repens
*Viola cornuta

NOTE.—Those plants suitable for growing in the shade are marked *.

CHAPTER XVI

WATER AND BOG GARDENS

THE WATER GARDEN

THE pond selected for the water garden can be large or small, it may be constructed in part of a river, or a tiny stream may afford the water supply. It is, however, useless to attempt water gardening unless a continuous supply of water, the year through, is available. A very small supply, even a trickle artificially laid on, will suffice, provided it is continuous, but a water garden which is liable to dry up in the summer is a sure source of disappointment. A low-lying piece of land should be selected, preferably one where a natural depression already exists; one should look down on the plants, not have to look up at them. The pond—assuming that one does not already exist—should be made about 3 feet in depth at the deepest point.

Making the Artificial Lily Pond

The aim is to copy nature as nearly as possible. Let the pond, therefore, occupy the lowest-lying part of the ground, and to assist in this striving for natural surroundings the water garden may often be advantageously associated with the wild garden, or the rock garden. Size can be made to suit requirements and the surrounding conditions. Shape is dependent upon space and the other features of the garden; naturalness must again be the aim and it should be remembered that a series of sharp and erratic curves will never produce a pleasing and natural outline. The design must be simple; curves may be used, of course, but they must be long, sweeping and natural. On the other hand, not a single curve need be used; the severely simple square or rectangular pool has a charm all its own. In such cases the garden becomes more formal, the pool may well be bordered by a paved walk, and in the crevices between the stones may grow small wall or rock plants. Where the more informal shape has been chosen the grass can well be allowed to clothe the gently sloping banks right down to the water's edge, and marsh plants can be planted in groups from the very brink up to the higher slopes, where bamboos and other shrubs should be used to form a screen and background.

Depth of Water Required

Few water plants, except very strong growers, which are better excluded even from the moderately large water garden, require a greater depth of water than 2½ feet.   To allow for the thickness of the pond lining and for the inclusion of soil to nourish the roots, it is necessary to excavate to a depth of somewhat over 3 feet. The actual walls of the pond itself are best cut perpendicularly if concrete is to be used (they must be left sloping if the pond is to be " puddled " with clay), but the earth should be thrown well back several feet from the pond so that the banks, on which the marsh plants are to grow, may slope very gently right down to the water's edge.

Now as to the impervious lining to keep the water in the pond.

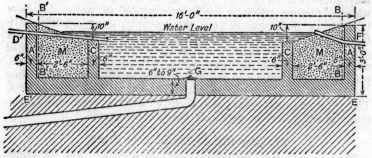

FIG. 19.—MAKING THE LILY POND.

A and *A'* are walls of concrete 6 inches thick ; *C* and *C'* are also of concrete and of the same thickness, but are 10 inches shorter than the outer walls. *B'* to *B'* shows the overall width of the pond ; *M* and *M'* are pockets of saturated soil for bog plants ; *D* is the inflow pipe, and *F* the overflow. The plug *G* enables the pond to be emptied and cleaned.

There are three materials that can be used, puddled clay, bricks, mortar, or concrete and cement.   We recommend the last as being the easiest to work and the most lasting.   Where the subsoil consists of a stiff, sticky, impervious clay, puddling, provided it is well done and is carried to a depth of about 10 inches, is a cheaper and equally successful process.

Digging out the Pond

It must be remembered that all constructional work will have to be hidden and that a permanently moist margin of soil some 2 to 3 feet wide round the pond to accommodate marsh plants will be desirable.   It will, therefore, be necessary to excavate to a width sufficient to allow for this ; that is to say, supposing it has been decided that the pond shall be 10 feet wide, a hole 3 feet deep all over and 16 feet wide will have to be dug ; this allows for a 2½ foot margin of moist earth, as well as 6 inches for the thickness of the wall on each side, if concrete is used. The bottom of the pond need not be more than 5 inches in thickness.

When the excavation is complete all loose soil must be dug out and the bottom made thoroughly firm by pounding with a heavy beater. If the soil over which the concrete is to be laid is left loose, it may shrink away and cause the concrete to crack.

Mixing the Concrete

A useful mixture consists of one part of cement, two parts of sand, and five parts of gravel, broken stone, or brick. Whilst still in the dry state, the materials should be turned over two or three times. The heap is then wetted with water poured over it from a large water-pot fitted with a fine rose, and the whole is mixed by again turning it over once or twice, so that the materials may be thoroughly amalgamated.

When well mixed and in a semi-liquid condition, place a layer of concrete 6 to 9 inches thick over the bottom of the pond and smooth it down firmly; next build a retaining wall of boards parallel to the earth walls, but 6 inches nearer the centre of the pond. The gap between the wood and the earth sides, when filled up with concrete, will form the two walls A and A'. The supporting boards B'B' and BB are, of course, not removed until the concrete is thoroughly dry. Now construct the two inner walls C and C', each 2½ feet from the outer retaining walls, but 10 inches shorter than them.

An inflow pipe D and an outlet pipe F should be inserted before the concrete work is completed. As soon as the concrete is quite dry it should be roughed over, wetted, and then thoroughly worked over with cement-wash, 2 inches in thickness, care being taken to see that the corners E and E' are perfectly watertight. A word of warning may here be given—it is unwise, apart from the shade cast and the dead leaves and twigs that will fall into the water, to construct a pond under or near trees, as their roots run a considerable distance underground, and are in time likely to crack the concrete unless it is very strong.

The Water Supply

For the great majority of aquatic plants a constant flow of water is not a necessity, the inflow pipe D may, therefore, be dispensed with, and water lost in evaporation may be periodically replaced by means of the hose or by bucket. It should be said that, if the border of marsh plants around the pond is to prove successful, the water must never be allowed to fall below the tops of the inner walls C and C', or the marshy conditions of the banks within the outer containing walls will not be maintained. Likewise the water level must be kept just below the tops of the walls A and A' or too much of the surrounding ground will become marshy. The outflow pipe F is, therefore, a necessity to carry off superfluous rainwater. A plug and outflow G at the bottom of the pond is a useful feature, the water may then periodically be drained away so that the pond can be cleaned and rearranged.

When the concrete is thoroughly dry the spaces M and M' between the retaining walls A and C and A' and C' are filled with a compost of loam and peat, or loam and leaf-mould, and banked up so that the tops of the walls A and A' are covered with soil and hidden from sight. The surrounding ground should slope up gently from this point so that turf may, in places, run right down to the water's edge whence the water and marsh plants may best be surveyed.

At other points rocks may be firmly cemented on the tops of the walls A and A', and sometimes just below the water level. These shelves under the water will form ledges on which aquatics can be planted, and the rocks, which can be built up as miniature cliffs on one side of the pond, will present an excellent contrast to the smooth turf running down to the water's edge on the other.

Planting

In the moist pockets M and M' are planted the bog or marsh plants, those requiring 4 to 6 inches of water over their crowns being planted under water lower down the bank, while a shade higher up the moist shelf should be grouped those plants flourishing on cool moist swampy banks. The bottom of the pond should be covered with a layer of soil some 12 inches deep, in which plants may root.

The best method of planting water plants in a pond or lake is in pans or flat baskets, in which the plants are placed in fibrous loam and a little cow-manure, the pans or baskets then being gently lowered into the water in the desired situation. A layer of enriched mud should cover the bottom of the pond, the baskets resting in this so that the roots of the plants can work out and ramble at will.

The borders of the pond should be hidden with such plants as spread out on the

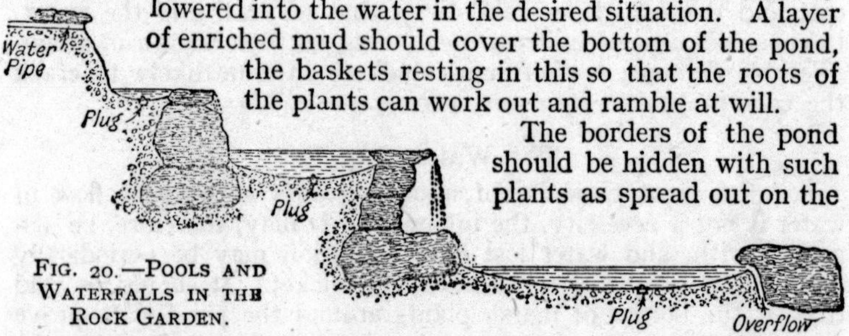

FIG. 20.—POOLS AND WATERFALLS IN THE ROCK GARDEN.

The rocks forming the pools in the above diagram must be set in cement to keep the structure firm; the pools are of concrete and lined with cement. A continuous trickle, artificially fed if necessary, will keep the miniature falls running.

THE FORMAL LILY POOL

Photo]   [*Malby*

In this type of garden flagged paths and " dry " walls harmonise delightfully
with the formal construction of the pools.   See page 141.

THE WATER GARDEN

surface of the water, while rooting in the firm soil at the margin. Among these are the water forget-me-not, *Myosotis palustris, Comarum palustre, Calla palustris*, and *Veronica Beccabunga*. These, prettily grouped, will clothe the actual margin, while beyond them the taller-growing plants, such as irises, spiræas, marsh marigolds, with the sedges, grasses, and rushes, thrive on the slightly swampy banks. Many of the ferns love such a situation as this, among them the beautiful *Osmunda regalis*, and the bamboos make effective backgrounds for smaller plants.

Care of the Water Garden

Once planted many aquatic and marsh plants are better if left undisturbed and only lifted and replanted when they appear to be unhealthy and ailing. Others, however, are much like hardy perennials in their requirements and thrive best if lifted, divided and replaced every third or fourth spring. Some of the water lilies make tremendous leaf growth, and consequently little bloom, cover the surface of the water, and prevent the sun's rays from warming it ; a function so essential to most aquatics, especially the nymphæas or water lilies. This strong growth must, therefore, be periodically cut away, and the roots should be divided if necessary.

Many people are troubled with an objectionable slimy green growth called Blanket weed. This covers the surface of the water in hot, dry weather, usually in spring and summer. It may be disposed of by adding 4 oz. of copper sulphate or 1 oz. of potassium permanganate to each 25,000 galls. of water contained in the pond. A second application should be made in a week's time, should the first be unsuccessful. This will harm neither plants nor fish.

Aquatic plants, as they are termed, are propagated some by seed and some by division of the roots. The seeds, when sown, must be placed under water. In other respects aquatic plants require the same general treatment as other herbaceous plants.

(*See also* the Alphabetical List of Plants, p. 207, for the culture of individual aquatics.)

THE BOG OR MARSH GARDEN

The site of the bog garden must be low-lying and where the surface drainage will naturally collect. If the subsoil is of sticky clay, a mere trickle of water will keep the soil in a swampy condition. Should the subsoil be light and well-drained, a certain amount of excavation will be necessary.

Dig out about 2 feet of the top soil and introduce a little clay to form a basis ; over this stretch a 5-inch bed of rubble or large stones and then a layer of coarse soil. Now fill the hollow, almost to the level of the surrounding land, with a compost of half loam and half leaf-mould or peat. Unless a natural flow of water is available,

an artificial trickle, just sufficient to keep the bog swampy, must
be introduced. As bog plants should never suffer from drought,
the marsh garden should be kept quite moist but must not become
stagnant, and for this reason slight bottom drainage is introduced.
The bog should never be more than 2 feet in depth; its extent, of
course, will depend on space available and taste. Make paths of
rough stones or bricks through the bog, and over these place flat
stepping-stones so as to make every part of the bog accessible.

Selecting the Plants

Almost any moisture-loving plant may be used, so may all the
plants loving the margins of streams and ponds. Do not overcrowd the plants, rather group together three to five plants of the
same kind, leave a space, and again plant a group of some different
colour, type, and height. If the area is small, greater variety and
beauty can be obtained by the use of small-growing species; while
among extensive surroundings full rein may be given to the freer-
growing varieties, many of which are invaluable as a background
where space permits. It is always necessary, however, to bear in
mind the size to which the plants will grow in two to three years'
time, and to arrange them accordingly.

PLANTS FOR THE WATER AND BOG GARDENS

NOTE.—For Cultural Details, and notes as to Colour, Height and Time of Flowering,
see the Alphabetical List of Flowering Plants, p. 207.

Water Garden.

Alisma Plantago
*Aponogeton distachyum
Butomus umbellatus
Calla palustris
Cyperus longus
Hottonia palustris
Limnanthemum nym-
    phæoides
Menyanthes trifoliata
Nuphar advena

Nymphæa alba plenis-
    sima
N. Attraction
N. Ellisiana
N. Gladstoniana
N. James Falconer
N. Laydekeri fulgens
N. Marliacea ignea, etc.
N. odorata maxima
N. odorata minor

N. odorata sulphurea
    grandiflora
N. pygmæa helvola
N. Robinsonii
N. tuberosa Richardsoni
Pontederia cordata
Ranunculus Lingua
Sagittaria latifolia and
    S. sagittifolia fl. pl.
Stratiotes aloides

Bog or Marsh Garden

Acorus Calamus and A.
    C. var. variegatus
Anagallis tenella
Arundinaria (Bamboo)
Arundo Donax
Astilbe (various)
Caltha palustris fl. pl.
Cortaderia (Pampas
    Grass)
Cypripedium spectabile
Fritillaria Meleagris
*Funkia (various)
Gentiana Pneumonanthe
Geum rivale

Gunnera scabra
Hemerocallis (various)
Iris aurea, I. cuprea,
    I. Kæmpferi, I. Monnieri
*Leucojum æstivum
*Linnæa borealis
Lysimachia clethroides,
    L. nummularia aurea
Lythrum Salicaria roseum
*Mimulus cardinalis, etc.
Osmunda regalis
Parnassia palustris
Phormium tenax
*Pinguicula vulgaris

Polygonatum multi-
    florum
*Primula Beesiana, P. Bul-
    leyana, P. Juliæ, P.
    rosea grandiflora, etc.
Ranunculus aconitifolius
Scirpus lacustris
*Spiræa Aruncus, S. palm-
    ata
Thalictrum (various)
Trollius (various)
Typha latifolia and T.
    stenophylla

NOTE.—Those plants marked * will grow in the shade.

CHAPTER XVII

WILD AND WOODLAND GARDENS

THE wild and woodland gardens may be considered in one chapter as, in many ways—mainly because they are both essentially wild gardens—their construction and upkeep are so similar. The wild garden must be free and natural in its character, it must have none of the formality and neatness so essential to some other parts of the garden. The flowers of the wild garden must not be those that have been increased in size and varied in colour by the horticulturist, rather must they resemble their relations of the hedgerows, and the manner of their planting and grouping must be as if executed by nature herself.

Plants chosen for the woodland garden must be those that will thrive in the shade or partial shade and under the drip of trees. They must also be able to withstand a certain amount of drought during the summer, as the trees themselves consume much moisture from the soil and, when in leaf, prevent much rain from reaching the soil. Woodland plants, therefore, usually have bulbs or thick tuberous roots, by means of which they are able to store up moisture and nutrition. The blue-bell is a good example of a woodland plant.

The plants selected for either wild or woodland gardens must be those that require little attention, no tying or staking, they must be those that will flourish in the soil the garden provides, and must be thoroughly hardy and suitable to the climate in which they must grow, year in year out. It is chiefly to the bulbous and perennial plants and hardy shrubs that we look for subjects for the wild garden, for there should be no annual replanting, no trenching and digging of the soil once the plants have been inserted, and there should be no need for protection during the winter. It may, of course, become necessary from time to time to divide some of the crowns of the more vigorous growing species. A point too often overlooked in choosing plants for the wild garden, is that they shall not be subject to such pests as slugs, caterpillars, and the various harmful flies. Some plants are exceptionally free from pests, and these should be selected.

The most usual mistake made in planting is to include too many specimens; only a few should be scattered about naturally, and these, if suitable to their surroundings, will rapidly spread and gorgeous masses of colour and foliage will result. Study the individuals and plant those loving partial shade round the edges of copses or in open glades. Shade lovers may be set further in the woods, while those thriving in full sun should be kept well in the open. It must be remembered that even the shade lovers also require plenty of air and light.

With regard to naturalizing bulbs in grass we would refer the reader to page 118 in our chapter on bulbs, where this fascinating subject is fully treated.

The following list, although by no means complete, as suitable subjects are almost innumerable, will give a very fair idea of plants that will look at home and which will thrive in the wild garden.

PLANTS SUITABLE FOR THE WILD AND WOODLAND GARDENS

NOTE.—For Cultural Details and notes on Colour, Height, and Time of Flowering, also the best Species and Varieties, *see* the Alphabetical List of Flowering Plants and Shrubs, p. 207.

Achillea (various)
*Anemone apennina
*Aquilegia (Columbine)
*Artemisia lactiflora
Arundinaria (Bamboo)
Asperula odorata
*Astilbe Davidii (Spiræa)
Azara microphylla
Buphthalmum speciosum
Camellia japonica (vars.)
Centaurea babylonica
Clematis (various)
Convallaria majalis
*Crocus (various)
*Cyclamen (various)
*Digitalis purpurea (Foxglove)
Doronicum plantagineum and var. excelsum
*Epilobium angustifolium
*Eranthis hyemalis
Eryngium bromeliæfolium and E. pandanifolium
*Fritillarias imperialis (Crown Imperials) and F. Meleagris
*Galanthus (Snowdrops)
Galega officinalis and G. patula

Galtonia candicans
Gentiana asclepiadea
*Gunnera manicata
*Hedera Helix (Ivy)
Helianthus (Sunflower)
Hydrangea paniculata and var. grandiflora
Impatiens Roylei
Iris fœtidissima and I. germanica
Kalmia latifolia
Kniphofia (various)
*Leucojum æstivum and L. vernum
Lilium croceum, L. giganteum, L. Martagon, L. pardalinum, L. pyrenaicum and L. regale
Lunaria annua (Honesty)
Lupinus polyphyllus
*Meconopsis cambrica
Monarda didyma
Montbretia (various)
Myosotis dissitiflora and M. pyrenaica
Narcissus (various)
Œnothera biennis var. grandiflora
Pæonia officinalis, P. albiflora, P. suffruticosa

Phormium tenax
Polygonatum multiflorum (Solomon's Seal)
Polygonum cuspidatum
*Primula acaulis (Primrose), P. Beesiana, P. officinalis (Cowslip), P. Bulleyana, P. japonica, P. sikkimensis, etc.
Rheum Emodii and R. officinale
Rhododendron
Rosa Moyesii, R. rugosa
Saxifraga peltata
*Scilla nutans (Bluebell)
Senecio clivorum
*Sibthorpia europæa
*Solidago (Golden Rod)
Thalictrum aquilegifolium, T. Delavayi
Tulips (various)
Valeriana officinalis
Verbascum phlomoides and V. pulverulentum
Viburnum Opulus
*Vinca major and minor
Viola odorata (Violet)
*Woodwardia radicans

NOTE.—The plants marked * will grow in the shade.

CHAPTER XVIII

FLOWERING AND ORNAMENTAL SHRUBS AND TREES

IN almost every garden shrubs have a very important part to play. As individual plants, often of considerable beauty, as providers of shade, as interesting backgrounds for smaller plants, as instruments for the division of the garden into its several parts, shrubs serve purposes the importance of which it is difficult to overrate. The variety which is now available of flowering and of evergreen shrubs is enormous. Yet to look at many gardens, one would think that the privet, the laurel, the elder, the euonymus and the rhododendron constituted the whole race.

Before planting, the ground should be deeply dug or trenched to a depth of 2 feet, enriched with well-rotted old manure and leaf-mould, and sufficient space should be allowed to each individual plant for the free and full development of its own peculiar habit of growth. The turf within a radius of 3 to 4 feet round bushes planted on lawns should be permanently removed so that the earth may be thoroughly broken up and exposed to the air.

Planting

As a general rule, plants of medium size for their kind should be planted rather than fully-grown specimens. They more readily take root and the proportion of losses is much smaller. While there is no hurry and planting is done with an eye to an effect which is to be produced several years later, it is often wise to plant even younger bushes. In this case it is possible either to fill the space with small bushes and to remove a proportion when they become over-crowded or each shrub may be allotted the full space it will require in later years, the bare soil in between being temporarily decorated by herbaceous plants. Usually the best time to plant deciduous shrubs is from the middle of October, when the leaves begin to fall, to the middle of November, or in February and March. Evergreens are best planted in September and early October, or better still, perhaps, in April and the beginning of May. Never plant evergreens in the depth of winter when their vitality is at the lowest, nor when cold drying winds are prevalent. Plants that have been grown in pots

149

may, of course, be planted out at almost any time during the year. In the case of both deciduous and evergreen shrubs it is usually wise, at the time of planting, to thin out and reduce the length of the branches by about one-third ; this will somewhat relieve the strain put upon the roots, at this time themselves considerably reduced.

For details as to how to plant, *see* Planting Fruit Trees, p. 323.

Grouping and Arrangement

The arrangement of shrubs naturally varies according to the purpose which they are to fulfil. If they are to serve as individual specimens on a lawn or similar situation, clearly no " arrangement " is required. If planted in groups it is usually desirable that several plants of a kind should be placed together, though even here full space should be allowed for each individual to develop. This grouping together of say, three to half a dozen specimens is not only more effective than scattering single plants about indiscriminately, but it makes it easier to give each group of shrubs the special soil in which they thrive best. (For soils suitable to each species *see* the Alphabetical List of Flowering Plants and Shrubs, p. 207.) The fact that we can have a continued sequence of bloom from flowering shrubs almost all through the year, provided they are carefully selected, is often overlooked. It is necessary, therefore, to select shrubs not only for the colour of their flowers, their suitability for their situation, but also for the time of year at which they flower. Care must be taken that specimens whose colours clash and which bloom simultaneously are not placed together. Associate shrubs whose blooms harmonize in colour and time of flowering, and allow the blooms of the specimens in flower to be set off and enhanced by the foliage of shrubs whose flowers are over or still to come. The stronger growers must be kept in check by periodical pruning or they may overpower the more beautiful, but perhaps less vigorous plants. As backgrounds to borders too great a regularity is usually to be avoided, and their fronts should not present a straight forbidding line. Rather should they afford projections and bays, now pressing out into the border, now forming recesses into which vigorous plants from the border may find welcome shade and shelter. During the summer the soil round the shrubs should be kept well hoed and should be forked over each winter, and where a shrub is seen to be doing badly or to be exhausted, well-decayed manure should be thoroughly worked into the soil round the roots.

Conifers

These are all handsome and graceful trees and among them will be found many species that may well be planted singly as specimen trees on the lawn. Among the best for this purpose are :—*Abies brachyphylla, A. nobilis,* or *A. pectinata* ; *Cedrus Deodara* ; *Cryptomeria japonica* ; *Cupressus Lawsoniana* ; *C. macrocarpa* and *C. obtusa* ; *Juniperus communis hibernica* ; *Picea excelsa, P. Morinda,* or *P. pungens glauca* ; *Pinus excelsa, P Laricio,* or *P. sylvestris* ; *Pseudolarix Kœmferi* ; *Pseudotsuga Douglasii* ; *Taxodium distichum* ; *Thuya japonica* or *T. orientalis* ; and *Tsuga Albertiana.*

Shrubs with Coloured Foliage in Autumn

In planting trees and shrubs it is well worth while to consider their appearance not only in the spring and summer, but in the late and early autumn also, for when the garden is at its most sombre, trees and shrubs may be made to give notes of cheerful and striking colour. A useful selection of these trees and shrubs will be found noted on the list, p. 154.

Pruning Shrubs and Climbers

The time for pruning depends on the season of flowering, and the method is dependent upon whether the bloom is borne on the new or the old wood. Where the new shoots, that is to say those of the current year, bear the flowers, some of the old and weak growth has to be cut in order that the new shoots may be encouraged. This may be done any time from October to November as the flowers are usually borne in late spring or early summer. Where, however, the plants flower on the old wood, generally in late winter or early spring, only the decayed and useless old wood must be cut away, which is usually done in late spring or early summer directly after flowering, as it is of vital importance to give the plants as much time as possible to form and ripen new wood before the winter sets in, as on this wood the flowers will be borne the next spring. Many such plants are only pruned sufficiently to keep them tidy and trim.

April is the best time to trim evergreens, except conifers, which are best trimmed in September or October. Conifers, however, except when grown as hedge-plants, are not usually pruned. When such conifers as the cupressus or yew are used as hedges, they can be pruned back to any height desired , the lateral branches also being trimmed in.

The aim of pruning is, firstly to let air and light to the wood so as to ripen it and thus encourage bloom on flowering shrubs ; secondly to train the plant into the shape and size required ; and thirdly to keep it tidy. There are also several ways of pruning, the most usual being the cutting back of the shoots. Side shoots are often " spurred " or cut right back leaving only three or four buds; plants requiring this treatment are usually late flowerers, such as the *Buddleia*. Again, the strong main shoots may be "topped" or cut back by about one-third to encourage sturdy growth, or may be only just "tipped" to keep the plant tidy and the growth within bounds; at the same time all old and weak wood is cut out. Another method of pruning, often required, is the removal of the seed-heads from such plants as the rhododendron. If these seed-heads are allowed to remain in position, a poor crop of bloom will result in the following year. Disbudding, the removal of superfluous buds, is also looked upon as pruning, for it increases the size of the flowers left on the plant.

More or less tender shrubs grown in the open in sheltered positions should never be pruned in autumn. This would lay them open to attacks by frost; they should be pruned in April, or even later when danger of severe frosts is past. The reader is referred to the *Alphabetical List of Flowering Plants and Shrubs*, p. 207, where full instructions for the pruning of each kind of shrub will be found. *See also* Pruning Fruit Trees, p. 328, and Clipping Hedges, p. 159.

PROPAGATION OF SHRUBS AND CLIMBERS
Seeds

When sowing seeds saved from the garden, they should not be gathered too early, but must be allowed ample time to ripen, and must be cleaned before being sown. The seeds of such trees as the chestnut, oak or holly are oily in nature and unless carefully stored in slightly moist sand or fibre are apt to shrivel. They are, therefore, best sown in the open, in the shelter of a wall or hedge, as soon as they are ripe, but the seeds of most other shrubs are better sown under glass, in well-drained boxes of sandy soil, in February or March, and when germinated and sufficiently high, should be thinned-out to $1\frac{1}{2}$ to 2 inches apart, the less hardy kinds being hardened-off in a cold frame and the hardy kinds planted out in nursery beds in the open. The seeds of most shrubs and trees germinate in a month or two; some, however, like the rose and thorn, take a year and even more. The seeds of most conifers must ripen in their cones on the trees for about a year, some require to hang for quite two years. When the cones have been gathered they are stored in a warm and dry place; the dryness opens the cones and the seeds are liberated and should be sown thinly in the open in March or April, and be only just covered with fine sandy soil, seeds from healthy trees only being used. Transplant from the seed-beds to rows in the nursery garden as soon as the seedlings are large enough to handle. It is wise to shelter the young seedlings from the sun.

Cuttings

This is undoubtedly the most popular method of propagating shrubs. It provides larger plants in a much shorter time, and ensures that the new plants shall be true to type, which cannot always be relied upon when raising from seed. This method is resorted to especially when propagating dwarf, variegated or rare shrubs. Strong sturdy shoots varying from 3 to 12 inches in length should be taken. During the spring, summer and autumn most shrub cuttings may be struck in the open, except the cuttings of most conifers, golden privet, and many evergreens which always require the protection and moist atmosphere that glass provides. (See also p. 189.)

Cuttings inserted in the autumn remain inactive through the winter and do not usually form roots until the following spring. They must, therefore, not be disturbed until the next autumn, when they may be planted-out 12 to 18 inches apart in a nursery bed.

Division of Roots

All the so-called " tufted " shrubs, or those that throw out suckers from their crowns or base may be propagated by division at the time of year when they are best transplanted.

Grafting or Budding

If the shrubs are grafted, it is usually effected by grafting under glass between January and early June, but many of them may be grafted in the open in April and May. Budding is usually effected in the open in July and August.

Layering

This method is usually employed in the spring or early summer.

The reader is advised to consult the *Alphabetical List of Flowering Plants and Shrubs*, p. 207, where he will find the best methods of propagating each individual shrub, the most suitable time, whether it is effected in the open or under glass, or whether artificial or bottom heat is necessary. Here also will be found full cultural details.

See also Propagation of Plants, p. 183.

SOME USEFUL TREES AND SHRUBS

Hardy Flowering Trees and Shrubs

NOTE.—For Colour of Flowers, Time of Blooming, Heights, Cultural Details, and the best Species and Varieties, *see* the Alphabetical List of Flowering Plants and Shrubs, p. 207.

Abelia triflora (D) and A. grandiflora (E)
Æsculus (D)

*Ailanthus glandulosa (D)
†*Amelanchier canadensis
Andromeda polifolia (E)

*Arbutus (various) (E)
*Aucuba japonica (E) *s*
Azalea (various) (E or D)

*Azara dentata, etc. (E)
*Berberis (Barberry)
Buddleia (various) (D)
Buxus sempervirens (E) s
Calluna vulgaris (E) r
Calycanthus floridus (D) s
Cassinia fulvida (E) r
Castanea sativa (D)
Catalpa bignonioides (D)
Ceanothus (various) (E)
Chimonanthus fragrans grandiflora (D) w
Chionanthus retusus (D) s
Choisya ternata (E) s
Cistus (Rock Rose) (E) r
†*Clerodendron trichotomum (D)
*Colutea arborescens (D)
*Cornus (D) w, r, s
*†Cotoneaster (E or D) r, s
†*Cratægus (Thorn) (D)
Cydonia japonica (D) w
Cytisus (D or E) r
Dabœcia polifolia (E) r
*Daphne (E or D) r
Deutzia (various) (D)
Diervilla (Weigela) (D) s
†Enkianthus (various) (D)
Erica (Heath) (E) r
Escallonia (E or D) s
Euonymus japonicus (E)
Exochorda grandiflora (D)
Forsythia (various) (D) s
Fraxinus Ornus (D)
Fuchsia (various) (D)
Garrya elliptica (E) w
*†Gaultheria procumbens and G. Shallon (E) r, s
Genista (various) (D) r
Grevillea rosmarinifolia r

Halesia carolina (D)
†Hamamelis (D) w
Hedera Helix (Ivy) (E) s
Helianthemum formosum
Hibiscus syriacus (D) s
Hydrangea (D) s
Hypericum (E or D) s
Itea virginica (D) s
Jamesia americana (D) s
Jasminum (various)
Juglans regia (D)
Kalmia (various) (E) s
Kerria japonica fl. pl. (D)
Laburnum (various) (D)
Laurus nobilis (E)
Lavendula Spica (E)
Ledum latifolium (E) r
Leiophyllum buxifolium
*Leycesteria formosa (D) s
*†Ligustrum (Privet) (E) s
†Liriodendron tulipifera
Lonicera (Honeysuckle)
Lupinus arboreus (D)
Magnolia (E or D)
Morus nigra (D)
Myrtus communis (E)
Olearia Haastii (E) r, s
Osmanthus aquifolium
†Parrotia persica (D)
*Pernettya mucronata (E)
Philadelphus (Mock Orange) (D) s
*Phillyræa media (E) s
Pieris floribunda and P. japonica (E)
Prunus Amygdalus (D)
Prunus Avium fl. pl. (D)
P. cerasifera (Cherry Plum (D)

Prunus Persica (Peach) (D)
P. serrulata (Japanese Cherry)
*Pyracantha Lalandei (E)
†*Pyrus (various) (D)
Rhododendron (E)
†Rhus (Smoke Bush) (D)
†Ribes aureum, R. sanguineum (D) s
Robinia hispida (D)
Romneya Coulteri (D)
*Rosa Hugonis (D)
*†R. rugosa (D)
Rosmarinus officinalis (E)
Rubus ulmifolius (D) s
Salix babylonica (D)
*Sambucus canadensis maxima (E) r
Santolina Chamæcyparissus (D) s
*Skimmia japonica (E) s
Spartium junceum (E)
Spiræa (various) (D) s, r
Staphylea colchica (D) s
*Symphoricarpus racemosus lævigatus (D) s
Syringa (Lilac) (D) s
Tamarix pentandra (syn. hispida æstivalis) (D)
Tilia dasystyla (D)
Ulex europæus fl. pl. (E)
Veronica (Speedwell) (E) r
†*Viburnum, (D or E)
†*V. Tinus (D) w, s
Vinca major elegantissima (Periwinkle) (E) s. r
Weigela (see Diervilla)
Yucca gloriosa (E)
Y. recurvifolia (E)

Hardy Ornamental Trees and Shrubs
Evergreen

Abies (Fir)
Artemisia Abrotanum r
Arundinaria metake s
Arundo Donax
Bambusa aurea, B. fortunei, etc. (Bamboo)
Cedrus (Cedar)
Cupressus (Cypress)

Elæagnus microphylla, s.
*Ilex aquifolium and vars. s.
†Juniperus (Juniper)
Ligustrum (Privet) s
Picea excelsa, etc.
Pinus (Pine)

Pseudotsuga Douglasii
Quercus Ilex
Sequoia gigantea
Taxus baccata and vars. s
Thuya (various) s
Tsuga Albertiana

Deciduous

†Acer (Maple)
Alnus glutinosa, etc.
Betula verrucosa, etc.
Elæagnus angustifolia, syn. hortensis (Oleaster)
*Euonymus latifolius
†Fagus (Beech)

Fraxinus excelsior pendula (Weeping Ash)
†Ginkgo biloba (E)
*Hippophæ rhamnoides
Larix europæa (Larch)
†Nyssa sylvatica (Tupelo)
Platanus acerifolia

P. orientalis
Populus alba Bolleana
†Pseudolarix Kæmpferi
Quercus Cerris
†Q. coccinea splendens
†Taxodium distichum
Ulmus Louis Van Houtte
U. montana pendula

NOTE.—* Denotes best Berry-bearing shrubs ; † Coloured Foliage in Autumn ; w, Winter-flowering Shrubs ; r, Shrubs for the Rock garden ; and s, Shrubs that will grow in the shade ; E = Evergreen ; D = Deciduous.

CHAPTER XIX

CLIMBING PLANTS

CLIMBING plants are often given but crude treatment, yet if they are to thrive it is scarcely possible to spend too much attention in the preparing and enriching of the soil in which their roots are to grow.

Choosing the Site

First as to site ; nearly all creepers do better if the air can circulate freely round their stems and shoots, but this does not mean that they enjoy cold draughts from the north or east. Most climbers will thrive better on a wooden trellis, provided it is sheltered from these cold blasts, than they will against a brick wall which throws back the sun's rays and is apt to scorch them. Many of less hardy nature, of course, demand the shelter of a wall and several require that this wall shall also face south to catch all available sunlight and warmth. In Chapter XXIV we have pointed out the preference as to aspect shown by each plant.

Planting

A creeper must not be planted with its roots right up against a wall, the roots should be placed some 18 inches from the wall, so that they may receive adequate air and moisture. In dry weather a good watering should occasionally be given to all wall plants, even though correctly planted with their roots some way from the wall. The creosote or paint used on the wooden supports of a pergola may be very harmful if it comes into contact with the roots, and this is another reason why the climber should not be planted too close to its support. *See also* the instructions for planting deciduous and evergreen shrubs in the chapter on Shrubs, *also* Planting Fruit Trees, p. 323.

The most valuable of our garden climbing plants are perennials, but annuals also furnish us with a number of beautiful climbers which, by their quick growth and easy culture, are often of the greatest value.

Full cultural details of the climbers mentioned in this chapter are given in the *Alphabetical List of Flowering Plants and Shrubs*, p. 207 ; for Pruning and Propagating *see chapter on* Ornamental and Flowering Trees and Shrubs, p. 149; and for Training *see* Garden Operations, p. 74.

SOME GOOD CLIMBING PLANTS

For Cultural Details, and for Colour of Flowers, Time of Flowering, Height, and the best Species and Varieties, *see* the Alphabetical List of Flowering Plants and Shrubs, p. 207.

Perennial and Shrubby

Ampelopsis. *See* Vitis
Aristolochia Sipho, S.W.
Azara microphylla (Warm sheltered), S.
*Berberidopsis corallina (Southern Counties only), S.W.
*Buddleia variabilis magnifica, S.W.
Calycanthus occidentalis, S.W.
*Carpentaria californica Southern Counties, S.
Ceanothus dentatus, S.
C. Gloire de Versailles, S.
C. rigidus, S.
*C. Veitchianus, S.
Celastrus scandens, N.E.
Chimonanthus fragrans (Winter Sweet), S.W.
*Choisya ternata, S.
Clematis flammula, E.W.
C. florida vars., E.W.
C. Jackmanni vars., E.W.
C. lanuginosa vars., E.W.
C. montana vars., N.E.W.
C. patens vars., E.W.
C. vitalba (Traveller's Joy), N.E.W.
C. viticella vars., E.W.
Cotoneaster horizontalis, N.E.
C. Henryana, N.E.W.
Cratægus pyracantha. *See* Pyracantha coccinea, N.E.   [E.W.
Cydonia japonica vars.,
*Eccremocarpus scaber, S. Treat as an annual
Escallonia exoniensis, S.
E. langleyensis, S.
E. macrantha, S.

E. montevidensis, S.
Forsythia suspensa (Sieboldii), S.W.
Garrya elliptica, N.E.W.
Hedera dentata, N.
H. Helix (Common Ivy)
Humulus Lupulus aureus (Golden Hop)
*Hydrangea petiolaris scandens, N.W.
Jasminum nudiflorum, N.E.W.
J. officinale, W.E.
J. primulinum, S.W.
J. revolutum, S.W.E.
Kerria japonica, S.W.
Lathyrus grandiflorus, S.W.
L. latifolius (Everlasting Pea), S.W.
Lonicera Caprifolium, E.
L. japonica flexuosa, N.E.
L. japonica aureo reticulata, N.E.
L. Periclymenum, N.E.
L. P. belgica (Early Dutch), N.E.
L. P. serotina (Late Dutch), N.E.
L. sempervirens, N.E.
Lycium chinense
Magnolia conspicua, W.
M. grandiflora, S.W.
Mutisia decurrens (Sheltered), S.W.
Myrtus communis, S.
M. lusitanica tarentina, S.
Passiflora cærulea and P. c. Constance Elliott (Passion Flower), S.W.
Polygonum baldschuanicum

Pyracantha angustifolia, N.S.E.W.
P. coccinea (Fire Thorn), N.S.E.W.
Rosa. *See* Rose, p. 296
Rubus laciniatus (Parsley-leaved Blackberry)
R. thyrsoideus fl. pl. (Double - flowered Blackberry)
R. ulmifolius, var. bellidiflorus
*Solanum crispum, S.W.
*S. jasminoides(Sheltered), S.W.
*Tecoma grandiflora (Trumpet Flower), S.
*T. radicans, S.
Trachelospermum jasminoides
Tropæolum speciosum (Flame Nasturtium), N.
Vitis Coignetiæ (Crimson Glory Vine), S.
V. Henryana (Sheltered), S.
V. inconstans (syn. ampelopsis Veitchii), N.S.E.W.
V. quinquefolia (syn. ampelopsis hederacea) [Virginia Creeper], N.S.E.W.
V. vinifera purpurea (Claret-leaved Vine) (Sheltered), S.W.
Wistaria multijuga, S. or S.W.
W. m. alba, S. or S.W.
W. sinensis, S. or S.W.
W. s. alba, S. or S.W.

Annual

*Cobæa scandens
Convolvulus major
*Cucurbita (Gourd)
Humulus japonicus
*Ipomœa coccinea

*I. grandiflora (Moon Flower)
*I. purpurea (Morning Glory)
Lathyrus odoratus (Sweet Pea)

*Mina lobata
*Tropæolum aduncum (Canary Creeper)
T. majus (Climbing Nasturtium)

NOTE.—N.S.E. or W. indicates the most suitable position, e.g. Wall facing North, South, East or West. E = Evergreen ; D = Deciduous ; *denotes Half-hardy.

CHAPTER XX

HEDGES, FENCES AND WALLS

HEDGES

CONSIDERING its importance, very little forethought is given, as a general rule, to the choosing and planting of a hedge, which can do much to make or mar the garden. Until quite recently it was the custom to plant the inevitable and monotonous privet or laurel, but of late years it has been realized that there are better subjects for the hedge. Of deciduous hedges, the beech, hornbeam, cherry plum, briar, and thorn are the most general, while the box, cypress (*Cupressus macrocarpa* and *Lawsoniana*), *Lonicera nitida*, evergreen oak, holly, thuya and yew are all evergreen.

Purposes of the Hedge

Whether the hedge is required as a shelter from the wind, as a screen, as a barrier, or purely as an ornament, are points which must be taken into consideration, and shrubs suited to the soil and aspect should also be chosen. Evergreens like holly, laurel, or yew, and leafy, quick-growing deciduous shrubs like the elder or privet, are excellent for shelter from cold winds. As a screen, cypress, escallonia, holly, laurel, Lonicera nitida, or yew are undoubtedly the best ; while flowering shrubs such as Berberis stenophylla and B. Darwinii, guelder rose, gorse, lilac, shrubby honeysuckle, or Viburnum Tinus, make an excellent ornamental hedge. Nothing is so suitable as a barrier as beech, hornbeam, myrobella plum, or thorn.

Forming the Hedge

In forming any hedge, it is, of course, necessary to take into consideration the aspect, the quality of the soil, and many other particulars. All plants will not suit all climates, all situations, and all soils. It is wise, therefore, to consider that though there are many ornamental plants and shrubs that will make good hedges, it is not all of these that may choose to flourish where we wish our hedge to grow. As a general rule, the knife may be used unsparingly on all things suitable for hedges, and the hedge itself will be greatly improved by its use. All hedges, but especially those that bear the shears or clippers, should be cut upwards to a narrow ridge, for by this means the lower part, not being overshadowed by the upper, will be kept thick, and the hedge will last sound much longer. After

157

they have been planted several years, hedges of most materials will require to be cut down, the soil renovated, and, perhaps, new plants introduced. This necessity, however, is very generally the result of neglect in early years, for where proper care has been bestowed and annual pruning given, hedges will last as long as brick walls.

Flowering Shrubs for Hedges

Many flowering shrubs make excellent hedges. The best of these are Berberis Darwinii, B. stenophylla, flowering currant, Cydonia japonica, gorse, guelder rose, lilac, and the shrubby honeysuckle. The hedge need not necessarily be composed entirely of one species ; a very ornamental hedge, sections of which will be in blossom almost the entire year through if the plants are carefully selected, can be made up of various species of flowering shrubs. Evergreens may be interspersed among the flowering shrubs, and the hedge will be all the firmer if a thorn or a cherry plum is inserted fairly frequently as a stiffener. The Sweet Briar and the Penzance Briars make a splendid hedge.

Planting

Many seem to think that a hedge will grow anywhere and however it is planted ; but it must be borne in mind that a hedge, once planted, is usually in position for many years, and that if it is to do well every care should be taken in its planting. A strip of ground 3 feet wide, in which the hedge is to be planted, should be trenched to a depth of at least 2 feet, and vegetable refuse, leaf-mould, and well-decayed manure should be forked in. Most hedge shrubs are best planted when from 2 to 3 feet in height, they then more easily establish themselves, are easier to train, and are also cheaper. The larger the shrub the more care necessary in planting. With the exception of the quicker or larger-growing shrubs, such as the evergreen oak or cupressus, most hedge shrubs are best planted out 10 to 15 inches apart ; if a very thick hedge is required two rows may be planted some 10 inches apart, the plants, as before, being 10 to 15 inches apart in the rows, but planted so that those of one row come opposite the middle of the gaps between those in the other row thus: · . · . ·

Long tap roots should always be shortened back before planting, and to ensure bushy plants, in the case of deciduous shrubs, 6 to 10 inches must be trimmed from the top of the newly-planted hedge when the buds begin to swell in spring. Evergreens are best cut back at planting time. Water well after putting the shrubs in, and once a week in dry weather until the roots are established. Should a very dry season follow, syringe the foliage of evergreens every evening if the plants do not appear to be thriving.   In late April or early May, during its first year, the hedge should be well watered and then mulched with a 2- to 3-inch layer of well-decayed manure and well-rotted leaf-mould.   Severe frosts during the first winter after planting will probably raise the bushes somewhat from the soil.   After frosts, therefore, newly-planted shrubs should be firmed back with the foot.   We refer the reader to the chapter on *Shrubs*, page 149, and to the table of *Shrubs for Hedges*, page 163, where will be found a wide choice of hedge shrubs, together with details as to the method and time of planting, and the manner of trimming.

For individual cultural details and particulars as to species and varieties, see Chapter XXIV.

Clipping Hedges

Most hedges are best trimmed twice a year, in May and again in August or September; few shrubs will make much growth after the autumn trimming and will remain tidy all the winter.   Hedge-clipping is not an easy matter for the amateur, and only the man with a very "straight eye" can trim successfully without some guidance in the form of a string stretched taut horizontally and at the required height.

All hedges, especially evergreen hedges, are best cut to a point pyramidically; for if the top is allowed to overhang the bottom, the lower shoots will invariably die off.   If carefully trimmed they may also be cut square at the top, as is necessary in the rose garden and some of the more formal parts of the garden, but the top must not overhang the bottom.   With hollies and laurels use the knife in pruning, to avoid the rusty appearance of the withering of half-cut leaves.   Privet, box, thorn, and all small-leaved shrubs may be clipped with the garden shears.

In winter the hedge and the soil round it should be thoroughly cleaned ; all dead wood should be cut out and any brambles and climbers should be removed.   The weeds must be taken out from the hedge bottom and the soil should be turned up.   Where insect pests and disease have been prevalent, the hedge should be sprayed with a caustic soda solution, which must not be too strong in the case of shrubs flowering in the early spring, or the blossom may be damaged.

Renovating Neglected Hedges

Few things afford stronger indications of the necessity of renovation in a garden than the state of the evergreens and hedges.   These are so easily and so insensibly allowed to grow wild, and are so seriously injured by want of care and the proper use of the knife, that neglect cannot go on very long without its ill consequences becoming manifest.   Portugal laurels and many other evergreens may be cut in ; but with the common laurel it is a saving of time to cut it down at once ; so also with the arbutus and sweet bay. Privet and holly hedges, which from years of neglect are found to be occupying too much space, must be cut in.   The former may often be cut down with advantage to within a few inches of the ground, and the latter cut close on all sides to the single stems.   In a few years new and fresh wood will fill up all vacant spaces, provided the soil is enriched and kept free from weeds.   This drastic cutting back is best done in April.

A Warning

Although hedges are delightful and useful features in a garden, since they help to produce the much desired "element of surprise," and are useful as screens, shelters or barriers, too many should not be planted in a small garden, as they take up a deal of room, keep sun and air from other plants and, worst of all, make a great demand upon the soil.   It is, therefore, useless to expect plants to thrive in close proximity to any hedge.

FENCES
Forms of Fences

Fences may be constructed of various materials and of many different patterns.

Close Wooden Fencing.—If privacy is desired, close-boarded oak fencing should be used.   This type of fencing is strong and will last a considerable time.   Split oak makes a more durable fence than sawn oak.   The usual heights are from $3\frac{1}{2}$ to 7 feet.   Fir, larch, pine, or deal are sometimes used in lieu of oak.   They are, of course, by no means so durable and should be creosoted to preserve them from the weather.

Wattle Hurdles make effective and quite artistic fences ; they are easy to set up and are comparatively cheap.   As a shelter from the wind they are hard to beat, and have the great advantage of being easily moved if required in another position.

Split Chestnut Fencing, in which the palings are wired together with strong strands of wire so that there is an interval of about 3 inches between each, makes an efficient and economical fencing, although it affords no shelter from the weather and no privacy. It forms a useful boundary fence of a temporary nature ; and is itself quite durable as a protection to a newly-planted hedge.   The fencing is stretched to posts some 10 feet apart.   The footings of these posts should be charred and tarred.

Rustic Fences are much used to separate one part of the garden from another.   They can be made of hazel, larch, spruce, and indeed

From the Painting by]   *[Ella du Cane*

A CORNER OF THE POOL

of any young trees. The bark should always be left on, and the more numerous and rougher the knots, the more rustic the fence will be. The bars of rustic trellis-work should be slightly notched one into another at the points at which they cross, so that they may have a better bearing one against another and a firmer holding than round sticks could possibly have if nailed together without notching.

Wire Netting.—There are many patterns and sizes of this " rabbit-netting " to choose from, and the size of the mesh and the strength of the wire used should be regulated by the purpose to which the netting is to be put. The closer the mesh of the netting, the higher in proportion will be the cost ; do not, therefore, use netting with an unnecessarily small mesh. Wire netting lasts quite well, but cannot be called very lovely. It is stretched on posts planted on an average 10 feet apart. Straining-posts will be needed every 100 feet and, of course, at each corner.

Iron Palings form a very durable fence. There are two favourite types : the park fencing, usually with three horizontal bars supported by uprights every 3 or 4 feet ; or upright iron spiked palings, 4 inches apart and held in position by two horizontal bars, one at the top, the other at the bottom. The latter type is more useful for keeping off intruders, but is rather more ugly than the park fencing. These palings require painting periodically to keep them in good condition.

WALLS

Kitchen Garden Walls

Garden walls have long been a subject for discussion, and will probably always remain so : like everything else connected with gardening, they depend on local circumstances. The walls which would be suitable for a moderate-sized kitchen garden, in a flat or thickly-wooded country, would be very unsuitable for a loftier site, on the side of a hill, or in an open, undulating country ; while a plot of small extent, enclosed by walls 14 or 16 feet high, would be inadmissible both on artistic and physiological grounds ; on the first, the walls would appear prison-like ; on the second, they would exclude the air, which is essential to the growth of plants.

A walled garden is usually designed as a parallelogram and not as a square. Besides the fact that the former shape is more pleasing, there is also the utilitarian reason that north and south walls are more useful than east and west walls and are, therefore, made longer. In addition, owing to the fact that the power of the sun in these colder latitudes is greatest an hour or so after noon, the south wall of a garden is generally so situated that the sun strikes it fully about 1 p.m. ; that is to say, the wall faces slightly west of south.

Best Heights for Walls

For this reason it is considered that for small gardens 8-feet walls are most suitable, provided the trees on them are planted so far apart as to admit of full horizontal extension. For gardens of larger size, 10-feet walls, and for an extensive garden 12, and even 14 feet, will not be too great. Where an acre of ground, in the form of a parallelogram is enclosed, on a gentle slope, a north wall might well be 14 feet high, and the east, west, and south walls only 10 feet; if the slope of the ground is considerable, the difference may be less. In gardens of greater extent—enclosures of four acres for instance—the walls may be higher, but in no instances more than 18 feet high for a north wall, 15 feet for east and west walls, and 12 feet for a south wall.

(*See also* Training Fruit Trees, p. 321.)

Flower Garden Walls

Walls are occasionally introduced into flower gardens, either for the shelter they afford in bleak localities, their architectural effect near houses, or for the culture of the more tender plants in the open air. They should seldom be more than 10 or less than 6 feet high. It would be worth going a hundred miles to see a wall 6 feet high and 50 yards long, covered with a collection of tea roses in full bloom. If the wall were mounted with a coping projecting 4 inches, so constructed as to prevent the drip of water, and the roses were slightly covered in winter with spruce branches, and sheltered with canvas covering from early spring frosts, such a sight might well be realized.

(*See also* Climbing Plants, p. 155, *and* Wall Gardening, p. 137.)

Preservation and Radiation of Heat

But besides the protection it affords, the properly constructed garden wall has other important duties. The wall and its coping prevent the radiation of heat. During the heat of the day it absorbs the sun's rays, and, in common with all heated bodies, it radiates its heat in a ratio proportionate to the square of its distance; so that if an object placed a foot from the wall receives 1° of heat from it, at 1 inch it will receive heat equal to 144°. The reflection, also, of all unabsorbed rays striking the surface of the wall greatly increases the temperature of the air in immediate contact with it. Besides this power of absorbing heat, moisture is also absorbed, both from rain and from the atmosphere, and, with the heat, is given out by radiation, tempering the atmosphere during the night. A wall is thus, in every sense, a source of protection; and it is of considerable importance that its height and form, as well as its workmanship and materials, should be well considered.

SHRUBS SUITABLE FOR HEDGES.

Note.—For Times of Flowering, Colour of Blooms, and Cultural Details, *see* the Alphabetical List of Flowering Plants and Shrubs, page 207.

Name.	Common Name.	Average Height in Feet or Form of Hedge and Time in Years to Make Good Hedge.	Height in Ins. at which to Plant	Number of Rows.	Distance in Inches between Plants.	Distance in Inches between Rows.	When to Trim.
Berberis (E) Darwinii	Barberry	5 ft. ; 6 yrs.	20	1 or 2	10	12	Shorten long shoots after flowering
B. stenophylla (E) [Simonsii	Barberry	5 ft. ; 5 yrs.	18–24	1 or 2	18–24	18	Shorten long shoots after flowering
Cotoneaster (E)	Rockspray	5 ft. ; 5 yrs.	18–24	1 or 2	18	18	August
Cydonia japonica	Japanese Quince	6 ft. ; 6 yrs.	18–24	1 or 2	18–24	18	Shorten long shoots after flowering
Cratægus (D) oxyacantha	Hawthorn or May	6 ft. ; 8 yrs.	12–20	2	6	15	April and August
Cupressus (E) Lawsoniana	Cypress	7 ft. ; 7 yrs.	12–24	1	24	—	April, trim with knife
Cupressus (E) macrocarpa	Cypress	9 ft. ; fast grower	12–20	1	25	—	May and Aug., twice yearly
Cytisus albus &c. (D)	Broom	6 ft. ; 5 yrs.	12	2	18–24	—	June
Euonymus (E) japonicus	Japanese Spindle Tree	6 ft. ; 6 yrs.	12–18	1	24	—	Trim with knife April and August
Fagus sylvatica (D)	Beech	Tall as Shelter ; 6 yrs.	18–30	2	10	20	August
Forsythia (D) intermedia vars.	Golden Bell	8 ft. ; 6 yrs.	12–18	1	12–18	—	Cut well back in May
Fuchsia (D) Riccartonii	Fuchsia	5 ft. ; 6 yrs.	12–18	1	12	—	Feb. or March
Ilex aquifolium (E)	Holly	Thick Boundary hedge. Slow grower first 3–4 years.	15	1 or 2	12	12	May and August
Lavendula Spica (E)	Lavender	2–3 ft. ; 5 yrs.	12	1	12	—	After flowering
Ligustrum (E) ovalifolium	Privet (Oval-leaved)	Screen. Fast grower	20	2	10	15	Whenever straggly
Ligustrum (E) ovalifolium folius aureus	Privet (Golden)	4 ft. ; fast grower	20	2	10	15	April and August
Lonicera (D) fragrantissima	Honeysuckle, Shrubby	4 ft. ; 5 yrs.	18	1	12	—	April, shorten long growths
Lonicera nitida (E)	Honeysuckle, Shrubby	5 ft. ; 5 yrs.	12–18	1	12–18	—	End June–August
Olearia Haastii (E)	N. Zealand Daisy Bush	4 ft. ; 5 yrs.	12–18	1	12	—	Trim straggly shoots
Osmanthus (E) ilicifolia		8 ft. ; 5 yrs.	9–12	1	18–24	—	August
Prunus (E) Laurocerasus var. pyramidalis	Laurel	6 ft. ; 5 yrs.	20	1	24	—	May and Sept., with knife
Prunus (D) cerasifera	Cherry Plum	Boundary ; 6 yrs.	20–40	2	6	15	June
Ribes sanguinea (D)	Flowering Currant	5 ft. ; 4 yrs.	18–24	1	18	—	Shorten shoots after flowering
Rosa rubiginosa (D) & Penzance Briars	Sweet Briar	6 ft. ; 4 yrs.	30	1	24	—	March and August
Tamarix gallica (D)	Tamarisk	6 ft. ; 5 yrs.	24	2	12–15	18	February, heavily
Taxus baccata (E)	Yew	5–10 ft. ; slow growing	30–60	1	24	—	May and August
Thuya plicata (E) (syn. gigantea)	Thuya	As background ; fast growing	30	1	18–20	—	April to Sept.
Thuya orientalis (E)	Thuya	do. ; 5 yrs.	24	1	24	—	April to Sept.
Thuya (E) occidentalis	Thuya	do. ; 5 yrs.	24	1	18–20	—	April to Sept.
Ulex europæus (E)	Gorse, double	5 ft. ; 6 yrs.	12–18	2	20	25	Trim or clip after flowering
Veronica (E) Traversii	Speedwell	3 ft. ; 6 yrs.	12–18	1	18	—	Little necessary
Viburnum Tinus (E)	Laurustinus	5 ft. ; 5 yrs.	12–20	1	18	—	Spring after flowering

Note.—D = Deciduous ; E = Evergreen.
Plant Deciduous Species from February to March or from October to November ; Evergreen Species from March to April or in September or October.

CHAPTER XXI

GARDENING UNDER GLASS

THE gardener who is fortunate enough to possess a "little glass" will find that he is able to attempt successfully many kinds of flower and fruit growing that without some form of glasshouse are either impossible or very difficult.

Situation and Aspect

If the greenhouse can be placed only in a shaded corner of the garden it is clearly hopeless to attempt to grow plants and flowers which need much sunshine. It is better to devote the space to growing ferns to which shade is not only not harmful, but absolutely necessary. If the greenhouse is to be used for fruit and flowers it should stand in full sunlight. Daylight and shelter from north and east winds are essentials.

Ventilation

Upon the proper ventilation and regulation of the heat and moisture of the greenhouse much of its success depends. It is very easy to kill, or at least gravely to injure, a house full of plants by injudicious opening or closing of all ventilators. Only in summer when the temperature is too high should top and side ventilators be opened simultaneously and then only in moderation, as a chilly draught between the two openings may cripple the less hardy plants. Only ventilators on the side opposite to that from which the wind is blowing should be opened, except in summer, when a mild wind can do little harm, provided a draught is not caused.

The amount of air admitted, of course, depends on the nature of the plants ; young growing plants and seedlings require a warm and moist atmosphere while plants in bloom require the air to be drier ; the moisture would, in many cases, injure the bloom. Where there is ample top ventilation there is far less need of side ventilation as well, indeed many experts now discontinue the use of side ventilators altogether, as they are held to make the atmosphere over-dry. In cases in which this dryness is desired, as it may be in a few houses built for particular plants, side ventilation may be employed by means of small sliding shutters placed in the side of the house and below the hot-water pipes. This latter position will ensure the slight warming of the air as it passes over the pipes and before it circulates in the house. It is important that the temperature of the house should be carefully watched, especially in the morning—the sun will often come out suddenly with surprising power, and unless the ventilation is regulated in time the heat will become intense. In order to avoid the risk of scorching, the ventilators, in mild weather, should be opened early, beginning with a little opening, which is gradually increased as the sun becomes more powerful, reversing the process towards evening as the temperature falls. Violent changes of temperature are as harmful to plants as to people, and the sudden check given to foliage which is in a state of great heat and transpiration on the sudden lowering of the temperature of the surrounding atmosphere will almost certainly give rise to mildew. If this occurs dry flowers of sulphur should be sprinkled over the plants affected.

Watering

Plants will need most water in the spring and summer, both because the air is then drier, and because the plant is in full activity and is using up water at a great rate. Water at least once a day, sometimes twice, will be needed at this season, and it is permissible in very hot dry weather to stand moisture-loving plants in saucers of water. Dormant plants and freshly potted plants are best kept rather dry until growth begins. A watering once a week will suffice for most plants in winter time; the soil must be prevented from becoming dust-dry. In the greenhouse, watering is often as useful for keeping the air in a proper state of moisture as for anything else, and in hot weather the walls, staging, and floor, should be frequently syringed. When the air is very hot and dry, the floor may with advantage be absolutely swilled with water, which will evaporate into the air and keep it moist. This is better than too much overhead watering with a rose, which tends to produce weak, insipid foliage.

In the summer, the watering of the plants themselves should be done when the sun's heat is at its lowest, early in the morning or in the early evening, but in spring, late autumn, and in winter it is essential to water in the morning so that excessive moisture may have drained off before the evening, otherwise there is great liability to " damping-off." Plants should never be allowed to become so dry as to droop, as this may cause irreparable damage, but if this has occurred, the whole plant, pot and all, should be stood in water deep enough to cover the pot. When thoroughly soaked, it should not at once be replaced on the staging, but put in the shade for an hour or two to recover. Nearly all plants, and especially those that have not recently been repotted, will be the better for a watering with liquid manure every ten days while the buds are forming. The manure water must be discontinued as soon as the flowers are out. *See also* Watering, page 77.

Shading the Greenhouse

During the summer, from about March to the end of September, the house will require shading from the strongest sunshine, or there is great risk of the plants being scorched and dried-up. No definite dates or hours when shading should be commenced can be given as everything depends upon the weather prevailing. The cool house, however, usually needs shading from about the end of February and should be shaded each day as soon as the direct rays fall on the house. The blinds may be removed as soon as the rays are passed. The plants in the warm house can do with more sun and heat. Let the rays play for half an hour or so on the house before shading it and remove the shading about half an hour before the sun's rays leave the glass, in order that the heat of the house may be maintained. Protection from the direct rays of the sun only should be given. Where constant attention can be given, an arrangement of roller blinds is, of course, the best, as the amount of light can be better regulated, and the blinds can be left up on dull and sunless days. Where, however, as is often the case, the greenhouse must of necessity be left to look after itself for a good part of the day, some other plan must be adopted. The simplest, and on the whole the most satisfactory method is to wash the glass over with a mixture of whiting and milk. It is far better to risk losing a little sun than to court damage from burning. The whiting solution is easily washed off when cloudy weather sets in and more light is necessary.

Cleanliness in the Greenhouse

Cleanliness inside the greenhouse is most essential. Aphides, thrips, red spiders, mealy bugs, scale insects and woodlice are the chief pests met with here. The manner of countering them is shown in the chapter on *Diseases and Pests*, where fumigation is described. Keeping every corner of the house and the stem of every plant as clean and free from rubbish as possible will do a great deal to keep down insect pests.

GREENHOUSE TEMPERATURES

It is not possible to give any fixed rules for the temperature of the greenhouse. This must of necessity vary with the plants grown and instructions in this matter will be found under the headings of the different plants. Greenhouses are, however, roughly divided into cold, cool, warm or intermediate, and hot houses, and as a rough guide the following may be taken as the mean temperatures of the last three:

HOT HOUSE	Summer	Day.	.	70° to 85° F.
		Night	.	65° to 75° F.
	Winter	Day.	.	65° to 75° F.
		Night	.	60° to 70° F.
WARM (INTERMEDIATE) HOUSE	Summer	Day.	.	65° to 75° F.
		Night	.	60° to 70° F.
	Winter	Day.	.	60° to 70° F.
		Night	.	55° to 65 °F.
COOL HOUSE	Summer	Day.	.	60° to 65° F.
		Night	.	55° to 60° F.
	Winter	Day.	.	55° to 65° F.
		Night	.	45° to 50° F.

The Cold or Unheated Greenhouse

This house depends solely on the heat of the sun for its warmth. Thus its temperature varies enormously at different times of the year. It requires no artificial heat even in winter. It must, however, be remembered that glass of itself will not keep out frost and the plants selected for the cold house must necessarily be hardy and able to stand a few degrees of frost. Much may be done by placing sacking and canvas over the glass to keep frost from the more tender plants and such hardy plants as bloom too early in the season to withstand the frost in the open.

Ventilation.—The cold house must have ample ventilation, but care must be taken to exclude all draughts. On warm summer nights the ventilators may be kept open all night; in cooler and damper weather it is best to ventilate thoroughly in the morning and to close the ventilators soon after lunch. *See* Ventilation, p. 164. For shading, the roller type of blind is best, as these may be pulled down as protection against frosts on winter nights.

Watering.—Watering requires a good deal of care and is best done in the morning ; the foliage and atmosphere will then have time to dry somewhat before the cold night air can cause " damping-off." This applies especially to watering in autumn, winter and spring ; in summer the watering may be done in the evening. **In hot** weather plants may be sprayed overhead and the paths and staging damped, as advised for the warm house, but this should be done with caution and only in the hottest periods, as the majority of cold house subjects are not lovers of a damp, and humid atmosphere. See list of plants, page 175.

The Cool House

The cool house will need artificial heat during the colder periods of the year only. Between October and March a day temperature of 55° F., with a night temperature of 45° F., is necessary. During April and May, in a normal year, a temperature five degrees above that of the outer air, both night and day, will be enough. The cool house provides a home for a very large number of tender and half-hardy plants, and will be found the best all-round house for the amateur.

The Warm (Intermediate) House

The warm, or intermediate, greenhouse requires a 55° F. night temperature, and a 65° F. day one all the colder part of the year and from 65° to 75° in the day all the summer and spring. The warm greenhouse will give the amateur a very wide range of choice, for many of the plants which have been included amongst those grown in the cold and cool houses can also be had in perfection in the slightly warmer house. The warm house also allows of very much greater scope in the matter of forced and out-of-season flowers. See list of plants, page 176.

The Hot House

The hot house requires considerably more heat. In winter the night temperature should never fall below 60° F., while the day temperature in summer should range between 70° and 85° F. The amateur is very prone to give too much heat in winter at a time when most plants are resting. Forcing them at this period will weaken them and impair the beauty and quantity of their flowers. Exposure to the open air and sun matures the wood and strengthens all plants. All except the more tender greenhouse plants should, therefore, be kept in the open from the end of May until early in September, having first been hardened-off for a fortnight in a cold frame and then shaded from the strong sun for their first ten days in the open. On returning the plants to the greenhouse before the first frost, they must be given very free ventilation. The plants are not usually taken out of their pots, but the latter should be plunged to their rims into beds, preferably not of earth, but of ashes or fibre, which will keep them well-drained and prevent worms from entering and attacking the roots.

HEATING THE GREENHOUSE

It is generally recognized that the hot-water system is the best method of heating the greenhouse. The fitting of a system of hot-water pipes requires considerable care and experience, and unless he is himself qualified to supervise the work, the amateur is advised to put the work in the hands of a reliable firm.

Fuels

Between coke and anthracite there is not much to choose. In the case of small, upright boilers, coke must be used, the anthracite being unsuitable, and the fuel must be broken into pieces of the size of a walnut before being used.

Lighting the Fire

To light the fire open the ash-tray door, pull out the damper and lay the fire with paper or shavings, dry wood and some small coal as for a house fire and close the fire-door. Light it and put on a little more coal as the fire burns up, then add the anthracite or coke and anthracite. Close the ash-tray door and regulate the draught by means of the damper. When the pipes are hot enough, push the damper in further to check the draught; if this does not regulate the fire sufficiently, open the fire-door a little. The more the latter is opened, the less the draught. The fire should remain thus until more heat is wanted in the late afternoon or evening when the final stoking up is given. For the last stoking before leaving the fire for the night the bars of the furnace should be raked thoroughly clear and the hot coke or anthracite raked down together. The furnace should then be filled with anthracite or with coke which has been slightly moistened and mixed with breeze or slack. The addition of the latter will help to liven up the coke fire. The door of the ash-tray should be opened and the fire-door closed and the damper drawn out, the fire will now burn up and if properly stoked should go well till next morning. When the fire has burnt up open the fire-door and leave it so during the night. Should the night be cold and windy push the damper almost right in and nearly close the ash-tray door, but if there is no wind, the damper should be half-way in, and the ash-tray door half open. In the morning close the fire-door, pull out the damper and open the ash-tray door, then rake out the clinkers after the fire has been stirred and had time to burn up a little. It may then be banked up to burn through the day.

PROPAGATION

Propagating Frame

A propagating frame is a most useful adjunct to the greenhouse, both for the purpose implied in its name and for bringing on plants and bulbs required for forcing and for greenhouse decoration. It saves a great deal of room in the house, as well as giving a home to all kinds of plants, cuttings, and seedlings which do not help the attractive appearance of the house.

Propagating Box

For raising seedlings, propagating cuttings, and such purposes a box within the greenhouse is very useful where a house cannot be set aside for this alone. This box may either be a fixture, in which case it should be built in such a position as to include within it some portion of the heating pipes, or it may be movable, if space is an object, so that it may be cleared out of the house when not wanted. Where the pipes are built in they should be covered with a good depth of coco-nut fibre, and the pots or boxes containing the plants to be dealt with plunged in the fibre.

The propagating box will need watching carefully while it is in use. The glass should have a sheet of paper thrown over it to shield newly inserted cuttings and seeds from the sun, and this paper should be kept in position until the cuttings have rooted, probably in about three weeks, or until the seeds have germinated. All decayed leaves must be frequently removed as they encourage " damping-off," and the condensation should be wiped off the glass every morning.

It may be here stated that the cuttings or seeds of nearly all cool house plants should be placed under glass in a temperature of 50° to 60° F. Warm house plants require a propagating temperature of from 65° to 75° F.

For special cultural details of individual plants *see* chapter XXIV, the Alphabetical List of Flowering Plants and Shrubs, p. 207 ; *the chapter on* Frames and Forcing, p. 170 ; *and the chapter on* Propagation, p. 183.

FRAMES AND FORCING

THE COLD FRAME

Span-roof frames are excellent, as the lights can be opened on either side and it is, therefore, possible to ventilate, whatever the direction of the wind. The span-roof frame should be placed so as to run north and south ; either side then gets its proportion of sun. Lean-to frames must face due south so that they may get full sun, unless shade and a low temperature are necessary, when the frames should face north.

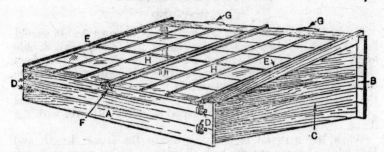

FIG. 21.—THE TWO-LIGHT FRAME.

A and *B* represent front and back respectively; *D* and *D* are mortices, tenons and pegs holding the frame together. The lights slide up and down on rebated ledges *E, E* and *F*. *H H* are flat iron bars which strengthen the lights; *G G* are iron handles.

The Bed or Foundation

The substance used to form the bed of the frame will depend upon the uses to which it is to be put. If pots or boxes are to be kept in it, a dry and hard bottom of ashes or shingle, some 3 inches deep, is admirable; this will keep out worms and other pests and will afford good drainage. If a seed-bed is made, support the four corners of the frame with bricks, place a layer of leaves at the bottom and cover with 6 inches of well-sieved compost consisting of loam, leaf-mould and sand. Make the bed firm and sprinkle the surface fairly liberally with coarse sand. (*See* Making a Seed-bed, p. 184.) The bed must, in any case, be made up so that the surface is not more than 6 to 9 inches from the glass, otherwise the plants will soon become weak and drawn-up.

(For Ventilation, Shading, etc., *see* Gardening under Glass, p. 164.)

THE HEATED FRAME

In the heated frame the heat is either supplied by means of 3 or 4 inch hot-water pipes along the front and back of the frame, or through the medium of a hot-bed upon which the frame is placed.

Management is in all respects identical with that of the cold frame, except that even more care must be given to correct ventilation and to the steady maintenance of an even temperature.

With a heated frame and a temperature of from 60° to 70° F. it is not only possible to raise plants for early transplanting to the open, but by careful management a sequence of crops of almost any vegetable can be had practically the winter through, until the vegetables from the open are ready to take their place.

THE HOT-BED

A quantity of stable dung not more than three weeks old should be collected, proportioned to the size of the frame; two double loads for a three-light frame are usually allowed. The dung should be thrown up into a heap and be turned over four or five times during a fortnight, and wetted if dry. In order to prevent the material from becoming too hot, and burning the roots of the plants, it is advisable to mix an equal quantity of leaves with the dung.

When the material is ready, measure the frame, length and breadth, and mark out the bed, allowing 18 inches more each way for the bed than the length and breadth of the frame. At each corner of the bed drive a stake firmly into the ground, and perfectly upright, to serve as a guide by which to build the bed. Then proceed to build the bed, shaking up the dung well and beating it down with a fork. The whole should be equally firm and compact, so that it is not likely to settle more in one part than in another; the bed should be about 4 feet high at the back and 3 feet in front. The frame and lights may now be placed in the centre, but the lights left off, so that the rank steam may escape.

When the rank steam has passed off, which generally takes five or six days, place a 9- to 10-inch layer of good loam under each light. By the next day this will be warmed to the temperature of the hot-bed, and the plants may be planted in it.

The heat of the hot-bed, if properly made, will last about two months but the bed will require watching. It is advisable to have a thermometer in the frame, and as soon as the heat gets below 70° F. apply a lining of fresh dung, which has been prepared as before, to the front and one side of the bed; and when the temperature again drops, add another to the back and to the other side. The bed can be kept at a growing heat for any length of time by this means, removing, at first, the old linings and replacing them by fresh. But after a time, the roots will penetrate the linings, when they must not be disturbed; fresh dung must then be added to them.

FORCING

Forcing is the process of making a plant flower or fruit out of its natural season. To effect this a suitable glass shelter and a means of applying artificial heat are necessary.

Vegetables and Fruit

Vegetables may be forced in a heated frame, or in borders and boxes in the warm greenhouse. For forcing fruit a greenhouse is necessary; cucumbers, figs, grapes, nectarines, peaches and tomatoes require a warm greenhouse, most other fruit can be forced in a cool greenhouse and is generally grown in pots. For cultural details and for the temperature required at the various seasons the reader is referred to the articles on the cultivation of the different fruits and vegetables in the chapters on *Fruit-growing under Glass* and *The Vegetable Garden*.

Flowers

Of the flowers most suitable for forcing are those of a woody and shrubby nature and those with bulbous or large, fleshy roots. All plants to be forced must be vigorous and fully matured or no blooms will result.

Bulbs

Bulbs for forcing must be firm and plump and are best of medium size. For cultural details *see* Bulbs in Pots, page 118. After forcing, the bulbs should be placed in a cold frame for a fortnight or three weeks to harden-off and for the foliage to die down. Bulbs are useless for forcing a second year, but if naturalized in the wild garden or in grass, they will soon regain their vigour and will bloom for many years. Lilies, however, can be forced year after year and will show little sign of deterioration.

The following are the bulbs most usually forced:—*Alliums, crocuses, freesias, hyacinths, lilies, narcissus, scillas, snowdrops, tuberoses,* and *tulips.*

Flowering Shrubs

Shrubs for forcing must, above all things, be vigorous and the shoots should be firm, well ripened and must show plenty of flower buds. Heat must be applied gradually, and too little rather than over much should be given. The shrubs are usually potted up in September and early in October and are placed in a cold frame until November. Early potting is essential. About the middle of the latter month transfer them to the greenhouse and place them in a

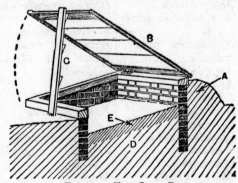

FIG. 22.—THE COLD PIT.

In the accompanying diagram *A* shows a bank of earth thrown up against the back wall to increase the warmth of the pit; *B* indicates the light supported by the notched stick *C* when raised to admit air; *D* is the soil in which plants are set; *E* the top-dressing of leaf-mould or fibre.

temperature of about 45° F. for the first fortnight; during this period syringing overhead twice a day will be necessary in fine weather. After the first couple of weeks the temperature may be raised to 60° F., and as soon as the plants break into active growth the temperature can be raised another ten degrees. When the colour of the buds begins to show, lower the temperature by five or ten degrees and maintain this level while the plants are flowering. After forcing, some of the old wood that has flowered should be cut away and any weak shoots should be cut right back; the aim being to let air and light into the centre of the plant so that the shoots shall become thoroughly ripened and be able to produce buds for the following season. After trimming, let the plants remain in the warm for three weeks or so and syringe overhead in fine weather with tepid water and feed once a week with weak liquid manure. Following this treatment they should be stood in the cold house or cold frame for a fortnight or three weeks to be gradually hardened-off preparatory to being set out in the open for the summer early in June.

Nearly all shrubs are the better if forced every alternate year only, and with lilacs this is essential. Roses, however, can quite successfully be forced for several years in succession.

For details as to the pruning and special cultural requirements of individual shrubs *see the* Alphabetical List of Flowering Plants and Shrubs, p. 207.

The following is a selection of hardy shrubs for forcing:

Acer japonica
Acer negundo variegata
Amelanchier canadensis
Amygdalus persica
Andromeda floribunda
Azalea mollis
Ceanothus
Cerasus pseudocerasus
Chionanthus
Choisya ternata
Clematis
Cytisus andreanus
Daphne

Deutzia gracilis and Lemoinei
Forsythia suspensa
Hydrangea paniculata and Mme. Mouillère
Jasmine
Kalmia latifolia
Kerria japonica
Laburnum
Lilac, see Syringa
Lonicera fragrantissima
Magnolia stellata
Philadelphus
Prunus sinensis, subhirtella, or triloba

Pyrus floribunda or spectabilis
Rhododendron
Ribes sanguineum
Rose
Spiræa arguta, media and thunbergii
Staphylea colchica
Syringa Charles the Tenth or Marie Legraye
Viburnum carlesii or opulus sterilis
Weigela
Wistaria

The treatment of roses differs slightly from that of other shrubs in that they must be established in their pots at least twelve months before forcing is to take place ; that is to say, they must not be lifted straight from the open ground to be forced. They can, however, be repotted in October if need be. Early in November they must be placed in a cold frame, pruned about the middle of December, and transferred to the greenhouse ; about a fortnight later the forcing heat should gradually be applied.

Other plants for forcing are : *Convallaria, Dielytra spectabilis, Polygonatum* and *Spiræa japonica.*

These roots should be potted-up at the end of October or early in November and kept in a cold but frost-proof frame to be transferred to the greenhouse, in batches as required, at any time from December to March or April. This will ensure a good show of bloom all through the winter from December until the end of May, when there will be no dearth of other flowers. The plants should be kept near the glass for some time after being taken into the house and ample water must be given, but the soil must not be allowed to become sour. Gradually remove the pots farther from the glass as the days become longer and the sun stronger, and to increase the time that they remain in flower shade the plants while in bloom.

SOME GREENHOUSE PLANTS

NOTE.—For Cultural Details, for Colour of Flowers, Time of Blooming, Height, and the best Species and Varieties, *see* the Alphabetical List of Flowering Plants and Shrubs, page 207.

The Cold House

Aquilegia cærulea	Dicentra spectabilis	Polygonatum multiflorum
Astilbe japonica	Fuchsias	Primula acaulis (Primrose)
Begonia (tuberous)	Godetia	P. auricula
Calceolaria (herbaceous)	Lobelia cardinalis	P. variabilis (Polyanthus)
Campanula pyramidalis	Matthiola (Intermediate	P. stellata
Chrysanthemum	Stock)	Schizanthus
Clarkia elegans	Myosotis palustris	Trollius asiaticus
Convallaria majalis	Pelargoniums	T. europæus
Dianthus Heddewigii	Phlox divaricata	Viola odorata (Violet)

Bulbs

Anemone blanda	F. Meleagis	L. tigrinum
A. fulgens	Funkia grandiflora	*Muscari botryoides
Anthericum Liliastrum	Galanthus (Snowdrop)	*Narcissus Bulbocodium
*Chionodoxa sardensis	Hyacinthus [cinth)	*Narcissus cyclamineus
Crinum Moorei and C.	H. candicans (Cape Hya-	N. Horsfieldi
*Crocus [Powellii	Iris alata	*N. minimus
*Cyclamen coum	*Iris stylosa	Ornithogalum arabicum
C. europæum	Ixia	*Scilla sibirica
*C. neapolitanum	Kniphofia Macowani	Trillium grandiflorum
Erythronium Dens Canis	Lilium candidum	Tritonia (Montbretia)
*Fritillaria aurea	L. speciosum	Tulips

* Denotes bulbs suitable for culture in the Alpine House. All small bulbs are best grown in shallow pans 5 to 6 inches in diameter ; not in pots.

THE COLD HOUSE (*continued*))—

FLOWERING SHRUBS

Amygdalus nanus
Azalea mollis
Berberis Darwinii
Camellia japonica
Ceanothus rigidus
Choisya ternata
Clematis Jackmanii
Cytisus kewensis (Broom)
Daphne Cneorum

Deutzia gracilis
D. Lemoinei
Erica carnea
E. mediterranea
Forsythia suspensa
Hydrangea hortensis vars.
Jasminum nudiflorum
Magnolia stellata
Pernettya mucronata

Prunus Japonica fl. pl.
Cydonia Maulei
Ribes sanguinea
Spiræa arguta
Syringa vulgaris (Lilac)
Veronica speciosa
Viburnum Tinus (Laurustinus)
Wistaria sinensis

The Warm House

Summer Temperature, 60°–70° F. ; Winter Temperature, 55°–60° F.

FLOWERING IN EARLY SPRING

Acacia armata (Mimosa)
Azalea mollis
Camellia japonica
Cineraria
Convallaria majalis
Cytisus fragrans (Genista)
Diervilla rosea (Weigela)
Erica hyemalis

Freesia refracta, alba, etc.
Kerria japonica fl. pl.
Laburnum vulgare
Lachenalia
Olearia stellulata
Philadelphus Lemoinei
Primula stellata
Prunus serrulata, etc.

Pyrus spectabilis, etc.
Ribes aureum
Ribes sanguineum
Spiræa Van Houtteii
Syringa vulgaris (Lilac)
Viburnum plicatum (Snowball Tree)
Wistaria sinensis

FLOWERING IN LATE SPRING

Calceolaria herbacea
Cineraria
Deutzia gracilis

Dicentra spectabilis
Eupatorium petiolare
Hippeastrum

Kalmia glauca
Lilium longiflorum
Pelargonium

FLOWERING IN SUMMER

Achimenes
Agapanthus umbellatus
Agave americana
Aloysia citriodora
Begonia
Campanula isophylla
Campanula pyramidalis
Canna indica
Celsia Arcturus
Cobæa scandens

Crinum Powellii and
C. Moorei
Dianthus (Malmaison Carnation)
Echeveria secunda glauca
Fuchsia
Gloxinia
Heliotropium
Hydrangea hortensis
Impatiens Balsamina

Lilium auratum
Lilium speciosum
Mimulus moschatus
Nerium Oleander
Oxalis
Pelargonium
Petunia violacea
Plumbago capensis
Schizanthus
Verbena

FLOWERING IN AUTUMN

Begonia
Bouvardia
Chrysanthemum indicum
Nerine
Polianthes tuberosa

Reseda odorata (Mignonette)

Salvia rutilans, S. involucrata var. Bethelii

Salvia patens and S. splendens vars.
Streptocarpus
Vallota purpurea (Scarborough Lily)

FLOWERING IN WINTER

Begonia (Fibrous-rooted)
Bouvardia
Chrysanthemum indicum
Cineraria
Cyclamen persicum
Daphne odora

Erica
Freesia [papyraceus
Narcissus Tazatta var.
Pelargonium zonale
Euphorbia pulcherrima
Primula stellata

Richardia africana (Arum Lily)
Solanum capsicastrum (Winter Cherry)
Sparmannia africana
Tropæolum Lobbianum

176

From the Painting by]   [*George S. Elgood, R.I.*

POPPIES, WHITE LILIES, VERONICA, AND
GIANT YELLOW SCABIOUS

CHAPTER XXII

THE ART OF POTTING

Washing the Pots

POTS that have been used should always be washed in hot soda water, otherwise any disease or fungus present in the old potting soil will be transferred to the next inhabitant of the pot ; besides, a dirty pot will not be porous, as it should be, to allow the air to permeate the soil. Even new pots should be put in water for at least half an hour, for a dry pot will draw away the moisture from the potting soil. The pot, however, must not be actually *wet* when used, as this would be almost as bad as using a dirty pot, for the soil and eventually the roots, would stick to it. For the winter always store pots in a dry, frost-proof place : if they are dry the frost will not hurt them ; if they are wet, however, when the frost comes it is almost certain that many of them will be ruined.

Pot Sizes

Pots are generally made in what are termed "casts"—that is to say, a certain quantity of clay is taken, from which one pot is made, or two, four, six, eight, twelve, sixteen, twenty-four, thirty-two, forty-eight, sixty, or eighty ; and pots are therefore known to gardeners as ones, twos, fours, etc., according to the number of pots made from a single cast.

The following table shows the inside measurements of the pot-sizes in general use.

Sizes.	Diam. Top in Ins.		Depth in Ins.	Sizes.	Diam. Top in Ins.		Depth in Ins.
Thimbles	2	..	2	Sixteens	$9\frac{1}{2}$	..	9
Thumbs	$2\frac{1}{3}$	..	$2\frac{1}{2}$	Twelves	$11\frac{1}{2}$	..	10
Sixties	3	..	$3\frac{1}{2}$	Eights	12	..	11
Fifty-fours	4	..	4	Sixes	13	..	12
Forty-eights	$4\frac{1}{2}$	..	5	Fours	15	..	13
Thirty-twos	6	..	6	Twos	18	..	14
Twenty-fours	$8\frac{1}{2}$	..	8	Ones	20	..	16

THE PRINCIPLES OF POTTING

Preparing the Compost

When it is considered that the compost is the medium whereby the roots receive nutrition, water and air, it will be realized what an important part it plays in the life of the plant, and for this reason every effort should be made to give the compost best suited to the needs of each plant. In our *Alphabetical List of Flowering Plants*, chapter XXIV, details as to the most suitable individual composts are given.

The most usual ingredients of potting composts are : loam, which generally forms the greater part ; leaf-mould ; sand ; old mortar rubble ; well-rotted manure ; and charcoal.

Mixing the Potting Soil

The potting soil must be moderately moist, that is to say, if a handful is taken up and pressed firmly together, it should become moulded to the shape of the hand, but at the same time it should be dry enough to crumble as soon as it is disturbed. Mix the ingredients well together, but do not sieve the compost ; this would rob it of much of its plant food and most of its porosity, large lumps must of course be broken up. Only for seeds and cuttings should the compost be sieved, and in this case through a quarter-inch mesh. Young plants with fine fibrous roots need a compost much finer in texture than do mature and vigorous plants being potted-on into their final pots.

As has been said before, the proportions in which the various ingredients are added to the compost vary in accordance with the requirements of individual plants and with the nature of the loam used, but the following may be taken as a suitable compost for the general run of the more common soft-wooded plants grown in our greenhouses.

$\frac{1}{2}$ part Fibrous Loam
$\frac{1}{4}$ part Leaf-mould
$\frac{1}{8}$ part Well-rotted Manure
$\frac{1}{8}$ part Coarse Silver Sand

The compost should be stored in the potting-shed, and where greenhouse subjects are to be potted-up, the compost should be stored in the warm house for at least twenty-four hours previously to potting, if possible, so that the compost may be warmed up to the temperature of the house.

When to Re-pot

The time at which a plant should be re-potted depends on whether the " ball " is to be broken up, as for instance when a plant from the open ground is to be potted-up or when a plant has to be re-potted because the soil is old and sour, or whether the "ball" is to be left practically intact as when a growing plant is to be "shifted" into a slightly larger pot. In the latter case the operation can be performed at any time when the plant is in fairly active growth, as the roots will at once go ahead and take possession of the new soil. Where the "ball" is to be broken up, however, repotting can only be undertaken just as the roots are beginning to come into active growth, at which time they will be able to penetrate the new compost; if the "ball" were broken up when the roots were not in their most vigorous state, the young root-matter could not fail to be badly damaged and in consequence would be unable to recuperate in sufficient time to penetrate the new soil before the "resting" period set in, and the new soil would become sour before it could be occupied.

During the growing season a plant or two of each batch of similar flowers, whether they are biennials being grown on for greenhouse use, soft-wooded perennials or hard-wooded plants, should be turned out of their pots so that it may be seen whether re-potting is necessary. As soon as the roots begin to wind round the sides of the pot a larger pot should at once be given unless the "resting" season is approaching when potting should be held over till growth again begins. Plants make most growth in April and May and again in August and September; the best time to re-pot, therefore, is just before this growth commences, that is to say about March and again in August and early September. March is the better time at which to re-pot established plants as the spring growth is more vigorous than the autumn growth, and new material will then be of more use to them.

The Size of the Pot

It is always advisable to put a plant into a pot slightly too small rather than too large. Unless the plant is very pot-bound, or is required to grow very quickly (as in the case of many young and growing plants), put the plant back in the same sized pot if possible. Many gardeners like to have about 1 inch of soil between the "ball" and the sides of the pot.

It is fatal to try to save work or to force a plant on by putting a small subject into a pot too large for it. The small roots will be unable to make use of all the moisture and plant food in the soil; this hangs about in the compost and it is a long time before any fresh air is able to enter, so that the soil becomes clammy and finally sour. For this reason pot-up into small pots, re-potting frequently as the plants grow and the roots become pot-bound. It is rarely necessary to move a plant into a pot more than two, at the most three, sizes larger than the old one. As soft-wooded plants are as a rule vigorous growers, they may usually be put into proportionately larger pots than would be advisable for the slower-growing hard-wooded plants.

Drainage

Over the hole at the bottom of the pot should be placed small pieces of broken pots, technically called " crocks." For cuttings, which are not intended to remain in the pot for any length of time after they have rooted, a single piece of crock, convex side uppermost, is sufficient, but when the time of tenancy is likely to be prolonged to months, and perhaps even years, it is necessary to fill one-sixth, and in some cases as much as one-fourth, of the entire depth of the pot with broken potsherds.

Inserting the Compost

The crocking being done and a little coarse mould thrown over them, some fine mould should be put in and shaken together by gently knocking the edge of the bottom of the pot against the potting-bench, or by striking the sides of the pot gently with the hand. This soil at the bottom of the pot should be just sufficient to lift the plant so that the top of the " ball," when set in the new pot is within $1\frac{1}{2}$ inches of the rim of the pot—when firmly planted and covered with $\frac{1}{2}$ to 1 inch of new soil, it should be 1 inch below the rim in a large pot and $\frac{1}{2}$ inch in a small pot.

Removing the Plant from the Old Pot

The most suitable times for re-potting the various kinds of plants will be found in the individual articles in the Alphabetical List of Flowering Plants, chapter XXIV.

The plants to be re-potted should, if necessary, be watered an hour or so before the work is to take place so that the " ball " of earth round the roots may be just moderately moist ; if too wet the fibrous roots may be torn ; if over-dry the small roots will find great difficulty in becoming established in the new compost. Now turn the pot upside-down, placing the first and second finger of the left hand so that the stem lies between them while the palm and fingers lie across the top edges of the pot, and grasp the bottom of the pot, which is now uppermost, with the right hand. Next tap the rim of the pot gently on the edge of the potting-bench, and the roots and soil will come out complete, being supported by the left hand, as the pot is removed by the right. Care must be taken that the plant and soil do not drop from the pot. Should the plant " ball " not come out of the pot, the finger or a small blunt-headed stick should be inserted through the drainage hole at the bottom of the pot, and if gentle pressure is applied, the " ball " will soon be moved from the pot.

Potting-Up the Plants

The crocks, any sour soil and dead roots, must be carefully removed so that the roots are not bruised, and some of the thickest roots should be drawn out from the "ball" with a pointed stick; these will establish themselves in the new soil round the sides of the larger pot. Now place the "ball" on the soil already in the pot so that the plant will be quite central, and pack the soil with the hand or trowel between the "ball" and the sides of the pot on the bench, consolidating the earth by knocking the pot on the bench, and pressing the compost down round the sides with a potting stick, or the thumb, which is more convenient when dealing with the smaller sizes of pots. Press the new soil firmly about the collar of the plant with the thumbs. Keep the new soil *level* with the top of the old "ball." The collar should not be raised above the general level, but to depress it beneath is certain death to hard-wooded plants. All plants, however hardy, should be kept warm and moist for a few weeks after re-potting, especially if they have received a large shift. The growth of the roots is thus promoted—a point of great importance at this stage.

Only remove from the "ball" that soil that is really sour; it is a mistake to disturb the roots if the soil is still fresh; if, however, the compost has become very sour, all the soil must be removed and the roots must be well washed through with luke-warm water, any dead or diseased parts being cut away.

Potting-on Seedlings and Cuttings

Cuttings and seedlings are best potted-up in the house in which they have hitherto been grown; they are delicate and if transferred to a cold draughty shed may receive a set-back. Once established in their new pots, they can gradually be hardened off to stand the temperature of their new house.

The size of the pot to be used naturally depends on the kind and size of the plant, but as a general rule 3 or 4 inch pots are suitable for the first potting-up of seedlings that have previously been pricked-off into boxes, round the sides of pots, or into thumb pots; the new pots should be just large enough to take the roots without their touching the sides; a larger pot will be needed with each shift as the plants grow. The size of the pot in which the plant is ultimately to be flowered bears closely upon the dimensions of the pot used for the first potting-up. If the ultimate pot is to be 8 inches in diameter, the first pot should usually be a 3½-inch one, the pot for the second shift being a 5-inch one. A 3-inch is generally large enough as a first pot when the eventual size is to be 6 inches, the intermediate shift being into a 4-inch pot. For the general run of biennials potted-on for greenhouse use three pottings in all (excluding the seed or cutting boxes and the prick-ing-off) are all that the gardener can afford to give, though in some cases more frequent potting is beneficial, if possible. Perennials are potted-on as they increase in size and as they become pot-bound.

The procedure is the same as for the potting-up of maturer plants, but the stem of the seedling must be buried nearly up to the two small seed leaves, or cotyledons. The young roots are very brittle and tender, so that the soil must not be pressed down with the thumbs and fingers as when potting maturer plants; the tapping of the pot on the bench and the watering afterwards should render the compost quite firm enough. Seedlings grown in boxes or close together in pots should be potted-off fairly early, that is, before their roots begin to intertwine.

How Firm to Pot

With the generality of plants it is desirable to pot firmly, not to ram the earth down hard, but sufficiently firm for the plant to offer resistance if slight pressure is applied to it to pull it upwards. The degree of firmness necessary varies with the age of the plant, the nature of the roots, and the character of the compost. Young plants, of all kinds, whose roots will expand need planting only moderately firmly, the soil being packed just tight enough to hold the plants in position; each potting must, however, be firmer. When mature, fibrous-rooted plants should be planted very firmly, the more sandy the compost the firmer must the planting be. Plants with large fleshy roots require a much looser compost. Between these two extremes there are roots of varying sizes and characteristics, and in each individual case the gardener must use his discretion. Although it may be necessary to firm the soil firmly round the roots, do not pack the surface down hard or the air will be excluded. Lastly, never fill a pot with soil right up to the edge, but only to about half an inch below the edge of smaller pots, and 1 inch for larger pots. This should be done in order to afford sufficient room for watering. Water must always be given through a fine rose directly after potting-up, so that the soil may settle round the roots, after which the plants should be kept rather dry in a close atmosphere for a week or so until estab-lished; soft-wooded plants should also be shaded from the sun. Plants which are rather top-heavy or whose roots do not grip the soil firmly must be staked—the stick should be thin, but strong, and should be pushed into the compost down the side of the pot to avoid piercing and damaging the roots. (*See* Staking *and* Tying, p. 71, and Potting Bulbs, p. 118.)

CHAPTER XXIII

PROPAGATION OF PLANTS

PLANTS may be propagated by several methods : they may be raised from seed ; cuttings may be taken ; they can be layered ; with a great number, especially herbaceous perennials, the roots may be divided ; of some, root-cuttings can be secured ; a few can be propagated by leaf-cuttings ; while others, mostly fruit trees and roses, are propagated by budding or grafting. Below we describe in detail the various processes.

SOWING SEED

Generally speaking, seeds retain full vitality for one or two years only in ordinary circumstances. From this we gather it is better to sow seed saved during the previous year, or, at the utmost, not more than two seasons old.

Weather for Sowing

Never sow in a cold, wet soil. Wait until the ground has dried sufficiently and until the weather really bids fair to be mild. It is false economy to sow before one feels sure of the weather, just on the off-chance of getting an extra early crop. Dry weather should, therefore, be chosen for seed sowing, and if seed can be sown just before a gentle shower, or when the weather is likely to be showery, so much the better. Of course, there is a proper time for sowing for every kind of seed (*see* chapter XXIV), but this cannot be specified in a series of general instructions which apply equally to all. The smaller the seed, the finer should be the soil in which it is grown. The soil in which seed is sown should be tolerably dry—dry enough to crumble lightly when worked with the hand. It must not clot together in a pasty mass. Place or position—that is to say, whether in the open air or under protection—also forms an important factor with regard to time.

Storing Seeds

Seed should be stored in a dark, cool place ; it should be kept dry and above all in an even temperature. It is best placed in tins with tightly fitting lids, in thoroughly clean glass bottles, if kept in the dark, or in glazed paper impermeable to moisture. Soft

183

absorbent paper is bad, as the seeds will either dry and shrivel up or, if kept in too moist a place, will get damp and will rot. Do not leave the seeds in their pods, as is so often advised, since after a time the pods dry up and draw both moisture and vitality from the seeds.

When saving seeds from the garden, they should not be gathered too early, but must be allowed ample time to ripen.

SOWING SEED IN THE OPEN

Preparing the Seed-Bed

The seed-bed should be situated in partial shade and should be sheltered from the north and east. The soil should be made as fine as possible, first by breaking up the lumps with a fork and then by raking it thoroughly until the earth is well pulverized. It should contain 10 per cent. to 20 per cent. of sand—this will make it porous and will enable the air to penetrate freely through it. If the soil is not made fine in this way many of the seeds will fall down in between the clods and will not germinate; those that do come up may have their tiny roots parched up, as there will be no fine soil through which they can work and so obtain nourishment and moisture. Too rich a soil must not be used as the seedlings would become tall and straggly, instead of short and sturdy, which is the ideal at which to aim. The bed must be pressed down firmly and left to settle for a few days before seeding. Water the bed thoroughly, if dry, and sow the seed thinly in drills running north and south, if possible, and about 6 inches apart (for times, depth to sow, and distances apart for the different flowers, vegetables, etc., *see* chapters XXIV and XXVIII). Sowing in drills is much better than the " broadcast " method, in which the seed is scattered over the entire surface of the seed-bed. It saves seed and makes their sowing more easy. Thick sowing means that the seedlings will get drawn up and will be sickly; thin sowing secures short sturdy seedlings.

Depth to Sow

Cover the seeds lightly with fine, sandy soil; the depth of covering required depends on the size of the seed. Minute seeds hardly need any covering at all, a mere sprinkling of sand is sufficient; medium-sized seeds must have a covering a little less than half an inch thick; and large seeds, such as those of the iris or pæony, and also those like the seeds of the hepatica and phlox, which do not sprout the first year after sowing, can do with $\frac{1}{2}$ to 1 inch of soil over them. Few seeds require a covering of more than 1 inch. Seeds may be sown slightly deeper out of doors than under glass, as the rain is liable to wash out any with too sparse a covering. A good rule is to cover the seeds with a layer of earth twice their own thickness. Do not pat down the soil after the seeds have been planted. Seeds sown in heavy soil must not be placed so deep as those planted in sandy loam, while in sandy soil a covering of nearly twice that given in a heavy soil will be required. Do not plant the seeds too deep, however, as if so planted and they ever reach the surface at all, they will have used up most of their strength and energy and will make weak, straggly seedlings. Should the soil of the seed-bed be very dry the seeds should be soaked overnight in warm water.

Watering the Seeds

As soon as the seeds have been covered, give them a good watering from a can with a very fine rose ; the rose must be very fine or the seeds may be uncovered and washed away. Keep the soil uniformly moist but not too wet ; over-watering causes the seeds to rot and is the most frequent cause of failure. A few strands of black cotton, supported on small sticks, should be stretched across the bed to keep the birds away. If, before planting, the seeds are steeped in a weak solution of paraffin, neither mice nor birds will trouble much about them.

Thinning-Out and Transplanting

In a month or so the seedlings should be about 2 inches high and will be large enough to be handled between finger and thumb and pricked-off. This should always be done at the earliest possible moment. Delay in thinning and transplanting means that the seedlings become drawn-up and weakly ; when they are eventually moved the fibrous roots become torn and the seedlings will take much longer to become established. They will, in fact, never make such sturdy plants as those transplanted at the right time. In order that the roots shall not be torn the seed-bed should be watered the evening before the day on which thinning is to take place.

The seedlings should be raised from the seed-bed by means of a small fork, each seedling may then be separated from its neighbours without any damage to its roots, and should be planted very firmly, by means of a small trowel, in a hole just large enough to receive the roots without cramping them or doubling them up, and care must be taken not to leave an air-pocket below the roots or they will soon be parched. Sturdy seedlings should be transplanted about 10 inches apart, smaller ones 6 inches apart. If, as in the case of carrots or onions, the seedlings are to be thinned and not transplanted, the fork is not used to raise them, but the unwanted seedlings are pulled up between the finger and thumb, a finger of the other hand being pressed upon the soil to keep the roots of the other seedlings in place. The soil should be firmly pressed back around those seedlings left in the seed-bed or they will be likely to die off. If transplanting is done in the evening, the seedlings will have the cool night in which to recover, and will not be so liable to be scorched as when transplanted in the heat of the day. The reserve garden into which the seeds are transplanted must possess a sunny aspect, should have been well dug and the soil, if poor, will be all the better for having had good, well-rotted manure mixed with the top 3 inches of its surface, which must be dressed with just sufficient soot to blacken the surface of the soil in order to ward off slugs. A further dressing of vegetable ashes will help to lighten the soil and furnish nourishment for the seedlings. In dry weather the reserve bed should be well watered the day before it is to receive the seedlings, but it must not be made too wet, as the seedlings will not grow if it is made to "cake." The bed should be again watered after the transplanting has been done. If transplanting can be carried out in showery weather, so much the better.

Care of the Seedlings

In dry weather, the seedlings should be watered (but not when the hot sun is on them) and the bed must be well hoed. Tepid water is far more congenial to them than cold water from the tap or a deep tank, and provided the soil is fairly rich the seedlings should receive no manure until they approach maturity. A dressing of sootwater is a sufficient stimulant and a protection from slugs, and lessens the risk of " damping off."

Wintering the Seedlings

In warm and sheltered districts the young plants may be left in the open all winter (annuals will, of course, have attained maturity, flowered and died down), but in colder districts it is safer to winter them in a frame, where they should be placed in October. Light, sandy soil and a southerly aspect best suit most seedlings. As much air as possible should be given, but care must be taken to exclude frost and damp.

In November of the second season or in March of the third year the plants can be put out in their permanent positions ; tender plants receiving protection during the second winter as afforded in the first. Slugs are the great enemy of young seedlings and some good soil fumigant should be used to keep these at bay. *See* page 54.

SOWING SEEDS UNDER GLASS

The less hardy plants must be raised under glass, and the soil for the seed pans or boxes should consist of a composition of two-thirds good loam and one-third leaf-mould, together with a good sprinkling of sharp silver sand. The compost should be sieved through a quarter-inch mesh and the soil for covering the seeds through a sieve even finer. Mix the compost thoroughly, press it gently into the pot or box, and make a level surface just below the rim of the pot. The seed pans or boxes should be drained by means of "crocks" or broken pots, an inch of crocks being required in a box or pot 5 inches in depth. Earthenware pots or pans are preferable, as the earthenware keeps the soil more evenly moist than the wooden box. The seeds must be sown thinly in February or March, and then be watered, not with a can but by immersing the pots or pans nearly to their brims, thus allowing the water to soak up from the bottom. Place the seed pans in a frame or greenhouse in moderate but steady heat (about 60° F.). A sheet of glass should be placed over the boxes and the glass in turn be covered with a sheet of brown paper to keep out the light. Each day the glass must be lifted so that the condensation may be wiped off, or the seeds will be kept too moist. No further water need, as a rule, be given until the seeds have germinated. As soon as the seeds are up (in about three weeks time) the glass and paper may be removed, and the boxes must be lifted by gradual steps up to within 6 inches of the lights. If the box is left some distance from the glass, weak straggling seedlings will result. In warm weather it is wise to water the seedlings in the evening, but in the colder weather the watering must be done before lunch time or there may be danger of the seedlings "damping off."

Sowing Seeds in a Frame

The seeds may be sown in a frame in exactly the same way as described for sowing in pans or boxes; the frame should be in a sheltered position, as it is essential to ventilate as much as possible when the weather is sunny and sufficiently calm.

Pricking-off

When the seedlings are from 2 to 3 inches high, they must be pricked-off, using a wooden label in place of a small hand-fork, from 1 to 3 inches apart so that the leaves do not touch (strong growing kinds 6 inches apart), and should be transplanted into boxes of light sandy soil and again put in a position some 6 inches from the lights. The wooden label should be inserted in the soil an inch or so from the seedling, whose roots may then be gently levered up without damage—never should seedlings be pulled up between the finger and thumb, as this will sorely damage the roots. The seedlings should be planted so that the first pair of leaves show just above the soil. They must be planted firmly and should have the soil pressed tightly down round the roots and stems, though care must be taken not to injure any part of the seedling. A thin dibble about the size of a pencil should be used to make the holes for the seedlings, and these must not be made too deep or the roots of the seedlings will not reach the bottom and the air-pockets left under them will wither their roots. Do not " firm " the seedlings by pressing the earth round the stems with the fingers, but use the dibble, inserting it into the soil, in three or four places round the seedlings, about half an inch from them, and to the same depth as when preparing the holes. This will firm the soil all round the seedlings, right down to the bottom of the roots ; the fingers would only press in the top and the roots would be left loose in the soil. Strongly growing seedlings can be potted up at once, the process of pricking-off being unnecessary. In the case of seeds that germinate irregularly, the first batch of seedlings should be pricked-off as soon as they can be handled, and the seed boxes should then be replaced so that the remaining seeds may germinate.

Such treatment is necessary with plants like the anemone, auricula, polyanthus or primula. After pricking-off keep the seedlings in a close atmosphere and shade from the sun for a few days until they are established in their new pots.

Hardening-off and Planting-out

In March or April the seedlings should be transplanted into the cold frame which should contain soil similar to that in the seed boxes. There they are hardened off by gradually allowing them more and more air until they are planted out very firmly in the reserve garden in May or at the beginning of June. Annuals will, of course, be placed in their flowering position.

Wintering

Half-hardy biennial and perennial seedlings, however, will require protection during the coming winter, and in early October must be lifted, then replanted close together in light sandy soil in boxes, to be stored in the greenhouse in a temperature of about 50° F., or in a cold frame. Give as much air as possible when the weather is fine and dry to prevent the plants from " damping off." Should there be any signs of this, take every opportunity of thoroughly ventilating on dry warm days and sprinkle the soil very finely with powdered charcoal. The following May the biennials should be set out in their flowering positions and the perennials must again be placed in the reserve garden. Half-hardy perennials will require protection during each winter and will again have to be lifted in October and wintered under glass. It is as well to look at the thermometer the last thing at night and to cover the lights with sacking if the frost is likely to be severe. These mats should not be removed too early in the morning.

Half-hardy perennials or biennials can, of course, be sown in the open in May or June and wintered as stated above. Hardy plants are frequently sown under glass to procure early and sturdy plants for bedding-out in the spring.

PROPAGATION BY CUTTINGS
Soil for Cuttings

Coarse sand is, perhaps, the best medium in which to strike cuttings. A light soil through which the air can pass freely is essential to the well-being of all cuttings. That aeration is necessary is proved by the fact that cuttings will strike readily in coco-nut fibre, a material that is extremely pervious to air and which retains moisture for a considerable period. Powdered charcoal also forms a good medium. Perhaps the free access of air through the excellent drainage in such a position is the reason why cuttings root more freely when placed close to the side of the pot.

How to Take the Cutting

Cuttings should be taken of shoots that have ripened or which are beginning to ripen, because in wood which is attaining or has attained maturity the callus so necessary to root formation is more readily induced to show itself. The side shoots of plants, low down on the stem, are the best for cuttings, and should be taken when the sap is in full motion, because its return by the bark tends to form the callus, or ring, of granular matter from which the roots proceed. The leaves of a cutting must never be cut off, except in so far as may be necessary at its base in order that it may be inserted in the soil. The leaves are the lungs of the plant, and if they are cut the sap that they contain will be lost to the cutting and prevented from passing downwards to form the callus. Cuttings of plants that are difficult to strike may frequently be induced to do so by making a ring round them, or by tying a piece of string round them for a short time before they are taken from the parent plant. The downward flow of the sap is arrested by the tightened ligature and a swelling is caused, which forms a callus from which roots are soon emitted. The cutting must be severed from the parent plant just below the ring or band, and the callus formed should be covered when the cutting is inserted in the soil.

In taking cuttings strong sturdy shoots varying from 3 to 12 inches in length should be removed from the plant, with a very sharp knife, by a clean straight cut just below a joint. If it is possible to take a "heel" or small wedge-shaped portion of the old wood and bark with it, so much the better, and it is then not essential to cut immediately below a joint. The joint need not necessarily be the junction of two stems; it may equally well be the "eye" from which a pair of leaves have sprung. When no "heel" is taken, the cut must be especially clean and just below a joint, but the joint itself must be left intact; in fact, about an eighth of an inch of wood should be left below the joint. The "heel," from which all ragged edges should be trimmed, when placed in contact with the ground provides a larger surface on which roots can form. The length of cuttings is decided by the distance between the joints; when these are, say, an inch apart, the cuttings must be 12 inches long and over half this length must be buried in the soil. Where the distance between joints is less, the cuttings may be shorter, but all hard-wooded cuttings should have at least 6 inches in the ground, and all cuttings must be inserted right to the bottom of the hole prepared for them.

Types of Cuttings

Cuttings of hard-wooded shrubs, such as the heath or myrtle, are more difficult to strike than those of soft-wooded plants, such as the geranium, and for this reason on hard-wooded cuttings the "eyes" on the part of the stem that will be placed underground should be carefully cut out; this will encourage the formation of roots at these places. Cuttings of free-growing hardy plants, such as the gooseberry, and the willow, strike freely without care or attention after being inserted in the soil. The position for all cuttings should, of course, be sheltered and shaded from full sun, and although not necessary with hardy plants, most cuttings when planted in the open do better if covered by a hand-light until the roots have formed. The less hardy and less vigorous plants should be struck in pots or boxes in a cold frame or under hand-lights, while the more delicate still require artificial heat or the bottom-heat of a propagating box. It may be taken as a general rule that cuttings of soft-wooded plants require more heat than those of hard-wooded plants. "Soft" cuttings, as a rule, should not be struck in the open as, apart from a little heat being desirable, the wind and sun would dry the moisture from their leaves and the roots would never form. A glass covering is, therefore, necessary. Cuttings of soft-wooded plants, such as the geranium, strike best when they have not too much foliage to bear, and should have the stems, shortened to two or three joints beneath the point from which the foliage springs. Never make the cuttings longer than necessary. In the case of the less hardy plants the soil should be stored in a warm greenhouse for a few days before the cuttings are inserted, and rooting will be more certain and prompt if the cuttings are watered with lukewarm water.

There are several plants like the pansy or the honeysuckle whose stems, when mature, are hollow and useless for ordinary cuttings. In such cases the young shoots must be struck, or with the honey-suckle both ends of the cutting may be inserted in the soil. There are other plants, such as dahlias and lupins, whose cuttings must be taken at the junction of the stems and the roots. These require a glass covering.

Cuttings of nearly all the less hardy and greenhouse plants require a propagating case, placed over the hot-water pipes. With the more hardy kinds no artificial heat is needed, except that provided by the glass, but the soil must be kept uniformly warm and moist.

Shrub cuttings may be taken at three distinct periods, firstly in autumn when the wood has hardened and is quite mature; secondly in September or August when the shoots have half-matured; and thirdly when the shoots are beginning to ripen in early summer; the latter time is perhaps the best of the three. With many of the hardier shrubs the cuttings may be struck in sandy soil in a sheltered bed in the open (*see* chapter XXIV), provided the wood is fully ripe. Half-matured cuttings, even of hardy shrubs, must, however, be treated like those of the less hardy natures and be struck under glass. Cuttings of hardy evergreen shrubs are also best struck under glass, not because they need heat, but because a close, steady and fairly moist atmosphere is required (*see* Propagation of Shrubs, p. 152).

When cuttings are struck in pots or boxes the latter should be well drained by an inch layer of crocks at the bottom, and must be clean. If they are dirty the mould will be likely to stick to them when the cuttings are turned out for transplanting and the tender new root fibres may be torn.

Making the Compost

A good compost for striking the cuttings of most plants can be made by mixing equal quantities of leaf-mould and well-sieved loam and by adding to this a good proportion of sharp silver sand, and then sieving the whole through a quarter-inch mesh. It is always well to sprinkle the surface of the soil which is to receive the cuttings with a layer of sharp silver sand about 1 inch thick, so that when the dibble is pressed down to form the hole for the cutting, some of the sand will trickle into it and be ready to encourage the production of roots. The sand keeps the soil porous and prevents the base of the cutting from rotting. The soil should be firmed down and the slips inserted at least 1½ inches apart; they must not be placed too close together or they may "damp-off." Press the earth well down round the cuttings, as they will not root if standing loosely in the soil. If the cuttings can be fairly easily pulled from the compost it may be taken as an indication that they are not planted sufficiently firmly.

Inserting the Slips

As has been said, cuttings strike more readily when placed at the side of a pot, than when inserted in its centre. Of ordinary plants about seven cuttings can be placed in a 4-inch pot. No cutting should be set too deeply, but as in the case of seeds, the depth will depend mainly on the size of the cutting; a good general rule is to set about two-thirds of the length of hard-wooded cuttings in the soil, with soft-wooded cuttings only one-third or one-half should be inserted. Leaves should not be permitted to touch the soil; if they do they will "damp-off." Water well after insertion.

When using pots or boxes, it is better, but not necessary, to sink these nearly to their brims in ashes or coco-nut fibre, which will keep the soil at an even temperature. Whether the cuttings are covered by plates of glass, glass bells or the lights of a frame, the condensation must be wiped off each morning. Once the cuttings have struck, ventilation must be given whenever possible, and decaying leaves must be removed to avoid any possibility of "damping off." The great thing is to keep the soil at the same temperature as the surrounding air.

Too much light, air, water, heat, or cold are alike injurious to cuttings freshly inserted under glass. A close equable temperature and a moderate degree of moisture should be maintained until the cuttings have "rooted." This condition is best attained by covering them with a bell glass or hand-light and by shading them if not placed in a shady situation. Once they have struck, which will be in about three weeks, the cuttings should be gradually given more ventilation and hardened-off until they can be potted up singly for the greenhouse, or planted out into the open.

Soft-wooded cuttings soon form roots, and can often be potted-off in a month or so's time; cuttings of hard-wooded shrubs, however, take root less quickly and should not be disturbed for at least a year (sometimes 18 months) after being struck. To give the cuttings ample room to grow they are usually planted at least 6 inches from each other in rows 10 inches to a foot apart.

HOW TO POT UP

1. Washing the pots. 2. Inserting the "crocks." 3. The plant potted up, showing the "ball" of the roots, the fine potting compost round it, the coarse soil below it, and the drainage. 4. Removing the plant from the old pot. 5. Working the fine soil round the roots. See page 177.

1. Suitable plant from which cuttings may be taken, preferably in June and July, The cuttings should be kept dry for 24 hours before potting. 2. The plant after the cuttings have been removed. 3. The cuttings, showing the straight cut just below a joint. 4. The cuttings struck, 1½ in. deep, round the sides of a 4-in. pot of light sandy soil. The pot should be placed in a shady position under glass. See page 283.

PROPAGATION BY LAYERS

This is an easy and very sure method of propagation, usually effected about July, though it may be effected at any season of the year. It consists in the production of roots on one or more of the lower shoots of the plant to be reproduced. An upward cut, just below a joint, is made in the layer or shoot ; the incision passes from the underside through to the centre of the shoot, and is from about 1 inch to 3 inches in length, according to the size and nature of the plant to be propagated. The aim is to produce a " tongue " of bark and wood that can be wedged open and pegged down into the soil ; the more the tongue is kept open when placed in contact with the earth the better the chance of rooting. The shoots chosen for layering must be perfectly healthy, and should be semi-matured. It is usual to layer several shoots at a time, and when the cuts have been made, as described above, the earth all round the plant is stirred up to a depth of 3 inches and the layers are pegged down firmly, so that the open tongues come well in contact with the soil. Little mounds of earth some 6 inches high are then piled up over the layers, which are pressed firmly down into the earth, and well watered. An addition of sharp silver sand to the soil (often in the proportion of 50 per cent. of its volume) as in the case of cuttings, helps the layers to root. The outer end of the shoot, beyond the cut, should be turned upwards to check the flow of the sap, and all buds not required to form shoots in the new plant should be removed. When the layers have rooted firmly, they may be cut away from the parent plant, potted up or planted out, preferably in autumn. The layers of soft-wooded plants, such as the carnation, will be found to root in six weeks or so, shrubs like the laurel or veronica will take two or three months to form roots ; while with hard-wooded shrubs, like the daphne or rhododendron, it will be a year or more before the layers can be severed from the parent plant.

PROPAGATION BY RUNNERS

This is, perhaps, the most simple method of propagation, though only possible with certain plants, namely those that throw out long thin stems or runners which grow out over the surface of the ground. The strawberry is a well-known example of the runner-producing plant. At intervals along the stems will be found joints, and wherever one of these joints comes in contact with the soil and so remains for some time, roots form and foliage is thrown up.

To assist in this method of propagation the earth should be stirred up to a depth of 2 or 3 inches all round the plant and the runners must be firmly pegged down into it, at the required number of joints. Young roots will form and after a few weeks they will be strong enough to support the new plant which may be cut away from its parent, and potted up or transplanted. A better method, but one entailing a little more work, is to sink to their brims pots of good sandy soil exactly under the joints of the runners and to peg the latter down firmly to the soil in the pots. This operation provides an easier way of transplanting and one beneficial to the young plant, as the roots are not so easily injured when replanting.

PROPAGATION BY OFFSETS

Offsets afford yet another means of propagation suitable to many herbaceous perennials and to many rock plants. These offsets are growths forming young crowns round the older central crown, and may be carefully separated from the parent crown when large enough and can be potted up into small pots or transplanted. About a month after the plant has flowered will be found the best time to accomplish the operation.

PROPAGATION BY DIVISION

Plants are best divided in October and November, or in March and April. The clumps should be lifted with their roots as entire as possible, that is, with a good "ball" of earth round the fibres. This is done by inserting two forks vertically downwards, one on either side of the plant and backs facing each other, and then by levering the clump and its roots gently upwards. When the plant has been lifted, don't, as is so often done, use a spade to cut the roots apart, but carefully divide the plant up into as many crowns as possible by means of a sharp knife which will do the minimum injury to the roots. The strong new outer crowns are those that should be retained and replanted ; the old inner roots being removed. The stems that have already borne flowers should be cut away from the new crowns, so that only the young and vigorous shoots from the base remain. Replant as described in the chapter on *The Herbaceous Border.*

PROPAGATION BY ROOT-CUTTINGS

This is another and easy method of propagation eminently suitable in the case of plants with fleshy roots. If the roots are examined in the early spring, they will be found to be covered with small whitish knobs or shoots ; these are the "eyes" from which the new growth will spring. Cuttings of these roots from 2 to 8 inches in length, in accordance with the virility of the plant, and each having an "eye," are taken. They are planted 1 inch deep and 8 inches apart in light sandy soil in partial shade, or in a cold frame with a warm close atmosphere. The cuttings are inserted vertically with that part of the root which was nearest the stem uppermost.

In propagating plants whose roots are fleshy, but rather more
fibrous in nature, the larger root-stems should be cut away from
the crowns with as many of the smaller fibrous roots as possible
adhering, and should be planted as advised above, but should be
left intact and not be cut up into small pieces. In the case of
plants whose roots creep horizontally just below the surface of
the soil, cut the roots into pieces from 1 to 6 inches in length,
each piece having an " eye " or bud from which shoots can spring,
and plant horizontally in the soil at the same depth as they were
before being dug up.

The root-cuttings will require frequent watering during the
following few months, and will be benefited by the occasional
application of a little weak manure water. It is essential to keep
the surface of the soil loose. The cuttings can be planted out in
the autumn or in the following March or April.

PROPAGATION BY LEAF-CUTTINGS .

Propagation by leaf-cuttings is a very interesting method not
often resorted to, and then only in the case of plants with succulent
or thick spongy leaves, and soft veins.

A perfectly healthy leaf must be selected, it is then taken and
planted, stalk downwards, and with the leaf proper just clear of
the soil, in a propagating case in equal parts of sandy loam and leaf-
mould. Roots will soon form and a young plant will grow from
them. In the case of a large and thick leaf, the veins on the back
may be slit at their junctions. The stalk is then planted in sandy
soil, and the whole leaf is pinned firmly backside-down, so that it
cannot move, on to the mould in the propagating case (temperature
70° F.), and allowed plenty of moisture, though the bed must be
well-drained and not be permitted to become stagnant, or the
leaves will rot. In a short time plants will grow wherever the veins
have been slit. The little plants can be transplanted or potted
up as soon as they have roots strong enough to support them.
This method of propagation, which may be resorted to at any
season when fully-matured leaves are available, is particularly
suitable in the case of such plants as the achimenes, begonia, and
the gloxinia.

RINGING

Hard-wooded plants which are difficult to propagate by other
methods may be increased by a process known as *ringing*, and which
consists in removing a small narrow ring of bark all round the
stem in the place in which the formation of roots is desired to take
place. Care must be taken not to cut deeply into the stem—indeed,
it is better to peel off the outer bark only, and not to cut into the
inner wood at all, no hindrance is then offered to the ascent of the

sap. A callus is formed on the bark which forms the upper edge of the ring, and this thickens as time goes on, and ultimately emits roots. Branches and trailing stems operated on in this way should be firmly pegged down, and earth should be drawn over the incision. Layers should be brought into as erect a position as possible, and they may be shortened back. (*See* also paragraph on layering, p. 193.)

GRAFTING AND BUDDING

THE USES OF GRAFTING

Grafting has been spoken of as "ennobling," the branch which is transferred being spoken of as the "scion," and the tree to which it is attached as the "stock." The scion becomes, as it were, parasitic upon the stock, and by carefully removing all branches which spring from the stock below the point of union, gardeners are enabled to divert to the scion all the energy produced by the roots of the stock. It is only possible to graft a scion on to a stock of a nearly allied species. Thus quinces, apples, pears, and medlars can all be mutually grafted on to one another as also can plums, peaches, apricots, and almonds, but it would be impossible to graft an apple on to an oak or a plum on to a willow.

Altering Habits

Much valuable time may be saved by grafting ; it might take some fifteen or twenty years before a tree raised from seed would bear fruit, whereas by grafting fruit might be had in three or four years. Better results are also often obtained by grafting a tree on to a stock and roots other than its own.

Another purpose for which grafting is employed is for the altering of the habit of a tree. Thus, pears and apples are dwarfed by grafting them respectively on the quince and the paradise stock, and dwarfed weeping trees are converted into tall standards by attaching a scion from the weeping variety to a tree with a tall, upright trunk.

Suitability to Soil

In the selection of a suitable stock attention should be paid not only to the readiness with which connection is able to be established between the scion and the stock, but to the soil in which the trees are to be grown. Thus, for example, in light soil, plums grown on their own roots rarely do well, but when grafted on the peach they usually thrive. *Vice versa*, peaches on their own roots rarely do well in heavy soils, and may often be made to succeed by grafting them on the plum. Again, on chalky soil, where the peach usually does badly, it can often be made to grow and fruit by grafting it on the mountain ash. It is certain, also, that in some cases the flavour of fruit can be modified by the stock on which the variety is grafted. Apples occasionally become more acrid by being grafted on to the crab, and the Angoulême pear is improved by being grafted on the quince.

Restoration and Development

Grafting is also occasionally employed to bring about the development of flowers or fruit from parts of a tree otherwise lacking in them. Sometimes, again, it is made use of for the purpose of restoring an exhausted tree ; and lastly it is employed to bring together on one stock the two sexes of monœcious plants—that is to say, plants which bear their male and female flowers on different trees—and so to facilitate their fertilization and consequent fructification.

THE PRINCIPLES OF GRAFTING

When to Graft

In order to effect a successful union by grafting it is necessary that the sap should be flowing in the portions of the wood used for the operation, and it is therefore possible to graft in the open between the first signs of growth in the buds at the beginning of spring until about midsummer, when the sap has risen fully. Under glass the time is somewhat earlier, being possible any time from January to March, and again from July till September. The operations of budding and grafting are not unlike, being, indeed, identical in theory, but whereas in budding a bud only of the current year's growth is employed, in grafting whole branches are used, while their buds are still dormant or nearly so. The time for grafting trees will, therefore, vary with the time of their breaking into leaf, those kinds which bud early being the first to be dealt with. Plums are generally the first to be ready in late March, next quinces and pears, followed by cherries and apples in this order ; but as the time of leafing varies with certain varieties the order is not without exceptions. To ascertain whether the stock is ready for grafting, the bark should be slit and if it is easily raised to expose the polished surface of the wood beneath, the stock is ready. If the bark tends to tear, the stock must be left for a week or so longer.

Preparation of Grafts and Scions

Grafting needs a certain amount of previous preparation. The stock or tree which is to receive the graft should be cut back or beheaded at about the end of January. Where the frosts are still very hard it is well to defer the operation till the weather loosens a little, but no risk must be run of movement having begun

in the sap. The object of the preparation of the grafts and scions
beforehand is that the last year's ripened sap should still be in
them, to supply life to the severed scion until union has been
effected, and to this end the scions, which must be well ripened
one-year-old wood and taken from prolific and healthy trees only,
should be cut in winter before there is any chance of movement,
while the buds are still absolutely dormant. Grafting must be
carried out when the scion is in the same state of vegetation as
the intended stock. It is necessary, therefore, where the grafts
selected are in a more advanced state of vegetation, to detach
them from the parent stems and to lay them with their stems
three parts buried in moist soil under a north wall until stocks
and grafts are in a similar state. In this position the grafts will
remain stationary while the stocks are advancing. When the
weather is so mild as to appear likely to cause movement of the
sap the scions should be pulled up occasionally, and left exposed
to the air for a little while in order to check growth. The scions
should be cut at about the same time as the stock is cut off. This
latter process consists in removing from the stocks, which should
be three-year-old plants, planted at least a year before grafting,
all the side branches together with the tops, and cutting down
the main stock to just above a bud within about 7 or 8 inches of
the soil. Where older plants are used as stocks, as in the case of
grafting on mature trees, these should be cut back throughout to
within from 3 to 6 feet from the stock, according to the size of
the tree. Enough wood should always be left to allow of the
removal of a further portion, as this will be necessary when the
actual grafting is proceeded with. If this cutting back is not done
until the actual time of grafting the junction is seldom so good,
and where the trees employed are stone-fruit trees—particularly
liable to this accident—gumming is very likely to result, with
consequent weakening of the trees. Stocks to be used as standards
must be allowed to grow to the height required. The time of
grafting varies according to the stock used. It should be ascertained with accuracy that the sap is really rising, and it is better
for that reason to be a little too late than too early, when there is
a chance that it has not yet begun to move. Usually May will be
found the best time for grafting on mature trees, and April for those
which are only in their third year.

THE PROCESS OF GRAFTING

The stock should be grafted, as in the case of budding, as near
to the ground as possible. To effect a union the inner edges of the
inner bark of the two parts must meet and remain in contact, this
inner layer of bark being the only portion of the wood which is

capable of uniting. The process consists in cutting the bark of the two portions so that this inner layer shall be in contact when the two pieces are pressed together, and in keeping them together and excluding air, which might dry the tissues, by means of wax or clay and ties of thread and wool.

Appliances and Materials

When grafting is to be undertaken, all materials should be got in readiness beforehand. The stocks and grafts should be prepared and at hand, together with a few tools such as a strong knife for cutting back the stocks, a saw, chisel, and mallet, a small knife with a narrow blade for fine operations, woollen thread and soft string for tying, and the wax or clay required. The clay needs careful preparation, and should be obtained some weeks before it is required for use, and beaten up into the consistency of mortar with water. This moistening and beating should be repeated every day for a fortnight, and a day before it is to be used it should be mixed with one-third of its own bulk of cow manure and about the same amount of hay. The hay should be cut up into lengths of about 3 inches, and thoroughly mixed into the other ingredients, and will prevent the clay from cracking off as it hardens, as well as materially assisting in keeping it moist.

It is simpler for the amateur to buy a good grafting wax than to prepare it for himself, and he is advised to obtain some such good cold grafting wax as Mastic l'Homme Lefort, an excellent French cold wax. A good substitute for grafting wax is the quick-drying varnish called "knotting." This is very quickly dry, and is impervious to wet and weather. It is applied with a brush over the part to be protected.

Tongue or Whip-Grafting

The method of grafting employed depends largely on the size and other conditions of stock and scion. Where the stock is a young one, and about the size of the finger, the kind known as tongue grafting is the most suitable. With this method of grafting the stock must be more advanced in its state of growth than the scion. The scion is prepared by taking a well-ripened one-year-old shoot some 6 inches long, and selecting a place on it where two good buds come on opposite sides of the shoot, one a little higher than the other. Beginning just below the upper of the buds, make a clean cut at one sweep through the wood in a downward slope, coming out just below the lower bud. It is essential that there should be a good bud just above the cut at each end. Now, beginning at the top of the cut just under the top bud, with a perfectly sharp knife cut a hollow curve in the wood, slop-

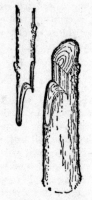

Fig. 23.— Tongue or Whip Grafting.

It is essential that there should be a good bud on the scion just above the cut at each end. The stock must also be cleanly cut off just above a good healthy bud.

ing the cut from the inner end of the curve down in a straight line to the tip of the cut by the lower bud. The bottom of the shoot, seen sideways, should now have a section like the letter J turned upside down. It is important that these cuts should be made firmly and without unevennesses, or the scion will not fit closely to the stock, and its chance of a perfect union will be lessened. Having prepared the scion, attention should be turned to the stock. This, as will be remembered, was cut back late in January to about 8 inches from the soil. Remove all side growth from the base and selecting a good smooth place about 3 or 4 inches from the surface of the ground, cut the stock cleanly off just above a good healthy bud. This bud's chief function will be to draw up the sap into the top of the cut parts while they are healing together, just as do the buds on the scion, but while the latter are allowed to grow and, indeed, become the real tree, the former should not be allowed to outlive its utility, and when perfect union has taken place it should only be allowed to grow two or three leaves, and then should be stopped out. Having cut down the stock, its top should be carefully measured against the scion, and cut in a curve corresponding with the curve on the scion. Where the scion has a long "tail," the tail of the " J " shape, a strip of wood and bark should be peeled from the side of the stock, with the greatest care to fit it, so that the stock and scion, when placed together, may fit with accuracy. The tail of the scion will be found to fit on to the peeled strip of the outside of the stock, though, owing to the different angle of the section, a narrow strip of the inner bark of the stock will show round the edge of the scion when applied. The important thing to arrive at is that the cut surfaces of the inner bark of both stock and scion should touch as much as possible. If it is found impossible to make these layers of bark meet on both edges, make them meet perfectly on the one. The tail of the scion should not in any case come

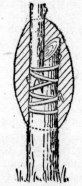

Fig. 24.— Binding the Graft.

When the scion and stock are properly fitted the junction is bound firmly with raffia or soft string; the whole junction must then be covered with grafting wax or clay.

below the end of the peeled piece of the stock, if anything it should err on the other side.

When both scion and stock fit perfectly, a further security should be obtained by making a small upward cut in the tail of the scion, in order to obtain a slip projecting towards the stock. In the stock itself, opposite this slip, should be made an incision into which the slip will exactly fit, thus holding stock and scion together during the operations of tying and covering with wax. This slip should be thin, or it may cause the junction to bulge, and the scion to be pushed away from the stock. When these two latter are fitted closely together, and it is found that their layers of inner bark are fitting closely and neatly, the junction should be made firm by tying with raffia, woollen thread, or soft string, the ligature being made firm enough to prevent movement but not tight enough to prevent the proper circulation of the sap beneath the bark. The last process is the secure covering of the whole junction—scion, stock, and ligature—with grafting wax or clay, and the graft is complete. The label should always be attached to the stock, not to the scion, as otherwise there would be an added risk of the scion being caught accidentally and pulled off before a union has been effected.

FIG. 25.—SUPPORT-
ING THE GRAFT.

The graft should be supported by a stake firmly bound to the stock.

Saddle-Grafting

Saddle-grafting is a kind much used for stocks of about the thickness of a broom-handle, the scion in this case being about the same thickness as the stock and cut with two tails, the one below the upper bud being shorter than that below the lower bud. The whole of the inner part of the wood below the buds is re-moved, and at the top the cuts are ended by a cross-cut beginning just behind the upper bud and sloping slightly upwards. The scion will now have two tails of unequal length, the shorter one having a bud at its upper extremity, and the longer one having a bud midway up its length. The stock should then be taken, and its top cut to slope slightly, at an angle corresponding with that of the cross-cut of the scion. A slip should be peeled corre-sponding with the long tail of the scion, and the latter laid over the stock, saddlewise, the long tail fitting its peeled slip, and the top angle of the stock fitting into the top angle of the cross-cut. The short tail of the scion will be found to cross the top of the stock

FIG. 26.— NOTCH
OR SLIT GRAFTING.

A pointed, wedge-
shaped incision is made
in the bark and wood of
the stock, beginning at
the cut edge of the bark
and sloping downwards
and outwards. Sloping
cuts are made on two
sides of the scion at an
angle corresponding with
that of the incision on
the stock.

and project a little. A slip should be cut off the side of the stock to fit this projecting piece of the tail, which should then be bent down on to it, and the graft is ready for tying and waxing. This system has the advantage that the scion unites on both sides of the stock, and is therefore not so liable to an accidental break during the healing process.

These methods of grafting are both employed for young stocks, but others must be used in the case of mature trees, where the branches are usually too large for either of the systems described—Cleft-grafting, Crown- or Rind-grafting, and Notch-grafting. The first system is not to be recommended, as it results in a crack being left right across the top of the stock, in which rain, insects, and fungi are apt to lodge and injure the tree.

Notch or Slit-Grafting

Notch-grafting is rather difficult, but is excellent when well done, and is used when the diameter of the stock is some four times greater than that of the graft. In this method the stock is first cut clean across, as in the other ways, and then pointed, wedge-shaped incisions are made in the bark and wood, beginning at the cut edge of the bark and sloping downwards and outwards. The scions are prepared by making sloping cuts on two sides of the wood, making an angle corresponding with that of the wedge-shaped incision in the stock, so that the scion, when fitted into the stock, fills the space closely, the outer layer of the bark of the scion being slightly lower—because thinner—than that of the stock. The best way of doing this is to make the first cut in the stock with a widely-set saw, and then sloping the sides of the cut slightly outwards with a sharp knife. The angle of the cut in the stock should not be quite so wide as that of the scion, as the latter will in this way be held tighter in the slit. The scion, when properly shaped, should be set into the cut and hammered lightly down into position with a small wooden mallet. It should then be tied and waxed as described.

Crown or Rind-Grafting

is the most popular and the easiest method of grafting on to mature trees when the stock is comparatively large, especially when renovating old fruit trees. In this system the scion is prepared much as for tongue-grafting, but the curve at the top is replaced by a sloping cut about $1\frac{1}{2}$ inches in length. The tail is quite thin, too much wood often being left by beginners when preparing scions for grafting. The stock should be cut off cleanly, and with a sharp knife a slit should be made in the bark of the same length as the tail of the scion. While the knife is still in the cut the blade should be gently pressed from side to side so as to loosen the bark in the immediate neighbourhood of the cut, and on withdrawing the knife the scion is slipped in between the wood and the bark, and pressed down until the surface left by the cross-cut at its head lies on the top of the stock. Any number of scions from two to four, should be placed on each branch over 4 inches in diameter so treated, as the more scions there are the better and more strongly will the sap be drawn up, and the quicker and better will the stock heal and effect a junction. When the grafts are growing well they should be supported by being tied to sticks fastened securely to the branches of the stock. Until the grafted tree has developed a good head of new grafted wood it is a great mistake to remove all the shoots and twigs of the old stock. A number of these should be allowed to grow for a long time, or the circulation of the tree will be impaired and its health affected.

After-care of the Graft

In May the grafts should have begun to make growth, and if this is the case the clay or grafting wax should be removed so that the binding may be undone before it " throttles " the new growth, which it will do if left in position. If the graft is not yet secure the binding must be replaced, but more loosely. The clay or wax should not be replaced. The graft should also be supported by a stake firmly bound to the stock. Laterals that form on the graft should be pinched off to encourage a good straight single shoot from the graft, and any shoots forming on the stock below the point of grafting must be rubbed off, once they have served their purpose in drawing sap up to the graft.

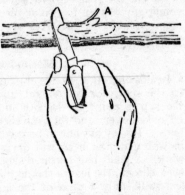

FIG. 27.—" TAKING " THE BUD.

In cutting the bud A out of the wood, the knife should enter the wood some half an inch above the bud and leave it at an equal distance below it, the knife making a curve behind the bud.

The wax may be found difficult of removal and in such a case care is required in order to get it off without damaging the junction. It is best done by placing a block of wood or some other firm thing on one side of the lump of wax, and lightly hitting the other side with a hammer, no unnecessary force being employed. The wax will crack off and may be removed with ease.

BUDDING

Budding is another method of improving or altering the nature of the fruit and flowers borne by a given tree, and it is based on the same principles as those which govern grafting. It is superior to the latter inasmuch as it produces a more perfect union, a proportionately larger surface of the inner bark coming in contact with that of the stock. In budding no wood at all is left on the bud employed, only the bud itself and a surrounding surface of bark being left on the " bud " when prepared.

When to Bud

A spell of showery or dull weather should be chosen for the operation of budding, as then the bark separates freely and easily from the wood, but if the year is very dry and hot, the stocks to be budded should be given a good soaking of water for a day or two before the operation. The best time for budding is between the early part of July and the end of September, and if the buds do not start until the next spring so much the better. New wood of the current year's growth is usually the best for budding upon, but young growths up to two or three years may be used, if otherwise more suitable. Fruit trees are best budded in July and August, while roses do best from the middle of July till early in September.

Method of Budding

In this operation, unlike grafting, the bud and stock are prepared on the spot, not beforehand, and a time should be chosen when the sap is rising freely both in stock and bud. The tree should be looked over, and the best shoot selected for the cutting of the buds. If they are not to be used at once the shoots should be put in water, or the bark will dry slightly and be more difficult to work. A good half-matured shoot of current year's growth having been chosen, the leaves should all be removed from it close to the leaf-stalk, only a piece of the latter being left on. If the leaves are left on they will draw and pass out the moisture from the bark and the bud, shrinking the latter. With a sharp knife the bud is then cut out of the wood, the knife making a curve behind it, leaving the bud midway on a thin strip of bark and wood. The knife should enter the wood some half an inch above the bud, and leave it an equal distance below it, leaving a piece of bark of the shape of a long shield, whence the name of "shield-budding" sometimes given to the operation. The woody part of this must now be removed, and in order to do this the piece is held by the leaf stalk and bud, starting the bark away from the wood at the top end with the tip of the knife, and then giving a sharp pull, when the bark should peel cleanly off the slip of wood. Occasionally, and generally when the bud is too forward when cut, the wood, when it pulls away, will leave a small hole in the bark behind the bud, as if it had pulled out a little bit of the inside of the bud with it. When this has occurred the bud is spoilt, and will shrivel and die before it has time to build up new cells to replace the missing ones. Such a bud should be thrown away and a fresh one, less developed, taken.

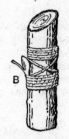

FIG. 28.—
SECURING THE
BUD.

When the bud *B* is fitted in the bark of the stock, bandage lightly with raffia or worsted above and below the eye, bringing the bark of the stock over the bud so that no opening remains between them.

The bud being ready, the stock must next be dealt with. A clean, smooth spot on the stem is chosen, and with the budding knife a cut about $1\frac{1}{2}$ inches long is made, only just sufficient pressure being employed as will pierce the bark without penetrating the wood beneath. At the top of this a cross-cut half an inch long should be made with equal precaution, and the bark on either side of the first cut raised from the wood by means of the blade of the knife, or its thin handle, slipped in between bark and wood. The point of the "shield" containing the bud is then inserted at the cross-cut, and gently pushed down under the bark until the bud is well down below the level of the cross-cut. The easiest way to do this is to hold the shield between the finger and thumb of the left hand, by the leaf-stalk, while holding the bark open with the knife held in the other hand. When the bud is well down, the projecting tip of the shield should be cut off with a cut exactly on a level with the cross-cut in the stock, so that the tip of the shield fits inside the bark. Afterwards bandage lightly with soft material —raffia, worsted or matting—above and

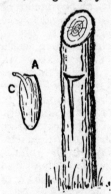

FIG. 29.— INSERTING
THE BUD.

The point of the "shield" *C*, containing the bud *A*, is inserted at the cross-cut on the stock, and gently pushed down under the bark until the bud is well below the level of the cross-cut.

below the eye, bringing the lips of the bark of the stock together again over the bud by means of the ligature in such manner that no opening remains between them. Above all, take care that the base of the eye is in free contact with the bark of the stock. As much rapidity as is consistent with thoroughness should be used, as much of the success of the operation depends on the moist condition of the bud and stock when brought into contact.

Selecting the Buds

In selecting buds for this purpose, particularly in the case of fruit trees, care must be taken to make sure that the buds are wood buds, from which a shoot will start, and not fruit buds, which will not make wood. These two kinds of bud are more easily distinguished in some kinds than in others, but as a general rule it may be taken that the wood buds are more pointed than are the fruit buds. The buds of some fruit trees, most usually in dry seasons, are troublesome to peel away from their wood, the wood very frequently pulling out the middle of the bud with it, as described above. When this is very marked, it is a good plan to pierce the wood just behind the bud with the point of the knife, so as actually to cut it away from the bud at that point, before beginning to peel it from the bark. The shoots selected for budding, whether for fruit or rose-trees, should be plump, firm and well-ripened. Watery shoots or buds are valueless.

After the budding process is completed the stock should be left untouched, neither leaves nor any other part being cut away until about November, when the binding must also be cut to allow the stock to grow. At this time the top of the stem which bears the bud may be cut back to about 3 inches above it. When the bud shoots in the spring—or possibly before—this three inches should be reduced to one, and all shoots springing from the stock should be cut away periodically through the summer. In autumn the "snag" above the bud may be cut away completely.

When the buds begin to grow they require to be protected from strong winds; otherwise they would be detached from the stem. This is done by driving a stake, A (Fig. 25), firmly into the ground, attaching it by a strong cord to the stem of the stock above and below the junction, as in the illustration, and tying the shoot of the young scion firmly to the stake above, protecting it by a bandage of hay or other substance to prevent the bark being injured.

These are general principles applicable to the majority of plants; for individual cultural details, *see* the Alphabetical List of Flowering Plants and Shrubs, chapter XXIV.

CHAPTER XXIV

ALPHABETICAL LIST OF FLOWERING PLANTS, AND ORNAMENTAL AND FLOWERING TREES AND SHRUBS

Showing the Detailed and Individual Culture, also the Best Species and Varieties

NOTE.—The words in the brackets following the varieties indicate first the colour of the flowers, then the time of blooming, and lastly the average height in inches to which the plants may be expected to grow.

Abelia.—Hardy and half-hardy evergreen and deciduous shrubs which in mild, sunny, sheltered positions may be grown out-of-doors. *Culture*— Take cuttings in late summer and strike in frame or layer in August. Plant-out in March or October in well-drained peat, loam and leaf-mould, or pot-up for the cool greenhouse. Trim to keep in shape only, cut off dead blooms and thin old wood after flowering. *Species.*— *A. floribunda* (Purple-rose, June–July, 48 in.); *A. triflora* (Pink-white, Aug.–Sept., 36–96 in.); and the hybrid *A. grandiflora* (Pink-white, Aug.–Sept., 36–48 in.).

Abies (Fir).—Handsome evergreen coniferous trees, which thrive in open positions in good loam. *Culture.*—Plant in April or October. No pruning is required. To propagate, sow in the open in March or April. *Species.*—*A. balsamea* (Balsam Fir); *A. brachyphylla* (Nikko Fir); *A. cephalonica* (Grecian Silver Fir); *A. grandis* (Giant Fir); *A. nobilis* (Noble Fir); *A. pectinata* (Silver Fir).

Abronia.—A small half-hardy annual trailing plant, thriving in sunny borders, or rock gardens, in light sandy soil. *Culture.*—Sow in pots under glass in spring and plant-out the following April or May. *A. umbellata* (Pink, Summer, 9 in.) is one of the best species.

Abutilon (Indian Mallow).—A handsome half-hardy shrub for the greenhouse, or sheltered beds and borders. *Culture.*—For bedding-out increase by means of cuttings of young wood struck in moderate heat (60° F.) during the previous autumn, or early in February, grow on, and, if for summer-bedding, plant out about the end of May. 2 parts fibrous loam to 1 part of peat and sand makes a suitable compost. Trim and cut out old wood in February. *Varieties.*—*A. Boule de Neige* (White); *A. Golden Fleece* (Yellow); *A. Red Gauntlet* (Dark Red); *A. Thompsonii* (Mottled Green and Yellow Foliage). All August to November, 18 to 24 inches.

Acacia (Mimosa).—Most of these evergreen trees and shrubs are green-house shrubs, not sufficiently hardy to plant in the open, except in warm sheltered borders during the summer months. *Culture.*—Sow seed when ripe, or take cuttings of half-matured wood with a " heel " and strike in a close frame in July or August. In the warm greenhouse *A. armata* will flower in early spring. Pot-up in summer after blooming, in 6 to 10-inch pots, and give liquid manure while growing. Stand in a sheltered position out-of-doors in summer and take in again in September. Cut back straggling shoots after flowering. For Hardy or Rose Acacias *see* Robinia. *Species.*—*A. armata* (Yellow, Jan.–March, 3–10 ft.) ; *A. Baileyana* (Yellow, Jan.–May, 3–20 ft.) ; *A. dealbata* [Mimosa] (Yellow, Jan.–May, 3–50 ft.) ; *A. hastata* (Pale Yellow, Feb.–April, 3–4 ft.).

Acæna (New Zealand Burr).—A genus of trailing plants, the dwarf-growing kinds of which are useful rock plants. They do well in sun or shade in ordinary light sandy soil. *Culture.*—Sow under glass in March, place cuttings in a cold frame in August, or propagate by division in April. Plant-out in spring or early autumn. *Species.*—*A. adscendens* (Purple, June–Aug., 6 in.) ; *A. Buchananii* (Yellowish-red, Summer, 2–3 in.) ; *A. microphylla* (Bright Red, June–Aug., 3 in.).

Acantholimon (Prickly Thrift).—Useful little rock plants, which like a warm dry sunny position and gritty well-drained loam and are best propagated by means of cuttings with a " heel " in July, in a cold frame, or by layering. *Species.*—*A. androsaceum* (White) ; *A glumaceum* (Pale Pink). Both July–August, 5 to 6 inches.

Acanthus (Bear's Breech).—A hardy perennial useful for beds, borders and cold greenhouse. It likes a sunny sheltered site with light soil. For culture, *see* Perennials, p. 128. *Species.*—*A. mollis,* var. *latifolius* (Rose, Summer, 24 in.) ; *A. mollis* (Lilac, Pink or White, Aug., 40 in.) ; *A. spinosus* (Purple-pink or White, July and Aug., 40 in.).

Acer (Maple).—Hardy deciduous trees for the pleasure grounds and park in positions with well-drained ordinary soil. *Culture.*—Plant in November. No pruning is required. Propagate by means of seed, layering and budding in the open in August.

Achillea (Milfoil, Yarrow and Double Sneezewort).—This genus includes a number of hardy perennials. The dwarf-growing kinds are useful for the rock garden. They like a sunny situation and light, dry, ordinary soil. For culture, *see* Perennials, p. 128. *Species.*—*A. argentea* (White, May and June, 3–4 in.) ; *A. filipendulina* (Yellow, July–Sept., 36–40 in.) ; *A. Millefolium* [Cerise Queen] (June–Aug., 24 in.) ; *A. tomentosa* (Yellow, June–Aug., 6–9 in.).

Achimenes.—A genus of tuberous-rooted plants, suitable for the living-room or greenhouse. *Culture.*—Use a compost of equal parts of leaf-mould, loam and silver sand. Plant 5 to 6 tubers an inch deep in a 5- or 6-inch pot in February, and place in the cool house. Shade from the hot sun and feed with liquid manure. To keep up a succession, commence starting them in heat in January and continue until May. Dry-off after flowering, lift rhizomes and store. Propagate by offsets in February, or by cuttings in May under glass. *Varieties.*—*A. Admiration* (Red-purple) ; *A. Celestial* (Pale Mauve) ; *A. coccinea* (Scarlet) ;

1. Cutting the "tongue" in the shoot to be layered. 2. Shoot prepared for layering, showing a cut through a joint. 3. Pegging down the layer with the "tongue" open and well in contact with the soil. The layering of carnations is best done in July and August. See page 227.

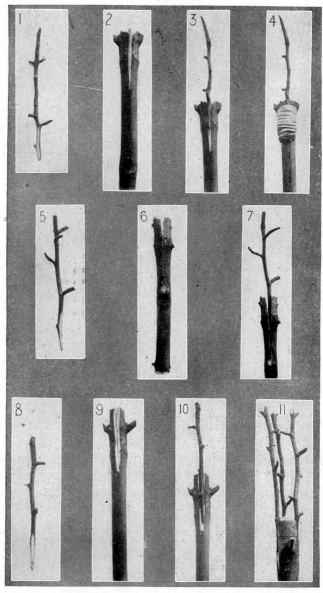

1. A scion ready for placing in the stock (2) which is prepared in the manner shown (notch-grafting). 3. Shows the scion inserted, and (4) the same, covered with clay and bound with bass. 5-7. Show the method of cleft-grafting. 8-11. Rind-grafting. See pages 196-204.

A. longiflora (Blue) ; *A. l. alba* (White) ; *A. Pink Perfection* (Rose-magenta). All July–September, 12–18 inches.

Aconite (Eranthis).—Winter Aconites like a shady position in moist sandy loam and leaf-mould. *Culture.*—Plant in October 2 inches apart and 2 inches deep. Do not lift from the ground. Propagate by means of division in October. *Species.*—*A. cilicica* (Yellow) ; *A. hyemalis* (Greenish Yellow). Both January–March, 4 inches.

Aconitum (Monkshood or Wolfsbane).—Hardy perennial, *poisonous* plants. For culture, *see* Perennials, p. 128. *Species.*—*A. Fischeri* (Pale Lilac-blue, Sept.–Oct., 36 in.) ; *A. Lycoctonum* (Yellow, July–Aug., 36 in.) ; *A. Napellus* (Blue and White, June–Oct., 48 in.).

Acorus (Sweet Flag, Sweet Sedge or Myrtle Grass).—A genus of hardy perennials 6–30 inches high, flowering in July and August. *Culture.*—Propagate by means of division in March and plant-out in sunny, marshy situation or in shallow water.

Adenophora (Gland Bellflower).—Hardy perennials which thrive in sunny borders, in well-drained ordinary soil. For culture, *see* Perennials, p. 128. *Species.*—*A. ornata* (24 in.) ; *A. liliifolia* (12–40 in.). Both have blue flowers from June–August.

Adonis (Pheasant's Eye).—A genus of useful rock plants, annuals and perennials, thriving in shade in a mixture of loam, peat and leaf-mould. For culture, *see* Annuals, p. 106, and Rock Plants, p. 135. *Species.*—*A. æstivalis* (Crimson, May–June, 12 in.) ; *A. annuus* (Blood Red, June–Aug., 12 in.) ; **A. amurensis* (Yellow, Feb.–April, 12 in.) ; **A. vernalis* (Yellow, March–April, 10 in.). Perennials marked *.

Ægle sepiaria (Hardy Orange or Bengal Quince).—A hardy deciduous shrub, which likes a sunny position in well-drained fibrous loam and leaf-mould. *Culture.*—Sow in March in a frame, or take cuttings of half-ripened shoots. Plant-out in March or October. After flowering (April or May) cut out dead wood and trim to shape only.

Æsculus (Horse Chestnut and Buckeye).—One of the most handsome of flowering trees. *Culture.*—Plant in November in a sunny position with ordinary soil. Thin out branches when overcrowded only. To propagate, sow in March, layer in autumn or graft in the spring. *Species.*—*A. carnea* (Red Horse Chestnut) ; *A. Hippocastanum fl. pl.* (Double Horse Chestnut) ; *A. Pavia* (Red Buckeye).

Æthionema (Burnt Candytuft).—A genus of dwarf-growing shrubby perennials that are excellent subjects for the rock garden. They thrive in the sun in gritty or sandy loam. *Culture.*—Sow under glass in March or insert cuttings in a cold frame in July. *Species and Varieties.*—*A. cordifolium* (Rose, June–July, 6 in.) ; *A. grandiflorum* (Rose, May–July, 12 in.) ; *A. var. Warley Rose* (Carmine-rose, May, 9 in.).

Agapanthus.—Beautiful African lilies blooming in August and September. They thrive in the open in warm sunny borders in rich sandy loam and leaf-mould, but are more suitable for the cool green-house. *Culture.*—Pot-up in March, using a 9-inch pot and compost of 2 parts loam to 1 part of leaf-mould, rotten manure and sand. A large pot or tub is required for several plants. During summer give abund-ance of water and liquid manure twice a week. In winter protect from frost and water sparingly. Large plants may be stood out during the

E.G O

summer. Sow seed under glass or propagate by means of division in March. *Species.—A. umbellatus* (Blue) ; *A. umbellatus albus* (White). Both August, 18–40 inches.

Agave.—The best known variety is the *Agave americana*, or American Aloe, which, in the cool greenhouse, usually grows from 20 to 40 inches high, though much larger plants are obtainable. *Culture.*—Pot-up firmly every 4 or 5 years in a well-drained compost of 2 parts of rich fibrous loam to 1 part of leaf-mould, sand and brick-rubble. The plants may be stood out-of-doors in summer. Propagate by means of seed in heat in February or by offsets in the summer. *Species.—A. americana* (Yellowish-green, Aug., 30 in.) ; *A. americana variegata* (Variegated) ; *A. densiflora* (Green, Sept., 40 in.).

Ageratum (Floss Flower).—A useful half-hardy annual for the rock garden, and for edgings to beds or borders. For culture, *see* Annuals, p. 107. *Species.—A. mexicanum* (Blue and White, May–Sept., 6–18 in.). *Named Varieties.*—Blue Perfection (Amethyst Blue) ; Imperial Dwarf (Deep Blue) ; Lavender Band (Lavender) ; Little Dorrit (Pale Blue) ; and Snowflake (White).

Ailanthus (Tree of Heaven).—A fine hardy deciduous tree, growing from 60 to 70 feet in height and flowering in August. *Culture.*—Plant in November in a sunny open position and ordinary soil. Thin out wood when overcrowded. To propagate, place root cuttings in a frame in August. *Species.—A. glandulosa.*

Alisma (Water Plantain).—Hardy perennials useful for bog or water margin in ordinary soil. *Culture.*—Sow in March in peat, or propagate by means of division in April, and plant in sunny position with from one to twelve inches of slow-moving water above the crowns.

Allium.—Attractive hardy bulbous plants which grow from 6 to 18 inches high, and bloom from May to July. They like a sunny position and light loam to which a little sand and leaf-mould have been added. *Culture.*—Plant in September or October 3 inches deep and 4 inches apart. Lift from the ground when overcrowded and replant immediately. Propagation is by means of seed in frame in slight heat in March, or by offsets in October. *Species.—A. Beesianum* (Blue) ; *A. cœruleum* (Blue) ; *A. Moly* [Lily Leek] (Yellow) ; *A. neapolitanum* (White) ; *A. roseum* (Lilac-rose). All May–July, 12–18 inches.

Alnus (Alder).—A deciduous tree which grows well in sunny open positions in moist swampy soil. *Culture.*—Plant in November. No pruning is necessary. Propagate by seed, layering or grafting.

Aloe.—A greenhouse evergreen plant, generally in the form of a rosette. Plant firmly in summer in pots or tubs in a compost of sandy loam, peat and well-rotted manure. Stand in a sunny position and water freely in summer, but sparingly in winter (Temp. 45° to 60° F.). Propagate by means of suckers in spring or sow seed in heat.

Alonsoa (Mask Flower).—A pretty half-hardy dwarf annual suitable for sunny beds, or for pot culture, in the cool greenhouse. *Culture, see* Annuals, p. 107. If " stopped-back " periodically through the summer some can be lifted and potted-up in September for flowering indoors, during autumn and winter. *Pot Culture.*—Pot-up in 5 to 6-inch pots, keep close for three weeks, then give ample light and air. Pinch out young shoots occasionally. Water carefully and give weak liquid manure until buds show colour. *Species.—A. linifolia, A. miniata,* and *A. Warscewiczii.* All Scarlet, July–August, 18 inches.

Aloysia (Sweet Verbena).—Only one kind of this sweet-smelling deciduous shrub is grown to any extent, *A. citriodora,* with purple blooms in August. It can be grown in the open or against a wall in the South and West of England and in other parts it is suitable for the cold greenhouse, but requires protection from the frost in winter, even under shelter. *Culture.*—Re-pot into a smaller pot in the spring, in rich mould, loam and sandy peat or leaf-mould for preference ; when well rooted transfer to a larger pot. It succeeds also in the warm greenhouse. Cut young shoots hard back to the old wood in February and pinch back the young shoots from time to time, but not later than June. Propagate by means of cuttings of young wood in gentle heat in spring.

Alstroemeria (Herb Lily or Peruvian Lily).—Tuberous-rooted perennials, some of which are hardy and suitable for sunny borders, in which the soil is well drained, rich and light, with a little old mortar, leaf-mould and sand mixed with it. They are also useful for pot culture. *Culture.*—Propagate by means of division in spring or autumn. Plant 4 inches deep and 10 inches apart. Water freely and mulch in summer when growing and protect from severe frost in winter. Do not lift the rhizomes. Seed may also be sown in gentle heat in January, the seedlings being planted out in May or June. *Species.—A. aurantiaca* (Orange-red, May–Aug., 30–36 in.) ; *A. chilensis* (Red, Pink or Yellow, July, 30 in.) ; **A. Pelegrina* (Pinkish with Purple Spots, July, 12–18 in.). Greenhouse species marked *.

Alyssum (Madwort).—Useful dwarf annuals and perennials for sunny beds, edgings, or rock garden with sandy soil. For culture, *see* Annuals, p. 106, *and* Perennials, p. 128. *Species.—A. maritimum* [Sweet Alyssum] (White, May–July, 4–6 in.) ; **A. montanum* (Yellow, May–June, 3 in.) ; **A. saxatile citrinum* (Yellow, May, 6–10 in.). Perennials species marked *.

Amarantus (Love-lies-bleeding, and The Prince's Feather).—Half-hardy annuals growing from 12 to 36 inches high and flowering from July to October. They thrive in sunny beds or borders with shallow, light soil, or in the cool greenhouse. For culture, *see* Annuals, p. 107. *Species.—A. caudatus* (Crimson, July–Oct., 10–40 in.) ; *A. c. var. ruber* (Crimson, with Carmine Foliage, July, 30 in.) ; *A. c. var. tricolor* (Crimson, with Red, Yellow and Green Foliage, July, 36 in.).

Amaryllis Belladonna (Belladonna Lily).—This beautiful species is very variable in the size and colour of its flowers, frequently producing flowers variously shaded from white to a reddish or purplish hue. There is only one species. Some of the varieties are *A. Belladonna rubra major, A. Belladonna pallida,* and *A. Belladonna Parkeri,* a cross between *A. Belladonna* and *Brunsvigia Josephinœ.* This plant succeeds out-doors in well-drained soil at the foot of warm plant-house walls. The bulbs should be planted during the summer, when they are dormant, being covered with about 6 inches of rich loamy soil mixed with leaf-mould and silver sand. If planted too deep they do not flower freely. The blooms are produced during August and September, and the leaves, in common with those of many South African bulbs, during the winter and spring. Leave the bulbs in the ground but protect with fibre in winter. *Greenhouse Culture.*— If grown in the greenhouse, they require very large pots or pans. Even so, they do not flower freely.

Amelanchier (June Berry or Service Berry).—Hardy deciduous trees and shrubs that thrive in sunny sheltered positions and in moderately light and moist soil. *Culture.*—Plant in October or November. Do not prune, but cut out dead wood and thin when necessary after flowering. Propagate by means of seed in March, by grafting on the thorn in March, by cuttings struck in the open in October or by layering. *Species.*—*A. alnifolia ; A. canadensis ; A. vulgaris* (Shrub). All White, April–May, 6–30 feet.

Ammobium alatum var. grandiflorum (Everlasting Sunflower).— A beautiful half-hardy biennial, growing about 18 inches high and blooming from June to August. Excellent for warm, sunny borders. For culture, *see* Biennials, p. 107.

Anagallis (Pimpernel).—Half-hardy annuals, suitable for a warm, sunny rock garden or greenhouse. For culture, *see* Annuals, p. 107. *Species.*—*A. arvensis, var. grandiflora* (Various, Summer, 6 in.) ; *A. tenella* (Bog Pimpernel), said to be perennial, (Pink, July, 3 in.).

Anchusa (Alkanet).—The annuals are unimportant. The half-hardy biennials and perennials like a sunny position, but do not require very rich soil. For culture, *see* Biennials, p. 107, *and* Perennials, p. 128. *Species.*—*A. capensis* (Blue, July, 20 in.) ; **A. italica var. Dropmore* (Rich Blue, June–Oct., 40–60 in.) ; **A. myosotidiflora* (Pale Blue, May–July, 12 in.). Perennials species marked *.

Andromeda (Marsh or Wild Rosemary).—Hardy, evergreen, heath-like shrubs, which thrive in the sun in boggy or moist peaty soil, and also make good pot plants for the cold greenhouse. *Culture.*—Plant in October. Propagate by means of ripe seed in pans or boxes under glass in October, divide the roots, or layer in September. *Species.*— *A. polifolia* (Rose-white, May and June, 20 in.). *Vars. angustifolia* and *major.*

Androsace (Rock Jasmine).—Perennial rock plants which like a moderately sunny position and a mixture of loam, peat and 30 per cent. grit. *A. foliosa* and *A. lactea* require some limestone and no peat in the soil. For culture, *see* Perennials, p. 128. *Species.*—*A. carnea* (Rose, May, 3 in.) ; *A. foliosa* (Rose-lilac, May–June, 6 in.) ; *A. sarmentosa* (Rose, White Eye, May–June, 4 in.).

Anemone (Windflower).—Anemones of both kinds, hardy fibrous-rooted herbaceous perennials and tuberous-rooted, thrive best in semi-shade in a moist, light, rich medium loam, but generally succeed in any which is well drained, well dug and manured. The dwarf-growing kinds are excellent for the rock garden, while *St. Brigid* anemones are favourites for beds and borders. *Culture.*—(Tuberous.) Plant from October to the end of March. Set the tubers about 3 inches deep and 5 inches apart. The roots are best left undisturbed, but may be taken up as soon as the leaves have died down for removal or for drying-off and replanting in the autumn. A change of position is recommended at intervals of two or three years. These anemones may be propagated by means of division of dry rhizomes from September to March. (Fibrous-rooted Herbaceous Perennials.) Sow in the reserve garden in April, thinly in drills a foot apart and ¾ inch deep. Shade from the sun until the seed is up. Thin-out the seedlings to 3 inches apart and leave them in the reserve garden until the leaves have died down after flowering the following spring, then lift, store, and replant in their flowering positions 8 inches apart early in September. *Greenhouse Culture.*—Plant in the autumn, using 6-inch pans and a compost of deep, rich sandy loam, and place in the cool greenhouse. Dress annually with fertilizer and lift the tubers when the foliage has died down. *Species.*—*A. alpina* (Cream, May–July, 18 in.) ; *A. Hepatica* (Blue, Red, Pink and White, March–May, 6 in.) ; *A. japonica* [*Charmeuse*] (White-Rose, Aug.–Oct., 30 in.) ; **A. apennina* (Blue or White, March–May, 9 in.) ; **A. blanda* (Blue, Pink, White, March–April, 6 in.) ; **A. coronaria* (Various, May–June, 12 in.) ; **A. fulgens* (Scarlet, May–June, 12 in.) ; **A. hortensis* (Purple-rose and Whitish, April, 10 in.) ; **A. nemorosa* (Blue or White, April, 6 in.). Tuberous species marked *.

Anthemis (Chamomile).—Hardy perennials that like a sunny border or rock garden with sandy loam. For culture, *see* Perennials, p. 128. *Species and Varieties.*—*A. montana* (White, June–August, 12 in.) ; *A. tinctoria* (Yellow, June–Oct., 18–24 in.) ; *A. tinctoria var. Kelwayi* (Pale Yellow, June–Oct., 18 in.).

Anthericum Liliago (St. Bernard's Lily).—Hardy tuberous-rooted perennials, which thrive in a warm, sunny border with moist, light, rich soil, or in a 6-inch pot in the cold greenhouse. They grow to a height of 30 inches and carry white flowers in June and July. For culture, *see* Perennials, p. 128.

Antholyza paniculata (African Corn Flag).—Hardy bulbous-rooted perennial, which thrives in a sunny position in well-drained borders with sandy loam, and grows to about 30 inches high, carrying scarlet and yellow blooms from June to August. *Culture.*—Propagate by offsets in March or October, and plant 5 inches deep and 6 in. apart.

Anthyllis (Kidney Vetch and Ladies' Fingers).—Pretty little rock plants which like a sunny position and warm, gritty loam. They flower in June and July and reach a height of 10 inches. For culture, *see* Rock Plants, p. 135.

Antirrhinum (Snapdragon).—These are grown both as biennials and perennials. They like a dry, well-drained, well-manured loam, and a sunny position, and are extremely useful for dry beds, borders, wall, rock and wild gardens. For culture, *see* Biennials, p. 107, *and* Perennials, p. 128. *Varieties.*—TALL.—*Cottage Maid* (Pink and White) ; *Crimson King ; Moonlight* (Apricot) ; *Primrose King ; Scarlet Prince ; Snowflake* (White, tinged Yellow) ; *Torch Light* (Orange-scarlet) ; and *Yellow King.* All flower from April to October, and grow from 30 to 48 inches in height. INTERMEDIATE.—*Amber Queen* (Yellow and Pink) ; *Black Prince* (Deep Crimson) ; *Bonfire* (Orange-red) ; *Bronze Queen ; Buff Beauty ; Coccinea* (Orange-scarlet) ; *Cottage Maid* (Pale Pink and White) ; *Mauve Beauty ; Pink Perfection ; Prima Donna* (Apricot and

White) ; *Rosy Queen* ; *The Fawn* (Apricot) ; and *Yellow Queen*. All flower from April to October, and grow from 15 to 30 inches in height. DWARF.—*White Prince, Yellow Queen*. Both these flower from April to October, and grow 6–15 inches in height.

Aponogeton distachyum (Cape Water Hawthorn or Pond Weed).— A hardy aquatic plant which produces masses of white flowers from May to October. *Culture.*—Propagate by means of offsets or division in March. Plant in a weighted basket in slowly-moving water with from 6 to 30 inches of water above the crowns.

Aquilegia (Columbine).—Hardy herbaceous perennials and biennials, that thrive in rather shady borders in moist, cool, well-drained, deep loam and leaf-mould. They are also useful for greenhouse culture and the dwarf kinds for the rock garden. For culture, *see* Perennials, p. 128, *and* Rock Plants, p. 135. *Species and Varieties.—A. alpina* (Violet-blue, May and June, 10 in.) ; *A. cærulea* (Pale Blue and White, May–July, 12–18 in.) ; *A. chrysantha* (Golden Yellow, May–July, 30 in.) ; *A. Skinneri* (Dark Scarlet and Greenish Yellow, May–July, 24 in.).

Arabis (Rock Cress).—Hardy perennial rock plants which like a sunny position in ordinary well-drained soil or sandy loam. For culture, *see* Rock Plants, p. 135. *Species.—A. alpina* (White, May–July, 6 in.) ; *A. albida fl. pl.* (White [Double], May–June, Trailer) ; *A. androsacea* (Rose, May, Trailer) ; *A. muralis rosea* (Rose, June, 6 in.).

Aralia.—Hardy shrubs which like a sunny position and sandy soil. *Culture.*—Plant in November. No pruning is required. Propagation is by means of root cuttings in autumn, or suckers in spring. *Species.— A. chinensis* (Angelica Tree) ; *A. spinosa* (Hercules' Club).

Araucaria (Chili Pine or Monkey Puzzle).—Coniferous trees which like a sunny position and well-drained, deep loam. *Culture.*—Plant in April or September. No pruning is necessary. Propagate by seeds under glass. These trees are unsuitable for town gardens. *Species.— A. imbricata. Pot Culture.—A. excelsa* (Norfolk Island Pine) is only suitable for the cool greenhouse. Pot-up in March, using two parts of sandy loam to one part of leaf-mould. Propagate by means of cuttings in heat in October, or by " ringing."

Arbutus (Strawberry Tree).—Evergreen shrubs which thrive in a warm, sunny, sheltered position in moist, well-drained peat and loam. Trim back the long straggling shoots in April and cut out dead wood. To propagate sow seed in a frame when ripe. Grow in pots till ready to plant-out and do not transplant more than necessary. Cuttings of young shoots may also be taken in July and struck in a frame. *Species.—A. Andrachne* (White, tinted Green, March and April, 10–30 ft.) ; *A. andrachnoides* (White, Winter, 15–30 ft.) ; *A. Menziesii* [Madrona], (White, May, 20–100 ft.) ; *A. Unedo* (Cream-pink, Sept.– Oct., 10–20 ft.).

Arctotis grandis.—Half-hardy annual for sunny, sheltered beds and borders. It grows about 24 inches high and carries pearl-grey, daisy-like flowers in summer. For culture, *see* Annuals, p. 107.

Arenaria (Sandwort).—Dwarf hardy perennial creeping plants, useful for carpeting, for the paved garden and for the rock garden. They like a moist, sandy, gritty loam. For culture, *see* Rock Plants, p. 135.

A. balearica likes a shady spot and ample leaf-mould in the compost, but *A. montana* loves to tumble over the sides of a rock in full sun. *Species.—A. balearica* (White, May and June, 3 in.) ; *A. montana grandiflora* (White, May–July, 3 in.) ; *A. purpurascens* (Reddish-purple, June and July, 3 in.),

Aristolochia.—A deciduous perennial climber. Some species, such as *A. Sipho*, the Dutchman's Pipe (Brown and Yellow, June–July, 20 ft.), are hardy in sheltered situations, but others are only suitable for the greenhouse. *Culture.*—Sow under glass in March, or take cuttings under glass in April. Plant-out in the following March (hardy species) or in the greenhouse in a mixture of light, sandy loam and leaf-mould. Thin-out the wood during the spring.

Armeria (Thrift, Sea Pink, Cushion Pink, etc.).—Dwarf hardy perennials mainly seen in the rock garden. They like a sunny, open position in dry, deep loam. For culture, *see* Perennials, p. 128. *Species.—A. cæspitosa* (Pinky-lilac, June, 4 in.) ; *A. maritima* (Rose, Red, Lilac, White, June–July, 6–12 in.) ; *A. plantaginea* (Rose, May–July, 18 in.).

Arnebia (Prophet Flower).—Hardy annuals and dwarf perennials which thrive in the sun in sandy loam and are excellent for border or rock garden. For culture, *see* Annuals, p. 106, *and* Perennials, p. 128. *Species and Varieties.—A. cornuta* (Yellow, Black Dot, June–Aug., 15 in.) ; *A. Griffithii* (Deep Yellow, June–Aug., 10 in.) ; **A. echioides* (Pale Yellow, Black Dot, May–Aug., 9 in.). * Denotes perennial.

Artemisia (Old Man, Lad's Love, etc.).—Hardy herbaceous perennials and evergreen and deciduous shrubs thriving in ordinary soil. Several of the dwarf-growing kinds make excellent rock plants. *Culture.*—Propagate by means of division in October, or by cuttings in July. *Species.—A. argentea* (Yellow or White, June–Sept., 20 in.) ; *A. lactiflora* (Cream-white, Aug.–Oct., 60 in.) ; *A. lanata* (Yellow [Silver Foliage], July–Aug., 6 in.).

Arum Lily (Richardia).—The Arum Lily is easy to cultivate either in the greenhouse or in a room. Re-pot every October in rich, light mould, preferably loam with equal parts of sand and cow-dung, the offsets having been removed, and the old soil well shaken out. A 6-inch pot may be used for each plant, or three may be placed in a 9 to 10-inch pot. From this time till June, or earlier if the plants have flowered, they should have abundance of water and occasional doses of liquid manure ; it is best to keep the pot always standing in a deep saucer full of water. After this, however, they must be planted-out in rich soil, or stood in the open in the semi-shade, kept moist, and be given occasional doses of manure water till October, when the same treatment should be repeated. Propagate by means of offsets. The yellow species are less hardy and thrive best in the warm greenhouse. Pot-up in February. Withhold water gradually after flowering and keep the pot in a frost-proof frame through the winter. *Species and Varieties.—Richardia africana* ; *R. africana Childsiana* (White, 24 in.) ; *R. africana Little Gem* (White, dwarf) ; *R. Rehmannii* (Rose) ; *R. melanoleuca* (Purple and Yellow) ; and *R. Elliottiana* (Yellow, Aug., 24 in.). The arum (except the yellow varieties) usually flowers in April.

Arundinaria.—A genus of bamboo, the species of which thrive in a moist climate in a deep, rich loam holding ample leaf-mould, and given protection from north and east winds. Of the hardy kinds *A. japonica* (Syn. Bambusa Metake), 10 to 15 feet, is the most generally grown. There are also many half-hardy species for the warm greenhouse. *Culture.*—Propagate by means of division in May and plant in sheltered positions. Cut out all dead wood in April. See also Bambusa. *Other Species (Hardy).*—*A. Falconeri* (25 ft.); *A. nitida* (10 ft.); *A. Simonii* (15 ft.); *A. Veitchii* (15 in.); *A. Fortunei* dwarf (20 in.).

Arundo (Great Reed).—A perennial which thrives in semi-shade on slightly swampy banks in light, rich loam, and grows to a height of 10 feet. *Culture.*—Propagate by means of division in May. *Species.*— *A. Donax* (Glaucous Foliage, 10 ft.); *A. Donax variegata* (Leaves Striped White, 10 ft.).

Ash (Fraxinus).—These well-known trees like a sunny position and ordinary soil. *Culture.*—Plant in November. Thin-out branches when overcrowded. To propagate sow in a frame in autumn.

Asparagus Fern (Sparrow Grass).—Hardy and greenhouse evergreen and deciduous climbing and trailing plants which thrive in a compost of two parts loam to one part of leaf-mould, peat and sand. *Culture.* —Pot-up in March using 6 to 10-inch pots. Syringe and water well in summer. Propagate by means of seed in March in heat, by cuttings in a propagating case at the same period, or by division in March. The hardy species do well in a warm, sunny position in rich, sandy soil. See also Smilax. *Species.*—*A. plumosus* and var. *nanus*; *A. retrofractus*; *A. Sprengeri*; *A. tennuissimus*; *A. verticillatus.*

Asperula (Woodruff).—Hardy annuals and dwarf-growing perennials useful for beds, borders, edgings, rock garden, etc. The annuals like semi-shade; the perennials a sunny site, and soil with ample grit in it. For culture, see Annuals, p. 106, and Perennials, p. 128. *Species and Varieties.*—*A. azurea* (Light Blue, June–Sept., 4 in.); *A. Gussonii* (Rose, May–Aug., 4 in.); *A. odorata* (White, May–June, 9 in.); *A. suberosa* (Pink [Silver Foliage], June and July, 3 in.).

Asphodel (Asphodelus).—Mostly hardy perennials that thrive in the sun in any soil, though rich, sandy loam is most suitable. For culture, see Perennials, p. 128. *Species.* *A. acaulis* (Pink, May–July, 12–24 in.); *A. luteus* (Golden-Yellow, May–July, 24–36 in.); *A. ramosus* [King's Spear] (White, May–July, 24–36 in.).

Aster. The China Aster (Callistephus).—A half-hardy, autumn-flowering annual particularly adapted for small beds, edgings, the rock garden, or for pot culture. All varieties thrive best in a deep rich light soil and in hot dry weather should be mulched with well-rotted manure, and frequently supplied with manure water. For culture, see Annuals, p. 107. *Pot Culture.*—Sow in the open in May. Pot-up three plants in a 6-inch pot in a compost of two-thirds fibrous loam and one-third well-decayed manure. Stand in the open on a hard bed of ashes or on slates and cover to the rims with fibre. Transfer under glass as soon as the buds begin to colour. *Species and Varieties.*— *Callistephus chinensis* [single] (18 in.); *Chrysanthemum-flowered* (12 in.); *Comet* [Broad Florets] (24 in.); *Dwarf Bouquet* (6–9 in.); *Giant Ray*

[Stiff and Prominent Florets] (18 in.) ; *Mignon* (10 in.) ; *Ostrich Plume* [Branching with Double flowers] (18 in.) ; *Quilled* (Tubular Florets) ; *Pæony-flowered* [Incurving Florets] (18 in.) ; *Victoria* [Double] (15 in.). (*See also* Michaelmas Daisy.)

Astragalus (Milk Vetch).—Hardy dwarf-growing plants of the broom genus, some of which make excellent subjects for the rock garden. They thrive in the sun in deep loam, sand and mortar. *Culture.*— Sow in the spring or summer, or propagate by division in autumn. *Species.—A. alpinus* (Purple, June–Aug., Trailing) ; *A. danicus albus* (White, May–July, 5 in.) ; *A. massiliensis* [*syn. Tragacantha*] (Violet-purple, May–July, 24 in.).

Astrantia (Masterwort).—Hardy perennials, which like a shady position with cool, moist loam and leaf-mould. The dwarf-growing kinds are excellent for the rock garden. Propagate by means of root division in spring or autumn. *Species.—A. major* (White, tinged Pink, May–July, 18 in.) ; *A. minor* (Pale Rose, May–July, 6 in.).

Aubrietia (Rock Cress).—Pretty evergreen perennial trailing plants, which are useful for edgings, or the rock garden. They thrive in the sun in dry, rich, sandy loam and leaf-mould. For culture, *see* Perennials, p. 128. *Varieties.—Bridesmaid* (Blush-pink) ; *Crimson King ; Dr. Mules* (Violet-blue) ; *Lavender ; Lilac Queen* (Rose Lilac) ; *Magician* Purple) ; *Warbarrow* (Rose). All April–June, 4 inches.

Aucuba (Spotted or Variegated Laurel).—A hardy evergreen shrub, well suited for shady places and well-drained ordinary soil. It may also be grown in large pots. *Culture.*—Plant in March or October. Cut back long weak shoots in May. To propagate, take cuttings and strike in the open in autumn, or sow seed in frame when ripe.

Auricula (Primula auricula).—Auriculas are divided into two classes, namely, Show Auriculas and Alpine Auriculas. The best compost is a good fibrous rather heavy loam, adding a little decayed manure and leaf-mould, with a liberal addition of silver sand, and a sprinkling of charcoal or wood ashes. *Culture.—(Show Auriculas.)* Sow in pans in a warm house on the surface of a compost of half loam and half leaf-mould and gritty sand, when ripe, or from January to March. Moist moss should be kept over the surface of the soil until the seedlings are up. When these have three or four leaves, transplant into 3-inch pots. Four to five-inch pots are large enough for full-sized plants. Where it is essential that the flowers shall come true to type and in the case of choice specimens, it is better to propagate by means of offsets or root division in February or March, or in August after re-potting. Offsets may be placed singly in 3-inch pots, or three in a larger pot. Keep the pots in the open in a cool, sheltered site and remove to the cool greenhouse at the end of September. The auricula blossoms, and is in full growth from February to June, when the plants should be removed from the glazed shelter under which they have been flowering, being placed in the open air on a shelf or stage having a north or north-east aspect, and if possible with some glass lights rigged up overhead. In August, when the fresh growth commences, the plants should be re-potted, the tap-roots being shortened with a sharp knife. In November place the plants under glass. Keep the plants within 18 inches of the glass, but shade from direct sun. Never allow water to fall on the foliage or to settle on the leaves at the base. Very little artificial heat is required and a close atmosphere is fatal. (*Alpine Auriculas.*) Sow seed in a light sandy soil in a little heat in March. Prick-off into boxes as soon as four leaves have formed. Harden-off in a shady cold frame at the end of May. Plant-out 6 inches apart in September or October in a partially shaded position facing north, in well-drained rather heavy loam and cow-manure. Lift, divide and re-plant triennially after flowering. *Varieties* (*Show*).— White Edged : *Acme* and *Heather Bell.* Green Edged : *Dr. Horner* and *Prince Charming.* Grey Edged : *George Rudd* and *George Lightbody.* Self : *Gordon Douglas* and *Harrison Weir.* (*Alpines*).—*Admiration, Day Dream, Firefly, Majestic, Roxborough, Silver Wood.*

Azalea.—Azaleas are distinguished as Ghents (deciduous), Mollis (deciduous), and Indian (evergreen). The former two are more suitable for open-air culture and the last for greenhouse decoration. A compost of sandy peat and loam or two-thirds fibrous loam and one-third leaf-mould is suitable for all species, but they will grow quite well in almost any soil which does not contain lime or chalk. *Culture.* —For outdoor culture, *see* Rhododendrons. *Pot Culture* (*A. indica and hybrids*).—Pot-up firmly from October to November using 6 to 10-inch pots and the compost mentioned above. Keep in a cold frame until late November, then move in succession into the house and gradually acclimatize to moist, warm conditions. After flowering prune straggling shoots and remove all dead blooms. Re-pot if necessary (usually every second or third year), place the pots in the warmest corner and syringe overhead. Stand in the open in a cool, sheltered position on a bed of ashes or shingle from June to September, and water liberally and syringe overhead morning and evening in dry, warm weather. In September return to the house. *A. mollis*, although hardy, is also useful for the warm greenhouse. *Forcing.—See* p. 173. To propagate, take cuttings of half-matured wood early in summer and strike in a frame (50° to 60° F.) ; sow in moist heat and fine sandy peat in spring ; or layer. *Species.*—(*Hardy*)—*A. mollis* (Red, Yellow, etc.) ; *A. nudiflora* (Pink or White) ; *A. pontica* (Yellow). All May-June, 3-6 feet. (*Greenhouse*)—*A. indica* (many shades of colour). They flower from December to May, according to the temperature of the house, and grow from 1 to 3 feet high. Named varieties are almost innumerable, and growers' catalogues should be consulted.

Azara.—Evergreen shrubs and climbers that are almost hardy, and which like a warm, sheltered position and well-drained sandy-loam. *Culture.*—Plant in March or October. Thin out the branches when necessary, but otherwise do not prune. Propagate by means of cuttings under glass in summer or by layering in spring. *A. microphylla* is a beautiful shrub with pale yellow flowers in early spring.

Balsam (Impatiens).—A pretty half-hardy annual for sunny beds or borders with rich soil or for the greenhouse. *Culture.—See* Annuals, page 107. Support with neat stakes. *Pot Culture.*—Pot-up as required, using 5 to 6-inch pots and a compost of half loam and half rotten cow-dung and leaf-mould with a little sand, and stand near the glass in a cool greenhouse. Syringe overhead, ventilate, and water liberally. As soon as the buds begin to form, water twice a week with a weak liquid manure. Do not " stop " back. When large specimens are desired, shift into 8 to 10-inch pots, using the richest compost available, and plunge the pots into spent hops or tan and feed with manure water. *Species and Varieties.—Impatiens Balsamina* (many vars.) ; *I. Holstii* (Vermilion) ; *I. Oliverii* (Mauve) ; *I. Sultanii* (Rose).

Bambusa (Bamboo).—There are three great classes of bamboos, namely, *Arundinaria, Bambusa* and *Phyllostachys.* Most species do well in the open, especially if the soil is of a moist, deep, light loamy nature, and has some peat or leaf-mould in it, but in exposed situations they require some protection. The dwarfer kinds are suitable as pot plants. *Culture.*—Propagate by means of division in May. Cut out dead canes in April. *Pot Culture.*—Pot-up in March in a well-drained compost of two-thirds loam and one-third leaf-mould and sharp sand. Water liberally, syringe well overhead in summer, and give weak liquid manure twice a week during the growing period. A moist and moderately warm atmosphere is essential. *Species.—(Hardy)—B. disticha* (2 ft.) ; and *B. quadrangularis* (4–8 ft.). *(Greenhouse)—Arundinaria Fortunei variegata* (Striped Silver, 2 ft.) ; *A. pumila* (1–2 ft.) ; and *Phyllostachys ruscifolia* (1–2 ft.).

Bartonia (Mentzelia Lindleyi).—A pretty little hardy annual for the border or rock garden. It grows to a height of 15 inches and bears yellow flowers from June to October. For culture, *see* Annuals, p. 106.

Begonia.—These plants thrive in sunny beds and borders with rich loam, and are also extremely useful in the greenhouse.

Culture.—(Tuberous-rooted Species.)—For bedding out or for greenhouse decoration June to October. Sow in February under glass (Temp. 65° F.) in a finely sifted and just moist compost of two-thirds loam and one-third leaf-mould and sand. Water before and after sowing and keep the seed-pan moist. Prick off the seedlings into shallow boxes. Pot-off singly into pots and plant-out in May or June, or pot-up into 5-inch pots for the greenhouse, keep near the glass, and shade when the sun is hot. Particular varieties may be propagated in spring by means of leaf cuttings. Ordinary stem cuttings may also be taken in summer. When starting tubers, they should be planted flat or hollow side uppermost in February or March, and just covered in shallow trays in heat (60° F.) with moist sandy loam and well-rotted manure for soil. Water in moderation until growth commences. If for summer bedding, harden-off in May in a cold frame and plant-out in June, or, if for the greenhouse, pot-up in 4-inch pots in a compost of two-thirds loam and one-third leaf-mould, well-rotted manure and sand, re-potting when pot-bound into 7-to 8-inch pots. Water well in summer, shade from hot sun, and once the roots have filled the pots, feed with weak manure-water twice a week. Stake any shoots that need support and pick off all dead blooms. Greenhouse temperature 55° F. winter to 70° F. summer. The tubers should be lifted in October when the frost has turned the foliage black. If they must be removed from the beds before this, lift them with a good " ball " of soil, pack in boxes, and place in a sheltered spot to finish ripening. Then shake the soil and foliage away from the roots, allow them to dry for a day or so and store in dry soil in boxes in a cool but frost-proof place. Tuberous begonias in pots must be gradually dried-off and stood in a frost-proof shed or frame for the winter.

Culture.—(*Fibrous-rooted Species.*)—This is a large and varied class, including as it does a large number of species and varieties of a sub-shrubby habit, which require an intermediate or greenhouse temperature. Some of them flower more or less all the year round, and a few of them may be used for summer-bedding. The most important for this purpose are the many beautiful varieties of *B. semperflorens,* which may be raised from seed sown during January in a temperature of 60° F., or by means of basal cuttings from plants lifted and potted up and kept in a warm house over the winter. The sub-shrubby and perennial species, generally, are propagated by means of ordinary cuttings, or by means of leaf-cuttings, in a temperature of from 60° to 70° F. The winter-flowering section, which is represented by *Gloire de Lorraine* and its varieties, may be increased by means of leaf-cuttings, or by young basal shoots. They are usually secured from plants that have flowered and that have been rested for a few weeks. These are then partly cut back and started in a temperature of from 65° to 70° F., cuttings being secured during March. The other winter-flowering section, which is represented by varieties raised from crossing the species *B. socotrana* with the tuberous-rooted varieties, are by no means easy to grow successfully, and require very careful management during their resting period. After flowering, they should be stood in a house with a temperature of from 55° to 60° F. They should have very little water at the root, on the other hand, they must not suffer from dryness. In May give more water, and when the young shoots are about three inches in length, they should be secured as cuttings, and inserted singly in small pots of sandy compost. They root readily in a close case with a bottom heat of 70° F. During the summer months they should be grown in an average temperature of from 55° to 65° F.

Culture of Ornamental and Variegated-leaved Species.—Pot-up in March or April in a compost as recommended above, keep in a moist atmosphere, never letting the temperature fall below 50° F., and shading from the strong sun. At that time, water liberally and give a little weak liquid manure. Decrease the water supply in winter, but do not dry off entirely. Propagate by means of seed, leaf-cuttings, or by cuttings of unflowered shoots (Heat 60° to 65° F.).

For species and varieties see growers' catalogues.

Bellis (Daisy).—Dwarf-growing hardy perennials, which thrive in the sun in moderately rich soil. For culture, *see* Perennials, p. 128. They grow from 6 to 12 inches high and flower in May.

Benthamia (Bentham's Strawberry Tree, Cornus capitata).—Half-hardy evergreen shrubs which may be grown in the open, in warm, sheltered situations in the south. *Culture.*—Plant in October or April in rich, moist loam. Propagate by means of ripe seed sown in a cool greenhouse, or by layering in September or October. *B. fragifera* (Cream-pink, Spring, 12 ft.) is the best-known species.

Berberidopsis corallina (Coral Barberry).—A half-hardy evergreen climbing shrub which thrives in a cool greenhouse, or in a border in the south in well-drained, light loam against walls facing south or west and partially shaded. It carries coral-red flowers in June, and grows to a height of 20 feet. *Culture.*—Take cuttings early in summer, or propagate by means of layering in October. Plant-out in April and October and thin-out branches when overcrowded.

Berberis (Barberry).—Beautiful hardy flowering shrubs, evergreen and deciduous. *Culture.*—Plant evergreens from March to April or from October to November ; deciduous, November to March, in ordinary soil or sandy loam. Thin-out shoots after flowering when overcrowded and trim to shape. Trimming should be delayed until the spring in the case of shrubs grown for autumn foliage. Most species are propagated by means of seeds in the open in October, by half-matured cuttings in a frame in July or August, or by layering in August. *B. stenophylla* must be propagated by cuttings or layering. *B. Darwinii* is useful for pot culture in the cold greenhouse. Pot-up in November using 8 to 10-inch pots and a compost of two parts of sandy loam to one part of leaf-mould and rotten manure. *Species and Varieties.*—(*Evergreens*)—*B. candida* (Yellow, April–May, 2 ft.) ; *B. Darwinii* (Orange, April–May, 8–10 ft.) ; *B. stenophylla* (Yellow, April–June, 8–10 ft.). (*Deciduous*)—*B. polyantha* (Yellow, May, 6–8 ft.) ; *B. Thunbergii* (Yellow, April–May, 3 ft.) ; *B. vulgaris* (Yellow, April–May, 4–15 ft.) ; *B. Wilsonæ* (Yellow, May, 2–4 ft.).

Betula (Birch Tree).—Plant in November in a sunny, open, moist position. All species will thrive in a poor, gravelly soil. No pruning is necessary. Propagate by means of seeds, layering, or grafting. *Species.*—*B. verrucosa* (Silver Birch) ; *B. v. var. laciniata* (Cut-leaved) ; *B. v. var. pendula Youngii* (Weeping) ; and *B. v. var. purpurea* (Purple Birch).

Bignonia (Trumpet Flower).—Some of these are fine half-hardy perennial climbers, closely allied to the Tecoma, *which see*. *B. buccinatoria* (syn. Cherere) is a greenhouse plant worthy of note.

Bocconia [*syn. Macleaya*] (Plume Poppy).—A hardy perennial which thrives in sunny borders and light, rich soil. For culture, *see* Perennials, p. 128. *Species.*—*B. cordata* (Whitish-cream, June–Oct., 70 in.) ; *B. microcarpa* (Creamy-bronze, June–Oct., 90 in.).

Boltonia (False Starwort).—A hardy perennial for border or wild garden, thriving in any moist and moderately good loam. For culture, *see* Perennials, p. 128. *Species.*—*B. asteroides* (White, July–Sept., 48–60 in.) ; *B. a. decurrens* (Whitish-pink, Aug.–Sept., 48 in.).

Boronia.—Evergreen shrubs which do best in the cool greenhouse in equal parts of sandy loam, peat, and leaf-mould. *Culture.*—Pot-up from April to May in 5 to 7-inch pots. Stop-back young plants, give ample air and liquid manure while growing. Prune after flowering, and stand outdoors from June to September. To propagate, take cuttings of young shoots in May and strike in sand, peat and charcoal under glass (60° F.). *Species.*—*B. elatior* (Carmine) ; *B. heterophylla* (Cerise) ; *B. megastigma* (Brownish-purple and Yellow) ; *B. serrulata* (Scarlet). All February to April, 12 to 24 inches.

Bouvardia (Jasmine Plant).—A winter-flowering evergreen shrub which likes a mixture of fibrous loam, leaf-mould, sand, and a little well-rotted cow manure. *Culture.*—Pot-up in March in 5 to 8-inch pots. Keep in a frame from June to September, water liberally and syringe. In September return to the greenhouse and give liquid manure once the buds begin to form. Cut hard back after flowering, and stop-back young shoots until August. (Temp. 50° to 60° F. winter to 60° to 65° F. summer.) Propagate by cuttings of young shoots or root cuttings in February and March in heat (70° F.). *Varieties.*— *Bridal Wreath* (White) ; *King of Scarlets* ; *Mrs. R. Green* (Single Salmon) ; *President Garfield* (Double Pink) ; *Priory Beauty* (Pink).

Box (Buxus).—Plant in April or September, in light, well-drained soil. Clip in May and August. Propagate by means of cuttings in August or September under bell-glasses, division in September or by layering in October. *Species.*—*B. sempervirens* (Common Box) ; and vars. *aurea* (Golden) ; *argentea* (Silver) ; *myrtifolia* ; and *suffruticosa* (Dwarf-growing).

Brachycome (Swan River Daisy).—A beautiful summer-flowering, dwarf-growing, half-hardy annual. For culture, *see* Annuals, p. 107. *Varieties.*—*White Star* ; *Blue Star* ; *Red Star.* All June to Sept., 8 in.

Bravoa (Twinflower).—A half-hardy bulbous plant which likes a sunny, sheltered position in rich, light soil mixed with old leaf-mould. It grows about 15 inches high and flowers in July and August. *Culture.* —Plant in a warm border or in the greenhouse in September, 4 inches deep and 6 inches apart, and protect with fibre during winter.

Brevoortia (Crimson Satin Flower).—Half-hardy bulbous summer-flowering plants, growing to a height of 30 inches. For culture, *see* Brodiæa.

Brodiæa (Californian or Missouri Hyacinth).—Hardy and half-hardy bulbous plants, that thrive in well-drained, deep, sandy soil mixed with leaf-mould, in sunny borders, in the cool greenhouse, or in the rock garden. *Culture.*—Plant in October, 3 inches deep and 5 inches apart. Protect with ashes during winter, and lift the bulbs from the soil every fourth year only. Propagate by means of offsets in October. *Species.*—*B. coccinea* [*syn. Brevoortia Ida-Maia*] (Dark Crimson and Green, Summer, 20 in.) ; *B. grandiflora* (Violet-blue, June and July, 15 in.) ; *B. ixioides* (Yellow, Summer, 6 in.) ; *B. uniflora* (White or Blue, April–May, 6 in.) ; *B. volubilis* [*syn. Stropholirion californicum*] (Rosy-purple, Summer, Climber).

Bryanthus.—A hardy trailing evergreen shrub that thrives in sunny or partially shaded positions in moist, but well-drained, sandy peat, but which will grow quite well in ordinary soil. *Culture.*—Plant in October or March ; no pruning is required. Propagation is by means of cuttings in a frame in October, or by layering at that time.

Buckthorn (Rhamnus).—These small trees will do well almost anywhere, provided they have shelter from the wind. *Culture.*—Plant in the late autumn or early spring, and prune in February. Propagate by means of cuttings in the open in September, by layering in October or March, or sow seed outdoors in September. *Rhamnus alaternus* (Evergreen, 12 ft.) is a good kind.

Buddleia.—Beautiful flowering shrubs. Most species are not quite hardy enough to endure severe weather out of doors, but flourish in well-drained, deep, ordinary soil or good loam in warm, sunny, sheltered positions, or in the greenhouse. *Culture.*—Plant *B. globosa* (Orange Ball Tree) in March or-October. Do not prune *B. alternifolia* or *B. globosa*, merely cut out a little old wood after flowering, but in the case of *B. variabilis* cut last year's shoots back to within 10 inches of the old wood in February. Propagation is by means of cuttings in a frame in late summer or autumn, or by means of seed when ripe. *Hardy Species.* —*B. alternifolia* (Pale Purple, June, 4–6 ft.) ; *B. Colvillei* (Rose, July, 20 ft.) ; *B. globosa* (Orange, June, 10 ft.) ; *B. variabilis* and *vars.* (Lilac, Aug., 15 ft.).

Bulbocodium (Spring Meadow Saffron).—A pretty little hardy bulb with crocus-like blooms which likes a well-drained sandy soil and a sunny position. *Culture.*—Plant in August 3 inches deep and 4 inches apart, or pot-up if for indoors. Lift from the soil every fourth year, and propagate by means of offsets in August. *B. vernum* (Purple-red, Jan.–March, 5 in.) is the best species.

Buphthalmum (Ox-eye).—A tall hardy perennial, which thrives in the sun in well-drained loam. For culture, *see* Perennials, p. 128. *Species.* —*B. salicifolium* (Yellow, July–Sept., 24 in.) ; *B. speciosum* (Golden Orange, July, 60–70 in.).

Butomus umbellatus (Flowering Rush).—A hardy aquatic perennial, which likes a warm, sunny position in a bog or on a muddy bank, or in sheltered still water, with from 1 to 12 inches of water above the crowns. It grows some 30 inches high and carries pink flowers from June to August. Propagate by means of division in March.

Cacalia coccinea [*syn. Emilia flammea*] (Tassel Flower).—A hardy annual which likes a light soil, with plenty of leaf-mould in it. In summer and autumn it bears orange-red, daisy-like flowers on stems 18 inches high. For culture, *see* Annuals, p. 106.

Cacti.—Nearly all species may be grown in a moderately-heated greenhouse. They like a compost of one-half fibrous loam and one-half a mixture of sand, broken bricks, and lime rubble, and a sunny position, except *Epiphyllums, Phyllocactus* and *Rhipsalis*, which prefer shade and a compost of two-thirds fibrous loam and one-third sand, peat and brick rubble. Pot-up firmly in February or March and re-pot every three or four years, keeping pots as small as possible. A few pieces of charcoal in the compost are beneficial. Give ample ventilation and syringe with tepid water twice a week from April to September. Decrease water supply from October to April. Propagate by means of cuttings (partially dried) in summer, by grafting in March, or by offsets. *Hardy cacti* should be planted in spring in a well-drained, sunny, sheltered site in the rock garden or on a wall or bank in light loam with a mixture of brick rubble, sand and gravel. *Cereus, Echinocactus* and *Mamillaria*, and those with stems likely to hold moisture, should be covered with glass in winter. *Species.*—(*Hardy*)—*Cereus Engelmanni* (Purple, June, 18 in.) ; *Mamillaria setispina* (Pink, Summer, 9 in.) ; *Opuntia pulchella* (Purple, Summer, 10 in.). (*Half-hardy*)—*Cereus flagelliformis*, Whip Cactus (Pink, June, 12–30 in.) ;

Echinocactus Simpsonii, Hedgehog Cactus (Red, June, 5 in.) ; *Echinopsis cristata purpurea* (Rose, July, 10 in.) ; *Epiphyllum Russellianum,* Leaf-flowering Cactus (Pink, Nov., 10–24 in.) ; *Mamillaria sulphurea* (Yellow, Summer, 3 in.) ; *Melocactus communis,* Turk's Cap Cactus (Red, June, 12–30 in.) ; *Opuntia Ficus Indica,* Prickly Pear (Yellow, June, 30 in.) ; *Phyllocactus Aurora boreale* (Orange, June, 18–24 in.) ; *Rhipsalis cassytha,* Mistletoe Cactus (White, April, 15 in.).

Calamintha alpina (Calamint).—A hardy aromatic plant forming a thick carpet of foliage, and carrying sprays of violet flowers all through the summer. Grow in a sunny site in gritty loam. Propagate by seeds in March, or by division in March or September.

Calandrinia (Rock Purslane or Portulaca).—Dwarf-growing, annual and perennial plants that thrive in the sun in sandy loam. For culture, *see* Annuals, p. 106, *and* Perennials, p. 128. *Species.—(Annual)—C. discolor* (Lilac, 12–18 in.) ; *C. grandiflora* (Rose, 18 in.) ; *C. Menziesii* (Purple, 9 in.). *(Perennial)—C. umbellata* (Crimson, 9 in.). All July–Sept.

Calceolaria (Slipper Flower).—There are three distinct kinds of calceolaria, the *herbaceous,* raised and reared under glass ; the *shrubby,* grown for bedding-out ; these thrive in fibrous loam mixed with leaf-mould and sand. The third type, being hardy perennials and annuals, make excellent subjects for the rock garden. *Culture.—(Herbaceous Calceolarias)—*Sow lightly and thinly in a propagating case in June. Pot-up singly in July and keep in a frost-proof frame ; re-pot into 3 or 4-inch pots in September and take into the greenhouse. Keep warm and moist at night and give a steady even temperature. Pot-up finally in February or March (before the flower buds begin to move), using 7 to 8-inch pots and a compost of two parts loam to one part of leaf-mould and sand, and keep near the glass in a cool greenhouse. Stake securely, shade from the strong sun, and do not over-water. Weak liquid manure should be given at fortnightly intervals, as soon as the buds appear. Seeds should be sown afresh each year to attain the best results. *Culture.—(Shrubby Calceolarias)—*Take cuttings of vigorous young basal shoots in September and strike under glass, or in a warm north border, and cover with a hand-glass. If the weather turns frosty, throw some covering over the hand-glass. About the middle of February, the cuttings must have their growing points pinched back. A fortnight later they may either be potted or kept as cool as possible 3 to 4 inches apart in the pit, and finally transferred to the flower garden about 9 inches apart towards the end of May or early in June. Seed may also be sown under glass in March (Temp. 50°–60° F.). Transplant the seedlings into boxes as soon as they can be handled and next pot-up singly into 3 to 4-inch pots. Transfer to a cold frame in May, and before the plants become pot-bound re-pot into 5 to 6-inch pots, if for greenhouse use, or if for summer bedding, harden-off and plant-out early in June. *Culture.—*(third type) Annuals, *see* p. 106, Perennials p. 128. All May to September, 9 to 24 inches.

Calendula (Pot Marigold).—Hardy annuals which thrive in beds or borders in almost any soil. For culture, *see* Annuals, p. 106. *Named Varieties.—Favourite* (Sulphur Yellow) ; *Lemon Queen* (Lemon Yellow) ; *Orange King* (Bright Orange) : *Prince of Orange* (Orange, striped Pale

FLOWERING PLANTS

Anchusa italica (*Blue*).
Primula Auricula (*Various*).
Helleborus orientalis (*Pink or
   Greenish-white*).

Fritillaria Meleagris (*White and Red*).
Bouvardia "Maiden's Blush."
Doronicum plantagineum (*Yellow*).

G.   P

FLOWERING PLANTS

Photos]

[Dobbie & Co., Ltd.; Kelway & Son;
C. Jones; C. W. Teager.

Arctotis stœchadifolia (*Light Blue*).
Achimenes.
Lychnis Flos-jovis (*Purple or
Scarlet*).

Arabis albida flore pleno (*White*).
Amaryllis Belladonna (Belladonna
Lily).
Ageratum mexicanum (*Blue or White*).

Yellow); and *Yellow Queen* (Golden Yellow). All double, flowering from June to October, and about 18 inches in height.

Calla palustris (Bog Arum).—Hardy aquatic plants which spread over the surface of shallow still water. They like a sunny position in firm soil at the margin of ponds. Propagate by means of division in March. White flowers June to August.

Callistemon (Bottle Brush Plant).—Greenhouse evergreens which thrive in full sun, in a cool house, in equal parts of sandy peat and loam. They carry crimson and golden flowers in May and June on stems from 3 to 6 feet in height. *Culture.*—Pot-up in 6 to 10-inch pots, stand out-of-doors from June to September, and trim after flowering. To propagate take cuttings of matured wood in the late spring and strike in a frame.

Calluna vulgaris (Ling-Heather).—A hardy evergreen shrub thriving in full sun in peaty non-calcareous soil. *Culture.*—Plant in October or April; trim-off dead flower-heads in April. To propagate, take cuttings in summer and strike in peaty soil in a frame, or layer. *See also* Erica. *Varieties.*—*C. v. var. Alportii* (Crimson-pink, July–Sept., 15 in.); *C. v. var. aurea* (Golden Foliage, July–Sept., 12 in.); *C. v. var. alba Serlei* (White [Double], July–Sept., 12 in.).

Calochortus (Butterfly Tulip, Star Tulip, and Mariposa Lily).—Half-hardy bulbous plants that thrive in full sun in sandy leaf-mould. *Culture.*—Plant in late October, 3 inches deep and 3 inches apart. Cover with straw or fibre in winter, and lift the bulbs when the leaves die down. *Pot Culture.*—Pot-up ten bulbs in a 4 to 5-inch pot in November in a compost of two-thirds sandy loam and one-sixth part each of peat and leaf-mould. Keep covered with fibre in a cold frame until late December, when transfer to the greenhouse; dry-off after flowering. Propagate by offsets in November. *Species.*— *C. Howellii* (White, July–Aug., 18 in.); *C. pulchellus* (Yellow-orange, July–Aug., 12 in.); *C. venustus* and *vars.* (Yellow and Red, July and Aug., 15 in.).

Caltha (Marsh Marigold).—A useful hardy perennial for the water-side or moist border. *Culture.*—Propagate by means of division of roots in March or July and plant-out in moist, rich soil and in full sun or partial shade. *Species.*—*C. palustris fl. pl.* (Rich Yellow [double], May–July, 12 in.); *C. cœrulescens* (Deep Yellow, Flushed Maroon, May–July, 15 in.); *C. polypetala* (Golden, May–July, 20 in.).

Calycanthus floridus (Carolina All-spice).—A hardy deciduous shrub which likes a partially shaded moist position, and carries purple-red flowers in May and June, growing to a height of 5 feet or more. *Culture.*—Plant in November, and cut-out dead wood after flowering. Propagate by means of cuttings or layering in summer.

Camassia (Quamash).— Hardy bulbous plants which thrive in moist, but sunny, borders in a mixture of loam, leaf-mould and rotten manure. *Culture.*—Plant in October 4 to 5 inches deep and 10 inches apart; and lift from the soil every fourth year. Propagate by means of off-sets in October, or by seed under glass in March. *Species.*—*C. esculenta vars.* (Purple-blue and Silver-white, May and June, 20–30 in.); *C. Leichtlinii* (Cream-white, May and June, 40–60 in.).

E.G.   P

Camellia.—Hardy evergreen shrubs which thrive in sheltered and semi-shaded positions and in practically any soil, provided it is lime-free. They are also useful for greenhouse culture. *Culture.*—Pot up firmly in May, using 8 to 12-inch pots. They do best when under-potted. Use a compost of one-half part turfy loam and a quarter part each of sand and peat or leaf-mould. As soon as re-established, gradually harden-off, stand out-of-doors in partial shade on a firm base of ashes or bricks, and keep the roots moist, but not too wet. Move the plants into cold frames or the cold house in September. Trim-back all straggling shoots after flowering, syringe daily, sponge the leaves occasionally, and disturb the roots as little as possible. Propagate by grafting in a close propagating frame in early spring, using seedling *C. japonica* as a stock, or cuttings of half-matured shoots in a frame in July or August. Seeds may be raised in a moist heat. *Named Varieties.*—*C. alba plena* (White, Double) ; *C. cuspidata* (White, Single) ; *C. Donckelaari* (Crimson and White) ; *C. Henri Favre* (Rose-salmon) ; *C. Jupiter* (Rosy-red, Single) ; and *C. Waltham Glory* (Scarlet). All bloom between February and May.

Campanula (Bellflower).—A genus, including annuals, biennials and perennials and providing plants for the greenhouse, border and rock garden. Almost all species thrive in an open position in sun or semi-shade in well-drained, light, sandy loam with ample grit and leaf-mould. For culture, *see* Annuals, p. 106, Biennials, p. 107, *and* Perennials, p. 128. *Pot Culture.*—(*C. pyramidalis*). Sow in small pots and place in a well-ventilated frame : move into 5 to 6-inch pots in October and keep in a frost-proof frame for the winter. Pot-up again in March, using 7 to 8-inch pots and a compost of two-thirds sandy loam and one-third leaf-mould, rotted cow manure, and a little old mortar rubble, harden-off, and stand in the open. Stake as the flower spikes form, move into the house about July, and give liquid manure when the buds form. *C. pyramidalis* and other tall species for the greenhouse may also be increased by means of cuttings in a frame in March or August. *Greenhouse Trailing Species.*—Propagate by means of seed in heat in March, by cuttings in a frame in August, or by division in March. *Species.*—(Tall). *C. dahurica* (Pale Purple, June–Sept., 18 in.) ; *C. lactiflora* (Pale Blue or White, June–Aug., 36–48 in.) ; *C. latifolia* (Pale Blue, June–Sept., 24–48 in.) ; *C. Medium* (Canterbury Bells) (Various, June–Aug., 10–50 in.) ; *C. persicifolia* (Blue and White, June–August, 24–30 in.) ; *C. pyramidalis* (Chimney Bellflower) (Blue or White, July–Sept., 40–70 in.). NAMED BORDER VARIETIES.—*Faerie Queen* (Pale Blue) ; *Fleur-de-Neige* (White, Double) ; *Newry Giant* (White, Semi-double) ; *Shirley* (Blue, Semi-double). ALPINES.—*C. alpina* (Violet, June–Sept., 4 in.) ; *C. cæspitosa* (Blue, June–July, 5 in.) ; *C. carpatica, vars.* (Purple, Blue or White, May–Sept., 6–12 in.) ; *C. garganica* (Mauve, White or Pale Blue, June–Sept., 4 in.) ; *C. kewensis* (Violet-purple, June–July, 4 in.) ; *C. muralis* (Purple-blue, June–Aug., 4 in.) ; *C. pusilla* (Deep Blue or White, June–Aug., 3 in.).

Canary Creeper (*Tropæolum aduncum*).—This well-known creeper flowers best in a rather poor, dry soil, and in a sunny position. *T. aduncum* (Yellow) is half-hardy. *Culture.*—Sow late in April very thinly in the open, or under glass in March in a cool greenhouse. If planted indoors, pot-off singly, harden-off, and plant out 12 inches apart in May, otherwise thin out when fit to handle.

Canna (Indian Shot).—Half-hardy perennials for the cool greenhouse, or for summer-bedding in warm sunny beds and borders with well-manured rich loam. *Culture.*—Sow seed ½ inch deep in sandy loam and leaf-mould in a propagating case (Temp. 75° F.), in February or March (the seed having previously been soaked for a day in warm water). Pot-up singly as soon as possible, or propagate by means of division of roots in spring, dividing them so that each section of root contains an eye. Pot-up early in March or April in single pots and, if for outdoor culture, plant-out in June about 24 inches apart. If for greenhouse culture, pot-up into 6 to 12-inch pots, using a rich and porous compost of one-half loam and one-quarter part each of rotten cow manure and sandy leaf-mould. At the end of September pot-up those grown out-of-doors and winter under glass. Keep moderately dry and allow the leaves and stems to die off gradually. *Named Varieties.*—*Assaut* (Scarlet); *Beethoven* (Orange); *Italia* (Orange and Yellow); *President* (Scarlet); and *J. B. Van der Schoot* (Yellow Spotted). All August to October, 3 to 6 feet.

Caragana (Altagana or Pea Tree).—Hardy deciduous trees and shrubs of the cytisus family, which thrive in sunny positions on dry banks in light sandy or ordinary soil. *Culture.*—Plant in October; cut out dead wood after flowering. Propagate by means of seed in the open in May, or by layering in July.

Carnation (Dianthus Caryophyllus).—Carnations, picotees and pinks, which are closely allied, are all propagated by seeds, layers and cuttings.

Carnations in the Border.—Three weeks before planting time the bed (well-drained medium loam) should be double-dug and a little well-rotted stable manure should be dug in to at least 6 inches below the surface, but manuring must not be overdone. Plant in September or early in October, but in heavy and cold soils it is often wise to keep the young plants in a frame until May and then plant-out. In April the flowering stems should be supported, and as soon as it is apparent that the principal bud is a healthy one, the less important ones should be pulled off. A small dose of weak liquid manure or soot-water twice a week after watering should be given from the time the buds begin to form until the colour shows. Carnations are perennials, and the beds should only be replanted every third year.

Carnations under Glass.—In September or early in October pot-up the young layers singly into 3-inch pots in a compost of two-thirds turfy loam and one-third well-rotted leaf-mould and coarse sand, well sifted and sterilized by baking (*see* p. 53). Then stand the pots in a cold frame for the winter. Keep slightly moist but no water must settle on the leaves. In March, re-pot into 6-inch pots, adding a little well-decayed manure and old mortar rubble to the compost. Keep close after potting until established, then give more air and finally remove the lights. In May, re-pot into 8-inch pots and return to the frame for a fortnight. Then stand in the open in a sheltered position, on a firm bed of ashes or on slates. Water liberally, syringe in dry weather, and stake, manure and disbud as advised for those in the open border. When the young plants are some 6 inches high, the heads should be pinched off, and as soon as the side shoots are from 6 to 8 inches in length they will in turn require pinching-back ; not later than mid-June, however, for ordinary July-flowering carnations, or mid-August for perpetual-flowering species. Transfer to a light position in the cool greenhouse as soon as the flowers show colour (about July).

Propagation.—Choice varieties should be raised from cuttings or layers. *Seed.*—Sow 1 inch apart in April or May in seed pans, in a compost of two-thirds loam from decayed turf, one-third well-decomposed cow dung and a little old mortar rubble and bonemeal, and place in a sheltered part of the garden. When the plants show five or six leaves plant-out from 10 to 15 inches apart in sunny, well-drained beds. Protect during winter with a cold frame. In cold and heavy soil, some gardeners prefer to sow in August, winter in a cold frame and plant-out in spring. *Layering.*—The season for this is in July or August, and the process is fully dealt with on p. 193. *Cuttings.*—Cuttings may be struck in a frame with a bottom heat of 60° F. at any time from November to February (the best time is January). Early in March these cuttings, if struck in January, will need potting on into larger pots.

Perpetual or Tree Carnations are invaluable for winter blooms. The cultivation and soil are much the same as for the ordinary carnation. The cuttings, which will be furnished by the side shoots, may be struck in silver sand in February, August or September in gentle heat (55° F.) or the non-flowering shoots of the old plant may be laid down in a cold shaded frame in September. When rooted (in about a month), pot-up in 2½-inch pots and winter in a cool greenhouse near the glass and give ample air. The following summer pot-on into 6-inch pots and then into 8-inch pots, potting being more firm at each move. Pinch back, stand outdoors, and stake as advised above. About the beginning of September the plants may again be taken into the house and watered occasionally with weak liquid manure or soot water as soon as the roots have filled the pots. Seed may be sown in gentle heat (55° F.) in February.

Malmaison Carnations require treatment as detailed for border carnations, but only require one " stopping," and a cooler atmosphere ; the winter temperature should rarely rise above 45° F. They should not be placed in the open in summer. Propagate by layers in a frame in July and August, or by cuttings in a propagating frame with bottom heat in May or June.

Clove Carnations are a hardy border type, best planted-out in April. *Varieties.*—BORDER. SELFS.—*Bookham Apricot* ; *Blush Clove* (Blush-white) ; *Bookham Clove* (Crimson) ; *Bookham Rose* ; *Bookham Scarlet* ; *Border Yellow* ; *Coral Clove* (Coral-pink) ; *Crystal Clove* (White) ; *Fiery Cross* (Scarlet) ; *Glamour* (Yellow) ; *Margaret Keep* (Blush-pink) ; *Purple Clove* ; *Royal Scot* (Scarlet) ; *Salmon Clove* ; *The Grey Douglas* (Heliotrope) ; *Trumpeter* (Rose-madder) ; *White Clove.*

FANCIES.—*Centurion* (Yellow and Scarlet) ; *Endymion* (Canary-yellow, streaked Blood-red) ; *Highland Mary* (Primrose-yellow and

Rose-pink) ; *Kelso* (Golden-apricot and Blue-grey) ; *Linkman* (Yellow and Scarlet) ; *Mona* (Buff and Rose) ; *Mrs. Hawksbee* (White and Rose-crimson) ; *Ravenswood* (White and Maroon-crimson) ; *Saracen* (Slate-grey, striped Crimson and Rose) ; *Steerforth Clove* (White and Crimson-maroon) ; *The Cadi* (Rose-madder, striped Blue and Scarlet) ; *Viceroy* (Yellow and Carmine-crimson).

PERPETUAL BORDER.—*Sussex Avondale* (Salmon-pink) ; *Sussex Beauty* (Heliotrope) ; *Sussex Bizarre* (Peach, flaked Heliotrope) ; *Sussex Crimson* ; *Sussex Maid* (White flaked Rose-pink) ; *Sussex Pink*.

PICOTEES.—(*Yellow ground*). *Equisite* (Scarlet Edge) ; *Her Majesty* (Purple Edge) ; *Margaret Glitters* (Rosy-scarlet Edge) ; *Mrs. J. J. Kean* (Rose-pink Edge) ; *Niel Kenyon* (Rose Edge) ; *Togo* (Crimson Edge).

TREE OR PERPETUALS.—*Baroness de Brienen* (Salmon-pink) ; *Edward Allwood* (Scarlet) ; *Eileen Low* (Salmon-pink) ; *Laddie* (Salmon-pink) ; *Lady Northcliffe* (Salmon-pink) ; *Mikado* (Heliotrope) ; *Mary Allwood* (Reddish-salmon) ; *Mrs. A. J. Cobb* (Crimson) ; *Saffron* (Yellow) ; *Tarzan* (Scarlet) ; *Topsy* (Scarlet) ; *White Enchantress*.

MALMAISONS.—*Baldwin* (Pink) ; *Calypso* (Soft-flesh) ; *Duchess of Westminster* (Rose-pink) ; *Maggie Hodgson* (Crimson) ; *Nell Gwynne* (White) ; *Princess of Wales* (Pink).

Carnations, Marguerite.—Half-hardy annuals which thrive in open beds in rich, gritty loam. They grow about 18 inches high and flower from August to October. If lifted before damaged by the frost they will furnish flowers in the greenhouse through the winter and spring. For culture, *see* Annuals, p. 107.

Carpentaria californica (Californian Mock Orange).—Half-hardy climbing shrubs which like a warm sheltered position and well-drained loam. They grow from 5 to 10 feet high and flower about mid-summer. *Culture.*—Propagate by means of cuttings of young wood in April in a frame, by layering in September, or by suckers in autumn. Plant in autumn and prune-out weak wood and dead flowers after flowering.

Carpinus Betulus (Hornbeam).—A hardy deciduous tree which thrives in sunny, open positions in almost any soil and makes a good hedge plant. *Culture.*—Plant from November to February ; no pruning is necessary. Propagate by seeds, graft in March on the common hornbeam, or layer.

Cassinia.—Beautiful evergreen flowering shrubs which like a sunny position in ordinary soil. They grow from 3 to 6 feet high and flower from July to September. *C. fulvida*, 4 feet, with creamy-white flowers, is a good species. *Culture.*—Plant from October to November, and thin-out branches when overcrowded. To propagate strike cuttings in a frame in August.

Castanea (Sweet Chestnut).—Hardy deciduous trees which thrive in full sun in light gravelly loam. *Culture.*—Plant in November and thin-out branches when overcrowded. To propagate sow in the open.

Catalpa (Indian Bean Tree).—Hardy deciduous trees which thrive in full sun and in moist, but well-drained rather light loam. They grow 25–50 feet high and flower in July and August. *Culture.*—Plant from November to February. When seeds are not available, take cuttings of leafy shoots in July and insert them in gentle bottom heat, or layer in July.

Catananche (Cupidone).—Hardy perennial or annual plants, which like a sunny spot in a warm dry border and ordinary soil. For culture, *see* Annuals, p. 106, *and* Perennials, p. 128. *Species.*—*C. lutea* (Yellow, July, 9 in.); *C. cœrulea* (Blue, July–Aug., 30 in.).

Ceanothus (Californian Lilac).—Half-hardy shrubs which like a warm sunny position and well-drained ordinary soil and leaf-mould. There are two distinct classes, one flowering in Spring, the other from July to September. The latter are hardy deciduous shrubs and the others evergreens, suitable for sheltered walls and mild localities. *Culture.*—Plant in March or October. Cut spring-flowering species back in May; late-flowering plants must be pruned in early spring. Evergreens grown as bushes will not need severe pruning. To propagate, take cuttings in July or August and strike in a frame, or layer during the same months. *Species.*—EVERGREEN, SPRING-FLOWERING: *C. dentatus* (Blue); *C. rigidus* (Purplish-blue); *C. thyrsiflorus* (Pale Blue); and *C. Veitchianus* (Bright Blue). HYBRID (DECIDUOUS), LATE-FLOWERING; *Ceres* (Rose-pink); *Gloire de Versailles* (Lavender); *Henri Defosse* (Dark Blue); *Indigo* (Indigo Blue); *Marie Simon* (Rose); and *Perle Rose* (Rose-carmine).

Cedar (Cedrus).—Hardy evergreen trees suitable only for large gardens. *Culture.*—Plant in Sept. or Oct. when from 1 to 4 ft. high, in a sunny position in well-drained, gravelly, chalky, or sandy soil. No pruning is necessary. To propagate, sow in March or April. *Species and Varieties.*—*C. atlantica* (Mt. Atlas Cedar, 80–100 ft.); *C. deodara* (Deodar, 150 ft.); and *C. Libani* (The Cedar of Lebanon, 100 ft.).

Cedronella cana.—This plant bears crimson-purple flowers in June on stems 3 feet high. For culture, *see* Perennials, p. 128.

Celastrus (Bitter Sweet, Staff Tree, etc.).—Hardy perennial climbing plants which thrive in most soils and positions. They carry hundreds of brilliant golden-yellow fruits exposing scarlet-coated seeds in autumn. *Culture.*—Cut out weak wood and tip stray shoots in February, and propagate by means of layering young shoots in October.

Celosia (Prince of Wales' Feathers, or Cockscomb).—Half-hardy annuals which thrive if planted out in June in a warm, sheltered situation in southern districts. Grown in pots in the greenhouse, they may, with a little management, be had in flower the whole winter. For culture, *see* Annuals, p. 107. *Species and Varieties.*—*C. argentea* (Silvery); *C. cristata* (Cockscomb) (Crimson, July–August, 18 in.); *C. c. coccinea* (Scarlet); *C. pyramidalis* (Scarlet, Crimson or Gold, July–Sept., 30 in.).

Celsia (Cretan Mullein).—Half-hardy biennials and perennials which thrive in the cool greenhouse, in a compost of sandy loam and a little leaf-mould. For culture, *see* Biennials, p. 107, *and* Perennials, p. 128. *Species.*—*C. Arcturus* (Deep Yellow, spotted Purple, June–Nov., 20 in.); *C. cretica* (Golden-yellow, spotted Brown, June-July, 60 in.).

Centaurea.—A large genus of hardy annuals, biennials, and perennials, all of which thrive in a sunny position in any good garden soil.

The perennials (Knapweed) make good border plants; *C. Cyanus* (Cornflower) and *C. suaveolens* (Sweet Sultan) are annuals. For culture, *see* Annuals, p. 106, Biennials, p. 107, *and* Perennials, p. 128. *Pot Culture.*—*C. gymnocarpa* (Dusty Miller) and *C. ragusina* are useful in the cold greenhouse. Sow in heat in January and August, or take cuttings in September. *Species and Varieties.*—HARDY ANNUALS—*C. Cyanus* (Cornflower) (White, Pink, Blue, July–Oct., 6–36 in.); *C. depressa* (Blue, Crimson Centre, July–Oct., 12 in.); *C. suaveolens* (Sweet Sultan) (White to Yellow, Rose and Purple, July–Oct., 20 in.). HARDY PERENNIALS—*C. babylonica* (Yellow, July–Sept., 6–8 ft.); *C. dealbata* (Rose, Silver Foliage, July–Sept., 24 in.); *C. macrocephala* (Deep Yellow, July and Aug., 50–60 in.); *C. montana* (Blue, White, Pink and Yellow, July and Aug., 24–30 in.); *C. ruthenica* (Sulphur Yellow, Aug., 50–60 in.); *C. Scabiosa* (Purplish, June–Aug., 18 in.).

Centranthus [syn. Kentranthus] (Valerian).—A hardy perennial, which likes a sunny position and dry, limy soil, and is useful for border, rock garden, or walls. For culture, *see* Perennials, p. 128. *Species.*— *C. angustifolius* (Crimson, May–July, 24 in.); *C. ruber* (Crimson, Rose, June–Aug., 24–36 in.); *C. r. var. albus* (White, June–Aug., 24 in.).

Cerastium (Mouse-ear, Chick-weed, Jerusalem Star).—A genus of dwarf-growing hardy perennials that are useful for carpeting or for the rock and paved gardens. For culture, *see* Rock Plants, p. 135. *Species.* —*C. Biebersteinii* (White, Silver Foliage, May–June, 6 in.); *C. tomentosum* (White, Silver Foliage, June–Aug., 6 in.).

Ceratostigma (Leadwort).—Low-growing rock plants which thrive in the sun in gritty loam. For culture, *see* Rock Plants, p. 135. *C. plumbaginoides* (Cobalt-blue, July–Sept., 9 in.) is the best-known.

Cercis (Judas Tree).—Tall deciduous shrubs or small trees which thrive in full sun in moist, sandy, and well-drained loam. In May they carry rose-purple pea-shaped flowers. *Culture.*—Plant in Oct. or Nov. To propagate, sow in a frame, or layer in September.

Charieis heterophylla (Cape Aster).—A pretty little hardy annual, very effective in beds, or rock gardens. It grows some 6 inches high and flowers from June to Sept. For culture, *see* Annuals, p. 106.

Chelone (Shellflower).—Hardy perennials, many species of which are now classed with pentstemons, which like a sunny or semi-shaded site in moist sandy loam with humus in it. For culture, *see* Perennials, p. 128. *Species and Varieties.*—*C. coccinea* (Red); *C. Lyonii* (Rosy Purple); *C. obliqua* (Pink). All June to September, 24 to 36 inches.

Chimonanthus fragrans (Winter Sweet).—A winter-blooming hardy deciduous shrub, which likes a sunny, sheltered position in deep, moist, sandy loam. It bears pale yellow flowers stained purple, and reaches a height of 7 feet on walls. *Culture.*—Plant in October or March, and when grown as a climber cut back side shoots to within five to six " eyes " of the main stems after flowering. Propagate by means of layering in August, or by suckers or seed in March.

Chionanthus (Fringe Tree).—Hardy deciduous shrubs or small trees, which like a sheltered position in well-drained, moist loam, and bear white flowers in June and July. *Culture.*—Plant from October to November, and trim to shape after flowering if required. Propagate by means of layering in September, or strike cuttings of half-ripe shoots in a close frame during July and August.

Chionodoxa (Glory of the Snow).—This bulbous plant requires similar treatment to that accorded to bulbs generally, and thrives in sun or shade and sandy loam in the border, rock garden or greenhouse. *Culture.*—Plant in October 2½ inches deep and from 3 to 4 inches apart. Propagate by offsets in October or raise from seed. *See also* Bulbs, p. 116. *Species.*—*C. Luciliæ gigantea* (Soft Mauve, Blue and White, March, 9 in.) ; *C. L. grandiflora* (Lavender-blue, White Centre, March–April, 9 in.) ; *C. L. var. sardensis* (Deep Blue, March–April, 7 in.).

Choisyaternata (Mexican Orange Blossom).—A half-hardy evergreen shrub which likes a sunny sheltered position in sandy loam. It grows from 6 to 10 feet high and from May to September bears small white flowers. *Culture.*—Plant in April or September, and in April cut out old wood or trim if required. Propagate by means of layering in August, or by cuttings in a frame in August. *Pot Culture.*—Pot-up in spring in a 6 to 8-inch pot and a compost of peaty loam, leaf-mould and sand. Prune straggly shoots after flowering and put out in the open, with pots sunk in ashes, from July to October.

Christmas Rose (Helleborus niger).—A hardy perennial which thrives in well-dug, light and moist soil in a border facing preferably east or west or in a cool house. For culture, *see* Perennials, p. 128. If for the greenhouse, pot-up in October in 6 to 8-inch pots in 2 parts fibrous loam and 1 part rotten manure ; select fresh plants annually, planting the old ones out in April or May. This and *Helleborus orientalis* [Lenten Rose] (Jan.–April, 18–24 in.) are the most popular species, there being many colour forms and varieties of the latter species.

Chrysanthemum.—The chrysanthemum is one of the hardiest plants, but owing to the fact that it flowers somewhat late its beautiful blooms are subject to injury from the weather when grown out-of-doors unless the protection of glass is provided. Chrysanthemums may be classified according to the time of their blooming, as early-flowering, blooming from July to October ; semi-early, blooming in September and October in the open ; and ordinary or late-flowering, blooming in November and December.

Culture of Indoor Chrysanthemums.—If seed is used it should be sown as soon as ripe (Feb.) in a pan of sandy soil in a temp. of 60° F. : transplant and pot-on as necessary. *Propagation by Cuttings.*—After the plants have finished blooming the stems and all weak shoots from the base should be cut down to within a few inches of the ground and the pots given a position in the cold greenhouse or a frost-proof frame. A half-inch mulch of fine loam and leaf-mould, and a little water, will help the old roots to throw up sturdy young shoots for cuttings. *See* Cuttings, p. 189. Grow in pots in a mixture of well-rotted leaf-mould, grit or silver sand and fibrous loam, in about equal parts, and a dusting of wood ashes, all well sieved. Once the cuttings are rooted (in from three to five weeks), stand the pots near the glass in a frost-proof frame, and give ample ventilation in fine weather. Cuttings of Japanese types must be taken in December or January. Nearly all growers differ as to the best time for striking cuttings of the " Decorative " types.

Some recommend November ; some succeed admirably by inserting them in May ; the latter date only when propagating plants to flower in small pots in December. Perhaps it is better to make a compromise by striking in February or March. *Potting-on.*—December-struck cuttings should be well rooted by the middle of February and should then be potted-up into 3 or 3½-inch pots, adding to the compost one-third part well-rotted manure. They should receive their next shift into 5 or 6-inch pots about the first week in April. Disturb the roots as little as possible, and add a little more manure and a dusting of bonemeal and powdered charcoal to the compost, which do not sieve. The cuttings should then be continued in a frame or on a shelf near the glass. Shade from the sun, then in about a fortnight's time harden-off, stand out-of-doors by the middle of May, and give a final shift a month or six weeks later. *Summer Treatment.*—The pots should be stood in the open on slates in a sheltered position, facing south or west. As soon as the pots are full of roots the plants should be placed in 8 to 9-inch pots ; about the middle of June is a good time to complete the final potting-up. No soil is better for them than a compost of two-thirds lumpy fibrous loam, one-sixth well-rotted cow-dung, and one-sixth leaf-mould and a little old mortar rubble and sharp sand liberally coloured with bonemeal and soot. There need not be much drainage. *Staking and Tying.*—The plants must be properly supported. *See* Staking and Tying, p. 71. *" Stopping " and Disbudding.*—If bushy plants are to be grown, pinch out the tip of the central shoot, when the plants are some 5 or 6 inches high. A second " stopping " will be necessary in early summer. If you grow blooms for exhibition only, no stopping will be needed until the " break-bud " appears in early summer. Pinch-out this bud and all the young shoots just below it, save the three strongest and best placed, and concentrate the whole strength of the plant into these stems and the strength of these stems into a single bud at the top. *Feeding and Autumn Treatment.*—From early in August the plants should be fed two or three times a week alternately with sulphate of potash and with weak manure water. Feeding must cease as soon as the blooms are three parts open, and early in October the plants should be moved under glass. This is a critical change for them, and the leaves should be kept well syringed, *except in dull, damp weather,* two or three times a day for a few weeks.

Outdoor Culture of Border Chrysanthemums.—Plant-out in March, or in the case of less hardy sorts, towards the end of May. They should receive the same general treatment in training and watering as those grown indoors, except that the majority should not be " stopped." The soil should be well-drained and well-dug in winter, but it must not be too rich. A mulch of well-rotted short stable manure in June is beneficial. In planting, 24 to 36 inches should be allowed between each plant, and an open, sunny, sheltered position is essential. Most varieties naturally form bushy plants, but with others it is necessary, from time to time, to pinch-back the tips of the shoots ; this pinching-back must not be continued after the end of July. If large blooms are desired the plants should be disbudded As soon as the flowers are over cut the plants down to the ground, lift them, shake the soil from the roots and place them, close together, in shallow boxes of light, sandy soil and store in a frost-proof place. In March divide the crowns, retaining the younger and more vigorous portions only, and plant-out again in the border, or take cuttings as advised for the indoor kinds. In light and warm soil it is not always necessary to lift the crowns in autumn.

Varieties.—GREENHOUSE, *Japanese Exhibition.*—*Aquitania* (Chestnut and Gold) ; *Bob Pulling* (Yellow) ; *Edith Cavell* (Orange-bronze) ; *Louisa Pockett* (White, tinted Pink) ; *Majestic* (Golden Amber) ; *Mrs. A. Holden* (Crimson-scarlet) ; *Mrs. John Balmer* (Indian Red) ; *Nan Luxford* (Silvery Pink) ; *Queen Mary* (White).

Japanese Decorative.—*Baldock's Crimson* ; *Blanche Poitevene* (White) ; *Exmouth Crimson* ; *Golden Marvel* (Yellow) ; *Heston White* ; *In Memoriam* (Crimson) ; *Jean Pattison* (Copper) ; *Pink Pearl.*

Incurved Varieties.—*Buttercup* (Yellow) ; *Embleme Poitevene* (Orange-yellow) ; *H. W. Thorpe* (White) ; *J. W. Streeter* (Primrose) ; *Mrs. Sidney Dove* (Silvery Pink) ; *Progress* (Silvery Mauve).

Single Varieties.—*Ceddie Mason* (Crimson) ; *Exmouth Pink* ; *Golden Mensa* (Yellow) ; *Kitty Bourne* (Yellow) ; *Lady St. Audries* (Crimson and Gold) ; *Mrs. H. Woolman* (Orange-yellow) ; *Mrs. W. Higgs* (Pink) ; *Nona* (White) ; *Phyllis Cooper* (Orange) ; *Portia* (Red).

Anemone-centred Singles.—*Elspeth* (Mauve) ; *Golden Nymph* (Yellow and Gold) ; *Mary Godfrey* (Pink) ; *Thora* (Rose) ; *Winsome* (Crimson).

Pompons.—*Billie Burke* (Golden Orange) ; *Ethel* (Red) ; *Golden West* (Golden Yellow) ; *Hilda Canning* (Bronze) ; *Nemo* (White).

HARDY BORDER VARIETIES.—*Almirante* (Chestnut Crimson) ; *Bronze Cranfordia* ; *Champ d'Or* (Canary Yellow) ; *Crimson Circle* ; *Daffodil* (Yellow) ; *Framfield White* ; *Goacher's Crimson* ; *Mrs. Jack Pearson* (Bronze) ; *Mrs. Phil. Page* (Red) ; *Normandie* (Pink).

Hardy Singles.—*Carrie Luxford* (Crimson) ; *Doreen Woolman* (Golden Flame) ; *Maidenhood* (Primrose) ; *Mrs. H. Woolman* (White) ; *Shirley Crimson* ; *The Dome* (Salmon and Gold).

Chrysanthemum, Annual (Corn Marigold, Crown Daisy).—These showy plants thrive in sunny beds or borders. For culture, *see* Annuals, p. 106. *Named Varieties.*—*Eastern Star* (Yellow Brown Eye) ; *Evening Star* (Golden Yellow) ; *Morning Star* (Primrose) ; *The Sultan* (Maroon) ; and *White Pearl* (Double). All June to September, 20 in.

Chrysanthemum, Perennial (Ox-Eye Daisy).—These, like the annual species, make a good show in sunny borders and ordinary soil. For culture, *see* Perennials, p. 128. *Species.*—*C. alpinum* (White, June-Sept., 5 in.) ; *C. arcticum* (White, tinged Pink, Oct., 18 in.) ; *C. coccineum* (Scarlet, June-Sept., 36 in.) ; *C. maximum* (White, July-Sept., 36 in.) ; *C. uliginosum* (White, Sept.-Oct., 3-5 ft.).

Cimicifuga (Bugwort, Bugbane or Snake-root).—A hardy perennial which thrives in a deep, moist loam and fairly sunny position. For culture, *see* Perennials, p. 128. *Species.*—*C. cordifolia* (Creamy-white, July-Aug., 36 in.) ; *C. racemosa* (Cream-white, July-Aug., 36-48 in.) ; *C. simplex* (White, Aug.-Oct., 36 in.).

Cineraria.—Beautiful greenhouse perennials which, by careful management, may be had in flower from November to May. They thrive in a compost of 2 parts fibrous loam to 1 part of leaf-mould, well-decayed cow manure and a little sand and old mortar rubble, and are best grown from seed. *Culture.*—The first sowing should be made in April in pans filled with equal parts of loam and leaf-mould and one-sixth part of sand, and placed in slight bottom heat. Cover with glass and paper and keep slightly moist. Stand the seedlings in partial shade, move into 3-inch pots as soon as possible, gradually harden-off, and remove the lights of the frame entirely by day from July to the end of September. Shift the young plants into 4½ to 5-inch pots as required, and give them their final shift in September into 6 to 8-inch pots. Keep moist and syringe every afternoon in hot weather, then towards the end of September the plants should be placed in a cool greenhouse, and weak liquid manure or soot water given alternately with water. Another sowing may be made in a cold frame in May, and a third in June. Pot-on as above, but at proportionately later dates. *Cineraria maritima* is a beautiful foliage plant for summer bedding, or decoration in the cold greenhouse. Sow under glass in March. *Species and Varieties.*—*C. maritima* (Silver Foliage, Summer, 18 in.); and *Senecio cruenta* (Cineraria), of which there are many varieties. (Various colours, Winter and Spring, 18–30 in.)

Cistus (Rock Rose).—Evergreen perennial shrubs mostly hardy in warm sheltered sites. They love the sun and do well in dry, well-drained sandy loam or ordinary soil to which ample lime-rubble has been added. *Culture.*—Do not prune, merely keep the shrubs in shape by means of "stopping" in March and by removing dead blooms. Propagate by means of layering in August, sow seed in April, or take cuttings of half-matured wood in August and strike in a shaded frame. Grow in pots till ready for planting-out. *Species.*—*C. algarvensis* (Yellow and Crimson, June–July, 24 in.); *C. ladaniferus* (White [Spotted Red], June–July, 48–60 in.); *C. purpureus* (Purple-red [Blotched Crimson], June–July, 36–48 in.), etc.

Clarkia.—Hardy annuals which thrive in fairly moist rich soil in the border or cold greenhouse. For culture, *see* Annuals, p. 106. For the greenhouse sow in a frame in August, and pot-up as required, using 6 to 7-inch pots for three plants. *Varieties.*—*Brilliant Rose* (Rose); *Firefly* (Crimson); *Marginata* (Pink, margined White); *Orange King* (Orange); *Scarlet Beauty* (Scarlet); *Purple Queen* (Purple); *Salmon Queen* (Salmon); and *Snowball* (White). All July to October, 24 in.

Claytonia (Spring Beauty).—Dwarf-growing hardy perennials which thrive in sun or shade and in any soil. *Culture.*—Sow in March where the plants are to flower. *Species.*—*C. sibirica* (Rose) and *C. virginica* (White). Both Spring, 6 inches.

Clematis.—Beautiful hardy climbers which do well against walls and on trellises, facing north, east or west, or in the greenhouse. A sunny position is most suitable, but the lower part of the stems require shade. Although not particular as to soil, they prefer light to heavy land if it has been well manured; a mixture of well-drained loam, well-rotted manure and old mortar rubble is most satisfactory. *Culture.*—Propagate by means of layering in summer and plant-out in March. Cut away dead and weak wood, giving ample light and air to the growths retained, and fasten the shoots up securely. Propagation may also be carried out by means of grafting, by cuttings or seed. Most varieties require pruning after flowering, but *C. vitalba* is best pruned in March, while *C. Jackmanii* and *C. viticella vars.* should be cut down to 6 inches in November or to a foot in spring. *Pot Culture.*—Pot-up in March, using 5 to 10-inch pots and a compost of 2 parts peaty loam to 1 part of leaf-mould, well-rotted manure and sand. *Varieties.*—EARLY-FLOWERING—(Florida Group) *Countess of Lovelace* (Lavender-blue); *Duchess of Edinburgh* (Double, White). LATE-FLOWERING—(Jackmanii Group) *Gipsy Queen* (Purple) and *Snow White* (White). (Lanuginosa Group) *Henryi* (Greenish–white); *Beauty of Worcester* (Blue-violet); *Fairy Queen* (Flesh Pink); and *Mrs. Pope* (Lavender). (Patens Group) *Duke of Edinburgh* (Purple–violet); *Miss Bateman* (White); and *The Queen* (Lavender); *C. montana* (White); and var. *rubens* (Rose); *C. tangutica* (Golden Yellow); and *C. Flammula* (White). (Viticella Group) *C. Ascotiensis* (Azure Blue), and *viticella alba* (White, Semi-double).

Clerodendron.—Beautiful deciduous shrubs or small trees, which thrive in a sunny sheltered position in well-drained, rich loam. *Culture.*—Plant in October or November. Propagate by means of seed, cuttings of half-ripened shoots in a frame, or by root cuttings. *C. fœtidum* is a good plant for the cold greenhouse. *Hardy Species.*—*C. Fargesii* (White, Red Calyx, 10–12 ft.); *C. fœtidum* (Purple, 3–6 ft.); *C. trichotomum* (White, Red Calyx, 10–12 ft.). All July to September.

Clianthus.—Evergreen climbing shrubs which succeed best in the warm sunny border of a cool greenhouse in sandy peat and fibrous loam. *C. puniceus* (Crimson), *vars. magnificus* (Red) and *carneus* (Flesh), Parrot's Bill and Lobster's Claw, blossom freely out-of-doors against a trellis or south wall. *Culture.*—Sow in February singly in pots, and when 3 to 4 inches high move into 4½-inch pots and keep in these until ready for planting-out in April, or, in the case of *C. Dampieri* (Glory Pea), into a border in the house. Syringe house plants daily in hot dry weather, and trim back straggling shoots after flowering. They may also be raised by means of cuttings in a frame (Temp. 70° F.) in May or June.

Clivia (Imantophyllum).—Beautiful evergreen plants with lily-like blooms, for the cool greenhouse. *Culture.*—Plant in February in 9-inch pots in a mixture of rich sandy loam, leaf-mould and old manure, keep in a cool place, and let the roots fill the pots, as the plants flourish best when root-bound. Water well in summer, keep cool and on the dry side during winter, and sponge the leaves occasionally with tepid water. Weak manure water should be given twice a week while the buds are forming. Propagate by means of division of suckers in February, or by seed sown when ripe. *Species.*—*C. citrina* (Yellow); *C. miniata* and *vars.* (Orange-scarlet); *C. nobilis* (Red and Yellow). All March to April, 20 inches. Clivias make very useful room plants.

Cobæa (Cup and Saucer Plant).—Beautiful evergreen climbers that thrive in the cool greenhouse. They grow to a height of 20 feet and flower from July to September. *C. scandens* (Purple and Greenish-white) will also thrive in the open in warm sheltered positions in the south and west of England; in more exposed positions it must be treated as an annual and be raised afresh each year. *Culture.*—Sow thinly under glass (Temp. 45° F.) in light rich soil in February, or propagate by cuttings of young shoots in January or February, and raise in a propagating case. Pot-up into 3 to 4-inch pots, harden-off, and if for growing in the open, plant out 24 inches apart in June in equal parts of loam, leaf-mould and sand, or grow on in pots and keep in the cool greenhouse. In February prune laterals back to two buds, and cut out all weak growth.

Colchicum (Meadow Saffron or Autumn Crocus).—Hardy bulbous *poisonous* plants usually grown in the rock garden. *Culture.*—Plant in July or August in full sun, 5 inches deep and 6 inches apart, in moist, cool loam. Lift from the ground (triennially) in August to increase. *Species.*—*C. autumnale* (Lilac-rose, Sept.–Oct., 6 in.) ; *C. montanum* (Lilac or White, Sept.–Oct., 4 in.) ; *C. speciosum* (Crimson, Purple or White Eye, Sept.–Oct., 10 in.).

Coleus Blumei.—Half-hardy annual and perennial foliage plants, useful for bedding-out or the cool greenhouse. *Culture.*—Sow thinly in heat (70° F.) in March. Named varieties must be propagated by means of cuttings at any time from spring to autumn, struck singly in pots sunk to their rims in fibre in a frame with good bottom heat (70° F.), and in a moist atmosphere ; the best time is March. These plants like a light, rich soil ; 2 parts of loam to 1 part of leaf-mould and sand being recommended. Place near the glass, but shade from strong sun. When rooted, re-pot into 3-inch pots, pinch-back, and pot-on till they are finally in 5 to 6-inch pots. *Varieties.*—*Beckwith's Gem* ; *Countess of Dudley* ; *Decorator* ; *Pride of the Market* ; *Sunset* ; and *Verschaffeltii* (largely used for bedding). All species flower in summer and grow from 6 to 24 inches in height.

Collinsia (Collin's Flower).—Hardy annuals for sunny beds, borders or the greenhouse. For culture, *see* Annuals, p. 106. *Species.*— *C. bicolor* (Reddish-purple and White, July–Oct., 12 in.) ; *C. grandiflora* (Purple–blue and White, July–Oct., 12 in.).

Colutea (Bladder Senna).—A deciduous broom-like shrub, thriving in almost any position or soil. *Culture.*—Plant in October or November, and in March cut the previous year's growth well back. To propagate, take cuttings in September, or sow in the open in spring. *Species.*—*C. arborescens* (Yellow, June–Aug., 10 ft.) ; *C. cruenta* (Red and Yellow, June–Aug., 6–8 ft.) ; *C. media* (Reddish-brown, June–Aug., 10 ft.).

Commelina (Day Flower).—Annual and perennial plants, which thrive in a sunny position in warm, well-drained borders and rich light soil. For culture, *see* Annuals, p. 106, *and* Perennials, p. 128. *Species.* —*C. cœlestis* (Rich Blue, June–July, 18 in.).

Convolvulus (Bindweed).—A large family of hardy annual and perennial climbing and trailing plants, most of which like a sunny position and rather poor soil. For culture, *see* Annuals, p. 106, *and* Perennials, p. 128. *Species.*—ANNUALS—*C. tricolor* (White to Purple and Blue, June–Oct., 8–9 ft.) ; *C. tricolor alba* (White, July–Oct., 12 in.). PERENNIALS—*C. Cneorum* (Soft Pink with Silver Foliage, June–Sept., 18 in.) ; *C. mauritanicus* (Blue, June–Sept., 12 in.).

Coreopsis (Tickseed).—Hardy annuals, biennials and perennials, most of which are best treated as biennials. The tall varieties are effective in mixed borders, and the dwarf kinds make fine bedding plants. A moist, sandy loam and a sunny position are most suitable, and ample water is needed in summer. For culture, *see* Annuals, p. 106, Biennials, p. 107, *and* Perennials, p. 128. *Species.*—ANNUALS —*C. coronata* (Orange and Brown, July–Oct., 18 in.) ; *C. Drummondii* (Golden Yellow, July–Oct., 24 in.) ; *C. tinctoria* (Yellow and Bronze, July–Oct., 18 in.). PERENNIALS—*C. grandiflora* (Golden Yellow, July–Oct., 24–30 in.) ; *C. lanceolata* (Yellow, July–Oct., 24–30 in.) ; *C. rosea* (Reddish–pink, July–Sept., 18 in.) ; *C. verticillata* (Golden Yellow, July–Sept., 24 in.).

Cornus (Cornel, Dogwood, Cornelian Cherry).—Deciduous shrubs and trees and hardy herbaceous perennials. *Culture.*—Sow under glass, or propagate by means of layering in October, or by suckers in November. Plant-out in spring or early autumn in the shade, in a mixture of moist leaf-mould and peat, or ordinary soil. *C. Mas,* the Cornelian Cherry (10 to 25 ft.), thrives quite well in a dry soil. Thin-out after flowering when the branches are overcrowded. *Species and Varieties.*—*C. alba sibirica variegata* (Silvery Variegation) ; *C. alba* var. *Spœthii* (Golden Foliage) ; *C. florida rubra* (Rosy-pink Floral Bracts) ; *C. Kousa* (White Floral Bracts), etc. All May, 7 to 10 feet.

Corokea.—Half-hardy evergreen flowering shrubs which thrive in a warm sunny position and in ordinary soil. *Culture.*—Plant in April or October, and prune only to keep in shape. To propagate, strike half-matured cuttings in a frame in August. *Species.*—*C. buddleioides* (White, April–May, 3–4 ft.) ; *C. Cotoneaster* (Yellow, May, 6 ft.) ; *C. macrocarpa* (Orange, May–June, 6 ft.).

Coronilla (Crown Vetch or Scorpion Senna).—Half-hardy evergreen or deciduous shrubs, and herbaceous perennials, which succeed well against a south wall with a little winter protection, also in the rock garden, or cold greenhouse. *Culture.*—Plant in March or October in well-drained ordinary soil, or in sandy loam (rock garden species). *Pot Culture.*—Pot-up in March, using 6 to 8-inch pots and a compost of 2 parts sandy loam to 1 part of peat. Prune into shape and cut-out old and dead wood in February, and stand in the open after flowering until September. To propagate, sow in a frame in March, or take cuttings of young wood in April or August (greenhouse plants) and strike in a frame (Temp. 60° F.) The rock garden species are propagated by seed as above, or by division of roots in October. *Species.*—*C. cappadocica* (*syn. C. iberica*) (Cream–yellow, July–Aug., 4 in.) ; *C. minima* (Yellow, June–July, 3 in.) ; *C. varia* (Lilac-pink, Aug.–Sept., 12–18 in.).

Cortaderia (Pampas Grass).—Perennial grasses which thrive in sunny, sheltered positions, and well-drained soil. They grow 6 to 8 feet high and flower in autumn. For culture, *see* Perennials, p. 128.

Cortusa Matthioli (Bear's Ear).—Dwarf-growing rock plants, closely allied to the Primula, which thrive in partial shade in rich, sandy loam and leaf-mould, and flower in July. *See* Rock Plants, p. 135.

Corydalis (Fumitory).—Hardy annual and perennial rock garden or border plants, which require shade and comparatively poor soil. For culture, see Annuals, p. 106, and Perennials, p. 128. Species.—(Perennials)—C. bulbosa (Purple and Rose, May, 9 in.) ; C. capnoides (Cream, May–Sept., 12 in.) ; C. lutea (Yellow, June–Sept., 6–12 in.).

Corylopsis.—Hardy deciduous shrubs which like a sunny, sheltered position, and well-drained, ordinary soil. Culture.—Plant in October or November. Little pruning is required. Propagate by means of layering in the summer. Pot Culture.—Pot-up from October to February, using 6 to 8-inch pots and turfy loam. Sink the pots in ashes in the open, from May to December, then take into the cold greenhouse. After flowering prune-out weak wood and dead flower shoots. Species. —C. Goteana ; C. pauciflora ; C. spicata and C. Willmottiæ. All Yellow, March to April, 4 to 8 feet.

Cosmos (Mexican Aster).—Half-hardy annuals and perennials which thrive in warm, dry borders and in ordinary soil. The early-flowering annuals should be chosen. For culture, see Annuals, p. 107, and Perennials, p. 128. Species.—ANNUALS—C. bipinnatus (Pink, White and Crimson, June–Oct., 30–70 in.) ; C. sulphureus (Yellow, June–Oct., 20 in.) ; C. tenuifolius (Purple, June–Oct., 24 in.). Named Varieties.— Early Dawn (Pink and White) ; Klondyke (Yellow) ; Rose Queen (Rosy Red) ; and White Queen (White).

Cotoneaster (Rockspray).—Hardy shrubs or small trees, most of which grow best in poor or chalky soil. Culture.—Plant from October to March. No pruning is necessary, though some species require thinning-out after flowering. To propagate, take cuttings of hard wood in a frame in July or August, or layer in September or October, Seed may be sown in the open in March or September. Species.—C. buxifolia (E) (White, April, 8–12 ft.) ; C. Franchettii (E) (White, May, 7–10 ft.) ; C. horizontalis (E) (Pale Pink, April, 2–4 ft.) ; C. humifusa (E) (White, April–May, prostrate) ; C. microphylla (E) (Rosy White. May, 2–3 ft.) ; C. salicifolia (E) (White, May, 6 ft.) ; C. thymifolia (E) (Pinkish, April, 18 in.). (E)=Evergreen.

Cotyledon (Pennywort).—Dwarf-growing rock plants which thrive in sun or shade in dry, gritty loam and sand, and which flower in June. For culture, see Rock Plants, p. 135. See also Echeveria.

Cratægus (Thorn).—Hardy deciduous trees or shrubs, useful for hedges, etc. Culture.—Plant in Oct. or Nov. in a sunny position and ordinary soil. Thin-out the branches when overcrowded. To propagate, sow seed when ripe, bud or graft. See also Pyracantha. Species. —C. Crus-galli (White) ; C. oxyacantha fl. albo pl. (White, Dbl.) ; C. o. fl. roseo pl. (Pink, Dbl.) ; C. o. punicea (Scarlet, Sngl.). All May, 15 feet.

Crinum (Cape Lily).—A half-hardy bulbous plant for the cool greenhouse. C. Powellii and C. album will grow outdoors in a sunny, sheltered, moist border, in well-drained, deep and rich sandy loam and peat. Culture.—Plant 6 inches deep in March, surrounded with coarse sand, and protect with fibre in winter. Do not disturb unless overcrowded. Pot Culture.—Pot-up in the spring (triennially) one bulb in each 9 to 10-inch pot in a compost of two parts fibrous loam to one part sandy peat. Propagate by means of offsets in March. Species and Varieties. —C. capense (White and Red) ; C. longifolium (Pink or White) ; C. Powellii (Rose-red or White). All June to August. 24 to 36 inches.

Crocus.—Besides those which bloom in the early spring, there are species and hybrids that flower in the autumn and winter. *Culture.*—They like a good light soil to which a little bonemeal has been added, and thrive in sun or shade in a warm rock garden, border, or in pots, and are also useful for naturalizing in grass or for the wild garden. Crocuses are increased by offsets or by seed, the former being the usual method. Offsets are treated the same as old bulbs and will bloom the second year. Seed should be sown in pans of light sandy loam as soon as ripe, and placed in a sheltered situation out-of-doors until late autumn. During heavy rain and cold weather protect with a cold frame. They may remain in the same pans during summer, but lift in autumn and plant in beds of mellow loam in the reserve garden, 2 inches apart and 3 inches deep ; here they will form strong bulbs and flower the third or fourth spring. Plant mature bulbs from 2 to 3 inches deep and 4 inches apart, autumn-flowering species from July to August ; spring-flowering species in September or October. Divide and replant every third year. *Pot Culture.*—Plant about seven corms half an inch deep in a 5 to 6-inch pot in autumn, using a compost of good, fairly light, sandy loam and leaf-mould, and keep covered with ashes or fibre in a frame until growth commences, then water and transfer to the cool house. Stand out in the open and keep dry in summer, and re-pot in September. *Species.*—EARLY SPRING—*C. aureus* (Golden Yellow) ; *C. biflorus* (White, veined Violet) ; *C. chrysanthus* (Orange-yellow and Red) ; *C. Imperati* (Lilac or Buff and Black) ; *C. Sieberi* (Lilac-blue and Gold) ; *C. Tommasinianus* (Lavender and Orange) ; *C. versicolor* (White, feathered Purple) ; *C. vernus* and *vars.* (Various). AUTUMN—*C. asturicus* (Purple) ; *C. iridiflorus* (Lavender) ; *C. ochroleucus* (Yellow) ; *C. pulchellus* (Lavender-blue and Orange Throat) ; *C. sativus* (Violet, Mauve and Orange) ; *C. speciosus* (Violet-blue and Orange) ; *C. zonatus* (Lilac-pink with Orange Throat). NAMED VARIETIES.—*Grandeur Triomphante* (White and Blue) ; *King of the Whites* (White) ; *Large Yellow* (Yellow) ; *L'Unique* (Lilac-pink) ; *Van Speyk* (Purple, veined White) ; and *Yellow Hammer* (Yellow). All 3 to 4 inches.

Cryptomeria japonica (Japanese Cedar).—Handsome evergreen trees which thrive in deep sandy loam in a sheltered, sunny situation. *Culture.*—Plant from September to November. No pruning is required. To propagate, sow in March or April or strike cuttings under hand-lights in August. The variety *elegans* is an attractive small tree.

Cucurbita (Ornamental Gourds).—Half-hardy climbing plants, many of which are very ornamental. Treated in a similar way to ordinary marrows, most will thrive in the open. Any good seedsman's catalogue will give several good varieties.

Cuphea (Cigar Flower).—Hardy and half-hardy annuals, perennials, and shrubs, all better treated as half-hardy. For culture, *see* Annuals, p. 106, *and* Perennials, p. 128. (*Shrubby Species*).—Propagate by cuttings of young wood in bottom heat (70° F.) in spring. Trim the following January, and re-pot if necessary in February.

Cupressus (Cypress).—Quick-growing conifers which thrive in sunny, sheltered positions in almost any soil. *Culture.*—Plant in April or September. No pruning is required, except in the case of hedge plants.

ASTERS

Photos]

[*Alexander & Brown (Perth); R. H. Bath, Ltd.;*
Dobbie & Co., Ltd.; and Ryders (St. Albans).

Marguerite Asters.
Victoria Aster.

Comet Asters.
Giant Californian Asters.

FLOWERING PLANTS

Photos]   [Alexander & Brown (Perth); Dobbie & Co., Ltd.; C. Jones.

Gilia androsacea alba (*White*).   Lavatera "Carmine Queen."
Malope trifida (*Purple-white*).   Lithospermum prostratum (*Blue*).
Lychnis (*Dwarf White*).   Mimulus (Large-flowered Perfecta
                                             Hybrids).

They may be propagated by means of cuttings in a frame in August or September ; some, however, are best raised from seed in March. For small gardens none are better than *C. obtusa* and vars. *C. tetragona minima* is a dwarf-growing form for the rock garden.

Cyclamen (Sowbread).—Tuberous-rooted plants, useful alike for rock garden, border, naturalizing in grass and for greenhouse culture. Of the hardy cyclamen there are two types, the spring-blooming and autumn-blooming. *Culture.—Hardy Species.*—Plant in August 2 inches deep and 2½ inches apart in a shady position in light sandy loam mixed with peat or leaf-mould and mortar. Protect with fibre in winter and top-dress annually with leaf-mould and rotten manure. Propagate by means of seed in gentle heat in spring, and do not plant the young corms in their permanent positions until of moderate size. *Pot Culture.—* (*C. persicum*).—Soak the pot and corm that have been dried-off in water and stand on a shelf in the greenhouse. Pot-up in August, placing one corm in a 5-inch pot in a fresh compost of rich sandy loam and leaf-mould, and keep close for a few days, then give ample air and not too much heat (60° F.). Moist, steady heat, and shade from strong sun, are essential. After flowering, decrease water supply, dry-off, and keep the roots cool and almost dry until next potting-up. Keep the plants indoors from September to May, and in a cold frame with the pots on their sides from June to August. Only use the same corms for pot-culture for two years in succession. One-year-old plants give the finest flowers ; cyclamen are, therefore, best raised annually from seed. To propagate, sow thinly in pans in a finely-sieved compost of two-thirds loam and one-third leaf-mould and sand from August to November, and place in a cold frame or on a shelf near the light in the cool greenhouse. Prick-off into pans, then pot-up singly into thumb pots and subsequently into larger pots until, in July, they are in 5 to 6-inch pots in which they may be flowered. *Species.—C. coum* (Purple, Red and White, Jan.–March, 3 in.) ; *C. europæum* (Red and White, July–Nov., 3 in.) ; *C. neapolitanum* (Rose, White and Purple Throat, Aug.–Sept., 6 in.) ; *C. persicum* (White to Crimson, Nov.–March, 6–10 in.).

Cydonia (Quince).—Hardy deciduous flowering trees and shrubs, which thrive in sunny positions in ordinary soil. *Culture.*—Plant in October or November. Cut-out old wood and shorten side shoots in June. Propagate by means of seeds, layering, suckers, or cuttings in October. *Pot Culture.*—Pot-up in November, in 8 to 10-inch pots, and take into the cold greenhouse. Sink the pots in ashes outdoors from May to November. *Species and Varieties.—C. japonica* (Orange-red), vars. *Aurora* (Rose, shaded Yellow) ; *cardinalis* (Rich Red) ; *nivalis* (White) ; and *rubra grandiflora* (Crimson). All March to June, 6 to 9 feet.

Cynoglossum (Hound's Tongue).—Annuals, biennials and perennials which thrive in rather poor, ordinary soil, and bear deep blue forget-me-not-like flowers from June to August. For culture, *see* Annuals, p. 106, Biennials, p. 107, *and* Perennials, p. 128.

Cytisus (Broom).—A genus of shrubs, mostly hardy and deciduous, which thrive in light ordinary soil, in a dry, sunny position. The species and hybrids *C. Ardoinii* (Deep Yellow), *C. Beanii* (Golden Yellow), *C. kewensis* (Cream), and *C. purpureus* (Rose-purple), flowering in May and June, are all prostrate or trailing, and suitable for the rock garden. *C. præcox* (Sulphur-yellow, April–May, 6 ft.) and the purple-flowered hybrids *Dallimorei, Donard Seedling*, and *Dorothy Walpole* (May, 5–6 ft.) are the best border species, while for pot culture *C. fragrans* (Yellow, 3 ft.) is the favourite. *Culture*.—Cut back all branches by at least a third and plant in October. Small plants give little trouble. Except when quite young only trim to keep in shape ; pruning must be systematic and regular so that it is not necessary to cut into old wood. Spring-blooming species should be trimmed and pruned directly after flowering ; late-flowering kinds must not be pruned until the following February or March. *Pot Culture*.—Pot-up in May, after flowering, using a compost of two parts turfy loam to one part lumpy leaf-mould and coarse sand. Prune hard back after flowering, then keep in the warm and syringe in fine weather. Harden-off and sink the pots in ashes outdoors from May to October, then move into the cool greenhouse. To propagate, sow in the open in September, take cuttings in March or August and strike in a frame and grow in pots near the glass until ready for planting-out. Young plants need occasional "stopping-back." The Genista is closely allied to the Cytisus.

Dabœcia (Irish Heath).—Hardy evergreen shrubs which thrive in sandy peat and loam with no lime in it. *Culture*.—Plant-out in March or October, and cut-off dead blooms in October. To propagate, strike cuttings in a frame in July or August, layer in September or sow seed. *Species and Varieties*.—*D. polifolia* (Rosy-purple) ; *D. p. alba* (White) ; *D. p. bicolor* (Purple and White). All June to Sept., 1 foot.

Daffodils.—The word *daffodil* is popularly applied to those types of narcissi with long, trumpet-like coronas. For culture, *see* Narcissus.

Dahlia.—The dahlia is easily grown in ordinary garden soil, and in warm districts can be left in the ground all winter if a heap of ashes or sand is placed over the tubers. It is somewhat tender, however, and it is better to lift it as soon as the plants have died down, and to store the tubers for the winter. The ideal soil is a rich, sandy loam containing sufficient humus to make it retentive of moisture.

Culture.—Dahlias may be multiplied by seeds or by dividing the base of the old stem in April, taking care that an " eye " and a tuber or two are attached to each portion. Another way is to cut off the young shoots at their base and strike them in small pots. *Seed*.—Sow about 1 inch apart in shallow pans or boxes in March. The soil should be light and sandy with a mixture of leaf-mould. Place the pans on a warm shelf, and in April pot-off either singly or round the edge of 6-inch pots. Place in a cold frame, gradually harden-off, and plant out 2 to 3 feet apart, early in June. After flowering, the young tubers are taken up and treated as old tubers. *Cuttings*.—In February, March or even the first week in April, tubers which have been wintered in a dry place are placed in shallow boxes containing a slightly moist compost of two-thirds finely sieved loam and one-third leaf-mould and sand, which does not quite cover them, and are set over a hotbed close up to the glass (Temperature 65° F.). A number of strong shoots soon appear ; when these are 3 to 4 inches long they are taken off and struck round the edges of 4-inch pots, filled with equal parts of sandy loam and leaf-mould. They should be watered, and again placed in the same hotbed, and shaded from the sun. Pot-up singly as soon as the cuttings have struck (about three weeks) and transfer to a cold frame. Pot-on as required, harden-off, and plant-out early in June.

Preparing the Ground and Planting.—In autumn the beds should be prepared ; they should be in an open, but sheltered, position and should catch the morning sun, but must have a little shade in the afternoon. Damp, low-lying situations should be avoided. Dahlias will be best displayed in beds 3 feet wide with alleys between. The beds should be marked by stakes placed at each corner, 4 inches of the surface soil being removed and 4 inches of thoroughly rotted manure and bonemeal at the rate of 3 oz. to the square yard being put in its place. The whole is then dug to a depth of 18 inches or 2 feet, and the manure thoroughly mixed with the soil. Towards the end of May, the soil should be top-dressed with wood ashes which should then be thoroughly raked in. The three foot beds will receive each a row of plants, and the four to five-foot stakes are firmly fixed at planting time 3, 4 and 5 feet apart, according to the size of the plants, which are planted 4 inches deep so that the crown is just above the surface. After planting a good watering should be given, and soot sprinkled around. Syringe every evening in dry weather, and search for slugs, earwigs and other pests. During June and July water as often as twice a week in hot dry weather, and assist the roots by stirring the soil with a fork every two or three weeks. Remove all dead or straggling shoots and keep the plant trim and well staked. A surface mulch of rotted manure, 3 inches deep, will help to keep the roots cool and moist ; if this is not applied, weak liquid manure should be given every third or fourth day throughout August and September. When dahlias are intended either for exhibition or for highly developed flowers, early in July, when the plants are 18 inches high, pinch-out the top, and thin-out the stems that form after this, to six at the most and leave only one bud on a shoot. Where a show of colour, or flowers for picking, is required, eight or nine main stems may be left ; constant thinning-out of stems is necessary. Flowers for exhibition should be protected both from the sun and rain. As the autumn approaches examine the shoots tied-up and slacken the raffia or bass where necessary. When the frost turns their foliage brown or black, take up the plants, leaving 6 inches or so of stem attached. Hang the tubers up to dry with the stem downwards for a few days, then plunge them with a little old soil still left on them into a box of ashes, fibre, chaff, or sand in order to preserve them from damp, frost, and heat.

Varieties.—CACTUS—*Alabaster* (White) ; *Border King* (Crimson-scarlet) ; *Empire* (Crimson, shaded Scarlet) ; *Harry Strutt* (Deep Crimson) ; *J. H. Jackson* (Crimson-maroon) ; *J. H. Reed* (Salmon-scarlet) ; *Masterpiece* (Cattleya Mauve) ; *Miss Eckert* (Pink and White) ; *Mrs. H. Blackman* (Pink) ; *Snow Bunting* (White). " CHARM " OR MINIATURE PÆONY-FLOWERED—*Aurora* (Crimson and Cherry Red) ; *Crimson Glow* (Crimson) ; *Dazzle* (Scarlet) ; *Gloria* (Orange Shaded) ; *Ladybird* (Salmon and Yellow) ; *Norah Bell* (Scarlet, Flame and Yellow); *Our Annie* (Shrimp Pink and Yellow) ; *Pink Pearl* ; *Radium* (Crimson-

scarlet and Golden-yellow) ; *Tangerine* (Orange and Scarlet). COL-
LARETTE—*Arran* (Rose-pink and White) ; *Doon* (Orange-scarlet and
Yellow) ; *Dunottor* (Scarlet) ; *Glen Sannox* (Vermilion-scarlet and
Yellow) ; *Grandeur* (Scarlet-crimson and Yellow) ; *Scarlet Queen*
(Scarlet and Yellow) ; *Scotia* (White) ; *Tiger* (Yellow, White and Red).
DECORATIVE—*Acclamation* (Rosy-cerise) ; *Bishop of Llandoff* (Crimson,
Dark Foliage) ; *Couronne d'Or* (Golden-orange) ; *Glory of Aalsmeer*
(White) ; *Glut* (Crimson) ; *Insulinde* (Deep Orange) ; *Jersey Beauty*
(Salmon-pink) ; *Moorcop* (Crimson-red) ; *Mrs. Carl Salbach* (Rosy-
pink and Cream) ; *Polar Bear* (White) ; *Porthos* (Bluish-violet) ;
Prestige (Orange) ; *Reg. Godfrey* (Crimson) ; *The Prince* (Crimson-
maroon). MIGNON—*Ada* (Yellow) ; *Avondrood* (Orange) ; *Coltness
Gem* (Crimson-scarlet) ; *Dinkie* (Yellow) ; *Lady Aileen* (Salmon-pink) ;
L'Innocence (White) ; *Maasland* (Dark Red) ; *Paisley Gem* (Orange-
scarlet) ; *Peter Pan* (Red). PÆONY-FLOWERED—*Creation* (Cherry-
red) ; *Fairy Queen* (Salmon-pink) ; *Joyce Goddard* (Scarlet-yellow) ;
Ruby ; *Salmonea* (Salmon) ; *Scarlet King.* POMPON—*Bacchus* (Scar-
let) ; *Cardinal* (Carmine-red) ; *Girlie* (Rosy-mauve) ; *Jewel* (Yellow) ;
Murren (Bronze and Rose) ; *Nerissa* (Rosy-pink and White) ; *Princess*
(Shell-pink) ; *Snow White* ; *Tommy Keith* (Red and White) ; *Wee
Gracie* (White and Lavender). SINGLE—*Beacon* (Yellow) ; *Lemur*
(Crimson, Dark Foliage) ; *Miss Willmott* (Crimson) ; *Prince of Wales*
(Pink) ; *Snowdrop* (White). STAR—*White Star* (White) ; *Yellow Star*
(Yellow) ; *Bronze Star* (Bronze) ; *Morning Star* (Carmine) ; *Autumn
Star* (Terra Cotta) ; and *Southern Star* (Crimson). All July to October,
18 to 72 inches.

Daphne.—Dwarf-growing deciduous and evergreen shrubs, which
thrive in a sunny sheltered position in well-drained, deep, sandy loam
and peat. *Culture.*—Plant in March or October. No pruning is
necessary. Propagate by layering in August, grafting in May, or seeds.
D. Mezereum (Purple, Rose and White, 2–4 ft.), which is usually propagated by means of seed, is the best known of the hardy deciduous
species. It thrives in ordinary garden loam, but needs shade from the
hot sun. If trimming is necessary, it should be done in April. For the
rock garden none are better than *D. alpina* (White, May, 1½ ft.), *D.
Blagayana* (Ivory, May, ½ ft.), and *D. Cneorum* (Purple-pink, May–Aug.,
1 ft.). They thrive in partial shade in sandy loam and peat or leaf-
mould. *Greenhouse Culture.*—*D. odora* (Pink, 2 ft.), and *D. o. alba*
(White), often but wrongly named *D. indica* in gardens, are too tender
for the open air, except in S.W. Pot-up in April, using 5 to 7-inch pots
and a compost of peaty loam and sand. Plunge the pots in a cool,
shady position out of doors from May to September, syringe daily in fine
weather, and keep just moist. Move into the house in September and
gradually give more heat. Treatment as advised for *Forcing*, p. 173,
will bring the blooms out by December. Propagate by means of
cuttings under glass from April to July.

Delphinium (Larkspur).—A large genus of hardy annuals, biennials
and perennials, which like a sunny site in deep, highly enriched and well-
drained friable loam, and need ample water in hot dry weather. If
flower stalks are cut down as soon as they have bloomed a second crop

of bloom will be obtained in early autumn. For culture, *see* Annuals, p. 106, Biennials, p. 107, *and* Perennials, p. 128. *Pot Culture.*—Pot-up in October or November in 5 to 6-inch pots, and winter well up near the glass in a cool house. *Species.*—(PERENNIALS)—*D. cardinale* (Scarlet) ; *D. cashmirianum* (Purple-blue) ; *D. nudicaule* (Orange-scarlet) ; *D. tanguticum* (Blue and White) ; *D. sulphureum* (Sulphur-yellow). All June to August, 24 to 60 inches. For named varieties *see* growers' catalogues.

Desfontainea spinosa.—These evergreen shrubs are almost hardy in England. They thrive in warm, sheltered borders or in pots in the greenhouse, in a well-drained compost of equal parts of loam and peat with a little sand added. They grow to a height of 10 feet and flower from July to September. *Culture.*—Plant in spring or autumn. Propagate by means of cuttings in slight heat in spring.

Desmodium (Tick Trefoil and Telegraph Plant).—Hardy perennials and shrubs, also greenhouse deciduous shrubs. The former thrive in sunny sheltered borders in ordinary soil, the latter in the cool greenhouse. For culture, *see* Perennials, p. 128. *Greenhouse Shrubs.*—Pot-up in March in a compost of sandy loam and peat. Propagate by means of cuttings in frame or from seed. *Species.*—*D. gyrans* (greenhouse) (White, July, 2 ft.), and *tiliæfolium* (Lilac, July–Oct., 3–4 ft.).

Deutzia.—Hardy deciduous flowering shrubs, which thrive in a sheltered, partially shaded position in rich, well-drained ordinary soil in the shrubbery, or in the greenhouse. *Culture.*—Plant in October or November, mulch annually after flowering, also thin-out well and cut away weak and old wood. To propagate, strike cuttings of soft wood in June in a frame with bottom heat. *Pot Culture.*—Pot-up from September to November, in rich, sandy loam, using as small a pot as convenient. Keep cool, but frost-proof, then in December or January move into the greenhouse and gradually raise the temperature to 65° F. As soon as the buds form, water with weak manure water, or dress with artificial manure once a week until the colour of the flowers is visible. Deutzias are well adapted for forcing, but should be exempted from this process every alternate year. *Species and Varieties.*—*D. discolor grandiflora* (Pink) ; *D. d. major* (White) ; *D. gracilis* (White) ; *D. longifolia Veitchii* (Rose-purple) ; *D. magnifica* (Dbl. White) ; *D. scabra (syn. crenata) fl. pl.* (Double Pink) ; *D. Vilmorinæ* (White). All May to June, 3 to 6 feet.

Dianthus.—A beautiful and extensive genus, which embraces the Carnation, Picotee, Pink and Sweet William (*see* separately).

Dicentra (Dielytra or Bleeding Heart).—Hardy perennials which thrive in a sheltered, sunny site and a light dry soil with ample leaf-mould in it. Although hardy it is safer to winter them in a cold frame. They are often forced in the greenhouse in late winter. *Pot Culture.*—Pot-up in September in well-manured sandy loam, stand in the cold frame, plunged in ashes, and keep just moist until November, then move into the greenhouse (55° F.). After flowering, continue water until the leaves die down, and stand in the open from May to September. Dicentras require ample water and, when making full growth, the pots may be stood in saucers of water. Propagate by division in

April or September, and plant-out during those months. In the open the flowers are borne from May to July. *Species.—D. Cucullaria* (White, 5 in.) ; *D. eximea* (Purple, 15 in.) ; *D. formosa* (Red, 9 in.) ; *D. spectabilis* (Red or White, 24 in.).

Dictamnus (Burning Bush, Dittany or Fraxinella).—Hardy perennials, suitable for sunny or semi-shaded borders and dry, light soil. For culture, *see* Perennials, p. 128. *Species.—D. albus* (White) ; and *D. a. var. purpureus* (Purple-red). Both June to August, 30 inches.

Diervilla (Bush Honeysuckle or Weigela).—Hardy deciduous shrubs which thrive in sun or shade in almost any soil, though moist fibrous loam and leaf-mould suits them best. *Culture.*—Plant in October or November, and after flowering cut out old and straggly wood. To propagate strike cuttings of soft wood in June in a frame, or matured cuttings in the open in October. *D. rosea* will flower in March in the cool greenhouse. Pot-up annually in October, using 8 to 12-inch pots, and a compost of two parts sandy loam to one part of leaf-mould and rotten manure. Plant-out in June after flowering, and don't re-pot for at least two seasons. Prune as above. *Species and Varieties.—D. amabilis* (Pale Rose, April–May, 6 ft.) ; *D. Abel Carrière* (Carmine-red, April–May, 5 ft.) ; *D. Eva Rathke* (Crimson-purple, May–Sept., 3–4 ft.) ; *D. florida* (Deep Rose, 5–6 ft.) ; and *D. f. candida* (White), etc.

Digitalis (Foxglove).—Handsome biennials and hardy perennials, that thrive in the shade in almost any fairly rich soil. For culture, *see* Biennials, p. 107, *and* Perennials, p. 128. *Species.—D. purpurea* (White and Purple) ; *D. gloxinioides* (Purple and Rose) ; *D. lutea* (Pale Yellow) ; *D. tomentosa* (Red). All June to Sept., 10 to 50 inches.

Dimorphotheca (Cape Daisy or Star of the Veldt).—A half-hardy annual which likes a sunny position in light soil and is useful for inclusion in the rock garden. It flowers from July to October and grows 12 inches high. For culture, *see* Annuals, p. 107.

Dodecatheon.—The American Cowslip, which thrives well in cool shady borders, or the rock or marsh garden in rich, deep loam. For culture, *see* Rock Plants, p. 135. *Varieties.—D. Hendersonii* (Rose, May, 6 in.) ; *D. Jeffreyi* (Purple-rose, June–July, 18 in.) ; *D. Media* (Lilac, Rose and White, May–June, 12–18 in.).

Dog's Tooth Violet (Erythronium).—A pretty little bulbous plant which does well in any light soil, and is useful as an edging to borders or in the rock garden. *Culture.*—Plant 4 to 6 inches deep and 4 inches apart in partial shade in September in moist, well-drained sandy loam and ample leaf-mould. Surround the tubers with about an inch of silver sand and do not lift more often than necessary, but mulch annually with well-rotted manure and leaf-mould. Propagate by means of seed in a frame in August. Thin-out, but do not plant the seedlings out until the third September after sowing. The plants are also increased by offsets. *Pot Culture.*—Plant in August in 5 to 6-inch pots, using a compost of loam, peat and leaf-mould, and keep in a cold frame during the winter, giving but little water until February. Then increase the supply and take into the cold greenhouse. *Species and Varieties.—E. citrinum* (Yellow) ; *E. Frans Hals* (Purple-rose) ; *E. revolutum* (Pink) ; *E. Hartwegii* (Creamy-white). All April to May, 10 inches.

Doronicum (Leopard's Bane).—Hardy perennials which thrive in sunny borders and ordinary soil, or under almost any conditions. Cut down the shoots that have flowered and dress with well-rotted manure to encourage a second crop of bloom. For culture, *see* Perennials, p. 128. *Species.*—*D. austriacum* (Golden-yellow, April–May, 18 in.) ; *D. plantagineum excelsum* (Yellow, March–June, 24–36 in.).

Draba.—Dwarf-growing rock plants which thrive in a moderately sunny spot, in well-drained gritty loam. For culture, *see* Rock Plants, p. 135. *Species.*—*D. Aizoon* (Bright Yellow) ; *D. Dedeana* (White) ; *D. pyrenaica* (Pale Mauve-pink). All March to May, 3 inches.

Dracocephalum (Dragon's Head).—Hardy perennials useful for cool shady borders, or rock gardens with light soil. For culture, *see* Perennials, p. 128. *Species.*—*D. grandiflorum* (Blue, 15 in.) ; *D. Ruyschianum* (Purple, 15 in.) ; *D. parviflorum* (Blue, 6 in.). All July and August.

Drosera (Sundew or Youthwort).—Curious dwarf-growing plants which thrive in a warm, sheltered position in the bog or wild garden. They grow some 3 inches high and flower about midsummer. Propagate by means of seed or root cuttings in March.

Dryas (Mountain Avens).—Evergreen trailing hardy perennials which like sun or partial shade and a cool gritty loam with lime and leaf-mould in it. They are excellent in the rock garden. For culture, *see* Rock Plants, p. 135. *Species.*—*D. Drummondii* (Golden-yellow) ; *D. octopetala* (White). Both June–July, 3 inches.

Eccremocarpus scaber.—A half-hardy climber which thrives in any well-drained light loam against south walls, trellises and pillars, and is also useful as a greenhouse climber. *Culture.*—Propagate by means of cuttings in a frame in autumn, or sow in heat in January ; plant-out in April. After flowering cut away dead wood and protect the roots in winter. *Species.*—*E. scaber* (Orange-red) and *E. s. var. roseus* (Red). Both flowering from July to September, 10 to 20 feet.

Echeveria.—Half-hardy dwarf-growing rosette-shaped plants which thrive in warm, sunny sheltered positions, but which must be brought indoors in October. The red and yellow flowers are borne on short stems. *Culture.*—Pot-up in March in 4 to 5-inch pots in a compost of loam and mortar-rubble. Propagate by means of offsets or leaf-cuttings in summer. *See also* Cotyledon.

Echinacea.—Hardy perennials which thrive in sunny borders and well-drained light loam. They reach a height of about 3 feet and flower in August and September. *E. purpurea* (Reddish-purple) is the best species. For culture, *see* Perennials, p. 128.

Echinops (Globe Thistle).—Hardy perennials that thrive in the sun in light loam, but do not like being disturbed. For culture, *see* Perennials, p. 128. *Species.*—*E. bannaticus* (Blue, July–Sept., 36–60 in.) ; *E. exaltatus* (White, July–Aug., 60–70 in.) ; and *E. Ritro* (Blue).

Edelweiss (Leontopodium).—A hardy plant which requires a sunny position, in sandy loam and old mortar-rubble. The cream-white, star-shaped flowers are borne from June to September on stems 6 inches high. For culture, *see* Rock Plants, p. 135.

Elæagnus (Oleaster or Wild Olive).—Hardy evergreen and deciduous shrubs which grow freely in full sun in almost any soil. *Culture.*—

Plant in March or from Sept. to Nov., and cut-out dead wood when required. To propagate, strike cuttings of matured wood in Oct. in a frame, or layer. *Species and Varieties.*—*E. argentea* (6–12 ft.) ; **E. glabra* (15–20 ft.) ; *E. multiflora* (6–10 ft.) ; **E. pungens* (10–15 ft.).

Enkianthus.—Beautiful flowering shrubs which like a sunny sheltered position and moist peat or non-calcareous sandy loam and leaf-mould. *Culture.*—Plant in Oct. or Nov. ; no pruning is necessary. To propagate, sow seeds or strike cuttings of mature shoots in a frame in October. *Species.*—*E. campanulatus* (Cream, Yellow and Red, May, 4–8 ft.) ; *E. japonicus* (White, April, 3–6 ft.).

Epacris (Australian Heath).—Heath-like winter-flowering evergreen shrubs that thrive in the cool greenhouse. *Culture.*—Pot-up when growth recommences (about May), using 5-inch pots and a compost of sandy peat. Keep close until established and then stand in a cool greenhouse during the summer months. Water moderately, and give liquid manure while growing, but do not syringe. Cut long shoots well back and thin-out after flowering. Propagate by cuttings of young wood with a little bottom heat in spring, or sow seed in pots in March.

Epilobium (The Willow Herb).—Hardy perennials, the dwarf-growing species of which are useful for the rock garden, and the marsh or water-garden. They do well in sun or shade in moist ordinary soil, but prefer a gritty loam with some peat in it. For culture, *see* Perennials, p. 128. *Species.*—*E. angustifolium* (Crimson, July–Aug., 36–40 in.) ; *E. obcordatum* (Rosy-purple, Aug.–Oct., 3–6 in.) ; *E. rosmarinifolium* (Rose-pink, June–Aug., 24–36 in.).

Epimedium (Barrenwort).—Dwarf-growing perennials which thrive in sun or shade in the rock garden in sandy loam with a little peat. For culture, *see* Rock Plants, p. 135. *Species.*—*E. alpinum* (Yellow and Crimson, April–July, 9 in.) ; *E. Musschianum* (White, May, 9 in.) ; *E. rubrum* (Rose, April–May, 10 in.).

Eremurus (Fox-tail Lily, Giant Asphodel, or King's Spear).—Tall hardy perennials which thrive in sunny sheltered borders in rich loam. For culture, *see* Perennials, p. 128. *Species.*—*E. Bungei* (Golden Yellow, June–July, 20–40 in.) ; *E. Elwesianus* (Soft Rose, June, 50 in.).

Erica.—An important genus of hardy and greenhouse evergreen flowering shrubs, often known as Heath or Heather. *Culture.*—(*Hardy Species*)—Plant in October in a sunny position in well-drained sand and peat, or in any light garden loam without lime in it (except *E. carnea*, which likes lime). Do not prune, but merely keep in shape by removing dead blooms from the spring-flowering species in June, from the summer and autumn bloomers in March, and from winter-flowerers in April. To propagate, strike cuttings of half-matured wood in July in a frame, sow seed in a frame in March, divide the roots, or layer in autumn. *Culture.*—(*Greenhouse Species*)—Propagate by means of cuttings of tender tops of young shoots in March or April or in Sept. (Temp. 50° F.) in well-drained pots or pans of sandy peat. Pot-up into 2-inch pots as soon as rooted. " Stop-back " to make " bushy " plants. Re-pot in September into 5-inch pots and transfer to a light, airy position ; re-pot into 6-inch pots, if need be, in March, and summer on a hard bed of ashes in a cold frame in full sun. Mature plants

Note.—* denotes evergreen species.

should be potted-up in September in 6 to 7-inch pots in a compost of sandy loam and peat in equal proportions and should be stood in the cold greenhouse. Trim after flowering. The winter-flowering kinds should be turned out into the frames after hardening-off in April ; the summer-flowering species in July, when they have finished blooming. In the cool house *E. gracilis* (Red-purple) flowers in Nov. and Dec., and *E. hyemalis* (Purple-pink) from Dec. to Feb. *See also* Calluna. *Hardy Species.*—*E. arborea* (White, Feb.–May, 15 ft.) ; *E. carnea* (Carmine-crimson and White, Nov.–April, ½–1 ft.) ; *E. cinerea* (Purple, Sept., ¾ ft.) ; *E. c. alba* (White) ; *E. darleyensis* (Rosy-red, Nov.–April, 1–1½ ft.) ; *E. lusitanica* (White, Jan.–April, 6–10 ft.) ; *E. mediterranea* (Lilac-rose, March–May, 3–4 ft.) ; *E. m. alba* (White) ; *E. vagans* (Rosy-purple, July–Oct., 1–1½ ft.), etc.

Erigeron (Fleabane).—The species grown are hardy perennials which thrive in sunny borders or in the rock garden in ordinary soil. For culture, *see* Perennials, p. 128. *Species and Varieties.*—*E. B. Ladhams* (Orange-rose, May–Sept., 30 in.) ; *E. Pink Pearl* (June–Aug., 18–30 in.) ; *E. Quakeress* (Pale Lilac, July–Sept., 30 in.) ; *E. alpinus* Purple, July, 10 in.) ; *E. aurantiacus* (Orange, July–Aug., 6–12 in.).

Erinus (Summer Starwort).—A hardy evergreen rock garden or wall plant thriving in sun or shade in sandy loam and old mortar-rubble. For culture, *see* Rock Plants, p. 135. *Species.*—*E. alpinus* (Lilac-rose and White) ; *E. a. carmineus* (Carmine). All May to July, 4 in.

Eritrichium.—Beautiful hardy alpines that grow best in sheltered, semi-shaded positions in a cool compost of gritty loam, leaf-mould, peat, and sand mixed with broken limestone and sandstone. Propagation is by means of division in April, or by seed. They need protection from frost and moisture in winter.

Erodium (Heron's Bill).—Partly hardy and partly half-hardy perennials which do well in sandy loam in dry, warm, sheltered situations in the rock garden. For culture, *see* Rock Plants, p. 135. *Species.*—*E. chamædryoides* (White, veined Pink, May–Sept., 3 in.) ; *E. hybridum* (Pale Crimson-purple, May–Sept., 10–20 in.) ; *E. macradenum* (White, tinged Rose, blotched Violet, June–July, 6 in.), etc.

Eryngium (Sea Holly).—Tall hardy perennials, which like a dry, sandy soil and a sunny position in a warm border. For culture, *see* Perennials, p. 128. *Species.*—*E. amethystinum* (Metallic Blue, June–Aug., 24 in.) ; *E. giganteum* (Bluish, July–Sept., 30–40 in.), etc.

Erysimum (Fairy Wallflower, Hedge Mustard).—Hardy annuals, biennials and perennials, excellent for sunny borders and rock gardens when grown in gritty and sandy loam. For culture, *see* Annuals, p. 106, Biennials, p. 107, *and* Perennials, p. 128. *Species.*—*E. Perofskianum* (Yellow and Orange, July–Oct., 12–18 in.) ; *E. linifolium* (Lavender, May–Sept., 6 in.) ; *E. rupestre* (Sulphur, June, 9 in.).

Escallonia (Chilian Gum Box).—Half-hardy evergreen (except *E. Philippiana*, which is deciduous and hardy) shrubs, which succeed in sheltered situations in well-drained soil. *Culture.*—Plant in Oct. or Nov., or in March or April. Cut-out old wood, shorten laterals after flowering (August), and trim to shape. Autumn-flowering species should not be pruned until the following March. To propagate, strike

cuttings of half-matured shoots in July or August in a frame. *Species.*
—*E. floribunda* (White, July-Sept., 5–10 ft.) ; *E. langleyensis* (Rose-
carmine, June, 10–15 ft.) ; *E. Philippiana* (White, June–July, 6–8 ft.) ;
E. rubra (Deep Red, Sept.–Oct., 6–12 ft.), etc.

Eschscholzia (Californian Poppy).—Hardy annuals which thrive in
sunny beds or rock garden (dwarfs) in poor, light soil. For culture,
see Annuals, p. 106. *Species.*—*E. cæspitosa* (Yellow, May–Oct., 9 in.) ;
E. californica (Orange and Yellow, Red, etc., May–Oct., 18 in.).

Eucalyptus (Gum Tree).—Half-hardy evergreen trees, which thrive
in the cool greenhouse in a compost of two parts of fibrous loam to
one part of leaf-mould and charcoal. *Culture.*—Pot-up in March, using
6 to 8-inch pots ; plant outdoors in a sunny position from June to
September. To propagate, sow in gentle heat (60° F.) in early spring,
or strike cuttings of mature shoots under glass in June.

Eulalia (Zebra-striped Grass).—Hardy perennial grass, suitable for
borders and cool greenhouses. It thrives in ordinary soil and is propagated by means of division in March or April.

Euonymus (Spindle Tree).—Deciduous and evergreen shrubs and
small trees, which like a sunny position and good loam. *Culture.*—
Plant evergreens in April or Sept. and Oct., deciduous from Nov. to
March. No pruning is necessary. Propagate in autumn by means of
cuttings from the previous year's growth, or by seeds. *Species and
Varieties.*—*E. alatus* (*syn. amurensis*) (D.), (Scarlet Leaves, Autumn,
6–9 ft.) ; *E. europæus* (Pink Fruit, Autumn, 10–25 ft.) ; *E. e. atropurpurea* (Purple Foliage, 6 ft.) ; *E. japonicus* (E.), (Deep Glossy Foliage,
6–10 ft.), etc.

Eupatorium (Hemp Agrimony).—Evergreen greenhouse shrubs and
hardy perennials. *Culture.*—(*Shrubs*)—Propagate by means of cuttings in heat in spring. Keep the cuttings warm and near the glass,
harden-off and plant outdoors in the sun in June. Stop-back occasionally until July, and cut old plants well back after flowering. Pot-up in
September, using 6 to 8-inch pots and a compost of rich loam with
some peat in it, and place in a cool house. (*Perennials*)—Propagate
by division of roots in March. *Species.*—*E. cannabinum* (Pink, June–
Sept., 48 in.) ; *E. perfoliatum* (White, June–Sept., 40 in.) ; *E. pur-
pureum* (Purple, June–Sept., 48–60 in.) ; *E. ianthinum* (Lilac, Jan.–
Feb., 15 in.) ; *E. petiolare* (White, April–May, 30–40 in.).

Euphorbia (Spurge).—The hardy perennials are the only ones worth
growing ; *E. epithymoides* (Yellow, 15 in.), and *E. Myrsinites* (Yellow,
6 in.), both like a gritty loam and full sun. *See* Perennials, p. 128.

Everlasting Pea (*Lathyrus latifolius*).—A beautiful hardy climber.
Moist, good soil and a sunny position suit it best. For culture, *see*
Perennials, p. 128. *Named Varieties.*—*White Pearl* (White), and *Pink
Beauty* (Carmine-rose). Both June to September, 6 feet.

Exochorda (Pearl Bush).—Hardy deciduous shrubs, closely allied to
the Spiræas. They thrive in sunny, sheltered positions in rich loam.
E. grandiflora (White, May–June, 5–10 ft.) is the best species. *Culture.*
—Plant in Oct. or Nov. and cut back straggling shoots after flowering.
To propagate, strike cuttings of ripe shoots in October in a frame.

Note.—D. =deciduous. E. = evergreen.

Fabiana (False Heath).—Half-hardy evergreen summer-flowering shrubs, suitable for outdoor culture in sandy loam with some peat in it in warm, sheltered situations. In northern counties they should only be grown in the cool greenhouse. *Pot Culture.*—After flowering, cut-back weak and straggling stems, pot-up, and summer in the open on a bed of hard ashes. Return to the house in September. Water liberally in spring and summer. Propagate in April or May by means of cuttings of young shoots in a warm frame, or sow in heat in March. The best-known species, *F. imbricata* (3–6 ft.), has white flowers.

Fagus (Beech).—This well-known tree thrives in chalk soils and is a good tree for woodland planting. *Culture.*—Plant in October or November. No pruning is necessary. Propagation of varieties is usually carried out in March by means of grafting on the common beech. *Species.*—*F. aureo variegatus* (Golden Beech) ; *F. sylvatica* (Common Beech) ; *F. s. cuprea* (Copper Beech) ; *F. s. pendula* (Weeping Beech).

Fatsia japonica (Japanese Aralia).—A semi-hardy evergreen shrub which thrives well in the cool house ; in good loam in warm, sheltered positions it will grow out of doors. It grows some 12 feet high and carries cream-white flowers in October and November. *Culture.*—Plant in March or April, or pot-up in March, using a compost of two parts of loam to one part of leaf-mould and sand. Water well, syringing in spring and summer, and shade from the sun. To propagate, sow seed when ripe in heat (70° F.), insert 2-inch pieces of stem in sandy soil in a propagator in spring or September, or increase by " ringing."

Ferns.—Hardy ferns thrive in sheltered and shady positions in moist but well-drained deep loam with plenty of leaf-mould, peat and coarse sand in it. Dead fronds should be left to act as a protection in winter. Half-hardy kinds require slight artificial heat in winter and tender ferns a temperature of 60° F. Pot-up in spring when growth commences in a compost of two parts fibrous loam and one part well-sieved manure, leaf-mould and coarse sand, keep moist and syringe. Propagate, preferably in March or July, by means of " spores " sown in the same manner as seed, in equal parts of loam, peat, leaf-mould, and sand (sterilized with boiling water, *see* p. 53), by division in March or April, or, in some cases, remove and pot-up the minute plants growing on the fronds. *Species.*—(*Hardy*)—*Adiantum pedatum* (Maidenhair Fern) ; *Aspidium aculeatum* (Hard Shield Fern) ; *Aspidium angulare* (Soft Shield Fern) ; *Asplenium officinarum* (Spleenwort) ; *Athyrium filix-fœmina* (Lady Fern) ; *Blechnum spicant* (*syn. Lomaria*) (Hard Fern) ; *Nephrodium dilatatum* (Broad Buckler Fern) ; *Osmunda regalis* (Royal Fern) ; and *Polypodium vulgare* (Polypody).

Forget-Me-Not (Myosotis).—There are annual and perennial species, some of the latter being grown as biennials. All thrive in the sun in ordinary soil, and are useful for bedding, for the rock garden and for the cool greenhouse. *Culture.*—*See* Annuals, p. 106, Biennials, p. 107, *and* Perennials, p. 128. *Pot Culture.*—Pot-up in October, using 4 to 5-inch pots and sandy soil, and keep in a cold frame through the winter ; move into the cool house in early spring. *Species.*—*M. cæspitosa Rehsteineri* (Blue, April–May, 2 in.) ; *M. dissitiflora* (Light Blue, April–June, 6–9 in.) ; *M. palustris semperflorens* (Sky-blue and Yellow,

May–Sept., 6–9 in.) ; *M. pyrenaica* (Blue, Pink and White, June–August, 6 in.).

Forsythia (Golden Bell Tree).—Hardy deciduous shrubs, thriving in ordinary soil and in sunny positions. *Culture.*—Plant from October to November, and cut well back after flowering. To propagate, strike cuttings of soft wood in a frame in June, or July, and layer. *F. spectabilis* is useful for the cold greenhouse. Pot-up from October to December, using an 8 to 10-inch pot and a compost of two parts of loam to one part of leaf-mould and sand ; sink the pot in ashes outdoors from May to October. *Species and Varieties.*—*F. intermedia vars. densiflora* and *spectabilis* and *F. suspensa* and *viridissima* (Golden Yellow, March, 6–10 ft.).

Fothergilla.—Hardy deciduous shrubs which like a moist, sandy loam and peat. They grow some 3 to 6 feet high and flower from April to June. *Culture.*—Plant from October to March. Propagate by means of cuttings in late summer, by layering in autumn, or sow in heat in spring.

Francoa ramosa (Bridal Wreath).—A graceful cool greenhouse plant with small white or rosy-red flowers in late summer. *Culture.*—Sow in March with slight bottom heat (55° F.), or propagate by means of cuttings under glass in June. Pot-up from February to March, using 6 to 8-inch pots and a compost of sandy loam and leaf-mould. Discard the old plants, and raise a fresh batch annually.

Freesia.—A species of almost hardy bulbous plants for the warm, sunny border or cold greenhouse. *Culture.*—Plant in August, 2 inches apart, in light, well-drained soil, protect with fibre in winter, and lift after flowering. *Indoors.*—Pot-up in succession from July to December, 1 inch deep and 2 inches apart, in equal parts of sandy loam, leaf-mould and rotten manure. Place the pots under a south wall, or in a frame in the case of coloured varieties, until the bulbs begin to grow (about six weeks). Then, if standing in the open, transfer to a cold frame, and in a fortnight place on a shelf near the glass. Thin stakes are necessary for support, and freesias require bi-weekly doses of liquid manure as soon as the buds form. The bulbs will bloom from January to April. Keep dry in a sunny frame from May to July, and shake clear of soil and pot-up each year. They can be increased easily from seed. Sow the seed when ripe, in August or September, in 5-inch pots in well-sieved sandy loam and leaf-mould, and place in a cool frame exposed to the sun's rays ; thin-out to leave five or six plants in each pot. Soak the seed for twenty-four hours before sowing. Freesias do not like transplanting. They may also be propagated by means of offsets in July or August. *Named Varieties.*—*Purity* (White) ; *Excelsior* (Cream) ; *Lemon King* ; *Orange King* ; *Rose Beauty*, etc.

Fritillaria.—Hardy bulbous plants, which succeed in any garden soil, although a dry, deep, rich (*F. Meleagris* moist), sandy loam gives the most satisfactory results. They are excellent for shady borders, the rock garden, for naturalizing in grass, and (some species) for pots. *Culture.*—Plant in October 4 inches deep and 7 inches apart (except *F. imperialis*, which should be 10 inches apart), and do not lift from the ground, unless overcrowded ; when necessary lift and re-plant immediately. *Pot Culture.*—Plant in the autumn in 4 to 5-inch pots in a mixture of loam, peat, leaf-mould, rotten manure, and sand, and give occasional doses of liquid manure when the buds form. Propagate by means of bulbous offsets in October. *Species.*—*F. aurea* (Golden Yellow, 8 in.) ; *F. citrina* (Yellow-green, 8–12 in.) ; *F. imperialis* (Red or Orange and Yellow, 30 in.) ; *F. libanotica* (Lilac and Yellow, 15 in.) ; *F. Meleagris* (Purple or White, 10 in.) ; *F. persica* (Persian Lily) (Violet, 24 in.). All April to May-flowering.

Fuchsia.—Fuchsias grow in almost any soil and are excellent for the cold greenhouse or the open border in summer. Feeding them with weak manure water of any kind is preferable to mixing manure with the soil, and after they are well rooted they should never be watered with clear water, but should always have a stimulant. A carefully-shaded house, guarded against the ingress of bees, is the best place for them when in blossom. *Culture.*—Sow in heat (70° F.) in the spring, but the more satisfactory way is to take cuttings in spring or autumn. Plants that have been at rest during the winter should be started in February or March and large early-flowering specimens will be produced by cutting down the old plants and re-potting them in good, rich compost. When re-potted, keep them in a temperature of 55° F., and syringe overhead daily in fine weather. Insert cuttings taken from these plants in pots filled with two-thirds fibrous loam and one-third leaf-mould, well-rotted manure, and old mortar-rubble, and plunge the pots in a bottom heat of 60° F. In three weeks they may be potted into 3-inch pots, and re-plunged in the same bed, keeping the temperature from 50° to 60° F. As soon as necessary shift into fresh pots, until they receive their final shift into 6, 9, or 12-inch pots towards the end of June ; or into the open about the end of May. Cuttings can also be taken of semi-matured wood in August. The plants should be kept close up to the glass and will require " stopping " at least six times, and careful training. Never " stop " a plant within two months of the time it is required to bloom. A regular, moist temperature must be maintained, and the foliage should be sprayed in warm weather. During bright sunshine the glass should be slightly shaded. In July or August, the plants should be stood in a sunny position in the open. *Species.*—(HARDY)—*F. corallina* (*syn. exoniensis*) (Purple and Red) ; *F. macrostemma* (Scarlet) ; *F. m. globosa* (Violet and Purple) ; *F. Riccartoni* (Bright Red). (HALF-HARDY)—*F. cordifolia* (Red and Green) ; *F. corymbiflora* (Scarlet) ; *F. excorticata* (Purple). All July to September, 5 to 6 feet. There are numerous named varieties.

Funkia (Plantain Lily).—Hardy herbaceous plants, suitable for the border, rock garden, shrubbery or cold greenhouse. They require rich, well-dug soil and thrive in sun or shade. *Culture.*—Propagate by means of division in spring or autumn or pot-up in March. *Species.*—*F. ovata* (Lilac-blue, July–Aug., 12–18 in.) ; *F. Sieboldiana* (Pale Lilac, July–Aug., 12–18 in.) ; *F. subcordata* (White, July–Sept., 18 in.).

Gaillardia (Blanket Flower).—Annuals and perennials, both kinds being usually treated as half-hardy. They thrive in any light, rich soil in sunny beds. For culture, *see* Annuals, p. 106, *and* Perennials, p. 128. *Named Annual Varieties.*—*The Bride* (White) ; *Crimson*

Glow (Crimson) ; *Lorenziana* and *Picta* (Red and Yellow). *Named Perennial Varieties.—Grandiflora* ; *Masterpiece* (Red) ; *The King* and *Sunset* (Red and Yellow). All June to October, 12 to 30 in.

Galega (Goat's Rue).—A hardy border perennial which thrives almost anywhere and in any soil. For culture, *see* Perennials, p. 128. *Species.—G. patula* var. *Hartlandii* (Pale Lilac-blue and White, June–Oct., 50 in.) ; *G. officinalis* (Lilac-blue, White and Pink, June–Oct., 48 in.).

Gardenia.—Evergreen flowering shrubs suitable for hothouse or warm greenhouse, and which require much heat and plenty of water when growing. They thrive in equal parts of peat, loam and rotten manure with a little charcoal added. *Culture.*—Prune into shape and pot-up in February or March, putting year-old plants into 5 to 6-inch pots ; 8-inch pots should be large enough for old specimens. Syringe daily, and give liquid manure when the buds form. Propagate in February or March by means of shoots with a " heel," in pots in sandy peat, in a propagating frame with a bottom heat of 70° to 80° F. *Named Varieties.—Florida* (Cape Jasmine) ; *Fortuneana* and *Thunbergia.*

Garrya (Californian Garrya).—Hardy evergreen shrubs with yellow or greenish-white flowers from November to March. *Culture.*—Plant in May in ordinary soil and a sunny, sheltered position. In May trim back long shoots a little and cut out dead wood. To propagate, strike cuttings in August in a frame, or layer. *Species.—G. elliptica* (6–12 ft. or more).

Gaultheria (Winter Green, Shallon, etc.).—A genus of evergreen shrubs, some of which are hardy and suitable for the woodland or rock garden. *Culture.*—Plant in April or October in cool, moist, ordinary soil and leaf-mould in a partially-shaded position. Thin-out old shoots when overcrowded. Propagate by means of seed in heat in March, division or layering in Oct. *Species.—G. procumbens* (White and Pink, July–Aug., creeping) ; *G. Shallon* (White and Red, May–July, 3–6 ft.).

Gaura.—Hardy perennials which are best treated as annuals, and thrive in light, warm, rich soil in sunny borders. They reach a height of 36 inches and flower from June to October. *See* Annuals, p. 106.

Gazania (Treasure Flower).—A showy summer bedding-plant with yellow and bronze flowers from June to October ; also useful for cool greenhouse. *Culture.*—Propagate by means of basal cuttings in summer in a cold frame. Plant-out in June in a sunny position. Protect from frost in winter. For indoors, pot-up in March in sandy loam and peat.

Genista (Broom).—The Genistas, which are closely related to the Cytisus, are hardy flowering shrubs, valuable for the greenhouse, border, shrubbery, or rock garden. *Culture.*—Plant in October in dry, light soil in a sunny position. The early-flowering types should have the old wood thinned-out and should be trimmed into shape directly after flowering ; the later bloomers should be cut hard back in February or March. Do not prune *G. ætnensis, G. cinerea* or *G. virgata,* merely keep in shape by " stopping " and removing dead blooms. To propagate, sow in a frame when ripe, or strike cuttings of half-matured wood in a frame during August and grow on in pots until planted-out, as they do not transplant readily. *Species.—G. ætnensis* (Golden-yellow, July–

Aug., 10–20 ft.) ; *G. cinerea* (Golden, June–July, 8–10 ft.) ; *G. hispanica*, the Spanish Broom (Golden, May–June, 1–3 ft.) ; *G. pilosa* (Yellow, May–June, trailer) ; *G. tinctoria fl. pl.* (Golden [Double], July–Aug., 1–2 ft.).

Gentiana.—Beautiful little rock plants which need as much approximation to alpine conditions as possible. A moist, but well-drained, gritty, peaty loam and leaf-mould, to which has been added a fair amount of old mortar-rubble, suits them well. Ample moisture is essential through the summer and most species do best in partial shade. For culture, *see* Rock Plants, p. 135. The Gentians are impatient of root division, and indeed of transplanting. *Species and Varieties.*—*G. acaulis* (Deep Blue) ; *G. Andrewsii* (Violet-blue) ; *G. decumbens alba* (White) ; *G. lutea* (Yellow) ; *G. septemfida* (Blue and White) ; *G. verna* (Deep Blue), etc. All April to October, 3 to 12 inches.

Geranium (Crane's Bill).—Ordinary garden soil, provided it is fairly light and well-drained, suits the hardy geraniums ; a sunny, open site is essential. The dwarf kinds are suitable for the rock garden, and thrive in poor, sandy and gritty soil. An autumnal dressing of granite chips will help them to survive the winter. *Culture.*—Sow in March or August (under glass), or in April in the open, or the plants may be increased by division from October to March. Cuttings of matured side-shoots can also be struck in August in a frame. For half-hardy greenhouse bedding-plants and show varieties, *see* Pelargonium. *Species.*—(HARDY)—*G. armenum* (Red-purple, 18–24 in.) ; *G. Endressii* (Rose-pink, 15 in.) ; *G. grandiflorum* (Blue, 18 in.) ; *G. pratense* (Mauve, Blue or White, 20–30 in.). (*Dwarfs*)—*G. Farreri* (Pink, 6 in.) ; *G. sanguineum* (Crimson-purple, 9 in.) ; *G. s. album* (White, 9 in.) ; *G. s. lancastriense* (Rose and Crimson, 6 in.). All June to September.

Geum (Avens).—Hardy perennials which thrive in sunny borders in almost any well-drained, light, rich soil ; the rock garden species love a deep, gritty loam, and *G. reptans* and *G. rivale* require plenty of moisture. For culture, *see* Perennials, p. 128. *Species and Varieties.*—*G. Borisii* (Orange-scarlet) ; *G. Lady Stratheden* (Double, Golden-yellow) ; *G. montanum* (Yellow) ; *G. Mrs. Bradshaw* (Bright Red) ; *G. Orangeman* (Orange) ; *G. reptans* (Golden-yellow) ; *G. rivale* [Leonard's] (Crimson-pink). All April to October, 6 to 24 inches.

Gilia (Ipomopsis).—Hardy annuals and half-hardy biennials which thrive in ordinary soil in warm, sunny borders. For culture, *see* Annuals, p. 106, *and* Biennials, p. 107. *Species.*—(ANNUALS)—*G. aurea* (Yellow, 5 in.) ; *G. densiflora* (Lilac-pink, 12 in.) ; *G. tricolor* (Pale Purple, White and Yellow, 10–20 in.). (BIENNIALS)—*G. aggregata* and *G. coronopifolia* (Crimson-scarlet, 24–48 in.). June to October.

Ginkgo biloba (Maidenhair Tree).—A hardy deciduous tree thriving in deep loam in a sheltered position. *Culture.*—Plant in October. No pruning is required. Propagate in March by means of seed in a frame. A good town tree growing 60 feet or more in height.

Gladiolus (Sword Lily and Corn Flag).—Gladioli are divided into two sections, namely, the early-flowering (blooming from June to July), and the late-flowering (blooming in August and September). They like a deep, well-dug, firm loam and a warm spot well exposed to the sun and sheltered from cutting winds. *Culture.*—Line the pocket in which the bulbs are to rest with a little coarse sand. Plant in March or April 4 inches deep and 4 to 6 inches apart, in rows 15 to 20 inches apart. Each flower spike will need staking securely. If seed is no object, the first flower stems should be cut down, when many of the bulbs will throw up a second flower-stem. The bulbs are taken up in October or November and stored. Prepare for planting in the following March or April by rubbing off the old roots and soil adhering at the bottom of the bulbs, and save the débris. *Propagation.*—Examine this débris, and thousands of little scaly-looking rubbish will be found, which are young gladioli bulblets. Draw a drill 2 to 3 inches deep on a bit of rich soil in the reserve garden, and sow the bulblets thinly in March. Keep moist and some of these will flower late in autumn, many the second year, and all the third year. These young bulblets require exactly the same treatment as the old ones. Gladioli may also be raised from seed in May in a cold frame. If, however, it is desired that all the young plants shall come " true to type," propagation must be effected by offsets. *Pot Culture.*—Place one corm 3 inches deep in a 6-inch pot in a compost of 2 parts sandy loam to 1 part of leaf-mould and rotten manure and ample sharp sand, in October or November ; cover with fibre till growth starts, and keep in a frame until March. Then put in a light airy position in a cold greenhouse to bloom. Dry-off after flowering, store, and keep dry from May to October. *G. Colvillei* is good for pot culture, and makes a good room plant. *Species.*—(EARLY)—*G. byzantinus* (Purple-red, 20 in.) ; *G. cardinalis* (Scarlet, White Spots, 30 in.) ; *G. Colvillei* (Purple, White Spots, 18 in.) ; *G. C. alba* (White, 18 in.). All June to July. (LATE)—*G. brenchleyensis* (Scarlet) ; *G. gandavensis* (Various) ; *G. primulinus* (hybrids) (Various) ; *G. ramosus* (Purple, Rose and White). All August to September, 24 inches. Named varieties are innumerable and catalogues should be consulted.

Globularia (Globe Daisy).—Dwarf-growing perennials, which thrive in the sun and in moist light loam. They are useful for the paved or rock garden. For culture, *see* Rock Plants, p. 135. *Species.*—*G. cordifolia* ; *G. trichosantha.* Both Blue, May to July, 8 inches.

Gloxinia.—Tender tuberous-rooted perennials which thrive in a fibrous peaty loam mixed with leaf-mould, cow-dung, sharp sand and charcoal. *Culture.*—Start the tubers in succession from January to April by placing them in a box in a 2-inch layer of the above compost (Temperature 60° F.). Keep just moist, and as soon as from 2 to 3 inches growth has been made, plant one tuber in each 4-inch pot. Maintain the same heat and moisture, shade from the sun, and water liberally when well rooted. Pot-up into 5-inch pots as soon as pot-bound, and again into 6-inch pots when the buds are forming. After flowering, dry-off and store the tubers in peat or coco-nut fibre. Propagate at the end of January by means of seed in a compost of peat, sand, and fine rich loam, thinly covered with coarse sand only, and exposed to a bottom heat of about 70° F. Prick-off 1 inch apart as soon as possible, and gradually reduce the temperature to 60° F. ; pot-up singly into 4-inch pots, and place near the glass. Maintain the temperature, and keep moist, but do not let moisture touch the leaves. Pot-up by stages, until the flowering pots (5 to 7 inches) are reached. Seed may also be sown in a cold house in June. Old tubers, when started in heat in February in boxes of damp fibre, supply shoots from which cuttings may be made ; these should be placed in a close propagating frame and subjected to moist and gentle heat. Another method of propagation is by means of leaf-cuttings taken at any time. *Varieties.* —*Mauve Queen* (Mauve) ; *Beacon* (Crimson) ; *Cyclops* (Rose-scarlet and White) ; *Pink Beauty* (Pink). All June to October, 12 inches.

Godetia.—Hardy annuals, useful for summer-bedding. (*See* Œnothera.) For culture, *see* Annuals, p. 106. *Named Varieties.*— *Duchess of Albany* (White) ; *Apple Blossom* (Pink) ; *Lady Albemarle* (Crimson) ; *Duke of York* (Red and White) ; *New Lavender* (Mauve) ; and *Azalea-flowered* (Various). All June to October, 6 to 24 inches.

Golden Rod (Solidago).—Hardy perennials which thrive in sun or shade in almost any soil. For culture, *see* Perennials, p. 128. *Species.* —*S. canadensis, S. elliptica, S. rigida, S. Virgaurea.* All Golden Yellow, August to October, 2–4 ft.

Gunnera.—Hardy perennial foliage plants, which thrive in rich soil and sheltered, shady positions. They are valuable for margins of lakes, and for shrubberies. The crowns require slight winter protection. *See* Perennials, p. 128. *G. scabra* (Crimson, Aug., 5 ft.) is the best.

Gypsophila (Chalk Plant, or Gauze Flower).—Hardy annuals and perennials which thrive in dry, well-limed loam, in sunny borders or the rock garden. For culture, *see* Annuals, p. 106, *and* Rock Plants, p. 135. *Species.*—(*Annuals*)—*G. elegans* (White [large], 18 in.) ; *G. muralis* (Pink, 6 in.). (*Perennials*)—*G. cerastioides* (White, veined Red, 3 in.) ; *G. paniculata* (White [Single and Double], 30 in.) ; *G. repens* (White and Pink, 4–6 in.). All May to September-flowering.

Haberlea.—Hardy perennials suitable for a shady spot in the rock garden in moist peat, leaf-mould and sand. For culture, *see* Rock Plants, p. 135. *H. rhodopensis* (Lilac, May–July, 6 in.) is a favourite.

Habranthus pratensis (Hippeastrum).—A genus of bulbous-rooted plants, suitable for sunny beds, rock garden or pot culture in the cool greenhouse, and which like a warm spot in light loam, leaf-mould and sand. They grow about 12 inches high and carry red, yellow or white flowers from May to August. *Culture.*—Plant in October 5 inches deep and 4 inches apart, only lift when the flowers become poor, and protect with fibre in winter. Propagate by means of offsets in October, or raise from seed when ripe, in a propagating case. *Pot Culture.*—Pot-up every third year in October, placing one bulb 2 inches deep in a 6-inch pot, and give bi-weekly doses of liquid manure when the flower buds form, and until the leaves die down. Ripen in a sunny frame, and dry-off in the pot until next potting time.

Halesia (Silver Bell or Snowdrop Tree).—Hardy deciduous summer-flowering trees or shrubs (8–30 ft.) which thrive in well-drained, moist sandy loam in a sunny, sheltered position. *Culture.*—Plant in October or November ; thin-out branches when overcrowded. To propagate sow in a frame in March, or take cuttings in October.

Hamamelis (Witch Hazel).—Small deciduous flowering trees or shrubs which thrive in sunny positions in moist but well-drained loam with peat and leaf-mould in it. *Culture.*—Plant October to November. Just thin-out and trim the branches in April when overcrowded. To propagate, sow seed when ripe in a frame, layer in late summer, or graft. *Species.*—*H. japonica* and *H. j. arborea* (Yellow, Jan.–Feb., 8–15 ft.); *H. Zuccariniana* (Pale Yellow, Dec.–Feb., 3–6 ft.); *H. mollis* (Golden Yellow, Dec.–Feb., 8–10 ft.).

Hebenstreitia comosa.—A half-hardy perennial, growing about 18 inches high, with fragrant semi-double orange-red and white flowers, from July to September. For culture, *see* Perennials, p. 128.

Hedysarum.—A genus of hardy biennials, perennials and shrubs, useful for borders and the rock garden. They thrive in the sun and in ordinary soil. For culture, *see* Biennials, p. 107, *and* Perennials, p. 128. *Species.*—(*Biennials*)—*H. coronarium* (Scarlet, June–Sept., 36 in.). (*Perennials*)—*H. capitatum* (Rose, Summer, 24 in.); *H. microcalyx* (Purple, June–July, 20 in.); *H. neglectum* (Purple-red, June–Aug., 6 in.). (*Shrub*)—*H. multijugum* (Purple-red, June–Sept., 36–72 in.).

Helenium (Sneezeweed).—Hardy perennials which thrive in sunny borders in rich, ordinary, well-drained soil. For culture, *see* Perennials, p. 128. *Species.*—*H. autumnale* (Yellow, July–Oct., 48 in.); *H. a.* var. *pumilum*; *H. Hoopesii* (Orange, July–Oct., 30 in.); *Riverton Beauty* (Yellow [Chocolate Centre], Aug.–Oct., 36–60 in.); *Riverton Gem* (Red [Shot Gold], Aug.–Oct., 36–60 in.).

Helianthemum (Sun Rose).—Shrubby evergreens which love the sun and do best on dry banks, or in the rock garden in sandy soil. For culture, *see* Cistus. *Species.*—*H. glaucum*, var. *croceum* (Yellow, May–Sept., 6 in.); *H. rosmarinifolium* (Yellow, June–July, 24 in.); *H. vulgaris varieties.*—*Fireball* (Red); *Rose Queen*; *Rubens* (Orange); *The Bride* (White); *tigrinum* (Salmon) and *venustum plenum* (Dbl. Scarlet).

Helianthus (Sunflower).—Hardy annuals and perennials which grow freely in a sunny site in any rich, well-dug soil. For culture, *see* Annuals, p. 106, *and* Perennials, p. 128. *Varieties.*—(ANNUALS). *Named Varieties of H. annuus*—*Golden Nigger* (Deep Yellow); *Langley Gem* (Primrose, flushed Pink, Double); *Primrose Dame* (Pale Yellow). All July to October. *Named Varieties of H. annuus cucumerifolius*—*Apollo* (Gold and Maroon); *Mars* (Golden Red); and *Venus* (Cream, tinged Yellow). (PERENNIALS)—*H. decapetalus* (Yellow [single **or** double], Aug–Oct., 60–100 in.); *H. mollis* (Orange-yellow, Sept.–Oct., 50 in.); *H. orgyalis* (Yellow [Black Centre], Sept.–Oct., 100 in.), etc.

Helichrysum (" Everlasting Flowers ").—These are mostly half-hardy or hardy perennials or annuals, which thrive in sunny positions and gritty loam and are mostly suitable for borders, or as pot plants indoors, while the dwarf species make excellent rock plants. For culture, *see* Annuals, p. 106, *and* Perennials, p. 128. *Species.*—(*Half-hardy Annuals*)—*H. bracteatum* and vars. (White, Brown, Red, Pink, and Yellow, July–Oct., 36 in.); *H. orientale* (Yellow, July–Oct., 24 in.). (*Hardy Perennial*)—*H. bellidioides* (White, July–Oct., 5 in.).

Heliotropium peruvianum (Cherry Pie).—Soft-wooded shrubs, for summer bedding, and pot-culture, and succeeding best in light, rich loam and leaf-mould. *Culture.*—Seed sown thinly in spring in moderate heat makes good plants for summer and autumn decoration. Pot-off in April into 4-inch pots, pinch-back when 3 to 4 inches high, harden-off and plant-out, about 12 inches apart, in June. The finest plants are obtained from cuttings taken in the same way as for verbenas and bedding calceolarias. Take the cuttings in spring or autumn (preferably late August) and strike in boxes in a frame in moderate heat ; syringe in hot weather, and in five or six weeks pot-up into 3 or 4-inch pots and move into the cool house. *Pot Culture.*—Pot-up annually in March, using 6 to 8-inch pots and a compost of two parts loam to one part of leaf-mould and sand. " Stop " back to make bushy, and prune well back in February. *Named Varieties.—Lord Roberts* ; *Mrs. J. W. Lowther* ; *President Garfield* ; *Swanley Giant* ; *The Speaker* ; and *White Lady.* All May to September, 12 to 36 inches.

Helipterum.—These half-hardy annuals, which now include the acroclinums and the rhodanthes, are everlastings, valuable alike for greenhouse (rhodanthes) and flower garden. They succeed best in a light, rich soil and warm sheltered positions. For culture, *see* Annuals, p. 107. *Pot Culture.—(Rhodanthes).* Sow ¾ inch apart in August (50° F.). Place the seedlings near the glass and keep fairly dry at first. Pot as soon as possible into the flowering pots. *Species.— H. Manglesii* (Rose and Silver) ; *H. M. var. maculata* (Pink, Yellow or White) ; *H. roseum* (Rose). All June to October, 12 to 18 inches.

Helonias (Stud Flower).—Hardy herbaceous plants which thrive in moist, sandy and peaty loam in semi-shade, and which grow about 15 inches high and flower in April and May. *Culture.*—Sow in a frame in April, or propagate by means of division in April or October.

Hemerocallis (Day Lily).—Hardy perennials which do well in moist, light, and deep soil in a shady border or marsh garden. Propagate by division in April or Nov. *Species and Varieties.—H. aurantiaca* (Apricot-orange) ; *H. Dumortieri* (Yellow and Red-brown) ; *H. Gold Dust* (Golden) ; *H. Sovereign* (Orange Yellow) ; *H. fulva, var. Kwanso fl. pl.* (Bronze-yellow). All May to August, 12 to 36 inches.

Heracleum (Cow Parsnip).—Tall hardy biennials and perennials most suited to the wild or woodland garden or to the shrub border. For culture, *see* Biennials, p. 107, *and* Perennials, p. 128. *Species.— (Biennial)—H. asperum* (3 ft.). *(Perennial)—H. Leichtlinii* (6 ft.) ; *H. persicum* (10 ft.). All carry white flowers ; the biennials blooming from May to July, the perennials from June to October.

Herniaria glabra and others are useful little creeping plants for the paved or rock garden. They like a sunny position and gritty loam, and are propagated by means of division in the spring.

Heuchera (Alum Root).—Hardy perennials which do well in warm, rich and light soil, in a sunny border. The dwarf species are useful for the rock garden. For culture, *see* Perennials, p. 128. *Species and Varieties.—H. brizoides gracillima* (Rosy-red) ; *H. hybrida* (Red to White) ; *H. sanguinea* (Coral Scarlet). All May to September, 20 to 30 inches.

Hibiscus (Rose, Shrubby, or Syrian Mallow).—Beautiful hardy and half-hardy plants, suitable for borders and indoor decoration. *Culture.* —Plant the hardy sorts in sandy loam in March in a sheltered position in sun or shade ; do not prune, merely keep in shape by " stopping " and removing dead blooms after flowering. Propagate by sowing seeds about April, by cuttings in a frame in Sept., or by grafting. Those intended for indoor culture require a compost of fibrous peat and rich fine loam with a large proportion of sand ; a little charcoal added is often beneficial. Propagate these from seeds sown over gentle heat, or by cuttings struck early in spring in a close frame. *Species.—(Hardy Annual)*—*H. africanus* (Yellow and Purple, June–Oct., 18 in.). *(Shrubs)*—*H. coccineus* (Bright Scarlet, Aug.–Oct., 4–5 ft.) ; *H. pedunculatus* (Rosy-pink, Aug.–Oct., 3 ft.) ; *H. syriacus and vars.* (White, Blue, Pink or Crimson, Single or Double, Aug.–Oct., 7 ft.), etc.

Hieracium (Hawkweed).—Hardy perennials, some of the dwarf-growing species of which thrive in ordinary soil in a sunny rock garden or border. For culture, *see* Perennials, p. 128. *Species.—H. alpinum* (Yellow, July, 6 in.) ; *H. aurantiacum* (Orange, June–Aug., 20 in.).

Hippophæ rhamnoides (Sea Buckthorn).—Hardy deciduous shrubs or trees (10–40 ft.) which thrive in moist ordinary soil in open positions (preferably near the sea). *Culture.*—Plant in Oct. or Feb. and cut back weak shoots in Feb. Propagate by means of seed in the open, suckers or layers in autumn, and by root-cuttings in spring.

Holly (Ilex).—Hardy trees and shrubs which thrive in sun or shade in almost any well-drained soil. Plant in May or Sept. ; prune with secateurs in April (hedges in May or August). To propagate, sow in March in shallow drills in the open. The seeds usually take two years to germinate, and many people prefer to strike cuttings of half-matured wood in August in a cold frame, or to layer in summer.

Hollyhock (Althæa rosea).—Though really perennials these are best treated as biennials. They like a sunny position in well-drained and deeply worked rich loam. In summer give a liberal supply of water, and a good mulch of well-rotted manure. A dose of weak liquid manure every ten days should be given as soon as the plants reach a height of 3½ to 4 feet. *Propagation.*—Sow seed thinly in drills 1 inch deep early in May in the open. When about 4 inches high transplant 8 inches apart in a nursery bed, and plant-out 3 feet apart in October. On cold heavy soils it is better to sow in boxes in May or June, pot-up in winter, place in a frame, and plant-out in April. For Staking and Tying, *see* p. 71. Cuttings may be struck in sandy soil under a hand-glass in spring or the plants can be increased by division just as the new growth is starting. *Species and Varieties.—A. alba superba* (White) ; *A. delicata* (Cream) ; *A. Queen of the Yellows* (Yellow) ; *A. Constance* (Pink) ; *A. James Vert* (Salmon) ; *A. Britannia* (Scarlet) ; *A. Palling Belle* (Silvery-pink) ; *A. King Albert* (Purple) ; *A. Black Knight* (Black) ; *American Fringed* (Various, Semi-double) ; *A. ficifolia, the Fig-leaved Hollyhock* (Red, Orange or Yellow, Single or Double). All flower from July to September and grow 6 to 10 feet in height.

Honesty (Lunaria annua).—Hardy biennials 24 to 30 inches high carrying purple, mauve or white flowers. They thrive in semi-shaded borders or wild garden in moderately rich soil. *See* Biennials, p. 107.

Honeysuckle.—(*See* Lonicera).

Horminium pyrenaicum (Pyrenean Clary).—A hardy perennial which grows about 10 inches high and bears purple-blue flowers from June to August. It does well in dry ordinary soil in sunny borders or in the rock garden. For culture, *see* Perennials, p. 128.

Humea (Incense Plant).—A handsome foliage plant which thrives in rich sandy loam and leaf-mould in sunny beds or borders and which may be grown in the cold greenhouse in an 8-inch pot. The best-known species is *H. elegans*, a half-hardy biennial. *See* Biennials, p. 107.

Humulus (Hop).—Hardy annual and perennial climbers, delighting in rich, deep, sandy loam. *H. Lupulus aureus* (Golden Hop) and *H. japonicus variegatus* (Silver Variegated Hop), both annuals, must have poor soil. For culture, *see* Annuals, p. 106, *and* Perennials, p. 128. Cut the latter down to the ground in late autumn.

Hyacinth (Hyacinthus).—Hyacinths can be divided into two classes : the *early-flowering Roman Hyacinths*, so useful for pot work and for forcing, and the *Dutch Hyacinths*, also good for pot work, but specially suitable for spring-bedding. The best soil for hyacinths is a well-manured, deeply-dug, sandy loam with leaf-mould in it, but they will grow in almost any soil or in coco-nut fibre, water or sand. *Culture.*—Plant in a sunny position from September to November about 4 inches deep, and from 5 to 10 inches apart, according to variety. *Pot Culture.* —To obtain bloom from December to April, plant in succession from August to November. A free, porous soil composed of two parts of turfy loam to one part of well-rotted manure, leaf-mould and sand, thoroughly incorporated and sieved, is necessary. For three bulbs a 5½-inch pot will be sufficient. *See also* general cultural details in the chapter on Bulbs, p. 116. *Named Varieties.*—(White) *L'Innocence* ; (Yellow) *City of Haarlem* ; (Pink) *Charles Dickens* ; (Red) *Roi des Belges* ; (Mauve) *Lord Balfour* ; (Blue) *King of the Blues* (dark) ; (Purple-blue) *Duchess of Westminster*.

Hyacinthus candicans (Galtonia, or Cape Hyacinth).—Tall hardy bulbous plants, flowering in August and September, and loving a sunny border and well-manured, deeply-dug, sandy loam and leaf-mould. *Culture.*—Plant in March or October from 4 to 6 inches deep and 15 inches apart, letting the bulbs rest on sand. If the soil is cold and heavy, the bulbs must be lifted annually. *Pot Culture.*—Place one bulb ½ inch deep in a 6-inch pot and set in a cold greenhouse. Only grow in a pot for one year, after which plant-out. Propagate by means of seed in the open as soon as ripe, or by offsets in autumn.

Hydrangea.—The common hydrangea—*H. Hortensia*—is a half-hardy summer-flowering deciduous shrub, which thrives in a sheltered position in well-drained and richly-manured sandy loam. *H. paniculata* and *var. grandiflora* (Creamy-white) are quite hardy. *Culture.*— The same treatment, both indoors and out, will suit these species, bearing in mind that although *H. paniculata* is quite hardy, *H. Hortensia* is not. The two species also require different treatment as to pruning. *H. Hortensia* should be pruned in the summer ; *H. paniculata* in March. Plant in March. *Pot Culture.*—Pot-up from February to March, using from 5 to 12-inch pots and a compost of two parts rich loam and one part of rotten manure and sand. When grown in small pots one stem only is encouraged. After flowering, stand in the open until September. *H. Hortensia* is also suitable for forcing in the warm greenhouse. Blue flowers may be procured by planting in a lime-free soil and by watering freely with a weak solution of alum : one tea-spoonful in one gallon of rain-water, or with 3 oz. of aluminium sulphate in one gallon of water. Both these solutions should stand for at least twelve hours before use. To propagate, strike cuttings of young wood in May, or of strong matured shoots that have not flowered in August ; both in a frame. Autumn-struck cuttings should be wintered in a frame with an even temperature of 40° F. *Named Varieties of H. Hortensia.*—*Etincelant* (Carmine) ; *Helge* (Dark Rose) ; *Le Cygne* (White) ; *La Marne* (Mauve) ; *Mme Moullière* (White) ; *Triumph* (Rose-pink). For bluing, *Blue Prince*, etc.

Hymenocallis.—Hardy and half-hardy bulbous plants from 12 to 24 inches high with white or yellow flowers from February to October. They require a light, rich loam. *Culture.*—Plant about 4 inches deep in September and protect with ashes or fibre in winter. Lift about every fourth year. Propagate by means of bulbils, or seed.

Hypericum (St. John's Wort, Aaron's Beard or Rose of Sharon).—This genus includes a number of hardy shrubs, evergreen and deciduous, as well as hardy annuals and perennials. The annuals are hardly worth growing, but some of the dwarf-growing perennials and evergreen shrubs make excellent rock or edging plants. Sandy loam and a sunny site suit them best. For culture, *see* Perennials, p. 128. (*Shrubs*)—Plant in November ; cut well back in March. Propagate by means of cuttings in July or sow seed when ripe. *Species.*—(*Perennial*)—*H. crispum* (12 in.) ; *H. gracile* (5 in.) ; *H. tomentosum* (6–9 in.). (*Shrub*)—*H. calycinum* (12–18 in.) ; *H. elatum* (48–60 in.) ; *H. Hookerianum* (*syn. oblongifolium*) (3–5 ft.) ; *H. Moserianum* (12–18 in.) ; *H. patulum Henryi* (18–36 in.). All carry yellow flowers from July to August, except *H. tomentosum*, which blooms from August to October.

Iberis (Candytuft).—Hardy annuals and perennials, both of which succeed in any soil with lime in it, but prefer dry, sandy loam and a sunny position. For culture, *see* Annuals, p. 106, *and* Perennials, p. 128. *Species.*—(*Annual*)—*I. umbellata* (Purple, Crimson and Pink, July–Oct., 12 in.). (*Perennials*)—*I. gibraltarica* (Lilac-pink, May–July, 12 in.) [this needs a warm, sheltered position] ; *I. sempervirens* (White, May–June, 6–12 in.).

Ice Plant (Mesembryanthemum crystallinum).—Useful half-hardy annuals and perennials for rock-work, thriving in fairly good soil, in a dry, sunny situation. For culture, *see* Annuals, p. 106 ; Perennials, p. 128.

Incarvillea.—Hardy annuals and tuberous-rooted perennials growing from 12 to 36 inches high and flowering from May to August. They thrive in well-drained rich loam in sunny borders. *Culture.*—Sow in pans in a frame in April, thin, and plant-out in spring or autumn. Seed can be sown in the open early in May ; increase also by division in March or Oct. *I. Delavayi* (Crimson-pink or Purple) is the most popular.

Inula (Fleabane).—Hardy perennials useful for sunny borders or for the wild garden. For culture, *see* Perennials, p. 128. *Species.*—*I. grandiflora* (Orange-yellow) ; *I. Hookeri* (Yellow) ; *I. Oculis-Christi* (Golden-yellow). All June to August, 24 to 36 in.

Ipomœa (Moon Flower, Morning Glory, etc.).—A large genus of half-hardy climbing plants, closely allied to the convolvulus, all requiring a rich, light soil. *Culture.*—(*Annuals*)—Sow seed singly in April in small pots under glass, and plant-out 24 inches apart in May or June against a trellis or sunny wall. (*Perennials*)—These are best propagated by means of cuttings of side shoots struck in a frame between March and August. *Varieties.*—*I. coccinea* (Scarlet or Yellow) ; *I. grandiflora alba* (White) ; *I. limbata* (Purple) ; *I. purpurea* (Various [Single and Double]) ; *I. rubro-cœrulea* (Sky–blue). All June to Sept., 8 to 10 feet.

Iresine.—Half-hardy ornamental foliage plants suitable for warm, sunny, and sheltered beds or for pot culture indoors. They grow about 18 inches high and thrive in ordinary soil. *Culture.*—Strike cuttings of young shoots in a frame in late summer or in spring. Plant-out in June 8 inches apart, or pot-up in March, using 5 to 8-inch pots and a mixture of peat, loam, leaf-mould and sand.

Iris.—A genus of hardy plants usually divided into two sections—namely the bulbous and the non-bulbous or rhizomatous-rooted. To the latter class belong the Flags or Bearded Irises, the Kæmpferi or Japanese group and the Sibirica Irises ; to the bulbous class belong the English, Dutch and Spanish Irises. The cultivation of irises is simple, the plants succeeding in a sunny position in any light, rich garden soil, though sandy loam with 50 per cent. peat or leaf-mould is most suitable for the bulbous species. The English Iris needs a heavier and cooler soil than the Dutch and Spanish species, and it is necessary to lift bulbs of the last two triennially, rest them for a few months, and then re-plant. For the tall bearded iris the soil should be deeply dug, well manured and should have some old mortar-rubble incorporated ; it will, however, grow in almost any well-drained soil. The Japanese irises love marshy land, require a position in full sun, and should occasionally be transplanted and divided in August after blooming. The three following types also belong to the rhizomatous group :—the *Evansia* section, the *Oncocyclus* or Cushion irises and the *Regelia* irises.

Culture.—(*Bulbous-rooted.*)—Plant 3 to 4 inches deep in September or October, with a little sand round the bulbs (Spanish, 4 inches ; Dutch, 5 inches ; and English, 6 inches apart). Most spring and autumn-flowering species require to be lifted from the ground in August ; summer-flowering kinds should be lifted every third year, in October, after the plants have died down. English irises should be left undisturbed ; the Dutch irises need just the same treatment as the Spanish. *Pot Culture.*—Many of the bulbous irises make good pot plants ; among these are *I. alata*, *I. persica*, *I. reticulata*, and the English and Spanish kinds. They need a compost of two-thirds fibrous loam, one-third leaf-mould and sand ; plant five bulbs in a 6-inch pot in September or October. They may be propagated by offsets in October.

Non-bulbous or Rhizomatous Species.—Sow seed in April in a cold frame, or propagate by division in August. Plant-out in August or September ; Bearded irises (tall) 20 inches apart ; (medium) 15 inches apart ; (dwarf) 5 inches apart. The upper part of the rhizomes should lie on the surface of the soil, so as to be exposed to the air and sun. The dwarf bearded rock species may be propagated by seed sown in

September under glass, by off-shoots in October, or by division in the spring after flowering. Lift and re-plant the rhizomes triennially.

Species and Varieties.—BULBOUS-ROOTED. SPRING-FLOWERING—*I. Histrio* (Lilac-blue and Yellow, Jan.–Feb., 6 in.) ; *I. orchioides* (Yellow, Lilac Spots, March to May, 20 in.) ; *I. persica Heldreichii* (Purple, Yellow and Green, March, 4 in.) ; *I. reticulata Krelagei* (Purple, Red and Orange, Jan.–Feb., 8 in.). SUMMER-FLOWERING—*I. xiphioides* (*English Iris*) (Purple, Mauve, Pink and Blue, July, 10–25 in.) ; *I. Xiphium* (*Spanish Iris*) (Blue, Yellow and White, June, 20 in.). AUTUMN-FLOWERING—*I. alata* (Sky-blue and Yellow, Nov.–Jan., 4 in.). NON-BULBOUS OR RHIZOMATOUS.—*I. cuprea* (*syn. fulva*) (Red-bronze, June-July, 20 in.) ; *I. fœtidissima* (Bluish-lilac or Yellow, June, 30 in.) ; *I. Kæmpferi* (Various, July–Sept., 18–30 in.) ; *I. Monnieri* (Yellow and White, June–July, 36–48 in.) ; *I. Monspur* (Light Blue, Lavender or Violet, July–Aug., 50 in.) ; *I. ochroleuca* (White and Yellow, June–July, 48 in.) ; *I. sibirica* (Blue, White and Yellow, May–June, 36 in.) ; *I. spuria* (Deep Blue, June, 40 in.) ; *I. unguicularis* [*syn. stylosa*] (Various, Nov.–March, 6–12 in.). Named varieties are innumerable and catalogues should be consulted.

Itea virginica.—Hardy deciduous summer-flowering shrubs (3–5 ft.) which like a moist, peaty soil and partial shade ; plant in October, and thin-out the branches when overcrowded. Propagate by means of seed in the open in April or by suckers in October.

Ivy (Hedera).—There are many kinds of this well-known climber. The common sorts thrive against walls in ordinary rich soil ; the variegated kinds prefer walls facing south or west, and like ample lime in the soil. *Culture.*—Strike cuttings in autumn in sandy soil in a shady border, or layer ; plant-out in showery weather between the following October and April. When established, old leaves and untidy shoots need clipping hard back in April. *Species and Varieties.*—*H. Cænwoodiana* (Small Green Leaf) ; *H. dentata* (Large Green Leaves) ; *H. Helix* (Common Ivy) ; *H. H. vars. angularis aurea* (Yellow) ; *hibernica* (Irish Ivy) ; *purpurea* (Bronze), etc.

Ixia (African Corn Lily).—Half-hardy bulbs which thrive in warm, dry, sunny borders or in the rock garden in rich, sandy loam and leaf-mould or peat, or in pots in the cold greenhouse. *Culture.*—Plant in September, 4 inches deep and 3 inches apart. Do not lift, but in winter cover the bulbs with ashes or fibre. *Pot Culture.*—Pot-up from August to September, placing six bulbs in a 6-inch pot in a compost of two parts turfy loam to one part each of leaf-mould, rotten cow-dung and sand. Dry-off after the foliage dies. Propagate by means of seed in a frame in September or by offsets in October. Seedlings take three years to flower. *Named Varieties.*—*Bridesmaid* (White) ; *King of the Yellows* (Yellow) ; *Queen of the Roses* (Rose) ; *Excelsior* (Red) ; *Azurea* (Blue, Purple Centre). All May and June, 15 inches.

Ixiolirion (Ixia Lily).—Half-hardy bulbous plants which grow about 15 inches high, flower in June, and do well in well-drained sandy loam in a warm, sunny border or rock garden. *Culture.*—Plant in September, 5 inches deep and 3 inches apart ; do not lift the bulbs, but protect them with fibre during the winter. If grown in pots treat as Ixia.

Jacobæa Lily (Hippeastrum formosissimum). Grow in pots in the warm greenhouse in well-drained, rich and heavy loam, to which bone dust and charcoal have been freely added. *Culture.*—Plant in February ; water well and give liquid manure when the buds appear ; and keep dry after flowering. Re-pot every three or four years, and propagate by offsets treated as old bulbs.

Jamesia americana.—A hardy deciduous flowering shrub which likes a damp rich soil and a sunny position. *Culture.*—Plant from October to November ; thin-out branches when overcrowded. To propagate, sow seed when ripe, or in autumn strike cuttings.

Jasmine (Jasminum).—*J. officinale*, the common white jasmine which blooms in June and July, is the best known ; *J. revolutum*, with yellow flowers in May, is better grown in bush-form ; *J. nudiflorum* has yellow flowers in winter and is useful outdoors or in the cold greenhouse ; there are also beautiful hothouse species. Hardy kinds like rich loam and most do well against walls and pergolas facing north or west. *Culture.*—Strike cuttings of ripe wood in summer in a frame, or layer. Plant-out from Oct. to March, and after flowering prune shoots that have bloomed. *Pot Culture.*—(*Cold House*)—Pot-up in February or March, using 6 to 8-inch pots and a compost of two-thirds loam and one-third leaf-mould and well-rotted manure with a little sand ; give weak liquid manure twice a week as soon as the buds form. (*Warm House*)—Pot-up in March ; keep moist and syringe frequently until the plants have bloomed ; then keep moderately dry.

Juglans (Walnut).—Hardy deciduous nut-bearing trees which thrive in well-drained loam in a sunny, open position. *Culture.*—Plant in October when three to four years old. Thin-out branches when overcrowded. To propagate, plant nuts 4 inches deep in the open.

Juniper (Juniperus).—Handsome evergreen shrubs which thrive in the sun in moist, well-drained and deep loam with mortar-rubble. *Culture.*—Plant in May or Sept. ; no pruning is required. To propagate, strike cuttings in a frame in September, or raise from seed.

Kalmia (American Laurel).—Hardy evergreen shrubs which should be treated as the rhododendron (*which see*) ; they are also suitable for gentle forcing. To propagate, sow in a frame in spring, strike cuttings in a frame in October, or layer in October. *Species.*—The best known are *K. latifolia*, the Calico Bush, or Mountain Laurel (Rose and White, June) ; *K. angustifolia*, the Sheep Laurel (Purple-red or White, June).

Kerria (Jew's Mallow).—Hardy deciduous shrubs, bearing orange flowers in March and April. *K. japonica* (4 ft., Single) and *vars. fl. pl.* (8–9 ft., Dbl.) and *aurea variegata* are usually grown ; as climbers they run up to double the heights mentioned. They do well in sandy soil in sunny positions against walls facing south or west. *Culture.*—Strike cuttings of young shoots in a frame in autumn, or propagate by division of roots in late autumn. Plant-out from October to March. About June or early July cut-out the oldest wood. *Pot Culture.*—In the cool greenhouse *K. j. fl. pl.* may be had in flower in February. Pot-up annually in October, using 8 to 10-inch pots and a compost of two parts of sandy loam to one part of leaf-mould and rotten manure. Prune after flowering and plant outdoors.

Kniphofia (Tritoma, Red Hot Poker, Flame Flower, Torch Lily).— Tall hardy perennials which thrive in well-drained and deep sandy soil in sunny or partially-shaded borders ; they may also be potted-up in April or November in 8 to 10-inch pots and grown in the cold green-house. For culture, *see* Perennials, p. 128. *Species and Varieties.*— *K. modesta* (White, May–Sept., 30 in.) ; *K. Northiæ* (Rose and Pale Yellow, May–Sept., 60 in.) ; *K. Uvaria grandiflora* (Orange-red, July–Sept., 70 in.). *Named.*—*Golden Spur* ; *Harkness Hybrid* ; *Mount Etna.*

Kochia (Summer Cypress).—Half-hardy annuals useful for summer-bedding, for borders and the cold greenhouse. *See* Annuals, p. 107.

Laburnum (Golden Rain or Golden Chain).—Hardy deciduous trees with yellow flowers in May ; almost any soil and a sunny position suit them well. *Culture.*—Plant in November ; trim back weak shoots after flowering and cut-out dead wood in winter. In the cool greenhouse *L. vulgare* will flower from February to April. *Pot Culture.*—Pot-up in October, using 8 to 10-inch pots and a compost of two parts sandy loam to one part of leaf-mould and rotten manure. Prune as above after flowering and plant-out in the open. Do not re-pot for forcing for two seasons. To propagate, sow in a frame in spring ; budding and grafting are sometimes resorted to. The seeds are *poisonous.*

Lachenalia (Cape Cowslip).—Beautiful bulbous-rooted flowering plants suitable for greenhouse culture. *Culture.*—Pot-up in August, ½ inch deep in a compost of peaty loam with decayed cow manure and sand. Put one bulb in a 4-inch pot, or five bulbs in a 6 to 7-inch pot. Keep in a cold frost-proof frame until early December, watering only when dry, then transfer to a shelf near the glass in the greenhouse (50° F.), and water as growth commences. Keep quite dry in pots from May to August. Propagate by means of offsets in August. *Named Varieties.*—*L. Nelsonii* (Golden Yellow) ; *L. pendula* (Red and Yellow) ; *L. luteola* (Yellow-green, tipped Red).

Lantana (Surinam Tea Plant).—Bushy evergreen half-hardy shrubs, 6 to 8 inches high, flowering from June to September. Useful for the greenhouse and flower garden. *Culture.*—Pot-up as soon as the young shoots break after pruning, using 6 to 7-inch pots and a com-post of two parts of loam to one part of leaf-mould, well-rotted manure and sand. Syringe in spring and summer. If planted out during the summer, they must be wintered indoors. Seeds sown in heat (75° F.) in March make the summer and autumn blooming plants. They are also propagated in spring or autumn by cuttings of half-matured wood in heat. *Varieties.*—*Drap d'Or* (Yellow) ; *Favorita* (Yellow and Red) ; *La Neige* (White) ; and *Magenta King* (Purple-red).

Lapageria.—Beautiful evergreen climbers for the cool greenhouse, which require a well-drained turfy loam plentifully mixed with sand, an equal portion of peat and a little charcoal. They grow to a height of 10 feet and flower in October and November. *Culture.*—Propagate by seed sown as soon as ripe in gentle heat or by layers after flowering, the latter being the best way. Pot firmly, or plant in border in March, shade and water well. Cut-out weak shoots only after flowering. *Species and Varieties.*—*L. rosea* (Rose) ; and *vars. albifolia* (White), and *Nash Park* (Rosy-red).

Larix (Larch).—One of the few deciduous conifers. It grows from 30 to 100 feet in height and thrives in a sunny position and in ordinary soil. *Culture.*—Plant in October. Remove dead wood when necessary. Propagate by means of seed in the open in November. *Species.*— *L. europæa* (Common Larch) ; *L. pendula* (Weeping Larch).

Larkspur (Annual Delphinium).—Showy hardy annuals ; the dwarfs (12 in.) excellent for edging ; and taller sorts in mixed borders. For culture, *see* Annuals, p. 106. *Species.*—*D. Gayanum* [syn. *Ajacis*] (Blue) ; *D. Consolida* (Purple) ; *D. cardiopetalum* (Blue).

Lathyrus (Everlasting Pea, Sweet Pea).—Annual and perennial climbing plants, the most popular of which are the Sweet Pea and the Everlasting Pea, *which see* under those headings.

Laurel (Prunus Laurocerasus).—Evergreen shrubs which thrive in almost any soil and are useful for hedges. Prune carefully in May and September with a knife—shears must not be used—and when some years old, cut-out old wood. Plant young bushes 2 feet apart in March or September, and cut the vigorous young shoots back below the level of the others. Propagate by means of cuttings and layering.

Laurus.—This genus includes two species only, viz. *Laurus or Lindera Benzoin* (deciduous) and *L. nobilis* (evergreen), the true Bay Laurel or Sweet Bay. The latter thrives in well-drained fibrous loam, leaf-mould and peat in a sheltered position in sun or shade. To propagate, strike cuttings in a frame in August.

Lavandula (Lavender).—The best-known species, *L. Spica* (Mauve to White), the common lavender, thrives in light and well-drained soil in sunny positions, grows about 3 feet high, and flowers in July and August. *Culture.*—Plant in March or September, and clip after flowering. To propagate, strike cuttings in October.

Lavatera (Mallow).—Hardy annuals, biennials and perennials, which thrive in the sun in any soil. For culture, *see* Annuals, p. 106 ; Biennials, p. 107 ; *and* Perennials, p. 128. *Species.*—ANNUAL—*L. trimestris* (Rose or White). BIENNIAL—*L. arborea* (Violet). PERENNIAL —*L. thuringiaca* (Blue). All July to September, 30 to 60 inches.

Layia (Tidy Tips).—Hardy annuals suitable for sunny beds, borders or rock gardens. For culture, *see* Annuals, p. 106. *Species.*—*L. densiflora* (Mauve and White) ; *L. elegans* (Yellow, margined White) ; *L. glandulosa* (White). All July to September, 10 inches.

Ledum (Labrador Tree).—Hardy evergreen shrubs which thrive in cool, moist loam deficient in lime in sun or semi-shade. *Culture.*— Plant in May or September. No pruning is necessary. Propagate in September by means of layering, or cuttings, or by seed in spring. *Species.*—*L. latifolium* (White, tinged Pink) ; *L. palustre* (Pink). Both April to May, 10 to 40 inches.

Leiophyllum (Sand Myrtle).—Hardy dwarf evergreen shrubs for the rock garden, that thrive in fibrous loam in the sun, and flower in summer. *Culture.*—Plant in April or September. Propagation is by means of seed in a frame in spring, or by layering in September.

Leptospermum.—Evergreen shrubs which thrive in the cool green house in a compost of two parts peat to one of loam and a little sand. *L. scoparium* (White) may be grown outdoors in a warm, sheltered situation. Propagate by cuttings (with bottom heat) in May, or by seed in slight heat in March. *Species and Varieties.—L. Donard Beauty* (Red, margined Rose, 50 in.) ; *L. grandiflorum* (White, 80 in.) ; *L. scoparium Chapmanii* (Rose Scarlet, 50 in.). June to August flowering.

Leptosyne.—Annuals and perennials which thrive in the sun in ordinary soil. For culture, *see* Annuals, p. 106, *and* Perennials, p. 128. *Species and Varieties.—*ANNUAL*—L. Douglasii* (12 in.) ; *L. Stillmanii,* (20 in.). PERENNIAL*—L. maritima* (30 in.). All Yellow, Summer.

Leucojum (Snowflake).—Hardy bulbs which thrive in any garden soil in semi-shade, and are useful for borders or the rock garden. *Culture.*—Plant in September 3 to 4 inches deep and 5 inches apart ; lift every seven years. Propagate by offsets or by seed. *Species.—* *L. æstivum* (White, spotted Green, May, 15 in.) ; *L. autumnale* (White, tinged Red, Oct., 10 in.) ; *L. vernum* (White, March, 9 in.).

Lewisia (Bitter-root).—Useful little rock plants for a dry sunny crevice and in gritty loam. Protect from wet in winter. For culture, *see* Rock Plants, p. 135. *Species.—L. Cotyledon* (Pink, striped Buff or White, May–June, 4 in.) ; *L. rediviva* (Pink and White, May–Aug.).

Liatris (Blazing Star, or Kansas Feather).—Hardy perennials, better grown as biennials. They thrive in almost any soil in a warm, sunny border. For culture, *see* Biennials, p. 107. *Species.—L. graminifolia* (Pink, 40 in.) ; *L. spicata* (Mauve-purple, 70 in.). All Aug. to Oct.

Libertia.—Herbaceous perennials for the border or rock garden. They need a light soil. For culture, *see* Perennials, p. 128. *Species.—* *L. formosa* (White, 20 in.) ; *L. grandiflora* (White, 20 in.) ; *L. ixioides* (White, 40 in.). All March to May.

Libocedrus (Incense Cedar).—Hardy and half-hardy evergreen coniferous trees, the most popular species of which is *L. decurrens.* It likes a well-drained loam and a warm, sheltered position. *Culture.* —Sow seed October to April, or strike cuttings in frame in September.

Ligustrum (Privet).—Hardy evergreen and deciduous shrubs, usually grown as hedge-plants, but poisonous to cattle. They thrive in ordinary soil and in full sun. *Culture.*—Plant from November to March ; clip in summer and cut-out dead wood. To propagate, strike cuttings in the open in autumn. *Species.—L. ovalifolium* (Common Privet) and *L. o. foliis aureis* (Golden Privet) are those most used.

Lilac.—*See* Syringa.

Lilium (Lily).—There are many different species and varieties of lilies, but they are for the most part hardy bulbous perennials requiring practically the same management. Lilies thrive in deep, well-dug garden soil, or in a moist, well-drained fibrous loam with well-decayed leaf-mould and gritty sand in it. A few, such as *L. auratum, L. giganteum* and *L. pardalinum,* love a peaty soil, but with the majority the presence of peat will cause failure.

Culture.—Plant in October in groups of five or seven, 4 to 5 inches deep (about three times their own depth), and from 6 to 12 inches apart, according to species ; the bulbs should, as a rule, when planted, rest on sand, and they should not be disturbed oftener than every three years. A yearly top-dressing of well-decayed manure each spring will be beneficial. Lilies which form roots from the base of the stem should be planted among low-growing shrubs ; these particular lilies may be planted at any time, and somewhat deeper than the non-stem-rooting kinds. When in bloom, all lilies must be carefully staked, and all dead flowers should at once be removed, but the stems must not be cut down until they have died off. *The Madonna Lily* (*L. candidum*) requires different treatment. Transplant this lily in August, only lift when necessary, and top-dress with well-rotted manure each spring.

Pot Culture.—Plant in late autumn ; a 12-inch pot will take six bulbs, a large bulb of *L. auratum* would require a 10-inch pot to itself. The bulbs should be covered by 1 inch of soil which should be made firm, and care must be taken that the bulbs do not touch the sides of the pots. They should be treated in their first stage of growth exactly as hyacinths grown in pots, except that the pots must be only partly filled with soil. The pots should remain buried in ashes or fibre, in a frame till the plants begin to grow, when, as the stems grow, the pots are gradually filled up to within about an inch of the rim. Those intended to flower early should be placed under glass, while late bloomers should remain out-of-doors in a sheltered situation. Propagation is carried out by means of offsets in October, by planting scales from bulbs in sandy soil in a cold frame, or seed in pans in cold frame in August. Seedlings of most species do not flower until they are 2 to 5 years old.

Species and Varieties.—*L. auratum* [Japanese Lily] (White, Yellow and Crimson, Aug.–Sept., 40 in.) ; *L. candidum* [White Madonna Lily] (White, June–July, 50 in.) ; *L. chalcedonicum* [Turk's Cap] (Bright Scarlet, July–Aug., 40 in.) ; *L. croceum* (Orange, July–Aug., 36– 60 in.) ; *L. longiflorum formosanum* [Trumpet Lily] (White, July– Aug., 30 in.) ; *L. Martagon* (Rosy-violet, Wine-red and White, July, 40 in.) ; *L. pardalinum* [Panther Lily] (Scarlet, Orange and Yellow, July, 60 in.) ; *L. regale* (White and Yellow, July, 24–40 in.) ; *L. testaceum* (*syn. excelsum*) [Nankeen Lily] (Nankeen Yellow, Anthers Scarlet, June–July, 60 in.) ; *L. tigrinum splendens* [Tiger Lily] (Scarlet-orange, dark Purple Spots, Aug.–Sept., 50 in.).

Lily of the Valley (Convallaria).—To grow Lilies of the Valley well the roots should be set in bunches a foot apart in a mixture of sandy loam, leaf-mould and old manure in a partially-shaded position ; they can hardly be treated too liberally. *Culture.*—Plant in October, only just covering with soil, and mulch with a 2-inch layer of leaf-mould, which should be removed in the spring. Dress annually in summer with leaf-mould and rotten manure, lift from the soil every fourth year, and propagate by means of division in October. *Pot Culture.*—Plump crowns should be potted-up 1 inch apart in November, using 5 to 6-inch pots and a compost of sandy loam and leaf-mould, and so that only the tops obtrude. Water well and keep in a cool frame for a few days, then take into the house in batches as bloom is required. The pots must be kept in the dark until the shoots are 5 to 6 inches in height, after this gradually admit light, raise the temperature to between 60° and 70° F., and give warm water in increasing amounts as growth goes on. After flowering, plant the crowns in the border.

Limnanthemum (Fringed Golden Buck Bean).—Hardy aquatic plants, flowering in July and August, and enjoying a sunny position in slow-moving water. Sow seed, or propagate by division in March, and plant with not more than 12 inches of water above the crowns.

Limnanthes.—Dwarf hardy annuals, which flower in summer, and are useful for edging or rock garden. For culture, *see* Annuals, p. 106.

Linaria (Toad Flax).—These are mostly hardy annuals and perennials. All species like a light sandy soil and a sunny, dry position; the rock garden species need a gritty soil. For culture, *see* Annuals, p. 106, *and* Perennials, p. 128. *Species.*—(ANNUAL)—*L. bipartita* (Red, White or Purple, 12 in.) ; *L. reticulata* (Yellow and Purple, 12–18 in.). (PERENNIAL)—*L. alpina* (Violet, blotched Orange, 3 in.) ; *L. Cymbalaria* (Mauve and Orange, Trailer) ; *L. dalmatica* (Orange and Yellow, 40 in.). All June to September.

Linnæa borealis (Twin-flower).—A hardy evergreen trailing shrub which thrives in a mixture of sand and peat in the shade on moist banks, and flowers in June and July. *Culture.*—Propagate by means of division in March or October or increase by layering.

Linum (Flax or Linseed-oil Plant).—Hardy annuals and perennials which thrive in dry, light soil in a sunny position. The rock garden species need the addition of ample grit. For culture, *see* Annuals, p. 106, *and* Perennials, p. 128. *Pot Culture.*—Pot-up in March or April, using 5 to 6-inch pots and a compost of loam and peat with a little sand mixed. In February or March prune back the previous year's growth to within an inch from the base. *Species.*—(ANNUAL)—*L. grandiflorum* (Crimson-scarlet, Black Centre, Oct., 12 in.) ; *L. usitatissimum* (Blue, July–Oct., 24 in.). (PERENNIAL)—*L. alpinum* (Blue, May–June, 6–9 in.) ; *L. flavum* (Golden, June–Sept., 10 in.) ; *L. hirsutum* (Blue and White, May–Sept., 9 in.) ; *L. narbonense* (Deep Blue, May–Sept., 12–24 in.) ; *L. perenne* (Pale Blue, May–Sept., 12–24 in.).

Liquidambar styraciflua (Sweet Gum).—Hardy deciduous trees, growing 40 to 80 feet high, and which like a cool, moist ordinary soil and a sunny position. Propagate by seed or by cuttings.

Liriodendron (Tulip Tree).—Tall deciduous trees, flowering in July and August, which thrive in well-drained soil in a sunny position. *Culture.*—Plant in November ; in autumn cut-out dead wood. To propagate, sow seed in a frame in March.

Lisianthus Russellianus.—A handsome biennial with purple flowers in July and August. For culture, see Biennials, p. 107.

Lithospermum (Gromwell).—Hardy trailing evergreen shrubs and perennials, which do well in a mixture of gritty loam and peat in moderately sunny positions, and are excellent for dry walls, rock gardens and for edging. For culture, *see* Rock Plants, p. 135. *Species.* —*L. graminifolium* (Sky Blue) ; *L. intermedium* (Deep Blue) ; *L. prostratum* (Blue). All June to September.

Lobelia.—A genus of half-hardy annuals and perennials, of which the low-growing kinds are suitable for edging, thriving in deep, well-manured and moist soil in sunny positions. *L. gracilis* is equally beautiful in pots or beds ; all varieties of the greenhouse perennial *L. Erinus* are valuable for edging and for hanging baskets or vases. Treat all these as half-hardy annuals. The tall perennial species are valuable in the mixed border. *Culture.*—(*Annuals*)—*See* p. 106. If required for greenhouse use pot-up singly into 3 to 4-inch pots in the compost mentioned below. (*Perennials*)—*See* p. 128. As soon as the foliage is dead in autumn, the stems are cut down and the roots lifted and stored in boxes of dry soil in a frost-proof frame ; water is given in March to re-start growth and late in April the roots are divided and planted-out. *Pot Culture.*—(*L. cardinalis and vars.*)—Pot-up in March, using 6 to 8-inch pots and a compost of fibrous loam, leaf-mould, rotten manure and sand ; keep in a frame on ashes until about to bloom, then transfer to the cool greenhouse. After blooming, cut down the flower stems, return to the frame in October, and cover with ashes for the winter ; give a good watering in February, and a month later divide and re-pot if necessary. *Species and Varieties.*—(ANNUAL) —*L. Erinus—Barnard's Perpetual* (Dark Blue and White) ; *Celestial* (Cobalt Blue) ; and *Imperial Blue* (Dark). All July to October, 6 inches. *L. gracilis* (Celestial Blue, 12 in.) ; *L. tenuior* (Blue, White Eye, 12 in.). (PERENNIAL)—*L. cardinalis* (Crimson-scarlet, 24–36 in.) ; *L. fulgens* (Scarlet, 30 in.) ; *L. syphilitica* (Blue and White, 24–30 in.). All June to Sept. *Named Varieties.*—*Kimbridge* (Magenta) ; *B. Lad-hams* (Scarlet) ; *Queen Victoria* (Red) ; *Purple Emperor* ; *Salmon Queen.*

Lonicera (Honeysuckle)—A genus comprising all the trailing and climbing hardy and half-hardy deciduous or evergreen plants known as Honeysuckles. These thrive in any good, moderately dry garden soil and frequently in shaded positions. *Culture.*—Strike cuttings of ripe shoots in the open in late summer ; let the cuttings stand in the bed for a year, then plant-out from October to April. If preferred, propagate by layering or from seed. After flowering cut away old wood and trim back shoots. For garden use *L. Periclymenum belgica* and *L. P. serotina*, the early and late Dutch honeysuckles, are excellent. *L. sempervirens* forms a beautiful greenhouse climber, and *L. Standishii* and *L. fragrantis-sima* (Bush Honeysuckles) flower early in February. *Pot Culture.*— Pot-up in late autumn in a compost of sandy loam, leaf-mould and rotten manure, and keep in a cold house until Feb., then move to a sunny posi-tion in the cool house ; the plants may be stood out from June to Oct.

Lophospermum.—Half-hardy annual climbers which thrive in ordinary rich soil in warm sheltered positions outdoors, or in the cool greenhouse. For culture, *see* Annuals, p. 107.

Lotus (Bird's Foot Trefoil).—The hardy perennial species of this plant, which grow well in ordinary soil, are well suited for sunny borders or for the rock garden. For culture, *see* Perennials, p. 128. *Species.*— *L. corniculatus* (Yellow, July–Aug., 6 in.) ; *L. Bertholotii*, syn. *pelior-hynchus* (Scarlet, June, 10 in.) ; *L. Tetragonolobus* (Purple, July–Sept., 6–12 in.).

Lupinus (Lupins).—Hardy annuals and perennials valuable for borders and wild garden ; the dwarf species are excellent for bedding. They thrive in light, rich and well-drained soil deficient in lime and in sunny positions. For culture, *see* Annuals, p. 106, *and* Perennials, p. 128. Stake the plants early, cut the stems to the ground after blooming, and mulch with well-decayed manure. *Species and Varieties.* —(ANNUALS)—*L. Hartwegii* (Pale Blue) ; *L. nanus* (Lilac Blue and White). (PERENNIALS)—*L. arboreus* (Yellow, White and Blue) ; *L.*

leucophyllus (Rose-pink) ; *L. polyphyllus* (Blue, White and Rose). All May to October, 12 to 60 inches. *Named Varieties.*—(White) *Snowbird* ; (Cream) *Mrs. Morris* ; (Yellow) *Sunshine* ; (Rose) *Wargrave Beauty* ; (Orange-fawn) *Flaming Torch* ; (Crimson) *Downer's Delight* ; (Blue) *Porcelain Blue* ; (Blue and White) *Admiration* ; (Purple) *Happiness* ; (Mauve) *Punchinello.*

Lychnis (Catchfly, Campion, Ragged-Robin, Rose of Heaven).— Hardy annuals, biennials and perennials which thrive in any good soil, especially in rich light loam, and like a sunny position ; the rock garden species need a gritty loam. For culture, *see* Annuals, p. 106, Biennials, p. 107, *and* Perennials, p. 128. *Species and Varieties.*—*L. alpina* (Rose, April–June, 6 in.) ; *L. chalcedonica* (Scarlet and White, June–Sept., 30 in.) ; *L. fulgens* (Salmon, June–Sept., 12 in.) ; *L. Haageana* (Crimson, July– Aug., 12 in.) ; *L. Viscaria splendens fl. pl.* (Rose, June–July, 12–18 in.).

Lycium chinense (Box Thorn).—Hardy deciduous climbing shrubs which thrive in shrub borders and against sunny walls. *Culture.*— Strike cuttings of ripe shoots, or layer in the open in October. Let the cuttings stand in the beds for a year, then plant-out from October to March. In winter cut-out weak shoots and top strong shoots.

Lysimachia (Creeping Jenny, Moneywort, or Loosestrife).—These herbaceous perennials do best in moist, rich, ordinary soil in semi-shade. The low-growing species make excellent subjects for carpeting in the rock garden ; the taller kinds for border or wild garden. *Culture.* —Propagate by means of division in April or October ; no protection is required during winter. *Species.*—(Tall)—*L. ciliata* (Yellow, 30 in.) ; *L. clethroides* (White, 30 in.). (Dwarf)—*L. Nummularia aurea* (Creeping Jenny) (Yellow, Trailer). All June to September.

Lythrum (Purple Loosestrife).—Hardy perennials thriving in rich, sandy soil in shady, moist borders, or in the wild garden. For culture, *see* Perennials, p. 128. *Species.*—*L. Salicaria* (Purple and Rose, 50 in.) ; *L. virgatum* (Rose Queen) (Rose, 40 in.). All June to September.

Magnolia.—Hardy and half-hardy deciduous and evergreen shrubs to which a good, deep, well-drained loam with ample leaf-mould and a sunny position are essential. Transplant as little as possible, and prune when required (which is but rarely) in summer. They grow from 15 to 60 feet high and flower spring and summer. *Culture* (*Hardy Species*).—*M. conspicua*, *M. Soulangeana*, and *M. stellata*, etc. Plant in April or October. Propagate by means of grafting under glass in spring, layering, cuttings and seeds. *M. grandiflora :* Plant in April or September. To propagate, sow seed in a frame, strike cuttings of matured wood of the current year in heat in July, or layer during that period. *Pot Culture* (generally *M. stellata*).—Pot-up in October or November, using 8 to 12-inch pots and a compost of sandy loam, leaf-mould and rotten manure. After flowering prune-out weak wood and dead flower shoots, and sink the pots to their rims in ashes outdoors from May to December when the pots should be moved into the house.

Maianthemum (Twin-leaved Lily of the Valley).—Beautiful little hardy perennials, useful for carpeting in the rock garden, and which like a mixture of loam and leaf-mould and a shady position. *Culture.* —Propagate by means of division in April or September.

From the Painting by]   *[Beatrice Parsons*

A BORDER OF PURPLE, MAUVE, PINK, WHITE AND BLUE

Malope (Mallow-wort).—Tall hardy annuals useful for sunny beds or borders. For culture, *see* Annuals, p. 106. *Species.*—*M. trifida* (Crimson, Red and White).

Malva (Marsh Mallow).—Hardy and half-hardy annuals and perennials which like a well-drained border of ordinary soil and a sunny position. For culture, *see* Annuals, p. 106, *and* Perennials, p. 128. *Species.*—(HARDY ANNUALS)—*M. crispa* (White, 60 in.). (HARDY PERENNIALS)—*M. Alcea* (Purplish-red, 50 in.) ; *M. moschata* (Rose and White, 30 in.). All June to September.

Marguerite (Chrysanthemum frutescens).—These popular half-hardy plants like a soil that is not too rich. *Culture.*—Sow under glass in April, or strike cuttings of young shoots in a cold frame in September ; protect in severe weather. Pot-up into 4-inch pots in March, harden-off and plant-out towards the end of May, or re-pot into 6-inch pots, harden-off, and stand on ashes in the open until September, then move into 7-inch pots and transfer to a cool, but frost-proof, house for the winter. Young plants grown on for pot culture should be " stopped " during the spring and summer. *Varieties.*—*Broussonetii* (White, Single) ; *Etoile d'Or* (Yellow) ; and *Queen Alexandra* (White, Double).

Marvel of Peru (Mirabilis).—A genus of greenhouse and hardy perennials which grow best in sunny positions and in a light, rich loam, but do well in any good garden soil. They are best treated in the same manner as dahlias, and can be grown from seeds sown in gentle heat from March to April, hardened-off and planted-out in May.

Maurandia.—Beautiful, but somewhat tender, deciduous climbers which will grow in the open in rich, ordinary soil in a warm, sheltered position. *Culture.*—Sow in heat in March, or strike cuttings of young shoots under glass in summer. Plant-out in June. *Pot Culture.*—Pot-up in March, using 6 to 7-inch pots and a compost of two parts of loam to one part of leaf-mould and sand. Trim straggly shoots in autumn. *Species.*—*M. Barclayana* (Violet-purple) ; *M. erubescens* (Rose) ; and *M. scandens* (Purple). All July to September, 10 feet.

Mazus.—Hardy creeping perennials that are excellent for the paved or rock garden, and which thrive in a mixture of well-drained loam and leaf-mould and in sunny positions. For culture, *see* Rock Plants, p. 135. *Species.*—*M. Pumilio* (Purple-mauve) ; *M. reptans* (Mauve).

Meconopsis.—The best of this genus are hardy herbaceous perennials or biennials. They thrive in gritty loam and peat, and in partial shade in borders or rock garden. For culture, *see* Biennials, p. 107, *and* Perennials, p. 128. *Species.*—(BIENNIAL)—*M. integrifolia* (Yellow, 15–20 in.) ; *M. Prattii* (Blue-purple, 20–36 in.) ; *M. puniceus* (Red, 15–20 in.) ; *M. Wallichii* (Pale Blue, 4–6 ft.). (PERENNIAL)—*M. cambrica fl. pl.* (Yellow, Orange, Dbl., 12–18 in.). All May to August.

Menyanthes trifoliata (Bog Bean).—A hardy perennial which thrives in ordinary soil and a sunny position in bog or in still, shallow water. It bears rosy lilac flowers from March to June. *Culture.*—Strike cuttings in mud in summer ; plant-out in March.

Mertensia (Lungwort and Oyster Plant).—Hardy perennials which thrive in almost any moist, cool soil with a little peat in it in shady borders or in the rock garden. For culture, *see* Perennials, p. 128.

E.G.   **S**

Species.—*M. echioides* (Blue) ; *M. maritima* (Pink, later Blue) ; *M. primuloides* (Deep-blue, Yellow Centre). All May to August, 4 to 24 inches.

Michaelmas Daisy (Starwort).—Hardy perennial asters which thrive in the sun in ordinary well-drained soil and are excellent for borders and wild gardens ; while the dwarf kinds make excellent subjects for the rock garden. They flower from July to November, and grow from 6 inches to 6 feet in height according to species. For culture, *see* Perennials, p. 128. NAMED VARIETIES OF A. AMELLUS.—*Beauté Parfait* (Dark Blue) ; *Beauty of Ronsdorf* (Mauve) ; *King George* (Purple-blue) ; and *Perry's Favourite* (Pale Pink). NAMED VARIETIES OF A. CORDIFOLIUS.—*Diana* (Lilac) and *Silver Spray* (Pale Lilac). NAMED VARIETIES OF A. ERICOIDES.—*Enchantress* (Pink) ; *Ophir* (Mauve) ; *Perfection* (White) ; and *Simplicity* (Blue). NAMED VARIETIES OF A. NOVÆ ANGLIÆ.—*Barr's Pink* (Pink) ; *Mrs. F. J. Rayner* (Crimson) ; and *Purple Prince* (Purple). NAMED VARIETIES OF A. NOVI BELGII.—*Aldenham Pink* (Pink) ; *Beauty of Colwall* (Blue) ; *Brightest and Best* (Purple-rose) ; *Climax* (Heliotrope-blue) ; *Elsa* (Rose-lavender) ; *J. H. Jones* (White) ; *King of the Belgians* (Pale Mauve).

Michauxia.—Tall hardy biennials which thrive in moist, sandy loam in sunny borders. *See* Biennials, p. 107. *Species.*—*M. campanuloides* (Pink, July–August, 50 in.).

Mignonette (Reseda odorata).—This sweet-scented perennial is commonly grown as an annual ; it likes a fairly rich soil with lime in it and a sunny position. For culture, *see* Annuals, p. 106. Seedlings grown in the open should not be transplanted. *Pot Culture.*—Sow in pots under glass in March, June, August and September, using a compost of two parts of loam to one part of rotted cow-manure and a little crushed lime-rubble and sand, and placing several seeds in each 6-inch pot. Thin to four plants in each pot and stand near the glass or grow in a frame. Cut-off all dead flowers, and prune back straggly shoots. *Named Varieties.*—*Crimson Giant* ; *Golden Gem* ; *Pearl* (Cream) ; *Machet* (Buff) ; *Salmon Queen* (Salmon-pink) ; *Giant Red* (Red). All July to September, 9 to 18 inches.

Mimulus (Musk or Monkey Flower).—Hardy and half-hardy annuals and hardy perennials. Seed of the annuals sown in spring makes good bedding plants, and seed sown in autumn produces early-flowering plants for the greenhouse. They like a shady site with moist, rich soil. The smaller species are useful for edging and for the rock garden. For culture, *see* Annuals, p. 106, *and* Perennials, p. 128. *Pot Culture.*—Pot-up in May, using 5 to 6-inch pots and a compost of two parts of loam and one part of leaf-mould, peat and sand. Pinch back to make bushy, and keep cool in winter. *Species and Varieties.*—HALF-HARDY ANNUAL.—*M. tigrinus* (Yellow, Spotted, June, 9 in.). HARDY PERENNIALS.—*M. Burnetii* (Pale Brown, 10 in.) ; *M. cardinalis* (Scarlet, 20 in.) ; *M. cupreus* (Orange, 12 in.) ; *M. luteus* (Yellow Spotted, 9 in.) ; *M. moschatus* (Yellow, 6 in.) ; *M. radicans* (White and Violet, 3 in.) ; *M. ringens* (Pale-blue, 10 in.). All June to August.

Mina.—Half-hardy annual climbers, which thrive in rich, well-drained soil in warm, sunny, sheltered positions. *See* Annuals, p. 107.

Mistletoe (*Viscum album*).—This parasite is easy to cultivate ; an incision should be made in the bark on the underside of a three-year-old branch of an apple tree—many other trees, such as the pear, plum, ash, birch, etc., answer equally well—and in February into this incision insert some ripe mistletoe berries, and carefully tie the bark over with a piece of bass, or woollen yarn. Growth is exceedingly slow.

Mitraria coccinea (Mitre Flower).—A half-hardy evergreen shrub that will grow outdoors during summer in warm, semi-shaded and sheltered situations. Plant in April in moist, peaty soil. *Pot Culture.*—Pot-up in March in a compost of two-thirds turfy peat and one-third sand. To propagate, strike cuttings of young shoots in a frame in summer.

Monarda (Bee's Balm, Horse Mint, Oswego Tea, Red Sage or Bergamot).—Useful perennials thriving in deep, moist loam in sunny borders. They will, however, grow anywhere. For culture, *see* Perennials, p. 128. *Species.*—*M. didyma* (Red, July–Sept., 24 in.) ; *M. fistulosa* (Pink, July–Sept., 24 in.).

Montbretia (Tritonia).—Hardy bulbous plants, which thrive in rich, sandy loam and leaf-mould in warm, sunny beds or borders, or in pots. *Culture.*—Plant in April 4 inches deep and 4 to 6 inches apart. Cover with fibre in winter, and lift every four years only ; half-hardy varieties must be lifted each October. *Pot Culture.*—Pot-up in April, placing five bulbs in a 7 to 8-inch pot, and using a compost of two parts of peaty loam to one part of leaf-mould and sand. Sink the pots in ashes in a frost-proof frame, and transfer to the greenhouse early in June. Re-pot every fourth year only ; propagate by means of offsets. *Named Varieties.*—*Drap d'Or* (Yellow) ; *Etoile de Feu* (Orange) ; *Lady Hamilton* (Apricot) ; *Lord Nelson* (Scarlet) ; *Phare* (Crimson) ; *rosea* (Rosy-pink) ; *Salmon King* (Salmon). All July to September, 2 to 4 feet.

Morina (Whorl-flower).—Half-hardy and hardy perennials, excellent for the border or rock garden. They like a warm, sunny position and a rich, gritty loam. In exposed districts winter in a frame. Sow in March, or propagate by offsets. *Species.*—*M. longifolia* (Rose-purple) ; *M. persica* (Red and white). Both July to August, 30 inches.

Morisia hypogœa (Mediterranean Cress).—Hardy little summer-flowering rock plants which thrive in well-drained, deep, gritty loam in an open and fairly sunny spot. *See* Rock Plants, p. 135.

Morus (Mulberry).—Hardy deciduous trees which thrive in the sun in deep, moist but well-drained ordinary soil. They grow 20 to 30 feet high and flower in May and June. *Culture.*—Plant in October, and do not shorten the long tap roots ; little pruning is necessary. Propagate by means of cuttings in September.

Muscari (Grape Hyacinth).—Hardy bulbous plants which thrive in good loam in warm, sunny borders or in the rock garden, or in pots. *Culture.*—Plant in October from 2 to 3 inches deep and 3 inches apart ; lift from the ground only when overcrowded. Propagate by means of offsets in October. *Pot Culture.*—Pot-up annually in October 1½ inches deep in 5-inch pots ; dry-off in a cold frame after flowering. *Species.* —(EARLY)—*M. botryoides* (Blue and White varieties, Feb.–March, 6 in.). (LATE)—*M. conicum var. Heavenly Blue* (Sky-blue, April–May, 8 in.). *M. racemosum* (Deep Blue, April–May, 6 in.).

Mutisia.—A hardy climbing plant usually grown in the cold greenhouse. *Culture.*—Pot-up in a large pot in a compost of two-thirds loam and one-third leaf-mould and ample sand. Water liberally and syringe from May to July, but keep only just moist during the autumn and winter. *Variety.*—*M. decurrens* (Orange-yellow, July, 12 ft.).

Myosotidium.—A half-hardy perennial which needs a warm, sunny position and a fairly rich and moist soil. Propagation is by seed sown in May and June, or by root-cuttings in October. *Variety.*—*M. nobile* (Blue and Cream, May, 20 in.).

Myrtle (Myrtus).—Beautiful evergreen greenhouse shrubs which will grow out-of-doors in warm, sunny and sheltered situations. *Culture.*—Plant in May or September in loam and leaf-mould ; the addition of a little peat is beneficial. Trim in April, not in autumn. *Pot Culture.*—Pot-up in March (triennially), using 5 to 12-inch pots and a compost of two parts of sandy loam to one part of leaf-mould ; stand outdoors from July to October, and prune in February. To propagate strike cuttings in a frame in July, or layer in September.

Narcissus.—Beautiful hardy bulbs which are excellent for beds, borders, the rock garden (most species), for naturalizing in grass, and for pots. Most species thrive in well-dug and well-drained ordinary soil, though some few, notably the *Hooped Petticoat*, the *Cyclamen-flowered* and the *Angel's Tears*, prefer warm, deep and moist sandy loam ; the *Polyanthus narcissi* like a rather stiff soil. Partial-shade is desirable, but they will grow well in full sun. *Culture.*—Plant from August to October, the sooner the better, 4 inches deep in heavy soil and 7 inches deep in light soil, and about 4 inches apart, making exception of small species which should be 2 to 3 inches deep, and the May-flowering double white narcissus, which must be not less than 9 inches deep in well-worked moist loam. If used for naturalizing, the bulbs should be left in the ground, but in beds or borders they should be raised triennially in July. *Greenhouse Culture.*—Pot-up from August to November, using a compost of half fibrous loam to a quarter part each of sand and leaf-mould or rotten manure, and place from three large to twelve small bulbs in a 4 to 5-inch pot and keep in the open in a cool, shady site under a 3-inch layer of coco-nut fibre until growth commences, then move into the cool house in batches. Dry-off when the foliage dies and plant-out in the open the following year. The bulbs of the Polyanthus Narcissus being large, a 5-inch pot will be needed for a single specimen. Daffodils will not stand forcing, and only gentle heat should be used. Propagate by means of offsets at lifting time, re-planting the offsets immediately in a reserve garden ; seed may also be sown in pans or boxes in August, but they take four to six years to flower. *See also chapter on* Bulb-Growing. *Named Varieties.*—TRUMPET (Trumpet as long as or longer than the perianth segments)—(White) *Peter Barr ;* (Yellow) *Golden Spur ;* (Bi-color ; White or cream perianth with yellow trumpet) *Horsfieldii.* SHORT CUP OR INCOMPARABILIS (Cup not less than one-third, but less than equal to the length of the perianth segments, outer petals yellow or white, cup yellow or red)—*Lucifer, Sir Watkin,* and *Vesuvius.* BARRI (Cup less than one-third the length of the perianth segments;

bright coloured cups, perianths yellow or white)—*Albatross, Conspicuous* and *Seagull*. LEEDSII OR EUCHARIS-FLOWERED (Outer petals white, with white or pale yellow or cream cups, sometimes tinged pink)—*Bridesmaid, Duchess of Westminster* and *White Lady*. TRIANDRUS OR "ANGEL'S TEARS" (Short cup and reflexed outer petals)—*Agnes Harvey, Queen of Spain* and *Venetia*. CYCLAMEN-FLOWERED (Pale yellow with darker and very narrow trumpet)—*cyclamineus*. JONQUIL-FLOWERED—*Buttercup, Jonquilla* and *N. odorus rugulosus*. TAZETTA OR POLYANTHUS (These are all bunch-flowered and white with yellow cups)—*Aspasia, Elvira* and *Paper White*. POETICUS OR POET'S (Petals white or yellow with red eye)—*Cassandra Epic, White Standard* and *Pheasant's Eye*. DOUBLE—*Argent, Butter and Eggs* and *Telamonius plenus*.

Nasturtium (Tropæolum majus and minus).—Many varieties are well known as climbers ; the dwarf varieties are useful for bedding or edging, and for the rock garden. *Culture.*—Sow thinly from March to June ¼ inch deep in light, poor soil, and thin-out to from 12 to 18 inches apart when fit to handle. The double varieties do not seed, and cuttings must be struck in a cold frame in August or September.

Nemesia.—Half-hardy annuals which make excellent bedding, rock garden or pot plants. For culture, *see* Annuals, p. 107. *Species.*—*N. floribunda* (White and Yellow) ; *N. strumosa* (Red, Pink, Orange, Yellow, Blue and White) ; *N. versicolor* (White and Mauve). *Named Varieties.*—*Aurora* (Red and White) ; *Blue Gem* ; *Cherry Red* ; *Orange Prince* ; and *Twilight* (Mauve and White). All June to Sept., 12 in.

Nemophila (Californian Bluebell).—Dwarf-growing hardy annuals for edgings to sunny beds, or for the rock garden. For culture, *see* Annuals, p. 106. *Species.*—*N. insignis* (Sky-blue, White Centre) ; *N. Menziesii* (Purple, Blue, White, blotched Black) ; *N. M. discoidalis* (Maroon and White). All July to Sept., 3 to 9 inches.

Nepeta (Catmint).—Hardy perennials which thrive in sunny positions and in ordinary soil, and are useful for edgings to large borders, or for the rock garden. For culture, *see* Perennials, p. 128. *Species.*—*N. curvifolia* and *N. Mussini*. Both Blue, May to Sept., 18 inches.

Nerine.—Beautiful bulbous plants which thrive in the cool greenhouse in rich loam, mixed with leaf-mould, cow-manure and sand. *Culture.*—Plant singly in August in 4 to 5-inch pots, water well when the flower buds appear and feed with liquid manure. Keep dry from June to August, with the pots exposed to the sun, and when the flower shoots again rise soak the pots and top-dress with fresh soil. Re-pot every fourth year, and propagate by offsets in August, or sow seed when ripe. *Species and Varieties.*—*N. Bowdeni* (Pink) ; *N. corusca* (Orange-scarlet) ; *N. Fothergillii major* (Scarlet) ; *N. pudica* (White) ; *N. sarnensis* (Pale Salmon). All September to December, 20 inches.

Nerium.—The best known of this genus of evergreen shrubs is *N. Oleander*, the Common Oleander. The blossoms and wood are *poisonous*. *Culture.*—Pot when required in Feb., using 6 to 12-inch pots and a compost of two parts loam to one of leaf-mould, peat and a little sand. Keep in a sunny position in the cool greenhouse, and sponge the leaves frequently. Remove the shoots at the base of the flower buds, and prune to within three buds of the old wood. Keep fairly dry during winter. To propagate, place cuttings of well-ripened shoots in bottles of water, in a sunny frame in summer ; when well rooted, pot-up in light soil and " stop " from time to time.

Nertera depressa (Coral-berried Duckweed).—A dwarf-growing creeping plant, for the rock garden, or for edging. It thrives in the shade in warm, moist, sandy loam and leaf-mould, but must be protected from frost. For culture, *see* Rock Plants, p. 135.

Nicotiana (Tobacco Plant).—Although treated as annuals, tobacco plants are perennials, and if the roots are protected from frost they will come up again year after year. Among the sorts usually grown are *N. alata* and *N. Sanderæ*. The first has white flowers, fragrant in the evening ; the second bears red or white flowers, but these are not so fragrant. They thrive in rich soil in sunny beds and borders. For culture, *see* Annuals, p. 106. For greenhouse use, seed sown in a frame in August will furnish bloom from January to March.

Nierembergia (Cup Flower).—Half-hardy perennials which thrive in moist loam in a sunny position. *N. rivularis*, with creamy-white flowers streaked with purple, from June to August, is a useful little rock plant. For culture, *see* Rock Plants, p. 135.

Nigella (Devil-in-a-Bush, Love-in-a-Mist, Jack-in-Prison).—Hardy annuals useful for sunny beds and borders. For culture, *see* Annuals, p. 106. *Species and Varieties.—N. damascena* (Deep Purple) ; *N. hispanica* (Pale Blue or White) ; *N. Miss Jekyll* (Deep Blue, double) ; *N. orientalis* (Yellow and Red). All June to September, 18 inches.

Nuphar.—A genus numbering but a few species, among which is *N. luteum*, the Yellow Water Lily. This is hardy and, like all of its kind, may be grown in a pond or slow stream, and managed in the same way as Nymphæa, *which see*. *Species.—N. advena* and *N. luteum*. Both Yellow, June to August, 12 to 18 inches.

Nuttallia cerasiformis (Osoberry).—A hardy deciduous shrub growing from 5 to 10 feet high, and bearing white flowers from February to March. *Culture.*—Plant in October or November in sun or semi-shade and in ordinary soil ; thin-out old wood when overcrowded.

Nymphæa.—A genus of water-lilies including the common White Water Lily. The hardy species have white, rose, orange, or yellow flowers. Most species like a sunny, sheltered position in slow-moving water ; those from hot countries require a hothouse. *Culture.*—Sow seed in spring in rich loam in a basket under water, or propagate by means of division from April to June and plant in rich loam, leaf-mould and cow-dung in weighted openwork baskets sunk so that there is from 12 to 60 inches of water above the crowns, according to species.

Nyssa sylvatica (Tupelo Tree).—A hardy deciduous tree thriving in moist deep loam, or any good soil in sunny positions. *Culture.*—Plant in November (as young as possible). No pruning is necessary. Propagate by means of seed or layering. It does not transplant well.

Œnothera (Evening Primrose, Godetia).—Annuals, biennials and perennials, for bedding, borders, or for the rock garden, and also grown in the greenhouse. All the species thrive in rich, sandy loam, or any good soil, and in sunny positions. For annuals, *see* Godetia, and for culture of the Evening Primrose, *see* Biennials, p. 107, *and* Perennials, p. 128. *Species.*—(BIENNIAL)—*O. acaulis* (White, tinted Rose, 10 in.) ; *O. biennis grandiflora* (Pale Yellow, 30 in.). (PERENNIAL)—*O. cheiranthifolia* (Pale Yellow, Trailer) ; *O. glauca Fraseri* (Golden Yellow, 20 in.) ; *O. missouriensis* (Yellow, Trailer) ; *O. speciosa* (White to Rose, 30 in.). All June to October flowering.

Olearia Haastii (New Zealand Daisy Bush).—Hardy evergreen shrubs from 4 to 9 feet high and bearing white flowers in late summer. They like a sheltered position and well-drained soil. *Culture.*—Plant in May or October. Trim to shape when necessary in March, and every four or five years, cut hard back. *Pot Culture of greenhouse species.*—In the cool greenhouse they may be had in flower in March. Pot-up when required in October, using 6 to 7-inch pots and a compost of two parts of sandy loam to one part of leaf-mould and rotten manure. Sink the pots in ashes in a sunny spot outdoors from May to December, then take indoors and keep fairly dry until growth starts. To propagate, sow in a frame in March, or strike cuttings in a frame in Sept.

Omphalodes (Creeping or Rock Forget-Me-Not, Navelwort).—Annual and perennial creeping plants for semi-shade in the border or rock garden and loving a moist sandy or gritty loam. For culture, *see* Annuals, p. 106, *and* Perennials, p. 128. *Species.*—(ANNUAL)—*O. linifolia* (White, July, 9 in.). (PERENNIAL)—*O. cappadocica* (Porcelain Blue, May–June, 9 in.); *O. Luciliæ* (Lilac Blue, June–Sept., 6 in.) ; *O. verna* (Porcelain Blue, April–May, 4 in.).

Ononis (Rest Harrow).—Hardy perennials which thrive in sunny rock gardens and in almost any soil. For culture, *see* Rock Plants, p. 135. *Species.*—*O. fruticosa* (Purple-pink, May–Aug., 24–36 in.) ; *O. spinosa* (Rose-purple, July–Sept., 10 in.).

Onosma (Alpine Comfrey).—Hardy perennial rock plants which thrive in well-drained, gritty loam, peat and sand on hot, sunny ledges. Sow under glass in March, or strike cuttings in summer. *Species.*—*O. albo-roseum* (White, tinged Rose) ; *O. cæspitosum* (Orange) ; *O. frutescens* (Lavender); *O. tauricum* (Lemon-yellow). All June to July.

Orange (Citrus—Dwarf).—The dwarf fruiting species which are usually grown in the cool greenhouse are grafted plants. They thrive in a compost of three-quarters turfy loam and one-quarter leaf-mould, rotten manure and sand. In winter they need full sun, but in summer should be shaded from direct sun. Trim to shape only. The trees may be propagated by seed in gentle heat (65° F.), by budding in July, or by grafting in March ; but cuttings struck in spring produce bushes which fruit earlier. The culture of the lemon (*Citrus limonium*) and the lime (*Citrus limetta*) is identical with that of the orange.

Orchids.—Besides the numerous beautiful orchids which may be grown in the greenhouse, there are many hardy species which thrive outdoors in sheltered borders, in the rock garden or bog garden, notably the *Calopogon, Calypso, Cypripedium* (*Lady's Slipper*), *Epipactis, Goodyera* (*Adder's Violet*), *Habenaria* (*Butterfly Orchid*). *Listera, Ophrys* (*Bee and Fly Orchid*), *Orchis, Serapias* and *Spiranthes* (*Ladies' Tresses*). Most of these thrive in moist, sandy loam and leaf-mould or peat and in semi-shaded positions ; the *Ophrys, Orchis* and *Spiranthes* like a sunny position. Propagate most species by division in spring or autumn; in some cases by offsets. Greenhouse orchids vary considerably in their requirements and need careful attention. Space does not permit of these being dealt with thoroughly, and the reader is referred to a work devoted to orchid-growing.

Ornithogalum (Star of Bethlehem).—Hardy and half-hardy bulbous-rooted plants, for warm borders, for the rock garden and naturalizing in grass, and (chiefly *O. arabicum*) for pots. They thrive in ordinary soil in sun or semi-shade. *Culture.*—Plant from September to October, $3\frac{1}{2}$ inches deep and 3 inches apart, and protect from frost in winter. *Pot Culture.*—Pot-up from August to November, placing three bulbs in a 6-inch pot, or singly in a smaller pot, and using a compost of two parts of turfy loam to one part of leaf-mould and sand; grow near the glass in a cold greenhouse. Propagate by means of offsets. *Species.* —*O. arabicum* (White with Black Centre, May and June, 30 in.); *O. nutans* [Wild Hyacinth] (Greenish-white, May, 15 in.); *O. umbellatum* (White, Green Streaks, May, 10–15 in.).

Orontium aquaticum (Golden Club).—Hardy aquatic plants which thrive in slow-moving water. Propagate by means of root division in March, and plant with from 6 to 12 inches of water above the crowns.

Osmanthus.—Hardy evergreen shrubs, some of which resemble hollies. *Culture.*—Plant in May or September in sandy loam in sun or partial shade. No pruning is necessary, but long straggling shoots should be cut back in June. To propagate, strike cuttings of ripened shoots in a frame in September, or layer in summer. *O. Delavayi* (White, March and April, 4–6 ft.) is the best species. *O. Aquifolium* has small fragrant white flowers in late autumn.

Ourisia.—Hardy perennial creeping plants which thrive in moist sandy loam in the shade, and are excellent for moist ledges in the rock garden. For culture, *see* Rock Plants, p. 135. *Species.*—*O. coccinea* (Scarlet, May–Sept., 9 in.) is the best.

Oxalis (Cape Shamrock, Wood Sorrel).—Hardy and half-hardy annuals, perennials, and bulbous plants admirably adapted for pots, warm borders, and the rock garden. They succeed in any well-drained light, sandy soil and leaf-mould; the rock garden species need a gritty loam and a position in semi-shade. For culture of Annuals, *see* p. 106, *and* Perennials, p. 128. (*Bulbous Species*).—Plant from September to November 3 inches deep and 10 inches apart. Hardy species should not be lifted from the ground, but half-hardy kinds must. In light warm soils, however, protection from frost by means of ashes or fibre will be sufficient. Propagation is by means of small bulbs removed from the parent and planted in Sept. *Pot Culture.*—Pot-up in March $\frac{3}{4}$ inch deep, in 5 to 6-inch pots in a compost of two parts of sandy loam to one of leaf-mould. *See* Bulbs, p. 116. *Species and Varieties.*—(ANNUAL)— *O. corniculata* (Yellow, Aug.–Oct., 4 in.). (PERENNIAL)—*O. adenophylla* (Lilac-pink, dark Eye, May–July, 5 in.); *O. enneaphylla* (White, May–Sept., 6 in.); *O. floribunda* (Red, Rose, Mauve or White, March, 6 in.); *O. lobata* (Yellow, Sept.–Oct., 4 in.); *O. purpurata* (Carmine, Aug.–Sept., 8 in.); *O. tuberosa* (Rose, Oct.–Nov., 6 in.).

Oxydendrum arboreum (Sorrel Tree).—Hardy deciduous trees, which thrive in a loamy or peaty soil and in a sheltered position. They grow some 20 feet high and bear white flowers in July and August. Plant in May or October. To propagate, sow in a frame in March.

Ozothamnus rosmarinifolius (Snow in Summer).—A dark evergreen half-hardy shrub (8–10 ft.), bearing white flowers in May and June, and which needs the protection of a wall. Plant in rich loam or peat in a sunny site, and propagate by cuttings of young wood in a frame.

Pæonia.—Pæonies are divided into two classes, the *herbaceous*, and the *tree or shrubby*. They are mostly hardy and thrive in sun or partial shade in sheltered beds, in well-dug loam enriched with rotted cow-dung, but they will grow in almost any soil. *Culture.—(Herbaceous).*—Propagate by means of division in April or October and plant-out 3 feet apart, with the crowns 3 inches deep. Transplant as little as possible, never oftener than every five years, and if root divisions are required, they should be cut out with the plant *in situ*. Mulch with well-decayed manure each spring. (*P. Moutan, the Tree or Shrubby Species*).—Plant in September or early October, and protect from frost. If given gentle forcing in pots, they will furnish early blooms, but force only in alternate years. Increase by means of layering or by grafting on *P. officinalis* stock. *Varieties.—*(HERBACEOUS). (Single)—(White) *Bridesmaid* ; (White and Pink) *Eastern Brocade* ; (Rose-pink) *Avant Garde* ; (Salmon) *Kelway's Gorgeous* ; (Yellow) *Lemon Queen* ; and (Crimson) *Victor Hugo.* (Double)—(White and Red) *Kelway's Glorious* ; (Rose-pink) *Albert Crousse* ; (Blush-white) *Lady Alexander Duff* ; (Coral-pink) *Kelway's David* ; (Crimson) *President Poincaré* ; (Scarlet) *Agida* ; and (Purple) *Louis Van Houtte.* All May to July flowering. *P.* MOUTAN (TREE PÆONY).—(Single)—(White) *Queen Alexandra* ; (Salmon-pink) *Countess of Crewe* ; and (Crimson) *Eastern Queen.* (Double) —(White) *Aphrodite* ; (Flesh-pink) *Duchess of Marlborough* ; (Rose) *Reine Elizabeth* ; and (Scarlet) *Eastern Prince.* All flower in June.

Palms.—Some species require a considerable amount of heat, but such species as the *Areca* (Betel-nut Palm), *Chamærops* (Fan Palm), *Corypha* (Cabbage Palm), *Kentia* (Curly Palm), and *Phœnix* (Date Palm), may be grown easily in a house merely protected from frost. Palms are usually bought by the amateur as small plants, and should be re-potted in a compost of fibrous loam and silver sand, or fibrous peat and grit. Spring or early summer is the best time for potting. The roots must not be injured and they must be planted firmly the same depth as before. Water well both summer and winter, sponge the leaves with warm soft water, and syringe morning and evening in spring and summer. Partial shade is required in hot weather, and a little liquid manure made from cow-manure and soot is beneficial, and should the foliage turn yellowish, a small lump of sulphate of iron on the surface of the soil will remedy this. Propagation is usually by means of division in April, by suckers in September, or by seed.

Pancratium illyricum and P. maritimum (Mediterranean Lily, or Sea Daffodil).—Semi-hardy bulbous plants which thrive in light rich loam and peat in sunny, sheltered positions in warm and well-drained borders.

There are also many stove and greenhouse species. Both plants bear white flowers in May and June on stems 18 inches high. *Culture.*—Plant in October or March, 5 inches deep and 10 inches apart. Do not lift, but protect with fibre in winter. *Pot Culture.*—Re-pot every third or fourth year (in March) in two-thirds loam to one-third well-rotted manure and a little sand. Dry-off gradually after blooming, and stand hardy species in the open from May to September. Propagate by means of offsets in October or March.

Pansy (Heartsease).—*See* Viola.

Papaver (Poppy).—Hardy annuals, biennials, and perennials which thrive in the sun in almost any soil, though a deep, rich soil is best. They are useful for beds, borders and the wild garden. *P. alpinum* is a useful rock species ; it needs a gritty loam and is raised from seed sown in autumn. All dead flowers must be picked off, or the season of blooming will be greatly reduced. For culture, *see* Annuals, p. 106, Biennials, p. 107, *and* Perennials, p. 128. The latter should not be lifted oftener than every three or four years. *Species.*—(ANNUAL) —*P. glaucum* (Deep Scarlet, June–Sept., 20 in.) ; *P. lævigatum* (Red, White and Black, May–Sept., 25 in.) ; *P. somniferum* [Opium Poppy] (Crimson, Mauve, Rose, Violet and White [Double and Fringed], July–Oct., 30 in.) ; *P. Rhœas* [Shirley Poppy] (Orange, Pink, Red, Lavender, Blue and White [Single and Double], June–Sept., 24 in.). (BIENNIAL)—*P. alpinum* (Yellow, Salmon, White and Orange, May–Sept., 6–9 in.). (PERENNIAL)—*P. bracteatum* (Scarlet and Black, May–Sept., 36–48 in.) ; *P. Meconopsis cambrica* (Yellow) (*see* Meconopsis) ; *P. nudicaule* [Iceland Poppy] (Orange, Yellow, Buff, Salmon and White, May–Sept., 6–24 in.) ; *P. orientale* (Various, May–June, 30–50 in.). *Named Varieties.*—(*P. orientale*)—(White) *Perry's White* ; (Cerise) *Ethel Swete* ; (Scarlet) *King George* ; (Crimson) *Nancy* ; (Orange) *Orange King* ; (Salmon-pink and Black) *Perry's Pigmy*.

Paradisea Liliastrum (St. Bruno's Lily).—Beautiful bulbs which grow about 20 inches high, bear white flowers in May and June, and grow in well-drained light soil in sun or partial shade in the border or wild garden. *Culture.*—Plant from 9 to 12 inches apart in October or March, and mulch with old manure in March. Propagate by means of division in September or October.

Parnassia (Grass of Parnassus).—Hardy perennials for the bog, marsh, or water garden, or for the moist shady border. *Culture.*—Sow in the open in autumn, or propagate by means of division in April. *Species.*—*P. fimbriata* ; *P. nubicola* ; *P. palustris*. All white, June to August, 5 to 10 inches.

Paronychia.—Little creeping plants for the paved or rock garden, which thrive in the sun in gritty loam and are propagated by means of division in March, by cuttings under glass, or by seed. For culture, *see* Rock Plants, p. 135.

Parrotia persica (Persian Witch Hazel).—Hardy deciduous trees growing from 30 to 40 feet high, and which flower in March. They like a dry ordinary soil, and a sunny, sheltered position. *Culture.*—Plant in November. No pruning is necessary. Propagate by means of layering in summer.

Passiflora (Passion-flower).—A genus of beautiful climbing shrubs, which grow in almost any well-drained soil, though sandy loam is best, and should be given a position against a sunny wall facing south or west; the root-run should be restricted to encourage flowering. *Culture.*—Strike cuttings of young shoots in a frame in summer. Plant-out in October or March; cut back shoots to half their length in February or March, and cut-out weak wood. *Greenhouse Culture.*—Plant in March in a compost of two parts of fibrous loam to one part of peat and sand, and syringe and water well in summer. Prune back to within two buds of the old wood in winter, and cut away all weak shoots in spring. *P. cærulea* (Blue, June–Sept., 25 ft.), is the most hardy; for the cool greenhouse, the white variety *Constance Elliott* (June–Sept., 25 ft.) is recommended.

Pelargonium.—There is frequent confusion over the names *geranium* and *pelargonium*. The former term covers both sections of plants, but is more generally assigned to the hardy perennial sorts (*see* Geranium). The term "pelargonium" includes all half-hardy greenhouse and bedding plants and the show varieties. All pelargoniums need a light airy position, but no draughts, and only sufficient artificial heat to keep out frost is needed. *Propagation.*—About six months after cuttings are struck the plants should come into bloom; June and July are the best months for taking cuttings. The pots are prepared in the usual manner, and filled with a compost of five-eighths of loam to one-eighth part each of sand, leaf-mould, and rotted cow-manure; a liberal sprinkling of bonemeal should be added. The cuttings should be taken in dry weather when the parent plant has had no water for some days, and they should be kept dry for twenty-four hours before potting. Place five cuttings round the edge of each 4-inch pot and about an inch or an inch and a half deep. If the cuttings are struck in August or September, the protection of a frame is not essential and the pots may be sunk in a sheltered south border, where they will require no shading unless the sun is very hot; if a frame is used, the lights should only be put on as a protection against heavy rain. Gradually harden-off the cuttings for potting-off into 3-inch pots as soon as they are rooted. If they grow too freely before it is time to take them into the house or frames (September), the top shoots should be broken off; these tops may be used to provide another batch of cuttings. Through the winter months, little water and only just sufficient heat (50° F.) to exclude the frost, should be given. Pick-off all flower-buds as they appear, and as the weather improves give more air. Late in March, or early in April, re-pot into 5 or 6-inch pots, so that they may be grown on to be hardened-off and planted-out late in May or in early June. From April onwards, plants grown for flowering in pots should receive weekly doses of weak liquid manure or soot water, and should be grown near the glass in a cool greenhouse, being pinched-back to make them bushy. Plants stopped-back not later than February will flower in May; when blooming is to be delayed until July, pinching-back may be continued until towards the end of April. After flowering, ripen the growth in the sun in the open, then cut the stems back to from 3 to 4 inches from the base in July and rest the plants with the pots on their sides in a frame for two months. Then pot-up in fresh soil, keep in the frame, and remove all buds until the plants are moved into the house early in September.

Plants for Autumn and Winter Flowering.—A further batch of cuttings taken from old plants "started" in gentle heat can, if desired, be struck in the spring (March), and potted-up singly into 3-inch pots about May. When these pots are full of roots, move the young plants into 4-inch pots ; harden-off in a cold frame ready for setting out in the open on a hard bed of ashes in June, or into the open beds, if for summer-bedding. Plants for flowering indoors in autumn and winter should be stopped-back in July, and all flower buds picked off until September. Early in August move them into 6-inch pots and transfer to a light and airy shelf in the greenhouse at the beginning of September ; as the season advances a little heat (55° F.) will make the plants blossom. Zonal, Ivy-leaved, and Scarlet-leaved pelargoniums, if treated in this way, will flower in autumn and winter ; Regals so treated, however, will not come into bloom until March, and will continue to flower until the middle of June. Plants may also be raised from seed, but this is rarely attempted by the amateur. *Varieties.*—(REGAL AND DECORATIVE)—*Beauty of Exmouth, Bridesmaid, Dazzler, Elsie, Godfrey's Pride, Market Favourite, Magpie, Mrs. W. J. Godfrey, Pictor, Pearl, Princess Mary, Queen of the West.* (ZONAL).—Single-Flowered for Pots—(Amaranth) *Amarantha* ; (Scarlet) *Canopus* ; (Vermilion) *Dick Smith* ; (Rose-pink) *Freyda* ; (Salmon) *Harry Wood* ; (Orange) *Janet Scott* ; (Pink) *Mrs. J. Foster* ; (Crimson-lake) *Ryecroft Gem* ; (White) *Snowstorm* ; Double for Pots—(Purple) *Fantome* ; (Salmon) *Madame Landry* ; (Crimson) *Ryecroft Pride* ; (White) *Ryecroft White.* Bedding —(Scarlet) *Paul Crampel* ; (Salmon) *Salmon Crampel* ; (White) *Dr. Nansen* ; (Red) *Decorator.* (IVY-LEAVED)—(Rose) *Madame Crousse* ; (Scarlet) *Scarlet Crousse,* and *Sir Percy Blakeney* ; (Cream) *Alliance* ; (White and Purple) *L'Elegant.* (SCENTED-LEAVED)—*P. crispum* ; *P. odoratissimum* ; and *P. quercifolium.*

Peltandra (Water Arrow Arum).—Beautiful hardy aquatic plants which thrive in the sun in ordinary soil at the water's edge. They grow from 24 to 36 inches high, and flower in July. Propagate by means of division of roots in March.

Pentstemon (Beard Tongue).—Useful and graceful perennials, both dwarf and tall. The dwarf species are excellent for the rock garden, while the taller species make beautiful bed or border plants if treated as half-hardy biennials. All kinds thrive in the sun in a warm, sandy loam with a third-part humus in it. For culture, *see* Biennials, p. 107, and Perennials, p. 128. *See also* Chelone. *Species and Varieties.*— *P. barbatus* (Scarlet) ; *P. Bridgesii* (Lilac-purple) ; *P. gentianoides* (Purplish-red) ; *P. Hartwegii and vars.* (Crimson) ; and *P. Menziesii* (Purple and Red). All June to October-flowering. *Named Varieties.*— (BORDER)—(Crimson) *Crimson Gem* ; (Pink) *Daydream* ; (Scarlet and White) *George Home* ; (Mauve) *Mauve Bedder* ; (Rose and White) *Mrs. Ed. Matthews* ; (Crimson and Violet) *Mrs. John Forbes* ; (Salmon-pink) *Montrose* ; (Pink) *Pink Beauty* ; (Crimson) *Southgate Gem* ; (Scarlet and Cinnamon) *Thos. H. Cook* ; (White) *White Bedder.* All 20 to 30 inches.

Perilla nankinensis.—Half-hardy annuals with purple foliage, useful for summer bedding and greenhouse. For culture, *see* Annuals, p. 107.

Pernettya mucronata (Prickly Heath).—Hardy evergreen shrubs which do well in moderate sun in cool and moist, well-drained peaty loam. *Culture.*—Plant in March or October ; no pruning is necessary. *Pot Culture.*—Pot-up in October or November, using 6- to 8-inch pots and a compost of two parts of peat to one part of leaf-mould and sand, and place in the cold greenhouse. Plant outdoors when the berries fall. To propagate, sow in a frame in March, take cuttings in summer, or divide roots in autumn. *Varieties.*—*P. m. alba* (White berries) ; *P. m. atrococcinea* (Purple Berries) ; and *P. m. speciosa* (Crimson). All July, 2 to 5 feet.

Petasites.—Hardy herbaceous plants, the most popular species of which is *P. fragrans*, the Winter Heliotrope, which grows some 10 inches high and carries whitish flowers in late winter. Almost any moist soil suits petasites well ; it needs partial shade. Propagate by means of division in February or March, or seed can be sown in May or June.

Petunia.—Half-hardy soft-wooded perennials, best treated as half-hardy annuals. They like a sunny position and a moderately rich, light soil, and may be used for borders, bedding and (double varieties) for pot culture. *Culture.*—*See* Annuals, p. 107. If pricked-off into pots for greenhouse use they must be potted-on frequently until in their flowering pots. Double varieties should be propagated by means of cuttings of young wood in a temperature of 60° F. in the spring, or of mature shoots in a cold frame in August. *Pot Culture.*—Pot-up in May, using 6 to 10-inch pots and a compost of two parts loam to one part of leaf-mould and dry, well-rotted manure, and keep in cool greenhouse. Pinch-back to five joints from the old stem as soon as established in the flowering pots. Early training and staking is essential. Flowering may be retarded by standing the plants in a cold frame or on a bed of ashes in the open any time after the middle of May. *Species and Varieties.*—*P. integrifolia (syn. violacea)* and *P. nyctaginiflora.* (Numerous varieties, see seed catalogues.) June–Oct., 12 in.

Phacelia.—Dwarf-growing hardy annuals, suitable for edging, for the border, or the rock garden. They like a sunny or semi-shaded position and ordinary soil. For culture, *see* Annuals, p. 106. *Species.* —*P. campanularia* (Deep Blue, 8 in.) ; *P. tanacetifolia* (Pale Mauve, 20 in.) ; *P. Whitlavia* (Deep Blue, 8 in.). All June to August.

Phædranassa chloracra (Queen Lily).—Half-hardy bulbous plants, growing about 18 inches high and flowering in spring. They like a well-drained, deep, sandy loam, and thrive in sunny, sheltered positions in warm borders, or in pots in the greenhouse. *Culture.*—Plant 6 to 9 inches apart and 5 inches deep in March or October, and protect with fibre in winter. Propagate by means of offsets in March or October.

Philadelphus (Mock Orange).—Beautiful hardy deciduous flowering shrubs frequently better known under the name of Syringa, a name which rightly belongs to the Lilacs. They thrive in any good garden soil and like a sunny position. *Culture.*—Plant in October or November. Thin-out the shoots well immediately after flowering and cut-back old and weak wood of the previous year to the young lateral growths at the base. If much overgrown, cut hard back in March. *Pot Culture.*—In the cool greenhouse, *P. Lemoinei* may be had in flower in March ; pot-up annually in October, using 8 to 10-inch pots and compost of two parts of sandy loam to one part of leaf-mould and well-rotted manure. Prune as already described, and sink the pots to their rims in ashes outdoors from May to December. To propagate, strike cuttings in a frame in July or August. *Species and Hybrids.*— *P. coronarius* (White) ; *P. microphyllus* (White) ; *P. Lemoinei* (White-pink) ; *P. Virginale* (White, Double) ; and *P. purpureo maculatus* (White Petals, stained Purple). All May to July, 3 to 15 feet.

Phillyræa (Mock Privet).—Hardy evergreen shrubs which thrive almost anywhere and in any soil. *Culture.*—Plant in May or September. Propagate by means of cuttings in a frame, or by layering in September. *Species.*—*P. angustifolia* (White, May–June, 9 ft.) ; *P. decora* (White, April, 6–8 ft.) ; *P. media* (White, May, 6–8 ft.).

Phlox.—A magnificent genus of annuals and perennials which need a certain amount of sun and enjoy an open position, but one sheltered from strong winds. The *Phlox Drummondii* varieties—half-hardy annuals—make splendid bedding and potting plants. *Phlox paniculata* syn. *decussata* and *P. maculata*, perennials, look fine in borders, while the dwarf perennials or *Mossy Phloxes* are excellent for rock garden. The annual and herbaceous kinds succeed best in deep, rich and moist but well-drained loam. Stake early and thin-out all weak growths. For culture, *see* Annuals, p. 106, *and* Perennials, p. 128. *Pot Culture.*— (*Perennials*)—Pot-up in October, using 5- to 6-inch pots and a rich, sandy soil. Stand in a cold greenhouse, and water freely from April to October, then decrease the water supply. Give liquid manure from May to September. (*Annuals*)—If seed is sown in a frame in August and the seedlings are potted-up and transplanted to the greenhouse, blooms may be had from January to March. *Species.*—(ANNUAL)—*P. Drummondii* (Various, June–Oct., 6–12 in.). (PERENNIAL)—*P. paniculata* [*syn. decussata*] (Various, July–Oct., 40 in.). *Named Varieties of P. paniculata*—(White) *Tapis Blanc* ; (Pink) *Elizabeth Campbell* ; (Pink with Crimson Eye) *Selma* ; (Flame and Crimson Eye) *Thor* ; (Salmon) *America* ; (Scarlet) *Coquelicot* ; (Crimson) *Imperator* ; (Mauve) *Albert Vandal* ; (Rose-crimson Eye) *Sherriff Ivory* ; *P. Arendsii* hybrids ; (Lilac) *Amanda* ; (Rose) *Hanna*. (*Alpine*)—*P. amœna* (Carmine-pink, May–July, 6 in.) ; *P. divaricata* (Lavender-blue, May–July, 6–12 in.) ; *P. ovata* (Red, May–July, 10 in.) ; *P. subulata and vars.* (Pink, Mauve, Blue and White, May–June, 4 in.) ; *P. stolonifera* (Rose-purple, June, 6 in.).

Phormium (New Zealand Flax).—Tall perennials which require a fairly sheltered, sunny position in well-drained loam, and flower from June to September. *Culture.*—Sow in a frame in March, or propagate by means of division of roots in April. *P. robustum* (Yellow, 60 in.) and *P. tenax* (Crimson, 70 in.) are the best species.

Physalis (Winter Cherry, Chinese Lantern or Cape Gooseberry).— Half-hardy and hardy perennials, growing from 20 to 40 inches high, and flowering from June to October. They like warm, light and rich soil, and a sunny position in a sheltered border. For culture, *see* Perennials, p. 128. *See also* Solanum capsicastrum.

Physostegia (False Dragon's Head).—Hardy perennials, growing from 20 to 40 inches high, and bearing red flowers in late summer. They like partial shade and a rich sandy soil. *See* Perennials, p. 128.

Phyteuma (Horned Rampion).—Hardy annuals, biennials and perennials. The smaller species thrive in the rock garden in rich, gritty loam ; the taller kinds in a deep, rich soil in the border and in a sunny position. For culture, *see* Annuals, p. 106, Biennials, p. 107, *and* Perennials, p. 128. *Species.*—*P. comosum* (H.A.) (Pale Blue, 3 in.) ; *P. Scheuchzeri* (H.B.) (Blue, 18 in.) ; *P. Halleri* (H.P.) (Violet, 6 in.) ; *P. spicatum* (Lilac). All May to June.

Picea (Spruce).—Hardy evergreen trees which thrive in well-drained loam and in sunny positions. *Culture.*—Plant from October to November or in March and April ; no pruning is required. Propagate by means of seed. *Species.*—*P. excelsa* (Norway Spruce, 50–100 ft.) ; *P. orientalis* (Oriental Spruce, 60 ft.) ; *P. pungens glauca* (Blue Spruce, Grey-blue foliage, 20 ft.) ; *P. pygmœa* ($1\frac{1}{2}$ ft.).

Picotees.—These are a kind of carnation, distinguished by a narrow, dark-coloured edging to the petals, or by the petals being covered with tiny dots ; the ground colour is usually white or yellow. Only the yellow ground picotees are grown in the open ; cultivation is in every respect the same as for the carnation, *which see*. *Varieties.*—[Yellow Ground] *Exquisite* (Scarlet Margined) ; *Her Majesty* (Purple Edged) ; *Margaret Glitters* (Rosy-scarlet Edged) ; *Mrs. J. J. Kean* (Rose-pink Edged) ; *Niel Kenyon* (Rose Edged) ; *Togo* (Crimson Edged).

Pieris (Lily of the Valley Bush).—Hardy evergreen shrubs, which like a moist peaty loam and sand and a sheltered position in sun or partial shade. *Culture.*—Plant from September to October. Do not prune, but keep in shape by means of " stopping " and removing dead flowers in May. Propagate by means of layering in autumn. Good kinds are *P. floribunda* (White, April–May, 3–6 ft.) and *P. japonica* (White, March–April, 4–10 ft.). *See also* Andromeda.

Pinguicula (Butter-wort, or Bog Violet).—Hardy perennial bog plants which thrive in moist peaty loam and in a shady position. *Culture.*—Propagate by means of division in April. *Species.*—*P. alpina* (White) ; *P. grandiflora* (Blue) ; *P. vulgaris* [Bog Violet] (Purple-violet). All April and May, 3 to 4 inches.

Pinks (Dianthus).—Beautiful hardy perennials closely allied to picotees and carnations, and requiring very similar cultivation. They are excellent border and edging plants. New varieties may be obtained from seed sown in April, May and June, and old plants may be increased by cuttings of basal shoots that have not flowered, struck 2 inches apart in a frame in July. When well rooted they should be planted in a bed in rows 6 inches apart and with 3 inches between the plants. If preferred the cuttings can be struck in a sheltered north border. Here they should remain till September, when they may be planted in a bed or pots, in a compost of two-thirds loam from decayed turf and one-third well-decomposed cow-dung. After being gently watered, the pots may be placed in a cold frame, the lights being closed for the following four-and-twenty hours. In March re-pot into 24's in which they are to bloom. The best soil for this potting is a mixture of good loam and well-rotted manure from an old hot-bed, with a little white sea-sand and old mortar-rubble added if the soil is at all heavy ; March is also the best time to plant border pinks out in the open.   These resent disturbance and should remain in position for several years ; the ground, however, should be limed periodically and an annual dressing with a phosphate manure must be given.   Pinks are also easily increased by division if lifted in September, or they may be layered in July and the young plants can be moved to their new flowering positions in autumn ; seed may also be sown under glass in July.   The biennial *Dianthus chinensis*, the Chinese or Indian Pink, is best raised from seed in the autumn, wintered in a frame, and set out in the following May ; a sunny position is essential and a well-limed or chalky soil is a great advantage.   Its variety *D. c. Heddewigii* and its named sorts are best treated as annuals.   Another delightful class includes the Alpine or rock garden pinks ; these are easily grown in a sunny position and in sandy soil.   Perpetual flowering pinks (*D. Allwoodii*), if lifted in autumn and potted-up, will continue to bloom in the greenhouse throughout the winter.   They are not particular as to soil, will stand the winter in the open border well, and are easily raised from cuttings or by layering in summer.   *See also* Carnation.   *Varieties.*—(PERENNIAL).   (*Border*)— (Pink) *Apple Blossom* ; (Carmine, Red Centre) *Bookham Pride* ; (Rose-pink) *Dainty Lass* ; (Salmon, Laced Red) *Fair Rosamund* ; (Salmon, Crimson Centre) *Jean Douglas* ; (Shell-pink, Crimson Centre) *May Blossom* ; (White) *Mr. Simpkins* ; (White, Margined Deep Maroon) *Peter Pan* ; (Salmon-rose and Carmine) *Rosemary* ; (Reddish-pink and Crimson) *Sunset* ; (Salmon, Laced Crimson) *Vera* ; (White) *White Ladies*.   Consult the catalogues for numerous varieties.   All May to July, 12 inches.   (Alpine)—*D. alpinus* (Pink or White) ; *D. cæsius* (Rose) ; *D. neglectus* (Reddish-pink).   All June, 5 inches.   (BIENNIAL). —*Named Varieties of D. Heddewigii and vars.*—*Aurora* (Salmon-red, Double) ; *The Bride* (White, Ringed with Purple, Single) ; *Crimson Bell* (Blood-red, Single) ; *Empress* (Crimson and Rose, Single) ; *Salmon Queen* (Single, Fringed) ; *Scarlet Queen* (Single, Fringed) ; *Snowdrift* (White, Double, Fringed) ; *Vesuvius* (Orange, Single, Fringed).   All July to October, 6 to 12 inches.

Pinus (Pine).—A large family of hardy evergreen trees growing, according to species, from 4½ to 200 feet high.   They like a sunny position and prefer light loam, but will grow well in most soils.   *Culture.*—Plant in May or September when from 2 to 3 feet high.   No pruning is required.   Never plant pines near a smoky city.

Piptanthus nepalensis (Himalayan Laburnum).—Hardy semi-evergreen summer-flowering shrubs, growing from 6 to 10 feet high, and which like a sunny, sheltered position and well-drained ordinary soil. To propagate, sow in a frame in March, strike cuttings of semi-matured wood in a frame in summer, or increase by layering.

Platanus (Plane).—Hardy deciduous trees, which thrive in sunny positions, in any well-drained soil.   *Culture.*—Plant in November. Prune in winter when the wood is overcrowded.   To propagate, sow in March, take cuttings in autumn, or layer.

Platycodon (Chinese Bell-flower).—Hardy perennials which thrive in

well-drained, deep sandy loam, in open, shady positions, and are excellent for the border or rock garden. They grow from 10 to 25 inches high, and flower in July and August. *See* Perennials, p. 128.

Platystemon (Californian Poppy, or Cream-Cups).—Hardy annuals which like a sunny position and light ordinary soil, and are useful for beds, borders, or for the rock garden. The yellow flowers are borne in summer on 10-inch stalks. For culture, *see* Annuals, p. 106.

Plumbago (Leadwort).—A genus comprising about ten species of plants, mostly perennials, some suitable only for the greenhouse and others hardy. The most noteworthy for greenhouse culture is *R. capensis*, an admirable pillar plant, with pale lavender-blue flowers in September. *Culture.*—Pot-up annually in March in 6 to 8-inch pots, or plant in the cool house border. A compost of two parts of loam and one part of leaf-mould and coarse sand is best. Water well and syringe in warm weather, but keep dry from October to March. Young pot plants (not climbers) should be pinched back once or twice ; with bushes, cut back the shoots to within 10 inches of the previous year's growth in October. Climbers should be trained in a single stem in much the same manner as a vine. Cut back all laterals of climbers to within 5 inches of their base after flowering, and prune-back again to within 2 to 3 inches from their base early in February, and if grown in the greenhouse border, mulch annually in spring with well-rotted manure. Propagate by cuttings of semi-matured side shoots in gentle bottom heat in spring or early summer. *See also* Ceratostigma.

Podophyllum (Duckfoot or May Apple).—Hardy perennials which thrive in partial shade in moist peaty loam, and are useful for the bog or rock garden. They grow from 10 to 30 inches high and carry purple or white flowers in May. Propagate by means of division in April.

Polemonium (Jacob's Ladder, or Greek Valerian).—Hardy perennials for sunny borders, or the wild garden, and requiring well-drained loam. Rock garden species need partial shade and a compost of gritty loam and leaf-mould. For culture, *see* Perennials, p. 128. *Species.*—*P. cæruleum and vars.* (Blue or White, June–Sept., 18 in.) ; *P. confertum* (White or Bluish-white, June–July, 6 in.) ; *P. reptans*, (Slate-blue, March–June, 12 in.).

Polianthes tuberosa (Tuberose).—Half-hardy bulbous plants growing from 24 to 36 inches high and flowering in Sept. They thrive in sunny positions in sheltered warm borders, in a mixture of sandy loam, leaf-mould, and well-rotted manure, or they may be flowered in pots in the greenhouse. *Culture.*—Plant in March 6 inches deep and 6 inches apart, and do not water until they begin to grow. *Pot Culture.*— Plant bulbs singly in 4 to 5-inch pots (African kinds) late autumn, (American kinds) early spring, and plunge the pots in fibre in a warm frame (bottom heat 65° F.). When their roots fill the pots, re-pot, and repeat the treatment until the buds appear. The bulbs only flower for one season. Propagation is by means of offsets.

Polyanthus.—These are generally classified as *Gold-laced, Fancies,* and *Selfs,* and make an excellent show, especially during April and May, in partially shaded beds and borders, mostly as edging plants. They need a moist, deep, good loam. There are innumerable named varieties. The *Munsted* strain is excellent ; the colours are numerous and the flowers are borne from March to June on 8-inch stems. *Culture.*— Sow under glass in April or May, prick-off into boxes, and place in a cold frame. Harden-off and plant out 9 inches apart in a shady and sheltered reserve border in June, and transfer to their flowering positions in October. Seed may also be sown in the open in July, or the poly-anthus can be propagated by division immediately after flowering. *Pot Culture.*—Pot-up singly in 8-inch pots in October and keep in a cold frame until just before bloom is required, when transfer to the cool house. *See also* Auricula.

Polygala (Milk-wort).—Useful little plants, mostly shrubby ever-greens or hardy perennials, which thrive in a mixture of cool, moist and gritty loam and peat, or leaf-mould, in partial shade in sheltered positions. They are excellent for the rock garden, border or wild garden. For culture, *see* Perennials, p. 128. *Shrubby Species* are increased by cuttings of young shoots struck in coarse sand in a propa-gating case in spring. *Pot Culture.*—(*Shrubby Species*)—Pot-up in March in a compost of one-half peat, one-quarter fibrous loam and one-quarter sand. Shade from direct sun and syringe. Remove all dead flower heads, and, after flowering, cut the shoots of the current year back to within 6 inches of the old wood ; then syringe and stand in the sun to ripen the wood. Remove to the house in September. *Species.*— *P. calcarea* (Purple, Blue, Mauve, or Rose, May–Sept., 5 in.) ; *P. Chamœbuxus* (Purple and Yellow, June–July, 3 in.).

Polygonatum.—Hardy perennials of which the best known is *P. multiflorum* (Solomon's Seal or David's Harp), and which thrive in almost any soil and situation. For culture, *see* Perennials, p. 128.

Polygonum (Knot-wort).—A large genus including hardy annuals, hardy and half-hardy perennials, shrubs, climbers and trailers. The tall hardy perennials are useful for the wild garden or border, and grow in any ordinary loam, and in partial shade. *P. affine* (Pink, July–Oct., 8 in.) is a rock species. For culture, *see* Annuals, p. 106, *and* Perennials, p. 128. In the case of shrubby species, do not prune, but cut-out old wood from the centre and trim away thin straggly shoots. *Species.*—(ANNUAL)—*P. orientale* (Purple-rose, June–Sept., 4–5 ft.). (PERENNIAL)—*P. campanulatum* (Pink, July–Sept., 3 ft.).

Pontederia cordata (Water Plantain).—Hardy perennial aquatics bearing blue flowers from June to October, and which like a sheltered position in good loam and still, shallow water. *Culture.*—Propagate by means of division of roots in April.

Poppy.—*See* Papaver.

Populus (Poplar).—A large genus of hardy deciduous trees suitable only for large gardens, and which thrive in moist loam in sunny positions. *Culture.*—Plant in November. No pruning is required. To propagate, strike cuttings of matured wood in the open in October. *Species.*— *P. italica* is the Lombardy Poplar and *P. tremula* is the Aspen.

Potentilla (Cinquefoil).—A genus of plants, some species of which bear a resemblance to the strawberry in flower, and have a similar manner of propagation. Many species are of a low-growing and shrubby nature, others are hardy perennials. All do well in sun or shade, in the border or rock garden (dwarf kinds), in deep, sandy soil. Sow seed in light loam in spring, increase by division in March or Oct., or strike cuttings of ripened shoots in a frame in autumn. The old and dead wood should be thinned-out in Sept. *Species and Varieties.* —(BORDER)—*P. argyrophylla var. atrosanguinea* (Crimson) ; *P. Gibson's Scarlet* ; *P. grandiflora* (Yellow) ; *P. Hopwoodiana* (Apricot). All May to Sept., 12 to 18 in. (ALPINES)—*P. alba* (White) ; *P. nepalensis var. minor* (Crimson) ; *P. n. var. Miss Willmott* (Rose) ; *P. nitida* (Pale Pink) ; *P. Tonguei* (Orange, spotted Crimson). All May to Sept., 6 to 9 in. (SHRUBBY)—*P. fruticosa* (Yellow) ; *P. Veitchii* (White) ; *P. Vilmoriniana* (Sulphur). All July to Sept., 3 to 4 ft.

Poterium (Burnet).—Hardy perennials which thrive in ordinary soil in sunny borders. For culture, *see* Perennials, p. 128. These plants grow from 10 to 30 inches high, and flower from July to September. *Species.*—*P. canadense* (Rosy-purple), and *P. obtusum* (Rose).

Pratia.—Hardy dwarf-growing rock plants, which thrive in sandy peat and leaf-mould in sunny positions on well-drained banks, and from May to August carry white or blue flowers on 3-inch stems. For culture, *see* Rock Plants, p. 135.

Primrose (Primula acaulis).—*See* Primula.

Primula.—A large genus, including some of the most popular flowers, the auricula, the cowslip, the polyanthus, and the primrose. In the greenhouse, in the rock garden or bog garden, in beds and growing wild in the woods, the primula is one of the most useful genera that exist. The majority thrive in rich deep loam and appreciate the admixture of leaf-mould and grit with the soil (except higher alpine species which appreciate the addition of old mortar rubble and full sun). They are all moisture-lovers, but must have a well-drained soil. The majority like partial shade unless unlimited moisture is available in hot weather. *Culture.*—Sow seed in pots or pans under glass in May, in a compost of equal parts of loam, leaf-mould and sand, all sieved through a ½-inch mesh, and well mixed. Cover thinly with fine sandy soil and keep in a temperature of 60° F. Prick-off 1 inch apart into pans as soon as possible and, in about three weeks, pot-up singly into 3-inch pots ; harden off, and keep on a bed of hard ashes in a shaded frame ; transfer to 5 to 6-inch pots in September. Propagate also by means of division in September or in spring. *Pot Culture.*—Pot-up firmly in September or October, using 5 to 6-inch pots and a compost of half loam and half leaf-mould, rotted manure and coarse sand, and keep in a frame until November, pinching-off any flower buds that form, then transfer to the cool greenhouse for flowering. A little soot water may be given from time to time while the buds are forming. Discard the plants after flowering, except choice varieties. *See also* Auricula, Poly- anthus, etc. Alpine primulas are of great value to the rock garden and the bog garden. The first group thrives among the rocks in rich loam ; the second class loves a cool, moist, but well-drained soil. Space does not permit us to deal more fully with these, but below, the first group are marked with an * and the second †. *Species and Varieties.*— *P. acaulis* (*Primrose*) (Various, April, 6 in.) ; *P. Auricula* (Golden Yellow, March–May, 6 in.) ; †*P. Beesiana* (Magenta. May–June, 20–30 in.) ; †*P. Bulleyana* (Orange Scarlet, April–May, 12–18 in.) ; †*P. denticulata* (Lilac and White, Feb.–April, 12–18 in.) ; †*P. farinosa* (Rose-purple, May, 6 in.) ; †*P. japonica* (vars.) (Various, May–Aug., 12–24 in.) ; †*P. Juliæ* (Magenta, April and May, 4 in.) ; *P. kewensis* (Pale Yellow, April, 15 in.) ; *P. malacoides* (Pale Mauve, Pink or White, Sept.–May, 12–24 in.) ; **P. marginata* (Lavender-blue, margined White, May, 6 in.) ; †*P. minima* (Rose-pink, May–June, 2 in.) ; **P. nivalis* (White, Feb.–May, 6 in.) ; *P. obconica* (vars.) (Various, Spring, 9–12 in.) ; †*P. pulverulenta* (Crimson-maroon, April–May, 20 in.) ; *P. Sieboldii* (vars.) (Red, Purple, Lilac, May–June, 12 in.) ; †*P. sikkimensis* (Sulphur-yellow, May–June, 20 in.) ; *P. sinensis* (Various, Sept.–April, 12 in.) ; *P. stellata* (Various, Sept.–May, 12–24 in.). Those without distinguishing marks are for the greenhouse.

Prunella (Self-heal).—Dwarf-growing hardy perennials, thriving in moist, light and rich soil, in the sunny border or rock garden. For culture, *see* Perennials, p. 128. *Species.*—*P. grandiflora* (Purple, Red, Blue or White, 8 in.) ; *P. vulgaris laciniata alba* (White, 6 in.). All July to September-flowering.

Prunus.—A large genus of hardy deciduous flowering, fruit-bearing trees, including *P. Amygdalus* (Almond), *P. armeniaca* (Apricot), *P. Avium* (Gean), *P. cerasifera* (Cherry Plum), *P. Persica* (Peach), etc. They do best in a deeply dug and well-manured soil rich in lime, or in localities with a chalk subsoil. *Culture.*—Plant in Oct. in sunny positions sheltered from N. and E. winds. To propagate, sow seed, or bud in the open in summer on plum stocks. *Pot Culture.*—*P. sinensis* is a useful species for cultivation in the cold greenhouse. Pot-up in Nov., using 6 to 8-inch pots and well-manured ordinary soil. After flowering sink the pots in ashes outdoors from May to Dec. In the main, pruning should be as for ordinary fruiting plum trees (*which see*), but prune-out weak wood and dead flower shoots after flowering. The Japanese Cherries, vars. of *P. Lannesiana*, *P. serrulata* and *P. triloba fl. pl.*, may be grown in the cool house. Pot-up in Oct. using 8 to 12-inch pots and a compost of two parts of sandy loam to one part of leaf-mould and rotten manure.

Pseudolarix Fortunei (Golden Larch).—Hardy deciduous coniferous trees which thrive in well-drained loam in sunny, sheltered positions. *Culture.*—Plant in Oct. or Nov. No pruning is required.

Pseudotsuga Douglasii (Douglas Fir).—Hardy evergreen coniferous trees, which thrive in full sun in a cool, moist soil, and reach a height of between 100 and 200 feet. *Culture.*—Plant from September to November. No pruning is required. Propagate by means of seeds.

Puschkinia scilloides (Striped Squill).—A hardy bulbous plant which grows about 6 inches high and flowers in April and May. It thrives in deep, rich, sandy soil, mixed with leaf-mould, in warm sunny borders or in the rock garden. *Culture.*—Plant in October 3 inches deep and 3 inches apart. Protect with fibre in winter, and lift triennially.

Pyracantha (Fire Thorn, Evergreen Thorn, or Cratægus Pyracantha). —Beautiful hardy evergreen bushes or climbing shrubs which thrive in good light loam in sunny positions and against walls facing south. All bear white flowers from May to June. *Culture.*—Sow seed when ripe, or strike cuttings in summer. Plant from Oct. to April ; trim to shape in early spring, but clip as little as possible. *See also* Cratægus.

Pyrethrum.—Hardy perennials, now included under the genus Chrysanthemums, and which thrive in cool, light, deep and moderately rich soil in sunny, open borders. For culture, *see* Perennials, p. 128. *P. aureum* (Golden Feather) is a popular foliage plant for summer-bedding, and grows about 5 inches high. *Varieties.*—(SINGLE)—(White) *Princess Marie ;* (Pink) *Hamlet ;* (Scarlet) *Langport Scarlet.* (DOUBLE)—(White) *Mont Blanc ;* (Pink) *Queen Mary ;* (Blush) *La Vestale ;* (Red) *Melton ;* (Golden Yellow) *Pericles.* All flower in May and June and again in August, 18 to 30 inches.

Pyrus.—A genus of hardy deciduous trees including the *Pyrus* (Pear), *P. arbutifolia* (Chokeberry), *P. Aria* (White Beam), *P. Aucuparia* (Mountain Ash), *P. Malus* (Crab Apple), *P. nivalis* (Snowtree), *P. sinensis* (Sand Pear), and *P. Sorbus* (Service Tree). *Culture.*—Plant in November in a sunny position sheltered from cold winds, in deeply-dug and well-manured ordinary soil. Thin-out the branches when overcrowded, and cut-out dead wood and weak shoots after flowering. *Pot Culture.*—Many of the species, when small, are useful for culture in the cool greenhouse. Pot-up annually in October, using 8 to 12-inch pots and a compost of two parts of sandy loam to one part of leaf-mould and rotted manure ; sink the pots in ashes outdoors, from May to Dec. Propagate by means of seed, grafting, or budding in the open.

Quercus (Oak).—A large genus of hardy deciduous and evergreen trees, the majority of which are too large for the average garden. There are, however, a few species from Japan, which here rarely attain more than bush-form, except in mild districts. *Culture.*—Plant young trees in October in a sunny position in deep, good loam ; thin-out the branches in summer when required. To propagate, sow ripe acorns in the open in Sept. or Oct., or graft in spring.

Ramondia (Pyrenean Primrose, Rosette Mullein).—A small hardy perennial rock plant which thrives in the shade, in a mixture of loam, peat and leaf-mould. For culture, *see* Rock Plants, p. 135. *Species.*—*R. Heldreichii* (syn. *Jankæa*) (Pale Blue, Grey Foliage) ; *R. pyreniaca* (Pale Purple-blue, Orange Centre) ; *R. serbica var. Nataliæ* (Deep Purple-blue). All May to August, 6 inches.

Ranunculus.—A large genus of herbaceous perennials and tuberous-rooted plants, including the common buttercup, most species of which thrive in partial shade, in moist, deep, well-dug rich sandy soil with ample leaf-mould in it. They are also useful for pot culture, and the dwarf-growing kinds for the rock garden. *Culture.*—(*Perennials*)—Propagate by means of division in November or April ; the plants should remain in position for several years. (*Tuberous*)—Plant the tubers, claws downwards, 2 to 3 inches deep and 4 to 6 inches apart, early in March, surrounding with sand and charcoal. Lift the tubers after flowering. *Species.*—(FIBROUS-ROOTED)—*R. aconitifolius fl. pl.* (White [Double], May–July, 24–30 in.) ; *R. acris fl. pl.* (Yellow [Double], May–June, 24 in.) ; *R. aquatilis* (White, May and June, 2–12 in.) ; *R. Lingua major* (Yellow, June–Aug., 30–50 in.). (TUBEROUS-ROOTED—*R. asiaticus vars.* (Persian, French and Turban) (Various,

May–July, 6 in.). (ALPINE)—*R. alpestris* (White, May–Aug., 4 in.) ; *R. amplexicaulis* (White, May–Aug., 10 in.).

Raphiolepis.—A vigorous evergreen flowering shrub which grows well in well-drained, ordinary soil ; in cold districts it should be given the protection of a south wall. Pruning is rarely necessary, but may be done in March. Propagation is by cuttings under glass. The best species are :—*R. indica* (Rosy-red, 4 ft.), and *R. japonica* (*syn. ovata*) (White, 3 ft.). All species may be forced in the greenhouse in spring.

Rheum (Rhubarb).—The ornamental rhubarbs, which thrive on moist, sunny banks or in the water garden in deep, rich loam, are grown chiefly for their foliage. For culture, *see* Perennials, p. 128.

Rhododendron.—Among the most handsome and finest of all our flowering shrubs are the hardy rhododendrons. Most hardy species thrive best in a position sheltered from north and east winds and in semi-shade, and prefer well-trenched and well-drained moist peaty loam, but will grow in almost any soil deficient in lime or chalk, providing it contains ample decaying vegetable humus, and is sufficiently porous. Most flower in May and June, but a few early varieties bloom from Christmas onwards. Rhododendrons bear frequent transplanting so long as the ball of earth round their roots is not broken. They are surface-rooters and will not grow on steep banks, where the roots will parch up in summer. Except in the case of such hybrids as *Bagshot Ruby, The Bride,* or *Pink Pearl*, which will grow in full sun, rhododendrons require some sun which should, however, be intermittent. These shade conditions are best supplied by trees and large bushes planted among the rhododendrons. In addition to the hardy and half-hardy species, there are choice greenhouse kinds, which require moist warmth all the year ; these are best grown in a cool house during the winter and kept under glass in summer (Temp. 50° F.). When purchasing rhododendrons, care must be taken that the species chosen are suitable for the climate. *Culture.*—Plant and " heel-in " very firmly in October or November, or at any time in winter and spring, up to May, providing the soil is not water-logged and that there is no frost. When planting add some well-rotted leaf-mould, and mix it well with the other soil. Fresh stable manure must not be used. If the weather is dry, soak the hole well before planting, and in any case, a little leaf-mould should be placed at the bottom for the roots to rest upon. Bushy species should be set 6 feet apart, and smaller lime-hating subjects, such as azaleas, kalmias, daphnes and heaths, can be used to fill the gaps until the rhododendrons have grown a bit. Do not prune young bushes, merely keep them in shape by means of " stopping " and removing dead blooms immediately after flowering. When it is necessary to cut back old and straggling plants, do so in April. Top-dress annually in March with good leaf-mould, and every second or third year give a 4-inch top-dressing of old hot-bed manure in May. *Propagation.*—To propagate hybrids, graft (stock *R. ponticum*) under glass from January to May, layer well-matured shoots in late summer, or take cuttings. Species may be increased by means of seed sown thinly in March or April in pans, in a compost of equal parts of well-sieved leaf-mould or peat and coarse sand in a cold frame. Most species may be raised from cuttings of semi-matured shoots, struck in a frame with bottom heat, and practically all species can be layered in summer. For Pot Culture, *see* Azalea. Species and varieties are innumerable (*see* growers' catalogues). A few good hybrids are—*Alice* (Deep Rose-pink); *Ascot Brilliant* (Deep Blood-red); *Bagshot Ruby* (Ruby-red); *Bernard Crisp* (Pale Mauve-pink, spotted Brown); *Charles Dickens* (Dark Scarlet); *Cunningham's White* (White, tinged Pink); *Doncaster* (Bright Scarlet, spotted Dark Brown); *Duchess of Connaught* (White, flecked Lemon); *fastuosum fl. pl.* (Pale Lavender [Semi-double]); *Mother of Pearl* (Blush-white, Red Stamens); *Pink Pearl* (Flesh-pink); *Sappho* (White, heavily spotted Maroon); *The Bride* (White, marked Green); and *Unknown Warrior* (Rose-crimson).

Rhus (Lacquer Tree, Venetian Sumach, Smoke Bush, or Stag's Horn, etc.).—Hardy deciduous trees and shrubs which like a sunny position and good loam. *Culture.*—Plant in October; cut-out all old and dead wood. To propagate, strike cuttings of matured shoots under bell-glasses in September, or layer in September. *Species.*—*R. Cotinus* [Smoke Bush] (Greyish Flowers from July–Sept., Crimson and Yellow Foliage in Autumn, 6–12 ft.); *R. cotinoides* (Crimson Foliage in Autumn, 8–20 ft.); *R. typhina* [Stag's Horn] (Greenish Flowers in June, Orange Foliage in Autumn, 10–25 ft.).

Ribes.—Hardy deciduous shrubs, akin to the currant and goose-berry, which thrive in the shade in ordinary garden soil, and are treated in exactly the same way as gooseberries and currants, *which see*. *Species.*—*R. alpinum* (Yellow), *R. sanguineum* (Flowering Currant) with rosy-red flowers in April, and *R. Grossularia* (Flowering Goose-berry) with greenish-yellow flowers, are the best known.

Ricinus communis (Castor-oil Plant).—Half-hardy plants which thrive in rich loam in warm beds or in the cold greenhouse. *Culture.*—Sow singly in pots in March under glass (Temp. 50° F.); pot-on into 5-inch pots, harden-off, and plant-out in June, or pot-on into 6 to 8-inch pots and keep indoors. One of the best varieties is *R. communis var. Gibsoni*.

Robinia (Hardy or Rose Acacia and False Acacia).—Hardy deciduous summer-flowering trees, which like a well-drained light soil, and a sunny, sheltered position. *R. Pseudacacia*, the Locust Tree or False Acacia (White, 50 ft.), is the most common. The most attractive species for the garden, however, is *R. hispida*, the Rose Acacia (Pink, 9 ft.). *Culture.*—Plant in October. Do not prune, but merely trim to keep in shape. Propagate by means of seed or by grafting.

Rocket (Hesperis, Dame's Violet).—Early spring-flowering hardy annuals, biennials and perennials, which grow freely in any light soil in a sunny position, and are excellent for the mixed border. For culture, *see* Annuals, p. 106, Biennials, p. 107, *and* Perennials, p. 128. *Species.*—(BIENNIAL)—*H. tristis* (Cream, Brownish-red, Purple, May–Sept., 12–24 in.). (PERENNIAL)—*H. matronalis* (White, Red, Rose, Purple [Single and Double], June–July, 20 in.); *H. violacea* (Violet, May–July, 18 in.).

Rodgersia.—Hardy perennials growing 4 feet high and bearing pink or white flowers in June or July, and which thrive in partial shade in a moist border or by water's edge in peaty soil. *See* Perennials, p. 128. *R. æsculifolia* (Pink) is a good species.

Romneya (Californian or Bush Poppy).—Deciduous flowering shrubs or shrubby perennials. They are almost hardy and thrive in the sun in well-drained, sandy, enriched loam, in a sheltered position or under a south wall. *Culture.*—Plant in March ; cut-out all dead wood in the spring and cut-back any weak growth. In severe winters protect with straw, bracken, or sacking ; in the north, these plants must be grown under glass. *Pot Culture.*—Pot-up annually in April, in a compost of sandy peat and leaf-mould in 6 to 7-inch pots. To propagate, divide the roots in March, or strike root-cuttings in a frame in the autumn. *R. Coulteri* (White, June–Sept., 5 ft.) is the best known.

Rosa (Wild Rose, Briar).—This name includes all the wild roses and the briars ; most species are strong growers. *Culture.*—Plant from November to March, in a sunny position and in ordinary soil. In March, cut away old wood and cut back long shoots. To propagate, strike matured cuttings in the open in October or November.

Roses.—Roses are divisible roughly into several groups or classes. The two largest classes, containing most of the garden and exhibition roses of to-day, are the Hybrid Perpetuals and the Teas. These two groups include sub-divisions ; thus the Hybrid Perpetuals are often held to include Hybrid Teas and Perpetual Bourbons, while the Noisettes are classed with the Teas.

Soil.—The very best of all soil for roses is a deep stiff loam. The worst soil for roses, after pure sand, or nearly so, is the black soil of the town garden, very porous, and over-full of organic matter. Peaty soils, if rich in character, are quite good for roses, a general rule being that the more gravelly or sandy a soil the less favourable for the rose. An essential for good rose soil is that it should be well drained, and this means a substratum of porous material, chalk or gravel, not many feet below the surface. Gravel has had a bad reputation for roses, but it is not altogether deserved. It is usually considered too dry and hot for roses to thrive in, but really, if a little care is taken to improve it, it will grow very good roses. Tea roses, for example, bloom in perfection on a gravel soil, and many of the briars and the newer hybrids enjoy just such a light dryish medium. Chalk, providing that it is deep enough below the surface, and that there is a good depth of soil on top, is not a bad sub-soil. It is well drained, and not too dry in hot weather. Where it is very close to the surface it is bad, and needs a lot of work and preparation if it is going to grow good roses. Eighteen inches of decent loam is the minimum for roses on chalk, and where the loam is shallower than this special places must be prepared for the plants and extra soil supplied.

Situation.—Roses like shelter, and they like an open situation. They dislike wind, although they like fresh air, and hate to be shut in by big trees. The spot to look for, then, is one sheltered from frosts and violent winds, and not close to high hedges or trees. Shelter is desirable from north and east winds, and if there is room for choice, the rose garden should be on the highest part of the available land, other conditions of soil and shelter being equal. " Frost falls," as the country people say, and where the roses are planted on a slope let the more delicate kinds be at the top.

Planting.—Early November is the best time of all for this operation, though it may be done right through the winter—should conditions be favourable—until the end of March.

First, the soil must be thoroughly broken up to a depth of at least 2 or 3 feet. Next, the soil must be thoroughly well drained. Before the roses arrive the soil should be re-turned to a depth of about 18 inches, and a good allowance of manure incorporated with it. The lowest layer of soil in the bed should consist of rich, fairly retentive soil, which will hold a certain amount of water, while the upper layers should be lighter and more friable, to encourage the plants to produce plenty of good fibrous roots. The holes to receive the roots should be dug, from a foot to 18 inches square and deep enough where bush roses or dwarfs are to be planted, for the point of junction of the scion and the stock to be covered when planted to a depth of about an inch. Where standard roses are being planted the holes should be about 6 inches deep. (*See also* Planting Fruit Trees, p. 323.)

Pruning Roses after Planting.—When roses are planted during the autumn and winter months their first pruning should be left until the spring, but when spring-planted it should be done at the time of putting in. The trees should be gone over carefully and all dead wood cut clean out, together with weak and sappy, unripened wood, and any shoots which have received injury. Standards should then be cut back to within about 4 inches of their union with the stock, bush trees being dealt with a little less severely, having about 6 inches of every shoot left above the ground. This pruning is only meant to be carried out the first time after planting. The subsequent treatment varies with the variety.

Pruning Established Roses.—The time of pruning roses differs with the variety. Hybrid Perpetuals, both dwarf and bush, as well as standards and Hybrid Teas, are pruned during March, bush and standard Teas and Noisettes during April, while the climbing roses, Hybrid Perpetuals, Hybrid Teas, Teas, and Noisettes should be looked over twice in the year, being well thinned as soon as they have flowered in the summer and pruned properly in March. (*See also* Pruning, p. 328.) Roses may be roughly divided into classes for purposes of pruning. The first with which we are concerned is that of the Hybrid Perpetuals, Hybrid Teas, Teas, and Noisettes, which require hard pruning. All dead, unripe, and weak shoots should be cut clean out, and the centre of the plant thinned well to allow good room either with a sharp knife or the fingers. The shoots retained should be cut back to from four to six buds. Examples of this type are : *Admiration, Earl Beatty, Lady Plymouth, Madame Constant Soupert*, and *Mrs. Henry Morse.*

The Hybrid Perpetuals, Hybrid Teas, Teas, and Noisettes which require moderate pruning are the next class. These should have the dead unripe and weak shoots cut clean away. The shoots which cross, or may cross when full grown, should be cut out, the plant never being allowed to get crowded in the middle. The strong, well-ripened last-year shoots which are left should be cut back to from six to eight eyes. Examples of roses needing this treatment are : *Betty Uprichard, Captain Hayward, Emma Wright*, and *Lady Hillingdon.*

There are also varieties of Hybrid Perpetuals, Hybrid Teas, Teas, and

Noisettes which require light pruning. They should be treated as the previous classes, but still less wood should be cut away. The centre of the plant should be kept open, but beyond this the strong shoots from the base should be left about 8 inches long, while the other shoots should be cut back till on their laterals or side shoots there are from one to three buds left. The base shoots should be left 12 inches long, while the laterals on the older wood may be reduced to four or five eyes. Roses, needing pruning of this kind are such plants as *Abel Carrière, Caroline Testout, Frau Karl Druschki, La France*, and *Maman Cochet*.

The next section includes the climbing kinds of Hybrid Perpetuals, Hybrid Teas, and Teas, as well as some of the other climbers. These roses need very little pruning, most of them doing best if left to grow naturally. The necessary thinning out of dead wood and of the shoots which are likely to overcrowd the plant, together with the worn-out wood of over two years' growth will keep the plants in full vigour and blossom. The removal of the old worn-out wood is as well done in the summer, directly after the plants have done blooming, and the young shoots should at once be tied in to take the place of those removed. It is at this time that any necessary re-shaping of the rose should be done, crowded growths being thinned and the branches re-spaced over the wall or trellis so as to keep as much flowering wood as possible. Where the base of the plant becomes bare, as often happens with climbing roses, the space may be filled either by bending down one or more of the lower shoots to cover the bare space or by shortening one or two of the base shoots to induce them to throw out laterals. Among these climbing roses are *Climbing Cramoisie* and *Gruss an Teplitz*.

Propagating Roses.—The most usual method of propagating the rose is by budding. The operation of budding is fully described on page 204, but in the case of the rose the selection of the bud is so important a part of the operation that it must be touched on separately. The bud must be taken from a shoot which is mature enough to have borne or to be able to bear a flower—what is called a " ripe " shoot. A ripe shoot may be selected by trying it with the finger, which should be gently rubbed over the prickles. If these latter fall off easily the shoot is in a fit condition for budding. Budding should be done in the summer, between June and September, the earlier season being good if enough really ripe shoots can be found. This is an important point, however, and if there is any doubt the budding should be put off. The stock is chosen with reference to the soil or situation in which it is to be grown. Certain kinds do best in light soils, others in heavy, some in dry, and some in moist ground. Some varieties of rose, again, do better on one stock than another; very few of the choicer kinds are grown on their own roots. Roses are often propagated from cuttings, and certainly where the roses do as well on their own roots they are easier to deal with than when budded. There is always a risk that the stock may shoot out vigorously and choke the more delicate scion. Climbers and ramblers, as a rule, do well grown in this way, as do a good number of the Hybrid Perpetuals. When making cuttings it is simplest and best to take cuttings from well-ripened wood, which carries a good number of strong healthy leaves, in the summer, after the roses have done flowering. These cuttings will root well in the open air. A shoot should be selected which has borne a flower, and should be cut off with about three or four leaves attached. The leaf nearest the flower should be removed, the shoot being cut off short above the second leaf and just below the lowest. If the cuttings are to be rooted absolutely in the open a bed should be prepared in a shaded situation, the soil being worked up a little with decayed manure, sand and leaf-mould. A frame is more satisfactory than the open ground, but is not essential. The cuttings should be set 3 to 4 inches apart, and should be well watered in, water being again given with a sprinkler morning and evening. The cuttings do as well or better planted in pots, as they seem to root more quickly. A hand light or a cold frame placed over them will help rooting. (*See also* Cuttings, p. 189.)

Where roses are grown from seed, a method only employed where new varieties are being raised, the chief essential point is that the seed should be allowed to ripen thoroughly and should never become dry. The pods should be left on the plant until they are almost dropping, and should then be picked, stalk and all, and the latter set in damp sand until the following November or December, when the seed is to be sown. The seeds often take a complete year to germinate, so that hope need not be given up if the seedlings show no signs of life for many months. Where seedlings are being raised for the sake of new varieties the tiny plants are budded on to briars even during their first year ; as soon, in fact, as it is possible to take a bud from them. The seedlings will usually flower in their first year, but a bud should in all cases be secured if possible, as the little plants often die after flowering, the effort seeming to exhaust them completely.

Varieties.—So innumerable are the varieties of the rose and so much depends on the taste and preferences of the individual that it is impossible, in the space available, to give any adequate list of varieties. The reader is, therefore, referred to the growers' catalogues.

Rosmarinus officinalis (Rosemary).—Hardy evergreen shrubby perennials, which like a sunny position and a light, dry soil, but which will grow almost anywhere ; they grow 3 to 6 feet high and flower in April and May. *R. o. prostrata* is a trailing rock plant. *Culture.*—Plant in March or September ; trim to shape after flowering. To propagate, sow in the open in April, or strike cuttings in July.

Rubus (Bramble, Raspberry, etc.).—A large genus of hardy deciduous flowering shrubs and climbers, including the ordinary blackberry, loganberry and raspberry. These like a shady position and rich loam. A few, such as *R. deliciosus* are grown in bush form ; many, as in the case of *R. thyrsoideus*, are selected for the beauty of their flowers ; some, such as *R. flagelliformis*, for the decorative value of their foliage ; and others again for their white stems in winter. *Culture.*—Plant in October ; cut-out old and dead wood after flowering. Propagate by means of suckers in the autumn.

Rudbeckia (Cone-flower).—Hardy perennials which like a well-drained ordinary soil and a sunny position. Stake early. For culture *see* Perennials, p. 128. *Species.*—*R. grandiflora* (Yellow and Purple,

July–Sept., 40 in.) ; *R. laciniata fl. pl.* (Golden-yellow [Double], Aug.–Sept., 60 in.) ; *R. purpurea* (Purple, July–Sept., 70 in.) ; *R. speciosa* (*syn. Newmanii*) (Orange, Purple-black Centre, July–Sept., 24 in.).

Sagittaria (Arrow Head).—Hardy aquatic plants which thrive in a mixture of clay, sandy loam, and rotted manure, grow from 10 to 30 inches high and flower from June to October. *Culture.*—Sow seed ¼ inch deep in April, or propagate by means of division in March. Plant in March in weighted baskets in shallow still water.

Salix (Willow).—A genus of hardy deciduous trees and shrubs, excellent for growing near a pond or stream. *S. babylonica* is the common Weeping Willow. There are a few species with brightly-coloured stems ; these are usually cut hard back annually in spring. *Culture.*—Plant in November in a sunny position and in moist soil at the water's margin or in deep, heavy loam. Pruning, except when the trees are cut hard back annually as mentioned above, is not necessary, but dead wood should be cut out. To propagate, strike cuttings of matured wood in the open in November or March.

Salpiglossis.—Half-hardy annuals suitable for a rich soil in sunny beds, or for pot culture. For culture, *see* Annuals, p. 107. *Species.*—*S. sinuata* (Purple, etc.). July to September, 18 inches.

Salvia.—There are many species belonging to this genus ; annuals, biennials and perennials, which are grown in the greenhouse or in the garden as ornamental bedding-plants ; all thrive in the sun in rich, ordinary soil. For culture, *see* Annuals, p. 106, Biennials, p. 107, *and* Perennials, p. 128. *Pot Culture.*—Sow in moderate heat in February, prick-off early, and pot-on as required, never allowing the plants to become pot-bound, and using eventually 6 to 8-inch pots and a compost of two-thirds turfy loam, and one-third coarse sand, leaf-mould and well-rotted manure. Grow on in an average temperature of 60° F., harden-off in a cold frame, summer with the pots plunged in ashes in the open, and take into the cool house early in October. Pinch-back occasionally till August, and syringe daily. After blooming, keep the roots fairly dry and cool till March, then give more moisture and slight heat. Rather than raise from seed, however, strike cuttings of young wood in April. *Species.*—(HALF-HARDY ANNUAL)—*S. carduacea* (Lilac-blue) ; *S. coccinea* (Scarlet) ; *S. Horminum* (Various). All June to September, 12 to 18 inches. (HARDY PERENNIAL)—*S. argentea* (Pale-rose) ; *S. glutinosa* (Yellow) ; *S. superba syn. virgata nemorosa* (Purple-blue). All June to September, 24 to 36 in. (HALF-HARDY PERENNIAL) —*S. patens* (Deep Blue) ; *S. splendens* (*var. Pride of Zurich*) (Scarlet). Both June to December, 18 to 70 inches.

Sambucus (Elder).—Deciduous shrubs or small trees bearing white flowers in summer. *S. nigra* is the Common Elder ; its two varieties, *S. n. albo-variegata* (silver-leaved) and *S. n. foliis aureis* (golden-leaved), are very attractive. *S. racemosus*, the Berried Elder, flowers a month earlier. The flowers are followed by large clusters of red berries. *Culture.*—Plant in October in partial shade, and in moist loam, or if need be in almost any soil and situation ; cut well back in spring. To propagate, strike cuttings in the open in October.

Sanguinaria (Bloodroot).—Hardy perennials which like sandy loam and a sunny position in the border or rock garden. They grow 6 inches high and flower in spring. For culture, *see* Perennials, p. 128.

Santolina Chamæcyparissus (Lavender Cotton, Holly Flag).—Hardy evergreen shrubby perennials growing from 10 to 24 inches high, and bearing yellow flowers from June to August. They like a dry ordinary soil and a sunny position. For culture, *see* Perennials, p. 128.

Sanvitalia procumbens.—A pretty trailing hardy annual carrying yellow flowers with purple centres from June to September, and useful for edgings and the rock garden. For culture, *see* Annuals, p. 106.

Saponaria (Soapwort).—Hardy annuals of tufted habit and perennials, the creeping species of which are excellent for edgings or for the rock garden, and bear cutting back if necessary for a late autumn display. The taller kinds are useful in the woodland and the wild garden. All like a sunny position and dry, light, gritty loam. For culture, *see* Annuals, p. 106, *and* Perennials, p. 128. *Species.*— (ANNUAL)—*S. calabrica* (Rosy-red, June–Oct., 6 in.) ; *S. Vaccaria* (Rose, June–Aug., 20 in.). (PERENNIAL)—*S. cæspitosa* (Rosy-pink, June–Sept., 4 in.) ; *S. ocymoides and alba* (Rose and White, May–July, 6 in.) ; *S. officinalis* [*Single and Double*] (Rose or White, July and Aug., 20 in.).

Sarcococca.—A low-growing and hardy evergreen shrub with fragrant flowers, and which may be planted in any soil in the shade and even under the drip of trees, but prefers a mixture of sandy loam and peat. Propagate by division, or strike cuttings of semi-matured wood under glass. *Species.*—*S. humilis* ; *S. ruscifolia* ; *S. saligna.* All bear white flowers in early spring and grow from 2 to 3 feet high.

Saxifraga (Saxifrage, Rockfoil).—A large genus, including numerous species of which there are many varieties, and the group is swelled by a seemingly endless number of hybrids.

Euaizoonias (Encrusted or Silvery Saxifrages) are happiest among limestone rocks or in the moraine, but will grow almost anywhere if given a rather gritty soil and a warm, sunny site. Seed can be sown when ripe in pans of light compost in a frame, or the roots can be divided in summer. *Species and Varieties.*—*S. aizoon and vars.* (Creamy-white, Yellow or Rose, 6–10 in.) ; *S. Cotyledon and vars.* (White, 18 in.) ; *S. Hostii* [*syn. elatior*] (White, Spotted Pink, 15 in.) ; *S. mutata* (Orange, 18 in.). All May to July.

Dactyloides (Mossy Saxifrages).—These plants will grow in almost any well-drained soil, but prefer a compost of gritty loam, leaf-mould and sand, and should be given a cool position in semi-shade. Increase by division of roots in summer, or sow seed in spring in gentle heat. *Species and Varieties.*—*S. Clibranii* (Crimson, 5 in.) ; *S. decipiens* [*syn. cæspitosa*] (Red to White, 6 in.) ; *S. hypnoides* (White, 5 in.) ; *S. Miss Willmott* (Cream, blotched Chocolate, 6–9 in.) ; *S. moschata and vars.* (Creamy-white, Rose, and Red, 2–6 in.) ; and *S. muscoides* (White or Red, 4 in.). All flower from May to June.

Kabschias ("Cushion" or Tufted Saxifrages).—These plants need an open and cool, but fairly sunny site, facing preferably east or west, in the rock garden. The most suitable compost consists of one-third stone chippings and two-thirds calcareous loam, leaf-mould and sand. Above all, the soil must be well drained, and ample moisture should be available in summer. Plants in the open must, in winter, be given the protection of a frame-light, or a sheet of glass. Increase by division of roots after flowering, by cuttings in the spring or autumn, or raise from seed in gentle heat in spring. *Species and Hybrids.*—S. *Boydii* (Yellow, March–May, 3 in.) ; S. *Burseriana and vars.* (White or Yellow, Feb.–April, 4 in.) ; S. *cæsia* (White, May–June, 3 in.) ; S. *corymbosa luteoviridis* (Yellow, April–May, 5 in.) ; S. *Elizabethæ* (Citron-yellow, March–May, 4 in.) ; S. *Grisebachii* (Crimson, April–May, 5 in.) ; S. *lilacina* (Lavender-rose, April–May, 2 in.) ; S. *marginata and vars.* (White or Yellow, March–May, 5 in.) ; S. *media* (Purple, April–May, 4 in.), and a host of others.

Porphyrions.—Give these plants a cool position in partial shade and a well-drained compost of moist, gritty loam and leaf-mould. Increase by division. *Species.*—S. *Hirculus major* (Golden, July–Sept., 5 in.) ; S. *oppositifolia and vars.* (Crimson-purple, March–May, 2 in.) ; S. *retusa* (Rose, May–July, 4 in.).

Megasea.—These thrive in sun or semi-shade in ordinary garden loam and may be propagated by seed (gentle heat) in the spring ; or by division in the autumn. *Species.*—S. *cordifolia* (Rose, 12–18 in.) ; S. *ligulata speciosa* [*syn. Megasea*] (Purple-rose, 12–24 in.) ; S. *Stracheyi* (Pink and White, 10 in.). All April to May-flowering.

Diptera.—This section likes a position in the Alpine house in light, gritty loam, or a sheltered situation in the rock garden. Propagate by means of seed, by division or layering. *Species.*—S. *cuscutæformis* (White, June, trailing) ; S. *Fortunei* (White, July–Sept., 10 in.) ; S. *sarmentosa* (Mother of Thousands) (Yellow or White, June–Sept., 10 in.).

Robertsonia.—These like a shady position in light, gritty loam. Propagate by means of seed (gentle heat) in the spring, or by division in the summer. *Species.*—S. *cuneifolia* (White, 5 in.) ; S. *umbrosa var. primuloides* (Rose, 5 in.) ; S. *umbrosa and vars.* (*London Pride*) (Rose and White, 10 in.). All May to June-flowering.

Trachyphyllum.—These thrive in semi-shade in moist, gritty loam. Propagate by means of seed (gentle heat) in the spring, or by division in summer. *Species.*—S. *aspera* ; S. *flagellaris.* All Yellow, flowering from May to June, 3 to 5 inches.

Scabious (Scabiosa or Pincushion Flower).—Annuals, biennials and perennials, which thrive in sunny, open borders and in well-drained rich and light soil. They also make good pot plants for bearing winter blooms if lifted and taken into the greenhouse in September. For culture, *see* Annuals, p. 106, Biennials, p. 107, *and* Perennials, p. 128. *Species.*—(ANNUAL)—S. *atropurpurea. Named Varieties.*—*Black Prince* (Maroon) ; *Coral Pink* (Pink) ; *Fairy* (Pale Lavender) ; *Fire King* (Crimson) ; *Scarlet King* (Scarlet) ; and *Yellow Prince* (Yellow). All June to Oct., 24 to 36 inches. (PERENNIAL)—S. *arvensis* (Lilac, June–Oct., 18 in.) ; S. *caucasica and vars.* ; S. *Pterocephala* (Mauve, June–Oct., 4–6 in.). NAMED VARS. OF S. *caucasica.*—*Annie* (Pale Lavender) ; *Collarette* (Violet) ; *Diamond* (Violet-blue) ; *Edith* (Silver-lavender) ; *Elsie* (Pale Blue) ; *Isaac House* (Deep Blue) ; *Mrs. House* (White) ; and *Princess* (Deep Lavender). All May to Sept.-flowering and growing to a height of from 24 to 36 inches. S. *lutea* (Yellow, June–Oct., 60 in.).

Schizanthus (Butterfly Flower, Fringe Flower, Poor Man's Orchid). —A half-hardy annual which thrives in a compost of two parts of fibrous loam to one part of leaf-mould and a little pounded mortar-rubble. The species chiefly grown in the open ground is *S. pinnatus*. *Culture.*—Sow thinly in the open in April or under glass with moderate heat in late February for summer bloom ; in August for spring flowers. Prick-off 3 inches apart, harden-off, and plant-out 9 to 12 inches apart in April. *Pot Culture.*—Sow several seeds in a 5-inch pot in September, keep in a temperature of 60° F., and moderately moist ; thin-out to five seedlings in each pot, and top the young plants occasionally. Winter on a sunny shelf near the glass in a cold greenhouse, and in February pot-up with three plants in 6 to 7-inch pots and stake carefully. In three weeks' time nip-out the heads ; only slight heat is needed to bring the plants into bloom. *Species.*—*S. Grahamii* (Scarlet) ; *S. grandiflorus* (Orange) ; *S. pinnatus* (Purple and White) ; *S. retusus and vars.* (Salmon-rose and Orange) ; *S. wisetoniensis* (Various). All March to October, 18 to 48 inches, except *S. pinnatus*, which flowers from June to September.

Schizopetalon.—A fragrant little half-hardy annual bearing white flowers on stems a foot high in summer. A succession of sowings should be made in the open in a warm, rich soil from May onwards.

Schizostylis coccinea (Kaffir Lily, Crimson Flag or Winter Gladiolus). —A half-hardy rhizomatous-rooted plant which grows from 20 to 30 inches high and flowers in October and Nov. It thrives in sunny, sheltered borders with a south aspect, and moist but well-drained, light, rich soil, and is also useful for pot culture in the cool greenhouse. *Culture.*—Plant in March or October ; protect with fibre in winter. Lift and divide the roots every few years in March, and propagate by means of offsets during that month. *Pot Culture.*— Plant in November in a compost of two-thirds loam and one-third leaf-mould, well-rotted manure and coarse sand and stand in a cold frame, giving no water until growth commences. Sink pots outdoors in a sunny position in summer, and late in September, when the buds show, transfer to the cold house.

Scilla (Squill).—Hardy spring-flowering bulbous plants, which do well in warm, sunny borders, in the rock garden, or in pots. *Culture.*—Plant in September or October, 2½ inches deep and 4 inches apart, in good garden or sandy soil. Propagate by means of offsets in September. *Pot Culture.*—Pot-up from August to November, placing about eight bulbs in a 5 to 6-inch pot, and using a compost of two parts of light, rich loam to one part of leaf-mould. Keep the pots in a frame and covered with fibre until growth starts, then transfer to the cold greenhouse. Plant-out in the open after flowering. *Species.* —*S. bifolia* (White, Pink, Blue, Feb. and March, 6 in.) ; *S. hispanica and vars.* (*Spanish Squill*) (White, Pink, Blue, April and May, 15–20 in.) ; *S. nutans* (*Bluebell*) (Blue, Rose or White, May, 15 in.) ; *S. peruviana* (Blue and White, May and June, 12 in.) ; *S. sibirica* (Blue, March, 6 in.).

Scirpus (Club Rush).—Hardy perennial marsh or aquatic plants, of which *S. lacustris*, the Common Bulrush, is the best known. *Culture.*— Propagate by means of division in March, and plant-out in shallow water at the edge of a pond or stream.   *Pot Culture.—S. nodosus* is a greenhouse species, thriving in a compost of two parts of loam to one part of leaf-mould and sand ;   pot-up in March in a 6-inch pot.

Scutellaria (Skull-caps).—These pretty little rock plants grow in poor, shallow and dry soil, and carry pink or purple flowers on 6 to 10-inch stems from August to October.   *Culture.*—Sow in the open in May or June, or increase by division in March or October.

Sedum (Stonecrop).—A large family of hardy plants, mostly perennials, the low-growing species being chiefly suitable for the rock, paved or wall garden ;   the taller kinds are useful in the border.   Sedums do well in a dry, light soil with lime in it ;   the summer-flowering kinds like a sunny position ;   autumn-flowering species do equally well in sun or shade.   The smaller kinds require the protection of glass in winter. For culture, *see* Perennials, p. 128.   *Species.—(Perennial)—S. acre aureum* (Yellow, May and June, 3 in.) ;   *S. dasyphyllum* (Pink and White, June–Aug., 3 in.) ;   *S. Ewersii* (Rose-purple, June–Aug., 6 in.) ; *S. spectabile* (Rosy-flesh, July–Sept., 12–18 in.).

Sempervivum (Houseleek).—A large genus of curious succulent plants, mostly hardy perennials, although some require the protection and warmth of a greenhouse.   They are well suited to sunny chinks or bare ledges in the rock garden, and thrive in sandy loam.   For culture, *see* Rock Plants, p. 135.   Except for *S. arachnoideum*, the Cob-web Houseleek, the hardy kinds need no protection in winter.   *Species.—S. arachnoideum* (Reddish-pink, June–Aug., 5 in.) ; *S. arenarium* (Yellow, June, 8 in.) ;   *S. tectorum* (Common Houseleek) (Red, July, 10 in.).

Senecio (Groundsel or Ragwort).—A large genus of annual and perennial plants, some hardy and others only suitable for the greenhouse.   Those in cultivation like a moist, deep and moderately light loam and a sunny position.   For culture, *see* Annuals, p. 106, *and* Perennials, p. 128.   *Greenhouse Culture.*—Pot-up in March in a compost of two-thirds fibrous loam and one-third sand, leaf-mould and a little well-rotted manure.   Propagate by cuttings struck in spring in a frame with slight bottom heat.   *Species.*—(HARDY ANNUAL)—*S. elegans and vars.* (Purple, Rose or White, June–Oct., 12–20 in.).   (HARDY PERENNIAL)—*S. Clivorum* (Orange, Aug.-Sept., 36–48 in.) ;   *S. pulcher* (Purple, Aug.-Oct., 20 in.) ;   *S. tanguticus* (Yellow, August–October, 3–6 ft.).

Sequoia.—Hardy ornamental evergreen coniferous trees which thrive in a sunny position and in well-drained deep loam.   *Culture.*—Plant in May or September ;   no pruning is required.

Shortia (Crimson Leaf).—Hardy dwarf-growing perennials which thrive in a moist but well-drained compost of two-thirds sandy peat and one-third loam together with some rough grit and charcoal.   A sheltered, shady position in the rock garden suits them.   In spring they carry white or rose flowers on stems 4 to 6 inches high.   For culture, *see* Rock Plants, p. 135.

Sidalcea.—Hardy perennial plants which do well in sunny borders and in a moist loam.   For culture, *see* Perennials, p. 128.   *Species and Varieties.—S. candida* (White) ;   *S. malvæflora rosea* (Pink) ;   *S. Rosy Gem* (Bright Pink).   All July to September, 36 inches.

EVERLASTING FLOWERS

Ammobium alatum grandiflorum (*Yellow and White*).

Helipterum (syn. Acroclinum) album (*White*).

Helichrysum bracteatum (Mixed) (*White, Brown, Red, Pink & Yellow*).

Xeranthemum annuum fl. pl. (*Purple, Rose or White*).

FLOWERING PLANTS

Photos]　　　　　　　　　　　　　[*Alexander & Brown (Perth) ; R. H. Bath, Ltd. ;*
　　　　　　　　　　　　　　　　　　　Dobbie & Co., Ltd. ; C. Jones.

Shirley Poppy " Double Queen."　　　Phacelia campanularia (*Blue*).
Iceland Poppy (*White*).　　　　　　　Oriental Poppy " Ethel Swete."
Double Poppy " Rose Queen."　　　　　Hymenocallis ovata (*White*).

Silene.—A genus containing a considerable number of species, including the plants known as the Campion and Catchfly. They are for the most part hardy annuals, biennials and perennials, excellent for borders or the rock garden, and like a sunny, open position and a well-drained sandy loam. Most of the alpine species need a moist gritty loam. For culture, *see* Annuals, p. 106, Biennials, p. 107, *and* Perennials, p. 128. *Species.*—(ANNUAL)—*S. gallica* (Pink, June–Aug., 18 in.) ; *S. pendula compacta* (Blue, White, Rose, Spring–Summer, 4–6 in.). (PERENNIAL) —*S. acaulis* (Pink, June–Aug., 2 in.) ; *S. alpestris* (White, May–June, 5 in.) ; *S. Elizabethæ* (Rose, June–Aug., 6 in.) ; *S. laciniata* (Scarlet, July–Aug., 20 in.) ; *S. virginica* (Crimson, June–August, 6 in.).

Sisyrinchium (Satin Flower).—Hardy perennials useful in the border, the rock garden, or the alpine house. A cool and fairly moist loam with one-third part leaf-mould and sand, or sandy peat, suits them best. *Pot Culture.*—Pot-up annually in September, and place in a sunny position in the cold house. After blooming, keep in a cold frame until re-potting. For culture, *see* Perennials, p. 128. *Species.*—*S. angustifolium* (Light Blue, May–July, 5–10 in.) ; *S. bermudianum* (Deep Blue, May–June, 10 in.) ; *S. grandiflorum* (Purple, March–May, 10 in.).

Skimmia.—Hardy evergreen shrubs which like a sunny, sheltered position and a deep rich loam. They grow about 3 feet high, flower in April and carry scarlet berries in autumn. *Culture.*—Plant in March or October, grouping one male plant with six females. No pruning is necessary. To propagate take cuttings, or layer in the summer.

Smilax (Asparagus medeoloides).—Beautiful evergreen climbing plants which thrive in the cool greenhouse in a mixture of two parts of loam to one part of leaf-mould and sand. There are also a few hardy species which may be grown in the open. *Culture.*—Pot-up in March, using 5 to 6-inch pots, stand in semi-shade, syringe and water well in hot weather. Cut old plants right back each March. Propagate by means of seed in slight heat (65° F.) in spring, or by means of division in March.

Snowdrop (Galanthus).—Snowdrops thrive in the shade in well-drained moist, gritty loam, and are excellent for beds, for the rock garden, for growing in pots or for naturalizing in grass. *Culture.*— Plant in August or September, 3 inches deep and 3 inches apart ; lift every fourth year only, and propagate by means of offsets. *Pot Culture.*—Plant 1 inch deep in September or October, using 4 to 5-inch pots and a compost of two parts of ordinary soil to one part of leaf-mould and sand, and keep in a cold frame covered with ashes or fibre until growth commences. Dry-off after flowering. *Species and Varieties.*—(EARLY)—*G. Elwesii* (White, marked Green, Jan., 8 in.) ; *G. nivalis* (White, Jan., 6 in.) ; *G. plicatus* (White, Jan., 12 in.). (LATE) —*G. Ikariæ* (White, March–April, 8 in.). (WINTER)—*G. Fosteri* (White, 8 in.).

Solanum capsicastrum (Berried Solanum or Winter Cherry).— Beautiful evergreen greenhouse shrubs which do well in a compost of rich loam, peat and sand, and in winter bear red cherry-like berries. *Culture.*—Sow in March (Temp. 60° F.), or strike cuttings of young growths after blooming (February) in moderate heat. Pinch-back when 4 inches high, pot-up in June in 5-inch pots, and stand outdoors in a sunny, sheltered position for the summer. Pinch-back again two or three times before July, and early in October move into the house, and place near the glass. Cut back shoots of old plants in February.

Solanum jasminoides (Jasmine Nightshade).—A half-hardy climbing perennial which should be grown in leaf-mould, sand and loam mixed in equal proportions and in warm and sheltered positions, or in a greenhouse in cold districts. It carries white flowers from June to October. *Culture.*—Propagate by means of cuttings of young wood in a frame with bottom heat during March. Cut back any weak shoots in February.

Soldanella (Moon-wort).—A pretty hardy perennial rock plant thriving in the shade, in moist gritty loam and peat, and which in winter must be protected with a pane of glass. For culture, *see* Rock Plants, p. 135. *Species.*—*S. alpina* (Violet-blue, May–June, 4 in.); *S. pusilla* (Violet, June–July, 3 in.); *S. pyrolæfolia* (Lilac, March, 6 in.).

Sophora.—Hardy deciduous shrubs and trees which thrive in sunny positions and in well-drained soil. *Culture.*—Plant in Oct. or Nov. Thin-out the branches when overcrowded. Propagate by means of seed; the bushy species can also be layered and cuttings rooted.

Sparaxis.—Half-hardy bulbous plants which may be grown in the open in sunny positions in warm sheltered borders and in well-drained sandy soil, or in pots in the greenhouse. *Culture.*—Plant in September or October 2½ inches deep and 3 inches apart, and cover with fibre in winter. *Pot Culture.*—Pot-up in September, placing six bulbs in a 5-inch pot, and stand in a cold frame covered with fibre until growth commences. The culture of these plants is very similar to that required for Ixias (*which see*). *Species.*—*S. grandiflora and vars.* (Violet, White or Crimson, April–May, 18 in.); *S. tricolor* (Orange-red and Purple, May, 20 in.).

Sparmannia africana (South African Hemp).—Greenhouse evergreen shrubs, which thrive in the cool house in a compost of two parts of sandy loam and peat to one part of rotten manure. Prune hard back in February. Pot-up from March to April, using 6 to 12-inch pots, and from June to September stand in the open. Propagate by means of cuttings of semi-matured shoots in heat (60° F.) in March or April.

Spartium junceum (Spanish Broom).—Beautiful evergreen shrubs which thrive in a sunny position in poor, dry or sandy soil. They grow some 8 to 12 feet high and carry yellow flowers from July to Sept. *Culture.*—Plant in October. Cut back long shoots in March. To propagate, strike cuttings of young wood in a frame in July, or sow seeds; grow the young plants in pots until ready to be planted out.

Specularia (Legousia, Corn Violet, Venus' Looking Glass).—Hardy little annuals which thrive in sandy loam and peat in the rock garden. Sow in autumn and thin-out to at least 6 inches apart. *Species.*—*S. falcata* (Blue); *S. hybrida fl. pl.* (Lilac or Blue); *S. perfoliata* (Purple and Blue); *S. speculum veneris* (Purple or White). All June to September-flowering.

Spiræa.—A genus of plants, both herbaceous and woody and mostly hardy perennials, which thrive in moist, rich loam and in a semi-shaded position. They are excellent in the border, for forcing indoors, and as room plants. *Culture.*—Propagate by means of division in March or October ; cuttings of young wood may also be struck in a frame in autumn. Thin-out the older wood of spring-flowering shrubs after flowering, if the bushes have become unshapely. Shrubs that flower between July and September should have all weak wood cut right away in February, and all other shoots that have flowered must be cut back by at least one half. *Pot Culture.*—Pot-up in October, using 8 to 10-inch pots and a compost of two-thirds sandy loam and one-third leaf-mould and a little well-rotted manure. Keep almost dry in a frost-proof frame till growth starts, then take into the cool house in succession as bloom is required. In a fortnight's time raise the tempera- ture by five degrees or so, and give bi-weekly doses of weak liquid manure. Stand in a saucer of water in hot weather. Prune as advised above, harden-off in a frame, and sink the pots in ashes outdoors from May to October, then re-pot, if necessary, and place in a cold frame. *Spiræa japonica* (Astilbe) is much used in the cool or cold greenhouse. *Species* (SHRUBS)—WHITE FLOWERS.—*S. arguta* (6–8 ft.) ; *S. bracteata* (4–8 ft.) ; *S. canescens* (6–10 ft.) ; *S. discolor* (8–12 ft.) ; *S. Lindleyana* (up to 20 ft.) ; *S. prunifolia fl. pl.* (6–8 ft.) ; *S. Thunbergii* (3–5 ft.). PINK. —*S. Douglasii* (4–6 ft.) ; *S. japonica Anthony Waterer* (1–2 ft.) ; *S. Margaritæ* (4–5 ft.) ; *S. Menziesii triumphans* (4–6 ft.). A compara- tively new race of hybrid pink and white-flowered HERBACEOUS PEREN- NIALS, obtained by crossing *S. Davidii*, *S. japonica* and *S. astilboides*, are being extensively planted in flower borders and the bog garden. They are April to September-flowering and grow to a height of from 1 to 9 feet.

Statice (Limonium, Sea Lavender).—These beautiful " Everlasting " flowers thrive in sunny borders or in the rock garden in well-drained sandy loam and leaf-mould. For culture, *see* Annuals, p. 106. Nearly all the annuals are better treated as half-hardy ; for Perennials, *see* p. 128. *Pot Culture.*—Pot-up half-hardy species in a compost of two- thirds fibrous loam and one-third peat to which has been added a little leaf-mould and sand and some well-decayed cow manure. Pot-on as the roots fill the pots, until 8 to 9-inch pots are reached. *Species.*— (HALF-HARDY ANNUAL)—*S. sinuata hybrida* (Mauve, White and Rose, June–Oct., 15–30 in.) ; *S. Suworowii* (Rosy-purple or White, June– Oct., 12–18 in.). (HARDY PERENNIAL)—*S. Gmelini* (Purple-blue, July– Sept., 18–24 in.) ; *S. incana* (Red or Pinky-white, July–Aug., 15 in.) ; *S. tartaricum* (Red, July–Sept., 20 in.).

Sternbergia (Yellow Star Flower, Winter Daffodil).—Half-hardy bulbous plants, which thrive in sunny positions in warm borders, in the rock garden or greenhouse, in sandy soil mixed with a little leaf- mould and mortar rubble. *Culture.*—Plant in April 4 inches deep and 5 inches apart ; *S. Fischeriana*, which flowers in February, should be planted in July or August. Protect from frost with fibre and lift from the ground triennially ; or pot-up in July and grow in the green- house. Propagate by means of offsets in April. *Species.*—*S. colchici- flora* (Yellow, Aug.) ; *S. lutea* (Yellow, Aug.-Sept.) ; *S. Fischeriana* (Yellow, Feb.-March). All grow about 10 inches high.

Stock.—Beautiful half-hardy annuals and biennials, which thrive in the sun in a rich and not too dry soil with lime in it.

Before being set out in their flowering positions, seedlings should be examined to see that they are double, the single-flowered being discarded ; seedlings that will produce double-flowered plants generally have long, pale green, concave leaves, while the foliage of the single-flowered are, as a rule, deeper in colour, somewhat convex and more rigid.

The Ten-weeks' Stock (Matthiola annua) is a favourite for bedding. This half-hardy annual grows 6 to 24 inches high, and usually blooms ten or twelve weeks after being sown.   For culture, *see* Annuals, p. 107.

Intermediate Stocks.—These furnish flowers in the borders from June to October and are excellent in a cold greenhouse for flowering in late winter and early spring.   For spring-flowering, sow thinly in light soil in boxes or pots in a cold frame in August.   Thin or transplant singly into small pots when fit to handle, using a compost of two parts of turfy loam to one part of well-rotted manure.   Stand the pots in the open until frost is imminent, then transfer to a frost-proof frame.   Pot-up from October to February, using 6 to 7-inch pots, transfer to the cold greenhouse in January and keep near the glass, or if for summer-flowering in the open, keep them in a frame until April, when harden-off and plant-out in May.   If preferred, treat as Ten-weeks' Stocks.

East Lothian Stocks.—These are half-hardy biennials which bloom from June to September, and are popular for bedding.   For early-flowering, sow during July in a compost of two-thirds loam to one-third leaf-mould and sand, in a cold frame.   Winter in cold frames, or pits, and plant out the following spring.   *See* Biennials, p. 107. If preferred, these stocks may be treated as half-hardy annuals.

Brompton or Giant Stocks.—These are half-hardy biennials flowering in May, June and July.   The seed should be sown in July thinly in drills about 6 inches apart in a light sandy bed with an east aspect. When about 3 inches high, thin-out the seedlings to 6 inches apart, winter in a cold frame and plant-out in March.

Nice or Winter-flowering Stocks.—For winter-flowering in the cool greenhouse sow in a cold frame in June, pot-up three seedlings in a 5-inch pot, grow on in a frame and transfer to the cool house early in Dec.   For spring-flowering, sow in a frame in August, grow as above and take into the house when winter-flowering plants are over.

Varieties.—BROMPTON—(White) *Cottager's White* ; (Rose) *Sunrise* ; (Scarlet) *Old English Scarlet* ; (Purple) *Cottager's Purple* ; (Green) *Improved Green.*   EAST LOTHIAN—(White) *White Wallflower-leaved* ; (Crimson) *Crimson Wallflower-leaved.*   INTERMEDIATE—(White) *Crystal White* ; (Lilac) *Queen Alexandra* ; (Scarlet) *Covent Garden.*   NICE OR WINTER FLOWERING—(White) *Mont Blanc* ; (White and Rose) *Riviera Market ;* (White, Rose, Salmon, Mauve, or Crimson) *Beauty of Nice* ; (Pale Yellow) *Yellow Prince* ; (Pink) *Empress Elizabeth* ; (Lilac) *Queen of the Belgians.*   TEN-WEEK—(White) *Snowdrift* ; (Primrose) *Princess Mary* ; (Salmon) *Salmon Beauty* ; (Pale Red) *Almond Blossom* ; (Crimson) *Crimson King* ; (Scarlet) *Fireball* ; (Mauve) *Mauve Beauty* ; (Violet) *Violet Queen* ; (Blue) *Celestial* ; (Various) *Giant Perfection, Perfection Ten-week,* and *Superb Bedding.*

Stock, Night-scented (Matthiola bicornis).—This most fragrant of hardy annuals likes a fairly rich soil, with lime or old mortar rubble in it. For culture, *see* Annuals, p. 106.

Stokesia (Stoke's Aster).—Hardy perennials which thrive in sunny borders and in light, well-drained soil, grow some 1 to 2 feet in height, and bear blue or white flowers in early autumn. *See* Perennials, p. 128.

Streptocarpus (Cape Primrose).—A lovely perennial suitable for culture in the cool greenhouse. *Culture.*—Pot-up annually in February or March, using 6-inch pots and a compost of equal parts of sandy loam and leaf-mould. Propagate by means of seed in gentle heat (60° F.) in February, by leaf-cuttings or by division in March. If seed is sown, the small plants should be pricked-off singly into small pots and gradually re-potted until in 6-inch pots. They must be kept moist and shaded from strong sun. *Species, etc.*—*S. caulescens* (Pale Blue); *S. Dunnii.* (Rose); *S. Galpini* (Mauve and White); *S. Rexii* (Blue); *S. Wendlandii* (Rose or Blue). All May to Oct., 10 to 20 ins.

Stuartia.—Hardy deciduous shrubs requiring a sunny, sheltered site and rich, sandy loam and leaf-mould. Cut away all dead and weak wood every two or three years. Propagate by means of cuttings of ripened wood struck under glass in late summer, or by layering. *Species.*—*S. Malachodendron* (Virginica) ; *S. pentagyna* ; and *S. pseudocamellia.* All Creamy-white, June to July, 6 to 10 feet.

Styrax (Storax).—Hardy deciduous shrubs or small trees, that like a sunny, sheltered position and a moist, rich, sandy loam. *Culture.*—Plant in October. In autumn thin-out any weak shoots. Propagate by means of layering in autumn. *Species.*—*S. Hemsleyanus* (10–20 ft.) ; *S. japonica* (8 ft.) ; *S. Obassia* (8 ft.). All White, June to July.

Sweet Pea (Lathyrus).—Sweet Peas enjoy a rich soil properly prepared prior to sowing. A trench 2 feet wide should be dug out to a depth of from 2 to 3 feet, while a plentiful supply of well-rotted horse manure should be worked into the lower strata some 10 inches below the surface. With the top spit may be incorporated a little leaf-mould, bonemeal, soot and lime, but no stable manure. Sweet Peas can be sown in the open on a dry day, generally early in March, but rather earlier in a warm, sheltered situation. It is often beneficial to soak the seeds in warm water overnight, especially if the weather is very dry. The seed should be sown 1½ inches deep and 3 inches apart and the surface dusted with soot. When about 4 inches high, thin-out to 6 inches apart and support by means of twigs. As the plants grow taller, stakes 7 to 8 feet in height should be placed in position. Wire peaguards or strands of black cotton should be used to keep the birds from the seeds. To secure the finest blooms, however, the seeds should be sown in late autumn or early in February in 5-inch pots, placing six seeds in each, or a single seed in a small pot. The seeds may also be sown some 2 inches apart in boxes about 4 inches deep, but the seedlings must be potted-off singly as soon as possible. A compost of two-thirds fibrous loam and one-third leaf-mould, to which a sprinkling of bonemeal, wood ashes and coarse sand have been added, will be found most suitable. Raise the young plants on a shelf near the glass in a cool greenhouse or in a frost-proof frame. Before being planted-out into the open, early in March, when the plants are about 4 inches high, the plants should be hardened-off in a cold frame. Not more than three growths should be allowed to spring from each root, and when the plants have grown to 3 or 4 feet high, they should be given, after rain or a soaking with clear water, a little soot-water or weak liquid manure (the colour of weak tea), once a week. The application of the latter must not be overdone. Water applied to sweet peas must have been exposed to the air for at least twenty-four hours ; stone-cold water may cause the buds to drop. Plants so raised should flower from early June to late September ; if desired, early May blooms may be had by growing the peas throughout in the greenhouse. The after-attention is very simple, but it is of prime importance to keep the plants free from seeds. If seeds are required, a portion of the row or one clump may be set apart for the purpose. The tips should be pinched-out when they reach 6 to 8 inches above the top of the stakes, and the soil between the plants should be kept continually stirred. Named varieties are innumerable and catalogues should be consulted.

Sweet William (Dianthus barbatus).—A beautiful hardy perennial, best treated as a biennial. For culture, see Biennials, p. 107. Sweet Williams can also be propagated by cuttings, by division of roots, or by layering. *Varieties.*—*Auricula-eyed* (Rich Colours and White Eyes) ; *Giant White* (Self) ; *Harlequin* (Multi-coloured) ; *Nigricans* (Deep Purple) ; *Pheasant's Eye* (Double Strain, Crimson and White Eye) ; and *Scarlet Beauty* (Self). All June to September, 9 to 18 inches.

Symphoricarpus (Snowberry).—Hardy deciduous shrubs which thrive in sun or shade and in ordinary soil. They grow some 5 feet high and flower in July and August. *Culture.*—Plant in October or November ; cut-out dead wood and weak shoots annually in March, and every few years lift the shrubs in autumn, divide the roots and replant the younger and more vigorous parts.

Syringa (Lilac).—Hardy deciduous shrubs which thrive in the sun in moist, well-manured, well-drained, and rather heavy loam. They grow from 5 to 15 feet high and flower in April and May. *Culture.*—Plant in October or November. Periodically cut away all suckers from the roots of grafted plants, disbud surplus buds in spring, and cut-out old and weak wood after flowering, but never trim away the young or half-matured shoots. Propagate by means of layering in June, by matured cuttings in the open in October, or by suckers in October. *Forcing.*—For decoration in the greenhouse, pot-up in October or November, using 6 to 10-inch pots and a compost of two parts sandy loam to one part of leaf-mould and a little sand and bonemeal, stand in a sheltered, frost-proof position, and move into the house in succession as bloom is desired. After flowering, remove all dead blooms, syringe and keep up the heat for three weeks or so, then harden-off and sink the pots in ashes outdoors from May until the October of the following year ; never force two years running. Prune as above. Named varieties are kept true to type by crown or cleft-grafting in March. For Mock Orange or *Philadelphus coronarius*, commonly called Syringa, see Philadelphus. *Named Varieties.*—(White) *Madame Lemoine* (Double) and *Marie Legraye* (Single) ; (Cream) *Jeanne d'Arc*

(Double) ; (Pink) *Virginite* (Double) and *Lucy Baltet* (Flesh-pink, Single) ; (Rose) *Emile Lemoine* (Double) and *Princess Marie* (Semi-double) ; (Deep Red) *Souvenir de L. Spaeth* (Single) ; (Blue) *Leon Simon* (Double), *Alphonse Lavallée* (Double, tinged Violet), and *President Grevy* (Double) ; (Purple) *Charles X* (Single) and *La Tour d'Auvergne* (Purple-violet) ; (Mauve) *Lemoinei* (Double) ; (Pale Lavender, Edged Rose) *Louis Van Houtte*.

Tagetes (African and French Marigolds).—Half-hardy annuals for warm, sunny beds and borders. *T. erecta* requires rich soil ; *T. patula* thrives in poor soil. For culture, *see* Annuals, p. 107. *See also* Calendula. *Species.*—*T. erecta* (African Marigold). *Named Varieties.*—*Giant Orange* (Double) ; *Lemon Queen* (Single). Both June to September, 20 to 40 inches. *T. patula* (French Marigold). *Named Varieties.*—*Cloth of Gold* ; *Yellow Bedder* ; *Star of India* (Crimson-red, Striped Yellow) ; and *Silver King*. All June to September, 9 to 18 inches.

Tamarix or Tamarisk.—Hardy deciduous or evergreen shrubs which do well anywhere in light ordinary soil, growing from 5 to 10 feet high and flowering from May to September. *Culture.*—Plant in October or November. Prune summer-flowering species in March, spring-flowering kinds after flowering. Strike cuttings in the open in October.

Taxodium distichum (Deciduous Cypress).—Hardy deciduous trees which thrive in full sun and in moist or swampy soil. *Culture.*—Plant from October to November. No pruning is required. Propagate by means of seed in a frame.

Taxus (Yew).—Hardy evergreen trees or shrubs which thrive in sun or shade and in ordinary soil. *T. baccata* is the Common Yew, usually used for hedges. *Culture.*—Plant in May or September. When necessary trim in May or August. Propagate by means of seed in the open in March, or by cuttings of young wood in a frame in September.

Tecoma (Trumpet Flower).—Evergreen climbing shrubs which thrive in well-drained, light soil on warm sunny walls or in the greenhouse. *Culture.*—Strike cuttings of ripe wood in a frame with bottom heat in autumn. Plant in dry, open weather between October and April. *Species.*—*T. capensis* (Orange-scarlet) ; *T. grandiflora* (Orange) ; *T. jasminoides* (White, striped Red) ; and *T. radicans* (Orange). All July to August, 20 feet or more.

Teucrium (Germander).—This genus includes some useful little herbaceous plants and a few evergreen shrubs. The herbaceous perennials thrive in the sun in gritty loam in the border or rock garden. For culture, *see* Perennials, p. 128. The shrubs need a warm, sunny and sheltered position ; a sandy loam suits them best. They are increased by cuttings of young shoots. *Species.*—(PERENNIAL)—*T. Chamædrys* (Bluish-red, July–Aug., 10 in.) ; *T. Marum* (Deep Pink, Aug.–Sept., 10 in.). (SHRUBBY)—*T. flavum* (Yellow, Aug.–Sept., 30 in.) ; *T. fruticans* (Pale Lavender-blue, March–Sept., 4–6 ft.).

Thalictrum (Meadow Rue).—Hardy perennials which thrive in well-drained, rich, sandy loam, in sunny or shady borders, or by the side of a stream. Dwarf kinds are useful rock plants. *T. minus var. adiantifolium* and *T. dipterocarpum* are excellent for cold greenhouse. For culture, *see* Perennials, p. 128. *Pot Culture.*—Lift from the open and pot-up in Nov. using 5 to 6-inch pots and a compost of equal parts of rich loam and leaf-mould. *Species.—T. minus var. adiantifolium* (Yellow, June–Sept., 20 in.) ; *T. alpinum* (Greenish, May–June, 5 in.) ; *T. dipterocarpum* (Rose, Purple, or White, June–Sept., 36–50 in.).

Thermopsis (False Lupin).—Hardy perennials which grow from 12 to 30 inches high and flower in summer. They do well in sheltered, sunny borders and in rich, sandy soil. *See* Perennials, p. 128.

Thunbergia alata.—Evergreen climbers carrying pretty flowers from June to September, and much used for hanging baskets and for greenhouse staging. They like a rich, fibrous loam mixed with leaf-mould and sand, and are raised from seed in March in sandy soil, in a temperature of 60° F., or from cuttings subjected to gentle bottom heat. Pot-on for flowering into 4 to 5-inch pots, or harden-off and set out in the open in June in a warm, sheltered bed.

Thuya.—Hardy evergreen trees often used instead of yew as hedge plants. They succeed in sunny positions in any moist garden soil. *Culture.*—Plant in May or September. No pruning is necessary. Trim hedge plants in April and September. Propagate by means of seeds in a frame, or by cuttings in a frame in September.

Thymus (Thyme).—Hardy trailing plants that are useful for the rock or paved garden, and which thrive in the sun in well-drained, sandy loam. For culture, *see* Rock Plants, p. 135. *Species.—T. nitidus* (Pink Flowers, 12 in.) ; *T. Serpyllum* (Purple Flowers, Grey Foliage, 3 in.) ; *T. S. album* (White, 3 in.) ; *T. S. citriodorus* (Purple Flowers, Trailing) ; *T. S. lanuginosus* (Grey Leaves, Purple Flowers, 5 in.) ; and *T. vulgaris argentea* (Silver Leaves, 8 in.). All June to August.

Tiarella cordifolia (Foam Flower).—Hardy perennials which like a shady position in the border or rock garden and a moist, ordinary soil. They grow some 9 inches high and carry creamy-white flowers from April to June. For culture, *see* Perennials, p. 128.

Tigridia (Tiger Iris).—Half-hardy bulbous plants which do best in a light, rich, sandy loam and leaf-mould, in a warm, sunny position in a dry border or rock garden, or in the greenhouse. *Culture.*—Plant about the middle of April 4 inches deep and 6 inches apart, letting the bulbs rest on sand. Lift from the ground in November. For Pot Culture, six bulbs may be placed in a 6-inch pot, the latter being kept in a frame or cool house until growth has started. Propagate by means of offsets in April. *Species.—T. conchiflora* (Yellow, Purple Spots) ; *T. grandiflora rubra* (Crimson, Scarlet and Yellow) ; *T. Pavonia* (Scarlet, Marked Yellow and Purple). All May to July, 12 to 18 inches.

Tilia (Lime).—Hardy deciduous trees, which thrive in sunny, sheltered positions and in moist, rich soil. They bear fragrant yellowish-green flowers from June to August. *Culture.*—Plant in October or November. Thin-out the branches when overcrowded.

Torenia.—Half-hardy annuals of trailing nature, which flower in August and are suitable for hanging baskets. They need a compost of sandy loam and leaf-mould. For culture, *see* Annuals, p. 107.

Trachelium cæruleum (Throat-wort).—A half-hardy biennial which thrives in leaf-mould and sandy loam in sunny beds or borders. It grows about 18 inches high and flowers in July and August. For culture, *see* Biennials, p. 107. *T. cœruleum* is a good pot plant for the cool house.

Tradescantia (Spider-wort).—Hardy and half-hardy perennial plants suitable for beds and cool greenhouse. They thrive in sun or shade in any good well-drained soil. For culture, *see* Perennials, p. 128. *T. reflexa* (Blue, June–Sept., 20 in.) and *T. virginica* (Purple, Red, Blue or White, June–Sept., 20 in.), the Common Spider Wort, and its varieties, are good representatives of the hardy species.

Trientalis (Starflower and Wintergreen).—Small hardy perennials, suitable for a light, rich, peaty soil, in a shady and moist position in the rock garden. They may also be used as a border edging. *T. americana* (Starflower) bears white flowers on 6-inch stems in June or July, and *T. europœa* (Wintergreen) in April or May. Propagate by means of seed in summer, or by division in spring.

Trifolium (Clover, Shamrock, Trefoil).—Hardy annuals and perennials which thrive in any light soil, and are easily raised from seed or propagated by means of division of roots.

Trillium (Wood Lily or Trinity Flower).—Hardy tuberous-rooted perennials, which thrive in well-drained, moist, peaty soil, in partial shade in border or rock garden, or in pots in cold greenhouse. *Culture.* —Plant in Oct. Lift from the soil when overcrowded. Propagate by means of seed sown in a frame in March, or in the open in June, or increase by division of roots in Oct. *Species.—T. grandiflorum* (Rose or White, June–July, 6–12 in.) ; *T. erectum* (Deep Purple, May–June, 5–10 in.) ; *T. sessile californicum* (White, May–June, 8 in.).

Trollius (Globe Flower).—Hardy herbaceous perennials, which thrive in rich, moist loam, in shady borders or in the marsh garden. For culture, *see* Perennials, p. 128. *Species.—T. asiaticus* (Yellow or Orange, May and June, 24 in.) ; *T. europœus var. napellifolius* (Orange, May–June, 30 in.) ; *T. Ledebourii* (Golden Yellow, April–May, 30–40 in.).

Tropæolum.—Beautiful climbers, mostly half-hardy annuals, invaluable for covering trellises out-of-doors and for training up pillars and rafters in the cool greenhouse. The best known are *T. aduncum* (Canary Creeper), *T. majus* and *T. minus* (Nasturtium) ; for cultural details *see* Canary Creeper and Nasturtium. For outdoor use, *T. aduncum* and *T. majus* are especially good, also the perennial species, *T. polyphyllum* and *T. speciosum* (Flame Nasturtium). *T. Lobbianum* blooms beautifully through the winter months in the greenhouse, and likes a light, but not too rich a soil. Pot-up from March to April in 6 to 10-inch pots and grow near the glass. Propagate by means of seed, or by cuttings in heat in March or April.

Tulips.—Tulips look best massed in beds or borders, carpeted with other spring flowers. The best tulip for all-round purposes is probably the *Keizer Kroon.* For planting permanently, the *Cottage* and *Darwin* tulips are best. *Culture.*—Tulips require a fair amount of sand in a well-drained, deeply-dug, rich loam with a cool, moist subsoil, and a sunny, sheltered position, not subject to draughts and cold winds. Plant early in November, from 4 to 5 inches deep and from 8 to 10 inches apart. It is best to lift the bulbs and plant them in a different bed each year. If this cannot be done, the soil should be well dug and improved by the use of bonemeal or well-rotted cow-manure. *Pot Culture.*—The early single and double dwarf *Duc Van Thol* tulips are excellent for this purpose. The former may be planted six or eight bulbs in a good-sized pot ; but of the latter, three bulbs are sufficient. All tulips require a good supply of water when in flower and should be shaded from the sun ; hard forcing will prevent flowering. The soil and treatment necessary for tulips grown in pots are the same as recommended for hyacinths. Propagation is carried out by means of offsets, separated from the bulbs when lifted in summer, and planted in September or October. *See also chapter on* Bulb Culture. Named varieties are innumerable and catalogues should be consulted.

Tunica.—Dwarf-growing hardy perennials for the rock garden and for edgings to borders. A sandy loam suits them best, in sun or shade. For culture, *see* Perennials, p. 128. *Species.*—*T. Saxifraga* (Pale Rose or White, June–Aug., Trailing).

Typha (Reed Mace, Bulrush, or Cat-o'-nine-tails).—A genus of aquatic plants, which thrive on a swampy bank, in the marsh garden, or at the edge of a sheltered pond with from 1 to 12 inches of water above the crowns. They grow some 6 feet high and flower in late summer.

Ulex (Furze, or Gorse).—Free-flowering evergreen shrubs bearing yellow flowers, and which like a sunny position and a poor, dry soil. *U. europæus fl. pl.* (5 ft.) flowering from March to June and *U. nana* (18 inches) flowering from September to December, are both useful for hedges. *Culture.*—Plant-out from pots at any time between March and October ; cut back when overgrown, and propagate by means of cuttings in a frame in August, or sow seed in a frame in March.

Ulmus (Elm).—Hardy deciduous trees which thrive in almost any soil and in practically any position. *Culture.*—Plant in October or November. Thin-out the branches in the summer when required. Propagate by means of seeds, grafting, or from sucker growths.

Vaccinium.—A large genus of shrubby plants which includes the Whortleberry or Bilberry (*V. Myrtillus*). There are several species grown for the beauty of their flowers, fruit and tinted foliage in autumn ; these require a moist, sandy and peaty loam. Propagate by means of cuttings struck under glass in spring and summer, by root-suckers, or by seed sown in autumn when ripe. Plant-out in March. *Species.*— *V. Arctostaphylos* [Bear Berry] (Greenish-white, 6 ft.) ; *V. corymbosum* [Blueberry] (Pale Pink or White, 5 ft.) ; *V. Myrtillus* [Whortleberry] (Pale Pink, 1½ ft.). All May-flowering.

Valeriana.—Hardy perennials of which the smaller species are useful for the rock garden. The best known are *V. officinalis* (All Heal), and *V. Phu.* They thrive in sunny borders and in any ordinary soil. For culture, *see* Perennials, p. 128. Both flower from June to October.

Vallota purpurea (Scarborough Lily).—Half-hardy bulbous plants, which thrive in a compost of two parts of sandy loam to one part of leaf-mould. They require the protection of the cool greenhouse or sunny window, and flower on stems from 1 to 2 feet high in August and September. *Culture.*—Plant in July or August singly in 5 to 8-inch pots, with the crowns 6 inches below the surface. Winter near the glass and give liquid manure when the buds form. Water moderately till the leaves die in spring, and keep fairly dry and exposed to the sun from May to September. Leave in the same pot for three or four years. Propagate by means of seed in spring, or by offsets in August.

Veratrum (False Hellebore).—*Poisonous* hardy perennials which thrive in deep, rich loam. For culture, see Perennials, p. 128. *Species.* —*V. album* (White) ; *V. nigrum* (Deep Purple) ; *V. viride* (Greenish-white). All July to September, 50 inches.

Verbascum (Mullein).—Hardy biennials and perennials which may be grown in sunny borders or in the wild garden in light, ordinary soil. For culture, see Biennials, p. 107, *and* Perennials, p. 128. *Species.*— (Biennial)—*V. olympicum* (Golden Yellow, Grey Foliage, June–Sept., 70 in.). (Perennial)—*V. Chaixii* (Yellow, Mauve Centre, June–Sept., 50–90 in.) ; *V. phœniceum* (Purple, White or Rose, June–Sept., 20–30 in.).

Verbena.—Half-hardy annuals, biennials and perennials, which do well in rich sandy loam, in sunny beds. For culture, see Annuals, p. 107, *and* Biennials, p. 107. (*Perennials*).—Sow in heat (Temp. 60° F.) in February and treat as biennials. With named varieties, at any rate, strike cuttings of sturdy shoots that have no flower buds in a frame in spring or early autumn. Autumn-struck verbenas are best left in the cutting pots until February ; and, unlike calceolarias, if sufficient old plants are kept over the winter for stock, spring-struck cuttings are best. Plant-out 10 inches apart in June. *Pot Culture.*— Pot-up in March, using 5 to 6-inch pots and a compost of sandy loam and leaf-mould, and a little well-rotted manure. Stop-back the young shoots to make bushy plants. *Named Varieties.*—(Half-Hardy Perennials)—(White, Scented) *Boule de Neige* ; (Pink) *Miss Willmott* ; *Crimson King* ; *King of the Scarlets* ; *Purple Emperor.*

Veronica (Speedwell).—Shrubby Species :—The evergreen shrubs of this genus are amongst the most valuable of summer and autumn blooming plants, both for greenhouse culture and for out-of-doors, where, with a dry subsoil and somewhat sheltered, sunny situation, the plants will generally stand uninjured through the winter. *Culture.*—Plant in April or September. Trim annually to keep in shape only, but it is usually necessary to prune hard back every few years. To propagate, strike cuttings of matured wood in a frame in August ; the young shoots should occasionally be pinched-back, but no " stopping " must be done after June. *Pot Culture.*—Pot-up in the early summer, using 6 to 8-inch pots and a compost of two parts of loam to one part of leaf-mould. Harden-off and stand in the open from May to September, then take into the cold house. After flowering, prune severely in March, and place the pots near the glass. Annual Species.—The miniature species, such as *V. glauca*, *V. syriaca* and *V. alba*, make very pretty plants for small beds and edgings. *Culture.*—Sow in the open in September, and thin-out to 5 inches apart as soon as fit to handle. Herbaceous Perennial Species.—These thrive in sunny positions and in any fairly good garden soil, especially if it is rather gritty. Every fourth year the plants should be lifted and divided, the younger outer crowns only being replanted. Propagate by means of division in March and (some species) in October. Some of the dwarf-growing species make excellent rock plants. For culture, *see* Rock Plants, p. 135. *Species and Varieties.*—(ANNUAL) —*V. alba* (White, Summer, 6 in.) ; *V. glauca* (Blue, Summer, 6 in.). (PERENNIAL)—*V. Allionii* (Deep Blue, May–July, 5 in.) ; *V. austriaca alba* (White, June–July, 12 in.) ; *V. caucasica* (Pale Red, June–Aug., 10 in.) ; *V. incana* (Violet-blue, Silver Foliage, June–Sept., 6–9 in.) ; *V. subsessilis* (Deep Blue, July–Sept., 20–30 in.). (SHRUBBY)—*V. Andersoni* (Purple or Blue, July–Sept., 2 ft.) ; *V. Autumn Glory* (Deep Violet, Sept.–Oct., 1½ ft.) ; *V. buxifolia* (White, June–Aug., 2 ft.) ; *V. cupressoides* (Violet-purple, July–Sept., 1 ft.) ; *V. Hectori* (Pale Lilac and White, July, 1 ft.) ; *V. speciosa and vars.* (Red, Rose, Purple, Mauve, Blue, July–Sept., 3–5 ft.).

Viburnum.—Hardy deciduous trees and shrubs which thrive in any soil, but prefer a moist, well-drained deep loam, and are most useful for shrubberies. The best-known shrubby species is *V. Opulus sterilis,* the Guelder Rose or Snowball Tree. *V. tomentosum plicatum,* a splendid border shrub, is also a useful sort for the greenhouse. Pot-up in October, using 7 to 10-inch pots and ordinary loam. Prune after flowering, and plant-out for two years in the open. *V. Tinus* (Laurustinus) is an evergreen species making a bush 8 feet in height, and best planted in sun or shade under trees and facing north. It flowers in autumn and all through the winter months. It is also useful for pot-culture indoors. In the latter case pot-up in the early autumn, using 6 to 10-inch pots and well-drained sandy loam. Cut well back after flowering, and put out in the open in semi-shade from May to October. Other good species are *V. Carlesii,* with pinkish-white flowers in April and May ; *V. fragrans,* pink or white, January to March ; and *V. tomentosum,* creamy-white, May and June. *General Culture in the Open.*—Plant in a sunny position, deciduous species in October, November, or March ; evergreens in May or September. Trim into shape annually and, when necessary, cut-out old wood in July (deciduous) and May (evergreen species). Propagate by means of cuttings in a frame in June, or layer in October.

Vinca (Periwinkle).—The hardy periwinkles are evergreen shrubs, which grow in any well-drained ordinary soil, and look well in borders or on rock-work. *V. major* (20 in.) and *V. minor* (9 in.) have purple-blue flowers from June to September. There are also mauve and white varieties. *Culture.*—Plant from March to October. Cut back straggling shoots in April. Propagate by means of division in March or Oct.

Viola.—The viola and pansy are so similar in their cultural requirements that we treat them under the one heading. Violas, sometimes called Tufted Pansies, are much used for bedding or as edging plants, where they will flower from May until well into November. Any ordinary, deeply-dug, moderately rich loam will suit them. A sprinkling of good compost and a dressing of soot or bonemeal should be scattered on the top. Heavy clay is not good for violas. A cool, but not damp, position in partial shade is best. *Culture.*—Violas may be propagated from seed, by cuttings, or by division of the roots. Seed intended for spring flowers should be sown in boxes in June, using a good light soil, and the box should be covered with a sheet of glass until the seeds are up. When fit to handle transplant 2 inches apart into other boxes; water liberally and shade from sun. As frosty weather approaches, the boxes should be placed in a cold frame for the winter. At the beginning of April, transplant about 9 to 12 inches apart into partially-shaded beds, keeping the " balls " as far as possible intact. Cuttings of new, but vigorous growths from the centre of the plant, may be struck in September in a shady frame and planted-out in March for blooming the following year. Propagation by cuttings may take place any time from April to the end of October, although August and September are the best months. For early flowering, it is best to propagate by division of old roots in September. The hardier kinds can be wintered successfully in the open in any shady nook in the garden, but not under trees. The less hardy kinds should be wintered in cold frames. Pansies bear larger and brighter flowers if raised from seed; violas, however, are more vigorous when propagated by cuttings. All dead blooms should be periodically picked-off. *Pot Culture.*—Strike cuttings in July or August, and when rooted, plant in 4-inch pots, and plunge in ashes or coco-nut fibre in a cold frame, where they should remain until the end of March. Then shift them into 8-inch pots, keep close for a few days, then admit air gradually. *Alpine Species.*—There are also many delightful alpine species which need similar treatment to that described for the bedding viola, but the soil should be somewhat more loose, gritty and moist. Named varieties are innumerable and catalogues should be consulted.

Violet (Viola odorata).—Violets may be grown in pots, by placing two or three runners or offsets in a pot in April or May, and keeping them in a frame, slightly shaded from the hot sun in summer; loam, leaf-mould and sand suit them admirably, but the violet is not particular as to soil. Russian violets, and sometimes the Neapolitan, will flower from September to April, if given the protection of glass; true violets flower in March and April. There are many varieties, but their culture is so similar that they may all be considered together. The grower should start with good stock from a reliable source, and, although the violet is a perennial, it is best to renew the stock each year.

Cultivation.—The violet should be propagated annually in June; when the plants have flowered, remove them from the soil, divide them into single crowns, cutting off all runners and dead foliage and selecting the finest outside crowns only; then plant-out the single varieties 15 inches apart each way, and the double kinds 10 to 12 inches apart and press the soil firmly round the roots, but do not bury the crown. A rich, well-dug and well-drained bed with an east aspect, where they can receive the morning sun should be chosen. When the plants show signs of growth, stir the soil about their roots with a small hoe, water liberally, and syringe them in the evenings of dry, hot days. Pinch-off all runners as they appear, and give a little shade from the sun in hot weather. Nothing more, save fortnightly doses of weak liquid manure or dustings with an artificial fertilizer and soot is required for their culture during the summer months. The double varieties should be wintered in pots under glass or in a frame. Violets may also be propagated by cuttings struck in a cold frame in September or October.

Pot Culture.—To obtain bloom during the winter months, the best compost is four parts of turfy loam to one part each of rotted manure, leaf-mould and sand, and a sprinkling of soot, well mixed together. In September raise the violets carefully from the bed in which they have been growing with as much earth on their roots as possible, and remove all side-shoots and runners. One strong plant should be put in each 6 to 7-inch pot with the crowns just above the soil. The pots should be well drained with broken bones instead of potsherds and after planting the pots should be well watered to settle the soil about the roots. A sufficient number of frames should be arranged in a sunny, sheltered southern aspect, placing them in such a manner that the lights will throw off rain quickly. Put in a layer of old tan about 4 inches thick, and in this the pots should be plunged in rows up to their rims. The bed of tan should be 6 to 9 inches higher at the back than at the front, and should be raised so that the plants are from 6 to 9 inches from the lights. Keep the frame almost closed for three or four days after planting, and shade if the sun is strong. After the first fortnight, and when the temperature is above 50° F., the lights may be removed during the day, and at night they should be tilted up at the back for the admission of air. When the temperature is below 50° F., the lights should be left on, but even then air should be admitted from behind during the daytime. If the temperature is below 40° F., the admission of air should be very partial, if it is admitted at all. At no time after the plants begin to bloom should the lights be entirely removed, except for the purpose of watering or gathering the flowers. When the weather is cold, a covering of mats should be applied at nights. In hard frosts, two mats should be put on as well as litter round the sides of the frame. Care must be taken to wet the leaves as little as possible.

Varieties.—(DOUBLE)—(White) *Comte de Brazza* ; (Lavender, Blue and White) *Marie Louise* ; (Violet Pink) *Madame Millet* ; (Pale Blue) *Duchesse de Parme* ; (Dark Blue, White Throat) *Mrs. Arthur.* (SINGLE) —(White) *White Czar* ; (Rose-pink) *Cœur d'Alsace* ; (Rose, Pink and White) *Rosea Delicatissima* ; (Rose and Lavender) *Mrs. Lloyd George* (Semi-double) ; (Purple) *Admiral Avellan* ; (Violet) *Prince of Wales.*

Virginian Stock (Malcomia).—Hardy annuals which thrive in sunny beds and in fairly light soil and which are useful for edgings. For culture, *see* Annuals, p. 106. *Varieties.*—(Crimson) *Fairy Queen* ; (Purple and Crimson) *Crimson King.* Both June to October, 6 inches.

Vitis (Vine).—Hardy deciduous climbers, including *Ampelopsis vitacea*, Virginian Creeper. They grow well in deeply-dug, moist soil with a little lime in it, and should be planted only in sheltered positions. *Culture.*—Strike cuttings in a frame in September. Plant in dry and open weather from November to March ; trim in winter. *Species.*— *V. Coignetiæ* is known as the Crimson Glory Vine ; other good species are *V. Thunbergii* and *V. vinifera purpurea*, the Teinturier Grape.

Wahlenbergia (Edraianthus, Tufted Harebell).—Dwarf-growing, hardy perennial rock plants, which like a sunny position and gritty loam, with a little lime-rubble. For culture, *see* Rock Plants, p. 135.

Species.—*W. gentianoides* (Blue, 10 in.) ; *W. pumilio* (Violet-blue, 2 in.) ; *W. serpyllifolia major* (Violet, 2–3 in.). All May to June.

Waitzia (Everlasting Flowers).—Half-hardy annuals, which can be grown in warm, sunny borders or in the greenhouse. For culture, *see* Annuals, p. 107. *W. aurea* (Golden-yellow, July–Sept., 20 in.) is best.

Wallflower (Cheiranthus).—Hardy biennials and perennials which may be grown in sunny, open beds or borders, in the rock garden or in the cold greenhouse, in dry, sandy loam with some lime in it. Double wallflowers, except German varieties, must be raised from cuttings. The perennial species are usually grown as biennials. For culture, *see* Biennials, p. 107. *Pot Culture.*—Pot-up in Sept., using 5 to 6-inch pots and ordinary soil, and keep in a cold frame until the buds appear. *Species and Varieties.*—*C. Allionii* (Bright Orange, 10 in.) ; *C. alpinus* (Pale Yellow, 6 in.) ; *C. kewensis* (Chestnut, 12 in.) ; *C. Marshallii* (Orange-yellow, 6 in.). All April to June. *Named Varieties.*—(C. Cheiri)—(Pale Yellow) *Primrose Dame* ; (Bright Yellow) *Cloth of Gold* ; (Golden) *Harpur Crewe* (Double) ; *Ivory White* ; *Orange Bedder* ; (Apricot) *Eastern Queen* ; *Blood Red* ; (Crimson) *Vulcan* ; (Brown) *Harbinger* ; *Purple Queen.*

Watsonia (Bugle Lily).—Half-hardy bulbous plants which should be grown in sunny positions in warm, sheltered borders and in sandy loam, peat, and leaf-mould, or in the cold greenhouse. *Culture.*—Plant in October or March, 3 inches deep and 4 inches apart. Pot plants should be kept dry in winter. Propagate by means of offsets in October. *Species.*—*W. coccinea* (Scarlet, 20 in.) ; *W. densiflora* (Pink, 15 in.). All June to August.

Wistaria.—Hardy May-flowering deciduous climbers that do well in any good garden soil, but prefer moist, deep and well-drained sandy loam. *W. chinensis (sinensis)*, of which there are three or four varieties, is the best known ; *W. multijuga* is a newer form with mauve, rose or white flowers, and longer racemes. *Culture.*—Propagate by means of layering young wood in the summer, and plant-out in permanent position in dry, open weather from October to April. Both winter and summer pruning are essential to promote flower buds, and straggling shoots should be cut away, but sturdy laterals should be encouraged to grow out some 3 feet from the main stems ; once the climbers are trained in this way, the young shoots should, in winter, be cut hard back to within a couple of inches of the old wood. *Pot Culture.*—In the cool greenhouse *W. sinensis* will flower from February to April ; pot-up in October, using 8 to 12-inch pots and a compost of rich, sandy loam. Prune in January or February, cutting back straggly shoots to within an inch of the base ; sink the pots to their rims in ashes outdoors in a sunny spot from May to December.

Wulfenia.—Hardy perennials which like a shady position in the rock garden in loam and peat. They carry purple-blue flowers in July and August on 9-inch stems. *See* Rock Plants, p. 135.

Xanthoceras sorbifolia.—Deciduous shrubs or small trees which need a sheltered position and a light, rich loam. They carry creamy flowers in April and grow about 12 feet high. Propagate by seed under glass.

Xeranthemum (Immortelles).—A showy class of everlasting flowers, all of which are hardy and thrive in sunny beds or borders and in rich soil. The best-known are : *X. annuum* (purple, rose, or white) and *X. inapertum*, (purple or white flowers) ; both grow 12 inches high and flower from July to September. For culture, *see* Annuals, p. 106.

Xerophyllum asphodeloides (Turkey's Beard).—Hardy perennials for the border, marsh, or wild garden. They love partial shade, and a moist gritty loam and leaf-mould. They carry spikes of white flowers 2 feet high in May. For culture, *see* Perennials, p. 128.

Yucca.—These are all practically hardy evergreen plants of quaint appearance, forming striking objects when planted on lawns, banks, or in the rock garden ; they are also useful for winter bedding. Yuccas do best in sheltered, sunny positions in well-drained ordinary soil. *Culture.*—Plant in March or April ; cut away dead leaves in March and dead flowers in October. *Pot Culture.*—Pot-up in a compost of two-thirds fibrous loam and one-sixth coarse sand, and one-sixth finely-crushed brick-rubble. Propagate by means of tops, with the leaves trimmed off, planted in pots of very sandy and porous soil, by rhizomes in spring, or by seed. *Varieties.*—*Y. recurvifolia*, one of the best species for the garden, carries greenish-white inflorescences in August and September ; *Y. gloriosa* is known as Adam's Needle, and *Y. angustifolia* is a hardy and more or less dwarf species.

Zauschneria (Californian Fuchsia).—Handsome perennials which thrive in gritty loam in the rock garden. For culture, *see* Rock Plants, p. 135. *Z. californica* (Scarlet, July–Sept., 12–18 in.) is the best-known.

Zea (Indian Corn or Maize).—Half-hardy annuals which thrive in ordinary soil in warm, sunny situations. For culture, *see* Annuals, p. 107. *Z. Mays* (3 ft.) is also useful for greenhouse purposes.

Zephyranthes (Zephyr Flower).—Bulbous-rooted plants, some species of which are sufficiently hardy to thrive in warm, sunny borders and in rich and well-drained peaty loam ; the more tender kinds should be grown in pots in the greenhouse. *Culture.*—Plant in October 4 inches deep and 3 inches apart with the bulbs resting in sand, and protect with fibre in winter. Lift when overcrowded, and propagate by means of offsets in October. *Pot Culture.*—Pot-up from August to November, placing four to five bulbs in a 5-inch pot in a compost of two parts of loam to one part each of leaf-mould and peat with a little silver sand. Dry-off gradually after flowering. *Species.*—*Z. candida* (White) ; *Z. carinata* (Pale Pink) ; *Z. rosea* (Rose) ; and *Z. texana* (Yellow). All May to September, 6 to 10 inches.

Zinnia.—Half-hardy annuals which thrive in light, rich soil. The dwarfer hybrid varieties are valuable for warm, sunny beds ; the taller kinds for borders and the cool greenhouse. For culture, *see* Annuals, p. 107. *Greenhouse Plants.*—Pot seedlings up singly in small pots in a compost of two-thirds fibrous loam and one-third dry, well-rotted manure and sand. Give ample light and ventilate freely, but do not let the temperature drop below 60° F., and avoid draughts. Re-pot before the plants get potbound, and as soon as the plants are re-established, reduce the temperature by about ten degrees and, as the buds appear, water weekly with weak manure-water and dress with bone-meal. *Species.*—*Z. elegans* (Various, 20–30 in.) ; *Z. Haageana* (Orange, 12 in.) ; *Z. pauciflora* (Red, 20 in.). All July to September.

ROSES

Photos]   [*R. H. Bath, Ltd. ; C. Jones.*

Polyantha Rose.   Moss Rose (*Pink*).
Single Rose " Dainty Bess."
Rose " Capt. F. Harvey Cant."   Rose " Rose Marie."

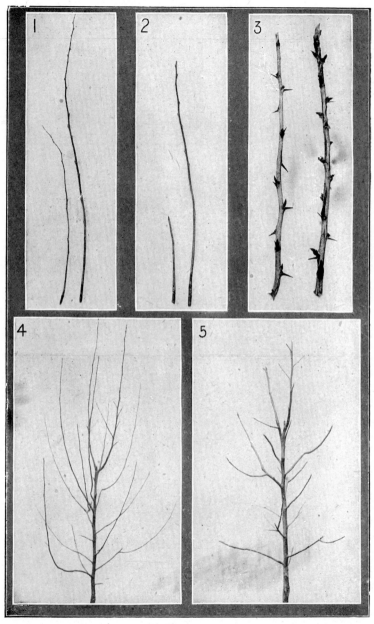

1. Strong and weak raspberry canes, before pruning.   2. The same, showing the weak cane cut back a foot from the ground and the strong with only the top removed.   3. Gooseberry shoots: on the left a one-year-old, and on the right a two-year-old.   4. Pyramid apple before pruning.   5. The same after pruning.

CHAPTER XXV

THE FRUIT GARDEN

Soil and Situation

DIFFERENT fruit-trees do best in soils and under conditions to some extent peculiar to each kind, their individual requirements are therefore noted in the paragraphs dealing with each kind of fruit. Much may be done to improve naturally unsuitable soils. (*See* p. 49.) On very chalky soil little success can be expected unless the chalk is taken out of the stations to a depth of 18 to 24 inches. Suitable soil must be substituted and renewed every few years.

Selection and Arrangement of the Trees

The grower with a walled kitchen garden can include in his selection of fruit-trees apricots, peaches and nectarines, which the orchard-grower would have difficulty in protecting adequately. In the mixed garden space is too valuable to allow of standard trees being planted. The bush and pyramid forms and the useful cordons and espaliers are here far preferable, as they can occupy spaces hardly larger than those required by, say, hardy perennials. Where standards are used in the mixed garden they are best planted upon any small lawn or grass-plot, where they will be seen to advantage.

THE BEST FORMS OF FRUIT TREES
Flat-Trained Trees

The Cordon.—An especially economical form is the cordon, where the fruit is borne on either side of one or two main stems, all branches but the main ones being rigorously suppressed. The cordon assumes three directions—the horizontal, the vertical or upright cordon, and the oblique cordon, which is mostly grown at an inclination of 45 degrees to the ground level. The cordon system of growing and training trees on supports is applicable to the apple in open ground ; and to pears, peaches, nectarines, apricots, gooseberries and currants, red or white, on walls or wires.

E.G.   321   X

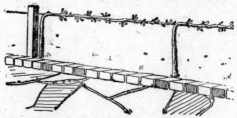

FIG. 30.—APPLES TRAINED AS HORIZONTAL CORDONS

The trees should be planted 4 to 5 feet apart and at least a foot from the path edging. The posts carrying the supporting wire, which should be about 18 inches above ground level, should be set 12 feet apart.

The Espalier.—In this form we have a central stem, from which branches extend horizontally sideways, giving the tree the form of a double ladder. Each of these branches is treated as a cordon and restrained to its one main stem, all side shoots being removed. There should be a space of about a foot between the tiers of branches. Where the espalier stands by itself a maximum height of five or six tiers is quite large enough, but where the tree is grown against a wall its size is practically only limited by the available space. Practically any fruit—especially apples and pears—that can successfully be trained as a cordon or bush may also be grown as an espalier. This system does not suit apricots, cherries, plums, nectarines or peaches. Espaliers should be planted 15 feet apart.

The Fan.—As its name implies, the fan is shaped with radiating branches like a fan, and, like the espalier, may stand away from or against a wall. Where it has support from a wall it may be much larger than where it has merely artificial trellises. The fan shape is excellently suited to plums, apricots, peaches, Morello cherries, and nectarines, the Morello cherry particularly enjoying a north wall. Fan-trained trees should be planted 15 feet apart.

Round-Shaped Trees

Of these, for a small garden, the bush form is generally considered the best. Standards are most suitable for orchards.

Bush and Pyramid Trees.—The bush tree and the pyramid are formed in much the same way, except for the fact that the pyramid has a central stem, running as straight as possible up the middle of the tree, from which the side shoots spring, while the bush tree has no central stem but branches from the side shoots, the middle being kept clear. The bush and pyramid forms are suitable to apples, pears, plums, and cherries. They should be planted 8 feet apart.

The Standard.—This form is a good one for apples, pears, plums and cherries. It is not, in our climate, so suitable for those fruits—peach, apricot, nectarine, and so on—which require more heat properly to ripen them.

Half-Standards are similar in form to standards, except that the main stem up to the first branch, is only 4½ feet high instead of the

6 feet in the standard. Large heads are formed, which produce a highly profitable crop.

Selecting the Varieties

The grower should make careful inquiries as to varieties and the types of trees—espaliers, standards or bushes, etc.—that thrive best in the locality and should also note the stocks that have been found most reliable and successful. A great failing is to have too many mid-season varieties ; early and late varieties should also be selected to extend the fruiting season as much as possible.

Many of the best varieties of apples, cherries, pears, plums are self-sterile, that is to say, they cannot fertilize their flowers with their own pollen, but require the pollen from another variety of the same kind of tree to enable them to set their fruit.   In selecting fruit trees for a garden or orchard, it is, therefore, necessary to have more than one variety of each particular kind of fruit. The different varieties must, however, be those that come into flower at approximately the same time. There are a few self-fertile varieties which can more or less effectively fertilize their own blooms and set a fair crop of fruit, but if good and regular crops are required, it is obvious that great care is needed in the selection of fruit trees. These self-fertile trees are marked with an asterisk in the tables showing the best varieties of fruit.

Planting Fruit Trees

Time to Plant.—The time for planting fruit trees is between early November and March, but the best of all is November. Planting should, if possible, cease before mid-December, to be continued if necessary, late in February when the worst of the frosts are over. In very heavy soils spring

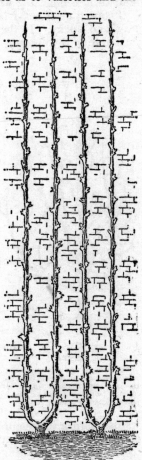

FIG. 31.—PEARS TRAINED AS DOUBLE VERTICAL COR-DONS

Although the *oblique* is the most convenient of all cordon forms, the double vertical cordon may be employed to suit the requirements of space or situation.

planting has certain advantages over autumn planting, but in the ordinary way, November planting is preferable. When trees are planted in spring, especially on light soils, it is absolutely necessary to keep the ground continuously moist by frequent watering and surface mulching with manure.

Planting must never be done during frost, or when the ground is wet and sticky. If the latter condition prevails when the trees arrive from the nursery, they must be " laid in " by the roots in a sheltered position, that is to say, they must have their roots well covered up with soil until the weather is suitable for planting. In frosty weather the trees cannot be "laid or heeled in"; they should be kept in a frost-proof shed with the roots covered with several thicknesses of sacking or paper.

Age of Trees for Planting.—Standards are best planted when three to four years old; half-standards as "two-year-old feathered trees," that is, " maidens " not pruned during the winter after their formation ; bushes and cordons as " maidens ", that is, trees that have made a year's growth after budding or grafting. Espaliers and fan-shaped fruit trees should be from three to four years old, while bush fruit, such as currants and gooseberries, should have made two years' growth after being struck as cuttings.

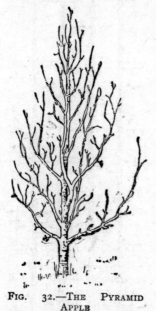

FIG. 32.—THE PYRAMID APPLE

The pyramid has a central stem, running straight up the middle of the tree, and from which the side shoots spring. This form is used for apples, pears, plums and cherries.

Pruning the Roots.—Prune the roots by taking off all the very small fibres and shortening the larger roots to about 6 inches from the stem. Bruised or broken roots should be removed entirely by a clean, sharp cut outwards and upwards. Two or three spurs are sufficient, but if there are more good ones they may remain after being carefully pruned. Should the roots be dry, soak them well in water until the bark has again become plump, then plant immediately. One great point in planting fruit trees is to keep the roots of the plants as little exposed as possible. A dry wind or a cutting, frosty air is fatal to them.

Planting.—The position is prepared by digging out a hole about 3 feet in diameter, and 2 feet in depth, in ground that has been well drained. In the bottom of this pit lay 10 or 12 inches of brick or lime rubbish, the roughest material at the bottom, and ram it pretty firmly so as to be impervious to the tap-root. The remainder of the pit should be filled in with earth suitable to the requirements of the tree. The tree should be placed upright in the centre of the hole and the lowest roots should be laid out horizontally. Fine earth should then be loosely thrown over them, and carefully pressed firmly over them. The next layer of roots should be treated in a like manner and so on until the whole of the roots are covered.

FIG. 33.—AN APPLE TRAINED AS OBLIQUE CORDON

Oblique cordons are usually grown at an inclination of 45 degrees to the ground level; all branches save the main stem must be suppressed. Plant 2 feet apart.

It is most important that the rootlets should, as far as possible, assume their natural position, thoroughly penetrating and permeating the surrounding soil. It is also most important to make the soil firm at each stage of the planting in order to minimize the depth to which the tree will sink. Firm planting is necessary in any soil and in light land it may be necessary to use a rammer.

Trees on strong-growing stocks should be planted to about the same depth as in the nursery garden; this depth can be seen from the marks on the stem. Fruit on dwarfing stocks, however, should be planted so that the union of stock and scion is just below the soil. It is rarely necessary to have more than 4 inches of soil over the upper roots; deep planting is the bane of fruit trees.

FIG. 34.—AN ESPALIER-TRAINED PEAR

Each horizontal branch is treated as a cordon, all side shoots being removed. There should be a space of 12 to 18 inches between the tiers of branches. Plant 15 feet apart.

Staking and Tying

The young tree should be supported with a strong stake reaching to the lowest branch but not higher, driven firmly into the ground, before the earth is filled in round the roots, and the stem tied to it with soft cord, after surrounding the stem with hay or straw or even a wrapping of old felt, so that the string will not cut into the bark. This cord should be renewed annually so that it may not eat into the bark as the tree swells. The stake should be rounded so as not to chafe the tree, should be pointed at the bottom, and have the lower 2 feet treated with creosote or tar. After the stake has been driven into the ground the burred-over top, caused by the mallet, must be trimmed up so as not to damage the bark of the tree. Water well after planting if the weather is dry, and apply a mulch of stable manure to protect the roots. (*See* p. 68.)

Manuring Fruit Trees

Trees, whether young or old, should only be manured when they are actually bearing a crop of fruit. It is no easy matter for the amateur to tell when the trees need generous or scanty treatment in the matter of manure, but the growth of the wood may be taken as a guide; if the wood has made an extension of 15 to 20 inches, it may safely be inferred that no manure should be given; should the trees have only made up to 5 inches of extension growth then they require liberal treatment; while anything between these growths indicates that manure should be given only in moderation.

Artificial Manures.—All fruit trees will thrive the better for the occasional application of wood ashes, a small amount of lime, and a good dressing of soot to the surface soil. Of the artificial manures proper, nitrate of soda, sulphate of ammonia, superphosphates, basic slag, and kainit are those most used. It must be remembered that potash and phosphates check growth and encourage excessive fruit production, all the more so when pruning is not severe. On the other hand, nitrogenous manures, especially when accompanied with severe pruning, produce much woody growth and tend to decrease the yield of fruit. (*See Table*, Manuring Fruit Trees, p. 327.)

Liquid Manure.—About the end of May liquid manure can with advantage be applied to all fruit trees. It should never be given too strong; the liquid manure from the farm yard should be diluted until it is pale amber in colour, and is best applied after rain or after the soil has been moistened a couple of hours beforehand. Liquid manure may be given more liberally on light, dry soils, than on cold, damp, heavy ground.

Farmyard manure contains nitrogen, phosphates and potash— the three essential plant foods—but to secure a large crop of fruit the trees should be given a little additional stimulant in the way of artificial manure. Farmyard manure is invariably spread during the winter; artificial manures are usually employed after pruning, when the fruit is set or in the spring, according to the special characteristics of the fertilizer selected.

The following table gives the quantities of the various manures for different fruits. (*See also chapter* Manures and Manuring, p. 60.)

TABLE OF FRUIT MANURING.
(Area ¼ acre)

NOTE.—3 qrs. per ¼ Acre is equal to 2 lb. to the Square Rod, or 1 oz. per Square Yard. The artificial manures are given in addition to the farmyard manure, which is applied in winter.

Fruit.	Farmyard Manure.	Artificial Manure.	When to Apply the Artificial Manures.
Apple . .	5 tons	Superphosphate, ¾ cwt. and	After pruning.
		Nitrate of Soda, ¼ cwt.	When fruit is set.
Apricot .	Mulch annually in May	1 lb. Bone Meal ⎱ per tree 5 oz. Nitrate of ⎰ Soda	Winter. When fruit is set.
Cherry . .	5 tons	Sulphate of Potash, ⅓ cwt. and	Winter.
		Sulphate of Lime, 1½ cwt. and	Winter.
		Nitrate of Soda, ⅓ cwt.	When fruit is set.
Cucumber .	4 cart-loads for a two-light frame in March	2 oz. Dried Fish Guano per sq. yd. *or* 1 oz. Sulphate of Ammonia per sq. yd.	Summer. Spring.
Currant and Gooseberry	5 tons	Sulphate of Ammonia, ¾ cwt., and Basic Slag, 3 cwt.	May. Autumn (triennially).
Damson (*see* Plum).			
Fig . . .	Mulch annually in May	Not required	—
Gooseberry (*see* Currant).			
Grape . .	A slight top-dressing	Apply Liquid Manure weekly from time the fruit sets until ripe	
Loganberry (*see* Raspberry).			
Medlar . .	5 tons	Superphosphate, ¾ cwt. and	After pruning.
		Nitrate of Soda, ¼ cwt.	When fruit is set.
Melon . .	Six loads for a three-light frame when bed made up	Tepid liquid manure	At weekly intervals from the time the fruits begin to swell until ripe.
Nectarine (*see* Peach).			
Nut . .	Not advised		
Peach . .	Mulch annually in May	1 lb. Bone Meal ⎱ and ⎰ per tree 5 oz. Nitrate of ⎰ Soda	Winter. When fruit is set.

Fruit.	Farmyard Manure.	Artificial Manure.	When to Apply the Artificial Manures.
Pear . .	5 tons	4 oz. Basic Slag and 1 oz. Kainit per sq. yd. of area covered by roots and	Autumn.
		2 oz. Superphosphate and 1 oz. Sulphate of Ammonia per sq. yd. of area covered by roots	Early spring.
Plum and Damson	5 tons	Bone Meal, 3 qrs. and Nitrate of Soda, 2 qrs.	After pruning.
Quince (see	Pear).		Spring.
Raspberry .	5 tons (decayed)	½ cwt. Nitrate of Soda, ½ cwt. Superphosphate, 1 cwt. Common Salt, ⅓ cwt. Kainit	Half in March, half in June.
Strawberry	5 tons	Nitrate of Soda, ¾ cwt.	May.
Tomato .	In Pots : ⅓ part of the compost (well decayed) In Beds : None	A pinch of Nitrate of Potash	At intervals through the growing season.

Propagation

For the propagation of fruit trees by means of Budding and Grafting, *see* Chapter XXIII.

PRUNING

The Objects of Pruning

There are three main objects at which we aim in pruning a tree. The first is to promote healthy growth of wood, and this is the chief aim of the grower in pruning his young trees. The second, and one almost equally important in the early life of the tree, is to give the form desired, a point of great moment in the future of the tree as regards fruit or flower. These two ends are attained by the same means : first, the tree is shaped in such a way that when fully grown it may be well balanced and well proportioned according to its natural habit ; secondly, the branches are so thinned as to allow of perfectly free circulation of air and light throughout the tree, thus promoting the ripening of the wood and keeping it healthy ; and thirdly, the tree is helped to produce good vigorous shoots and thus to come to maturity as soon as possible, by means of judicious cutting back of weak shoots and shortening of strong ones. The third main object is the increase of fruitfulness which of course means increase of flowers in plants grown for their blossoms.

The Pruner's Instruments

Clean cutting is the first thing to aim at in pruning. Two pruning knives will be required : one, very strong, for winter-pruning, where the wood to be removed is all hard and well-ripened ; and another lighter and with a thinner blade, for the removal of young green shoots in summer-pruning, where the passage of a thick blade might bruise the young wood unnecessarily. The secateurs are used for certain operations, and for the amateur are useful, as they do away with the possibility of injury to other shoots by the slipping of the blade. Instead of a clean cut, the secateurs are apt, however, to pinch and flatten the wood. This damaged end frequently withers, and if the cut has been made in the position which in pruning with the knife would be the correct one, the injury affects the bud, which is thus destroyed, and the pruning must recommence lower down. To obviate this difficulty, when pruning with secateurs, a piece of wood about half an inch long must be left above the bud. This wood will subsequently dry up and wither, and must be removed the following year. The only other instrument needed is a small hand saw for the removal of branches too large for the knife. All these instruments must be kept very sharp, or they will bruise the wood and leave unhealthy wounds. If it is necessary to cut away a branch altogether, no portion of it should be left on the main stem, as this stump would decay and encourage fungi and pests. The cut should be as nearly perpendicular as possible, smooth, and slightly bevelled, thus presenting the smallest possible extent of wounded surface. To avoid tearing the bark, should the branch fall before it is completely severed, it is wise to make a small cut on the underside of the branch before the main cut from above is commenced. Where the cut surface is very large it should be covered with the composition known as " grafting " mastic.

Method of Pruning

Making the Cut.—The way in which the cut is made is most vital. It should be as nearly as may be straight, and should not leave a surface slanting upwards from below the bud, with its lower edge below the spring of the bud and its upper on a level with it. This weakens the bud, which does not receive its full nourishment, and it results either in the shoot budding strongly from an undesirable bud lower down, or in the bursting of a new strong bud just below the one chosen, necessitating the re-pruning of the shoot down to that level. On the other hand, the cut should not be made too far above the chosen bud, or the wood left will wither up, and have to be removed the following year. The perfect cut begins on the side of the shoot opposite to the selected bud, and slants ever so slightly upwards across the shoot till it ends immediately above the tip of the bud. It should be clean and unbruised. Always prune back to a wood-bud, not a fruit bud, and see that the bud faces in the right direction, that is, usually outwards.

The first thing to be done before undertaking the operation of pruning is to study the trees to be dealt with, and make up your mind clearly as to what effect you wish to produce. Where you are dealing with young trees it is certainly not a good plan to prune for fruit, the trees are as yet weak and not firmly established, and their vigour should be devoted to the formation of good healthy, well-ripened wood, a well-shaped head, and healthy roots.

Fruit-Bud or Leaf-Bud ?—When pruning, it is an essential but easy matter to differentiate between fruit-buds and leaf-buds; the latter are thin and pointed and usually spring from the end of a spur, while the fruit buds are globular and have a plump appear-

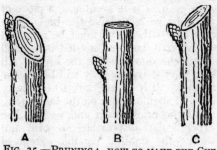

A   B   C

FIG. 35.—PRUNING : HOW TO MAKE THE CUT

The perfect cut (*A*) begins on the side of the shoot opposite the selected bud, slants slightly upwards, and ends just above the tip of the bud. In *B* (incorrect), the cut is made too far above the bud; if cut as in *C* (incorrect), the bud will be weakened.

ance and generally sprout from the old wood and from near the base of the young shoot. In summer the fruit buds are surrounded by a cluster of leaves. Several of these fruit-buds will be found in the fruit-spur, a short shoot springing naturally from the old wood and usually terminating in a leaf-bud. Fruit spurs may be formed artificially by summer-pruning. (*See* p. 331.)

Thinning Fruit Spurs.—After a few years the fruit spurs are likely to have grown too big and may need thinning, or the fruit will gradually decrease in size. This thinning is accomplished in two stages as shown in Fig. 37. In the first year, the spur is pruned back to A, A, which will encourage new growth nearer the base. The next year the spur is cut back to B and will, in consequence, have greatly improved fruiting capacity.

When to Prune.—All pruning of young trees should be done before the buds have burst, but when they are well swelled and plump. When this state is reached—that is to say, the end of February or the very beginning of March in ordinary years—the pruner can select the best bud and cut back to that without fear that the bud will dry up or become blind. Where young trees are concerned any summer-pruning beyond that absolutely necessary to keep them in shape should be barred. Where the new growth shows some defect in shape, such as a bad side shoot or a very lopsided branch, it may be removed in summer, but the less done in this way the better. Only very hardy and well-established trees should be pruned actually during winter, as fresh wounds render the trees much more apt to be affected by frost, and a tender tree may be easily killed in this way.

Summer-Pruning

The operation consists in going over the trees on two or three occasions in summer, and pinching off with the finger and thumb nail, a few at a time, the soft ends of the side shoots to about three leaves. This, if done too early, will result in fresh sub-lateral shoots being formed from the upper buds, which must again be pinched back to one leaf, making four in all. Leading shoots should never be summer-pruned. The result of this pinching is the concentration of the sap in the young leading shoot and the gradual change of the leaf buds upon the remainder of the side

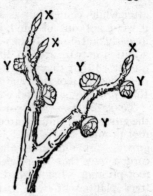

FIG. 36. — DISTINGUISHING BETWEEN FRUIT AND LEAF-BUDS

Leaf-buds are thin and pointed, and usually spring from the end of a spur ; fruit-buds are globular and generally sprout from the old wood and from near the base of the young shoot.

shoots into fruit buds. The best time to summer-prune varies with the variety of tree, soil and climate. Fruit on light soil can usually be pruned in July ; trees on heavier land a month later. Prune early enough to prevent shoots from making excessive growth, but not so early that a mass of sub-laterals are formed. Black currants, raspberries, Morello cherries, nectarines and peaches must not be summer-pruned, as the fruit forms along the whole length of the previous year's growth. The above remarks refer to all forms of fruit trees except the standard, this latter it is inadvisable to summer-prune.

Root-Pruning

Root pruning should not be needed where the trees have been grown on proper stocks and have been well looked

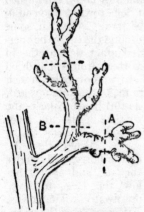

FIG. 37.—THINNING FRUIT-SPURS

Thinning is accomplished in two stages ; in the first year the spur is cut back to A,A ; this will encourage new growth near the base. The next year the spur is cut back to B.

after while young, but as a remedial measure where trees have, as it were, got out of hand, it has great uses and is best carried out in early autumn. It has much the effect of top-pruning, but in addition may be used to direct the roots towards the surface of the ground so that they may lie in the upper layers of soil, these being the fullest of moisture and nourishment as well as the best aerated. Root-pruning of old and young trees differs in method.

Young Trees.—Young trees should be completely lifted out of the ground and transplanted. This process will in itself be sufficient root-pruning and should be done to those trees whose summer growths are numerous and fruit buds few. Bush, espalier and cordon trees that are pruned in hard, are those most likely to need root-pruning. Established standards but rarely need it. Young trees planted in deep, rich soil may also require root-pruning. Trees with short healthy growth and plenty of fruit spurs are best left alone; they do not need root-pruning. Never root-prune unless it is quite obvious that the operation is a necessity. A sharp spade should be used in lifting the young tree, so that the rootlets may be cut cleanly and not broken and bruised, and all cut ends should be trimmed with the knife before replanting. Try the soil about 3 feet from the tree, and thence in towards the trunk until fibres are found. Then dig down below the tree and lift it out bodily. Tap roots which are striking straight downwards may be removed before the tree is replaced.

Large and Established Trees.—Root-pruning of large, established trees is a more difficult matter, and is best done towards the end of the season, when the leaves are still on the trees. A trench, some 3 feet wide and 2 to 3 three feet deep, is dug round the tree to be operated upon; the fibre roots should be preserved intact, tied together in bundles, and covered with sacking to keep them from being dried up by the sun or exposure to the air. All strong roots over an inch in diameter are cut off, care being taken to make the cuts upward, as this helps to keep the rootlets in the top layer of soil. A very sharp spade should then be driven horizontally under the tree, and $1\frac{1}{2}$ feet below the base, to sever downward-striking roots. This completes the work, and the trench should then be filled up with good loam, mixed, if possible, with some spent

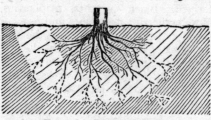

Fig. 38.—Root-pruning

The lightly-shaded section shows the position of the trench to be dug round the tree, and where a sharp spade should be driven horizontally $1\frac{1}{2}$ feet below the base of the tree to sever the downward-striking roots, shown by the dotted lines.

manure—some that has been
used in a hotbed is best, as it
will not be too strong. If it is
found that the fibrous roots are
not very numerous it will be
advisable only to root-prune
one side of the tree at a time,
the other side being operated
upon in the same manner the
following autumn. Should the
tree be of considerable size

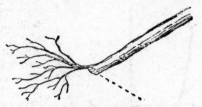

FIG. 39.—ROOT-PRUNING

In root-pruning, always make the cuts upwards,
as this keeps the rootlets in the top layer of soil.

the branches must be reduced, and side shoots should be cut-in
before root-pruning is attempted. A pretty safe guide as to the
position of the trench for root-pruning is the old saying that the
roots of a tree spread as far as its branches.

Pruning Newly-Planted Trees

Speaking broadly, a young and vigorous tree should have its
branches shortened to one-third of their length. Where the planting
is done fairly late in the season the necessary pruning may be done
at once, where it is early the operation may well be deferred for a
week or two, that the buds may be past the danger of drying up,
and the best ones may be more easily selected. Thin out all the
feeble shoots, so selecting them that the head when finished may be
balanced and evenly filled. The remaining one-year shoots should
then be cut back to a good bud, care being taken to see that it is so
placed on the stem, inwards or outwards, that the shoot produced
from it may occupy a suitable position in the general " design " of
the tree. The final shapeliness of the full-grown tree depends much
on this first selection of shoots, and for the first year, at least, more
thought must be given to the future shape of the tree than to the
immediate production of fruit.

Much also depends on the judgment of the pruner in the matter
of the amount to be cut from the young tree. The leaves and roots
are interdependent ; if the leaves are too few the root growth will
be feeble : if they are too many the roots will be unable to feed them
properly. The amount varies with the kind of tree. The peach
readily reproduces new shoots, so that it may be cut back freely
with safety, from two-thirds to nine-tenths of the last season's
shoot being removed to the advantage to the plant. The grape,
too, is a vigorous grower, and may be heavily cut back, while the
cherry, on the contrary, is very sensitive, and young trees have been
severely injured and even killed by too hard a summer-pruning.
Shoots of the cherry should not be cut back in the spring more than
half their length at the most. The pear and the apple are between

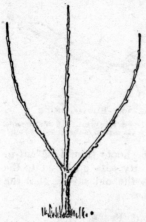

FIG. 40.—YOUNG TREE TO BE
TRAINED AS AN ESPALIER

It is in this state that the young
trees are usually received from the
nursery.

the two, and must be moderately pruned, without excess, but should usually be cut back by quite a half. The amount of cutting to be done varies also with the size of the fruit, and with other special conditions. For example, plum trees may be left fuller of wood than may apples, as the latter fruit is very much heavier, and the strain of a large crop much greater than in the case of the smaller plum. Again, the apple, to reach perfection, needs sunshine while on the tree ; therefore the shoots must be so thinned that the sunshine may penetrate as freely as possible, while the pear, whose fruit may be, and usually is, ripened after removal from the tree, may carry its shoots more closely packed.

Black currants, newly planted, should be cut hard back to two buds from the base ; this applies to all the shoots. Red and white currants and gooseberries should have all the weak shoots cut back to within two buds of the base, but all strong growths should be shortened back by about one-half only.

Pruning Established Trees

As a rough rule, the rapid formation of leaves and wood is adverse to the production of fruit. Obviously the tree has only a certain amount of energy and nourishment, and if this is all, or nearly all, expended on the formation of leaves there will be little left over for the fruit. On the other hand, a certain amount of leaf growth is necessary for the proper nourishment of the fruit and the tree itself. On the whole, the slow growth of wood favours the production of fruit and blossom, and should be the end to be aimed at. Where trees have been summer - pruned, winter-pruning will consist in little more than cutting back laterals to

FIG. 41.—PRUNING THE ESPALIER : FIRST
YEAR

The side branches are trained horizontally, and pruned to two-thirds of their length, with a bud immediately below the cut. The stem is pruned to 12 to 18 inches above the side branches, leaving three buds immediately below the cut —one on each side, well placed, and a third in front to continue the stem,

within two or three buds
of their base and in shortening the main shoots
back to a good leaf-bud.
*Standards, Bush Fruits
and Pyramids.* — With
standard, bush and pyra-
mid trees, it is merely
necessary to keep the
trees in shape, usually
cutting back to an out-
ward-facing bud so that
the resulting shoot may
grow out from the centre
of the tree, to admit of
plenty of air space.
Crossing branches must,
of course, be cut out.

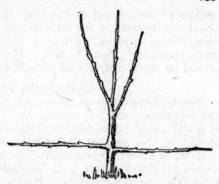

FIG. 42.—THE ESPALIER IN ITS SECOND YEAR

By the autumn of the second year the tree should have attained this form ; a central stem and two extra untrained side shoots.

Cordons, Espaliers, etc.—The "leaders" of cordons, espaliers,
and fan-shaped trees should be allowed to grow until they have
reached the desired length. All laterals should have been pinched
back in summer (*see* Summer-pruning), and must again be winter-
pruned to one or two buds. In trees trained up against a wall any
shoots growing out to the front must be cut right out. For detailed
instructions for pruning the different kinds of fruit trees, *see* under
the various headings, e.g.—*Apple, pear, cherry, etc.*, in the following
pages.

Thinning-Out the Fruit

This is a most important matter, firstly, because if too much fruit
is left on a tree all will be small, and secondly, because over-cropping
weakens the trees. A heavy crop ripened one year almost certainly
means but little fruit the
following. E s p e c i a l l y
necessary is it for young
trees to be heavily
thinned. Sturdy bushes
or cordons may bear just
a few fruit in their third
year—say one fruit to
each spur. With older
trees only just as much
fruit as the tree can
m a t u r e satisfactorily
should be left on the
branches ; the larger the

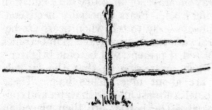

FIG. 43.—PRUNING THE ESPALIER : SECOND
YEAR

The new side shoots are trained horizontally and are pruned to two-thirds of their length, and the main stem to from 12 to 18 inches above them as before, having three well-placed buds to form the next tier. The first (lower) pair of laterals are pruned to two-thirds of the year's growth.

probable eventual size of the fruit, the smaller the number that should be allowed to remain, and the more vigorous the tree the more it may be permitted to bear. In thinning, all misshaped and badly placed fruit should be removed, and the operation of thinning should be performed, not all at once, but in two or three stages.

GATHERING FRUIT

Ripe fruit always leaves the tree upon a gentle touch, that is to say, the fruit-stalk parts easily from the twig on which it grows if the fruit is gently raised to the horizontal position. Fallen or bruised fruit should never be mixed with that which is to be stored.

When to Gather.—Fruit which ripens in summer and autumn should be gathered just a shade before it is ripe. A single day before they are perfectly ripe suffices for peaches and other delicate stone fruit; a week for apples and pears; but cherries are only gathered when completely ripe. Those apples and pears, which arrive at maturity in winter, are best gathered at the moment when the leaves begin to fall. Of cooking apples, only a few should be picked before they are actually ripe, and this should be done in the process of thinning-out the fruit. Fruit that has been damaged by insects and fungus will drop a considerable time before the other fruit, and this must not be taken as an indication that the sound fruit is ripe.

Weather for Gathering.—All gathering should take place in dry weather, and the late morning and afternoon will usually be found the best time, as all the fruit should be quite dry.

STORING FRUIT

Apples and Pears.—These must be kept in an even temperature of about 45° F., and looked over periodically once a fortnight, so that any decaying ones may be removed. They should first be sweated, i.e., laid in heaps and left to heat for ten days or a fortnight, and then be stored away on trays, or in a dry dark cellar in heaps, uncovered except during frost. Pears especially need constant inspection. It is not always easy to tell when pears are beginning to ripen. With several varieties, however, the skin becomes a golden yellow or the tinge of red, if present, will become brighter.

Grapes.—Cut the grapes when quite ripe so that the laterals removed with the bunches are about nine inches long. These should be inserted into wine bottles almost filled with water and containing a few lumps of charcoal. The bottles are then placed in racks or secured to the wall at an angle of 40 degrees, so that the grapes will hang naturally. The room in which they are stored must be kept cool and dark, but well aired. Bunches so kept will last almost into the new year.

1. Pyramid Plum before pruning.   2. The same after pruning.   See page 353.
3. Pyramid pear before pruning.   4. The same after pruning.   See page 351.

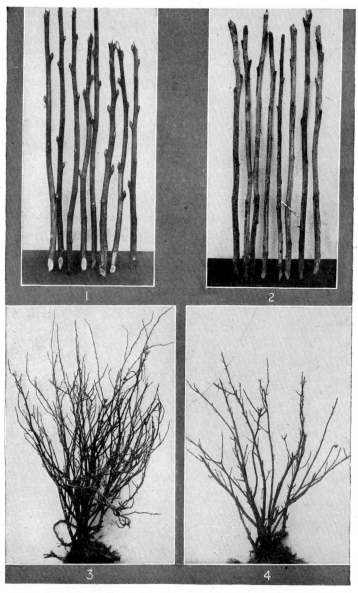

1. Black currant cuttings prepared for planting. 2. Red currant cuttings prepared for planting, showing the lower eyes removed from stem ; currant cuttings should be from 9 to 12 inches in length and are struck in the open in October. 3. An old black currant bush before pruning. 4. The same after pruning. See page 342.

CHAPTER XXVI

INDIVIDUAL FRUIT CULTURE

THE APPLE

SOIL and Situation.—The apple does well in any well-drained, moderate loam, providing the situation is not too low-lying, too exposed, or, on the other hand, too much shaded from the sun.

Forms of Trees.—In planting apples in an orchard on grass land what is known as the standard form (*see* p. 322), is undoubtedly the one to be selected. For most purposes, however, **the** bush or the pyramid (*see* p. 322) form of apple-tree is well suited. Apples are also sometimes grown as cordons or espaliers, trained against a trellis or wire fence. Apples are propagated by budding in July, or by grafting in March or April, on Paradise or Crab stocks.

Planting.—Standard trees should be allowed a space of 20 to 25 feet in all directions from tree to tree. Bush trees should be planted 8 feet apart. The process of planting fruit trees is described in detail on p. 323.

Winter-Pruning. Newly Planted Trees.—For general instructions for pruning newly planted trees the reader is referred to the section on *Pruning*. In the case of the apple, newly planted standards, bushes or pyramids, should have their main shoots cut back to about one-third of their length. Trees trained fan-wise and as cordons must be shortened by about a quarter.

In espaliers the "leader" must be shortened to 12 to 18 inches above the top pair of side-branches, which must be cut back by a half; any lower pairs of side-stems need only be slightly shortened, unless they have grown very rank. Laterals, on the main shoots, in all cases must be cut back to within two or three buds of their base. The pruning should be done in March.

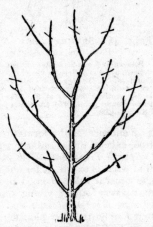

FIG. 44.—PRUNING **THE** ESTABLISHED BUSH APPLE

The main branches should be cut back by one-third of the growth made in the previous year and all laterals to two buds; prune preferably in December and January.

E.G.

Y

FIG. 45.—SUMMER AND WINTER PRUNING THE APPLE

Between July and September laterals should be stopped, a few at a time, to five or six leaves, as shown at *S*. Between November and March, prune main branches by one-third, and all laterals to two or three buds as at *W*. Standards are never summer-pruned and are winter-pruned as little as possible.

Winter - Pruning Established Trees.—Winter-pruning can be done any time between November and March, but is best done in December and January. Standards should be pruned as little as possible, only sufficient to keep them in shape and form ; dead and diseased wood and all sucker growth must, of course, be cut out. Bushes and pyramids will do best when their main branches are cut back by one-third, while trees trained on walls, espaliers and cordons, require only slight shortening until they have covered the desired space. In all forms, except the standard, laterals should be cut back annually to two or three buds. Short twigs 3 to 4 inches in length need not be pruned back as they will probably carry fruit ; when they have borne fruit they may be cut back to two buds like the more vigorous laterals.

Summer - Pruning is carried out in July and August, and again in September, the laterals or side-shoots being pinched back, a few at a time, to five or half-a-dozen leaves. Fresh shoots that develop after the "pinching back" are again stopped to two or three leaves. This encourages the formation of fruit buds and applies to all forms of tree, except the standard, which is not summer-pruned.

Special Treatment.—The varieties differ so much in habits of growth that what is excellent for one may be bad for another, within, however, the general rules of good pruning. Thus, some of the kinds usually make very strong young growth, and for these, of which *Blenheim Orange, Newton Wonder* and *Bramley's Seedling* are typical, after the first four years after planting severe pruning is not advised, as it leads them to form a mass of strong young shoots, which take all the tree's vigour. These varieties should be lifted at two years old and be replanted, to check their over-vigorous root action. When young they are best checked for their first season by tipping the shoots and removing any flowers before the fruit is formed.

The opposite tendency to this is shown by another class, of which

Bismarck, Grenadier and *Stirling Castle* are types. This kind has a tendency to spend all its early strength on the production of fruit, leaving insufficient nourishment for the formation of healthy young wood. The result is early crops of small fruit, and a dwarfed and stunted tree. The remedy for this is the removal of all fruit the first season, and the limiting of the crop to a small one in the second.

A few apples—for example, *Lady Sudeley, Mr. Gladstone,* and *Irish Peach*—bear fruit on the ends of the young wood. In such cases the tree should be pruned with a view to encouraging healthy side shoots, as by cutting these back in the autumn to six leaves and in the spring to two or three buds, good healthy young wood may be secured all over the tree. With such varieties, therefore, summer-pruning will consist in topping crowded shoots in the centre of the fruit tree, also any lateral shoots that it is necessary to shorten to keep the tree in shape. All other shoots should be allowed to grow.

Thinning.—Each cluster should be thinned to two or three fruits, those at the centre usually being retained. Varieties bearing large fruit must be more severely thinned than this, one or two apples to each spur being sufficient. (*See also* Thinning, p. 335.)

Gathering the Fruit.—Different varieties of apples ripen in different months, and early varieties should, of course, be picked when they are ripe. Most of the later kinds, however, have to be gathered before they are strictly ripe in order to be stored before the frosts. October is the great month of the apple harvest. (*See* Storing Fruit, p. 336.)

Varieties.—By careful selection a supply of apples may be had almost the year through, at any rate from July to May. For those who are handicapped by a heavy soil the following list may prove useful, all the varieties being comparatively able to withstand this unfavourable condition : *Bramley's Seedling, Lord Grosvenor, Wellington* and *Worcester Pearmain.* (*See also* Manuring, p. 326 ; Mulching, p. 68 ; and Root-Pruning, p. 331.)

SOME OF THE BEST APPLES

Dessert

Name.	Season.	Name.	Season.
(S) Allington Pippin . .	Oct.–Dec.	(I)* James Grieve . . .	Sept.–Oct.
(S) Blenheim Orange. .	Nov.–Jan.	(I) Lady Sudeley . . .	Aug.–Sept.
(I)* Charles Ross . .	Oct.–Nov.	(S)* Ribston Pippin . .	Nov.–Jan.
(S) Cox's Orange Pippin .	Nov.–Jan.	(S) Sturmer Pippin . .	March–May

Cooking

Name.	Season.	Name.	Season.
(S) Bramley's Seedling .	Oct.–Mar.	(S)* Newton Wonder . .	Oct.–Mar.
(I) Grenadier . . .	Aug.–Sept.	(S) Norfolk Beefing	March–May
(S) Lord Derby . . .	Oct.–Nov.	(I)* Stirling Castle .	Sept.–Oct.

(S) = Storing.   (I) = Immediate Use.   * = Self-fertile Varieties.
Allington Pippin, Bramley's Seedling, Cox's Orange Pippin, Lady Sudeley, Lord Derby, Newton Wonder, Stirling Castle, and Sturmer Pippin make an excellent combination for cross-pollination.

Fig. 46.—Pruning the Apricot

Summer-prune all side shoots to four leaves, as at *S*. When the leaves fall, stop all leading shoots and prune all shoots not needed to fill spaces, to two or three buds as at *W*.

APRICOT

Soil and Situation.—The apricot is most suited to cultivation on a south wall or under glass, thrives in a good well-drained calcareous loam, and is best planted in October. Water liberally in dry weather; a mulch of well-rotted manure early in June is very helpful. Netting of about ½-inch mesh which hangs in front of the trees, is the best method of protection from frost. Care must be taken that the wind cannot blow the netting against the flowers. Thin, partially, all fruit where it is thickly set, but reserve the final thinning, to 5 inches between fruits, until the fruit has stoned.

Pruning.—The apricot flourishes best trained as a fan with its main branches set some 9 inches apart. It will tend to produce spurs, which contain both wood and fruit buds, fruit buds proper borne on short growths not unlike spurs, and true wood buds, which should be thinned out to two or at the most three on each spur in April; good young shoots at the base of old wood being retained to train in where there is room between the main branches of the fan as the ends of the main branches tend, as they grow, to diverge from each other. If the laying-in of good young wood is neglected the tree will obviously become thinner and more sparse as it grows. All side shoots from this young wood should be cut back to four leaves in the summer to encourage them to bear fruit buds and spurs.

In winter-pruning, which should be done when the leaves fall, stop all leading shoots and cut back to two or three buds all shoots not required to fill up vacant places on the wall. Useless wood should be cut away and young shoots should be nailed in to replace them. All shoots which push out forwards from the wall should be removed. The apricot is propagated by budding in July or August on the St. Julien plum stock.

Varieties.—*Large Early* (July–August) ; *Shipley's Blenheim* (August) ; *Moor Park* and *Powell's Late* (August–September).

BLACKBERRY

The blackberry thrives in deep and well-manured soil, though in any soil it will do fairly well ; the ground must be moist, but well-drained. The best plan is to train it espalier style, 4 feet being allowed between plants, and to prune rigorously at planting time. In after years pruning should be done as soon as the fruit is gathered; the old canes are cut out and four or five new ones, some 10 inches apart, are tied to the support to replace them, and must have their long, weak ends cut off about 12 inches above the stake. The blackberry is propagated by cuttings or layers in March, and bears for from seven to fourteen years. The best varieties are the *Parsley-leaved* and the *Himalayan*.

THE CHERRY

Soil and Situation.—Cherries require a well-drained, moderately deep loam, and do well on soil overlying chalk. They do not thrive on dry gravelly soils, nor on heavy clay. They like an open situation, facing west or south, though Morellos and Kentish do well on a north or east wall. Protection from birds and from frost in the early spring is desirable. Cherries may either be grown as standards or against walls—trained horizontally—or as bushes or cordons.

The details of planting and manuring are given on pages 323 and 326.

Pruning.—Much cutting causes the tree to "gum," and for this reason it is best, wherever possible, to form the young tree carefully and then confine all pruning to summer stopping of shoots to five or six leaves, with the finger and thumb. Any further pruning with the knife that is found needful should be done not later than October, when the sap is still in the wood; laterals being shortened to three or four buds. If pruning is done later than this the tendency to gumming will be greater. Should the tree show a tendency to use up its energy on the formation of luxuriant wood and no fruit buds, it should be lifted and replanted, the check thus given to the root action being usually enough to remedy the bad habit. The cherry easily forms good fruiting spurs, and when the tree has a sufficient number of these to secure a good, but not exhaustive crop, it should be let alone as much as may be.

The cherry is propagated by budding in July or August on stocks of the Mahaleb cherry, or in the case of standards, by grafting in March on stocks of the wild cherry. Trees for training on walls are generally worked on the St. Lucie plum.

It must be remembered that most cherries

FIG. 47.—PRUNING THE CHERRY

Summer-prune to five or six leaves, as at *S*; further pruning should be as light as possible, because of the tendency to "gumming" and should not be done later than October, laterals being shortened to three or four buds, as at *W*.

are self-sterile and require the pollen from another variety of cherry to set their fruit; more than one variety must, therefore, always be planted.

(*See also* Fruit-growing under Glass, p. 357.)

SOME OF THE BEST CHERRIES

Name.	Season.	Name.	Season.
(D) Black Heart .	July	(C) Kentish Red . . .	July
(D) Early Rivers . . .	June–July	(D) May Duke. . . .	June
(D) Frogmore Early Bigar-reau	Early July	(C)* Morello	Aug.–Sept.
(D) Governor Wood . .	Early July	(D or C) Royal Duke . .	July

(C) = Cooking.
(D) = Dessert.
* = Self-fertile.
Note.—At least four varieties should be planted together for cross-pollination purposes (see page 323).

CHESTNUT

(*See* Nuts.)

COBNUT

The Cobnut requires the same treatment as the *Filbert* (p. 345).

CURRANTS

Soil and Situation.—Red and white currants require the same treatment, which differs in several respects from that needed by the black variety. Ordinary deep loam, deeply dug and fairly well manured, and an open, sunny site, answer the purpose well for both red and white; but black currants require a cool, moist, rich soil, and a shady situation.

Planting.—Currants should be planted 5 feet apart so that the highest roots shall be but an inch or so below the surface. (*See* Planting, p. 323.)

White currants are not such vigorous growers as the red varieties, they should, therefore, not be planted in between the latter or they will be crowded-out. Each variety should be planted separately. Currant bushes need liberal water in hot dry weather, and a mulch of rotted manure applied in May will do much to keep the roots cool and moist, and will help the fruit. Every branch of newly-planted black currants should be cut hard back to two buds the following March to encourage the growth of vigorous shoots during the following summer and fruit the next year.

Suitable Forms.—For general purposes, the bush or standard form is most useful, but red and white currants also do well when trained as cordons or against a wall. In forming these bushes, which are best if trained cup-shape, three main shoots are first grown, the second year these are each cut hard back so that two strong shoots will take the place of one, forming six in all. Cut back these main shoots some 6 to 10 inches each winter, until the bushes are the required size. The subsequent pruning is described below.

Pruning.—Red and white currants fruit on spurs, and consequently, young " lateral " shoots should, early in July, be pinched back to five or six leaves, and in October be cut back to about three buds from the base.

The " leaders " should not be cut back by more than one half, or the fruitfulness of the bush will be endangered, and care must be taken to cut back close to a good healthy bud. Old wood must periodically, though not too frequently, be cut away to permit young shoots to be trained in to take its place. Do not summer-prune too rigorously at one time; do a little each day. The " leader " must not be summer-pruned, but must be left intact. White currants are less vigorous than the red kinds and therefore do not require to be pruned quite so severely.

Black currants differ from red and white currants in that their fruit is borne on one-year-old shoots only. Old wood should, therefore, as far as possible, be cut well back to the base every year, and the more thoroughly this can be done, the more vigorous will be the young growths on which the following year's crop depends. These young growths, which should be encouraged from the base of the bushes, must, of course, not be summer-pruned, as advised for the red and white currants, as they are the fruit-bearers for the next year. Black currants should not be grown on very light soil, and, like the raspberry, the soil must not be deeply worked between the bushes or the roots will be damaged. The hoe must, of course, be used to keep the weeds down and the soil moist. Manure should be applied as described in the table on page 327. Birds are troublesome when the fruit is ripening, so before this time the bushes should be netted with muslin or other protective netting.

Propagation.— Currants are propagated by cuttings 9 to 12 inches long, taken in October and planted out in the open. Any buds below soil level being removed, except in the case of black currants when these buds must be

FIG. 48. — PRUNING RED AND WHITE CURRANTS

Early in July pinch back young laterals to five or six leaves, and in October cut back to within three buds from the base. " Leaders " should not be summer-pruned and must not be winter-pruned by more than half. Cut out old wood periodically.

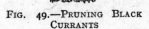

FIG. 49.—PRUNING BLACK CURRANTS

Cut old wood well away to the base as at *B–B* each year. Do not summer-prune, as the young growths are the next year's fruit-bearers.

allowed to remain. The bushes will bear fruit for some fifteen **or** twenty years.

Varieties.—(Red) *Cherry, Red Dutch* and *Mammoth*—Early, Mid-season and Late. (Black) *Boskoop Giant, Goliath* and *Baldwin*—Early, Mid-season and Late. (White) *White Versailles* and *White Dutch*—Early and Mid-season.

THE DAMSON

Damsons require exactly similar treatment to that advised for plums. The trees will bear for about twenty-five years.

Varieties.—*Bradley's King of the Damsons, Shropshire, Farleigh, Aylesbury Prune,* and *Merryweather.*

THE FIG

Soil and Situation.—The fig should have a sheltered and sunny wall facing south. Its rooting space should be somewhat limited. Indeed, the actual hole, which should be about 3 feet deep and 4 feet square, is often walled in by bricks and cement. At the bottom of this hole should be placed about a foot of broken bricks or gravel. On this should be laid about a foot of turves, grass side downwards, and the top foot should consist of a mixture of fibrous loam and broken mortar rubble. No manure must be added at planting time, but a good mulching of stable manure should be given in May, and the borders should be liberally watered every ten days in summer. Fifteen to twenty feet should be allowed between trees.

Pruning.—The fig may be trained against a wall in a fan-shape, as advised for peaches. Fix to the wall as many permanent leaders as are required at from 10 to 15 inches apart ; get rid of all unnecessary wood by disbudding, and stop the fruit-bearing shoots back to five or six leaves, at the end of August or beginning of September, according to the habit of the tree and the nature of the season. This stopping, the object of which is to induce the formation of fruit for the ensuing season, is a matter of much nicety. A too early stopping with most trees will cause a too early development of fruit, the consequence of which will be that it will not stand through the frost of winter. The fruit for next year must not be much larger than a pea when winter sets in. Other pruning is not much required, except so far as is necessary to maintain the shape of the tree, and to prevent overcrowding. The fruits mature principally on one- or two-year-old wood. Old wood should, therefore, be cut out in October where it is possible to train in well-ripened shoots of the previous year's growth. Each year a couple of vigorous young shoots from the base of the tree must be trained up to replace old and worn-out branches. When a tree is not bearing as well as it might be it should be lifted in October and root-pruned (*see* Root-pruning, p. 321). Figs are propagated from suckers or cuttings of one-year-old wood in October. The trees will bear for thirty to forty years.

(*See also* Fruit-growing under Glass, p. 358.)

Varieties.—(Early) *Castle Kennedy.* (Mid-season) *Black Ischia, Brunswick* and *White Ischia.* (Late) *Bourjasotte Grise.*

THE FILBERT

Soil and Situation.—Filberts are easily grown in well-drained, deeply-dug soil. The filbert, though smaller than the cobnut, has much the better flavour. The cultivation of both is the same. When planting a filbert plantation a site should be chosen which is sheltered from east and north-east winds. A shrubbery or hedge of evergreens will do this quite satisfactorily. The nuts are best grown in the form of bushes, with a crown of five to six main shoots supported by a sturdy stem some 15 inches high. The main shoots should not be allowed to grow to more than 6 feet in height. Plant the trees 15 feet apart in October.

Manuring.—A light dressing of organic manure, preferably shoddy or feathers, should be spread round the trees, and the soil should be well dug-over each year, preferably in December. To prevent the ground from becoming stale give a dressing of lime triennially.

Pruning.—As soon as the pollen is shed, usually early in March, pruning may be begun. Cut back vigorous side shoots to a catkin a few inches above the base, and cut out some of the oldest wood each year. Leave in the small, twig-like wood of the previous year's growth, for this bears the fruit. Wood that has borne fruit the previous year should be cut hard back to two or three buds. All sucker growth must be twisted off from the roots, and the centre of the trees kept well open. Nuts should not be gathered until they are perfectly ripe and brown, late in September. If they are to be stored, they had better hang on the trees until they fall naturally.

Propagation.—This is usually accomplished by layering two-year-old wood in autumn, but grafting is sometimes effected in March.

Varieties.—The *Kentish White* and *Prolific* are among the best Filberts, whilst the *Kentish Cob*, the *Emperor Cob* and the *Cosford Cob* are among the best Cobnuts.

THE GOOSEBERRY

Soil and Situation.—Though the gooseberry will grow on the poorest soil, it will not produce really fine fruit unless planted in a deep, rich, well-drained loam, and treated generously. Fresh air and sun are essential to the gooseberry.

FIG. 50.—PRUNING THE GOOSEBERRY

In July stop all unneeded shoots to two or three leaves; in January shorten main shoots to seven or eight buds and side shoots to two or three, and cut out old and weak wood.

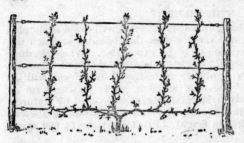

FIG. 51.—A GOOSEBERRY TRAINED AS A CORDON

This method provides the branches with ample sun and air, and is very economical of space.

Planting.—Early and late varieties should be planted in separate groups as they will want netting from the birds at different times. Weak growers must not be planted among varieties of more vigorous growth, or they may be overwhelmed by the latter plants. Plant the bushes 5 feet apart, and cut the bushes back moderately hard after planting.

Pruning.—Gooseberries bear on the young as well as on the two-year-old wood, generally upon small spurs arising along the sides of the branches. Young growths required to form future laterals should, therefore, be allowed to make their full length. Young shoots not needed should, in July, be pinched back to two or three leaves to form fruit spurs. In winter-pruning gooseberries, for which January is a favourable season, cut out the weaker of the young shoots and gradually remove the old wood so as to keep the tree thin of branches, but let those left be trained to some regular shape, and never be permitted to grow across each other. They should radiate in a cup-like shape, if trained as bushes or standards, so as to be 6 or 8 inches apart, leaving the centre of the bush open. The young shoots which are retained should merely have their soft ends cut off, just beyond a bud pointing upwards. Main shoots should be shortened down to seven or eight buds and the side shoots to two or three buds. In the case of many varieties there is a distinct tendency to a weeping habit, and this should be fought against by pruning back to upward-pointing buds only, as the fruit is liable to become earth-stained.

Every year liberal top-dressings of manure should be given in winter, and every third or fourth autumn apply a dressing of basic slag in the proportion of 5 oz. to every square yard of soil.

Protection from Birds.—If the bushes are dusted over with a mixture half of slaked lime and half soot early in March, the birds will be discouraged from picking off the buds. The best plan for protecting the fruit from birds is by encircling the bush with wire netting, and covering the top with a piece of string netting, which can be removed when the fruit is to be gathered.

Gathering the Fruit.—A start can usually be made in June. First gather all the fruit from the centre of the bush, then the large fruit on the lower branches ; after this the fruit is picked in successive gatherings as it swells and ripens. No preliminary thinning is necessary.

Propagation.—Young bushes should be raised from cuttings so as to build up a stock to replace a few of the old trees each year. Cuttings should be struck in spring or autumn. Select short-jointed, sturdy shoots of the previous year's growth, each some 8–10 inches long, not root suckers. To secure a clean stem and prevent the formation of suckers, remove with a knife every bud from the base to within 3 or 4 inches of the top. (For the method of striking cuttings, *see* p. 189.)

Varieties.—(Red) *Crown Bob, Red Champagne* and *Lord Derby*—Early, Mid-season and Late. (Yellow) *Gipsy Queen, Golden Gem*, and *Yellow Ball*—Early, Mid-season and Late. (Green) *Gunner* and *Thumper*—Mid-season and Late. (White) *Cheshire Lass* and *White Lion*—Mid-season and Late.

THE GRAPE
Cultivation in the Open

Soil and Situation.—A situation at the base of a wall facing south, south-east, or south-west should be selected. Manure should not be added unless the soil is very poor indeed, but it is well instead to incorporate with the soil a reasonable portion of gravel, wood ashes, old mortar, and rotten refuse.

Planting.—It is well to plant the young vines as single cordons 4 feet apart, about 6 inches distant from the wall with the roots about 4 inches below the surface, late in October.

Pruning.—Cut the rod down to within 12 inches of the ground in January, and during the first year only superfluous shoots should be removed, the young shoots intended to remain being allowed to grow to their full length. In the following November these should be pruned back to two buds, with the exception of the leading shoot which should be pruned back to about 30 inches from its base. Spurs will result, and the young shoots which grow thereon must, at an early stage, be reduced to one in each instance. Each of these shoots allowed to remain must subsequently be pinched back to two leaves beyond a bunch, if there is one, if not to five or six leaves, and the little shootlets that branch from it must be pinched back just beyond the first leaf, as soon as this appears. The following November these laterals are cut back to one bud and the main shoot to 50 inches. In successive years the treatment is the same. The vine may also be trained horizontally and then vertically as also advised for culture under glass. The branches must at all times be kept carefully and closely attached to the wall or fence. Muslin bags should be used for protecting the ripened grapes from the attacks of flies and wasps. *See* Fruit under Glass, p. 358.

Varieties (Out-door). —(Black) *Black Cluster*. (White) *Chasselas Dorée, Grove End Sweetwater* and *Royal Muscadine*.

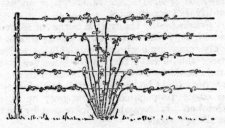

FIG. 52.—TRAINING THE LOGANBERRY

The loganberry is usually trained fan-wise on a trellis or wire fence. It may also be trained up fir-poles in the same way as rambler roses and will reach a height of 10-12 feet.

THE LOGANBERRY

Planting.—The loganberry loves a moist but well-drained, deep, rich loam, and is best planted 5 feet apart in October. It is usually trained fan-wise or as an espalier on a trellis or wire fence.

Pruning.—In June the clumps should be thinned-out, and all young shoots except half a dozen of the strongest should be cut away. Those that remain must be tied up to the supports and not allowed to straggle over the ground. They must, however, be kept clear of the fruiting canes. As soon as the fruit is gathered, cut out the old branches and tie in the new ones to replace them.

Propagation.—The loganberry is best propagated by layering in August. The new plant may be severed from its parent and transplanted in November to its fruiting position. The loganberry may also be increased by division of roots in October. The plants will bear fruit for ten to fifteen years.

THE MEDLAR

Soil and Situation.—The medlar is easily grown in any good, well-drained, but retentive soil. It requires an open situation where it is protected from cold winds, and should be planted with 10 feet between the trees.

Cultivation.—The cultivation of the medlar, so far as pruning is concerned, is almost identical with that advised for the apple. The fruits should be gathered about the middle of November, and should be stored in a single layer, " eye " downwards, on some dry silver sand. It is usually necessary to store the medlars for at least a fortnight before they are ripe for eating.

Varieties.—*Nottingham* and *Royal.*

THE MULBERRY

Soils.—The mulberry tree should be planted in October, 25 to 30 feet from tree to tree, in deep, well-drained and moist loam. In the south of the British Isles the mulberry can be grown in the open as a bush or standard, but in northern districts it should be grown on a warm south wall. Do not cut away any of the roots when planting or the tree may be spoiled. The mulberry is an attractive tree, but is rarely cultivated for its fruit.

Pruning.—As the fruit is borne on spurs and on short-jointed young wood, it is well to cut back young shoots to about four or five buds, only removing such as are calculated to lead to overcrowding. Wall-trees should have their main branches trained some 15 inches apart, and should be allowed to grow until they have covered the wall. Side shoots should be cut back in July to five or six leaves. The mulberry is easily propagated by cuttings or layers which root readily in October. It may also be increased by budding in August on a white mulberry stock.

Varieties.—The *Large Black* is one of the best varieties.

THE NECTARINE

The nectarine requires exactly the same treatment as the peach. (*See* p. 349. For best varieties *see* list, p. 350.)

NUTS

The principal nuts cultivated for their fruit in England are the Walnut, the Cob, the Filbert, and the Sweet Chestnut. The latter, however, is grown primarily as an ornamental tree, its fruit-bearing in this country being irregular and unreliable.

The walnut is raised from seed in November and is easily grown in almost any sandy loam or in limy soils, but does not thrive in damp, peaty soils. It will bear fruit for between fifty to a hundred years, but takes a great many years from the time of planting to the time of fruiting. Little pruning is necessary, only sufficient to keep the trees in shape, and is best done before the leaves fall.

(*See also* the Filbert, p. 345.)

PEACHES AND NECTARINES

Soil and Situation.—In the South of England, both peaches and nectarines may be grown in the open in sheltered situations against walls or fences facing south, south-east or south-west, where ample protection from spring frosts can be given by means of blinds or a double thickness of fish netting. The blinds or netting should be raised each morning, except when the weather is very severe, to allow the bees to approach and pollinate the blossom. They like best a calcareous, well-drained soil somewhat on the heavy side and previously well manured. When grown against a wall they should be planted in autumn, about 4 inches from the wall at a sufficient depth for all the roots to be covered with at least 6 inches and not more than 9 inches of soil. Not less than 18 feet width of wall space should be allowed to each tree. The fan-shape is the most satisfactory for both these trees.

Pruning and Disbudding.—The peach and nectarine are so closely related that the one description will cover the pruning of them both. Bearing their fruit mainly on the young wood of the previous year, the beginner will often be confronted with the apparently insoluble problem of how to remove a sufficient quantity of the old wood after the year's crop, while at the same time leaving enough of it to bear the young shoots for next year, as it does this mostly at the ends of the fruiting shoots.

The novice is apt to err on the side of leniency, and consequently his tree, after four or five years, will be found

FIG. 53.—PRUNING PEACHES AND NECTARINES

Summer-prune laterals to nine or ten leaves as at *S*, and winter-prune to seven or eight buds, as at *W*. Over-vigorous laterals, such as *B*, and extension shoots, as *C*, are neither summer nor winter-pruned. *D* shows a previous year's shoot in fruit; shoot *A* has been allowed to grow from the base to replace it when cut away after fruiting.

nearly barren, except at the extreme end of its branches. This may be prevented by the simple method of leaving, when the established shoot is disbudded as the spring growth starts, a good wood bud at the base of the shoot as well as one at the top, as this bud at the base will have to replace the fruit-bearing branch when the latter is cut away in the following winter. Should this shoot grow to more than 2 feet in length during the summer its top should be pinched out. This shortening will probably cause the formation of sub-laterals which must again be pinched back to one leaf. It is well to leave an "extension" bud at the upper end of the shoot, as it serves a useful purpose in helping to draw up the sap, and thus ensures a full supply of nourishment to the fruit buds on the intermediate part of the branch, but the top bud must be pinched back if it begins to extend too far—that is, shortened back to five or six leaves—and should be cut off with the old wood after fruiting and the lower one left to make the new wood. Buds must, of course, be left on where there are gaps to be filled, and as far as possible, new shoots from the top of the old wood should be trained in to fill these spaces. The cutting out of the old wood may be done at any time after the fruit is removed.

This "disbudding" should be performed gradually, but vigorously, quite five out of every six young shoots will need to be removed. The work should be begun in April, before the buds are an inch long, and should extend over a month. All wood buds which push forward from the wall should be rubbed out, and with them all those which obviously will not easily be made to fill a convenient space in the tree. As soon as the young shoots are long enough to handle they should be placed in position, some 4 inches apart, and secured. A tree which makes much wood and bears little fruit should not be disbudded too severely. If a good deal of strong young wood is laid in, the tree will soon cease to produce wood buds as freely as before, and a good crop will result. On the other hand, a weakly tree should be sternly dealt with. As soon as the fruit is set the ground should be well watered. Liquid manure may, with advantage, be given at this period.

Thinning.—The fruit should be exposed to as much air and sunshine as possible ; this is done by tying back the foliage that shades it. It is best to thin out the fruit as soon as it is the size of a filbert, starting with the smallest and most crowded on the underside of the branch, and removing a few at intervals of a week or so. A final thinning should be given as soon as the fruit has stoned so as to leave two peaches to every square foot of wall space, that is, about one fruit on every year-old shoot.

Propagation.—Peaches and nectarines are propagated by budding on an almond or plum stock in July.

(*See also* Fruit-growing under Glass, p. 363.)

Varieties.—PEACHES.—(Early) *Amsden June, *Waterloo, Royal George, *Crimson Galande and *Hale's Early. (Late) *Barrington, Golden Eagle and *Sea Eagle.

NECTARINES.—*Dryden, Early Rivers, *Lord Napier, *Pineapple and *Victoria.

* Denotes those kinds which will grow on a south wall in the open.

THE PEAR

Soil and Situation.—
The best soil is a sandy, slightly clayey loam with a clay sub-soil. The least suitable are light soils over gravel or chalk and cold, damp clays. (*See* Manuring Table, p. 328.) It is useless to plant in a north aspect, even as espaliers or fan-shaped trees against a wall. Shelter is, of course, required on the east and north. In the case of trees grown against walls, protection from frost may easily be afforded by hanging netting about 9 inches from the face of the wall. Abundance of sunshine and warmth is also essential. The pear is propagated by budding in July and August, and by grafting in March and April.

Planting.—See p. 323.

FIG. 54.—PRUNING THE PEAR

Shorten side-shoots in July to five or six leaves, as at *S*; leaders must not be stopped back. In spring, cut side-shoots back to two or three buds, as at *W*. Standards must not be severely pruned.

Summer-pruning.—Pears should be kept to their regular number of well-spreading branches, each branch kept thin like a cordon, with the side-shoots, which must not be less than 8 inches apart, shortened in July to five or six leaves. This summer-pruning must start from the top of the tree and should be carried out gradually, at intervals of two or three days, until the shoots at the bottom of the tree are finally pinched back. Do not stop-back the leading shoots. The *Jargonelle* pear and one or two other varieties fruit on the tips of the young shoots and not on spurs. Such varieties should be carefully summer-pruned ; only shoots in the crowded centre of the tree being " stopped." Well placed young shoots should be encouraged to grow and thus form vigorous branchlets to bear fruit the following season.

Winter-pruning, which is carried out in the early spring, consists in cutting the side-shoots back to two or three buds, always cutting back to an outward-pointing bud to preserve a good shape in the tree. All dead wood and any branches growing across other wood must be cut away, and where the fruit spurs are too numerous for the tree to mature all the crop, or where the fruit is too crowded, some of the spurs should be cut right out. Where spurs have aged and become weak they should also be cut clean away, as fresh ones will spring from their bases. Where the pear is grown as a pyramid or as a trained tree it will require lifting every two or three years to check rampant growth, or the tree will run to wood. As with apples, standard-trained pears must not be so severely pruned as fruit grown in the cordon, espalier, or bush form. The fruit buds of the pear are smaller than those of the apple, while its wood buds are smaller still, and darker in colour.

Thinning.—Each fruit should have ample room to develop. Varieties bearing large fruit naturally need thinning more drastically than the smaller fruiting kinds, which may be allowed to carry two or even three pears on each spur.

Gathering and Storing.—The fruit of the early kinds should be gathered before it easily separates from the tree. Early fruit should then be laid out singly and allowed to ripen for a few days and eaten at once, as few of the early varieties will keep. Choice fruit should be protected whilst still growing on the tree from the attacks of birds and wasps by means of thin muslin bags. (*See* Storing, p. 336.) Late dessert pears, especially, need care, and should be allowed to hang on the trees until the middle of November and then must be stored as above directed. Most of the fruit, however, should be gathered before the beginning of November.

SOME OF THE BEST PEARS
Dessert

Name.	Season.	Name.	Season.
(I) Beurré Superfin .	Oct.	(I) Doyenne du Comice	Oct.–Nov.
(I) Bon Chretien (William's)	Sept.	(I) Jargonelle . . .	Aug.
(I)* Conference . .	Oct.–Nov.	(S)* Josephine de Malines.	Dec.–Jan.
(I)* Durondeau .	Oct.–Nov.	(S) Pitmaston Duchess	Oct.–Nov.

Stewing

Name.	Season.	Name.	Season.
(S) Bellissimo d'Hiver ,	Nov.–March	(S) General Todleben . .	Nov.–Jan.
(I) Beurré Clairgeau .	Nov. Dec.	(S) Verulam	Jan.–Mar.
(S) Catillac . . .	Dec.–May	(I) Vicar of Winkfield . .	Nov.–Jan.

(S) = Storing.   (I) = Immediate Use.   * = Self-fertile (see page 323).

THE PLUM

Soil and Situation.—The plum likes best a fairly deep, well-drained loam, providing it contains lime or chalk in some form or another. It does not thrive in sandy or gravelly soils, though by heavy manuring (*see* table, p. 328) and the addition of a quarter of a bushel of lime for each tree much may be done even with these. Undrained soil in which stagnant water remains and low-lying sites suit plums no better than pears or apples. At any rate for the dessert varieties, a southern aspect is necessary, but for cooking kinds a north or north-east aspect

PRUNING GOOSEBERRY BUSHES

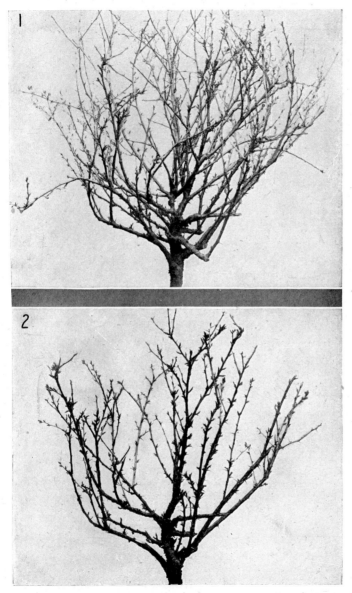

1. A bush before pruning. 2. The same after pruning. The weaker of the young shoots are cut out in January and the old wood is gradually removed to keep the bushes thin of branches. Young shoots retained should have their soft ends cut off just above a bud pointing upwards. Shorten main shoots to 7 to 8 buds and side shoots to 2 to 3 buds. See page 346.

1. A vine spur before pruning.   2. After pruning.   3. A vinery cleared and pruned in readiness for starting, and showing the tops of the vines bent down to ensure an even flow of sap.   See page 359.

will often serve. Shelter should be afforded from the east and north, and the shade of buildings or trees must be avoided. Plums are grown, apart from on walls, as standards, pyramids, and bushes.

Planting.—In any case they should be planted in October or February, and not too deep. In the first nine or ten years the plum is apt to make too much woody growth. This can be got over by growing the plums in the form of bushes or pyramids. In this form they may be lifted, root-pruned and replanted every third or fourth year, during the first dozen years, to ensure adequate fruit-spurs. Mulching, manuring, watering, and thinning are as necessary in the case of plums as in the case of other fruit trees. As many plums are self-sterile more than one variety blooming at about the same time should always be planted in the garden or orchard.

Pruning.—The plum fruits on spurs and on the previous year's wood. It has the habit of producing an intermediate kind of shoot, neither quite a shoot nor quite a spur, which is generally called a " stub." The shoots proper, those which extend from the framework of the tree, usually bear no fruit buds, and are found in great quantity on young trees. The pruner should select from among them those which he needs to form his tree. Where this is already well shaped and filled, the shoots may be left untouched, as they will then merely lengthen, but where the tree is thin and " unfurnished," the tips of some few selected ones should be cut back, that they may break sideways and fill the vacant places. The useful growths in a plum tree are the " stubs " which do not make long wood. A tree which produces these in number is a good bearer, and they should be touched as little as possible With standards, pyramids and bushes, once the tree is properly formed all buds not wanted for training in to replace old wood should be rubbed off in spring. In July all useless side-shoots should be stopped back, and in winter the " stubs " should be pruned back to two to three buds. All old, broken and diseased wood must be cut out, the mere process of keeping the tree open usually secures a good supply of healthy ripened wood, and this will produce fruit-bearing spurs spontaneously. Wall-trained fruit has a tendency to make vigorous growth towards its top and for the base of the trees to become bare. During July and August stop the side shoots of these wall-trained trees to six to eight leaves to encourage the formation of fruit spurs, and again cut them back to two to three buds in winter, at which time shorten the main shoots a little each year until the trees have covered the wall, training the lower branches well downwards, Plums require thinning and a start is usually made in June or early July. (*See* Thinning, p. 335.)

Propagation.—Plums are propagated by grafting in March and by budding in July on the St. Julien, the Mussel, or the Common Plum stock, according to variety.

The plum will bear well for twenty to twenty-five years.

Varieties.—(Cooking) *Belle de Louvain* and *Monarch.* (Dessert) *Coe's Golden Drop* and *Early Transparent Gage.* (Cooking and Dessert) *Pond's Seedling* and *Victoria.*

* Denotes self-fertile varieties.

THE QUINCE

Soil and Situation.—The quince requires a somewhat moist, deep soil of moderate richness, and enjoys an open situation. Although it does well in our southern counties, in the more northern parts it seldom ripens its fruit. (*See* Manuring Table, p. 328.)

Pruning.—The quince and the pear are very closely related, and they require much the same kind of pruning. The quince should be judiciously thinned as to the main branches, and have unproductive or straggling wood cut out ; this is best done in early autumn. The quince may easily be propagated by means of layers, cuttings or suckers in October.

Gathering and Storing.—The fruit of the quince should not be gathered until the end of October, unless the autumn is unusually frosty. When gathered they should be stored by themselves (they will affect the flavour of other fruit) in a cool, frost-proof place on layers of straw on a shelf, until they have turned yellow, when they are fit for use. Here they will keep for from two to three months.

Varieties.—The three existing varieties of quince are known as the " *Apple-Shaped*," the " *Pear-shaped*," and the " *Portugal*."

RASPBERRIES

Soil and Situation.—Raspberries do best in partial shade in rather damp, but well-drained, soil. Early in the autumn this soil should be dug to a depth of 2 to $2\frac{1}{2}$ feet, and a liberal dressing of manure (preferably cow or pig dung) should be incorporated with it. (*See* Manuring Table, p. 328.)

Planting.—The canes, which should be young ones, are best planted in November, though when this has been impossible they may be planted in February, they may be planted singly, 2 feet apart, in rows 5 feet from one another. The top roots should be but an inch below the surface. It is usually well to cut down the cane in March to about 10 inches from the soil. In the following year new rods will be produced from the base, and these will bear the year after.

Pruning.—In June the bushes should be gone over and all suckers removed, except about six of the strongest. It is only on the one-year-old shoots that fruit is borne, so that in autumn all old canes that have borne fruit should at once be cut down to the ground, and burned. All weak young shoots should be cut out at the same time, leaving about four of the strongest to bear fruit the following season. The only other pruning that is required consists in cutting off the sappy curved tops of the young mature canes in March to encourage the formation of laterals on which the berries are borne. The ground in which raspberries are grown should not be broken up, as the roots remain near the surface, but a liberal dressing of manure should be given as a mulch early in the spring and again in June. If the weather is hot while the fruit is swelling water the canes liberally and use the hoe constantly. The autumn varieties should have their canes cut down to about 4 inches from the ground in February.

Supporting the Canes.—Raspberries need some form of support, the simplest and most useful consisting of three wires strained horizontally at heights of about 2 feet, 3½ feet and 5 feet from the ground. To these wires the canes should be tied in autumn some 9 inches apart from each other. They should not be tied up during the summer as they ripen better if left untied.

Raspberries are propagated by division of roots in October. The canes will bear well for from seven to fourteen years.

An Autumn Crop.—By a little management raspberries may be made to bear a crop of fruit during September and October. For late bearing, as soon as suckers show themselves in June the old canes should be cut away entirely, so as to prevent summer fruiting ; and by a mulch of well-rotted manure in June encouragement should be given during July and August to such suckers as show blossom-buds, for these will bear fruit in autumn. Autumn-bearing raspberries must be kept thin or they will not prove successful. Water liberally in dry weather and apply liquid manure.

Varieties.—(Summer Fruiting) *Baumforth's Seedling, Devon, Guinea, Hornet, Laxton's Bountiful, Queen of England* and *Reader's Perfection.* (Autumn Fruiting) *Belle of Fontenaye, Hailsham Berry, November Abundance, October Red* and *Surprise d'Autumne.*

FIG. 55.—SUPPORTING A RASPBERRY CLUMP

Alternatively to planting in rows, raspberries are often planted in clumps of three roots, each clump being set 3 to 4 feet apart.

STRAWBERRIES

Soil and Situation.—Strawberries do best in a deeply-dug, well-drained loam which has been well dressed with manure some two or three months previously to planting. (*See* Manuring Fruit, p. 328.) In many gardens the strawberry crop is all too soon over. By using early and late varieties and by planting in borders with different aspects strawberries may be had in fruit for quite a long time. Those in the south border will be ready early in June ; those in a border facing north will form the late crop. An open, sunny position is essential.

Planting.—Planting should take place during the latter half of September ; late planting will give the strawberry little chance of becoming established before the winter sets in, and results in small and scanty fruit. Just previous to planting, the soil should be well watered and made firm. Plant so that the crown is left just above the surface of the soil. The plants should be watered in their pots before planting and water should be liberally given for a few days if the weather is dry. (*See* Planting, p. 69.) Every October a liberal top-dressing of manure should be given between the rows and forked in early in March. In May, before the flowers open, the ground between the plants should be well hoed, dusted with soot, or nitrate of soda at the rate of 1 oz. to the square yard, and then covered with fairly short straw to keep the fruit from being splashed with mud. If late frosts are severe this straw may be pulled up over the bloom to protect it. About 18 inches should be allowed from plant to plant, and 2 feet to 2 feet 6 inches between the rows. After the fruit has been gathered remove the straw, the oldest of the leaves, and all the runners except those required for layering, and loosen the surface of the soil gently. The plants should not be allowed to bear their first year or they will be lastingly weakened. For Forcing, *see* p. 172.

Propagation.—As a rule, strawberries crop best in their first season in the beds and deteriorate very much, in size if not in quantity, after their second or third year. About a third of the bed should, therefore, be laid down, on a fresh site, with fresh runners each year, so that no plants shall become more than three years old. The usual and the best method of propagation is by layering early in July. Early and vigorous runners with good compact centres from one-year-old, heavy-fruiting plants should be selected. (*See* Layering, p. 193.) It is best to peg the layers down into 3 to 3¾-inch pots rather than into the ground. Transplant these potted layers into their permanent positions in August or September.

Autumn-bearing Strawberries.—The *St. Fiacre* is large–fruited and of fine flavour, and is one of the best varieties of this kind of strawberry, which, if well-manured late in June bears in summer in the ordinary way and again in September.

Alpine Strawberries also bear in the autumn ; they are usually planted some 10 inches apart in March as edgings to borders. Cultivation is similar to that of ordinary strawberries. Two of the best varieties are the *Bergère* (red) and the *Improved White*.

See also Fruit-growing under Glass, p. 363.

Varieties.—(Early) *The Duke, King George V*, and *Royal Sovereign*. (Mid-season) *British Queen, President*, and *Veitch's Perfection*. (Late) **Dr. Hogg, Givon's Late Prolific, Latest of All, *Sir Joseph Paxton* and *Waterloo*.

* Denotes varieties suitable for heavy soil.

VINES

(*See* Grape.)

CHAPTER XXVII

FRUIT-GROWING UNDER GLASS

INSTEAD of repeating our remarks on heating, ventilation, and the general management of the greenhouse, we refer the reader to the chapter entitled *Gardening under Glass*, and to the details as to the temperature, ventilation, and cultural requirements of each fruit given in the following pages.

APPLES—PEARS—PLUMS

These fruits require no artificial heat and may all be successfully grown in the cold greenhouse. Cultural details are here unnecessary and the reader is referred to the chapter on *Potting* and to the separate articles describing the culture of these fruits in the open, pp. 337, 351 and 352.

THE CHERRY

Soil.—The cherry thrives best in a compost of two-thirds loam and one-third old mortar rubble, wood ashes, bone-meal and charcoal. For Potting, *see* Chapter XXII.

Temperatures.—Only slight heat should be applied and that very gradually ; until the flowers open, the thermometer should not be allowed to drop below 40° F. at night, but it must not rise above 50°–55° F. by day. Once the fruit has set the temperature may be allowed to rise to between 45° and 50° F. by night and 55° and 60° F. by day.

Pollination.—When the flowers are out dust them over daily about noon, when the air is driest, with a rabbit's tail to ensure good pollination ; this is an important point. While the fruit is setting syringe the trees twice daily in fine weather, and keep a good look out for insect pests. As soon as the fruit has set a top-dressing of ½-lb. of a mixture of one part nitrate of soda, two parts superphosphate, and three parts kainit, may with advantage be given.

Pruning.—See p. 328.

See also article on the Cherry, p. 341.

CUCUMBER

(*See* The Vegetable Garden, p. 393.)

THE FIG

The first crop is borne on the shoots of the previous year, the second on the growth of the current year, and the third on the sub-laterals from the current season's shoots. The third crop, however, is rarely of any value and, to avoid weakening the tree, should be picked off as soon as it forms. Artificial heat will only be necessary when fruit is required before August. When no artificial heat is used full advantage should be taken of the sun's heat, and the house should be closed early in the afternoon. When plants are started in January and plunged in a hot-bed with a temperature of about 75° F., and are given an air temperature of 60° to 65° F. by day and 50° to 55° F. by night, increasing gradually to some 10° above this, the fruit should be ready in June. The second crop will be ripe in August.

Compost and Planting.—As the roots should be confined, small pots should be used (*see* Potting, p. 177). For suitable compost and for border-planting details, *see* p. 344. February is the best time for planting. Until the plants break into active growth but little moisture is required, but once moving, ample moisture must never be lacking, even in winter, or the fruit will shrivel and drop. During the ripening period the water must be somewhat withheld or the fruit may crack ; if this happens ventilate more freely and sprinkle the floor instead of syringing the foliage.

Where artificial heat is used the leaves should be freely syringed twice a day to keep the atmosphere moist, and the house should be shut early in the afternoon to ensure a high night temperature.

Pruning.—To avoid overcrowding all unnecessary growth must be removed as early as possible, and as soon as the fruit has set, the shoots should be pinched back to five or six leaves. At the winter-pruning it will only be necessary to cut out old and useless wood. This pinching back, in summer, is very necessary in the case of the fig, as if this is not done, the extension grows very fast and diverts the nourishment from the fruit which is very liable to turn yellow and drop.

Thinning.—As soon as the fruits are the size of a pea they should be thinned out so that, on an average, not more than three remain on each shoot. Once the fruit commences to ripen syringing should be discontinued and more ventilation is required.

See also Fig Culture in the Open, p. 344.

GRAPES

Soil.—The border should be dug out to a depth of from 2½ to 3 feet, and should, where space is available, be about 10 feet wide. At the bottom of the border place about 6 inches of broken-up chalk or concrete. On this base should be laid a mixture of two-thirds fibrous loam with one-third wood ashes, lime rubble, charcoal, and a little soot. A hundredweight of crushed bones may be added for each load of loam. On the broken chalk and other drainage, turves a couple of inches thick should be laid, grassy side downwards, and on this the mixed soil should be placed.

Planting.—The vines should be planted 3 to 4 feet apart, if grown

as single stems, 1½ to 2 feet from the front wall, and about 1 inch
deeper in the soil than the old planting mark. The surface of the
ground should be covered with about 3 inches of short manure as soon
as planting has taken place. A good time to plant indoors is early in
January, when the canes should be cut back to about 18 inches long.

Training, Pruning and Disbudding.—During the first year the main
shoot only should be allowed to grow to its full length, other shoots
must be removed. When the vines have shed their leaves, the leading
shoot should be cut back to about 2 feet from the start of the current
year's growth. Each year the same treatment should be carried out,
except that after the first year of growth side-shoots are allowed to
form on the wood that has been cut back the previous winter ; these
laterals are cut back to one bud from the base to form spurs. When
the main shoot is sufficiently strong and has reached the top of the
house, no young growth is allowed to form at the top of the main
stem, but is rubbed off to
promote vigour in the fruiting spurs below ; these are
annually cut back to one bud
shooting outwards. Only one
shoot is desired from each of
these spurs, therefore, when
the young shoots push out in
spring the most vigorous one
only is retained. The inex-
perienced gardener, however,
should wait until the small
bunches of fruit are visible on
these shoots; at this stage

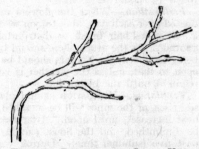

FIG. 56.—PRUNING THE GRAPE VINE

In winter, prune the side shoots made the previous
summer to within one bud (shooting outwards) of the
base. Cut back the main shoot annually to about
2 feet from the start of the current year's growth.

they look like crinkled peas at
the base of the third or fourth
leaves of the shoots, then he
should select the best bunch
and discard all the other shoots. When a rod has not been fruiting
well it is a good plan to train in another shoot from the bottom to take
its place, the old rod being cut out when the young growth has reached
the top of the house. The young shoot should be cut back when some
3 feet long and then be treated as advised above for the young vine.

The above method of training is applicable when several vines are
grown in one house ; where only one vine is planted, instead of training
one shoot to run vertically up the glass, two shoots are grown horizontally, running in opposite directions to each other, and are pruned as
for the single vertical stem. Laterals are allowed to form from the
upper side of these stems and are trained vertically upwards at intervals
of 3 to 4 feet, these eventually being pruned and trained as for the
single main-shoot. The vines should be tied to wires, fixed 9 inches
apart, and kept 18 inches from the roof-glass. The rods frequently
produce shoots from their tops before any young growth has formed
near the base. To encourage this lower growth the rods must be
unfastened from the wires and should have their heads bent down

towards the ground. This will arrest the flow of sap and young growth will soon form at the base. When the laterals all up the rod are in an even state of growth the rods may again be tied to the wires in an upright position. Vines should not be allowed to bear grapes the first year. If the vine is a strong one, a few bunches of fruit may be taken off during the second year, but not until the third season should anything like a crop be allowed to mature.

Temperatures.—Newly-planted vines should be allowed to become well established before any unnecessary heat is employed, fires being only lit to exclude frost. When the fruit is required in July or August the temperature may be raised to a minimum of about 55° F. early in March, and from the middle of April onward the temperature from sun heat alone may be allowed to rise to 85° F., a night-temperature of about 55° F. being afforded. From the time the young leaves are fairly developed until the grapes are in flower, a night temperature of 65° F. to 70° F. should be given.

Fertilization.—When the flowers are open they should be lightly dusted over each day, about noon when the air is warm and dry, with a soft camel-hair brush to distribute the pollen from one flower to another. As the atmosphere should be kept dry while the blooms are being fertilized, the borders should be well watered before the flowers open so that, unless the weather is very hot, water will not again be required until the bloom has set.

Ventilation.—Ventilation should always be started just before the sun rises, or the vines will be scorched, and should be increased as the heat increases, until noon. After two o'clock the ventilation should be diminished, and the house should be finally closed at about half-past five (summer-time). During very hot weather, and when the grapes are beginning to colour a little top ventilation should be afforded at night. Should the weather be cold and dull while the grapes are ripening, heat should be given, but ventilation should be provided. Except when the grapes are colouring, when the heat must be somewhat reduced and more air given, the floor and walls should be freely damped several times a day during the hot weather. When the grapes are colouring, however, a good damping twice a week is sufficient. As soon as the grapes are well coloured more ventilation may be given and the heat must be reduced to the minimum to avoid "damping-off." As the laterals grow they must be gradually bent down, a little at a time, before they touch the glass and first loosely tied to the wires with raffia, being later more securely fixed when they have become more used to the position. It is a job that must be done gradually as the stems are brittle and will snap if treated drastically. The shoots must be evenly distributed over the wires so that each receives ample sun and air. Water when the vines are "starting," shortly before the flowers open, while the fruit is stoning, liberally while the grapes are swelling and after the fruit has been harvested. Application of liquid manure should be given weekly from the time the fruit sets until it is ripe.

Thinning.—As soon as the bunches have set their berries it should be decided how many bunches are to be left, and how many grapes on each bunch. It has been estimated that each foot of rod of a well-matured

THE MELON

vine should bear about 1 lb. weight of grapes. Thus a fully-established vine about 20 feet long of such a variety as *Muscat of Alexandria* or *Black Hamburgh*, should not be allowed to bear more than about seven or eight bunches, averaging 3 lbs. a bunch, whilst of such varieties as *Trebbiano* or *Grosse Guillaume* not more than three or four bunches, each averaging from 6 to 7 lbs. in weight, are as much as it should be permitted to hold. No lateral should be allowed to carry more than one bunch, and the bunches retained should be compact and neat in form, not long straggling ones. Surplus bunches should be removed as early as possible, and on the bunches that are allowed to remain the grapes should be thinned-out at an early stage so as to make shapely bunches, thinning the centre especially and allowing ¾ inch from berry to berry. Grape-thinning scissors and a forked stick some 10 inches long to separate the grapes should be used. as on no account must the grapes be touched by the hand. Care must be taken that the scissors do not injure the grapes.

Propagation.—To propagate, several eyes or buds, that is, short pieces of the previous year's side growth some 2 inches in length each with one good bud upon it and having a slanting cut ½ inch long directly under the bud, are planted in January horizontally with the bud just above the soil in large pots, in a compost consisting of loam with one third leaf-mould and a liberal addition of sand. The pots are placed in a mild hot-bed and the soil kept moist and shaded. The eyes start growth quickly under these conditions, and should then be moved to a cooler, but light position. Repot singly into 6-inch pots as soon as the roots have well filled the pot. Stake carefully as the vines grow and by midsummer the plants will be about 6 feet in height. Move into 8-inch pots then again into 10-inch pots. Keep in the open from September to November and plant in the house in January.

Storing Grapes.—See Storing Fruit, p. 336.

See also Grape-growing in the Open, p. 347.

Varieties.—*Black Alicante, Black Hamburgh* and *Gros Colman* (all black); *Muscat of Alexandria* (amber); and *Cannon Hall Muscat, Foster's Seedling* and *Mrs. Pearson* (all white).

THE MELON

Preparing the Bed.—Make the hot-bed as described on p. 172, then cover it with about 6 inches of good, stiff garden loam, with an admixture of a little old mortar rubble, sand and a few handfuls of crushed charcoal. This should bring us to about the end of March.

Sowing.—Seed may be sown in the bed itself, or young plants may be raised two in a pot of sandy soil in a temperature of about 70° F. early in March, and be planted out, 2 feet apart, as soon as an even temperature of about 80° F. may be counted upon. Double as many seeds should be sown as plants ultimately required.

Pruning.—If grown in a frame the main shoot should be pegged down on to the soil and stopped when about 2 feet in length. Three or four laterals should be permitted to form. Train these evenly over the bed and pinch them back when sufficient flowers are visible. In a house allow the plant to grow up as a single cordon supported by a cane and stop it back when 3 feet high ; laterals will be thrown out and should be trained along horizontal wires 10 inches apart and be stopped when some 18 inches long.   The female flowers have small globular growths at their base, and four or five of these on each plant require " setting." This is done by picking the male flower, which has no globular formation at its base, removing the yellow petals and by pressing the pollen-covered remainder into the female flower.   The best time to do this is early in the morning when the sun is shining and the plants are dry. While the fruit is ripening it is essential to allow the shoots from beyond the fruits to thrive so that nourishment may be drawn out to the fruit ; all unnecessary side growth, however, must be stopped to avoid crowding.   Allow only one fruit to each lateral.

Watering and Ventilation.—During the early periods of growth the plants must never be allowed to be dry at the root, and twice a day in bright weather the leaves should be syringed with water ; preferably in the morning and again when closing the house for the night, tepid water should always be used.   When the flowers open very little water at the roots should be given, and the plant should not again be syringed overhead until the fruits begin to swell.   During the whole period of growth air should be liberally afforded, a careful eye being, of course, kept on the temperature, which should not fall below 60° F. at night, or below 70° F. by day.   Should the thermometer rise above 85° F. while the sun is shining, ventilate a little more until the temperature has dropped.   It will be difficult to maintain these temperatures when frames are used, but much may be done by covering the lights closely with mats and sacking on cold nights.   Throughout their whole lives melon plants require free ventilation and an abundance of light, and this is especially true during the period of fruit ripening.   Once their roots are established they cannot have too much sun.

Ripening the Fruit.—Fruit sown in March takes some four months from the time of sowing to ripen, later-sown fruit will only require three months.   As soon as the fruits begin to swell fertilizers should be applied or tepid liquid manure should be given at weekly intervals.   As the fruits swell more water, which must be tepid, is needed and more syringing in bright weather until they begin to ripen when the syringing and water supply must be diminished and more air given, but the plants must never be allowed to flag.   The fruit is heavy and when the size of a tennis ball, arrangements should be made for supporting it by means of small wooden " rafts " suspended from the roof by means of nets.   Ripeness is indicated by the stalk appearing to separate from the fruit.

Second and Third Crops.—Where artificial heat is available by planting a strong young plant as soon as the fruit has been gathered from the old one, three crops of melons may often be obtained in one season.   Seed sown in January will bear fruit in June, the plants put in at this time will ripen their fruit in August, and the last crop should ripen off by October.

Varieties.—*Blenheim Orange, Countess of Lathom, Emerald Gem, Golden Beauty, Hero of Lockinge* and *Imperial.*

PEACHES AND NECTARINES

The cultivation of these fruits under glass is essentially similar to their outdoor culture. Keep the house very cool until the first or second week in February when a temperature of 45° to 50° F. should be given. After ten days raise the temperature by about 10°. Ample ventilation should be given when outside conditions are suitable. In order to ensure fertilization dust over the flowers about noon with a soft camel's hair brush or a rabbit's tail. No syringing should be done while the trees are in bloom, but should be continued twice daily with soft water as soon as the fruit has set, when the temperature should be raised to 65° F. The ground should also be sprinkled with water three or four times each day while the fruits are forming and swelling. Not more than one fruit for every 9 inches square of wall space should be allowed.

Ripening the Fruit.—As the fruit approaches the ripening period it should be fully exposed to the sun and given as much ventilation as possible. Keep the shoots laid in closely, remove obstructing leaves, and mulch with manure. Syringing should cease as soon as the fruit begins to colour, as a drier atmosphere is needed at this period. Once the fruit is gathered give the roots ample water, and dress the border liberally with lime. Syringe the foliage and ventilate very freely.

For methods of planting, training, pruning, thinning, etc., *see* p. 349.

THE STRAWBERRY

Compost and Potting.—The young plants should be propagated as described on p. 356, and should be potted-up about the middle of August with the crowns appearing just above the soil in 6-inch pots in a compost consisting of a mixture of three parts coarse turfy loam, one part well-rotted manure, one part brick rubble and broken pieces of lime ; the whole should be well mixed together and then dusted over with a good sprinkling of bonemeal and soot. Drainage must be good. (*See* Potting, p. 177.) The pots should be stood on a floor of hard-rammed ashes or brick rubble, in a position in which they will be protected from the full sun. In fine weather syringe the plants three or four times daily, and never allow the roots to become dry, but do not let the soil become sodden. In ten days' time, when the roots are fully established, transfer the pots to a position where the plants will have full sun, give them soot water every three or four days, and syringe the foliage morning and evening in fine, warm weather. Any runners that form should immediately be cut off, as they only divert nourishment from the plants.

Wintering in Frame.—In November, or earlier should the frosts become severe, place the pots in a cold frame for the winter. Let the pots be sunk to their rims in ashes, but the foliage must come close up to the glass. Give free ventilation in fine weather and never let the pots become dry.

Forcing.—Early April is about the earliest that we can expect good fruit from forced strawberries, and to have fruit ripe by this time some of the pots should be moved from the cold frame about the middle of January, to be placed on shelves near the glass in the vinery or peach house, if a special forcing house is not available, or in a heated frame. Every three weeks, until the middle of March, a few more pots should be brought into the heat ; this will provide a succession of fruit from April until the open-air fruit is ready in June.

The Use of Bottom Heat.—A mild hot-bed will stimulate the root action and thus produce more vigorous plants and crops, so that where this is available the pots should be plunged into the hot-bed when moved from the cold frame, and before removal to the house, the first batch about the middle of January, and be left there for about a month, when the flower spikes will have formed. Each morning a little air should be admitted and when fine and bright the foliage should be syringed daily early in the afternoon, at which time the frame should be closed to preserve the heat of the sun through the night. Once the flower spikes have formed the plants should be transferred to shelves, about 15 inches from the glass of the house, or so placed in the heated frame that the plants are that distance from the lights.

Temperature and Ventilation.—The heat should, at first, be gradually applied, a temperature of 50° F. being quite sufficient at night, rising 5° to 10° F. by day in accordance with the heat of the sun. The atmosphere should be kept dry while the plants are in flower, and each day about noon, when the air is driest, the flowers should be gently shaken, or better still the centre of each should be dusted with a rabbit's tail, to ensure cross-pollination and consequent fertilization. Once half a dozen to eight fruits have set on each plant keep the atmosphere moist and allow the temperature to rise gradually to 60° F. by night and 65° to 70° F. by day. Syringe the plants and damp the floors early each afternoon when fine and warm. The house should be closed early in the afternoon to preserve the heat through the night. As free ventilation as possible should be given during the morning but the temperature must not be allowed to drop below the figures mentioned above. Green-fly are liable to appear at this period and careful watch must, therefore, be kept, and the house thoroughly fumigated on the first sign of them. If the undersides of the leaves are syringed daily, when fine, there should be little trouble from red spider. When the weather is very hot, water may be required twice or even three times a day.

Thinning and Ripening.—Should more than eight berries have formed on any plant they must be thinned out, retaining only the largest and best shaped berries. Once the fruits commence to swell weak liquid manure should be applied once a week. As soon as the fruit begins to turn colour the temperature must be gradually lessened, freer ventilation should be given, and syringing and the application of manure water must stop.

The berries may be prevented from becoming soiled by contact with the soil by being each supported on a short prong of wood pushed into the soil below the berry. When the fruit has been gathered, take the plants out of their pots and plant them out in the open where, if watered and well cared for, they will in all probability be induced to fruit again in the early autumn. *See also* Fruit-growing in the Open, p. 355.

FRUIT-GROWING AT A GLANCE

Fruit	Form of Tree	Distance between Rows	Distance between Trees	Most suitable Aspect	Best Soil	When to Plant	When to Prune	Time and Method of Propagation	When Ripe.
Apple	Cordon (Vertical), Bush, Half-Standard, Standard, Pyramid or Espalier	—, 8 ft., 20 ft., 25 ft., 10 ft.	2 ft., 15 ft., 20 ft., 25 ft., 10 ft.	Any; open best	Medium, Moist Loam, on Stiff Sub-soil; Sandy Loam	Oct. and Nov., Feb. and March	Winter-pruning March, Newly-planted Dec. and Jan. Established; Summer-pruning July and Aug.	Budding, July; Grafting, March and April	July–May
Apricot	Pyramid in Houses; Fan on Wall	—, 15 ft.		East by South to West	Good Loam	Oct.–Feb.	Winter-pruning, July, and Aug.; Summer-pruning, October.	Budding, July and Aug.	June–Sept.
Blackberry	Espalier	4 ft.	4 ft.	Any	Any Soil	Oct.–Feb.	Summer-pruning, May; After Fruit is Gathered	Cuttings or Layers, March	Sept.–Oct.
Cherry	Standard, Pyramid or Bush, Cordon (Vertical), Fan on Wall or Espalier	30-40 ft., 10-12 ft., —, —	30-40 ft., 10-12 ft., 2 ft., 15 ft.	East, South and West	Light, Sandy Loam; Chalky Soil	Oct.–Feb.	Winter-pruning, Sept.–Oct.; Summer-pruning, May–July	Budding, July and Aug.; Grafting, March	June–Sept.
Currant	Standard, Bush, Cordon (Single), Cordon (Double), Cordon (Treble), Espalier	6 ft., 5 ft., —, —, —, —	8 ft., 6 ft., 2 ft., 3 ft., 4 ft., 9 ft.	Any	Red and White, Good Loam; Black, Cool Moist and Rich	Oct. or Nov.	Winter-pruning, Sept.–Oct.; Summer-pruning, July	Cuttings, Oct. (Open)	July–Sept.
Damson	Standard or Half-Standard	20-25 ft.	20-25 ft.	Any	Strong Loam	Oct.–Feb.	Winter-pruning, Early Spring; Summer-pruning, July–Aug.	Budding, July; Grafting, March	Aug.–Oct.
Fig	Fan on Wall		15-20 ft.	South or South West	Well-drained, Fibrous Loam and Broken Rubble	Oct. to Feb.	Winter-pruning, Oct.; Summer-pruning, Aug.–Sept.	Suckers or Cuttings, Oct.	July–Sept.
Gooseberry	Standard, Bush, Cordon (Single), Cordon (Double), Cordon (Treble), Espalier	6 ft., 5, —, —, —, —	8 ft., 6 ft., 2 ft., 3 ft., 4 ft., 9 ft.	Any	Medium Loam	Oct. and Nov.	Winter-pruning, Jan.; Summer-pruning, July	Cuttings, Oct. or March (Open)	May–Sept.
Grape	In House		3-4 ft., if Grown as Single Stem	—	‡ Fibrous Loam, ‡ Wood Ashes, Lime Rubble, Charcoal and a little Soot. Also Crushed Bone.	Oct. to Feb.	Winter-pruning, Dec.; Summer-pruning, June	Budding, Jan.; Inarching, Spring; Bottle-grafting, Spring	April–June (heat from Nov.); July–Dec. (heat from March)

FRUIT-GROWING AT A GLANCE—*continued*

Fruit.	Form of Tree.	Distance between Rows	Distance between Trees.	Most Suitable Aspect.	Best Soil.	When to Plant.	When to Prune.	Time and Method of Propagation.	When Ripe.
Medlar .	Standard	10 ft.	10 ft.	Any	Any Good Soil; Deep-dug and Well-drained	Oct. to Feb.	Winter-pruning, Early Spring; Summer-pruning, July	Grafting, March–April	Oct.–Jan.
Nectarine .	Fan on Wall Cordon on Wall	— —	15 ft. 2 ft.	East to South-West	Open, Deep Calcareous, not too Moist	Oct,	Winter-pruning, Autumn; Summer-pruning, April–May	Budding, July	May–Sept. (glass); July–Sept. (open), according to Variety
Peach . .	Fan on Wall Cordon on Wall	— —	15 ft. 2 ft.	East to South-West	Open, Deep Calcareous, not too Moist	Oct,	Winter-pruning, Autumn; Summer-pruning, April–May	Budding, July	May–Sept. (glass); July–Sept. (open), according to Variety
Pear .	Cordon (vertical) Bush Standard Pyramid Espalier or Fan	— 8–12 ft. 20–30 ft. 12–18 ft. —	2 ft. 8–12 ft. 20–30 ft. 12–18 ft. 15 ft.	Any; East and West for Wall Trees	Deep Loam on Clay Sub-soil	Oct.–Feb.	Winter-pruning, Early Spring; Summer-pruning, July	Budding, July and Aug.; Grafting, March and April	Aug.–March, according to Variety
Plum . .	Espalier Fan Bush Standard Pyramid (see Cordon Bush)	— — 10–15 ft. 25–30 ft.	15 ft. 20 ft. 10–15 ft. 25–30 ft.	Any; South or West for Wall Trees	Strong, Well-drained Loam, not too Deep, containing Lime and Chalk	Oct.–Feb.	Winter-pruning, Early Spring; Summer-pruning, July–Aug.	Budding, July; Grafting, March	Aug.–Oct., according to Variety
Quince .	Cordon Standard Pyramid	— 20–30 ft. 8–12 ft.	2 ft. 20–30 ft. 8–12 ft.	Any	Moist, Deep, Medium Loam	Oct.–Feb.	Winter-pruning, Early Spring; Summer-pruning, July	Cuttings or Layers, Oct.	Sept.–Oct.
Raspberry	Canes Clumps of Three	5 ft. 6 ft.	2 ft. 4 ft. between Clumps	Any	Deep, Rich, Moist Loam	Oct.–Feb.	Winter-pruning, Oct.; Summer-pruning, June	Division, Oct.	June–Sept.
Strawberry	—	2½ ft.	1–2 ft.	South or South-West	Deep, Rich, Well-drained Loam	Aug.	Not needed	Runners, July	June–Sept.

CHAPTER XXVIII

THE VEGETABLE GARDEN

Planning the Vegetable Garden

A SIMPLE rectangular form is the most suitable and economical to adopt. All paths and borders and divisions should follow straight lines and form right angles with each other. The paths should be strong and solid, and the garden should be well drained and sheltered. The shadier parts of the garden should be the home of vegetables that do not primarily require warmth, such as rhubarb, seakale, Scotch kale, and the many varieties of salad. The pulses, potatoes and cabbages require more sun, and it is a safe rule to follow that where the cabbage will grow to perfection almost any vegetable will do well. The sides of any available walls which face east and south and west should have borders at their base in which fruit trees may be placed, and here also, owing to their more genial situation, early crops of all kinds may be nursed. The width of such borders depends upon the amount of sunlight that visits them, and while they should in no case be so wide as to render cultivation difficult, those which get most sun may be wider than those whose aspect is less sunny. A bed should be given up to herbs, and since so many of these are beautiful in form and sweet-smelling, the strip they occupy may be placed as near the house as is convenient.

Varieties Grown

It is, of course, impossible to say definitely what are the best varieties to grow as some kinds thrive on a moderately heavy soil, but do poorly on light soils and vice versa. Certain varieties are best for the early crop, others for the main crop, others are preferable for late sowing. At the end of the articles devoted to the individual vegetables, we have given varieties suitable for the various crops; some of the selections loving a light soil, others thriving in heavy soils.

367

Rotation of Crops

With a few exceptions only, it will always be found a good plan to vary the crops taken from any given plot, never growing the same kind of plant on it for two seasons running. Each crop takes out of the soil certain elements and leaves it enriched by others. Thus, for example, leguminous crops, as peas, are able to extract nitrogen from the air, and besides using a part of it themselves, leave the soil richer in nitrogenous constituents than they found it. The nitrogen is stored in the roots, which for this reason should always be left in the soil. This is a good moment to sow in this soil plants such as the onion, which demand a good supply of nitrogen in the soil ready for their use. It is a good rough rule that tuberous or bulbous-rooted plants should come after fibrous-rooted ones, and vice versa. Crops so similar in habit and nature as cabbages, broccoli, sprouts and kale should not follow one another. Plants with shallow roots as the pea, the lettuce and the cabbage should be grown alternately with deep-rooted plants like the beet, the carrot or the parsnip. The soil should not be freshly manured for root-crops, manuring for the previous crop being sufficient. If manure has not previously been given, it must be dug in very deeply to encourage good straight roots. Fresh manure should never come in contact with the roots. Related crops usually suffer from the same diseases; this is another reason for a rotation, as the contaminated soil would be likely to infect a plant of similar kind. (*See* Table, p. 370.)

It will be found that much time will be saved if the rotation is worked out and decided upon well before the planting time. The following table, showing a strip of land divided into three plots, with a rotation on each covering three years, is a useful guide. It can, of course, be extended indefinitely both with regard to the number of plots used or the successive number of years.

Plot.	1st Year.	2nd Year.	3rd Year.
A	Cabbages	Peas	Turnips
B	Leeks	Carrots	Seakale
C	Brussels Sprouts	Onions	Celery

Succession of Crops

Space is valuable and it is, therefore, essential to plant another crop as soon as the previous one has been cleared. The chief crops that are over early and permit of second cropping are early turnips, onions, cabbages, potatoes and early peas. Quickly maturing crops useful to form the second crop to follow these are spinach, lettuce, onions, shorthorn carrots, turnips, cabbages or broccoli for use the following spring. In selecting these crops consideration must be given to the correct rotation of crops. (*See* Table, p. 370.)

Catch-Crops

These are fast-maturing crops that may be planted between the rows of slower-growing vegetables or even in the rows between the individual plants. Before the main crop has matured and claimed its full space these " catch-crops " will have matured and have been cleared. Suitable catch-crops are shown in Table, page 370.

Sowing

On fairly dry soil, in warm situations, the sowing in the open may begin about the end of February—a few early peas, early beans, early horn carrots, and lettuce may then be sown. In March some parsnips, onions, beets, turnips and more peas, beans and carrots may be sown. In order to obtain a succession of vegetables through the year and not gluts at one time and none at another, it is desirable to sow the seeds of most vegetables in successive small quantities so that crop may follow crop. Always sow in drills, not broadcast ; it is then possible to keep the hoe busy between the rows. (*See also* Sowing, p. 184.)

Thinning and Planting-out.—Where crops are sown thinly, little thinning will be necessary, but as soon as the plants can be handled thin out to the distances advised for each vegetable.

Watering Vegetables

Seedlings.—Late in April and early in May while many seedlings are still tender we often experience hot, dry weather that would scorch up many of the seedlings unless they are watered. The hoe should be used unsparingly among the seedlings after watering. This will help to keep the earth moist, and will let the air into the ground. It is almost always essential to water transplanted seedlings thoroughly to make the soil firm about their roots.

Maturer Plants.—Crops whose roots spread out near the surface of the soil and do not descend very deeply will need liberal watering every day should the summer be very dry ; lettuce is a good example of this type of plant. There are other crops which, in spite of the fact that their roots run down fairly deeply, need copious supplies of water in dry weather ; beans, peas and celery may be instanced in this case. On the other hand root crops and many plants of the cabbage tribe, provided they are planted in deeply-dug, well-worked soil, will rarely need watering or mulching, even in the driest seasons. (*See also* Watering, p. 77.)

Blanching and Mulching

For these important operations *see* pp. 66 and 68.

ROTATION OF CROPS

The following table shows what crops a certain vegetable may follow and what it may *not* follow. It also shows what crops a vegetable may be followed by and the crops that should not come after it.

PRINCIPAL CROP.	CROPS IT MAY FOLLOW.	CROPS IT MAY NOT FOLLOW.	CROPS IT MAY BE FOLLOWED BY.	CROPS IT MAY NOT BE FOLLOWED BY.	CATCH-CROPS WHICH MAY BE PLANTED BETWEEN ROWS.
Beans.	Asparagus, borecole, broccoli, cabbages, turnips, parsnips, carrots, potatoes.	*Leguminous plants of its own natural order, i.e., peas, etc.	Beet, carrots, celery, leeks, lettuces, parsnip, salsify, turnip, and any of the Cabbage tribe.	*Leguminous plants of its own natural order, i.e., peas, etc.	Borecole, Brussels Sprouts.
Beet.	Cabbage tribe, and any crops but those specified in next column.	Spinach, turnips, parsnips, carrots, salsify, and scorzonera.	Peas, beans, cauliflower, lettuces, onions and any spring-sown crop except those in next column.	Spinach, turnips, parsnips, and carrots.	Nothing.
Borecole and Brussels Sprouts.	Peas, beans, lettuces, potatoes.	*Cruciferous plants of own order, i.e., any of Cabbage tribe, turnips, etc.	Peas, beans, beet, carrots, parsnips, onions, potatoes, kidney beans, celery, salsify, leeks, lettuce, endive, shallots, spinach.	*Cruciferous plants of own order, i.e., any of Cabbage tribe, turnips, etc.	Beans.
Broccoli	Peas, beans, kidney beans.	*Cruciferous plants of own natural order.	Any crop to be sown or planted when cleared off.	*Cruciferous plants of own natural order.	Nothing.
Cabbages.	Peas, beans, kidney beans, potatoes, lettuces, onions, leeks, celery, etc.	*Cruciferous plants of own natural order.	Peas, beans, kidney beans, potatoes, lettuces, carrots, parsnips, beet, salsify, celery, seakale, onions, leeks, radishes, endive, shallots, spinach, etc.	*Cruciferous plants of own natural order.	Coleworts.
Carrots and Parsnips.	Cabbage tribe and any crops except those in next column.	Any crops except root crops and *umbelliferous plants, as celery, parsley, etc.	Any crops except those in next column.	Any crops except root crops and *umbelliferous plants, as celery, parsley, etc.	Nothing.
Cauliflower.	Peas, beans, potatoes, celery, kidney beans, onions, carrots, lettuces, beet.	*Cruciferous plants of own natural order.	Peas, beans, potatoes, celery, kidney beans, carrots, leeks, salsify, endive, shallots, lettuces, beet, parsnip.	*Cruciferous plants of own natural order.	Spinach, lettuces, endive.

Celery.	Any crop except those in next column.	Parsnips, carrots, Parsley.	Peas, beans, kidney beans, onions, potatoes, turnips, and any of the Cabbage tribe.	Parsnips, carrots, parsley.	Lettuces, endive, dwarf early peas, French beans.
Endive and Lettuce.	Asparagus, potatoes, peas, beans and any of the Cabbage tribe.	Chicory, salsify, scorzonera, artichokes, cardoons, and any plants of the natural order *Composita.*	Peas, beans, potatoes.	Chicory, salsify, scorzonera, artichokes, cardoons, and any plants of the natural order *Composita.*	Nothing.
Kidney Beans and Peas.	Potatoes, carrots, parsnips, turnips, broccoli, and any of the Cabbage tribe.	Beans and *leguminous plants of own natural order.	Broccoli, cabbages, of any kind, spinach, turnips, potatoes, late celery, parsnips, beet, salsify, onions, leeks, lettuce, endive, shallots.	Beans and *leguminous plants of own natural order.	Summer spinach, radishes, lettuce, broccoli, turnip, early carrots; borecole and Brussels sprouts between dwarf sorts.
Leeks, Onions, Shallots, etc.	Cabbage tribe, celery, potatoes, peas, beans, kidney beans, lettuces, endive, spinach.	Garlic, chives, and any crop of the onion tribe.	Cabbages, carrots, coleworts, celery, cauliflower, parsnips, potatoes, peas, beans, beet.	Garlic, chives, and any crop of onion tribe.	Nothing.
Potatoes.	Any crop except those specified in the next column.	Carrots, parsnips, beet, salsify, scorzonera.	Any crop requiring a loose, clean, well-worked soil, and all *cruciferous plants, peas, beans, etc.	Root crops generally, as carrots, parsnips, beet, etc.	Brussels sprouts, cabbages, borecole, broccoli, and late celery if there is space enough for trench.
Seakale.	Potatoes, peas, beans, carrots, parsnips, beet, celery, etc.	*Cruciferous plants of own natural order.	Potatoes, peas, beans, carrots, parsnips, beet, celery, etc.	*Cruciferous plants of own natural order.	Nothing.
Spinach.	Peas, beans, kidney beans, cabbage, cauliflower, lettuces, etc.	Beet.	Peas, beans, kidney beans, cabbage, cauliflower, lettuces, etc.	Beet.	Nothing.
Turnips.	Potatoes, spinach, peas, beans, lettuces, etc.	*Cruciferous plants of own natural order.	Potatoes, spinach, peas, beans, lettuces, beet, carrot, parsnip.	*Cruciferous plants of own natural order.	Nothing.

*NOTE.—To save space in the table the above group names have been used and are here explained.
*Cruciferæ.—Cabbage, cauliflower, broccoli, colewort, turnip, radish, cress, seakale, mustard, horse-radish.
*Leguminosæ.—Peas, beans.
*Umbelliferæ.—Carrot, parsnip, parsley, celery, fennel, carraway.
*Compositæ.—Globe artichoke, Jerusalem artichoke, scorzonera, salsify, endive, lettuce, chicory.

NOTE.—A Dressing of 3 qrs. per ¼ Acre is equal to 2 lb. to the Square Rod, or 1 oz. to the Square
is applied in the Autumn or Spring according to

Name of Vegetable.	Farmyard Manure.	Artificial Fertilizers.*	
Beans	Moderately heavy, 3-4 tons	Basic Slag	3 qrs.
		Vegetable or Wood Ashes	3 qrs.
Beetroot	Organic manure for preceding crop only	Ammonium Sulphate	1½ qrs.
		Potash Salts	1½ qrs.
		Peruvian Guano	2 qrs.
Cabbage (including Broccoli, Brussels Sprouts, Cauliflower, Kale, etc.)	Moderately, 3 tons	Salt	2½ qrs.
		Steamed Bone Flour	2½ qrs.
		Nitrate of Lime	1½ qrs.
		Sulphate of Potash	1 qr.
Carrots	Organic manure for preceding crop only	Ammonium Sulphate	1½ qrs.
		Kainit	3 qrs.
		Salt	2½ qrs.
Celery	Moderately, 3 tons	Ammonium Sulphate	1½ qrs.
		Potash Salts	1½ qrs.
		Salt	2½ qrs.
Leeks	Moderately, 3 tons	Ammonium Sulphate	1½ qrs.
		Potash Salts	1½ qrs.
		Steamed Bone Flour	3 qrs.
Lettuce	Moderately, 3 tons	None necessary	
Onions	Moderately, 3 tons	Ammonium Sulphate	1½ qrs.
		Kainit	3 qrs.
		Soot	1 cwt.
Parsnips	Organic manure for preceding crop only	Ammonium Sulphate	1½ qrs
		Kainit	3 qrs.
Peas	Moderately, 3 tons	Basic Slag	3 qrs.
		Potash Salts	1 qr.
		or Wood or Veg. Ashes	3 qrs.
		Nitrate of Soda	1½ qrs.
Potatoes	Fairly heavily, 5 tons	Ammonium Sulphate	1½ qrs.
		Basic Slag	3 qrs.
		Potash Salts	1½ qrs.
		or Wood or Veg. Ashes	3 qrs.
Radishes	Moderately, 3 tons	None necessary	
Spinach	Moderately, 3 tons	(a) Ammonium Sulphate (heavy soil) or	1½ qrs.
		(b) Nitrate of Soda (light soil)	1½ qrs.
Turnips	Organic manure for preceding crop only	Ammonium sulphate	1½ qrs.
		Kainit	3 qrs.
		Steamed Bone Flour	3 qrs.

* In each case, *all* the fertilizers quoted should be used if the best

VEGETABLES

¼ acre.)

Yard. Unless otherwise stated the artificial manures are given in addition to the farmyard manure which the soil; heavy in Autumn, light in early Spring.

When to Apply Artificial Fertilizer.	Remarks.
Autumn and Winter Spring	No farmyard manure is needed unless the soil is exhausted. On heavy soil substitute 2 qrs. of Superphosphate for the Basic Slag, and apply when the crop is maturing.
Spring. When sowing „ „ „ Before sowing When growing When growing When growing as top-dressing Early Spring Spring. When sowing Spring or Autumn, according to soil When growing	Soil should have been well manured with organic matter for previous crop, which crop should not have been a root one. Farmyard manure should be well dug in in Autumn in heavy soil, or in early Spring in light soil. On light soil Nitrate of Soda should be substituted for the Nitrate of Lime. Soil should have been well manured with organic matter for previous crop, which crop should not have been a root one. On heavy soil substitute 1 qr. of Sulphate of Potash for the Kainit and apply early in Spring.
When sowing When growth commences When growing When sowing When growth commences When growing	Farmyard manure should be well dug in in Autumn in heavy soil or in early Spring in light soil. Farmyard manure should be dug in in Autumn in heavy soil or in Spring in light.
When sowing Spring or Autumn according to soil When growing	The farmyard manure should be well dug in in Autumn in heavy soil or in Spring in light soil. On heavy soil 1 qr. Sulphate of Potash should be substituted for the Kainit, and applied in early Spring.
When sowing Spring or Autumn according to soil Autumn and Winter Spring, when sowing When growing When planting Autumn or Winter When preparing soil	Soil should have been well manured for previous crop, which should not be a root one. No farmyard manure is needed unless soil is exhausted. On heavy soils 2 qrs. Superphosphate should be substituted for the Basic Slag, and applied when the crop is maturing. Soil should be deeply worked and the farmyard manure incorporated in the Autumn. On heavy soil 2 qrs. Superphosphate should be substituted for the Basic Slag, and applied when the crop is maturing.
(a) When sowing (b) When growing	No artificial should be necessary if the farmyard manure has been dug in.
When sowing Autumn or Spring, according to soil When growth begins	Soil should have been well manured for previous crop, which should not have been a root one. On heavy soil substitute 2 qrs. Superphosphate for the Steamed Bone Flour and apply when the crop is maturing.

results are desired. One fertilizer is, however, better than none.

INDIVIDUAL VEGETABLE CULTURE

ARTICHOKES

Chinese Artichoke

This artichoke requires space and a well-drained, well-manured, deeply dug soil. The tubers should be planted in March, in drills 6 inches deep, allowing 12 inches between the plants in the rows and 12 to 24 inches between the rows. The surface of the ground between the rows should be kept well hoed, and early in July a liberal top-dressing of manure should be given. During July and August water should be freely afforded. In light soil the tubers may remain in the ground through the winter, and be dug as required. Or they may be raised about the middle of November and stored under sand or fine soil covered with litter.

Globe Artichoke

Full exposure to the sun is desirable, and frost is less harmful than damp. The ground should be trenched and heavily manured in the autumn, and the planting should be done about the beginning of April. The best method of propagation is by root division or suckers, as seeds cannot be counted on to come true. No plants should be kept after three or four years old, and it is well to make a small fresh plantation each year. The flower-heads should be picked when about half-grown and closed. Liberal watering and mulching, and, if necessary, staking, are the principal parts of its summer treatment. At the approach of winter some ashes or sand should be banked round the plant, and before frosts are expected the plant should be covered with litter or leaves. About the middle of March this should be removed, and the earth between the rows lightly forked and dressed with manure.

Jerusalem Artichoke

The Jerusalem Artichoke does best in a somewhat light soil, deeply dug, and in an open situation. The tubers should be planted early in March in drills 3 inches deep, 18 inches being allowed between the tubers, and 3 feet between the drills. In very heavy soil it is well to plant only just below the surface and to mix plenty of ashes with the soil.

Storing.—The leaves should be cut down early in November and the tubers may be left in the ground through the winter and dug as required.

Varieties.—Good varieties are *Old Red* and *White.*

ASPARAGUS

On clay soils the cultivation of asparagus presents somewhat of a problem, though even here, by throwing up the soil into ridges, by the addition of burnt rubbish and leaf-mould, and by surface manuring, asparagus of no mean quality can be raised. Where, however, the soil is of a more sandy nature, and the natural drainage is efficient, every one, with a little care and attention, may easily grow this excellent vegetable.

Soil and Situation.—A warm situation should be selected, preferably with a southern aspect. Protection from the prevailing winds must be afforded. The soil, whether light or heavy, should be deeply dug, and while in the case of heavy soils it is well only to enrich the top foot or so of soil so as to keep the roots near the surface; in the case of medium and light soils the ground should be heavily enriched with decayed farmyard manure, preferably to a depth of 4 feet or more.

Planting.—The ground being dug and levelled, divide it into 5-foot beds, with alleys 2 feet wide between each bed. Strong one-year-old plants, without tops, should be selected and in April planted 1½ to 2 inches deep in three rows in each 5-foot bed, the rows a foot from each side of the bed, and the plants 2 feet apart in the rows. Water well after planting if the weather is dry. Throughout the summer the principal work must consist in keeping the surface of the ground broken up by means of the hoe, and in destroying weeds as soon as they appear. Under no circumstances should any other crop be raised between the plants. About the end of January a mulch of stable manure may be laid on the surface and a sprinkling of earth used to cover it; or alternately a little nitrate of soda or guano may be applied in May. About the second week of February each crown should be covered with a few inches of soil or preferably sand, or sand mixed with soil. Shoots may be cut, or better, broken, as low as possible, when about 8 inches in length, being careful not to injure young shoots not yet fit for cutting. In the case of first-year plants, the cutting should not be too severe, and should not be continued after May. Moreover, a few of the smaller shoots should be allowed to grow up from the start of growth. In the case of older plantations it is unwise to cut asparagus after the middle of June. Cut down all stems in autumn.

Forcing.—See p. 172.

Varieties.—*Perfection*; *Connover's Colossal*; and *Early Giant Argenteuil.*

BEANS, BROAD

Soil.—Broad beans like best a deep, somewhat heavy soil, which should be deeply dug and moderately heavily manured in the autumn before sowing.

Sowing.—The earliest sowing may be made in a warm and sheltered situation at the end of October or early in November. Seed should be sown in the open for main crop purposes in February and March, successional crops being obtained by sowing a few each month right up to May or June. About 9 inches should be allowed from seed to seed, and 2 feet between the rows. A little earth drawn up to the roots when the seedlings are 3 to 4 inches high induces them to put out fresh roots. When the stem is covered with about 18 inches of flowers the top should be pinched off to encourage the growth of the pods. All laterals should be removed as they appear. Should the black fly attack the beans, immediately pinch-back all young shoots; this may arrest the pests. If this is not successful the plants must be syringed with a solution of soft soap.

Varieties.—Earliest crop, *Mazagans* or *Early Green Longpods* ; Main crop, *Giant Windsors*.

Dwarf Broad Beans grow some 12 to 18 inches high, are bushy in form, and occupy no more space than the tall varieties. *Little Marvel* is a popular variety.

BEANS, FRENCH OR KIDNEY

Soil.—Dwarf Kidney Beans or French Beans like a deep, rich soil, which should be deeply dug and manured in the autumn. They should be grown in an open, unshaded situation.

Sowing.—By sowing partly in the open and partly under glass, French Beans may be obtained during practically every month of the year. In the open the first sowing should be made under a south wall about the middle of April, sheltering the young plants as soon as they come up with a little loose litter. The principal out-door sowing should be made early in May, but it is well to sow a few seeds at weekly intervals right on to the beginning of July. Seed should be sown 6 inches apart in drills 2 inches deep, 2 to 3 feet being allowed between the rows.

Thinning and Transplanting.—When the young plants appear they should be thinned or transplanted so as to allow at least a foot from plant to plant in the rows. The pods must be gathered before the seeds are formed and the period of bearing will be prolonged if the pods are picked as soon as they are fit. *See also* Forcing, p. 172.

Varieties.—Early sowing, *Ne Plus Ultra* ; followed by *Negro Longpod*, followed again by *Canadian Wonder* and *Perfection* ; latest sowing the *Newington*.

BEANS, RUNNER

Soil.—The Runner Bean does best in a deep moderately retentive soil, which has been well manured and deeply dug in the autumn.

Sowing.—The earliest seed should be sown in a sheltered situation about the middle of May. Successional crops may be obtained by sowing in the open until the middle of June. Sow in drills, 2 inches deep, 5 inches being allowed from seed to seed in the rows and 6 feet from row to row. Water and syringe liberally in hot weather. A weekly soaking with liquid manure as soon as some of the pods have set will increase the crop.

Training.—As soon as the plants have formed their first leaves, tall poles 8 feet in height and firmly set in the ground should be provided. Dust the young plants liberally with soot to keep away slugs. The pods should be gathered as soon as ready, or they will become hard and stringy.

Varieties.—Earliest planting, *Earliest of All* and *Tender and True* ; later, *Scarlet Giant, Scarlet Emperor, Best of All*, and *Mammoth White*.

BEETROOT

Soil.—The soil should be deep and of medium texture. No manure should be added just before sowing, but the beet should follow a crop, preferably leeks, for which the ground has been heavily manured.

Sowing.—For early use, the turnip-rooted kind, of which *Sutton's*

Globe and *Crimson Ball* are good varieties, may be sown on a mild hot-bed in a frame from the beginning of January to the end of March, or about the first week in April, in a warm border in the open, in drills 1 inch deep and 15 inches apart. A little salt dusted into the drills at the time of sowing, and sprinkled between the plants occasionally during June and July, will materially improve the roots. The soil should be made firm after sowing, and the young plants should be thinned to about 9 inches apart. Dust the young shoots with soot or lime to protect them from the birds. The turnip-rooted kinds may also be used for later supplies, where the soil is too poor or shallow for the long-rooted kind. Where the soil is suitable, however, the long-rooted kind are to be preferred for all but the earliest crops. These should be sown in May under similar conditions to those suggested for the turnip-rooted kinds. *Cheltenham Green-top* or *Galloway Purple* are perhaps the best varieties of all this group. *Pineapple* and *Nutting's Old Dwarf Red* are excellent.

Storing.—Any roots that remain in the ground should be lifted before the middle of October, the leaves should be twisted off, the roots dried and carefully packed away in dry sand in a cool but frost-proof place. If carefully and periodically looked over the roots will remain in good condition until the following April.

BORECOLE

The Borecole or Kale is one of the most popular of our vegetables, for it is in season from October till April.

Soil.—A rather stiff, deeply-dug, and well-enriched soil is desirable. The manure should be added some time previously to planting.

Sowing.—The seeds should be sown from March to May in drills about 1 inch deep. The seedlings should be thinned out to 4 inches apart where necessary as soon as they appear.

Planting-out.—The plants may be planted out when about six to eight weeks old, about 2½ feet being allowed from plant to plant in all directions. Water liberally until the roots are firmly established.

Varieties.—Autumn supply, *A1.* and *Dwarf Green Curled* ; for Christmas, *Curled Scotch, Drumhead* and *Read's Improved Hearting* ; for early spring, *Asparagus Kale, Welsh Kale,* and *Cottager's Kale.* The spring varieties, instead of being sown the previous May, may be sown in early autumn, often with advantage.

BROCCOLI

The broccoli, with care, will supply a succession of heads from November till June.

Soil.—A well-tilled rich soil is necessary, as rapid growth is essential.

Sowing.—The seeds should be sown in an open position in drills ½-inch deep, 1 foot being allowed between the drills. The ground should previously be finely prepared, dressed with soot and rendered very firm.

Thinning and Transplanting.—Thin out to 6 inches apart as soon as possible, and finally to 2½ feet apart. Broccoli flourish in ground that has been used for another crop and not retrenched. If the soil has been well manured, it should be beaten down hard round the roots.

This will encourage hard stems and prevent too much leaf forming. The plants should be kept well supplied with water until properly established, especially the autumn-flowering varieties, and these must also be liberally watered in all stages of their growth during dry hot weather. Before severe weather sets in, the spring kinds should be laid over, with their heads facing the north. This operation checks the action of the roots and the plants consequently become less succulent and better able to resist frost. They are also put in the best possible position for covering with stable manure or any other litter when such protection becomes necessary.

Varieties.—Mid-winter supply, *Sandringham Winter White, King's Large* and *Superb Early White* ; to succeed these *Purple* and *White Sprouting Broccoli, Leamington, Late Queen,* and *Model.*

BRUSSELS SPROUTS

Brussels Sprouts require a deeply-dug and previously heavily manured soil, well-trodden before planting.

Sowing.—The seed may be sown in a warm situation in drills about ¾-inch deep, and about 10 inches apart, at the end of February or the beginning of March. Cover the surface with loose litter until the plants are well up.

Planting-out.—Late in April the young plants should be moved either to their permanent quarters, or to fresh ground, about 8 inches apart, so that they can easily be again transplanted 3 feet apart. Water well after transplanting. For the earlier supplies seed may also be sown very thinly early in August, the young plants being moved to their permanent quarters the following April, having been once transplanted in October. For a late supply seed may be sown in rather rich soil about the end of April. If the plants are developing too quickly a few of the leaves should be cropped back to stumps in the autumn. This also greatly encourages the production of sprouts. The top growth should be left intact until all the sprouts are cleared, when the top may be cut and used as greens. Should some of the lower leaves turn yellow in autumn they must be removed or the sprouts may rot. Do not cut the tops or heads till late winter or the stems will stop growing and the production of sprouts will cease.

Varieties.—Early sowing, *Dwarf Gem* and *Matchless* ; general crop, *Aigburth, Exhibition, Market Favourite.*

CABBAGES

Soil.—The ground should be deeply dug and moderately enriched a few months previous to planting. Cabbages should be liberally supplied with water at all stages of their growth.

Sowing.—For an early spring supply, seeds should be sown about the end of July, and again about the middle of August. Sow a little seed at frequent intervals, so that the crop may mature successionally. The seeds should be sown thinly in rows 8 inches apart and about 1 inch deep. Keep the beds moist and give a liberal dusting of lime, salt, or soot now and then.

Planting-out.—About six weeks from the time of sowing the plants may be placed in firm ground which has not been newly dug but has been prepared some two or three months earlier. Fifteen inches should be allowed from plant to plant in the rows, and 20 inches between the rows. Thoroughly soak the ground after planting and give liberal supplies of water, especially for the first few days.

Varieties.—*Ellam's Early, Flower of Spring, Harbinger* and *Favourite*.

For a summer supply, such kinds as *Main Crop, Sutton's Favourite,* and *Miniature Marrow* may be sown at intervals during the second half of April and the whole of May. They should be treated much as advised in the case of spring cabbages, but they should be planted out into somewhat richer soil, as their growth is much more rapid.

For autumn crops we may rely largely on the Coleworts. They may be sown in May and the first two weeks of June, and treated very much as recommended for spring cabbage.

For late autumn, and winter and early spring use, savoys and hardy winter cabbages may be sown during the end of May and first half of June. The small-headed kinds have the best quality, though the drumheads are large and hardy. Two good winter cabbages are *St. Martin* and the *St. John's Day*. For later use *New Year* and *Bijou* may be grown. Do not cut savoys before November.

Red cabbages are grown almost entirely for pickling. The cultivation resembles that of other cabbages. Seed is best sown in March ; good compact heads may then be obtained ready for pickling in the autumn. The red cabbage should only be gathered when the head is thoroughly formed, the stem being thrown away as valueless. Useful sorts are *Dutch Blood-red* and *Dwarf Blood-red*.

CARDOONS

The prickly Tours cardoon, the red-stemmed Marseilles, and the large-growing Puvis are all much better than the Spanish variety.

Sowing.—Seed should be sown in a cold frame or under glass without heat early in April. Seed may also be sown early in June in the open.

Planting-out.—Early in May trenches, some 18 inches apart, should be dug to a depth of not less than 18 inches, about 6 inches of thoroughly decayed manure being placed at the bottom of the trench and dug in and thoroughly incorporated with the soil. Plant out the seedlings about the end of May.

Blanching.—When the plant is 18 inches high fasten it to a stake, and tie the leaves lightly to it, earthing up the stem at the same time like celery. Throughout the summer water copiously and frequently with soft water and a little guano to prevent flowering. In September the early crop will be fit for use.

THE CARROT

Soil.—A rather light, sandy soil which has been recently enriched by the liberal incorporation of well-rotted manure suits carrots best.

Where the soil is cold and heavy it may be greatly improved by being well trenched and by the liberal addition of wood ashes, leaf-mould or old potting soil. If these ingredients are not available the soil may be broken up and then drawn with the rake into ridges a foot high, on which the seeds may be sown.

Sowing.—The first sowing may be made in a warm border at the end of February, *Early Shorthorns* or *Gem* being chosen. They are best sown about 1 inch deep in drills 15 inches apart, thinning to about 8 inches from plant to plant. Further seed may be sown in April and May, the *Scarlet Horn*, the *Nantes Horn*, and *James's Intermediate* being selected for this sowing. It is worth while to make a small sowing of *Early Nantes* about the end of June with a view to obtaining some nice small roots in the early months of the year. In all cases, but especially in the case of these June sown carrots, it is wise to add a fairly liberal dressing of soot and lime to the soil in order to reduce the attacks of insect and other pests to a minimum.

Storing.—Carrots may be drawn for the table as soon as large enough ; but the main crop for storing should not be taken up till the end of October, or even later, unless severe frosts set in. Remove the carrots carefully so as not to damage the roots and store in a frost-proof and fairly dry place. A covering of straw or sacking should be given against severe frosts.

CAULIFLOWER

The cauliflower is in season from June to November.

Sowing.—In order to maintain a succession three or four sowings should be made, the first being made on a slight hot-bed (*see* p. 172) in February or very early in March. Good kinds for this early crop, which is ready about June, are *Sutton's First Crop* and *Snowball*. The seedlings should be thinned out, hardened off and planted out in the open in April. Early in April a second and larger sowing should be made in the open ground. For this crop such varieties as *Dwarf Mammoth*, *Autumn Giant*, *Erfurt*, *Pearl*, *Purity* and *Favourite* may be sown, young plants being planted out in May and June. A third sowing should be made about the middle of August to stand through the winter. For this third sowing such kinds as *Walcheren* will be found best.

Planting-out.—When the plants are large enough to be handled they should be transplanted 4 inches apart in rich and well-manured soil. In June the April sowings will be fit to plant out where they are to grow ; in September they will be heading, and will continue to improve until the frosts of early winter.

When the heads begin to appear, shade them from sun and rain by breaking down some of the larger leaves so as to cover them. Water well in dry weather.

Wintering.—On the approach of winter, the plants in flower may be taken up with as much earth at their roots as possible and laid in by the roots on their sides in a light sandy soil, in some frost-proof place.

Autumn-sown plants are generally pricked out under frames for protection during winter, giving plenty of air in fine weather.

CELERIAC

Celeriac is hardy and of easy culture, growing well in almost any rich garden soil.

Sowing.—Seed should be sown in March, over moderate heat. The seedlings should be pricked out as soon as capable of being handled, and should be potted in 3-inch pots.

Planting-out.—About the end of May the plants should be transferred to the open. The ground intended for their reception should have been deeply dug and well enriched and should have been made firm previous to planting. Planting should be shallow, as at no stage should any earthing-up take place. Rather, indeed, should the soil be gradually drawn from the bulbs so that they may almost stand on the surface as do onions. Liberal supplies of water should be given throughout the summer, and it is well to keep the surface of the ground between the plants covered with a little leaf-mould or litter. From 12 to 15 inches should be allowed from plant to plant in the rows, and about 18 inches between the rows.

Storing.—At the approach of winter the roots should be taken up and stored like beetroots (p. 377).

CELERY

Soil. Celery prefers a soil not too light. In any case, deep cultivation is a necessity, and manure and water must be liberally afforded.

Sowing.—Seed should be sown under glass over a heat of about 70°. March is the month for the principal sowing, but a pan of early seed may be sown in February. As soon as the seedlings are able to be handled, about 2 inches high, the young plants should be pricked out singly into 3-inch pots, containing soil rich with well-rotted manure. From this time bottom heat is unnecessary, and the pots may be placed in a cold frame. Later the plants may be transplanted into bigger pots preparatory to the final planting in beds or trenches.

Planting-out.—The ultimate planting-out, when about 6 inches high, takes place for the main crop about the end of June, the earliest plants from the February sowing being put out about the end of May and the late crop about the end of July.

The trench system of growing celery is that usually adopted. A common mistake is to make the trenches too deep. They should, it is true, be deeply dug, and even the sub-soil should be broken up to some extent, but it should be left in position, covered with a layer of manure, and manure should be liberally incorporated with the soil itself. When actually ready for planting, the trenches should be 4 feet apart, about 16 inches wide, and 4 inches deep. In the trenches the young plants should be placed at intervals of about a foot and firmly trodden in. In addition to the stable manure celery will do all the better if a dressing of $\frac{1}{2}$ oz. each of ammonium sulphate and potash salts to every square yard of soil is well dug into the ground before planting. Water should be liberally given at once, and some shade afforded. The soil between the plants should be kept mulched with old manure so as to afford additional nourishment and to check evaporation. As growth proceeds, earth should be gradually hoed up round the plants, about 4 inches at a time, and patted down firmly to keep out the rain, though the principal earthing-up, which must be done in dry weather, should take place about a month before the celery is required. The leaves should be held together while the earthing-up is in process, so that no soil may be allowed to enter between the stalks. The hearts must be kept well above the earthing-up, and any side growths should be removed. The last earthing-up in the case of the general crop should take place about the end of October.

Varieties.—For early use *White Gem*. For main crop, *Superb White*, *Standard Bearer*; *Sulham Prize* and *Mammoth Red* are good red varieties,

CHICORY

Apart from its uses as a salad, Chicory affords two possibilities for culinary use. Its early growth may be forced and blanched after the manner of sea-kale (p. 388), and its unforced green leaves may be used in spring much as spinach is used.

Sowing.—Seed may be sown from the middle of April to the middle of June in fine soil which has been well manured for a previous crop, in rows 15 inches apart, the seedlings being thinned to about 9 inches apart in the rows.

Forcing.—About the end of October the roots should be lifted, packed in deep boxes in moist light soil, and blanched in perfect darkness. A little forcing should be applied if an early supply is wanted. Discard the roots after forcing. The *Witloof* and *Christmas Salad* are good kinds.

COLEWORT

(*See* Cabbage, p. 378.)

COUVE TRONCHUDA

The culture and treatment of this variety of cabbage are the same as for the ordinary cabbage. It is fit for use, like savoys, after frosty weather sets in.

ENDIVE

(*See* Salads.)

KALE

(*See* Borecole, p. 377.)

KOHL-RABI

The Kohl-rabi is especially useful as an alternative to the turnip where the soil is light, as it will stand severe drought—frost has no effect upon it. The roots are most palatable if eaten when half grown.

Sowing.—For a summer supply, sow the seed in March in drills about ¾ inch deep, and 18 inches apart. The young plants should be thinned as soon as possible to about 10 inches apart. Transplanting is undesirable. For autumn and winter supplies seed should again be sown towards the end of July. (Store as for Turnips, p. 391.)

Varieties.—*Short Top Green, Earliest White* and *Early Purple*.

LEEK

Soil.—Very deep, rich soil is essential.

Sowing.—For an early crop the seed may be sown in boxes early in February (with a layer of rotted manure at the bottom of the boxes) and kept in moderate heat. When some 2 inches high the seedlings must be pricked off 2 inches apart. Keep in a moderate heat till the middle of April when transfer to a cold frame, harden-off and plant out in May. Seeds may be sown thinly in the open successionally in a warm border from the end of February till the end of March, ½ inch deep in drills about 6 or 8 inches apart. The seeds should be soaked in luke-warm water for about 12 hours previously to being sown.

Planting-out.—As soon as they are large enough to handle the young plants should be thinned out, and may be transferred to their permanent sites when about 1 foot high about June. They must be planted firmly with their lower leaves just resting on the ground. If the ground is rich and moderately heavy, the leeks may be planted on the flat in rows, 2 feet apart, about 12 inches being allowed from plant to plant. When the soil is not so rich and heavy it is desirable to grow leeks in trenches. These should be about a spade's width wide, about 2 feet apart, and about 15 inches deep, and at the bottom of each should be placed a liberal dressing of well-rotted manure. On this should be placed a little soil, in which the plants should be planted. Give liberal dressings of liquid manure in late summer ; and at all times keep the roots moist.

Blanching.—As they grow, earth is to be thrown into the trench so as to keep an increasing portion of the stem buried and consequently blanched. When grown on the flat they must be kept well earthed-up by means of the hoe. (*See* p. 67.)

Storing.—The leeks can remain in the ground through the winter and be dug as needed, or they may be stored in sand in a dry shed.

Varieties.—*Dobbie's Model* and *Holborn Model*.

MUSHROOMS

Soil and Situation.—Mushrooms merely require a supply of horse manure, and a certain degree of warmth and moisture. If the manure when crushed in the hand binds, but no excess liquid is pressed out, it contains the required proportion of moisture. During the months of summer and autumn, mushrooms may, perhaps, most conveniently be grown in the open air, but during late autumn, winter and spring, some building or frame is necessary.

Making the Bed.—As a rule, about six to nine weeks must be allowed from the commencement of operations to the gathering of a crop. The longest litter should first be shaken out of the manure, retaining all up to the length of about a foot. This should then be made up into a heap about 2 or 3 feet high and from 4 to 6 feet wide, and is best made on a gentle slope. In winter-time this heap should be made up under cover, or the heat will too quickly evaporate. Every second day the heap should be thoroughly turned, so as to bring the central portion to the surface and the surface to the centre, and during this process all lumps should be broken up. This turning should be continued for about a week in winter and about two weeks in summer. The manure should then be placed in position and well trodden down. The temperature of the heap should be taken by means of a thermometer plunged to a depth of about 8 inches.

Sowing the Spawn.—As soon as this temperature gets to about 75°

or 80° F., the spawn, which must be fresh and which is bought in bricks composed of a mixture of manure and soil, containing dry mycelium of the mushroom, should be inserted in pieces about 2 inches square. These pieces should be firmly planted by means of a trowel about 2 or 3 inches deep in the manure, and about 8 inches apart. The heap of manure is then at once to be covered with about 2 inches of well-sieved sandy loam. Old garden soil is totally unsuitable for the purpose. This soil should be just, and only just, moist enough to hold together, and should be beaten firm with the flat of the spade.

The whole must then be covered over with a layer of straw, 15 inches in thickness, or with other material to exclude all light. Additional protection should be afforded by mats or sacking, if the spawn is planted in winter.

Care of the Bed.—Little or no water should be given to the bed until the mushrooms begin to come up. As soon as the mushrooms appear, however, a moderate supply of tepid water may be given once a week, and it will be found that a little common salt, or, better still, saltpetre, will be beneficial.

So far as possible, the temperature of the air of the building in which mushrooms are being grown should be kept at from 55° to 60° F.

If the bed is to retain its health mushrooms should not be cut but should be twisted off, separating the stalk as near the base as possible. Fresh soil must be added to fill the holes made by picking, and the bed must again be covered with straw.

Pests.—Woodlice play great havoc in mushroom beds. Traps baited with carrot or potato will do much to keep this pest within bounds.

ONION

Position and Soil.—Onions require a sunny, open position, and prefer a rather strong, deep and rich friable loam, though they grow quite well in any good light soil. Clay is not very suitable, while a newly broken soil is impossible as the foliage grows at the expense of the bulbs which are also open to attack by insect pests, always present in freshly broken soil. The ground should be liberally dressed with lime and with plenty of well-rotted manure buried deeply, trenched deeply, and ridged in early autumn. Dress the top spit liberally with soot or wood ashes (4 cwt. to the acre). On a light soil kainit (3 cwt. to the acre) and ammonium sulphate ($1\frac{1}{2}$ cwt. to the acre) are the most suitable manures.

Sowing in the Open.—The main crop should be sown as soon as the ground is in working condition, between January and mid-March. Make the seed bed (*see* p. 184) and sow thinly in drills $\frac{3}{4}$ inch deep and 12 inches apart. Seed may also be sown under glass in a temperature of 60° F. early in January. Harden off in April, and plant out early in May.

As soon as possible after appearance of the plants the surplus should be pulled out, without loosening those which remain. At least 3 inches should, at the first thinning, be left from plant to plant. Water well during the summer if the weather is dry.

1. Cutting seed potatoes; the potatoes may be cut into two or more parts, but each part must possess an eye. 2. Placing the sprouted potatoes, 15 inches from each other, in a trench 5 inches deep and with 3 feet between the rows. 3. A trench fully planted. See page 386. 4. Sowing turnip seeds; the seed is held between the thumb and first finger, and may be sown from March to May, and thinned to 6 inches apart as soon as possible. See page 391.

1. A row of carrots before thinning. 2. After thinning; carrots should be thinned to about 8 inches from plant to plant. See page 379. 3. A row of lettuces before thinning. 4. After thinning; thin to 6 inches apart as soon as the plants are large enough to handle; thin again finally to 12 inches apart. See page 394.

A sowing in the open should also be made about the middle of August to furnish young onions during the winter, and for use in summer before the main crop is ready. The seedlings are allowed to remain where sown until the end of February, when they should be planted out in a moderately but not too rich soil.

Storing.—Towards the end of September the bulbs should be well formed and the tops show indications of ripening. Where this is not the case go over the crops, bending or breaking them down with the back of a wooden rake, and repeat this as often as may be necessary to check the growth of the tops. As soon as the bulbs seem to be properly matured, which will be known by the decay of the leaves, take them up, spread them in an airy shed or sunny situation in the open air until thoroughly dried, and then tie them up in what are called ropes, hang them on a shady outside wall, and protect them from the wet.

Varieties.—Spring Sowing : *Bedfordshire Champion, Improved Reading* and *Up-to-Date* ; Autumn Sowing : *Carter's Record* and *Giant Rocca* ; Winter Sowing : *Ailsa Craig* and *Excelsior.*

PARSNIP

Soil.—To grow the parsnip properly, deeply dug, rich, sandy soil, which has been previously well manured, is desirable. If manure is used it should be well rotted, short farmyard manure, well buried to draw the long tap roots deep down and to discourage the production of side roots encouraged by the use of manure on the surface. The ground should be trenched 2 feet 6 inches, and ridged up as long as possible before sowing.

Sowing.—Seeds may be sown at intervals from February to May, the best-flavoured, though not the largest roots, being obtained by sowing at the later date. Drills should be made ¾ inch in depth and 18 inches apart. In these seeds should be sown thinly, lightly covered, and well trodden in, and when the young plants appear thinning should be begun, until ultimately not less than 6 inches remain between plant and plant. As soon as they are large enough, they may be pulled and used.

Storing.—During the winter the roots are best left in the ground as when growing, but any that remain over should, after having had their tops trimmed off, be lifted and stored in sand in the dark early in March before growth restarts. Should the winter frosts prove very severe, the crowns should be protected by a layer of ashes, bracken or straw.

Varieties.—*Student, Tender and True, New Century* and *Hollow Crown.*

PEAS

Soil and Position.—Peas require deep loam, which has been well enriched and deeply dug or trenched in the autumn. It is a good plan to dig a shallow trench on each side of the rows, so that during the summer months manure and water can be easily supplied.

Sowing under Glass.—The very earliest peas are obtained by sowing early in December at the rate of nine or ten seeds in a 5-inch pot in a cold frame. The plants should be thinned to six per pot. They must have little or no artificial heat, abundance of light, and free ventilation on every possible opportunity. These plants, after being hardened off, should be planted out in a warm, south border about the second week in March, in deep drills.

Sowing in the Open.—The first sowing in the open may be made towards the end of February, providing the land is not too wet. To secure a succession sow once a fortnight from this time up till the end of May, or even the middle of June. The seeds should be sown 2 to 3 inches apart in flat based drills 3 inches deep and 4 inches wide. Before sowing the drills should be dusted with wood ashes.

Dwarf peas should be planted in rows about 2 feet apart ; medium, 4 feet ; and tall, 12 feet.

A handful of potash salts to every twelve plants, dug into the soil just before planting, will materially help the crops.

Sticking.—Stick the peas when 3 inches high and between the main sticks small twiggy sticks should be inserted to give the peas a start. After sticking, they should be well mulched. (*See* p. 68.) In hot, dry weather, peas require a copious supply of water, and syringing overhead.

The peas should be gathered directly they are fit, and if it is wished to prolong the fruiting period no pods should be allowed to remain on the vine beyond this stage.

Varieties.—For earliest sowings : *Sutton's Seedling* and *Chelsea Gem* ; for early sowing in the open : *Early Giant, Marvellous* and *The Pilot*. To follow these *Telephone, Duke of York* and *Duke of Albany*. These may be followed by *Best of All, Windsor Castle* and *Veitch's Perfection*. These should carry us well into August. Following these we have the so-called late peas, such as *British Empire, Ne Plus Ultra* and *Carter's Michaelmas*, success with which can only be hoped for in favoured localities.

POTATO

Soil.—Potatoes do best in a deep, sandy, well-drained loam. Before Christmas farmyard manure should be applied at the rate of about 20 tons per acre. This manure may well be supplemented by a mixture of 1½ cwt. ammonium sulphate applied in the drill at the time of planting, and 3 cwt. basic slag and 1½ cwt. potash salts when preparing the soil.

Sprouting.—Tubers which are intended to be used for " seed " should be selected at the time of lifting. They should be evenly shaped and should weigh from 2 to 3 oz. each. They should be spread on the floor in an open shed until the skin is set and hard, and should then be packed in single layers in trays and stored in a room inaccessible to frost, where, nevertheless, they are fully exposed to air and light. In the case of very early potatoes these trays may be placed under the stage in the greenhouse or other warm place. A little fine soil may also be sprinkled over the potatoes, which should be slightly watered. By this means a certain amount of growth results, and the potatoes, if carefully planted out without damage to the new rootlets, will be more forward than others not treated in this way. In all cases seed potatoes placed in boxes should be arranged with their crowns upwards. The eye in the centre of the crown is that from which growth should be encouraged, as it is much the more prolific, and makes the strongest plant. Only three or four shoots should be encouraged, the others should be rubbed off as soon as they appear.

For the earliest potatoes a south border, preferably sheltered by a wall, should be chosen. The potato is peculiarly susceptible to frost, and it is therefore generally useless to plant before the middle of February even in such a situation. In heavy soils it is generally better to plant after the middle of March. For the main crop March is the best month to plant, but some late kinds should also be planted in April.

Planting.—The soil having been prepared and levelled, drills should be drawn about 5 inches deep and 3 feet between the rows. The tubers should be laid at the bottom of the drills, at a distance of about 15 inches apart, and should then be covered by the hoe. When planting the early kinds only 2 feet need be left between the rows. When the plants are 5 to 6 inches high the first earthing-up should take place, and this should be continued every three or four weeks until the plants are nearly full grown.

Digging and Storing.—Except in the case of early potatoes for immediate use, which are dug up as required, the tubers should not be dug up until the tops are quite dead. One plant should be dug up as a trial; if the potatoes are ripe the skin of the tubers will be set and the potatoes ready for eating. If they are to be stored they should be left in the ground three weeks to a month longer. They are best lifted with a fork inserted deeply under the tubers, which will then not be likely to be damaged. They should be cleared of earth, dried by exposure to the sun for a day or two, then stored in a dry cellar or other dark frost-proof building. Where no building is available, they may be piled up, interspersed with layers of straw, on some raised site, and covered with straw and then a thick layer of earth.

RHUBARB

Soil and Situation.—To produce really good stems a deeply-dug soil somewhat heavily manured with farmyard manure, or if not obtainable with bone manure. The situation should be sheltered from east winds.

Planting.—Carefully selected roots should be planted 5 feet apart in spring with the top bud 2 inches below the surface. Cut no stems during the first season. Do not weaken the plants by pulling too many stems from any one plant in any one year. Any flower heads should, however, be immediately cut away.

Forcing.—A mild degree of forcing can be effected by covering the young shoots (of plants at least two years old) in the early spring with sea-kale pots or drain-pipes, and surrounding these with a heap of fermenting manure. A large dressing of well-rotted manure should be dug in about the roots as soon as one has finished pulling the leaves. The roots should be lifted and divided every three to four years. Propagate by division of roots.

Varieties.—*Daw's Champion*; *Victoria* (for summer use); *Champagne* (for early use) and *Stott's Monarch*.

SALSIFY

Soil.—Salsify does best in a deep, sandy soil. The manure should be buried 9 or 10 inches deep, the surface only having been enriched either for a previous crop such as celery or peas or by the addition of some well-spent hot-bed soil or old manure.

Sowing.—Sow thinly about the end of April in drills 1 inch deep and 12 inches apart. As soon as the seedlings are about 2 inches high they should be thinned to 5 or 6 inches apart. They will be ready for use in the early part of November.

Lifting and Storing.—The roots are best left in the ground throughout the winter and pulled as required for use. If the frosts are severe the roots should be protected with ashes, straw or bracken. Any roots that remain in February must, however, be lifted before the growth recommences, and stored under sand or earth and straw as advised in the case of beetroot.

Variety.—Giant French.

SAVOY

(*See* Cabbages.)

SCORZONERA

Scorzonera requires similar treatment to that advised for Salsify.
Variety.—Giant Russian.

SEA-KALE

Soil.—The ground intended for a permanent plantation should be deeply dug, and a very liberal dressing of manure should be incorporated, the top of the sub-soil being broken up and left *in situ.*

Sowing.—Sow thinly in March or April in drills about 2 inches deep, 18 inches being allowed between the drills. As soon as the seedlings have made six leaves they may be transplanted to rows 18 inches apart, allowing 9 inches from plant to plant. Water liberally and apply liquid manure frequently in hot weather. The following spring about 2½ feet should be allowed from plant to plant in every direction.

Propagation by Root Cuttings.—Far better than propagation by means of seed is propagation by root cuttings. Small roots, or rather pieces of root, about the size of the little finger, 5–6 inches long and ½-inch thick should be planted vertically about the end of March, bud-side upwards, the bud or the top of the piece of root—where there is no bud—being cut straight and planted just on a level with the surface of the ground. The bottom end of the cuttings should be cut slant-wise. Eighteen inches should be allowed between the rows in which these are planted, about 15 inches being allowed from set to set. The surface between the rows should be kept broken up by the hoe, and 2 or 3 inches of manure may be used as a top-dressing. On light soil a dressing of salt, about ½ lb. to the square yard, may also be given with advantage. Early in May all weak growths should be cut away and any flower stems must be removed, so that strong crowns may be formed for forcing in the winter. Water should be liberally given throughout the summer.

Forcing and Blanching.—If intended for early use the roots should be lifted about the end of November, as soon as the leaves part readily from the crowns. These roots can be packed closely together in light soil, the crowns being on a level with, or just below, the surface. They should be placed in a dark cellar or darkened part of the greenhouse, a large case placed under the staging being excellent for this purpose, and exposed to a continuous temperature of about 60° F. or a few degrees less. The soil in which the roots are packed should be gently watered and then covered with a layer of dry leaves or straw. The kale should be cut when about 7 inches long, and for a continuous supply it is important to place a fresh lot of roots under the forcing conditions weekly. The roots which have been lifted for purposes of forcing and which are not wanted for the moment may be stored away in soil crown uppermost, so that they can be placed in the forcing-house as required. Forcing takes about three weeks.

If it is intended to force sea-kale where it stands in the open the plants should be covered with sea-kale pots (or large drain pipes covered with slates) about the second week in November, and the space between the pots piled up with leaves, or, if these are unobtainable, with fresh manure. Enough leaves should be used to cover the pots. They should be lightly trodden down. Every fortnight a fresh supply of plants should be subjected to this process so as to yield a continuous supply. As soon as the crop has been cut the bulk of the heating material should be cleared away, but a little should be left as protection against frost.

Sea-kale should be cut when about 7 inches in length and care should be taken to remove not less than ½-inch of the old wood at the same time. *Lily White* is a good variety.

SHALLOT

Soil.—Shallots do best in an open situation, and in a medium well-drained soil that has been deeply dug and well manured for previous crops. The ground should have ¼ lb. of superphosphate to every square yard forked into it and must be made fairly firm before planting.

Planting.—The bulbs, which should be of medium size, should be planted in February or early in March just deep enough to make them firm, but should not be quite covered with soil. Six to 9 inches should be allowed from bulb to bulb and 12 inches between the rows. At the beginning of July the soil should be drawn away from the bulbs so that they may ripen and about the end of July or early in August, when the stems begin to die down, the bulbs should be pulled up and dried, after which they should be stored in a dry, moderately light room.

Varieties.—*Russian* is a good variety, and *True Shallot* for pickling.

SPINACH

Soil.—A deeply-dug, rather moist soil is to be preferred, a sandy, gravelly soil or sloping situation being unsuitable. If the soil is not moderately rich, a light dressing of well-decayed manure should be applied, but this should be kept some distance under the surface.

Sowing.—It is a good plan to soak the seed in water for twenty-four hours before sowing. Sow thinly in the permanent quarters, in drills 1 inch deep and 1 foot apart. When some 3 inches high the seedlings should be thinned out to 6 to 8 inches apart. Sowing in the open may take place at three-weekly intervals from the end of February to early in May. The *Victoria Roundleaved* is as good a variety as any. In gathering spinach, pick only the largest leaves ; do not pick the whole of the leaves from any one plant.

New Zealand Spinach.—If autumn or winter supplies of spinach are desired the *New Zealand* or *Prickly Spinach* should be sown early in August, 3 inches apart in drills with 18 inches between the rows, and must be liberally watered. Of this variety the shoots and not the leaves are used. For a winter crop a light, sandy soil is the most suitable. Early in February use the hoe among the winter spinach and give a liberal dressing with liquid manure.

Varieties.—Autumn supply : *New Zealand* and the *Carter* ; winter supply : *Victoria* and *Long Standing*.

TOMATO

In the southern parts of England tomatoes of moderate quality can, in favourable seasons, be grown in sheltered situations in the open air. But in most districts of England, and in average seasons in almost all districts, some kind of glass structure is necessary if ripe fruit is to be obtained.

Sowing.—Sow at weekly intervals through February and March, sowing ¼ inch deep and 1 inch apart in pans covered with glass and paper and placed close to the glass in a warm greenhouse or moderately warm frame. (Night temperature, 60° F. ; day temperature, 70° F.) They should be shaded from the strong sun till the seeds germinate. Seed sown in February should produce fruit in July. As soon as two leaves appear on the seedlings they should be pricked-off singly into thumb pots, a good half of the stem being buried in the soil. In a small greenhouse it is well that these young seedlings should be kept near the glass, to keep them short-jointed. As they grow they should be moved on into larger pots, and in about 10 or 12 weeks they should be ready for planting out into borders, 18 inches apart in the row, or into the final pots, some 10 inches in diameter, in which they are to be fruited. The first truss of bloom must be formed before the plants are finally planted out. Potting must be very firm.

Soil.—The soil required for the successful growing of tomatoes is fibrous loam, mixed with a little sharp sand, together with leaf-mould and some well-decayed manure. Do not give too much soil at first, start the plant in a small mound of soil, well-up near the light, and add to it as the roots grow and demand fresh compost. Over-manuring definitely tends to unfruitfulness, and no manure must be used which has not fully fermented. It is desirable to add a pinch or two of kainit or nitrate of potash at intervals through the growing season.

Cultivation under Glass.—Generous watering is essential at every period of growth, though a permanently saturated condition of the soil is, of course, undesirable. Under glass 3 feet should be allowed from plant to plant. Wires 9 or 10 inches from the glass may be employed to run the plants along under the glass. All side shoots must be nipped off, only the flower trusses being allowed to break from the main stem. The plants should have their heads pinched out as soon as they reach the top of the wires. To " set " the fruit pass a rabbit's tail over the flowers each day. Although warmth is necessary, over-heating is to be avoided. A night temperature of 55° to 60° F. and a day temperature of 60° to 70° or 75° F. should mark the extremes. Ample ventilation should be given. (*See* p. 164.) Seeds may be sown in June and July to furnish tomatoes through the winter.

Cultivation in the Open.—When it is proposed to grow tomatoes in the open-air, seeds should be sown in March under conditions similar to those already suggested. Suitable varieties, such as *Evesham Wonder* or *Ideal* should be selected for the purpose. The young plants, when some 15 inches high, should be cautiously hardened, and should be planted out about the end of May. A medium loam is the most suitable soil, and good drainage is essential. The best situation for tomato plants is against a south wall fully exposed to the sun. For the first week or so the plants should be protected at night by means of sea-kale pots or drain-pipes. They should be well watered with liquid manure to keep up a rapid growth. As soon as the blossom-buds appear watering should cease. Stop the side-shoots by nipping off the tops, and throw out all those sprays that show little signs of fruit, and do not allow the plant to grow much over 3 feet high. Water only to prevent a check in case of very severe drought. In dry weather a mulching with manure is very beneficial.

If the fruit will not ripen cut off the branches on which full-grown fruit is found, and hang them in a warm, dry greenhouse to mature.

Varieties.—*Britain's Best, Best of All*, and for early sowing *Orange Sunrise.*

TURNIP

Soil.—The most suitable soil for this vegetable is a sandy loam which has been deeply dug and well manured for a previous crop.

Sowing.—Successional sowings may be made in the open in March, April, and May, the *Red* and *White Milan* varieties, the *Early Paris Market* and the *Snowball* being chosen. The plants should be thinned to at least 6 inches apart as soon as possible. Turnips intended for autumn and early winter use should be sown in an open situation in July, the *Redtop Mousetail* and *Veitch's Red Globe* are most suitable. Sown the first week in August for mid-winter crops, *Orange Jelly* and *Golden Ball* are good mid-winter kinds.

Storing.—When frost sets in the turnips should be covered with a few inches of leaves or litter and left in the ground. In the spring any roots left will send up a crop of young green shoots—" turnip-tops " —which have considerable value as a green vegetable.

VEGETABLE MARROW

Soil and Situation.—This vegetable requires a deep, light, rich soil and a fairly sheltered position, where ample water can be supplied in dry weather.

Early marrows can be grown in frames after the manner of cucumbers, but as they require less heat, it is well to let the fermenting mass consist half of leaves and half of stable manure. The temperature at which these early frame marrows should be kept should vary from 55° F. to about 70° to 75° F. When the plants begin to bear fruit 1 oz. each to the square yard of superphosphate and sulphate of ammonia should be applied or well watered in. If slugs are tiresome a dressing of soot over the soil will keep them away. But the majority of marrows will naturally be grown in the open air.

Sowing.—Two seeds should be sown 1 inch apart early in April in each 3-inch pot or pan, filled with light, sandy soil, covering the seeds about 1½ inches. The seeds are placed flat, on their sides, not vertically in the soil. Place near the glass in gentle heat and keep fairly moist, and as soon as the plants are sufficiently strong to handle pot them off into 7-inch pots, putting two plants in each, and replace them near the glass in the warmth. When well established, remove to a cold frame, and gradually harden-off. Towards the end of May, or as soon as the weather is warm and appears to be settled, plant them out and protect them for a time by handglasses or other means and water well until the roots get hold of the soil. Train and regulate the shoots, so as to prevent them from growing too closely together, and stop them, if necessary, to forward the growth of the fruit. After a few of the marrows have set, but not before, a weekly dressing of liquid manure should be given, or artificial manures may be applied as advised for frame marrows. If it is impracticable to sow under glass seeds may be sown in May on the bed itself. Three seeds are usually planted 1½ inches deep and 9 inches apart in the form of a triangle, each seed or patch of seeds being covered with an inverted flower-pot, the hole being covered with a piece of tile. When the young plants are up they should gradually be hardened by the removal of the pots for increasing periods during the daytime. Two of the three seedlings in each group should be removed as soon as the rough leaves have appeared.

Making the Bed.—The bed for marrows grown in the open should be made up in about the second week in May. A shallow trench about 4 feet wide should be dug, and about 18 inches depth of an equal mixture of leaves and half-rotten stable manure should be laid in this. This fermenting mass should then be covered with the soil taken out from the trench.

Cutting.—Marrows should be cut while the skin can still be broken by the thumb-nail, the earliest to be cut usually being some 9 inches long.

Varieties.—The Melon, Moore's Cream, Tender and True and Long White.

SALADS

CORN SALAD

Sowing.—Sow in drills, about 3 to 6 inches apart, in light, rich soil in a warm situation. Successional sowings between February and

September will give a supply almost all through the year. Water liberally. The leaves should be eaten when they are young and tender; that is when the plant has about four leaves. Protect from severe frost with a covering of hay or straw.

CRESS

Sowing.—Sow four days earlier than the mustard in order to have both ready at the same time. Sow thickly and cover very lightly with soil in the open in March or April in a sunny spot and every fortnight for a succession from April to September in a moist and sheltered position. The seed leaves only are eaten. For winter use, sow from October to March in boxes placed in a greenhouse or window.

CUCUMBER

Soil.—Early in March a hot-bed should be prepared. (*See* p. 172.)

Sowing.—In a few days, when the steam generated by the hot-bed has been allowed to escape, seeds may be sown in the bed, rather more being sown than plants are required. The seedlings will make their appearance above ground in two or three days.

Cultivation and Training.—As soon as the plants appear, a day temperature of about 80° F. and a night temperature of 60° F. should be aimed at. The temperature should be regulated by the opening of the lights so as to admit air. Should the night temperature much exceed 60° F., it is well to wedge up the lights about $\frac{1}{2}$-inch when shutting for the night and during hot weather this amount of night ventilation may be increased. When the plants are grown in a frame and have made two leaves pinch out the point above the second ; each plant will then send out two lateral shoots above the second leaf on each shoot ; pick off the top. After that, stop them above every fruit, and as the plants grow add fresh soil to keep the roots covered till the whole bed is level, taking care that the soil is of the same temperature as that in the bed. If the cucumbers are grown in the greenhouse, stakes should be placed to lead the stems up to the first wire and until this is reached all side-shoots must be pinched out. The main-stems must be stopped when the top of the roof is reached. The laterals are run along the wires until they are some 2 feet in length when they must also be stopped. Liberal supplies of tepid water are essential, but the leaves should be watched as should they turn yellow it is an indication either that too much water is being given or that the temperature is too cold. Twice, or, in hot weather, three times a day, the plants and bed should be well wetted, either from the watering-pot by means of a fine rose, or by means of a garden syringe. In cold weather the lights should be covered with matting at night to exclude the frost.

From two to four plants will be sufficient for a two-light frame. Liberal dressings of guano are very beneficial. (*See* p. 327.)

The cucumbers should be gathered as soon as they have attained adequate size, and malformed ones should at once be removed to encourage the formation of fresh fruit.

Varieties.—*Tender and True* and *Improved Telegraph.*

DANDELION

Sow from March till June in drills a foot apart, the seedlings being thinned to 9 inches apart in the rows. In November the roots may be lifted and stored in sand until they are wanted, when by planting in boxes and the application of a little heat in a dark place, nice blanched growths are obtained (*see* Forcing, Sea-kale, p. 388.) When used as a vegetable the plant may be left out of doors, and the young leaves gathered from March till June. The improved thick-leaved and improved broad-leaved are both good varieties.

ENDIVE

Soil.—Endive thrives in light moderately rich soil. The ground should be trenched to a depth of 2 feet and thoroughly manured.

Sowing.—The first sowing should be made about the middle of May. For the main crop sow in the middle of June, and again about the middle of July. Plants to stand the winter should be sown early in August. Sow thinly 1 inch deep in drills 12 inches apart and the plants, when ready, should be thinned out to 9 inches. Plenty of water should be given in dry weather, and liquid manure occasionally.

Blanching.—When nearly full-grown, the plants should be blanched. In the case of the earlier crops and the broad-leaved kinds tie them up loosely when dry, after the same fashion as Cos lettuce, and draw the soil up about each plant. But as late crops intended for winter use are liable to be injured by frost these and the curly-leaved kinds should be blanched by covering the plants with inverted pots, the hole in which should be closed with a cork. Blanching should be done at intervals, so as to have a continuous supply. The August sowing should be planted out in some sheltered situation. In many localities these plants require the protection of glass to winter them safely.

Varieties.—*Large Ruffec, Green Curled*, and *Green Batavian*.

LETTUCE

Lettuces are of two kinds—those coming under the heading of Cabbage lettuces, which are short and globular in shape, and the Cos kind, which have long leaves.

Soil.—Both kinds like a light, rich and deep soil. For the main crop of summer lettuces a piece of ground that has already been well cultivated should again be trenched, incorporating in the process plenty of good fresh stable manure. The layer of manure should be placed a spade's depth below the surface. This process will prevent many of the lettuces from " bolting," as is so apt to occur in hot, dry weather. Abundance of moisture at the roots and ample room for leaf growth are essentials.

Sowing.—Lettuces may be sown under glass any time from January to March, but it is unsafe to sow them in the open until after this date, when successive sowings once a fortnight until August should be made in the bed in which the majority of them are to remain. Transplanting is necessary in the case of part of the crop, but the best plants are obtained by sowing in the permanent position.

Sowing in the Open, Thinning and Planting-out.—Early in March the seed should be sown thinly in drills a foot apart and ¾-inch deep on the bed prepared as above, and when the plants are big enough to handle they should be thinned to about 6 inches apart, the thinnings being themselves planted out at the same interval elsewhere in the plot. Final thinning to 12 inches apart must be made if good lettuces are to be grown, and it is better to leave too few plants than too many. For two or three weeks after planting out the young seedlings must be well dusted with soot to keep off the slugs. Ample moisture will now be required.

Winter Lettuces.—Winter lettuces are obtained partly from special sowings and partly by the preservation of part of the late summer crop. Sow in successive lots from August to the latter part of October, the earlier sowings being made both in the open and in frames, but the later ones—those sown in October—in frames only. Fine soil, well mingled with old rotted manure, is necessary for the seedlings when pricked out. Of these seedlings some should be planted in frames on light soil, not too far from the glass, at 3-inch intervals, and when the young plants touch each other they should be thinned out by pulling for use and for planting out. These thinnings may be planted out in a warm border at 6-inch intervals, leaving a crop still in the seed bed. All the crop in frames needs careful handling, plenty of moisture being allowed, or warm, bright weather will cause the plants to bolt. Slight protection given to the outdoor crop will keep them safe through the hard weather, and it is probable that the plants will be crowded enough to need the removal and transplanting of every other one, a process which needs and is worth extreme care. If placed in March in a good warm sunny border, the lettuces will be useful in the very early summer.

Tying and Blanching.—Tie the leaves of Cos lettuces with raffia just above the centre when nearly ready for cutting, so as to blanch their hearts. Cabbage lettuces do not need tying.

Varieties.—*Holborn Standard, Paris White* (Cos), *Favourite* (Cabbage), *Giant White Cos, Black Bath Cos, Webb's Wonderful* and *Tom Thumb* (for frame).

MUSTARD

Mustard is grown in the same manner as cress. (*See* p. 393.)

ONIONS

(*See* Vegetables, p. 384.)

RADISH

The radish may be grown successfully all the year round by sowing the seed in a hot-bed (*see* p. 172) in frames from October to February, and in the open ground at fortnightly intervals during the remainder of the year.

Soil.—Radishes thrive best in a light and slightly limed loam, manured for a previous crop.

Sowing.—Sow thinly in drills 1 inch deep, from 3 to 4 inches apart for long radishes, and from 4 to 6 inches apart for the larger sorts, as the *Spanish*. Any seedlings that press on their neighbours should be at once thinned out. Early sowings, about February, will require to be protected from frost by a covering of litter, but this must be removed every mild day as soon as the plants appear above ground. Sheltered positions facing south are best for the early crops. When the weather is hot and the ground dry, water before sowing ; some days before drawing water the beds well, and keep the soil moist until the crop is finished. (*See also* Forcing, p. 172.)

Varieties.—*Red Globe Short Top* (early use), *French Breakfast* (summer use), *Turnip Red*, *Turnip White* and *Black Spanish* (winter use).

RAMPION

Sow in drills about 10 inches apart in March or April for use in autumn, and in May for a winter supply. Thin out to 4 to 8 inches apart in the rows. Lift all remaining roots in November and store in sand in a dry frost-proof shed. A rich soil in a shady position is necessary.

WATERCRESS

This salad plant is best grown in a stream of pure running water with a good gritty bed. Vigorous shoots 15 inches long should be placed evenly over the surface of the bed in March. If the water is then gradually admitted these shoots will form roots in a few days, when more water can be let in as the plants become established, but care must be taken not to admit the water too rapidly or the plants will be torn from their young roots. The watercress will be ready for cutting about August. Provided the soil is kept very moist watercress can be grown in deep trenches, the seed being sown in May. By growing *Brown Winter Cress*, which is planted in August or September, watercress may be had almost all the year round.

HERBS

BORAGE

This is a good plant for bee-keepers, whilst its flowers are used in claret-cup and its young leaves in salads. It grows in any good, ordinary soil, and should be sown in March or April, in shallow drills 15 inches apart, the seedlings being thinned subsequently to 10 inches apart.

CHERVIL

Chervil well repays careful cultivation, deep digging, and moderate enrichment of the soil. In the warmer parts of the country seeds may be sown early in September in a warm, dry situation, the seedlings being thinned to about 6 or 7 inches apart. This crop will need the protection of mats fastened on bent sticks when the nights are frosty. In other parts of the country the seed may be mixed with fine soil or sand in the autumn, and the boxes containing the mixture may be placed in a frost-proof room for the winter. About the end of the following February seed and soil may be sown together in drills in the situation that they are permanently to occupy.

CHIVES

Chives is of the onion tribe, and its shoots are used in soups and salads.

It likes a good garden soil, and is propagated by division in March or October. The plants should be in rows a foot apart, with six inches between the plants. The bed will need replanting each third year. Seed may be sown in the open in April.

FENNEL

Fennel likes a rich soil, and is propagated by seed and root division. Sow in April in drills an inch deep, the drills being 18 inches apart, and when the plants are about 3 inches high they should be transplanted and set 9 to 12 inches apart. Root division is done in March, the plants being replaced a foot apart in rows at the distance of a foot. The flower stalks should be cut off as soon as they appear.

GARLIC

Garlic requires to be treated in the same manner as shallots (*which see*).

HORSERADISH

Planting.—Trench the ground in late autumn to a depth of 2 to 3 feet applying very little manure, as a heavy dressing encourages a tendency to fork. Then take up some old roots, cut off the crowns about 1½ inches long, and remove all fibrous roots. Next, with a dibble, which is marked 2 feet from the lower end—that being the depth the crowns are to be planted—make holes 10 to 12 inches apart in rows 18 inches apart. This done, take a lath-stick split at the end, insert the crown in the slit, thrust it down to the bottom of the hole, and push it out by another stick which is thrust down for the purpose. It is unnecessary to fill up the holes, as they gradually fill as the horseradish nears the surface. If a fresh row is planted every spring, and another taken up, the crop will be kept in good condition, and a fresh piece of improved ground offered every year for other crops. The roots will be ready for digging in November two years hence, when the roots should be dug up and stored in sand until required.

LAVENDER

Soil.—Lavender needs good drainage and deep cultivation, together with a fair enrichment with old manure. A south aspect is best.

Propagation.—The best method of propagation is by offsets or slips, pulled off with a " heel " (*see* Cuttings, p. 189) in October, the plants being placed a foot apart, and transplanted a year later to 3 feet apart.

MARJORAM

Soil and Situation.—Marjoram likes a sunny spot and good soil. It is of two kinds, sweet marjoram, which is the most common kind, an annual, which should be raised from seed sown in gentle heat in March and planted out in May 9 to 12 inches from plant to plant, and pot marjoram, which is a hardy perennial and is raised from seed in the same way or increased by root division. Both kinds can also be sown out of doors in April, the seedlings being thinned later to their proper intervals of 9 to 12 inches, the plants increased by root division needing an interspace of a foot. The pot marjoram, as it outlives the winter, needs a dry soil and a warm position, or a cold winter may injure it.

HERBS

MINT

Mint will do well in a not too sunny corner of the garden, though not in full shade.

Propagation.—Lift the roots in March, divide them, and replant 9 inches apart in trenches about a couple of inches deep. Liberal supplies of water are needed.

Drying.—Each autumn when the plants are about to bloom the shoots should be gathered for drying and the plants should then receive a top dressing of well-rotted manure. Towards the close of autumn all the stalks that remain should be cut down to the ground. The mint should be replanted every third year.

PARSLEY

Soil.—Parsley requires light, rich, deeply-dug loam, with a good admixture of leaf-mould, sand and a little old mortar.

Sowing.—Two sowings should be made, one for the summer crop, sown in April, the other for winter and spring, sown in July. Sow thinly in drills 15 inches apart and an inch deep. Not until about seven or eight weeks after sowing will the seed begin to show above ground, when it must be kept carefully weeded and well watered. The seedlings should be thinned out when old enough to handle to 6 to 9 inches apart. Any flower-buds should be nipped off at once. The crop required for winter use should be picked close in September when a fresh crop of leaves will shoot up.

Winter Protection.—If a frame is available the plants for the winter supply should be transferred to it in August or September ; plant about 5 inches apart, and cover the frame with matting in frosty weather.

Parsley runs to seed in the second year, even when sown as late as possible in the previous season ; it is therefore necessary to make a sowing every year. Parsley needs semi-shade.

ROSEMARY

Rosemary likes much the same conditions as does lavender, and may be propagated by cuttings taken in April, and planted in a semi-shaded situation. They may be transplanted from the nursery bed in September or the following April.

RUE

Sow in gentle heat in April, or take slips in June and September. The rows should be 18 inches and the plants 12 to 18 inches apart.

SAGE

Sowing.—Sow in a sunny, sheltered spot in late March or early April, the seedlings, when large enough, being transplanted to a nursery bed about 4 inches apart, and later re-transferred to their final bed : this at about a year old.

Cuttings.—Cuttings with a " heel " may also be taken in April. Fresh beds should be made every three to four years.

SAVORY

Savory likes a rich but not too heavy soil, and the summer kind should be sown in April in drills 12 inches apart, subsequently thinning the seedlings to 9 inches apart. The winter savory may be raised in the same way, or the old plants may be divided and replanted in March. The winter savory is the simplest to grow, as it does not need yearly renewal; but both kinds should be grown for a continuous supply.

TARRAGON

Soil.—A sheltered position and a light loam are needed.

Propagation.—The plants are propagated by root division in March, the little plants being put in drills 3 inches deep and 18 inches apart. There should be 9 to 12 inches from plant to plant. The surface of the bed should receive a dressing of well-rotted manure, and another dressing again each year in autumn, when the stems should be cut down.

THYME

Thyme enjoys full sun and a light, rich soil. It is best raised by division in April, setting the roots at intervals of a foot in each direction. Seed may also be sown in March or April, or cuttings taken in summer. It is advisable to remake the beds each year.

VEGETABLE GROWING AT A GLANCE

Name	When to Sow or Plant	Amount of Seed or Number of Roots required for 50 Foot Row	Depth to Sow or Plant in Inches		Time of Germination in Days	Time to reach Maturity in Weeks
			Light Soil	Heavy Soil		
Artichoke, Jerusalem	March	7 lb. Tubers	3	1	—	30
Artichoke, Globe	Feb. (Heat) April (Open)	7 lb. Tubers	1	¾	—	70
Asparagus	March	½ oz. or 7 Plants	2	1½	14–25	170
Bean (Broad)	Feb.–May	1 Pint	3	2	7–14	15
Bean (Kidney or French)	May	½ Pint	2	1½	7–14	12
Bean (Runner)	May	1 Pint	3	2	7–14	15
Beetroot	April–May	1 oz.	2	1	9–18	17
Borecole or Kale	March–May Sept. (for Spring Use)	¼ oz.	1½	1	8	20
Broccoli	April–May	1 oz. for 8 Square Yards	½	¼	6–10	20
Brussel Sprouts	Feb.–March	¼ oz.	¾	½	5–12	25
Cabbage	March–July	¼ oz.	1	½	6–10	18
Capsicum	Feb. (Heat, 65° F.)	¼ oz.	½	¼	12	30
Cardoon	April (Cold Frame) June (Open)	½ oz.	1½	1	15–20	24
Carrot	March–May	½ oz.	1	¾	10–20	24
Cauliflower	Feb. (Hot-bed)	½ oz.	½	¼	6–12	20
Celeriac	April and Aug. (Open)				15	
	March (Heat, 65°F.)	¼ oz.	½	¼		24
Celery	Feb. (Heat, 70° F.)	¼ oz.	¼	⅛	10–20	32
Colewort	June–Aug.	½ oz.	½	¼	5–10	24

VEGETABLE GROWING AT A GLANCE—*continued*

Name	When to Sow or Plant	Amount of Seed or Number of Roots required for 50 Foot Row	Depth to Sow or Plant in Inches		Time of Germination in Days	Time to reach Maturity in Weeks
			Light Soil	Heavy Soil		
Kohl-rabi	March and July	¼ oz.	¾	½	6–12	30
Leek	Feb. and March	½ oz.	½	¼	6–12	28
Onion	Jan.–March; July–Sept.	½ oz., or 1 Bulb per Foot of Row	1 Only cover	¾ half-Bulb.	10 10 (seed)	30 30 (seed)
Parsnip	Feb.–May	½ oz.	¾	½	12–18	32
Pea	Feb.–June	1 pint	3	1½	7–12	15
Potato	1st Early: Feb.–March 2nd Early: March Main Crop: April	1st Early 8½ lbs. 2nd Early 4 lbs. Main Crop 3½ lbs.	6	4	14–21	16
Rhubarb	Feb.	10 Crowns	2	1	—	108
Salsify or Scorzonera	April	½ oz.	1	¾	6–12	28
Savoy	April	¼ oz.	¾	½	5–10	24
Sea-kale	March–April	1 oz.	2	1	15–20	90
Shallot	Feb.–March	1 oz.	¾	½	10	25
Spinach	Late Feb.–Early May	½ oz.	1	½	10–20	12
Swede	March–June	½ oz.	½	¼	12	30
Tomato	Feb.–March (Glass)	3 Seeds for every Plant required	½	¼	7–14	15
Turnip	March–Aug.	¼ oz.	1	¼	6–12	12
Vegetable Marrow	April (Glass) May (Open)	3 Seeds for every Plant required	1½	1	7–14	12

SALAD GROWING AT A GLANCE

Name	When to Sow or Plant	Amount of Seed or Roots required for 50 ft. Row	Depth to Sow or Plant in Inches.		Time of Germination in Days	Time to reach Maturity in Weeks
			Light Soil	Heavy Soil		
Chicory	April–June	¼ oz.	1	¾	6–15	25
Corn Salad	Feb.–March and Aug.–Oct.	½ oz.	½	¼	9	10
Cress	April–Sept.	1 oz. for 2 Square Yards	⅛	⅛	5	1½
Cucumber	Feb.–May	4 Seeds for every Plant required	1	1	7–14	15
Dandelion	March–June	¼ oz.	½	¼	7–10	32
Endive	May–Aug.	¼ oz.	1	¾	6–12	16
Lettuce	March–Aug. (Open) Jan.–March (Glass) Aug.–Oct. (Glass)	¼ oz.	¾	½	6–12	10
Mustard	April–Sept.	1 oz. for 1 Square Yard	⅛	⅛	5	1½
Radish	Feb.–Sept. (Open) Oct.–Feb. (Frame)	½ oz.	1	¾	6	7

The times at which to plant-out, the distances to which to thin-out the seedlings, and the most suitable soils will be found in the paragraphs on the culture of the individual plants, pages 374-399.

1. Planting crocus corms in September or October, showing bulbs in position (2 to 3 in. deep and 4 in. apart) before covering with earth. See page 240. 2. Early garden peas showing 9 to 10 seeds in 5-in. pots, before covering with fine soil early in December. Thin to 6 seedlings in each pot and plant out in March. 3. Section of a row of garden peas, showing the seed in place, 2 to 3 in. apart, in drills 3 in. deep and 4 in. wide, before covering. See page 385.

1. The ingredients of the compost correctly proportioned previously to mixing. 2. "Crocking" the seed box. 3 & 4. The seeds in position. 5. Covering the seed with fine soil. 6. The box covered with glass and paper to keep off the sun. 7. Seedlings placed up near the glass to keep them short-jointed and sturdy. See page 167.

CHAPTER XXIX

DISEASES AND PESTS

Prevention and Control

IN order that the diseases and insect pests of plants may be adequately controlled it is essential to understand the nature of the complaint, whether it is due to insects, fungi or bacteria, and it cannot be too strongly impressed that every effort should be made to detect the presence of disease at the earliest possible moment and to treat it immediately. All diseases are easily controlled at their earlier stages, while if allowed to run unchecked they soon become quite uncontrollable. All trees and bushes should be kept free from mosses and lichens, which harbour pests, by periodical spraying in winter or early spring, with one of the cleansing washes given on p. 405. Most amateurs are willing to spend time and money in spraying their fruit trees in spring and summer, when they can actually see the damage being done, but few seem disposed to give sufficient time to winter cleansing washes at a period when the pests are unseen, though still present. We would impress upon the reader the importance of winter spraying and the great value of preventive measures, which are far more effective than treatment once the damage has been commenced.

It must be remembered that all insects are not harmful to the garden. Many, too, are not only harmless but helpful ; the centipede, for instance, devours soil grubs, the hover-fly attacks greenfly, the ichneumon fly, while in the grub stage, devours the flesh of other caterpillars, and the ladybird, like the hover-fly, is a great enemy of the green-fly. The gardener should, therefore, learn to recognize these friends and must encourage them.

Insect Pests

The habits of the pest will determine the most effective methods for its prevention and extermination. Insect pests may be divided into two classes, firstly, those like aphides (green-fly) that puncture the bark and tissues of the young shoots and fruit, and suck the sap, thus reducing the vitality of the plant, and secondly, those that feed on the outer tissues of shoots and leaves. In this latter class are included most beetles and caterpillars. The former class, the suckers, must be controlled by the use of " contact " insecticides, that are sprayed actually on to the bodies of the insects themselves. These insecticides poison the pests through the breathing pores in the bodies, the soap in the solutions also helping to clog the pores ; they should be applied with considerable force in a spray from a moderately coarse rose. The second class of pest, the eaters and biters, are more easily controlled, for it is possible to cover their food with a thin film of poison ; if the whole plant is sprayed they will sooner or later be forced to eat the poison. To ensure that every particle of available food shall be poisoned, both sides of the foliage and all parts of the branches must be thoroughly covered with the solution. This must be applied in a mist-like form from a sprayer with a very fine rose, so as to produce an even film over the leaves and twigs ; as soon as the insecticide begins to drip from the foliage the spraying must cease. The actual insecticide employed depends upon the pest to be controlled and the season of application, for the poisonous effects of some solutions if they come in contact with fruit or vegetables are very lasting ; such poisonous washes must not be used within a certain time of the harvesting of the crop. *See also table*, p. 405.

Fungous Diseases

Fungi, once established, develop rapidly, and in the later stages little can be done to remove them. Efforts should, therefore, be directed rather at prevention than cure, and if the fungus does become established the earliest possible opportunity should be taken of controlling it. When trees have been attacked by fungus in the previous season all dead wood and " mummied " fruit should be cut out in winter and burned, care being taken always to cut back to healthy wood. The fungus finds its way into the tissues of the wood, and there passes the winter, where no amount of spraying can affect it. In early spring, the trees should be syringed with a fungicide projected on to the twigs and branches in a very fine spray. This will form a film that will prevent the establishment and germination of fungus spores blown at this season by the wind or carried by birds from affected trees.

If an attack occurs in spring or summer, a fungicide must be used in the same way, all parts likely to be attacked—foliage, bark and fruit—being sprayed until the solution commences to drip off. It may be found necessary to make a second, or even third, application at intervals of about three weeks. Two of the most useful fungicides are Bordeaux Mixture and Lime Sulphur (*see* p. 405).

Cleansing and Winter Washes

These are applied not only to destroy what insect and fungous pests they come in contact with, but also to remove lichen and moss from the bark of trees. The use of these washes is a most necessary, but unfortunately a much neglected operation, as the lichen and moss form an ideal hiding-place for insect and fungous pests. Caustic soda and lime sulphur (*see* p. 405) are excellent cleansers and can be applied at any time while the trees are dormant in winter and early spring, but not later than February; they must be used before the buds break into blossom.

Dusting Powders

It is generally preferable to spray affected trees and plants with liquid insecticides and fungicides, but powders applied in the dry form may be used, especially when dealing with the various forms of mildew. The powders must be dusted over the affected parts in the morning while the foliage is yet wet with dew and preferably in hot, dry weather. As the powder must be very fine and evenly distributed, it is advisable to use special dusting bellows or a "sulphurator." "Flowers of sulphur" is the powder most frequently used; hellebore and pyrethrum powders are also effective for certain diseases. (*See* p. 406.)

Grease Banding

is used to prevent the winter moth and other insects from crawling up the trunks of fruit trees to lay their eggs. The stems are encircled early in September with bands, ten to twelve inches wide, of some material which the crawling moth will be unable to pass; such materials as brown paper coated with cart-grease mixed with tar, or any other coarse grease of the kind; special bands may also be purchased. The bands, if possible, should be placed from four to five feet from the ground to prevent the females from being able to get over them. If the bark is rough and uneven, which would enable the pests to crawl up between the band and the stem, soft putty should be smeared over the bark to be covered by the band and should then be well rubbed in till an even surface is formed to take the band. Do not forget also to grease-band the stake supporting the tree—a point often overlooked. The bands should remain in position until the following May. In the case of bush fruit, when the bands cannot be placed at this point, spraying is the better method. The bands should be kept greased at intervals throughout the winter and early spring months, as the grease frequently becomes hard and will allow the pests to pass. Strips of sacking and haybands, some six inches wide, may also be tied round the stems of the trees, about a foot from the ground, to catch the caterpillars of Codlin moths, climbing up in June and July. It is best to remove them at the end of September or early in October, replacing them by the bands of grease used as preventatives of the attacks of the Winter moth. All bands removed should be burned at once to kill the larvæ that have hibernated in them, and all refuse lying round the trees should be picked up and burned. *See also* Soil Fumigation and Sterilization, p. 52.

Fumigation

The best time for this important operation in the greenhouse is the evening in calm, fine weather, or in the morning on a dull, windless day. To prepare a house for fumigation, shut all ventilators, and cover with damp matting all broken or cracked lights and all roof ventilators, which are likely to leak at all. Where convenient, plants which are in full flower should be removed during the actual process. Most gardeners will find the fumigating or vaporizing materials sold ready for use with the necessary apparatus for burning, highly satisfactory; the makers give detailed instructions which should be closely followed. Where the house is badly infested with any insect pest, it should be dealt with two or three times on successive evenings; this is almost always necessary when extirpating red spider. The next morning, or when the fumes have thoroughly cleared, open the doors and ventilators and go round the house with the syringe and warm soft water, and free all plants from dead insects, washing the bodies off the stems and leaves.

INSECTICIDES AND FUNGICIDES
When and How to Use

Preparation.	How to Make.	How to Apply.	Principal Use.
Arsenate of Lead.	Dissolve 1 oz. arsenate of soda, 2½ oz. sugar of lead in 14 gallons of rain-water, then add 1½ lb. black treacle. Harmless to foliage. (*Poison.*)	During spring in fine spray on fruit trees, as soon as petals have fallen and leaves have formed. Garden flowers and roses, by means of knapsack machine. This insecticide poisons the food of the pests. As it is poisonous never use where the spray is likely to fall on vegetables or fruit.	Fruit tree caterpillars, winter moth, lackey moth, magpie moth, tortrix moth, slug-worms, cherry saw-fly, beetles, goat moth and gooseberry sawfly.

PREPARATION.	HOW TO MAKE.	HOW TO APPLY.	PRINCIPAL USE.
Bordeaux Mixture.	Dissolve 1 lb. sulphate of copper in boiling water; then slake 1 lb. freshly burnt quick-lime in a little boiling water; mix well and dilute to 12 gallons with water. Stir well, and use at once.	Apply to potato plants when half-grown early in summer; to other plants at same time. An excellent fungicide. If necessary make second and third applications at intervals of 3 weeks.	Potato blight, apple scab, leaf curl, leaf spot, onion mildew, tomato canker, and vine mildew.
Carbolic Emulsion.	Dissolve ½ lb. hard soap in ½ gallon water, add ¼ pint carbolic acid, boil, stirring meanwhile. Dilute with 25 parts water as wanted. Label bottle "Poison."	Useful for summer spraying and as fungicide. Good surface spray.	Turnip fleas, bean and pea weevils, cabbage moth larvæ, eelworms, and leatherjackets.
Caustic Soda.	Dissolve 12 oz. caustic soda and 9 oz. pearlash in 8 gallons water, then add 8 oz. soft soap. Use rubber gloves.	A good cleansing winter wash applied by means of knapsack sprayer. Cleans bark and destroys scale. Use only when trees dormant.	Aphis, apple sucker, codlin and winter moths, fungi, mealy bug, red spider, weevils, wither-tip and brown rot.
Cleansing Washes.	See Caustic Soda, and Lime Sulphur.		
Copper Sulphate Wash.	Dissolve ¼ lb. of copper sulphate in 10 gallons of water.	For winter use only.	Die-back in gooseberries.
Hellebore Emulsion.	Dissolve ½ lb. of hellebore powder and ½ lb. of soft soap in a little hot water and dilute to 5 gallons. Mix thoroughly.	Used when arsenate of lead not practicable, owing to possible poisoning of fruit.	Fruit tree caterpillars, especially those of sawflies and the magpie moth.
Lime Sulphur.	Boil 5 gallons slaked lime and 5 lb. flowers of sulphur in water for about 1 hour, stirring meanwhile; make up to 25 gallons. Harmless to foliage.	Summer spraying on foliage; makes good combination with arsenate of lead. Strain solution before use, and do not use apparatus having copper fittings. Give second and third applications at 3-weekly intervals. A good fungicide, insecticide, and cleanser.	Apple scab, apple sucker, black beetles, blister mite, flower beetles, mildew, brown rot, red spider scales scab, weevils and woolly aphis.
Lime Wash.	Slake 6 lb. of quicklime with a little water, then dilute to 5 gallons. See that the lime is not air-slaked before use. Stir well.	A wash for applying to the trunks of fruit trees just before the bloom opens. A good insecticide. also an excellent cleansing wash. Strain two or three times before use in sprayer.	Aphides, lichen and mosses on tree trunks.

Preparation.	How to Make.	How to Apply.	Principal Use.
Liver of Sulphur	Dissolve 3–5 oz. potassium sulphide (liver of sulphur) in 10 gallons water, add ¼ lb. soft soap. Does not affect zinc paint.	For outdoor and greenhouse use as summer spray. Make fresh as wanted.	Bean canker, cucumber and melon leaf blotch, gooseberry, rose and vine mildew, red spider.
Naphthalene Emulsion.	Dissolve ¼ lb. naphthalene, after crushing, in ½ gallon paraffin; boil 1 lb. soft soap, stirring in other ingredients. For use, dilute with 50 parts water.	Spray for summer use. Mixed with liver of sulphur for red spider, should be repeated in three days.	Ants, bean and pea weevils, cabbage moth larvæ, eel-worms, leatherjackets, and turnip fleas.
Nicotine Emulsion.	Nicotine 98% ½ to ¾ oz., soft soap ½ lb., and soft water 10 gallons. Boil the soap in 1 gallon of water, add the nicotine, and make up to 10 gallons. (Poison.)	Reliable insecticide for use at all times; on fruit trees as soon as blossom has fallen and leaves have formed. Apply as coarse spray. One of the most effective "contact" poisons. Must be used at least 14 days before fruit or vegetables are to be gathered.	Aphides, apple sucker, black fly, celery fly, green fly, sawfly grubs, caterpillars, white fly, leaf-miners and woolly aphis.
Paraffin Emulsion.	Boil 1 lb. soft soap in 1 gallon rain-water, while hot mix in 1 gallon paraffin by means of syringe. When required for use dilute with rain-water to 20 gallons, mixing well.	Stringent summer wash and soil spray.	Apple sucker, aphides, bean and asparagus weevils and beetles, mussel scale, onion and carrot fly, red spider, turnip fleas and woolly aphis.
Pyrethrum Powder Emulsion.	Dissolve 1 lb. of pyrethrum powder and ¼ lb. of soft soap in a little hot water for about 4 hours, dilute to 5 gallons and mix thoroughly.	Apply as fine spray.	Ants, aphides, beetles, caterpillars, and weevils.
Quassia Emulsion.	Steep 1 lb. quassia chips in 1 gallon water for 12 hours, melt ½ lb. soft soap and add, make up to 8 gallons with water	For use in warm weather after showers.	Black fly, green fly, hop aphis, red spider, and woolly aphis.
Soda-Resin Wash.	Boil 1 oz. caustic soda and 8 oz. powdered resin in 1 pint of water; dilute to 1 to 2 gallons.	Spring wash, hinders insects coming to life.	Brown currant scale, mealy bug, mussel scale, oyster scale and woolly aphis.
Winter-washes.	See Caustic Soda, and Lime Sulphur.		

SOME COMMON DISEASES AND PESTS

American Blight.—*See* Woolly Aphis.

Ants.—The best time to get rid of ants is in the early spring, when all the young brood is hatched and food is greatly in demand. Sprinkle sugar round their haunts and they will reveal their nest by carrying the sugar into it. Saturate the nest with paraffin or some strong disinfectant, or destroy it with boiling water. Empty honey jars or old treacle tins make good traps for the little pests, and hundreds may be easily destroyed by plunging the infested traps into boiling water. Old pieces of sponge dipped in syrup are equally efficacious. *Plants Most Usually Affected.*—A great variety of plants, especially when attacked by Aphis and Mealy Bug, the ants acting as carriers.

Aphides.—The common name for all the many species of aphis is "Green-fly," probably from the brilliant green of the aphis affecting the rose. Many kinds of aphis are, however, coloured differently : white, reddish, and black aphides being as common as the green. Aphides are sucking insects, not chewing ones, so that in order to deal with them, it is not enough merely to poison the surface of their food plant, as is the case with caterpillars and such creatures. The aphides pierce right through the poisoned surface and suck the juices of the plant, so that, to deal with them at all effectually, the insecticide has to be applied directly to their bodies. The best way to do this is to spray the plants on which the aphides are found with a solution of soft soap and quassia chips, with nicotine water, or with paraffin emulsion (*see* p. 406), the spraying being done directly on to the insects themselves and as soon as possible after the pests are discovered. All these insecticides are better used slightly warm. The spraying should be fairly violent, so as to dislodge as many of the creatures as possible. A mere solution of soft soap and warm water, or even, in some cases, warm water alone, will do a good deal towards the cleansing of the plants. Where possible, as in the case of choice rose trees, they should be gone over with a stiff paint-brush, all the aphides being either brushed off or killed by squashing with thumb and finger. Alternatively, the infested shoots may sometimes be turned down and actually immersed in the insecticide.

The insect which deposits the sticky substance known as " Honeydew " is an aphis, and on this gummy substance a fungus grows, which is known as "sooty mould," and does a great deal to weaken the plant by blocking up the pores on the surface of the leaves, and thus suffocating the plant. A lime wash applied in March is especially vulnerable to these honey-dew producing aphides. The black fly is especially common on the broad beans, where the tips of the shoots and undersides of the leaves are affected, and it also delights in the large Oriental and other poppies. Special efforts should always be made to exterminate aphides in spring and autumn. If roses or other plants under glass are attacked by green-fly, they must never be sprayed, but should be fumigated (*see* p. 404). *Plants Most Usually Affected.*—Apples, plums, cherries, currants, roses, broad beans, cabbages and Brassic generally, also many indoor plants.

407

Apple Aphides.—There are several kinds of these aphides, mostly purple, pink, or green in colour. The eggs, which are laid on the small twigs of the trees, hatch out in April. The foliage becomes badly curled and turns reddish-brown. In severe cases the foliage drops, the fruit is deformed, stunted and useless and the tree will take a year or often more to recover. *Treatment.*—Spray the trees all over in April with a nicotine and soap solution as soon as the pests appear, and repeat the operation frequently at short intervals. A winter wash also should be applied in December or early in January.

Apple Blossom Weevil.—This is really a little winged, brownish-grey beetle about a quarter of an inch long. The insect is distinguished by a yellowish-white, V-shaped mark across the back. It spends the winter in the earth or under the tree bark, and attacks the unopened flower-buds early in spring. It pierces the bud, laying its egg in the hole, never attacking the opened flowers. The grubs eat the ovaries of the flower, which is thus rendered sterile; the petals turn brown and remain on the trees for some time. The perfect insect appears in midsummer. It has the habit, common to all the weevil family, of dropping to the ground if alarmed, and much may be done to thin it out by spreading sheets of tarred paper on the ground under the affected trees on a warm summer day and shaking the trees suddenly. Many of the insects will fall on the papers and be trapped. In May the trees should be banded with greased paper, which is removed and burned in October, when the beetles will have finished crawling up the trunks to hibernate.

Apple Blossom Wilt and Wither Tip.—In this fungoid disease the blossom and young shoots wither and turn brown a short time after the buds have opened. In addition to the withering of the flowers and the consequent loss of fruit, the disease will at times find its way through the flower stalk to the fruit spurs and thence even far into the older wood, which it causes to become cankered and to die back. The leaves turn brown, shrivel, and usually hang on the trees during the winter. When the old wood is thus attacked, greyish pustules form on the bark in winter. These, in spring, produce powdery spores, which are carried by the wind and infect the opening buds, and thus spread the fungus. *Treatment.*—In summer all the brown and shrivelled shoots must be cut away and burnt, pruning well back to sound, healthy wood; in winter any affected shoots must be similarly cut out and burnt. In January, or early in February, a winter wash of caustic soda should be applied. *Plants Most Usually Affected.*—Apples.

Apple Brown Rot.—The first signs of this fungus are small, brown patches of decay in the tissue of the fruit. The putrefaction spreads rapidly, and concentric but irregular rings of pustules appear beneath the skin. These break through and become covered with a greyish-yellow powder. The skin of the fruit shrivels and the apples dry up and wilt, and unless picked, may remain on the tree through the winter as " mummified " fruit, which is the most frequent cause of the spreading of the disease. The fungus also attacks stored fruit. Cherries, pears and plums also suffer from this disease in another form, which does not infect apples. *Treatment.*—Go over the trees at intervals in summer and pick off all tainted fruit, and at the same time cut out any diseased shoots. In winter remove and burn all diseased wood and mummified fruit ; spray with Bordeaux Mixture in spring when the buds are beginning to open, and twice subsequently at intervals of three weeks. *Plants Most Usually Affected.*—Apples, Cherries, Plums.

Apple Canker.—Few diseases are more destructive than canker. The fungus enters through a wound in the bark, however small ; it often gains access through the punctures made by the woolly aphis. The point of entry is usually at the base of a bud or where two shoots or branches join. The disease is first apparent as small, concave patches on the bark. These increase in size and become elongated, the bark of the branches swells, cracks and large, deep wounds are formed. Concentric rings appear on the bark round the wound, and if these encircle the branch completely, the latter soon dies. Low-lying, ill-drained, heavy soil predisposes the trees to attack, but there must be a wound in the bark for the fungus to enter. *Treatment.*— Spraying is of no avail. All affected shoots and branches must at once be cut back to sound, healthy wood, and the diseased parts must immediately be burned, the cut surfaces on the trees being painted with Stockholm tar, white paint, grafting wax or clay. Badly cankered trees should either be taken right down and burned or should be cut hard back and grafted with an immune variety. Low-lying, damp, heavy soil should be drained, and every effort must be directed towards warding off woolly aphis. *Plants Most Usually Affected.*—Apples. Some varieties are more prone to attack than others ; a few, including *Bramley's Seedling*, seem almost immune from the disease.

Apple Capsids.—It is only during recent years that Capsid Bugs have become a menace to fruit growers. They must now be regarded as the most dangerous insect pest of the apple in England, and also one of the most difficult to control. Until recently the only harmful species was the Apple Capsid. Within the last few years a second species of capsid, the Common Green Capsid, has shown signs of attacking apples. Capsid Bugs feed on the sap of the plants, first attacking the young growing leaves. The punctures show as small brown spots. As the leaves become larger, parts round the punctures die and fall out, with the result that the attacked leaves are deformed and under-sized. The shoots are also attacked and are thus seriously checked or even killed. The injury to the fruit is, however, most serious. The apples attacked by the bugs are usually deformed, the skin showing rough, russeted patches, and having scattered pits and pimples due to the original punctures. Really bad specimens are rough and shape-less, often with deep cracks, and the whole surface is so rough and corky that the fruit is of little or no value for the market The crop is much reduced, as many of the fruits may fall off before they reach maturity. The eggs of the Apple Capsid are oval, white in colour, are laid under the bark of the apple twigs, and are practically invisible unless the twig is peeled. Towards the end of April, the eggs produce small green insects, which might be mistaken for aphides (Green-fly). They are, however, much more active. The young capsids, as soon as hatched, creep in between the developing leaves and flower buds, where they commence their work of destruction, feeding on the leaves, shoots and young fruit. From the end of May to the middle of June they become full-grown. The full-grown bugs are winged and bright green in colour, and, as in their younger stages, they are very active and fall off the trees when disturbed. The eggs are laid from the middle of June to the middle of July, sometimes later. They remain through the autumn and winter and give rise to bugs the following spring. *Treatment.*—This pest is very difficult to control. So far a nicotine and soft soap emulsion has proved most effective. The following formula has proved satisfactory : Nicotine (95–98 per cent.), 3 oz. ; soft soap, 4 lb. ; water, 40 galls. A coarse rose should be used and every part of the tree must be thoroughly wetted, as a few bugs are capable of causing a lot of damage. The time to apply the spray will vary with the season, but generally it is best applied a week or ten days before flowering. A watch should be kept for the first spotting of the leaves. After allowing ten days for the majority of the bugs to hatch out, the spray should be applied. In bad cases a second spraying may be necessary after the petals have fallen. Although most tar distillate winter washes have so far given indifferent control, a new form recently developed has proved more successful. *Plants Most Usually Affected.*—Apples, Black and Red Currants and less frequently Gooseberries.

Apple Mildew.—In this disease, which is due to a fungus, the buds, leaves and small shoots are affected in spring ; they become covered with a whitish mould and eventually shrivel up. If conditions are favourable to it, the disease quickly spreads by means of spores blown from leaf to leaf. *Treatment.*—Spray the affected parts with lime sulphur, and cut out all diseased portions in autumn while the effects of the mildew can still be seen. The following spring any buds still affected must be pinched off and burned, and as a preventive measure the trees should again be sprayed.

Apple Sawfly.—This sawfly is about a quarter of an inch in length, is reddish-yellow in colour with the upper parts of the head and body black. It lays its eggs in the blossoms, and the whitish maggots enter the young fruit through the side and eat out a large hole in the centre. When mature, the maggots drop off the trees, pass the winter in the ground, and emerge as complete sawflies the following April or May. The affected fruit remains small and generally falls to the ground in June or July. *Treatment.*—Remove all young fruit pierced with holes, and allow poultry to range through the summer over the ground under the infested trees. This pest can also be successfully controlled by spraying with nicotine and soft soap. The spraying should be started five or six days after the petals have fallen; in bad attacks a second spraying in seven days' time may be necessary.

Apple and Pear Scab.—Of fungoid diseases of the apple and pear, that popularly known as Scab is very common. It is very disfiguring to the fruits, making large, dark yellowish-green, roundish patches, and attacking both them and the leaves, which are usually attacked first. The spores on these leaves are carried by the wind on to the young shoots and fruit, and will thus rapidly spread. If the disease appears early in the season, the fruit will become cracked or malformed and will probably fall from the tree. *Treatment.*—Trees attacked by it should be sprayed with weak Bordeaux Mixture, not more than half its full strength, in the beginning of the flowering season, just as the buds are opening ; and the operation should be twice repeated—once when the petals are falling, and again when the young fruits are just beginning to grow, and are about the size of a pea. Pears should not be sprayed until the fruit is just setting and again a month later. The underside of the foliage must be well sprayed. All diseased wood, which will be seen to be blistered and rough, should be cut away in winter before the tree breaks into fresh growth in the spring. Fruit affected with Apple Scab is apt to rot, does not keep well, and will cause decay in fruit with which it comes in contact. *Plants Most Usually Affected.*—Apples and Pears.

Apple Sucker.—The larvæ of the Apple Sucker are provided with peculiar mouths, with which they suck the juices from the buds and young shoots. In spring they emerge from the whitish, oval eggs, which are usually fastened to the bark of the fruit spurs—the perfect insects being seen in July—and secrete themselves in the buds. They are, when perfect, about an eighth of an inch long, and though they vary a little in colour during the course of the season, they are generally green. The perfect insects live on the leaves and the blossom stems, causing the buds to turn brown and to remain on the tree, a characteristic sign of this disease. *Treatment.*—Spraying is the best means of combating this pest. The trees are sprayed when dormant with a tar distillate wash. Besides exercising a general cleansing effect on the trees, it destroys the eggs of Aphides, Apple Suckers and various other pests. A nicotine and soft soap wash should also be used shortly before the blossoms open. This is best applied with a coarse jet. *Plants Most Usually Affected.*—Apples.

Asparagus Beetle.—This beetle is a deep bluish-green in colour and has yellow and red wing-cases. In spring it lays its eggs on the young shoots on which the resulting yellowish-green larvæ feed. When mature the caterpillars fall to the ground and turn into pupæ, from which the complete beetles emerge in three weeks' time. *Treatment.*—Spray the infested shoots, when the caterpillars are active, with a solution of arsenate of lead, and remove all badly affected shoots.

Asparagus Fly.—In spring and early summer this little fly lays its eggs in the tops of the young shoots of the asparagus plant. The larvæ eat their way into the young shoots and stem, gradually working downwards to the subterranean portions of the stems, where they pass the winter. The flies, which emerge from the pupæ in spring, are brown in colour and have four lighter coloured bands across the body and over the wings. *Treatment.*—Remove and burn all affected stems. Sticky fly-papers, hung on short sticks inserted in the beds, will account for many of these pests.

Bark or Trunk Borer.—These shiny, brownish-black beetles bore small round holes into the twigs, branches and trunks of trees, especially the plum. The females lay their eggs in a gallery between the bark and the wood. The larvæ hatch out, first bore at right angles to the gallery, and then along the branches or trunk, always keeping between the bark and the wood. They then pupate, and when the complete beetles emerge, they bore their way out through the bark to attack another part of the bark or some other tree. The bark is often so riddled that the tree dies ; in any case, its vigour is greatly sapped. *Treatment.*—All affected wood must be cut out in autumn and burned. Badly infected trees should be destroyed altogether. If the damaged wood is not burned before the following spring, the pests will migrate to other trees. Where the damage has not gone too far, methylated spirit may be squirted into the holes, which must immediately be stopped with clay or grafting wax. *See also* Shot Borer Beetle. *Plants Most Usually Affected.*—Plums, and less frequently, Apples, Pears, Cherries, Peaches, Apricots and Quinces.

Bean Aphis.—The eggs are laid in the interstices of the bark of the Euonymus shrub in late summer. In spring the eggs hatch out and produce female aphides, which reproduce rapidly without laying eggs and without fertilization from the male. Certain winged females are produced and these fly to the beans, or other plants usually attacked, and quickly multiply, forming the black masses of " blight " which often infest beans in early summer, covering them with a sticky substance known as " Honey-dew." If the summer is warm, the aphides multiply all the more quickly. *Treatment.*—The young shoots at the top of the plant are those first affected ; if, therefore, the beans are sown early, they will already be well-grown by the time the insects appear and may, therefore, have the infested shoots pinched out and destroyed before the pests can spread far down the stem. Once the infestation has spread, spray with nicotine or paraffin emulsion. *Plants Most Usually Affected.*—Broad Beans.

Bean and Pea Beetles.—These beetles must not be confused with the Bean and Pea Weevil (which *see*). There are three varieties that cause most of the damage ; these are the *Spanish Bean Beetle* (the largest), the *Pea Beetle*, and the *American Bean Beetle* (the smallest). The last-named beetle is brown, the other two being black flecked with grey. The *Pea Beetle* is nearly a quarter of an inch in length. All three beetles have very similar habits. The eggs are laid on the young pods early in summer, the grub bores its way into the young seed and there feeds and grows until late in the summer, when it pupates. The beetle emerges, but usually remains inside the seed during the winter, though it may sometimes come out and spend the winter in the store-room, or even in a sheltered nook in the open. *Treatment.*—Look over the seeds, and any bearing a round, semi-transparent spot should be pricked with a pin over this spot to kill the beetle in the seed. Where there is a hole in the seed, it may be assumed that the beetle has left it. This treatment is impossible where large quantities are concerned and the seeds must then be fumigated for 40–50 hours with carbon bisulphide at the rate of $\frac{1}{4}$ oz. of carbon bisulphide to every 3 cubic feet, in an air-tight tin or case. A cloth saturated with the required amount of fumigant is placed over the seeds and the lid is then placed on the container. As the fumigant is highly inflammable, the operation must take place away from the house and away from a light of any kind. The seeds should be exposed to the air after fumigation. *Plants Most Usually Affected.*— Peas and Beans.

Bean and Pea Thrip.—The adult insect is black and about a sixteenth of an inch in length, with a pointed tail. The four wings are narrow and fringed. The young thrips are orange in colour and the pointed tail is black. They have no wings in this stage. In June the eggs are laid in the seed pods. The young thrips feed on the flowers and the seed pods for about a month, and then go down to the soil, where they lie until the following May, when they emerge as complete insects. *Treatment.*—Soil on which an affected crop has been grown should be dressed with naphthalene or lime and must be well dug over in the winter. Spray with a nicotine and soft soap wash on the first signs of attack. No bean or pea crops should be planted on the same or adjacent ground during the following season. *Plants Most Usually Affected.*—Beans and Peas.

Bean and Pea Weevil.—This is a small brown beetle, about a sixteenth of an inch in length, striped with golden brown. It emerges in July or August from the earth where it has lain as a pupa and lives on the foliage of the bean and pea. In autumn the weevil hides in the grass or among any rubbish, and there passes the winter, emerging in March and eating out little semicircular pieces from the leaves of the young peas or beans. It lays its eggs, and the resulting grubs feed upon the nodules of the roots of the plants and then pupate. Provided the young plants are vigorous, they soon outgrow the damage done to them, but where they are weak, the damage will frequently prove fatal. *Treatment.*—Dust the young seedlings with a mixture of lime and soot after rain or a heavy dew, and before sowing or planting have the soil broken up very fine. Spray with a weak emulsion of paraffin. *Plants Most Usually Affected.*—Beans and Peas.

Bean Pod Canker.—This disease attacks chiefly the pods of Scarlet Runners and French Beans, and is first seen as brown, sunken patches on the pods. *Treatment.*—Remove and burn all affected parts.

Bean Rust.—This disease attacks the young shoots and leaves, which become covered with a fine, rusty-coloured dust. If unchecked, the whole plant will become affected. *Treatment.*—All affected plants must be taken up and burned in the autumn. Another crop of these beans must not be sown on the same site the following year, as the ground is certain to be contaminated. *Plants Most Usually Affected.*— Broad Beans.

Beet and Mangel Fly.—Two or three broods of this fly may be hatched out in one season. The fly appears from late spring to early summer and lays her small white eggs on the underside of the leaves. The larvæ hatch out in a week or so, eat their way into the leaves and cause them to become blistered. When mature, the grubs drop to the ground. Here they go through the pupa stage, and the complete flies emerge to repeat the sequence of reproduction. *Treatment.*— Spray the leaves with nicotine emulsion. *Plants Most Usually Affected.* —Beets and Mangels.

Big Bud.—In this disease the buds swell up to an abnormal size and die off. The cause is a small mite which enters the bud and multiplies. The mite breeds chiefly in autumn and spring, at which times it rapidly spreads from bud to bud and from plant to plant as in Currant Bud Mite. *Treatment.*—Badly-diseased plants should be rooted up and burned ; less severe cases should have all affected buds removed and burned, the buds immediately above and below the diseased ones being picked off on trees and bushes that are only slightly affected. Spray the soil with a strong insecticide. If the invasion has been so heavy that most of the bushes have had to be destroyed, it is safer to make a new plantation on a different site. *Plants Most Usually Affected.*—Currants (Black and Red).

Black Aphis.—*See* Aphides.

Black Rot.—This disease chiefly attacks kale, turnips, cabbages, cauliflowers and their kind. Irregular yellow patches first appear on the leaves, these areas turn brown, streaked and spotted with black, and may spread over the whole surface of the leaves. Young plants, when attacked, remain dwarfed and eventually succumb. *Treatment.*—Remove and burn all affected plants, and endeavour not to grow a similar crop on the same ground for four or five seasons. Disinfect the soil with a solution of 1 lb. of commercial formalin in 25 gallons of water, applying 9 gallons of solution to every square yard of soil, which should be loosely dug up and dry before the solution is applied. After application, turn the soil several times, nothing being planted for a fortnight. *Plants Most Usually Affected.*—All plants of the Cabbage Family.

Black Spot.—This fungus causes large purple-black spots to appear on the leaves, which are greatly disfigured and eventually fall to the ground. *Treatment.*—Collect and burn all diseased leaves and shoots, remove a couple of inches of the top soil, and dress the ground liberally with slaked lime. Import fresh soil to replace that removed, and dress again with lime. Spray with Bordeaux Mixture, or with liver of sulphur. Dusting with flowers of sulphur and lead arsenate powder has given good results. *Plants Most Usually Affected.*—Roses, some varieties, especially many of the Pernetiana varieties.

Brown Tail Moth.—This moth lays its eggs in September on the leaves of fruit trees, roses and other shrubs. When they hatch out, each larva or caterpillar weaves itself an envelope in which it passes the winter. In spring the caterpillars emerge and build large silken cases in which they congregate. The mature caterpillars are dark brown in colour, with two fine red lines along the back and white spots on either side, and are covered with reddish-brown hair. Early in July the larvæ become chrysalides enclosed in cocoons spun among the leaves. The moth, which is pure white and has a greyish spot on the front wings, emerges in August. When the wings are open, they measure an inch and a half across. *Treatment.*—Spray the foliage with arsenate of lead solution in summer, and cut away and destroy the silken envelopes. *Notification of an attack by this moth must be given to the Ministry of Agriculture and Fisheries. Plants Most Usually Affected.*—Fruit trees, Roses and other shrubs.

Bulb Mite.—This dirty, reddish-white mite attacks bulbs and tubers and causes the foliage to turn yellow and the bulb eventually to rot. *Treatment.*—Soak the bulbs for some 20 minutes in soapy water at a temperature of 125° F. *Plants Most Usually Affected.*—Hyacinth, Lily, Hippeastrum, Eucharis and other bulbs grown indoors under glass.

Cabbage Moth.—This moth is of a dirty, greyish-brown colour; the fore-wings are spotted and lined with white. The first batch of eggs are laid in the food-plants in June, and from these the small, pale-green caterpillars emerge, and soon play havoc with the leaves of the plants. As they grow older they may change colour and become a good deal darker. After about five weeks, when they will be just over an inch in length, the caterpillars crawl down the stems to the earth and there become shiny, brown pupæ. During August and September a few moths will emerge from the pupæ and will produce a second brood of caterpillars. *Treatment.*—Examine the plants from June to September, while the moths are active, and pick off and destroy any eggs or young caterpillars. Spray thoroughly, so that the plants are drenched, and as soon as the pest is noticed, with a solution of 3½ oz. of soft soap and two gallons of water, which must be worked into a good lather before application. The leaves, when damp, may also be dusted with a mixture of soot and lime. Search for the pupæ both on surrounding plants and flowers and in the ground when it is being dug over. *Plants Most Usually Affected.*—The caterpillars are general feeders, for in addition to all members of the Cabbage Family, they attack Tomatoes, Tobacco plants, Lettuce, Onions, Maize, etc.

Cabbage Root Fly.—This fly is ashen-grey in colour and can easily be mistaken for the house-fly. It first appears early in May and lays its eggs just under the ground round the principal roots of the plants attacked. This is a most destructive pest. The fly itself is harmless, but the maggot attacks chiefly plants of the cabbage and turnip tribe. The roots are eaten away, which causes the plants to be stunted, and the leaves to become discoloured and droop. *Treatment.*—Place prepared tarred discs, which can be obtained from any seedsman, round the bottom of the stems to prevent the flies from laying their eggs near the roots. These must lie flat on the ground, and should be adjusted immediately the young cabbages are planted out. Do not allow any soil to lie on the surface of the discs or eggs will be laid in it. When the plants are vigorous and well-grown, the soil may be pulled up over the discs. As an alternative, saturate 3 lb. of powdered chalk with 1 oz. of creosote and sprinkle a little round the stem of each cabbage when planted out, and again on two or three occasions at intervals of a fortnight. Do not plant any crops of the cabbage or turnip tribe on infected soil until two or three seasons have expired after the attack, and dig the soil over in winter to enable the birds to get at the pupæ. Pull up and burn all cut stumps. *Plants Most Usually Affected.*—Cabbages and Cauliflowers are the principal sufferers, although all Cruciferæ are liable to attack.

Cabbage White Butterfly.—The oval, yellow eggs are laid in spring and summer in groups on the leaves, where they are quite visible. The caterpillars, which hatch out in about a fortnight, congregate and eat voraciously. They are a deep bluish-black in colour, yellow along the sides, and have a yellow streak down the back. In about four weeks' time they become black-spotted, yellowish or greyish chrysalides suspended by the tail in various positions near the food plants. The butterflies emerge in August and produce a second generation of caterpillars, which are very destructive during August and September. The chrysalides of these caterpillars remain dormant through the winter and produce the spring butterflies that lay the eggs from which the earliest brood of caterpillars hatch. *Treatment.—* See that given for *Cabbage Moth. Plants Most Usually Affected.—* Cabbages, but all members of the family are liable to attack.

Canker.—*See* Apple Canker, and Bean Pod Canker.

Carrot Fly.—This fly is of a metallic, dark greenish-black colour and has a large yellow head with black eyes. It lays its eggs in the ground in spring in convenient proximity to the young carrots, the natural food of the grubs which will hatch out from them. A carrot attacked by the grub will turn reddish and wither at the top, and the root, if lifted, will show iron-mould-like spots, and, if badly attacked, deep cracks. As there are several broods of this fly in the course of a single season, the carrots are often rendered quite rotten and unfit for use by their repeated attacks. *Treatment.—*Wood ashes dug well into the soil, and also paraffin in the proportion of a quart of paraffin to a barrow-load of ashes as a top-dressing when the plants are still quite small is a good preventative. The surface of the soil should be kept hard, so as to make it difficult for the female fly to penetrate it in order to lay her eggs. All affected carrots should at once be burned. *Plants Most Usually Affected.—*Carrots, Celery and Parsnips.

Caterpillars.—The caterpillars of numerous moths, notably the *Brindled Beauty, Brown-tail Moth, Buff-tip Moth, Lackey Moth, Leaf-roller Moth, Mottled Umber Moth, Pale Tussock Moth, Tortrix Moth, Vapourer Moth,* and *Winter Moth,* all cause havoc in the garden. They are all biters, and their food is easily poisoned by means of spraying. *Treatment.—*Spray the foliage with arsenate of lead solution in summer, or, if preferred, careful hand picking may be resorted to.

Celery Fly.—This fly is yellowish-brown in colour and has iridescent wings banded with reddish-brown and mottled with transparent spots. The flies hatch out in April, and in summer lay their eggs singly in the tissues of the underside of the celery leaves. The larvæ hatch out and feed on the tissues of the leaves and after a fortnight turn into pupæ, from which the complete flies emerge in a few days' time. Several broods appear in the course of a season. The pupæ of the last brood lie buried in the earth during the winter and produce the earliest flies. Celery and parsnips may be attacked from early in May until late in November, the grubs eat into the leaf tissues and produce blister-like patches which soon turn brown, and cause the leaves to shrivel. The stems fail to develop, or if badly attacked, the plant dies. *Treatment.—*Directly the grubs are observed, the affected leaves should be picked off and burnt. Some degree of protection is

CAMELLIAS, GLASGOW

afforded by the repeated sprinkling of the leaves from April onwards with fine, dry soot, three parts, and lime, one part, or by the occasional syringing of the seedlings with paraffin emulsion. But here, as with most other diseases of plants, perhaps the most important measure for securing health is to obtain good seeds, and by the proper preparation of the soil and general good treatment to secure steady and continuous growth. As a preventive measure, burn all leaves and stems left about on the soil after the plants have been dug. *Plants Most Usually Affected.*—Celery and Parsnips.

Celery-Stem Fly.—The maggots of the Celery-stem Fly bore into the stems, causing them to rot, and as the larvæ are hidden right inside the stems, they are extremely difficult to get at. *Treatment.*— The only useful measures are preventive ; that is to say, wherever the maggot is known to have been found, the young celery plants should be sprayed with a paraffin emulsion ; and all parts of diseased plants should at once be burnt. For both this fly and the Celery Fly a good preventive step is the dressing of the soil with quicklime after the plants are lifted. *Plants Most Usually Affected.*—Celery.

Chafer Beetles.—Three species of chafer beetle are usually found in the garden. Firstly, the Cockchafer, which is about an inch long and appears in May and June. Secondly, the Summer Chafer, which is about two-thirds of an inch in length and appears in June and July. And thirdly, the Garden Chafer, which is about half an inch in length, appears in June and July and feeds on the petals and stamens of the blooms. The eggs of all three species are laid in the ground and the grubs, which are a dirty white in colour with brownish heads and tails, feed on the roots of plants and trees. *Treatment.*— In spring or autumn dig naphthalene into the soil at the rate of 2 cwt. to every acre. Pick out all grubs while the soil is being dug over, and make a trap by placing a piece of turf upside-down on the ground ; the grubs will collect under the turf. *Plants Most Usually Affected.*— The grubs eat the roots of all kinds of farm and garden crops, including Strawberries and Fruit Trees, often proving very destructive to young nursery stock.

Cherry and Pear Sawfly (Slugworm).—As with the Gooseberry Sawfly, it is the larvæ that do the damage. They devour the soft tissue of the leaves of cherry, pear and certain other trees, leaving nothing but the ribbed veins and the hard skin of the leaves which turn brown and wither up. In bad cases, where every leaf may be attacked, the fruit will not be able to mature, or if the attack occurs later in the season, the fruit buds for the next year will have no opportunity of forming. The tiny slug-like larvæ are white when hatched, later they become greenish-black ; the mature flies have four transparent wings and are black in colour. The life-history is practically the same as that described for the Gooseberry Sawfly. *Treatment.*— Spray with arsenate of lead as soon as the damage is noticed, but not later than seven weeks before the fruit is to be gathered. Hellebore Powder solution and nicotine wash can be used up to within three weeks of picking the fruit. Naphthalene should be dug into the soil round the trees in the autumn (1½ lb. to the square rod).

E.G.   D D

Cherry Moth.—A great deal of the loss which is ascribed by many cherry growers to frosts, cold winds, and the like causes, in the shape of the falling of the fruit just as it is set, is really due to the depredations of the caterpillar of the Cherry Moth, which enters the tiny fruit just as it is fertilized and remains in for a fortnight or so, falling to the ground with it as it drops. The Cherry Moth is very inconspicuous, of a light brown colour with a dark band and light or whitish edges to the wings. The moth may be identified by its curious position when at rest, the tail being elevated as if the insect were standing on its head. The eggs are laid on the shoots and do not hatch out till spring, although laid in middle and late summer. *Treatment.*—As the caterpillars remain in the fallen fruits and pupate in them, hatching out as perfect insects, it is a good plan to sweep up all fallen fruit and burn them. In this way many of the pests are destroyed and birds will help to keep down the remainder. Once the eggs are laid on the shoots, nothing much can be done by way of remedy.

Cherry Scab.—Where this disease attacks the cherries early in the season, the fruit remains dwarfed. Dark green spots become visible on the fruit when the disease manifests itself late in the season. *Treatment.*—Immediately the disease appears spray the trees thoroughly with a solution of lime sulphur.

Club Root.—In this disease, which is common and very injurious, parts of the roots swell into irregular, knotted lumps, which though small at the outset may grow until the swelling is three or four inches in diameter. The flesh first becomes grey, spotted with dirty white, then goes brown and decays. The foliage turns yellow, makes little new growth or remains dwarfed. *Treatment.*—See that drainage is good, as a wet, stale soil encourages the disease, and on land that has been affected arrange a rotation of crops so that none of the plants susceptible is planted for at least four years after an attack. Weeds must be suppressed. Burn all diseased plants as soon as the disease is discovered. Take care not to transmit the spores to clean ground by using contaminated tools or by transferring infected soil to sound beds. In autumn dig in thoroughly ¾ lb. of powdered and newly-slaked lime to every square yard of infected soil. On ground in which club root is anticipated this dressing should be repeated every five years. *Plants Most Usually Affected.*—Turnips and all plants of the Cabbage Family.

Cockchafers.—*See* Chafers.

Codlin Moth.—Several moths attack apple trees, one of the most destructive as well as the commonest being that named from its habitat, the Codlin Moth. " Worm-eaten " apples are those which have been spoiled by the larvæ of this insect. The moth lays its eggs singly, one in the eye of each fruit, and fixes it inside the calyx with a gummy fluid. As the little apple grows and swells, the grub eats its way further and further in, until a little before the fruit would normally be ripe, the maggot has reached its core, feeding upon the pips, a proceeding which causes the fall of the fruit. The caterpillars, released from the fallen apple, creep up the tree-stem until they find a sheltered crack, in which they pass the other stages of their life till the perfect moth

emerges in the following spring to repeat the process. *Treatment.*—
The chief preventive operation is banding during June with old sacking, folded paper or ropes of hay (*see* p. 403). Gather and destroy
all prematurely-fallen fruit and spray the trees with insecticide as soon
as the blossoms fall in spring. *Plants Most Usually Affected.*—Apples,
Pears, Quinces and Walnuts.

Coral Spot.—So called from the masses of pink spores on the woody
stems of the plants affected. The disease procures a footing through
a cut in the stem or through dead shoots. *Treatment.*—Remove and
burn all dead and diseased branches, leaving none of the affected
wood in the tree. Care must be taken while pruning not to injure
the branches, and all wounds or jagged surfaces should be coated
with tar or grafting wax. No dead wood or rubbish should be allowed
to lie about in the vicinity of the trees. *Plants Most Usually Affected.*—
Apples, Currants, Gooseberries, and Pears.

Crown Gall.—This is a disease that does not greatly harm matured
trees and bushes. It attacks chiefly young plants and sometimes
proves fatal to them, although they usually live for some time, remaining stunted and unhealthy. The damage varies with the position
of the gall. When a plant contracts this disease, hard, round swellings
of various sizes appear on the roots, stems, or branches, though the
disease usually makes its appearance in the neighbourhood of the
" crown." The swellings are first white, but later become dark in
colour. *Treatment.*—Since the bacteria causing the disease enter
through a wound in the bark, great care should be taken not to injure
the stems in any way. The cutting out of a gall will not invariably
effect a cure, as the disease may break out in another place and the
operation may be so drastic that the plant is killed. Badly diseased
plants should, therefore, be discarded and destroyed, but where the
malady is local, such as on the roots, cut away the affected parts
and burn them. *Plants Most Usually Affected.*—Roses and Fruit
Trees, also some species of Chrysanthemum.

Cuckoo Spit.—A yellow insect known as the frog hopper causes this
trouble. The female hopper lays her eggs on the plant, and the grubs
suck the sap from the stems and leaves, covering themselves mean-
while with the well-known frothy substance known as " spittle " or
" spit." They are prevalent from May to July and greatly retard
the development and growth of the plants. *Treatment.*—Spray with
nicotine or paraffin emulsion. Project the spray as forcibly as possible
to wash away the covering of froth and thus enable the substance used
for spraying to come in actual contact with the insects. *Plants Most
Usually Affected.*—A great variety of garden plants are subject to
attack.

Currant Bud Mite.—*See* Big Bud.

Currant Clear-Wing Moth.—This is a moth whose larva pierces the
shoots of the currant bushes, causing them to wither off. The moth
is about three-quarters of an inch across, with the wings expanded,
and its wings are clear, like those of a fly, except for the veins, the
wing tips, a spot on each wing, and a border, all of which are blackish
in colour. The moths appear on sunny days in July. Their bodies

are black, banded with fine yellow stripes. *Treatment.*—It is almost impossible to prevent the attacks of this pest. The only thing possible is to go carefully over the bushes, removing and burning all dead or dying shoots. *Plants Most Usually Affected.*—Currants.

Currant Leaf Spot.—In this disease the upper sides of the leaves become covered with minute pimples and have a patchy appearance. *Treatment.*—On first signs of the disease spray thoroughly with Bordeaux Mixture, as, once established, the disease is very difficult to overcome. *Plants Most Usually Affected.*—Currants.

Currant Moth.—*See* Magpie Moth.

Currant Sawfly.—*See* Gooseberry Sawfly.

Currant Scale.—Currant Scale's characteristic sign is the white cotton-woolly material which it exudes as a protection, and which contains both the eggs and the young scales. This, unlike the Currant Mite, attacks all kinds of currants, and it should be dealt with by spraying as soon as its presence is detected. *Treatment.*—Spray with a warm solution of carbolic soft soap, putting 2 oz. of soap to the gallon of hot water. Spray over both sides of the leaves. *See also* Scale.

Currant-Shoot Moth.—This insect selects its host with care. It only attacks, so far, the red and black currants, none having, up to the present, been found on the white varieties. As, however, it was at first believed to be confined to red currants, it is possible that its tastes are widening. The larvæ attack the young shoots which are noticed to be withering. The moth and its larvæ are extremely small, and easily escape notice unless they are searched for. The perfect insects are flying late in May, and lay their eggs inside the berries of the plant attacked. They are of a brownish colour, with a purple sheen in some lights, the wings being naked and spotted with yellow. The skin of the fruit in which the eggs are laid is first pierced with an appendage borne by the female moth, who then deposits the eggs within it. Here they hatch out, and the larvæ feed on the fruit and the seeds, which wither and dry up. At the end of June they leave the berry, and spin themselves small, white cocoons on the shoots, from which they emerge in the following spring, and bore into the young shoots. When once they have bored into these, they cannot be touched by insecticides, and the caterpillars themselves are so minute that they are almost invisible to the eye. *Treatment.*—All prunings from suspected bushes should be burned, and the bushes should be sprayed thoroughly with a soft soap insecticide. *Plants Most Usually Affected.*—Currants, Red and Black.

Diamond-Black Moth.—This moth makes its appearance in May and June. It is greyish-brown in colour and has three triangular, whitish splashes on each front wing. These meet when the wings are folded, and form diamond-shaped marks. The hind wings are greyish and fringed. Eggs are laid on plants of the cabbage kind. The green caterpillars make a thin web on the underside of the leaves. They feed voraciously for about a month, and then weave white cocoons on the stalks and become pupæ, from which moths emerge in about a fortnight. Several broods appear through the summer, the last brood remaining as pupæ throughout the winter and spring to produce moths in the early summer. *Treatment.*—Watch for the moths and caterpillars on the underside of the leaves in June and July. If the caterpillars are present, dust the underside of the leaves with a good insecticide powder. Keep down weeds, especially charlock. When the leaves are touched, the caterpillars drop and hang in the air on silken threads, so that, if the underside of the leaves is brushed, the larvæ will be knocked on to the ground, where they can be crushed. *Plants Most Usually Affected.*—Cabbage Tribe, both wild and cultivated.

Die-Back (Fruit Trees and Bushes).—This disease, caused by various fungi, attacks most usually the apple, cherry, gooseberry, peach and plum. Although the general symptoms are the same in all cases, that is to say, the branches wither and " die-back," the different kind of trees are attacked by different species of fungus, and the first symptoms vary somewhat. In the apple the older wood is usually first attacked, large cankerous wounds, surrounded by purple patches of rough bark, are formed. If unattended, the cankers will soon kill the tree. The yellowing and shrivelling of the leaves on the younger branches are the first signs of the disease in the cherry. The bark then cracks and from the wounds, " bleeding " of the gum occurs. The branch dies and the disease spreads downwards to the older wood and the trunk. When the wood has been dead some time, little pustules form beneath the bark, these soon burst and broadcast the fungus spores. Die-back in the gooseberry affects leaves, young shoots, branches and fruit. The leaves become margined with yellow, and later with greyish-white. If this discoloration spreads over the whole leaf, the latter soon drops. The older wood is usually first attacked just above the ground, and grey tufts of woolly fungus appear on the withered and cracked bark. The fungus extends up the branches, and eventually kills the entire bush. When the fruit is attacked, the skin first becomes brown and as the flesh rots, the grey, woolly tufts of fungus form on the skin. When the peach is attacked, the foliage wilts, the young shoots take on a deep purple hue, and the bark of the smaller branches also turns purple, hardens and shrivels, and soon becomes covered with fungus spores. The disease affects the plum in very much the same way as the cherry, except that there is not the " gumming " and only one branch is usually affected at a time, although the whole tree is later attacked. *Treatment.*—All affected branches should be pruned out, care being taken to cut right back to sound, healthy wood. The prunings must be burned immediately and the cut surfaces should be painted over with a dressing of tar. Badly-diseased trees should be cut down entirely and burned. In the case of gooseberries, the above treatment should be applied, but the bushes should also be thoroughly sprayed the following spring, just before the buds commence to open, with a solution of copper sulphate. This will prevent the spread of the disease if any spores have been left on the bushes.

Earwigs.—Earwigs are easy to trap, owing to their propensity to hide in any sheltered spot during the day. Thus, a handful of straw, shavings, or hay, pushed lightly into a flower-pot and stuck on a stick will be found full of earwigs in the morning, if they are about in any numbers. Crumpled paper, pieces of corrugated cardboard, hollow stalks, and all such things make effective earwig traps. *Plants Most Usually Affected.*—Dahlias and Chrysanthemums.

Gall Fly.—The large, woolly, greenish or reddish galls which are sometimes encountered on rose bushes and trees are produced by a species of gall fly (*Rhodites rosea*). *Treatment.*—The parts affected should be cut right away and should be burnt at once.

Goat Moth.—This moth, in its caterpillar stage, does much damage to several kinds of fruit trees. The female lays its eggs on the trees, usually on isolated specimens. These eggs hatch out into caterpillars that make large, oval burrows in the trunks, which, if the pest is not checked, will eventually kill the trees. Until they pupate, the caterpillars feed on the trees. They then make cocoons of sawdust and small flakes of wood in the burrow, near the outside. This takes place about May, and the moths appear during June, July and early August. The caterpillars are from 3–4 inches in length, are of a deep, pinkish-yellow beneath and down the sides, while the back is a deep mahogany red, and carries stiff hairs on each segment; the head is black. The moth has a hairy thorax of greyish-brown, banded in rear with a much deeper brown; the abdomen is large and plump, and is grey, ringed with white. The fore-wings are light brown, splashed with grey and with irregular greyish-black transverse lines; the hind-wings are of a deeper shade of grey-brown, flecked with a darker colour. The wing expanse in the male measures from 2 to 3 inches, but from 3 to 3½ inches in the female. The peculiar goat-like smell which the moth exudes gives it its name, and is a clear indication of its presence. *Treatment.*—Badly-infested trees, if of no great value, should be cut down and must at once be burned; where branches only are affected, these should be cut back to sound wood, the trimmings being also burned. Where the holes are not too numerous, sodium cyanide (*poison*) should be inserted in them, the opening then being sealed with clay. *Plants Most Usually Affected.*—In addition to Fruit Trees, many other trees, such as the Elm, Beech, Lime, Sycamore, Walnut, Poplar, Willow, Birch, etc., are attacked.

Gooseberry Moth.—*See* Magpie Moth.

Gooseberry Sawfly.—It is in the larvæ stage that this pest does the most damage. The larvæ of the first brood hatch out about May, and first feed in colonies, making small round holes in the leaves, and then disperse over the bush and, if unchecked, will completely strip the plant in the course of two to three weeks. When fully grown, the larvæ fall to the ground, pupate in oval, earthy-brown cocoons, from which the flies emerge in two or three weeks. There are three, sometimes four broods during the season, the last passing the winter as pupæ in the soil and emerging as mature flies in April or May to lay their eggs on the underside of the leaves. These hatch in about six days and so the circle is completed. The young larvæ are pale-green, slightly spotted with black, there are blue and yellow markings on the flanks, and deep yellow on the neck and tail. As the larvæ grow they gradually lose their black and blue markings, and when fully grown are nearly an inch in length. In the mature fly all four wings are transparent; the thorax is black and yellow in both sexes, but the abdomen in the female is orange, and almost black in the male. *Treatment.*—Pick off and burn all leaves as they are seen to be attacked. If the bushes have not blossomed, spray immediately with lead arsenate solution. When the fruit has formed before the attack is noticed, it is necessary to wait until the fruit has been gathered and to spray immediately afterwards. Hellebore Powder may be dusted over the bushes, *but not less than three weeks before the fruit is to be picked.* The pest spreads at an alarming rate unless checked in the early stages. In the autumn naphthalene should be dug into the soil round the bushes at the rate of 1½ lb. to the square rod. *Plants Most Usually Affected.*—Gooseberries and Red and Black Currants.

Green-fly.—*See* Aphides.

" Honey-dew."—*See* Aphides and Bean Aphis.

Lackey Moth.—There are several moths which attack fruit trees, the commonest of them being the Lackey Moth, which lays its eggs in rings round the bark of a branch or twig; the caterpillars, which hatch out about April, live in colonies and cover themselves with webs spun over the leaves. The caterpillars are black, or nearly so, when first hatched, but as they mature, become brightly-coloured and have a white stripe down the back, flanked on either side by three orange lines separated by black and blue streaks. They also become covered with long brown hairs. The caterpillars feed on the foliage, doing great damage, and early in July pupate. The moths, which are brown in colour, emerge in July and August. They can be recognized by the two pale stripes on each fore-wing. *Treatment.*—To keep them down, the trees should be looked over in May and June, all infested leaves being picked off, shoot and all, and dropped into a bucket of strong insecticide. If a dull, damp day is chosen, the caterpillars will all be inside their little webs, and will be more easily dealt with. The trees may also be sprayed with lead arsenate, but this must be done as soon as the blossom has dropped. *Plants Most Usually Affected.*—Apple, Cherry, Plum and Pear, among fruits, Oak, Alder, Elm, Hawthorn, Willow and Rose among trees and shrubs.

Leaf Curl.—*See* Peach-Leaf Blister.

Leaf-Cutter Bees.—These are best destroyed by means of spraying affected foliage with arsenate of lead solution. *Plants Most Usually Affected.*—Roses.

Leaf Miners.—These maggots hatch from the eggs of small flies that frequent the leaves of plants and eat into the foliage, making pale streaks across the surface of the leaves, or causing brown, shrivelled patches. *Treatment.*—Spray with paraffin emulsion, or nicotine and soap wash, as a deterrent, and pick off and burn badly-infested leaves. *Plants Most Usually Affected.*—Celery, Parsnips, Chrysanthemums and Cinerarias.

Leaf-Roller Moth (Leaf Tortrix).—The caterpillar of this moth, like that of the Winter Moth, spins together the leaves and blossoms of the trees it attacks. The caterpillars may be distinguished from those of the Winter Moth by their habit of quickly wriggling backwards if their heads are touched; they also crawl flat along the leaves and have not the "looping" movement characteristic of the caterpillars of the Winter Moth. It is essential to differentiate between these two pests, as the Leaf-Roller Moth cannot be combated by banding. There are several kinds of Leaf Tortrix or Leaf-Roller Moth ; all are small, and the caterpillars are green, yellow, brown or red. *Treatment.*—Affected foliage should be pinched between the finger and thumb to kill the caterpillar. All damaged foliage must be burned, and the bushes sprayed with nicotine and soap solution. *Plants Most Usually Affected.*—Practically all fruit and many forest trees.

Leaf Scorch.—Yellow patches appear on the leaves, later turn brown, and become surrounded with a purple margin. *Treatment.*—Remove and burn all affected leaves, and in winter thoroughly spray the bushes or trees and the soil round about with Bordeaux Mixture and with a lime-sulphur solution. *Plants Most Usually Affected.*—Apples.

Leather Jackets.—These are the grubs of Daddy Longlegs. During summer, winter and spring they do great damage to the roots of many plants, feeding just below the soil and working their way right into the centre of large roots, and, in damp weather, and at night, attacking the stems of the plants. The Leather Jacket is so called because of its hard, leathery skin. It has no legs, is cylindrical in shape, and of an earthy-brown colour. The head is black and the tail-end is blunt with several short finger-like projections. *Prevention and Treatment.*—Break up new land thoroughly in the summer, as the grubs will soon die if exposed to hot sun and dry soil, and where possible keep weeds well in check by constant hoeing. Dig naphthalene, at the rate of 2 oz. to the square yard, thoroughly into the soil and water well. *Plants Most Usually Affected.*—May attack all farm and garden crops. Strawberries are badly attacked and Grass and Cereals.

Magpie Moth.—The pretty black and white markings on the wings of the Magpie Moth render it unmistakable, and when the moths first appear in July, they may be caught with tolerable ease and can be destroyed, thus checking the egg-laying. The caterpillars are also marked with black and white, with yellow along each flank. They feed on the leaves of the bushes, sometimes stripping them almost bare, which in the case of fruit means a great weakening of the crop. The eggs are laid on the leaves in July, and the caterpillars begin to feed in August. They live through the winter in sheltered nooks, and continue feeding in the spring, turning into black and yellow chrysalides in June. *Treatment.*—In the winter, all material which might harbour the caterpillars should be removed, preferably when the pruning is done, and with these fallen leaves and prunings about an inch of the surface soil should be raked off and burned. The remaining caterpillars should be picked off by hand in the spring, while spraying with Hellebore is effective, but it must be used at least three weeks before the fruit is picked. Pyrethrum is non-poisonous and may be used at any time. Lead arsenate may be applied before flowering and again during August. *Plants Most Usually Affected.*—The Magpie Moth is one of the chief enemies of both Gooseberries and Currants. It also attacks the Apricot, Plum, Euonymus and Laurel, as well as various other plants.

March Moth.—In the male of this moth the fore-wings are greyish-brown, banded with a slightly deeper colour, the hind-wings are a dirty white with an irregular grey band running across them. The female is brown, has no wings, and lays her eggs in bands round the twigs. The caterpillar is yellowish, and along the back has a deep green streak flanked on either side by yellow lines. When fully fed, it lets itself down to the ground, where it pupates and emerges as the perfect insect in March. *Nature of Damage and Treatment.*—*See* that for Winter Moth. *Plants Most Affected.*—Fruit, Forest Trees and Shrubs.

Mealy-Bug.—The mealy-bug is so called because a white, downy material grows on the bodies of the female insects. *Treatment.*—If present in large numbers, fumigation with hydrocyanic gas is sometimes necessary, but usually a good spraying with nicotine and soap solution, and subsequently the application of a little methylated spirit to the mealy-looking patches where the females congregate, will be sufficient to wipe them out. *Plants Most Usually Affected.*—Mealy-bugs attack chiefly Vines, Grapes, Figs and many other plants under glass.

Mildew.—*See* Apple Mildew.

Millepede.—The millepede attacks all bulbs and roots ; it eats away the skin or hollows out the inside. Decay sets in and other pests get to work. *Treatment.*—Dig powdered naphthalene into the soil, allowing $1\frac{1}{2}$ oz. to every square yard of land dressed. Water after application. Place a turnip with the centre scooped out just under the surface of the soil, the millepedes will enter this and feed. The trap should be frequently inspected so that the pests may be destroyed.

Mottled Umber Moth.—This pest is destructive to plum-tree foliage, attacking, also, many other orchard trees. It is very troublesome in dry seasons, and is only to be dealt with by using the same precautions as those indicated in the case of the Winter Moth (which *see*), namely, the affixing of unsurmountable bands of greasy material to the stems of the trees, to prevent the wingless female moth from climbing them.

Nut Sawfly.—Amongst the enemies of the nut, the caterpillars of the Nut Sawfly are most destructive to nut-trees in the orchard, and if unchecked, will strip the trees of leaves, only the mid-ribs remaining. They are large, and of a lovely blue-green colour, with a yellow tip to the body and numerous black spots. They have a curious habit of jerking their bodies on the approach of danger, twitching themselves spasmodically when disturbed. This odd habit, together with their manner of feeding in groups on the same leaf, renders them unmistakable at first sight. The Nut Sawfly in the perfect state makes its first appearance in May, and the eggs hatch out at the end of June or the beginning of July. When full-grown, they drop off, and pass their chrysalis state in the soil. *Treatment.*—The best method of dealing with them is to spread under the trees sheets of paper covered with some sticky substance and then to shake or gently sweep the insects off on to the paper, which should then be gathered up and burned. A spraying of lead arsenate all over the trees will do some good, whilst the grubs should be dealt with by lightly pointing in a dressing of lime and soot around the roots of the trees during the winter and again in early spring. *Plants Most Usually Affected.*—Nuts.

Onion Fly.—This fly is very like the house-fly. It is grey and has four brown streaks on the thorax and dark triangular patches on the abdomen. It is first seen in May and June, when it lays its eggs on the young shoots of the onions or in the ground close by. After three or four days, dirty-white grubs hatch out, burrow through the earth to the bottom of the young onions on which they feed for some three weeks and then become oval brown pupæ from which the flies emerge in the autumn or the following spring. Three batches are reared during the season in May and June. The maggots eat the bulbs of the young plants, and will destroy a whole crop. Where the attack matures late, the longest leaves turn yellow, droop, and become bleached, or the leaves may retain their natural colour, but will lose their firmness. If the bulbs are examined, they will be found to contain a number of the grubs and will be quite useless. *Treatment.*—The more advanced the crop the less the damage inflicted by the pest. Every effort should, therefore, be made to produce early plants. Sow in the open in autumn, under glass in February, or plant young seedling bulbs, saved through the winter, in spring, and apply sulphate of ammonia to encourage vigorous growth. Dust the young onions over early in spring, before the eggs are laid, with washing soda and sprinkle the ground liberally with soot. Dissolve ¾ of a lb. of soft soap in half a gallon of boiling water and to this add 2 pints of paraffin, mix thoroughly by syringing the liquid back into itself. Add 5 gallons of water, and again mix thoroughly before use. This makes an excellent solution with which to spray the plants and the adjacent soil. All infested plants should at once be removed and burnt, and to prevent future infestation, grow no plants of a similar nature on the same soil for at least three years.

Onion Mildew.—This is a whitish mould, turning to purple, which first forms over the upper parts of the leaves about the end of June, the mildewed patches being rough to the touch. The mildew soon spreads over the whole leaf, making it wither up, and checking the growth of the bulbs. It is encouraged by damp, sunless weather. If the attack has been severe, it is often followed by a black mould which makes all the diseased areas turn black. *Treatment.*—As soon as the mildew appears, dust the leaves, in the early morning while the dew is still on them, with a mixture of sulphur and lime in the proportion of 3 parts to 1 respectively. Remove and burn all affected foliage. No crops of onions should be planted on the same site for several years.

Onion Smut.—This is a fungoid disease which occurs mainly in spring and early summer. It is first seen as black streaks or spots on the leaves and bulbs ; from these fissures masses of powdery, soot-like spores emerge and eventually fall to the ground and contaminate the soil. It is through the soil alone that the plants can be infected, the fungus spawn gradually spreading from the lower stems up to the higher leaves. Infection cannot take place from leaf to leaf above ground, and since only quite young plants are attacked, healthy onion seedlings of moderate size can safely be planted even in contaminated soil. *Treatment.*—Remove and burn all infected plants immediately the disease is noticed, and never sow crops of leeks, onions, or shallots on ground once tainted with the disease. Do not contaminate the soil in other beds, by importing infected soil on the boots, or on the tools used. These must be carefully cleaned. *The presence of this disease must be notified to the Ministry of Agriculture and Fisheries.*

Pea and Bean Beetles.—*See* Bean and Pea Beetles.

Pea Mildew.—This is most frequently found on light ground after hot, dry weather. A thick white mould forms on the stems and causes the plants to turn brown and die off. *Treatment.*—Burn all affected stems in autumn. Plant all future crops in a deeply worked soil, and mulch in hot, dry weather to keep the roots cool and moist.

Peach-Leaf Blister.—One of the greatest enemies of the peach and nectarine is the Peach-leaf Blister, or Peach-leaf Curl, which is caused by a fungus, and gives rise in early spring to ugly and injurious blisters and bulges on the leaves and young shoots, curling them up from side to side. *Treatment.*—The diseased leaves turn yellow and often red, and later become thickened and covered with spores which appear like a " bloom " over the upper side. Eventually the leaves drop off and are usually replaced by fresh foliage. If the attack is severe, the fruit will fall before it is properly formed. The appearance of the disease is well known to most gardeners, but the conditions which help the pest to flourish are still undiscovered. There seems to be no peculiar atmospheric or other condition which assists it, though it has been noticed by some observers that exposure to cold winds, especially from the east or north-east, often coincides with a bad attack. Shelter is the best preventive of the disease, and a south wall should be given to peach trees in consequence. Hard pruning to beyond the point of infection, together with the removal and immediate burning of all infected leaves, is the best check on the spread of the disease. Spray when the leaf-buds are just beginning to open, and again repeat the process in three weeks or so with Bordeaux or Burgundy Mixture. A solution of liver of sulphur used at the rate of 1 oz. to 3 gallons of water is also a good control, and helps by rendering the tree immune from infection by wind-borne spores. *Plants Most Usually Affected.*— Peaches and Nectarines.

Pear-Leaf Blister Mite.—Blister-mites secrete themselves during the winter under the enveloping scales of the young buds. They are extremely minute, and hide there throughout the winter, attacking the young leaves as soon as they unfold, and causing pale-green, blister-like spots on both surfaces. These blisters soon become pink, and later brown, after which the whole leaf turns black and dies off in July and August. In the underside of the swelling there is a minute hole, through which the insects emerge and move to a fresh spot, repeating their process of damage, and in severe cases attacking the young shoots and fruit, which usually becomes deformed and falls from the trees while quite small. *Treatment.*—In cases where the attack has persisted through two or more seasons, spraying in November, or just before the buds open, with lime-sulphur must be resorted to, but as the creatures are hidden securely within the buds, they are practically safe from all insecticides, so that hand-picking of the diseased leaves is almost the only remedy. These should be burned at once, and if this is thoroughly done, it should greatly check the ravages of the mite. *Plants Most Usually Affected.*—Apples and Pears.

Pear Midge.—When attacked by this pest, the young fruit at first grows rapidly, then stops suddenly, does not develop and becomes distorted and deformed. The fruitlets drop when about half an inch in diameter. The female midge pierces the still unopened bud and lays its eggs deep down in the blossom. The larvæ hatch out and eat into the developing fruitlets from which they emerge when full-grown to pupate in the soil, where they remain until the following spring. *Treatment.*—All deformed fruitlets should at once be picked off and burned. In the autumn a good soil fumigant, such as naph-thalene at the rate of 1½ lb. to the square rod, should be dug into the soil round the trees, which should be thoroughly sprayed with nicotine wash just as the buds are breaking the following spring. Poultry allowed to roam in the orchard in spring and early summer will account for numbers of the pest.

Pith Moth.—In the spring the larvæ of this moth crawl into and devour the young shoots of the trees affected, causing them to wither suddenly and without apparent reason. If blisters pierced by holes are noticed at the base of the shoot buds, all wood having these must be cut away and burned at pruning time, as the larvæ hibernate under these blisters. Infested shoots must be taken off as soon as the disease is noticed. *Plants Most Usually Affected.*—Apples and Pears.

Plum-Tree Rust.—This disease affects the underside of the leaves, covering them with small reddish-brown spots, which in bad cases spread and almost cover the surface. The leaves, where badly injured, turn yellow, fall and check the tree, often doing great harm. *Treatment.*—Spraying with Bordeaux Mixture in the spring, and if necessary, later also, will usually prove effective. All fallen leaves should be swept up and burned. This latter step will be needed also if the plum suffers from Plum-leaf Blotch, which appears in the same way as the foregoing on the under surface of the leaves. The damson and sloe suffer much from this. *Plants Most Usually Affected.*—Almond, Apricot, Cherry, Peach and Plum.

Potato Black Leg.—This is a common disease and causes great losses in damp seasons. The disease first appears about the middle of June, the foliage becoming yellow or pale-green. The plants are liable to be stunted and the leaves on the higher shoots become dwarfed and stiff, and point straight upwards. It will be found that the affected stems are easily pulled from the soil, and will be seen to be black and rotten ; the tubers may also be diseased. At a later stage the foliage turns brown and the stems rot away ; if any tubers have been produced, they will probably be affected. *Treatment.*—Dig up and burn all affected plants as soon as possible, removing also all tubers from the soil ; the sound ones may be eaten, but must not be stored, or kept for " seed." Never plant doubtful " seed." Do not plant potatoes in contaminated land for at least two seasons.

Potato Blight.—This most destructive of all potato diseases is due to a fungus. It usually first makes its appearance in June or early

July. Black patches appear on the leaves and a whitish mould forms on the under surface; this latter mould is a characteristic by which this disease may be distinguished from all others that attack the potato. The leaves curl up and decay, the haulm becomes black and rotten, and later the tubers become infected. Purple-brown, sunken patches appear on the skin of the tubers, and the flesh below becomes diseased, purple-red in colour, and gradually decays. Damp, humid conditions are favourable to the spread of the disease ; dry weather will check its ravages. Fungus spores are blown from the white mould on the leaves to other plants, which quickly become infected. The spores also fall to the ground, and in this way infect the tubers ; these are also contaminated when being dug if the diseased haulms are allowed to lie about over them. The inception of the disease is due to the use of infected " seed " potatoes, it being practically impossible to tell when the tubers are slightly tainted ; care must, therefore, be taken to use " seed " only from a clean crop. *Treatment.*—Spray early in July with Bordeaux Mixture, again about three weeks later, and finally about a fortnight or so after the second application. Any diseased and blackened stems should at once be removed. Boxed tubers form a means of control, as affected tubers may sprout prematurely or not at all, or they may bear poor, weakly sprouts. Such tubers should not be planted.

Potato Leaf Roll.—Plants frequently show no sign of the disease for some time after infection, often not until it becomes evident in the young plants of the following season, when the symptoms will be very marked. The edges of the lower leaflets curl upwards and inwards, this spreads to the young shoots and eventually to the entire foliage. The plants may become stunted, assume a rigid and erect appearance, and the leaflets get thick and brittle, and may take on a reddish tinge. *Treatment.*—As soon as diseased plants are seen, they should be pulled up and should be destroyed. If affected early, no young tubers will have formed ; should the attack take place later on, the tubers must be dug up and should also be destroyed. Never save " seed " from diseased plants, nor from plants grown in close proximity to them. Where green-fly are present, spray them with a good insecticide, or if on the shoots of " sprouting " tubers in the store-room, fumigate. (*See* Aphides or Green-fly.)

Potato Mosaic.—*Symptoms.*—The leaves become faintly mottled with various shades of green and the edges of the leaves may be crinkled. If the attack is severe, the plants will be dwarfed or may cease to grow altogether. If infection takes place early in the year, the leaves will show the mottling that season; if infected late in the season, it may not be apparent, but will be transferred through the " seed " potatoes to the next year's crop. According to the severity of attack, the decrease in yield may be from 15 to 35 per cent. In gardens and allotments where local and home-saved seed is used, the losses may be even more serious. *Prevention.*—Obtain " seed " tubers from unaffected districts, preferably from the north of England or from Scotland or Ireland. Seed tubers should never be saved from infected plants or from fields or gardens where the infection is bad. Varieties that are particularly subject to the disease should not be grown. The following varieties have been proved to be specially susceptible, viz. : *Golden Wonder, Langworthy, Burnhouse Beauty, Tinwald Perfection,* and in a lesser degree *Arran Chief, Boston Kidney (Dargill Early), Irish Chieftain* and *King Edward.* In a small way, spraying with soft soap and nicotine should prove a good control.

Potato Powdery or Corky Scab.—This disease first appears as small, white swellings or pimples on the skin of the young potatoes. If the tubers are removed from the soil, these pimples soon turn brown. These swellings grow, the skin bursts, and frees masses of spores, which contaminate the soil, and cause outbreaks in following years. This mild form of scab does not injure the flesh of the potato, and does not greatly harm the crop. Should the attack become severe, however, the flesh will be eaten into and will assume a cankerous form, which is encouraged by overmuch lime in the soil and by damp, badly-drained ground. *Treatment.*—Do not grow potatoes on contaminated land for five years after an attack ; if it is essential, look to the drainage and dress the soil with flowers of sulphur at the rate of 3 oz. to the sq. yd. Infected tubers should not be used as seed. Steeping them for three hours in a weak solution of formalin ($\frac{1}{2}$ pint of formalin to 15 gallons of water) or rolling them when moist in flowers of sulphur has proved a good control.

Potato Scab.—This is a very common fungoid disease among potatoes, and is especially prevalent on land which has been much dressed with ashes, lime, road sweepings, and similar substances of an alkaline nature. It is also frequently met with in light, gravelly or sandy soils. The scabs are seen as small, dark spots of cork-like material, scattered over the surface of the tuber, or large patches of the outer skin may be eaten away. The scabs grow and may eventually almost cover the surface of the potato. The interior flesh is undamaged and good for consumption, although the appearance of the tubers is spoiled. *Treatment.*—Do not use potatoes affected with scab as "seed." Dress alkaline soils with flowers of sulphur at the rate of 1 oz. to every square yard of ground. Gravelly and sandy soils should be treated by digging in the mowings from the lawn or rotted leaves, before the seed is planted. A barrow-load of lawn-mowings to every five square yards should be sufficient.

Potato Stalk Disease.—This fungoid disease is first seen early in July as white patches on the stem of the plant. These patches swell out to the size of peas, become round or oval in shape, and gradually harden and turn black on the exterior. After a time they fall to the ground. The fungus also penetrates the stem and causes the tissues to wither and the stems to die and crack. The balls of fungus, or spores, lie dormant in the ground until the spring, when they form a kind of cup on the surface of the soil, from which spores are projected, to be carried by the air to the foliage of the plants, the older leaves of which they infect *Treatment.*—Injured tubers or roots from affected plants must be discarded, and plants liable to infection of this disease must not be grown in contaminated or even neighbouring soil for four years after an attack. Burn all affected parts of the plant as soon after the appearance of the attack as possible. *Plants Most Usually Attacked.*—Artichokes, Beans, Carrots, Cucumbers, Marrows, Potatoes, Tomatoes and Turnips.

Potato Storage Rot.—This is a fungoid disease appearing first in December among stored potatoes, and increasing in severity until late spring. A dark, sunken patch is seen on the skin of the potato, the surrounding skin becomes wrinkled and corrugated, white or pinkish spots of fungus appear, and the flesh eventually becomes shrivelled, brown and hard. *Treatment.*—Examine stored tubers frequently, and remove diseased ones. Burn badly-affected tubers. Dig and handle the tubers carefully, and avoid all injury. Early varieties should be put in the "sprouting trays" in October. Stored potatoes must have ample light and ventilation and must be kept cool. Never use tubers affected with storage rot, nor potatoes that may have been in contact with them, for "seed."

Potato Wart Disease.—The warts first appear on the "eyes" of the tubers, they grow, become very irregular in form, and frequently join up into large, rugged and shapeless masses. The growths turn from white to black, putrefaction sets in, and a dark liquid oozes from the excrescences and infects the soil with fungus spores, which remain there for many years. Where a plant is badly diseased, warts may also be found on the lower foliage. *Treatment.*—On infected soil grow varieties such as *Dargill Early* (early), *Arran Comrade* (second early) or *Rhoderic Dhu* (late), which are immune from the disease. Burn all diseased tubers and do not use infected tools or appliances on pure soil. *Appearance of this disease must be notified to the Ministry of Agriculture and Fisheries. Under the Wart Disease of Potatoes Order of* 1923 *Wales and adjacent central counties of England have been declared "Infected Areas."* Gardeners in these and neighbouring districts should acquire and study this Order. No fungicides have been found effective on badly-contaminated soils.

Raspberry Beetle.—Perhaps the most destruction is done to raspberries in the garden by the larvæ of the Raspberry Beetle. The grubs hatch out from eggs laid by the female in late spring within the buds or half-expanded flowers. They are small and yellowish, and when fed fully upon the flowers and young fruit, take refuge in cracks of the bark and spin themselves cocoons, from which they emerge in the following spring. In the perfect stage the beetle is covered with either a yellowish or a grey down or wool. Tarred paper should be laid under infested bushes, then, if the latter are smartly shaken, many of the beetles will fall and can be destroyed. The operation should take place early on a spring morning and preferably in dull weather. The old canes that are cut down after fruiting is over should be burned. *Plants Most Usually Affected.*—Raspberries, Hops, and young grafted stock of Fruit Trees.

Raspberry Moth or Shoot Borer.—When raspberry canes are attacked by the larvæ of this moth, the young shoots, usually those high up the canes, wither and prevent the development of the flowers and consequently the fruit. The moth appears towards the end of May and lays its eggs actually in the blossom. Its fore-wings are of a shiny, deep purple-brown spotted with yellow, the hind-wings are grey. *Treatment.*—Pick off and destroy all dead shoots. In autumn cut back and burn all canes and at the same time remove and burn all rubbish round the base of the canes and fork naphthalene, at the rate of 1½ lb. to the square rod, well into the soil. Spray thoroughly with paraffin emulsion in winter, and the new shoots with lead arsenate in April. *Plants Most Usually Affected.*—Raspberries.

Raspberry or Clay-coloured Weevil.—This weevil is most commonly found in the adult state in May and June, and in this form it devours the buds, blossom, leaves and bark of raspberries and young fruit trees. The adult weevils are blunt-nosed and nearly one-third of an inch in length, and although they are actually a deep, rich brown in colour and flecked with paler brown, they appear of an earthy hue, as they soon become coloured by the soil in which they usually hide during the daytime. These weevils are timid, and fall to the ground if disturbed by a light or if the tree is shaken. *Treatment.*—Lay tarred cloths or paper under the trees or plants and shake the branches, just before it gets dark. Numbers of weevils will fall and stick to the tar. Spray the foliage in summer with arsenate of lead. Clear up and destroy all rubbish in the neighbourhood, and in autumn dress the soil with a fumigant, such as naphthalene at the rate of 1½ lb. to the square rod. *Plants Most Usually Affected.*—Raspberries and young Fruit Trees.

Red-footed Beetle.—This is a mischievous insect which lives on the leaves of apple and pear trees, the leaves affected by it looking as if they had received a shower of small shot. The insect is black with red feet, and it is often found in numbers on the young leaves in spring. *Treatment.*—The female lays her eggs in the ground at the foot of the trees, and by lightly forking into the soil in the autumn and again just before spring a dressing of soot or lime, many of the insects may be destroyed as they hatch out. When they appear on the leaves a sheet may be laid on the ground below the tree, and if the latter is shaken a number of the insects will fall and may be gathered up and destroyed. An insecticide may be sprayed over the tree.

Red Spider.—The red spider eats into the underside of the foliage and sucks at the sap, causing the leaves to turn yellow and later, if the attack is severe, whitish. The pest is encouraged by drought in the open, or by excessive heating and drying of the atmosphere of the greenhouse, and may be kept under by remedying these conditions. *Treatment.*—Plants in the open that are attacked should be sprayed with paraffin emulsion or lime-sulphur, but this must be done early before the trees or bushes are badly damaged. On the first discovery of red spider in the greenhouse, all affected leaves should be sponged with soapy water and the house should be fumigated (*see* p. 404). *Plants Most Usually Affected.*—Apples, Plums, Peaches and Nectarines, Vines, Carnations and a great variety of Greenhouse Plants.

Rose Beetle or Golden Chafer.—This small and beautiful golden-green beetle does much injury to roses, especially to the blooms. The eggs are laid in the soil or in decomposed manure. The frequent turning of the surface soil and of any litter lying on it will expose the grubs to the attacks of birds, their natural enemies. A spraying of quassia solution is also helpful.

Rose Maggots.—The maggots of several species of moth attack rose foliage and buds in summer, frequently spinning the leaves together. They should all be treated in the same manner as caterpillars. Where buds are noticed to be badly infested, they should be picked off and burnt immediately. *Plants Most Usually Affected.*—Roses.

Rose Rust.—In spring an orange-coloured fungus sometimes appears on the shoots like small patches of powder ; in autumn the fungus becomes brown, flecked with black spores, and is also seen on the underside of the leaves. *Treatment.*—Pick off and burn all affected shoots and leaves, and spray the plants with liver of sulphur.

Rose Tortrix.—Among the moths the Rose Tortrix is distinguished by the rich golden-yellow of its breast and fore-wings. This colour is slightly clouded with orange, and is barred with purple-brown; there are also silvery scales. This moth, in the caterpillar state, is very destructive to roses. The moths deposit their eggs in the summer in the incipient buds. Round these leaves others grow in distorted shape, whilst the caterpillar revels on its core, devouring the petals of the flower as well as the leaf. When disturbed, the caterpillar drops down, suspended by a thin web which it spins, and by which it is able, when the danger disappears, to resume its former position. *Treatment.*—The only method of destroying these insects is by sharply pinching, in the early spring, the buds where they are suspected to be. This will relieve the plant and will enable it to throw out fresh leaves. If allowed to arrive at maturity, the moths should be destroyed as soon as they appear, and before they can deposit their eggs.

Rosy Rust Moth.—The caterpillars of this moth feed on the stems of potato plants and cause the shoots to wither. The best treatment is to snap off and burn the affected shoots.

Sawflies.—Numerous sawflies attack rose and fruit trees from June to September. The most commonly seen is the rose sawfly, whose maggots are dark green and spotted with white. For treatment, *see* Apple Sawfly, Cherry Sawfly, Currant Sawfly, Caterpillars and Maggots.

Scale (The Oyster-shell Scale).—This is an insect that infests and does much injury to the wood and leaves of many trees and plants. The tiny insects pierce the bark and suck the sap from the plants, attacking first the older wood. They infest the young shoots only after all the larger branches have been covered. Badly affected trees and bushes lose their leaves early in the season and rarely carry good flowers ; the sucking of the sap soon drains their vitality. The males are in the form of small flies. The females look like little plates or scales—whence the name—fixed to the bark and sometimes to the leaves. *Treatment.*—Scale is destroyed by scrubbing or by thorough spraying during winter with lime-sulphur or a strong paraffin emulsion. Miscible oil is also effective. As much of the old wood as possible should be cut away. The solutions should be applied in winter and special attention should be given to the undersides of the branches. *Plants Most Usually Affected.*—Plums, Cherries, Apples, Pears, Peaches, Apricots and Nectarines, also Currants and many shrubby plants.

Shot Borer Beetle.—These are small brownish-black beetles which bore into the branches and trunks of fruit trees, as do the Bark or Trunk Borers, with the exception that their burrows are flat in section and run right into the wood itself. They attack the same trees as the Bark and Trunk Borers, and must be prevented and dealt with as advised for these (which *see*).

Silver Leaf.— The fungus enters the wood through an injury in the bark, and causes the leaves to take on a silvery hue ; the diseased branches sometimes recover naturally, but more frequently die off, till the whole tree is killed if the attack is not arrested. The fungus later shows itself as a purple, leathery coating over the under parts of the dead wood, or in the form of horizontal lines of purple crust on the side of the trunk. *Treatment.*—As soon as the disease is discovered, cut the branches back to healthy wood, and paint the cut surfaces with Stockholm Tar ; this dressing should be renewed at intervals. Burn all diseased parts, also all old wood lying about near the trees. The soil should be well limed and faulty drainage should be rectified. *Plants Most Usually Affected.*—Of the fruit trees, Apples and Plums are especially susceptible to this disease, though Apricots, Cherries, Currants, Gooseberries, and Peaches are often attacked.

Slugworms.—*See* Cherry and Pear Sawfly.

Slugs and Snails.—Do not allow rubbish to accumulate in odd places ; keep the garden tidy. Encourage frogs and toads and insectivorous birds, such as the thrush, which devour snails and slugs, and where feasible allow poultry to range over the land. Dust young growths over with a mixture of soot and lime to prevent the pests from devouring them. At night or early in the morning sprinkle lime thickly on the soil and repeat the process two or three days in succession,—this will kill numerous snails; others may be trapped in orange skins, lettuce leaves, or bran, of which they are very fond. Much may be done by diligent searching in the early morning or evening. A ring of cinders round choice plants will do a great deal to discourage the attentions of slugs and snails. There are several anti-slug and snail powders on the market ; most are very effective.

Small Ermine Moth.—The caterpillars of this moth, which are greenish-grey and spotted with black, feed on the leaves of fruit trees. They spin large webs from leaf to leaf and from twig to twig, and if unchecked will cover the whole tree, denuding it of its leaves, and causing the fruit to fall before it is ripe. Early in July cocoons in which the larvæ pupate are formed, and the mature moths emerge about the end of the month and lay their eggs on the twigs. The front wings of the moths are greyish-white with numerous black spots, the hind pair of wings are grey. *Treatment.*—Spray the trees very thoroughly with a solution of arsenate of lead as soon as the blossom has wilted. *Plants Most Usually Affected.*—Apples, Pears, Cherries, Plums, Hawthorns, Euonymus, Mountain Ashes and other allied plants.

Social Pear Sawfly.—Certain of the sawflies attack the pear as well as the plum and the cherry. The Social Pear Sawfly is one of these, living in colonies on the leaves, which the grubs cover with a protecting web. Like all the sawflies, the grubs finally let themselves down into the earth, where they pass the winter, sometimes remaining two entire seasons in this condition, emerging only in the next year but one to their hatching. *Treatment.*—Picking off of the colonies with the leaves which harbour them and dressing the surrounding ground as advised for Pear Midge are the two best remedies. *Plants Most Usually Affected.*—Pears, Plums and Cherries.

Swift Moths.—There are five species of this moth in Great Britain, but only two do sufficient damage to warrant attention. These are : 1. *The Ghost Swift Moth.*—The male and female of this species have a wing expanse of 2 inches or more. In the female the fore-wings are buff, marked with pink, and the rear pair of wings are greyish. The hind wings of the male are sometimes greyish, but as a rule all four wings are silver-coloured and fringed with pink. 2. *The Small Garden Swift Moth.*—This is a much smaller moth and varies greatly in colour ; the fore-wings in the male are usually buff, marked with creamy-white ; the rear wings are grey-brown. The female is similar in colour, but the markings are usually much less pronounced and often absent. The caterpillars are similar in both species, except in size, being dirty-white in colour and having reddish-brown heads. The moths are seen in June and July hovering over plants at dusk. The female lays her eggs as she flies, these fall to the ground, hatch, and the young larvæ feed on the roots of plants near at hand. They eat at the roots till the following April, when they turn into chrysalides, the complete moths appearing in June or July. Many plants are attacked, shrubs, trees and numerous herbaceous plants being the chief sufferers. *Treatment.*—Dig over the soil as frequently as possible, and replant herbaceous borders every three or four years. Dig naphthalene, at the rate of one ounce to every square yard, thoroughly into infected soil before planting.

Thrips.—These are small, blackish-grey insects that infest and injure the flowers, leaves, and shoots, causing them to appear spotted, warped, and twisted out of place. The best remedy against thrips is the plentiful application of salt water, tobacco water, strong soapy water, or any of the insecticides that are sold for the purpose of destroying insect life. Thrips are most active in very dry weather. *Plants Most Usually Affected.*—Vines, Peas, Beans, Palms, also a great variety of Greenhouse Plants.

Turnip Flea Beetle.—The principal pest to which the turnip is liable is the Turnip Flea. There are several varieties of this beetle, most of them quite small and black in colour. They jump like a flea and are not easy to locate. They feed on any plants of the cabbage tribe, being especially fond of young seedlings, of which they often destroy whole crops. *Treatment.*—As with most other diseases and pests, the most important measure consists in frequent changes of soil, and its proper preparation. Liberal dressings of lime, soot, wood-ashes or Pyrethrum Powder may be given to the growing crop in the early morning while the dew is on the leaves, and frequent hoeing should be performed between the plants. The best method of prevention is to keep down the plants known to harbour it, as these nourish the insect and shelter it until the young turnips are ready for the attacks. Among these " host plants " are the charlock, the hedge-mustard and shepherd's purse. If the young turnips are vigorous and quick-growing, they are more likely to escape the pest, so that the use of a good, fresh, trustworthy seed is essential. As a safeguard, soak the seed in turpentine for a few hours before sowing, using one fluid ounce (about two tablespoonfuls) of turpentine to every seven pounds of seed. Mix the seed with sand, and sow in the ordinary way. An effective mixture for spraying the infested leaves may be made by dissolving 1 lb. of soft soap in a gallon of boiling water and adding two pints of paraffin. Mix thoroughly, using a syringe, and add rain-water to make the solution up to ten gallons. Stir before using.

Turnip Moth.—In this moth the front wings are a greyish-brown, marked with darker brown or black ; the hind wings are white. The caterpillars are also greyish-brown in colour, and have dark brown spots along their sides. The moths lay their eggs on the stems and leaves of various plants in June. The caterpillars, or " Cutworms " as they are called, feed mostly by night on the stems and leaves of the plants, especially potatoes and turnips, doing great damage. By day they lie hidden in the grass, among stones or in the soil. *Treatment.*—Hand pick the grubs from the soil and the stems when they are active at night, and by day hoe between the rows. This will kill many, and enable birds to account for more. Provided the plants are small, and that much root has still to form, spray with arsenate of lead if the foliage is being attacked, but great care must be taken in the use of this insecticide, *as it is poisonous to domestic animals and to human beings.*

Turnip Sawfly.—The grubs of this fly are quite small, black, and do great harm to the turnip crop. They may be brushed off the plants with a birch broom, after which the turnips and soil below should be well sprayed with paraffin emulsion.

Vapourer Moth.—There are frequently as many as three broods of this moth in a single season. The eggs, a dirty-white in colour, are usually deposited in masses on the empty cocoon of the female moth. The caterpillars are hairy and of a nondescript colour composed of a mixture of chestnut-red and yellow, with two reddish spots on each segment. They are to be found all through the summer. The female moth is yellowish-grey in colour, hairy and wingless ; the male is a deep chestnut-brown with darker markings. The moths are found in late summer and autumn. The caterpillars feed on the leaves of fruit trees, etc. *Treatment.*—In summer, all caterpillars should be picked from the trees, which should also be sprayed with arsenate of lead, but at least six weeks before the fruit is to be gathered. In winter destroy as many eggs as possible.

Vine or Black Weevil.—The mature weevils are found throughout the spring and summer and do considerable damage to the young shoots of the grape vine. These weevils also attack plants grown in the open, especially strawberries. They grow to about one-third of an inch in length, and in colour are black flecked with yellow. Plants attacked by them soon assume a sickly colour and fail to develop properly. *Treatment.—See* Raspberry Weevil.

Wasp Traps.—The best kind of trap for wasps is a bottle containing some kind of syrup, or sugar and beer mixed together, with a cord round its neck, from which issue other pieces of string attached to hooks of wire, by which the bottle can be suspended to a branch of the tree on which the fruit is ripening.

White Fly.—The Greenhouse White Fly, also known as the " Ghost Fly," is well known to most cultivators of greenhouse plants, especially to tomato growers, to whom it has caused considerable financial loss. It is essentially a greenhouse pest, and being a native of a warm country, it cannot live outdoors during our winters, except possibly in very mild districts. The white colour is due to a covering of mealy wax which acts as a protection and is very difficult to wet with spray. *Life History.*—The female White Fly lays her eggs, usually in an incomplete circle, but sometimes in groups, each egg being stalked, with the stalk inserted in a slit in the leaf and presenting the appearance of small black pegs. The eggs hatch in from 11 to 14 days, according to the temperature, and produce pale-green, flattish larvæ which crawl about for several days and then settle down with their sucking apparatus driven into the plant, remaining stationary until later on they become adult White Flies. *Methods of Control.*—Where this pest is not present, great care should be taken in introducing fresh plants to see that they are not infested by White Fly. Spraying has so far proved of little use against this pest. Fumigation by means of hydrocyanic acid gas and tetrachlorethane has proved most effective. The last is less poisonous than hydrocyanic acid gas and, therefore, more suitable for the amateur; although effective and safe for tomatoes, it proves injurious to many greenhouse plants. Hydrocyanic acid gas is the most satisfactory control, as it can be used safely with mixed collections of plants. Sodium cyanide or calcium cyanide is generally used, the last-named, a more recent compound, being mostly used, as it is in the form of a powder which only requires to be sprinkled on the floor of the house or houses. In good air-tight houses ¼ oz. to 1,000 cubic feet is regarded as the standard dose; in old houses more may be required. Fumigation should take place in darkness, it is important that there shall be no moisture on the foliage, and the plants should be as dry as possible at the root. *It must always be remembered that sodium cyanide, calcium cyanide, and hydrocyanic acid gas are all deadly poisons,* and great precautions must be taken to prevent accidents. The Board of Agriculture and Fisheries issue a leaflet with full instructions for fumigating by this method. *Natural Enemies.*—It has recently been discovered that White Fly has a natural enemy in two very small chalcid wasps. One of them, *Encarsia formosa,* has been bred in large quantities at the Experimental Station, Cheshunt, and quantities have been distributed to growers. This parasite has proved a complete control for White Fly on tomatoes and many indoor plants.

Winter Moth.—The Winter Moth attacks the foliage of the apple as well as that of most other fruit trees, and does enormous damage. The female moth is not fully-winged and, being unable to fly, crawls up the tree-stem to lay her eggs. The grubs hatch out early in April, begin at once to feed upon the young leaves, and when fully-fed let themselves down from the tree by spun threads and bury themselves in the ground to pass the next stage of their life. *Treatment.*—The eggs are laid all through the winter, and the best method of prevention is the encircling of the stems of the trees early in October with bands, about 8 inches wide, of some material which the crawling moth will be unable to pass. Such materials as grease-proof paper coated with cart-grease mixed with tar, or any other coarse grease of the kind. The bands, if possible, should be placed about 4 feet from the ground to prevent the females from being able to get over them. In the case of bush fruit, where the bands cannot be placed at this height, spraying is the better method. The bands should be kept greased at intervals throughout the winter and early spring months. Spray the trees with lead arsenate. This is best used in the paste form, 4 to 5 lb. of paste being added to 100 gallons of water. The spray should be applied as soon as the leaves begin to appear and before the flowers open. If necessary, a second application may be made after the petals have fallen. *Plants Most Usually Affected.*— Practically all Fruit Trees, as well as most Forest Trees and Bushes.

Wood Leopard Moth.—The caterpillars of this moth tunnel into the branches of fruit trees such as the apple, pear, plum and cherry, and at times do much damage. These caterpillars attain a length of two inches, are yellowish-white in colour spotted with black, and have a black head and tail. The pupæ are brown and enclosed in silver cocoons flecked with bark shavings. The mature moths appear about midsummer. The body is white spotted with bluish-black, so are the wings. *Treatment.*—*See* that advised for the Goat Moth.

Woodlice.—Woodlice congregate in rubbish, at the bottom of pots in a hot-bed and round the sides of wood edgings, fences, and stones. They should be searched for every morning and destroyed by having boiling water poured over them. They may be trapped by means of small flower-pots filled with dry manure or old hay. Powdered borax sprinkled in infested places will also do much to keep down this pest.

Woolly Aphis, or American Blight.—These aphides are usually dark purple in colour and are very difficult to get rid of. They derive their name from the masses of downy white wool with which they cover themselves. *Treatment.*—Immediately the fruit has been gathered, spray the affected trees with a paraffin emulsion or with any good insecticide. (*See* p. 406.) In autumn, too, the soil round the trees should be dressed with naphthalene at the rate of 1½ lb. per rod. A spraying with caustic soda wash or improved Woburn Wash in January is also a more or less complete control.

Yellow Underwing Moth.—In this moth the front wings are brown and spotted with a darker colour, the hind wings are a deep yellow ochre with a border of black. The caterpillars, or " Cutworms " as they are called, vary greatly in ground colour, from a greyish green to a reddish brown. They are darker on the underside than above and a strip of paler colour runs along each side. Except that this moth appears a little later than the Turnip Moth, its habits are practically identical and need not here be described. *Treatment.*—*See* that for the Turnip Moth.

INDEX

439